Project Management

Fifth Edition

Harvey Maylor
Neil Turner

Pearson

Harlow, England • London • New York • Boston • San Francisco • Toronto • Sydney
Dubai • Singapore • Hong Kong • Tokyo • Seoul • Taipei • New Delhi
Cape Town • São Paulo • Mexico City • Madrid • Amsterdam • Munich • Paris • Milan

PEARSON EDUCATION LIMITED
KAO Two
KAO Park
Harlow CM17 9NA
United Kingdom
Tel: +44 (0)1279 623623
Web: www.pearson.com/uk

First published in Great Britain in 1996 (print)
Second edition published 1999 (print)
Third edition published 2003 (print)
Third edition published 2003 with MS Project 2005 (print)
Fourth edition published 2010 (print)
Fifth edition published 2022 (print and electronic)

ISBN: 978-1-292-08843-3 (print)
   978-1-292-08847-1 (PDF)
   978-1-292-08844-0 (ePub)

British Library Cataloguing-in-Publication Data
A catalogue record for the print edition is available from the British Library

Library of Congress Cataloging-in-Publication Data
Names: Maylor, Harvey, author. | Turner, Neil, 1970- author.
Title: Project management / Harvey Maylor, Neil Turner.
Description: Fifth edition. | Harlow, England ; New York : Pearson, 2022. |
   Includes bibliographical references and index.
Identifiers: LCCN 2021033340 (print) | LCCN 2021033341 (ebook) | ISBN
   9781292088433 (paperback) | ISBN 9781292088471 (ebook) | ISBN
   9781292088440 (epub)
Subjects: LCSH: Project management.
Classification: LCC HD69.P75 .M3796 2022 (print) | LCC HD69.P75 (ebook) |
   DDC 658.4/04—dc23
LC record available at https://lccn.loc.gov/2021033340
LC ebook record available at https://lccn.loc.gov/2021033341

10 9 8 7 6 5 4 3 2 1
26 25 24 23 22

Front cover image: wellsie82/Moment Open/Getty Images
Cover designed by Kelly Miller
Print edition typeset in 9.5/12.5pt Charter ITC Pro by Straive
Printed in Slovakia by Neografia

NOTE THAT ANY PAGE CROSS REFERENCES REFER TO THE PRINT EDITION

Brief contents

List of figures and tables — xiii
Guided tour — xviii
Preface — xx
Acknowledgements — xxi

Making sense of the project context — 1

1 Introduction — 2
2 Structures and frameworks — 25
3 Projects and organisations — 57

Managing the project process: the 4-D model — 83

D1: Define it — 83

4 Setting up for success — 84
5 Planning for success — 109

D2: Design it — 143

6 Time planning and scheduling — 144
7 Making time planning robust: Advanced Project Thinking (APT) — 170
8 Building a business case for a project — 195
9 Engaging stakeholders — 222
10 Managing risks and opportunities — 243

D3: Do it — 269

11 Organising people in the project — 270
12 Leading people in projects — 295
13 Monitoring and controlling the project — 317
14 Procuring, contracting, and working with supply chains — 343
15 Problem-solving and decision-making — 369

D4: Develop it — 393

16 Completing projects and learning to improve — 394

Index — 430

Publisher's acknowledgements — 444

Contents

List of figures and tables   xiii
Guided tour   xviii
Preface   xx
Acknowledgements   xxi

Making sense of the project context   **1**

1 Introduction   2

Introduction   3
1.1   Basic definitions   4
1.2   Importance of successful project management to an organisation and to you   10
1.3   Project management past and present   14

Summary   19
Key terms   20
Project management in practice: *Four managers with distinctly different roles*   20
Topics for discussion   22
Further information   22
References   23

2 Structures and frameworks   25

Introduction   26
2.1   Describing the project context: high-level frameworks   27
2.2   Describing the project process: activity models   31
2.3   Describing the project management challenge: managerial complexity   42

Summary   46
Key terms   46
Relevant areas of the Bodies of Knowledge   46
Project management in practice: *The rescue of Crossrail*   50
Project management in practice: *Using the 7-S approach in the review of a real project*   50
Topics for discussion   54
Further information   55
References   56

3 Projects and organisations   57

Introduction   58
3.1   Organisational strategy and projects   59

3.2   Portfolios and programmes   64
3.3   Project roles and governance   70

Summary   75
Key terms   76
Relevant areas of the Bodies of Knowledge   76
Project management in practice: *The Airbus A380 development*   76
Project management in practice: *Selecting a personal project*   79
Topics for discussion   80
Further information   80
References   81

Managing the project process: the 4-D model
D1: Define it   83

4 Setting up for success   84

Introduction   85
4.1   Stakeholders: success and failure   86
4.2   Managing strategic choices   95
4.3   Benefits analysis, value and justification   100

Summary   102
Key terms   103
Relevant areas of the Bodies of Knowledge   103
Project management in practice: *Managing stakeholders at European
       transport infrastructure provider*   104
Project management in practice: *A new campus for the University
       of Rummidge (with apologies to David Lodge)*   105
Topics for discussion   107
Further information   107
References   108

5 Planning for success   109

Introduction   110
5.1   Models of planning   111
5.2   The planning process   116
5.3   Basic project landscapes: stages and gates, activities and maps   123

Summary   132
Key terms   132
Relevant areas of the Bodies of Knowledge   133
Project management in practice: *Norway's QA process for major
       project procurement*   134
Project management in practice: *The Mini project – the brief and the PID* 135
Topics for discussion   141
Further information   141
References   141

**Managing the project process: the 4-D model
D2: Design it**   **143**

6 Time planning and scheduling   144

Introduction   145
6.1   Deconstruction of a project   146
6.2   Constructing a time plan   150
6.3   Using Gantt charts   159

Summary   163
Key terms   164
Relevant areas of the Bodies of Knowledge   164
Project management in practice: *The Balti Experience*   165
Project management in practice: *The mobile phone development*   167
Topics for discussion   167
Further information   168
Reference   169

7 Making time planning robust: Advanced Project Thinking (APT)   170

Introduction   171
7.1   Limitations of current approaches to project planning   172
7.2   Managing by constraints in projects   177
7.3   Using the APT approach   183

Summary   186
Key terms   187
Relevant areas of the Bodies of Knowledge   187
Project management in practice: *A major road project delivered early –
    success with APT*   187
Topics for discussion   193
Further information   193
References   194

8 Building a business case for a project   195

Introduction   196
8.1   Basics of a cost planning process   198
8.2   Business case development   206
8.3   Challenges for the received wisdom   213

Summary   216
Key terms   217
Relevant areas of the Bodies of Knowledge   217
Project management in practice: *Justify IT!*   218
Topics for discussion   218
Further information   219
References   219
Appendix: Present value of £1   220

9 Engaging stakeholders   222

Introduction   223
9.1   The concept of quality and quality management   224
9.2   Quality performance and conformance   230
9.3   Towards quality improvement   236

Summary   238
Key terms   239
Relevant areas of the Bodies of Knowledge   239
Project management in practice: *Adopting a standard for project
    planning – useful discipline or unnecessary constraint?*   240
Topics for discussion   241
Further information   241
References   242

10 Managing risks and opportunities   243

Introduction   244
10.1   The nature of risk and risk management   245
10.2   Qualitative and quantitative approaches   249
10.3   Opportunities management   258

Summary   259
Key terms   260
Relevant areas of the Bodies of Knowledge   260
Project management in practice: *It's a risky business*   262
Topics for discussion   263
Further information   264
References   265
Appendix: PERT factor tables   266

Managing the project process: the 4-D model
D3: Do it   269

11 Organising people in the project   270

Introduction   271
11.1   Teams   272
11.2   Structures   279
11.3   Managing people   283

Summary   288
Key terms   289
Relevant areas of the Bodies of Knowledge   289
Project management in practice: *Matrix management at Cardiff Bay
    Development Corporation*   290
Project management in practice: *Alternative options for problem solving –
    open innovation and crowdsourcing*   291
Topics for discussion   292
Further information   293
References   293

12 Leading people in projects 295

Introduction 296
12.1 Leadership in projects 297
12.2 Leading and motivation 300
12.3 Leading and you 306

Summary 312
Key terms 313
Relevant areas of the Bodies of Knowledge 313
Project management in practice: *Doesn't time fly?* 313
Topics for discussion 315
Further information 315
References 316

13 Monitoring and controlling the project 317

Introduction 318
13.1 The concepts of monitoring and control 319
13.2 Techniques of control 324
13.3 Limits of control 334

Summary 336
Key terms 337
Relevant areas of the Bodies of Knowledge 337
Project management in practice: *The Lifter project* 338
Topics for discussion 340
Further information 341
References 342

14 Procuring, contracting, and working with supply chains 343

Introduction 344
14.1 The supply chain 345
14.2 Purchasing and contracts 347
14.3 Modern approaches to supply chain management 355

Summary 360
Key terms 360
Relevant areas of the Bodies of Knowledge 360
Project management in practice: *Heathrow Terminal 5* 362
Topics for discussion 366
Further information 367
References 368

15 Problem-solving and decision-making 369

Introduction 370
15.1 Structuring problems 371
15.2 Problem analysis 377
15.3 Decision support 382

Summary 385
Key terms 386

Relevant areas of the Bodies of Knowledge   387
Project management in practice: *The use of cause–effect–cause analysis*   387
Topics for discussion   390
Further information   390
References   391

Managing the project process: the 4-D model
D4: Develop it   393

16 Completing projects and learning to improve   394

Introduction   395
16.1   Completion and handover   397
16.2   Reviews and learning   401
16.3   Improving and maturing   412

Summary   420
Key terms   421
Relevant areas of the Bodies of Knowledge   422
Project management in practice: *IT all goes pear-shaped at VCS*   423
Topics for discussion   428
Further information   428
References   429

Index   430

Publisher's acknowledgements   444

List of figures and tables

Figures

1.1	Project characteristics	7
1.2	Volume versus variety and projects	9
1.3	Project organisational structure (for internal project)	12
1.4	Innovation and maintenance activities in project and line management	13
2.1	Describing the project environment: the 5-C model	28
2.2	The project as a conversion process	31
2.3	Four phases of project lifecycle	34
2.4	Graph showing how level of activity varies with time	35
2.5	Graph of cumulative expenditure against time – the S-curve	36
2.6	Project lifecycle example from IDeA in Armenia	39
3.1	Organisational strategy process	59
3.2	Traditional versus strategic approaches	60
3.3	Projects and organisational strategy	62
3.4	Arrangements of projects in programmes	69
3.5	Basic project governance structure	71
3.6	Relationship between the project and the project office	72
3.7	Comparative size of Boeing 747 and Airbus A380	77
3.8	Sourcing the components of the A380	78
4.1	Stakeholder groups	88
4.2	Stakeholder grouping for World Cup 2022	89
4.3	Power: interest stakeholder map	94
4.4	Trade-offs in project management	96
4.5	Time priority project	96
4.6	Quality priority project	96
4.7	Cost priority project	97
4.8	Time AND quality priority	97
4.9	Benefits map for PPM capability improvement	101
4.10	Stakeholder map	104
4.11	Outline structure – University of Rummidge	106
5.1	Initial planning	111
5.2	Concept development in NPD	112
5.3	Scope creep	114
5.4	Balancing costs and benefits (1)	116
5.5	Balancing costs and benefits (2)	118
5.6	Activity model using ICOMs	119
5.7	The project planning process	120
5.8	Stage-gate model of projects	124
5.9	Conventional approach to new product development	128
5.10	Effect of miscommunication on new product development	128
5.11	Engineering activity	128
5.12	Sequential versus concurrent models for new product development	129
5.13	The use of FFM/DFC in planning the introduction of a new coating material	131
5.14	Work breakdown structure	136
5.15	Four fields map	137
5.16	Gantt chart	140

6.1	Core planning elements	147
6.2	Example of a work breakdown structure (WBS)	148
6.3	Organisational breakdown structure	149
6.4	Product breakdown structure	149
6.5	Task dependency	151
6.6	Logical activity linkages	152
6.7	Representing multiple dependencies (1)	152
6.8	Representing multiple dependencies (2)	152
6.9	Representing multiple dependencies (3)	153
6.10	Activity notation	153
6.11	Activity network with durations included	154
6.12	Results from the forward pass	155
6.13	Results of the forward and reverse passes	156
6.14	Completed network analysis including floats and highlighted critical path	156
6.15	Microsoft Project output	157
6.16	Schedule development process	158
6.17	Horizontal bar chart: Activity A starts at Time 1 and finishes at Time 3	159
6.18	Project plan in graphical form	160
6.19	Logical links indicated by arrows	161
6.20	Planning the launch of a new food project	166
7.1	Activity completion profiles – assumed and actual	173
7.2	Components of a time estimate	174
7.3	Activities completed in strict sequence	176
7.4	The effects of multi-tasking	176
7.5	Resource contention	179
7.6	Plan with resolved resource contention	180
7.7	Five focusing steps applied to projects	182
7.8	Buffering the feeder paths	185
7.9	APT implementation	188
7.10	Weekly project management process	191
7.11	Improvement effect throughout the project – Months 0–3	192
7.12	Improvement effect throughout the project – Months 6–9	192
8.1	Top-down and ground-up approaches to costing	199
8.2	Learning curve effects on time taken	203
8.3	Elements of cost	204
8.4	Cost build-up	205
8.5	NPV profile	210
8.6	NPV profile: large discount rate range	210
8.7	Multiple benefit and payment points	211
9.1	Bridge model of project quality management	226
9.2	Trade-off options	229
9.3	Quality planning process	231
9.4	RACI matrix	233
10.1	Risk management schema	246
10.2	Probability impact chart	250
10.3	Examples of the use of Monte Carlo analysis	253
10.4	Network showing optimistic, most probable and pessimistic times	254
10.5	Distribution of estimated times for an activity	255
11.1	Management silos	272
11.2	Classic hierarchical pyramid	273
11.3	Effectiveness profile of team lifecycle	276
11.4	Spectrum of team/group performance	278
11.5	Project organisation	279
11.6	Mixed organisational structure	282

11.7	The nine team roles	285
12.1	The role of leadership and management	298
12.2	Main theories of work motivation	301
12.3	Maslow's hierarchy of needs	303
12.4	Effects of time management on the behaviour of individuals	309
13.1	Basic model of cybernetic control	320
13.2	Instability	322
13.3	Stable system	322
13.4	Hierarchy of control systems	323
13.5	Buffer penetration	329
13.6	Bar chart showing work completed	333
13.7	Control limits applied to progress in budget spend	334
13.8	A summary of the project against the baseline set on 31 August 2020	339
13.9	Cost control curves for Lifter project	340
14.1	Scope of influence of purchasing, materials management and supply chain management	346
14.2	Example of a purchasing process for materials	348
14.3	Establishment of contracts	354
14.4	BAA's approach to risk	363
15.1	Systematic problem-solving model	372
15.2	Pareto analysis	378
15.3	Ishikawa/fishbone diagram applied to late delivery problem	379
15.4	Entity A	381
15.5	IF A THEN B	381
15.6	IF A THEN B AND C	381
15.7	IF A AND B THEN C	381
15.8	Logic diagram for Bill's performance	381
15.9	Decision tree: project X versus project Y	382
15.10	Force-field analysis on standing for election	384
15.11	Current reality tree	388
15.12	Future reality tree: selling effectiveness	389
16.1	Project knowledge framework (adapted from Turner et al., 2014)	402
16.2	Process improvement	403
16.3	Performance groups	414
16.4	The three pillars of change	416
16.5	Complex information flow around systems	419
16.6	Simplified information flow through system	419

Tables

1.1	Accidental profession or profession of choice?	11
1.2	Project versus general management	12
1.3	Historical development of project management	15
2.1	The 7-S of project management	30
2.2	The four phases of project management	35
2.3	Development of the project lifecycle	37
2.4	Supply of a management information system to a hospital project	37
2.5	Comparison of approach (adapted from Dybå and Dingsøyr, 2008)	41
2.6	The complexity framework	44
2.7	Assessing project complexity	45
2.8	The APM Body of Knowledge 7th edition (2019) and the relationship with topic coverage in this text	47
2.9	The PMI Body of Knowledge and the relationship with topic coverage in this text	48

3.1	Strategy deployment table	63
3.2	Definitions of 'programme' (PMI 'program')	68
3.3	Strategy matrix	70
3.4	PMO roles	73
3.5	Relevant areas of the APM Body of Knowledge	76
3.6	Decision matrix	80
4.1	Stakeholders, requirements and measures	86
4.2	Input, process and outcome requirements	90
4.3	New product development (NPD) metrics	90
4.4	Conventional versus participatory project monitoring and evaluation	91
4.5	Conformance versus performance: attributes of time, cost and quality	98
4.6	Relevant areas of the APM Body of Knowledge	103
4.7	Relevant areas of the PMI Body of Knowledge	103
5.1	Stage gate questions based on the IDeA Foundation	125
5.2	Relevant areas of the APM Body of Knowledge	133
5.3	Relevant areas of the PMI Body of Knowledge	133
5.4	Risk assessment and management	140
6.1	The nature, role and accuracy of estimate types	151
6.2	Relevant areas of the APM Body of Knowledge	164
6.3	Relevant areas of the PMI Body of Knowledge	164
6.4	Project activities, precedence and duration	168
6.5	Project activities, precedence and duration	168
7.1	Relevant areas of the APM Body of Knowledge	187
8.1	Improvement over time	204
8.2	Recommended cost uplift for different project types	215
8.3	Relevant areas of the APM Body of Knowledge	217
8.4	Relevant areas of the PMI Body of Knowledge	217
	Present value of £1	220
9.1	Perspectives on quality management	227
9.2	Manufacturing and service approaches to quality	231
9.3	Management of expectations and perceptions	235
9.4	Communication plan	235
9.5	Quality cost categories	236
9.6	Relevant area of the APM Body of Knowledge	239
9.7	Relevant areas of the PMI Body of Knowledge	239
10.1	Numerical analysis	251
10.2	Sensitivity analysis	252
10.3	Three-point estimates for tasks	255
10.4	Three-point estimates and variances for tasks	257
10.5	Probabilities of completing tasks	257
10.6	Relevant areas of the APM Body of Knowledge	260
10.7	Relevant areas of the PMI Body of Knowledge	260
10.8	Simple risk management table	262
	PERT factor tables	266
11.1	Team lifecycle	276
11.2	Requirements of team structure	278
11.3	Relating project structures to project objectives	281
11.4	Relevant areas of the APM Body of Knowledge	290
11.5	Relevant areas of the PMI Body of Knowledge	290
12.1	Time usage analysis	310
12.2	Techniques to keep to a plan	311
12.3	Relevant area of the APM Body of Knowledge	313
12.4	Relevant area of the PMI Body of Knowledge	313

13.1	Project overrun data	318
13.2	Tasks and budgets	326
13.3	Weekly plan	331
13.4	Weekly review	332
13.5	Relevant areas of the APM Body of Knowledge	337
13.6	Relevant areas of the PMI Body of Knowledge	337
14.1	Examples of supply chains	346
14.2	The advantages of centralised and localised purchasing	349
14.3	Adversarial versus partnership relationships	356
14.4	Relevant areas of the APM Body of Knowledge	361
14.5	Relevant areas of the PMI Body of Knowledge	361
15.1	The use of mathematical modelling techniques	378
15.2	Supplier selection using unweighted attributes	383
16.1	Review and audit criteria	410
16.2	Elements of quality cost	412
16.3	Project management maturity stages	414
16.4	Key change issues	416
16.5	Lean principles applied to project management	418
16.6	Relevant areas of the APM Body of Knowledge	422
16.7	Relevant areas of the PMI Body of Knowledge	422

Guided tour

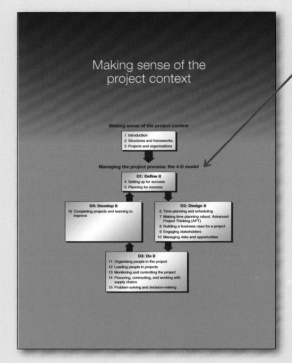

Each part opening page contains a **part diagram** mapping the structure of the book, which allows you to get a clear picture of how the book is set out and how each part and chapter in the book relates to each other.

A list of **Principles** sets forth and defines the fundamentals of what will be covered in the chapter.

A **chapter diagram** serves as a reminder of where you are in the book and the relation of the chapter to the other parts of the book.

A bulleted list of **Learning Objectives** will enable you to focus on what you can expect to learn from the chapter.

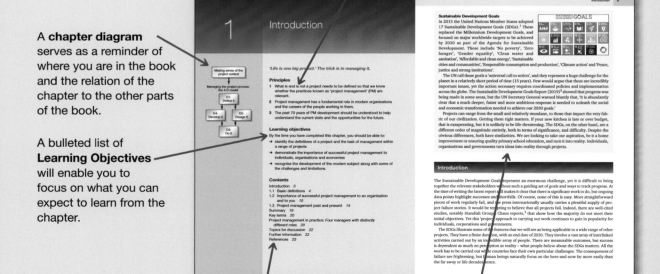

For quick and easy reference, a brief **Contents** list of the topics covered within each chapter with corresponding book page numbers is provided.

Short **Case Studies** explore the topics introduced in the chapter and enable you to put the information into context.

Real World boxes show how the theory discussed in the chapter relates to and can be applied to cases in the real world.

To help you consolidate your learning, the **Summary** section reflects on what the chapter has covered and provides an important revision tool.

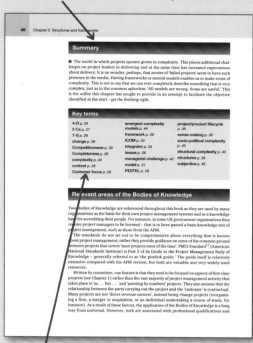

The **Key Terms** list is another useful revision aid and helps you create a bank of essential terminology.

Project Management in Practice boxes at the end of the chapter provide you with a practical function of the points learned throughout the chapter.

Topics for Discussion offer a set of useful questions and tasks for self-assessment and revision.

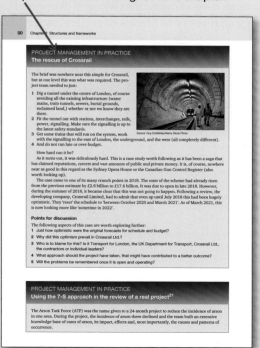

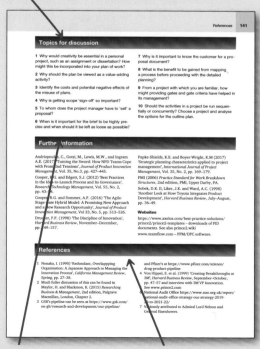

Further Information and **References** suggest books, websites and journals that may be of interest to you; information about the references used throughout the chapter is brought together here.

Preface

Projects are hugely important to the world. Our recent analysis showed that global annual spend on projects is in the region of US$22 trillion. For countries, whether it is delivering on climate change or any other aspect of policy, projects are the means by which society changes. For organisations, the success or otherwise of their projects will provide key determinants of their futures. And for individuals, either leading or contributing to projects is almost certain to feature at least once in their career, even if it is not their specialism.

The first edition of this book was published in 1996. Back then, the title was obvious as it reflected the thinking of the time – projects needed managing, we had a growing group of people who were identifiable project managers, and 'Project Management' was the 'field' in which we worked. The world, our thinking about it, and how we operate in it, have all changed significantly. Today, the title of so many courses is still 'Project Management' but our field is widely known as 'Project Studies', reflecting a broadening of the interests of those involved in the field. We could entitle this book 'realising strategy' or 'delivering benefits' or 'leading change'. Regrettably, we cannot change the title but this doesn't mean that we don't recognise that leadership in projects is active – and it should be a verb, not a noun.

Since the last edition, our thinking has developed, our analysis gets more powerful, our databases of experience fuller. Projects are not just process sets, but human systems of activity. In addition, I am reminded that a synonym for 'project' is 'enterprise'. The original promises of project management included delivering both discipline and enterprise. It is notable how often the very skills of the entrepreneur are needed, but neither recognised nor developed. I trust that this will come through here, showing that we need to respond to the complexities inherent in projects through all three of our facets of project leadership: managerial, relational AND entrepreneurial.

Finally, this 5th edition was very close to not happening. The level of copyright theft experienced with the fourth edition obliterated any financial rationale for spending many hundreds of hours updating the content. Fortunately, my co-author believed in the project and was prepared to look beyond this. Neil – you are a star!

We wish you great projects. After all, they are hugely important.

Harvey Maylor
Oxford
August 2021

Acknowledgements

We wish to acknowledge the many individuals, events and conversations that have had an impact on the thinking reflected here. Many of the individuals are participants on our programmes, whose willingness to question and share insights is always so much appreciated and both energises and supports the ongoing development of our work. Events such as the pandemic have raised great questions about the very way that we work and conversations around the future of the field always raise so many possibilities.

We are immensely grateful to all of the contributors to this edition. Mark Winter from Manchester Business School, Anne Live Vaagaasar from BI Norway and Cuong Quang from Octant AI deserve special mention.

Making sense of the
project context

Making sense of the project context

> 1 Introduction
> 2 Structures and frameworks
> 3 Projects and organisations

Managing the project process: the 4-D model

> **D1: Define it**
> 4 Setting up for success
> 5 Planning for success

D4: Develop it
16 Completing projects and learning to improve

D2: Design it
> 6 Time planning and scheduling
> 7 Making time planning robust: Advanced Project Thinking (APT)
> 8 Building a business case for a project
> 9 Engaging stakeholders
> 10 Managing risks and opportunities

D3: Do it
> 11 Organising people in the project
> 12 Leading people in projects
> 13 Monitoring and controlling the project
> 14 Procuring, contracting, and working with supply chains
> 15 Problem-solving and decision-making

1 Introduction

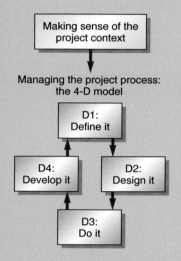

Making sense of the project context

Managing the project process: the 4-D model

D1: Define it

D4: Develop it

D2: Design it

D3: Do it

'Life is one big project.' The trick is in managing it.

Principles

1 What is and is not a project needs to be defined so that we know whether the practices known as 'project management' (PM) are relevant.

2 Project management has a fundamental role in modern organisations and the careers of the people working in them.

3 The past 70 years of PM development should be understood to help understand the current state and the opportunities for the future.

Learning objectives

By the time you have completed this chapter, you should be able to:

→ identify the definitions of a project and the task of management within a range of projects

→ demonstrate the importance of successful project management to individuals, organisations and economies

→ recognise the development of the modern subject along with some of the challenges and limitations.

Contents

Introduction   *3*
1.1 Basic definitions   *4*
1.2 Importance of successful project management to an organisation and to you   *10*
1.3 Project management past and present   *14*
Summary   *19*
Key terms   *20*
Project management in practice: *Four managers with distinctly different roles*   *20*
Topics for discussion   *22*
Further information   *22*
References   *23*

Sustainable Development Goals

In 2015 the United Nations Member States adopted 17 Sustainable Development Goals (SDGs).[1] These replaced the Millennium Development Goals, and focused on major worldwide targets to be achieved by 2030 as part of the Agenda for Sustainable Development. These include 'No poverty', 'Zero hunger', 'Gender equality', 'Clean water and sanitation', 'Affordable and clean energy', 'Sustainable cities and communities', 'Responsible consumption and production', 'Climate action' and 'Peace, justice and strong institutions'.

The UN call these goals a 'universal call to action', and they represent a huge challenge for the planet in a relatively short period of time (15 years). Few would argue that these are incredibly important issues, yet the action necessary requires coordinated policies and implementation across the globe. The Sustainable Development Goals Report (2019)[2] showed that progress was being made in some areas, but the UN Secretary General warned bluntly that, 'It is abundantly clear that a much deeper, faster and more ambitious response is needed to unleash the social and economic transformation needed to achieve our 2030 goals.'

Projects can range from the small and relatively mundane, to those that impact the very fabric of our civilization. Getting them right matters. If your new kitchen is late or over budget, that is exasperating, but it is unlikely to be life-threatening. The SDGs, on the other hand, are a different order of magnitude entirely, both in terms of significance, and difficulty. Despite the obvious differences, both have similarities. We are looking to take our aspiration, be it a home improvement or ensuring quality primary school education, and turn it into reality. Individuals, organisations and governments turn ideas into reality through projects.

Introduction

The Sustainable Development Goals represent an enormous challenge, yet it is difficult to bring together the relevant stakeholders without such a guiding set of goals and ways to track progress. At the time of writing the latest report still makes it clear that there is significant work to do, but ongoing data points highlight successes and shortfalls. Of course, none of this is easy. More straightforward pieces of work regularly fail, and the press internationally usually carries a plentiful supply of project failure stories. It would be tempting to believe that all projects fail. Indeed, there are well-cited studies, notably Standish Group's Chaos reports,[3] that show how the majority do not meet their initial objectives. Yet this 'project' approach to carrying out work continues to gain in popularity for individuals, corporations and governments.

The SDGs illustrate some of the features that we will see as being applicable to a wide range of other projects. They have a finite duration, with an end date of 2030. They involve a vast array of interlinked activities carried out by an incredible array of people. There are measurable outcomes, but success is dependent as much on perception as reality – what people *believe* about the SDGs matters. All the work has to be carried out while countries face their own particular challenges. The consequences of failure are frightening, but human beings naturally focus on the here-and-now far more easily than the far away or life decades hence.

We will explore success and failure and some of the reasons for each in future chapters. For now, this is a good example of the art and science of managing a project and the importance of projects in general to the world in which we live. The nature of the SDGs means that many forms of innovation are required by the individuals and project teams involved. In later chapters we will address the many opportunities as well as the challenges that come with projects.

In this chapter, we will begin with **definition**, stating what constitutes 'a project' and 'project management'. This is vital as it is possible, quite literally, to frame almost any activity as a project. Indeed, we can go as far as to say that the opening quotation of 'Life is one big project' – 'life' does fit many of the accepted definitions of 'a project'. The challenge is more aptly stated as 'finding what is not a project' so that it is possible to discuss with some clarity the range of human activity that this covers. In the case of organising work to support the sustainability goals, there are many issues that require significant coordination. We will explore the role of a project manager in outline here and the careers of project managers. Second, projects are important. They represent a significant part of all economic activity, being important to the individuals who carry them out, their organisations and, in many cases, society as a whole. Lastly, project management as a subject is developing fast. By understanding its history and the opportunities for the future development of this subject, we hope to show that rather than being fixed, pre-determined or staid, there is a lively conversation around how we should run projects in the future that is worth joining, as we certainly do not have all 'the answers' and as the statistics show, there are plenty of problems for projects.

1.1 Basic definitions

Does it matter what activities do and do not constitute **projects**? Almost any activity can be claimed to be a project. One practitioner put it to us very simply: '*a project is whatever I call a project*'. One step on from this is the most basic of accepted definitions: *a project is a task that has a beginning and an end*. This is insufficient, as the two examples below will demonstrate.

Environmental health manager

The role of the environmental health department in a local authority (a county council in this case) includes visiting food premises (restaurants, cafés, school canteens and mobile catering outlets) to determine whether the practices that they are following in the preparation, storage and serving of food meet legal requirements. Inspectors have considerable powers (including closure of the premises) where deficiencies are identified. The manager of the department was convinced that he was a project manager. Each inspection lasted for several hours and was, therefore, an activity with a start and a finish. QED in his view it was a project.

Delivery Team leader – UK Ministry of Defence – ship procurement

The prime role of the team leader is the management of the process from initial concept or identification of a requirement for a new capability, through the stages of approval, development, delivery into service, ongoing maintenance and finally disposal. The role is central to integrating the requirements (both current and future) of users, while making sure any equipment is compatible with other technology being used across the military. The provision of what is termed *through-life support* is vital, with upgrade paths being required for all equipment. The duration of the project was that of the ship. In the words of one team leader: '. . . end to end, this is a 60-year project.'

Both an inspection and the ship's life have a beginning and an end. However, it is not useful to define either of these as projects. Consider the requirements for managing each of these tasks. The first is relatively straightforward and would not require the input from the kind of approaches that will be discussed as 'project management' – they would simply be too cumbersome and costly for such a task. The process that was followed each time (arrange visit, visit, report and follow up) was the same and each inspector was visiting one or two premises a day. This was **operations** rather than project **management**.

It was, however, only one part of that manager's role. Other parts included planning and executing the response to public health issues, such as an outbreak of a particular disease (e-coli poisoning, for example). These were fortunately rare events and each one had its own characteristics. They also had to be pre-planned, so that no time was wasted when they did occur. Other projects included regular initiatives to highlight particular aspects of public health – such as an autumn campaign of promoting influenza vaccination. The role of this manager was therefore split between the **general management** associated with the ongoing activities and the project management of both initiatives and reactions to 'crises'. He was advised to look to operations management as a subject to help with the management of the day-to-day tasks, but to build a relevant knowledge base and set of practices for the projects he ran.

The second case is a hugely complex task that will change significantly in nature over the 60-year period. Each part (e.g. designing the ship, building it, trials, hand-over, maintenance, refurbishing and disposal) is a project or series of projects in its own right, with each project needing appropriate management. This task is clearly very different from that of the inspections.

It clearly does matter what we call projects, as when they have to be managed, it is useful to know something about the approach that should be taken to the management task. To help clarify this task, a comparison of the following definitions is useful.

> Association for Project Management (UK's largest professional body for project managers), 2019: A unique, transient endeavour undertaken to bring about change and to achieve planned objectives.

> Project Management Institute (one of the world's largest professional associations), 2017: A project is a temporary endeavour undertaken to create a unique product, service or result.

> British Standard 6079, 2019: Temporary management environment, usually undertaken in phases, created for the purpose of delivering one or more business outputs or outcomes.

> PRINCE2 2017 (PRojects IN Controlled Environments – UK government standard for project management): A temporary organisation that is created for the purpose of delivering one or more business products according to an agreed business case.

Some common themes are evident here:

1 **Unique**: the exact project has not been performed before. The project has a degree of novelty, in terms of time, place, team carrying out the task, product or service being provided. However, something like it has almost certainly been done by someone somewhere before. For this reason, projects are said to have *aspects of uniqueness*.
2 **Temporary**: the project does have a beginning and an end, as in our earlier definition, and requires a group of people to carry out the task (the establishment of a temporary organisation). When the project finishes, the team moves on. The financial resources available to the project are also temporary and almost always finite – when the project is completed the funding ceases.
3 **Focused**: the task of the project is to deliver a particular product, service or result (the specific mission). This is not to say that every project starts out with a complete and clear idea of exactly what will be achieved and how.

PRINCE2 2017 says that projects require the production of a specific **business case**. While this is evident in many organisations (and required for UK government-funded information technology (IT) projects), there are still many areas where this is not appropriate. For instance, when an earthquake and subsequent tsunami struck the Fukushima Daiichi nuclear power plant in March 2011, disabling the cooling systems for the plant, it started the second worst nuclear disaster in history. In addition to the task of bringing the reactors back under control, was the humanitarian project to help people (mainly local residents) whose lives had been changed forever by the disaster. There was not the time to prepare a business case and indeed, given no financial return was envisaged, it is inappropriate to use this term, and the more generic notion of achieving a particular **mission** is more useful. It is useful to look further than this, with the mission being a means to an end. We say that projects are undertaken to **deliver benefits**. This characteristic is evident in both commercial and non-commercial projects.

In many relief projects, both for this disaster and others, relief workers often remark that, 'We don't know what we will encounter until we get there.' This illustrates a further characteristic of many projects – that of **emergence**. The high-level benefits that the projects were undertaking were known (save lives), but the exact objectives and means to achieve them could be determined only once a certain amount of work had been done. These included assessments of the needs of different groups of people (for instance, some needed medical treatment, others needed shelter). Not all standards and processes recognise this emergence. The language in PRINCE2 (*delivering business products according to an agreed business case*) is inappropriate when the urgent requirement is to save lives. The exact timescale, budget and tasks are all unknown at the outset, but project management is still very much appropriate in addressing the evolving situation. Although disaster relief is an extreme example, it is a fact that many projects start with a limited or high-level view of what will constitute their performance measures and it is quite normal for such criteria to evolve as the project progresses.

Related to this characteristic, **uncertainty** is another fundamental of projects. The future cannot be predicted with certainty, and in many cases nor can the response to activities carried out in a project. Where emergence referred to the requirements of the project, uncertainty covers all of the environmental conditions in which a project has to operate. For instance, there may be uncertainty about costs of people or materials, or whether some part of the project is indeed achievable. We may not know how long tasks being undertaken for the first time will take. All of these provide the project manager with a major challenge: how they will work with such uncertainty.

A recent extreme example of this was the Covid-19 pandemic of 2020. Managers' plans across the world were thrown into turmoil by the crisis. The immediate concern was, of course, to safeguard lives, but projects were suddenly faced with massive uncertainty. Economies were being put on hold, throwing business cases into disarray. How long would this last? Weeks, months? Would the project still be viable afterwards? No one really knew. Hotels or restaurants in the middle of construction became somewhat more doubtful as the leisure and tourism industries ceased to function. As we will see within this book, there is a need both to plan the project and control the work so that it meets that plan, yet also a requirement to adapt to new circumstances should the situation need it. This can be a delicate balancing act, requiring both an inward focus on doing the work, while simultaneously looking out at the wider environment. Developing this judgement is important for a successful project manager.

In addition to having uncertainty, projects have another characteristic – they usually involve **change**. It used to be the case that an IT project such as an organisation adopting cloud computing would be viewed as a technical implementation of a new computer-based system. It is more usual now to consider it as an *IT-enabled change* project – the change brought about by any new system goes beyond the technology, to impact the way that people work.[4]

The change issue leads us to another facet of projects – they are not machines but are groups of people carrying out a (hopefully linked) set of tasks. We say that unlike a machine that is real and tangible, a project is a **social construction** – it was literally devised by people. It involves people and systems of people, both in the project team and associated with the project as customers, for instance. It is intangible. This has implications for the way that we consider projects.[5] For instance, treating a project as a mechanical system that responds easily to changes may be inappropriate. Because there are people and groups of people involved, there are going to be complex, dynamic interactions between those people and groups. The 'people challenge' is likely to be harder if the work includes a high level of uncertainty and emergence, as this implies a lack of stability which people can find unsettling.

It is not just people though that interact through a project. Sometimes major changes need to include the integration of the major, distinct, elements. Consider the introduction of electric vehicles to replace petrol cars. There is an underlying technical challenge in developing the technology (e.g. obtaining sufficient driving range from the batteries), yet this needs to be considered in light of the bigger picture. Electric vehicles need an appropriate charging infrastructure if they are to be adopted. Cars without a widely available charging network will remain a niche market, but neither governments nor private providers are keen to invest in a major network roll-out without a clear view of how many users they need to support. The growth of infrastructure needs to be in line with demand – if there is always a queue at the local charging points then few will upgrade their car. The incentives need to be aligned so that consumers are offered solutions that are practical. This needs to include the vehicle, its operation, and ongoing support such as servicing. If the change as a whole does not appeal, the new technology will not be adopted. Uncertainty is a major factor here, and although organisations will develop plans, these may need to be modified in light of events as they unfold.

The characteristics and their implications are shown in Figure 1.1. They either describe the nature of the task (aspects of uniqueness, mission focused, involving change, having

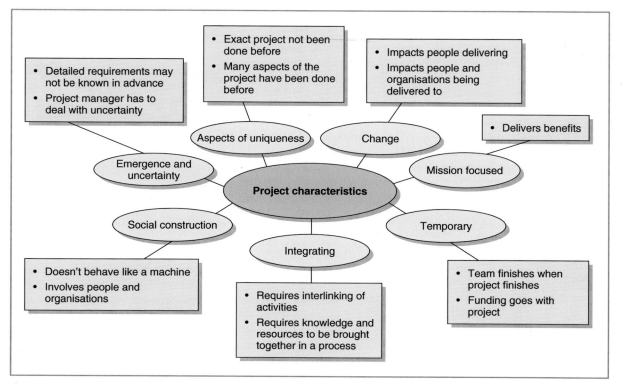

Figure 1.1 Project characteristics

emergence and uncertainty) or the means by which it is delivered (through a temporary organisation, which is a social construction involving integration). Further exploration of the means for delivery shows that this is rarely entirely random and that managers use combinations or systems of activities, people and organisations to deliver the project. Such a system of delivery is termed a **process**. The process is the main unit of analysis here.

A project as a process

The characteristics described above are useful to determine what is and is not a project. Further description of a project comes from analysing the system of delivery, including consideration of how activities in the project are identified, planned and executed, and how issues such as change and uncertainty are handled by the project team.

There are significant advantages to considering projects in this way (see Real World box).

A basic classification of processes considers **volume** and **variety**.[6] Volume is the quantity of throughput for that process. For a petrochemical plant, this is very high, whereas for a chauffeur service, it is low. The variety is the number of different variations of process possible. For instance, a petrochemical process is likely to have relatively little flexibility, while for a small operation such as the chauffeur service, the process will have far more flexibility to respond to the needs of individual passengers.

The relationship between volume and variety is shown in Figure 1.2. As you can see, there is generally an inverse relationship between volume and variety. For example, a noodle bar has a high-volume, low-variety process – it provides a high volume of products with very limited variety in the process for preparing the noodles and serving the customers. A strategic management consultancy, meanwhile, may operate at the other end of the scale, providing a low volume of services, with the process tailored to the needs of each client, and is therefore a high-variety process.

REAL WORLD   Benefits of the application of process thinking

It is now possible to build a McDonald's drive-through restaurant in just 24 hours. One project went from 'clear site' to 'open for business' in less than 48 hours, including foundations. Whatever your views of the proliferation of these outlets, they do represent a good case of what can be achieved when the true level of uniqueness of a project is assessed. The contractors who actually build the outlets are Yorkon and Britspace, and they have done so over 300 times in the UK alone. If each one had been considered to be a unique project, then we could reasonably expect the build time to be very long – months would be completely normal for such a space to be constructed. Recognising that

Source: Mark Richardson/Alamy

this was likely to be a project that was repeated meant that it was worth the companies investing in finding ways to improve the *process*. So, instead of trying to build a unique store on each site, the firms considered the opportunities for making the building *modular* and *manufacturing* the modules off site. One store typically consists of six modules and these are shipped to the site and 'assembled' on site, rather than involving traditional building techniques. Each time it was done, the processes for carrying this out could be improved.

Source: Alex Segre/Alamy

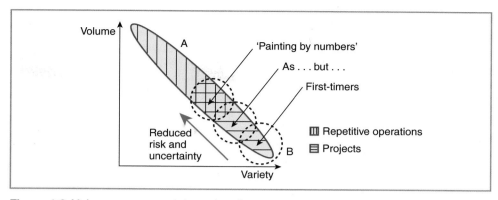

Figure 1.2 Volume versus variety and projects

The traditional project management area is low-volume, high-variety processes, where the notion of *uniqueness* prevails. These are indicated on the figure as **first-timers**. Examples of these are the first moon landing and the development of the first computer. It is noticeable with the wider adoption of project management that individuals and organisations are running projects, often over time periods as short as a few weeks or months, and that these are being carried out on a regular basis as part of ordinary business activity. Here, the end product may be different, but the process by which it is delivered is often repeated over time. Two further scenarios are identified here. The first is where there is some similarity to previous work, in terms of either the process followed or the product being delivered. These are referred to in Figure 1.2 as '**as . . . but . . .** 's, that is, *as* the job we did last time, *but* with the following differences. The second of these is where there is a high degree of commonality in both process and outcome. These are termed **painting by numbers** projects[7] because the process and the outcome are well known. The project team has the task of following the path to the required outcome. Projects such as carrying out a financial audit of a company will be project-based, but the processes and the outcomes (a set of reports and accounts) are well known in advance. Marketing research projects are similarly painting by numbers projects in many instances and the construction of the drive-through also fits in this category.[8]

Moving away from considering all projects as first-timers can be beneficial. The more like repetitive operations a project is, the less the risk and uncertainty. This is certainly the view from many organisations who prefer the relative reliability that can come from projects that are 'painting by numbers'. However, it can be a considerable challenge for many project managers to agree that their project is a 'painting by numbers.' There is something about projects that are first-timers that many managers will insist on, possibly for the allure of the more complex, difficult or risky, and therefore their skills as project managers need to be appreciated.

The two example projects used earlier in this section are classified as shown in Figure 1.2. The environmental health 'projects' are at the point marked 'A' on the diagram, in the region where the primary area of interest is in *repetitive operations* rather than projects. The 60-year product lifecycle 'project' is marked at point B, similarly outside the *projects* area.

For the purpose of this book, a project is from one of the three of the categories of projects from Figure 1.2. However, the nature of the work may not always be as evident as we would like. Sometimes it is not completely clear whether a particular undertaking is a project or repetitive operations. Take, for example, training to win the Hawaii Ironman Triathlon World Championships, quite likely the most gruelling sport going. The 2.4-mile swim, 112-mile bike leg and 26.2 mile marathon will tax even the strongest athlete. Chrissie Wellington has won this race four times, smashing numerous records in the process, and the event will be the focus of many athletes' training over the year. Is that a project? Probably. Next consider Serena Williams, winner of 23 Grand Slam tennis singles titles. Is each Grand Slam a different project? Likely not. They will be scheduled and planned for, but as part of the annual cycle. These athletes are among the greatest of all time and have been hugely successful in their chosen sports. Ultimately, we need to focus on the work being done and the outcomes we achieve from our projects, rather than worrying unduly about specific labels. There is a great deal of (sometimes rather esoteric) debate about the classification of different pieces of work. This can indeed be interesting, but the value is in the work that we do and the benefits we deliver, not necessarily what we choose to call it.

1.2 Importance of successful project management to an organisation and to you

For many organisations, projects are fundamental to the way they operate. The major management consultancies earn over 90 per cent of their revenues from projects. Whole sectors of industry are **project-based organisations** (PBOs), including much of the engineering and construction sectors, consultancy, many public-sector bodies and much of the IT industry. Construction alone makes up in the region of 8 per cent of gross domestic product in the European Union. Government, from local up to European Union level, carries out a significant proportion of its business through projects. Projects are central to our economies. So, just how important are they to an organisation? The Real World box demonstrates the extent of the impact of project performance to one organisation.

An APM report[9] in 2019 looked at the contribution of projects to the UK economy. Their data showed over 2 million full-time equivalent workers (7.9 per cent of UK employment) and over £150 billion of gross value added (GVA), representing 8.9 per cent of UK GVA. Economically, it is estimated that project activity comprises c.35 per cent of GDP for some countries,[10] an indication that this is a significant field of activity. Nonetheless, numerous industry bodies regularly lament that there is a shortage of project managers, indicating that there will be a demand for project management skills for the foreseeable future.

The economic impact of project management is undeniable, but there is more to it than just the numbers. It is not overstating it to say that project managers make the world a better place. They do vital work, be it in the building of key infrastructure, developing new products, implementing public policies, or helping disaster zones recover. This is important, meaningful, work that improves real people's lives. Managers we work with are proud of what they do, and rightly so. Doing it well brings benefits to people faster and more cost effectively. This is hugely positive and personally rewarding, but it is not always easy.

Projects and you – from accidental to professional PM

Who are these 'project managers'? There is one group which has the title – these are relatively easy to identify. Others examples are not so obvious. Organising a festival or a sporting event is a project (Glastonbury in the UK, Oktoberfest in Germany, Tour de France). Festival organisers may not give themselves the title of 'project manager', but many recognise the skills base is highly appropriate for what they have to do. Similarly, for the medical consultant given the job of managing the opening of a new local hospital, or a politician the job of launching a new policy, PM is core to what they are doing.

For many years PM was regarded as the **accidental profession** – people got into it by accident. Typical in this respect is the scenario described in Table 1.1. This role change,

REAL WORLD   Sometimes, it takes more than projects . . .

The product that has led to the revival of Apple Inc's fortunes is the iconic iPhone. Launched in 2007, like most new products its development was managed through a *portfolio* of work – that is, a coordinated set of projects with a common goal. These included:

1 The development of the hardware – from the electronics to the 'look and feel' of the product. The phone itself is refreshed regularly with new features, and is now accompanied by a range of complementary products including the iPad and the Apple Watch.
2 The development of the software – the user interface, and the firmware. Again, this is updated regularly to add functionality.
3 The production set-up – tooling up to produce prototypes to production of the final product and its subsequent upgrades. This now extends to a complex worldwide supply chain and outsourced production capability.
4 Establishing the product *ecosystem* – the success of the product (and its derivatives) was dependent upon the content that could be loaded onto it and this has developed significantly over time. Apps, music, films, a network of content creators – all of these add value. The newest incarnations of the hardware offer far more than the original iPhone (and its predecessor, the iPod), yet the fundamental offering remains similar.

Source: New Africa/Shutterstock

5 The marketing – from identification of market needs to promotion of the product.

This is not all within Apple's control. The evolution of the wireless networks on which the iPhone operates (now at fifth generation, or 5G) enables vastly more, and faster, data than in 2007. The product evolution is to some extent dependent upon this wider innovation so that new services can be designed and released.

While all of these aspects had to function together for the original product to be a success at its launch, the collaboration and the projects did not stop there. In order to keep up with a highly innovative and competitive market, there needed to be continual refreshing of the product, new versions and cost-reduction projects on the existing versions. Ability to deliver this depends on Apple Inc's ability to manage its projects, not just the ethos or brand image of the firm. This is not only dependent upon its internal competence, but also on the ability to manage a multitude of external suppliers. In addition, Apple both drives and responds to wider industry innovation (e.g. payment systems, and ongoing changing consumer expectations and behaviour). What will this look like in five or ten years? It is unclear. So although long-term plans need to be made, these need to be flexible enough to respond to world events and technology trends as they unfold.

Table 1.1 Accidental profession or profession of choice?

Accidental profession	*Profession of choice*
Engineering Projects Manager:	IT Programme Manager:
'I did my degree in engineering and all my professional exams to get chartered. I still really want to be an engineer – it's the technology that I find really interesting. But I was in the office one day and the MD walks in – "You OK to manage this next project?" he says. Couldn't really say no.'	'I started as a technical specialist, but was frustrated at how fast we could move things along and so really wanted to be running the project. I did my first PM professional qualification and then joined the programme management office. After a short time as a planner, I moved into project management. I did further management qualifications while working and recently championed our change programme on excellence in project management.'

from a technical role (in this case, engineering, but could equally well be from marketing, finance, IT, managerial or any technical specialism) to a project management role, used to be a transition that you were expected to achieve, often with little by way of development and support. But this has changed. For instance, during the 1990s, around 10 per cent of a class group of practicing managers being taught would have participated in formal training on project management. Today, it is more likely that most of the group will have that.

So how does this **project management career** fit with the traditional career path structure?

PM and line management

Figure 1.3 shows a conventional management hierarchy, with the lines representing lines of reporting or responsibility. At the head of each of the major functions or departments within an organisation there will be functional or line managers. These managers have the responsibility for the people who work under them in their departments.

A project manager may have a line-management role as well, but is responsible for projects that may run across several functions. The figure shows the project manager being responsible for people drawn from every function in their activities in relation to that project. As we will see in later chapters, this is only one type of project organisational structure. Projects also take place within single functions and across multiple organisations. The example of this internal project begins to illustrate the kind of organisational challenges that project managers face – having to work across internal organisational boundaries.

The project manager's role differs from that of the line manager in the nature of the task being carried out. Table 1.2 establishes the major differences.

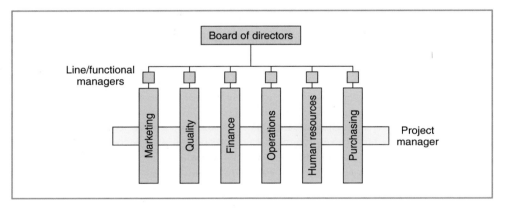

Figure 1.3 Project organisational structure (for internal project)

Table 1.2 Project versus general management

General management	Project management
● Responsible for managing the status quo	● Responsible for overseeing change
● Authority defined by management structure	● Lines of authority 'fuzzy'
● Consistent set of tasks	● Ever-changing set of tasks
● Responsibility limited to their own function	● Responsibility for cross-functional activities
● Works in 'permanent' organisational structures	● Operates within structures which exist for the life of the project
● Tasks described as 'maintenance'	● Predominantly concerned with innovation
● Main task is optimisation	● Main task is the resolution of conflict
● Success determined by achievement of interim targets	● Success determined by achievement of stated end-goals
● Limited set of variables	● Contains intrinsic uncertainties

As Figure 1.4 shows, the split between tasks that can be considered as **maintenance** (maintaining the status quo) and **innovation** is changing. In the figure, the trend is for the line AB to move downwards – increasing the degree of innovation activities required from line managers. The result of this is a change in the role of line managers and a reduction in the difference in the roles of line and project managers. Indeed, as already stated, this blurring of project management into general management provides for considerable confusion. Reference back to the definitions of projects will show those activities that are and are not project-based. Table 1.2 illustrates this.

Many managers today have both project-management and line-management responsibility and it is frequently quoted that the project-related proportion is in excess of 50 per cent of their time. Their line responsibilities (finance, marketing, design) involve them in a variety of day-to-day activities plus longer-term projects. The skills and techniques used in the line-management function will differ from those required in projects, as we shall see. The more enlightened organisations will provide a basic skills grounding in the best ways to run projects, and help, coach and mentor individuals in recognising and developing their project roles.

Lastly, there are many other professional roles associated with the project manager. We see many organisations using project management offices (as in Table 1.1) or project support offices. These are additional functions, often included in the organisation in the same manner as another internal function, alongside human resources, operations, finance and marketing. This gives recognition to the importance and prevalence of the roles required to support projects, described further in the next chapter. Indeed, we have seen four distinct career paths emerge in this area:

1 **Project manager.**
2 **Programme manager.**
3 **Project or Programme support office manager.**
4 **Portfolio manager.**

For a project manager, the addition of a project-management function in this way provides a route for promotion as they develop their skills, knowledge and experience in managing projects. Without this, there is seen to be little continuity in the careers of project managers and crucial knowledge can leave with a manager when a project is completed. Career development could lead to positions of project director, programme manager, senior responsible owner, sponsor and others (we will be looking at these roles in more detail in future chapters). However, it is clear that the main career paths do require fundamentally different skillsets and approaches to managing.[11]

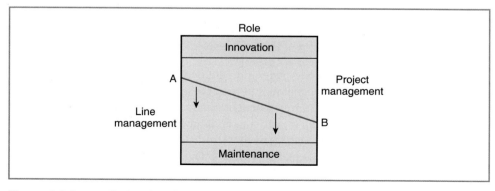

Figure 1.4 Innovation and maintenance activities in project and line management

1.3   Project management past and present

History

History should provide us with lessons that we can draw upon to improve our management of the present and the future. That is, we should be able to learn from how humans have managed projects since the start of civilisation. Projects are rarely totally unique and should avoid repeating the mistakes of the past.[12] However, there appears to be relatively little that has been gleaned from millennia of this type of human activity – great construction projects, movements of people, engineering achievements and so forth. Perhaps the evidence is there, just without obvious signs and indicators to the provenance of the ideas that are so accepted today as 'project management'.

There are other explanations for the apparent lack of learning. For one, the constraints are hardly the same today as they were. One very successful civilisation – the Roman Empire – did not have the same resource constraints that project managers face today. As one historian pointed out, if they wanted any more resources to complete their projects, they simply had to go and conquer the region that had those resources and take them. Maybe this is more reminiscent of industrial practice today than we credit . . . In later history, we see that project timescales were much longer and expectations were much less. For instance, construction of some of Europe's great churches was accomplished over many decades or longer. Lastly, we do have a 'survivor bias' for projects carried out by our ancestors – we do not find so much evidence of their failures as of their successes.

For the present, the most identifiable influences on project management come from work carried out in the 1950s. Obviously, small- and large-scale projects were undertaken before the 1950s. Individuals managed events and other situations. The Pyramids were constructed, wars were fought and products were developed, but not formalised as a 'project management process' until this time. Table 1.3 shows the progression of ideas in this area – from first-generation processes, developed for large engineering projects during the 1950s to the 1980s, through the development of a much wider range of approaches for many different projects in the 1990s, through to the third- and now fourth- and fifth-generation processes of today. The features of each **generation of project practices** are described.

During the 1950s, formal tools and techniques were developed to help manage large, complex projects that were uncertain or risky. The chemical manufacturer Du Pont developed techniques (critical path analysis (CPA) – see Chapter 6) for scheduling maintenance shutdowns at the company's production facilities. In the same period, the defence contractor RAND Corp. created its tool (Programme Evaluation and Review Technique or PERT) for planning missile development. These tools focused almost exclusively on the project-planning phase and there were no close rivals for their use. The methods survived and became accepted practice. The principles of these will be the subject of the discussion in Chapter 7.

The second-generation PM became evident in the 1990s, with an expanded array of tools and techniques beyond those of the first-generation processes. This was accompanied by the development of standards for PM processes in the US and Europe. Leading the development of such standards have been the major professional associations – specifically the Project Management Institute (PMI) in the US and the Association for Project Management (APM) in the UK. The International Project Management Association (IPMA) was founded in the 1960s as a networking group and since then has taken a greater coordinating role between over 70 national professional bodies from around the world. The emergence of PM as a recognised profession with definable knowledge requirements to enter the profession began.

Table 1.3 Historical development of project management

Time	Development	Generation
Pre-1950s	No generally accepted methods or recognised processes. Much industry-specific custom and practice	
1950s	Development of planning processes and numerical methods for quantifying uncertainty in high-profile, military projects, predominantly in the US	First-generation PM
1960s	Further development of techniques and wider acceptance of their application. 1965 IPMA, 1969 PMI founded	
1970s	Recognition of role of project manager in large-scale projects, formation of UK's APM (as now known)	
1980s	Continued interest in project management as a formalised means to manage large-scale engineering and construction projects	
1990s	Increasing recognition of role of **standards** in many industries and the profession as a whole, more work undertaken called projects[13] beyond engineering and construction. PMI and APM publish their **Bodies of Knowledge**[14]	Second-generation PM
2000s	Widespread acceptance of need for developing PM, burgeoning consultancy sector, further professionalisation including minimum standards required for taking the role of a project manager, development of ideas beyond traditional tools and techniques.[15] Rethinking project management takes place.[16] Development of lean and agile approaches to PM. Programme management becoming norm in organisations	Third-generation PM
2010s	Building on the previous generations, it is now acknowledged that contextually-dependent approaches to PM are more important than one-size-fits-all. New challenges posed by working in the cloud, crowdsourcing and increasing use of groups without formal coordination mechanisms. Technology revising traditional approaches	Fourth-generation PM
2020s	Integrating agile (an iterative approach to organising a project) and waterfall (a step-wise approach) (see Chapter 2). Development of project leaders and project entrepreneurs as well as project managers. Greater integration of different approaches (lean, agile, theory of constraints). Identification and better management of complexity. Use of AI and systems to guide planning and help to manage project data. These ideas are discussed in later chapters	Fifth-generation PM

The third-generation processes recognised the requirement for a strategic approach to the design of the project process rather than the highly reactive approach that was prevalent. The variety of practices evident under the heading of 'project management' increased significantly, with the best organisations and managers continuing to develop new approaches and many more starting their 'project management journeys'.

Conventional methods developed to manage large-scale, direct-value-adding projects with timescales of years, such as heavy engineering, are too cumbersome when projects require short timescales to exploit market openings quickly, in particular in an information-based economy.

The third stage of project management emphasised the strategic role of projects, especially those processes that the project manager must put in place to deliver the end objective of the project and satisfy the needs of all the project's customers. In this new approach, project managers became project *integrators*, responsible for integrating the required resources, knowledge and processes from the project's beginning to end. This third stage has also been greatly influenced by the changes that occurred in the context in which modern projects operate. In particular, the ready availability of technology (especially communications technology) led to the emergence of *virtual teams* as a means of running projects. Similarly, there was considerable development of powerful project planning software and the computer-processing power to support it. Both of these changed the way that we worked in projects. In addition, as mentioned in the previous section, we have seen the emergence of the career paths of project, programme, portfolio and project support office managers.

Changes in work modes in some (certainly not all) industries in more recent times has left managers facing what has been described as 'the perfect storm of complexity,' with massive uncertainties and change in the requirements of some projects, no direct authority over the people working in them, and the rise in outsourcing and offshoring of work. One single approach to managing projects is never going to fit with this diversity of settings in which work is carried out. If we consider what is happening in publishing, for instance. While there is still demand for conventionally published books, the demands of electronic publishing and the use of crowdsourcing mean that the traditional long publishing cycles (this book, for instance, took 9 months from completion of manuscript to being on sale) are incompatible. People working in such environments have different roles and expect to be included in the decision processes, rather than responding to hierarchies. This fourth generation of PM is a fundamental shift in thinking and acting for those involved, and is termed 'Project Management 2.0' by some. Most importantly though, there is no explicit rejection of PM 1.0 (previous generations of PM practice) as many of the principles still hold; they just need to be applied in different ways that fit with the context in which people are working. The requirement to manage a portfolio of potentially disparate projects within an organisation requires a different set of skills, and careers can be developed within this area where such a profession was barely recognised in earlier decades.

This consideration of the evolution of the subject brings us to the issues that practitioners and academics are facing today. This is the fifth-generation of PM and opens up a range of new challenges to which solutions are not evident. Multiple project management approaches are now available, with no clear guidance on the optimum choice, or how combination of choices may be identified. The greater scope of work in which project techniques can be applied offers new opportunities as well as further questions, and the role of new technology such as AI is the subject of much discussion with many opinions regarding realistic benefits and potential pitfalls.[17]

Perennial issues

There are many areas where project management proves to be a huge challenge for individuals and organisations. Some of these are reflected in the list below:

> *'Ready, fire, aim.'* A project is started with no clear objectives. The motto is *'shoot first – whatever you hit, call it the target'*. While we accept that emergence is a characteristic of projects, and some will be deliberately exploratory (but necessarily limited), this approach to managing projects is not associated with any great success for the organisation. However, if you do work in such an environment, setting your own targets at the end of the project is the easiest method for the project manager, without a doubt!

'It's all in my head.' The project manager will set out with all the information in their head. This may work well where the project is very small, but the lack of any system will soon start to tell on the individual and the results if there are any problems or if the scale of the project escalates. Here, the application of the structures and systems will greatly help, enabling better-grounded decisions to be made and avoiding many problems to which this approach will inevitably lead. It remains a challenge for many individuals and organisations to move away from this usually random approach to managing projects. This links to the next point.

'We work in a nanosecond environment, we don't have time to do this stuff.' This was a regular quotation from senior managers in fast-moving e-commerce firms in the late 1990s. Given the demise of so many of these, one can only speculate on the impact that the lack of good project management had on those businesses. Undoubtedly, changes to the basic practices of project managers are required under such circumstances, but this is more adaptation than radical re-invention. This scenario is in sharp contrast to the next one.

'Project management – we have a procedure for that.' Having procedures or a documented set of processes for projects provides a highly structured approach that is favoured in some industries. Indeed, there are many where the slavish dedication to highly restrictive methods is necessary as part of the requirements of customers (military procurement and areas where safety considerations are paramount are two such areas). The result is high levels of documentation (the procedures manual for projects at one international bank ran to several thousand pages) and considerable bureaucracy associated with it. Decision making can be very slow and the overhead costs associated with such systems significant. This represents the other end of the formalisation scale from the previous scenarios; it is a challenge for project managers to deal with this high degree of formalisation and yet try to engender creativity into the project and the people working on it. It is a constant theme among project management professionals just how much formalisation is required in systems. While some will have the levels specified by the requirements of the project, the vast majority, particularly for smaller projects, require an approach that is more appropriate to the particular situation.

'It's all just common sense, isn't it?' Well yes, but that depends on what you mean by common sense. If you mean 'the obvious after it has been explained',[18] then possibly. However, this statement usually just shows that things about which little or nothing is known appear obvious, as exemplified by the bar-room philosopher with easy answers to life, the universe and everything, if only they would listen . . . This is a great challenge for project management today. The past 70 years of the subject will be shown to have provided a substantial knowledge base for project managers to use. The art is in knowing the relevant parts of that base and tailoring that knowledge to the particular environment.

'I've got the badge, therefore I am a project manager.' The card-carrying project-management expert is a relatively recent phenomenon. Short courses, including PRINCE2, provide some knowledge, at the end of which participants take an exam. If they pass it, they have the status of project management practitioner. This is regardless of whether they can actually apply any of the knowledge gained from their course or its relevance to their context. Such courses are valuable as first steps on the way to becoming a professional project manager and many people have benefited from them; however, they are only a starting point.

'We've done this lots of times before. It never worked then, why should it this time?' Here we see the experienced project worker showing the exasperation that comes with the application of many different approaches, only to be regularly confronted with the same results – projects running late, over budget or delivering less than was required of them. This is not at all uncommon, because organisations rarely address the real causes

of failure. The failures deserve more careful study – they are a significant opportunity for learning and are generally very costly: to individuals, the organisation or both.

'It won't work here!' Lastly, a challenge for new methods that have been developed in other areas of business is to find how they might be applied with benefit to the project environment. These must overcome this often-heard rejection of anything new as it was 'not invented here, therefore it cannot be of any relevance to us'. The pressure for change in most organisations is such that ideas need to be brought in from wherever possible and adapted for projects and then the particular application. Examples of changes that are having an impact on the project environment include taking operations initiatives (including *lean* and *agile*) and applying the principles to the project environment. There is no longer just one best way to run a project; now there are many possible options (the real thesis of fourth and fifth generation / Project Management 2.0) and it is this choice of processes that will be discussed in subsequent chapters.

Overall, projects are a challenge to work in and the nature of that work for many people is changing.

Academic subject

Alongside practice, what has been written and taught about project management has evolved considerably over the recent past. At one time, a project management course was a relatively novel addition to an engineering programme of study. Today, it is thriving field of study and is taught extensively in management, engineering and science schools. Further, there is a growing band of academics researching, writing, teaching and consulting in the area, and more relevant papers appearing in a wide range of academic and practitioner journals.[19] The following Real World box describes a recent study that has been influential both in setting out the current state of the art in project management and in defining requirements for the future.

REAL WORLD Project X and the role of MSc content

'Project X'[20] was initiated by the Infrastructure and Projects Authority in the UK and funded via the Economic and Social Research Council. Its remit is to investigate the issues within major government projects and, through rigorous research, find ways of delivering savings in project delivery and enhance the project management capability across government departments and industry. It has six key themes:

A - **Defining value, understanding and measuring success and the identification of critical success factors**
B - **Front- and back-end management practices and their influence on project performance**
C - **Data quality and use and their connections to project performance**
D - **Assurance, reviews, reporting and governance and their connections to effective decision making**
E - **Capability & knowledge management**
F - **Spotlight on transformation**

This is an important initiative, and highlights the ongoing commitment the UK government is showing to improving the delivery of major projects. Published reports (e.g. from the UK National Audit Office) highlight the difficulties often faced within these pieces of work, and performance is often below expectation. Our experience teaching and working with senior civil servants is that they are smart and dedicated individuals, but that their projects are highly complex endeavours not amenable to any 'prescriptive' solutions. Although, as mentioned, there is a wealth of excellent material on how to manage projects, it does need a wide set of skills and a willingness to embrace the complexity they inevitably face.

To support both private- and public-sector managers in understanding the challenges and building a 'toolkit' they can deploy in a range of scenarios, many universities offer specific Masters courses in project management.

Although PM is often included within more 'generalist' MBA degrees, an MSc focused on the subject offers a more in-depth learning experience. These can be sector-specific (e.g. construction or defence), part- or full-time, and tailored for the experienced manager or those just starting out. Content varies significantly with institution. Key PM elements are always included, but a range of other complementary aspects such as finance, leadership, or systems thinking, can help develop a more 'rounded' approach. As we will see, effective project managers need a solid understanding of the wider business environment in which they work.

The most powerful academic research into project management is both highly rigorous, yet also highly relevant to practicing managers. It offers insight into, and explanations of, processes and outcomes. Additionally, it helps practitioners conceptualise their work differently, and think more critically. Our experience is that this aids them in dealing with the complexities they encounter and enables more nuanced solutions to be identified.

Summary

■ Projects are important issues to both individuals and organisations. There are some key questions to be answered if we are to understand the meaning and potential of the subject and profession of project management and the activity of managing projects today. The first is: what is it? For some people, the image that is conjured up is of large-scale construction projects (for instance, High-Speed 2 or Crossrail rail projects in the UK). The second is: what is the role of management in this? For many, project management is often associated with its basic tools and techniques or a particular software package. These views are limiting and do not do justice to the range or scope of project management today. To counter the first point, project management is a live subject – going on around us all the time, and not just in organisations that undertake large-scale projects. On the second point, rather than just being a limited set of tools and techniques, it is also a true profession, with a growing recognition of its contribution to all walks of working life. The role of project management covers the entire spectrum of management knowledge, making it a broad-based study, not confined to tools and techniques or technical issues.

■ On a business level, there are projects ongoing in every organisation. These are vital as they are the execution of all the visions, missions and strategies of that organisation. There are many books and distinguished articles written on strategy, but relatively little on how to deliver it. On a personal level, we all have a number of projects ongoing – pursuing a course of study, buying a house or organising a holiday. The level of complexity differs, the underlying principle of delivering the result at a given point in time is the same. At a commercial level, the effectiveness of the project management process will determine whether or not those projects play a role in providing a source of competitive advantage (or even continued existence) for an organisation. But this is not usually the case, as the opening of the chapter showed. There is a problem with projects and their management, as demonstrated by the large percentage of projects that run late, cost more than was expected, or fail to deliver what was required of them.

■ The first step on the way to understanding projects was their definition. This showed that there was a considerable diversity in the characteristics of projects, and that these require different approaches to their management. After we identified the nature of projects, the next discussion was to see how we arrived at the current state of the subject. Having emerged from the 'one best way' era of project management, we are faced with a large number of challenges, not least in terms of where the subject is going now. This is both helped and constrained by the current knowledge base, with high-profile bodies of knowledge being at the core of the professional discipline.

Key terms

accidental profession *p. 10*

as . . . but . . . *p. 9*

Bodies of Knowledge and standards *p. 15*

business case *p. 6*

change *p. 6*

definition *p. 4*

deliver benefits *p. 6*

emergence *p. 6*

first-timers *p. 9*

focused *p. 5*

general management *p. 5*

generation of project practices *p. 14*

innovation *p. 13*

maintenance *p. 13*

mission *p. 6*

operations management *p. 5*

painting by numbers *p. 9*

career *p. 12*

process *p. 8*

programme/project/ portfolio/project support office manager *p. 13*

project-based organisations *p. 10*

projects *p. 4*

social construction *p. 7*

temporary *p. 5*

uncertainty *p. 6*

unique *p. 5*

volume and variety *p. 8*

PROJECT MANAGEMENT IN PRACTICE
Four managers with distinctly different roles

1 The site manager of a housing development

'I am in charge of the construction of the buildings you see around you [he gestured with his hand to the mixture of partially and fully completed properties] and of making sure they go from this stage [he indicates a pile of drawings and building schedules] to the point where we can hand them over to the sales people to sell. Most of the work is supervisory, ensuring that orders are placed and materials arrive on time, people turn up, do the job properly and get paid for it at the end of the week. There are always arguments between the various tradespeople to resolve and problems just get dumped on the desk. Some of the toughest problems come with the people you have to work with. Some of them will do any-thing to try to get one over on you – they'll tell you a job is finished when you can see it is only half done. Unless you go and check it yourself you're in trouble. Also, they don't give a damn for my schedule. How do you get a roofer, at four o'clock in the afternoon when it is raining rather heavily [not the words actually used] when you know he has a long drive home, to get back on the roof and finish the job he is doing so that other jobs which rely on this being completed can start at eight o'clock the following morn-ing? It wouldn't be the first time we had to block his car in with a pallet of bricks to stop him leaving.'

2 Implementing Total Quality Management – the Quality Director

'The Quality Director was appointed with the brief to introduce Total Quality Management [TQM] to the company. It was his responsibility to put the proposal as to how it could be done, and then to carry it out. As he described at the outset of the project "[this] is one of the most complex projects that we could undertake at this time". The complexity came because the project would hopefully change the way that everyone in the company thought and worked [i.e. both attitude and procedures]. This would have to be done through consultation, training and the demonstration through piloting small-scale improve-ment activities, that the move towards TQ was worthwhile. The initial phase as part of the proposal process was to carry out a company-wide quality audit to determine attitudes, knowledge and current practice. The results paved the way for the carrying out of targeted efforts where needed most. The first phase of execution was to take the Board of Directors of the company on awareness training – showing them how working under a TQ environment would benefit them, and what changes would be needed. The next level of management were then trained, and so on, down the hierarchy until the middle management level. These managers then trained their own people – a process known as "cascading". The project to introduce the new philosophy to the company took several years, and has now moved on to become an accepted way of working. The Quality Director was initially involved in the management of the introduction process, where the employees and suppliers needed to be convinced that this was a good route for the company to take. His role then became one of project sponsor of a variety of improvement projects, which may be considered as subprojects of the main one.'

3 Manager in financial management system implementation

This was a manager responsible for a large-scale IT change. She was in charge of a multi-year piece of work with numerous interlinked IT projects that needed to be completed to bring about an update and consolidation of her organisation's (rather old and previously fragmented) IT systems.

'The main roles of the job include:

- organisation – from the design of the system to determining support issues and providing training;
- anticipation of future requirements of the system;
- monitoring of progress of the implementation;
- communication and information – providing progress reports to local team members and national common-interest groups;
- audit – ensuring the housekeeping, procedures and system security are in order.

The initial system design work involved coordinating with external system designers, the providers of the software and the in-house IT group. Our local area network [LAN] needed upgrading to run the new system. Other organisational issues were the role that consultants would play in the system design and training of users and the allocation of the budget between activities.

Anticipation was required as the requirements of the system would change over its life. For example, higher-level monthly indicators of financial performance would need to be provided where they had not been needed before. In addition, a management accounting system would be required to provide budgetary controls.

The monitoring system we used for the project was PRINCE2 2017. This provided a basic set of planning tools, and we filled in the blanks on the planning sheets. A team was set up to monitor progress against the plan.

Training was one area where I was personally involved with the users, showing them how to use the system. People are very frightened of technology and do not always grasp immediately ideas you think are very simple. This is where the greatest attribute of the project manager was needed in plenty – patience.'

4 Portfolio manager in Government

It is common practice to group projects with a common purpose into a portfolio. This allows a number of benefits if managed well. The UK leaving the European Union in 2020, meant that UK could no longer rely on trade deals established by the EU as its basis for trade. From 2017 onwards, a portfolio of projects was established to begin discussions on trade with a raft of countries and free-trade bodies, including the CPATPP (the Comprehensive and Progressive Agreement for Trans-Pacific Partnership). This portfolio was under significant pressure to deliver, as ministers who had supported EU exit wanted to be able to show the benefits of UK being able to negotiate its own deals in future.

The nature of international trade means that it is essential that there is coordination between the various trade deals and is one of the reasons this particular portfolio leader was so important. The commitment to a particular condition with one country may preclude a deal with another. So, while one project or negotiation in the portfolio might be important, it needed to align with the others, both current and future.

The portfolio leader faced one other major challenge. The UK had been a part of the EU for decades, and had not done any of its own trade deals. As a result, it did not have a pool of UK-based international trade negotiators on which to draw. **There was also a very limited departmental resource to support such negotiations. The portfolio of projects therefore also included having to design a department to provide the logistical and legal support.**

The leader, an experienced and very senior civil servant, was faced with significant novelty in establishing the portfolio.

Points for discussion

1 Identify the title which might be given to the management role in each case.

2 Describe the role of the manager in each of the cases.

3 Describe the desirable characteristics of each manager.

Topics for discussion

1 Carry out an Internet search to find more examples of project success and failure. From your search, are there any common themes in each? What are the implications of success and failure in each case?

2 Was the last Olympic and Paralympic Games a success? Carry out a search of the news of the time and the relevant websites to identify the characteristics of the project management that led to the success. Compare with the example of failed projects you found in the answer to 1.

3 Explain the differences between project and general management.

4 In what you are doing at the moment, which parts are 'project' and which are 'ongoing or repetitive operations'?

5 Identify five managers that have the title 'project manager' and another five that are project managers but don't carry the title. Do you notice any differences in their roles?

6 Select a sector of interest. For this sector, identify the likely pressures on project managers and the implications for them as a result of these.

7 Find examples of projects that fit into each of the categories of project – 'first-timers', 'as . . . but . . . s', and 'painting by numbers'. Briefly discuss how the category would influence how you would expect to manage the particular project.

8 Consider the definitions of 'project' provided by each of the professional bodies. What are the similarities and differences?

9 Does it matter what we call a project?

10 'A project manager should not have other managerial responsibilities.' Discuss.

Further information

Organisations of interest

Project Management Institute – see www.pmi.org for information about the Institute and referral to national organisations (known as *Chapters*).

The Association for Project Management (UK) – see www.apm.org.uk.

International Project Management Association – see www.ipma.world (including a full list of national associations and relevant websites).

Reference Material

APM (2019), *APM Body of Knowledge*, 7th edition, Association for Project Management, High Wycombe, UK.

PMI (2017) A Guide to the Project Management Body of Knowledge, 6th edition, PMI, Upper Darby, PA.

PRINCE2 2017 – see www.prince2.com for details associated with PRINCE2 and associated qualifications.

Managing Successful Programmes, 5th edition (2020), see https://www.axelos.com/best-practice-solutions/msp.

ITIL – see www.itil.org.uk – if you are involved in the IT field, worth checking out ITIL's standards and guides.

BS ISO 21500:2012, *Guidance on Project Management*, BSI Standards Publication.

BS 6079:2019, Project management – Principles and guidance for the management of projects, BSI Standards Publication.

Other PM sources

Project Management Today – www.pmtoday.co.uk

marketplace.pmi.org

www.apm.org.uk/book-shop/

www.apm.org.uk/resources/find-a-resource/research-series

Podcasts

The APM Podcast.

The Project Management Podcast.

Projectified (from PMI).

HBR Ideacast (Harvard Business Review).

Books of interest

Andersen, E. (2008) *Rethinking Project Management*, Financial Times Prentice Hall, Harlow.

Davies, A., and Hobday, M. (2005), *The Business of Projects,* Cambridge University Press, Cambridge UK.

Hodgson, D. and Cicmil, S. (eds) (2006) *Making Projects Critical*, Palgrave, Basingstoke.

Kerzner, H. (2017) *Project Management, A Systems Approach to Planning, Scheduling and Controlling*, 12th edition, Wiley, Hoboken, New Jersey.

Lock, D. (2013) *Project Management*, 10th edition, Gower, Aldershot.

Meredith, J.R., Mantel, S.J. and Shafer, S.M. (2015) *Project Management: A Managerial Approach*, 9th edition, Wiley, New York.

Morris, P. (2013), *Reconstructing Project Management,* Wiley, Chichester, UK.

Morris, P, Pinto, J.K. and Söderlund J. (eds) (2012), *Oxford Handbook of Project Management*, OUP, Oxford.

Murray-Webster, R. and Simon, P. (2009) *50 Lucid Thoughts: Shedding Light on Current Project Management Practice*, Lucidus, London.

Pinto, J. (2019) *Project Management: Achieving Competitive Advantage*, 5th edition, Pearson, New York.

Shenhar, A. and Dvir, D. (2007), *Reinventing Project Management*, Harvard Business School Press, Harvard, MA.

Turner, J.R. (2014) *Gower Handbook of Project Management*, 5th edition, Gower, Aldershot.

Turner J.R. (2014) *The Handbook of Project-Based Management*, 4th edition, McGraw Hill, New York.

Turner, J.R., Huemann, M., Anbari, F., and Bredillet, C., (2010), *Perspectives on Projects*, Routledge.

Journals of interest

International Journal of Project Management – published eight times a year by Elsevier.

Project Management Journal – published six times a year by Wiley.

International Journal of Managing Projects in Business – published four times a year by Emerald.

PM Network – monthly publication of PMI.

Project – quarterly publication of APM.

References

1   Available at unstats.un.org/sdgs/report/2019/The-Sustainable-Development-Goals-Report-2019.pdf

2   See sustainabledevelopment.un.org

3   See www.standishgroup.com

4   See for example Coombs, C.R. (2015) 'When planned IS/IT project benefits are not realized: a study of inhibitors and facilitators to benefits realization', *International Journal of Project Management*, Vol. 33, No. 2, pp. 363–379.

5   See for instance Teo, M. M and Loosemore, M. (2017) 'Understanding community protest from a project management perspective: A relationship-based approach', *International Journal of Project Management*, Vol. 35, No. 8, pp. 1444–1458.

6   For a fuller description of process and various classifications, see Slack, N. and Brandon-Jones, A. (2019) *Operations Management*, 9th edition, Pearson, Harlow.

7   See Obeng, E. (1994) *All Change: The Project Leader's Secret Handbook*, FT Pitman Publishing, London.

8   Turner, J.R. and Cochrane, R.A. (1993) 'Goals-and-methods Matrix: Coping with Projects with Ill Defined Goals and/or Methods of Achieving Them', *International Journal of Project Management*, Vol. 11, No. 2, pp. 93–102.

9   See Association for Project Management (2019) 'The Golden Thread: A study of the contribution of project management and projects to the UK's economy and society' at www.apm.org.uk/goldenthread/

10 Schoper, Y. G., Wald, A., Ingason, H. T., and Fridgeirsson, T. V. (2018) 'Projectification in Western economies: A comparative study of Germany, Norway and Iceland, *International Journal of Project Management*, Vol. 36, No. 1, pp. 71–82.

11 Partington, D., Pellegrinelli, S. and Young, M. (2005) 'Attributes and Levels of Programme Management Competence: An Interpretive Study', *International Journal of Project Management*, Vol. 23, No. 2, pp. 87–95.

12 Williams, T., (2008) 'How do organizations learn lessons from projects—and do they?' *IEEE Transactions on Engineering Management*, Vol. 55, No. 2, pp. 248–266.

13 This phenomenon is known as *Projectification* after Midler, C. (1995) 'Projectification of the Firm: The Renault Case', *Scandinavian Management Journal*, Vol. 11, No. 4, pp. 363–375.

14 PMI Body of Knowledge first published as a white paper in 1987. First edition formally published 1996. APM Body of Knowledge first published 1992.

15 See Hodgson, D. and Cicmil, S. (eds) (2006) *Making Projects Critical*, Palgrave, Basingstoke.

16 Winter, M., Smith, C., Cooke-Davies, T. and Cicmil, S. (2006) 'Directions for Future Research in Project Management: The Main Findings of a UK Government-funded Research Network', *International Journal of Project Management*, Vol. 24, No. 8, pp. 650–662.

17 Brock, J. and von Wangenheim, F. (2019) 'Demystifying AI: What Digital Transformation Leaders Can Teach You about Realistic Artificial Intelligence', *California Management Review*, Vol. 61, No. 4, pp. 110–134.

18 We are indebted to Keith Sutton of Chelmsford Technical College for this definition.

19 See 'Further information' for the main project management journals.

20 See www.bettergovprojects.com

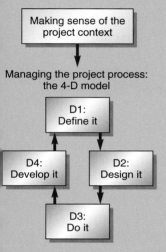

2 Structures and frameworks

Making sense of the project context

Managing the project process: the 4-D model

- D1: Define it
- D2: Design it
- D3: Do it
- D4: Develop it

Get the thinking right first. The rest is detail.

Principles

1 Structures and frameworks are necessary to enable us to construct mental models of complex systems of human activity.

2 Well-developed structures and frameworks exist that assist in making sense of projects.

3 The nature of the managerial task in projects can usefully be described by assessing the complexity of that task.

Learning objectives

By the time you have completed this chapter, you should be able to:

→ describe the environment that a project operates in and some of the challenges facing project managers

→ use a framework to identify elements of a project

→ assess the managerial complexity of a project and the implications of this for the project manager and the organisation.

Contents

Introduction *26*
2.1 Describing the project context: high-level frameworks *27*
2.2 Describing the project process: activity models *31*
2.3 Describing the project management challenge: managerial complexity *42*
Summary *46*
Key terms *46*
Relevant areas of the Bodies of Knowledge *46*
Project management in practice: The rescue of Crossrail *50*
Project management in practice: Using the 7-S approach in the review of a real project *50*
Topics for discussion *54*
Further information *55*
References *56*

The Big Carpet Company

The Big Carpet Company is a firm that makes a range of floor coverings. Its former CEO recognised that the firm would have to do something very different from their competitors, if they were to survive. While BCC had parity with their competitors in having a green policy (energy use, waste-water recycling etc.), he had become aware of a substantially different concept that the business could adopt – Cradle to Cradle (C2C) – where products were made out of materials so pure that they could be endlessly recycled. Following a strategy of C2C would mean a radical change for the firm, its products, and supply chain. For instance, they would need a 'reverse logistics' operation, to bring unwanted floor coverings back to plants for recycling. Their suppliers had to change too, developing new products and processes that were suitable for C2C. Their own portfolio of products, including some that were the core business for the firm, would have to change.

Source: Tim Scrivener/Alamy Stock Photo

The firm went ahead and engaged in a **change programme**. Like other change programmes, its intent was clear (100 per cent C2C products) but this would be achieved in a series of phases (or **tranches**) over many years. They became viewed as a world leader in C2C, had a clear unique selling point for their products, and saw their business thrive even when Europe had been in recession. Just as importantly, the firm set itself to be a sustainable business with the aim of leading others to this end.

Introduction

The case above is a great example of how a project was used to **change** fundamentally the way that things are done – in this case the business model for an entire organisation. However we write the story of BCC, there are many pieces of the reality of making this change that will not be included – there are too many parties involved, key decision points, and daily challenges that have been faced. We have to have a way of making sense of it and this is the purpose of this chapter. Talk to many project managers and they have had to make sense of considerable complexity in order to deliver their projects. Without this **sense-making** process,[1] project activities can appear to be 'too difficult' and the project process nothing more than an apparently random series of actions.

This chapter starts with a basic model of the project environment. It then considers the **issues** that project managers will face using the 7-S framework. It will be shown that the nature of the project management task is usefully described by its **complexity**.

As described in Chapter 1, important developments in the subject of project management in recent years have included the provision of documented 'Bodies of Knowledge' by the professional institutes. These are outlined at the end of the chapter, and points of reference with this book are identified.

The project environment

The challenges faced by project leaders do not seem to reduce year by year. Indeed, there is evidence that these challenges get harder. This context or environment is dynamic and a fundamental of project leadership is being able to work with this dynamism.

We observe that the number of international collaborative ventures increases year on year, with globalisation still on the corporate agenda. This has had a considerable impact on the nature of work carried out, due to the challenges of shifting geopolitical tensions and ongoing trade issues resulting in increased uncertainty. It is not unusual that project work will be undertaken internationally involving *virtual teams* (where the team members are geographically dispersed and communicate digitally). Furthermore, some specific drivers for this include:

- Legislative changes – restricting not just what can be done but how it can be done.
- Businesses' complexity – fewer are providing a commodity, product or service but instead provide a 'package' which meets an entire need rather than just part of that need.
- Contractual arrangements – projects are being delivered through a wider variety of contractual arrangements – with different roles for the client organisation in how much control they exert over the delivery process, or through complex financing arrangements (e.g. the financing of public projects through public private partnerships or private finance initiative arrangements in the UK and in many other countries).
- Ethical concerns and the impact of Corporate Social Responsibility is being both implemented through projects, and asking questions of projects more generally.
- Sustainability as a key concern for many organisations, as shown in the opening case. This can add an additional layer of requirements that have to be considered in the justification and delivery of many projects.[2]

Multiple changes in the environment in which the majority of organisations operate are continually impacting the way in which projects are managed. Indeed, one of the consistent characteristics of projects is that they are highly dynamic environments. Change will be happening both as a result of the project (e.g. BCC case) and to the project (e.g. Global Financial Crisis, 2008; Coronavirus pandemic of 2020), and external factors can increase uncertainty for many years (e.g. the UK EU exit plan after the 2016 referendum). The arrows in Figure 2.1 are two-way to reflect this – a project will have an influence back on its environment, as well as being influenced by it.

In addition, over the past 20 years, we have seen step changes in the way that many firms run their repetitive operations, with productivity, product quality and delivery reliability having improved steadily. As a result, the opportunities for improvement in performance in these systems without significant investment are declining. Projects are therefore a major source of competitiveness that many organisations have yet to realise.

The environment in which projects operate may be summarised by the **5 Cs**. These are:

- *Context* – the external general influences on the organisation in which the project is taking place;
- *Complexity* – the level of difficulty or complication of a piece of work called 'a project';
- *Completeness* – how much of the end requirement a project will deliver;
- *Competitiveness* – how many other organisations will be competing to deliver that work;
- *Customer focus* – the expectation that customers will have their needs met by the project.

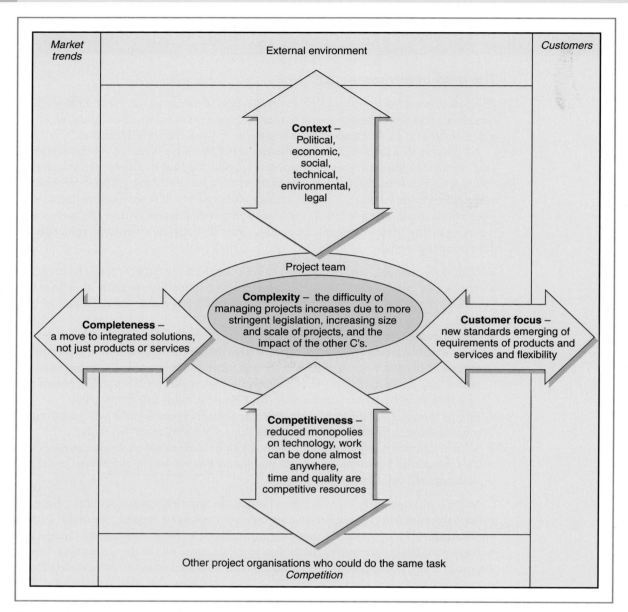

Figure 2.1 Describing the project environment: the 5-C model

These are shown in Figure 2.1. Complexity is more fully described later in this chapter. The **context** can be described in many ways. One acronym that is widely used to describe context is **PESTEL**:

- *Political influence* – in government organisations this may be Political (capital P), where, for instance, a change in policy or the party in power, may have significant ramifications for what government does, what it funds and, just as importantly, what it decides not to continue funding. All organisation have politics, hierarchies and a requirement at least to recognise where the power in that organisation really lies.
- *Economic* – the influence of general and local economics. For instance, during a period of economic 'boom', there may be challenges recruiting staff or obtaining contractors even to bid for work. During economic 'bust' times, the picture changes radically.

- *Social* – the influence of social changes on the project environment, for instance on methods of communication, use of social media, and the impact on relationships.
- *Technical* – changes in technology will challenge the viability of some projects and create the need for others, in addition to determining the way in which those projects are delivered.
- *Environmental* – an assessment of environmental impact is mandated for many projects now as part of corporate social responsibility.
- *Legal* – from the regulations affecting intellectual property to the requirements of major pieces of anti-trust (US) or government procurement (EU) legislation, legal pressures place an ever-increasing bureaucratic load on most aspects of economic activity. Recent challenges have included data-sharing (GDPR) and uncertainty over international trade rules.

Completeness refers to the increased scope of interest of many organisations and their projects. In particular, the service sector has significantly overtaken manufacturing in importance for many countries. Firms frequently provide a complex product and service offering, not just the product. For instance, a firm that sold flight training simulators twenty years ago, now provides a full suite of flight training: the simulators, the instructors, the training aircraft, and maintains the venue at which the training takes place. In projects, we often see major projects being contracted to deliver a solution for a given period. The UK and many other governments have pursued contracts for major pieces of national infrastructure, under *private finance initiatives*, in which typically a consortium of firms will design, build, operate and maintain an asset (e.g. schools, roads, hospitals and bridges) over a given life-time (often 25 years) for an annual fee (or allowing them to collect the revenue) after which the asset becomes owned by the state again.

Customer focus applies to both the outcome and the process by which it is delivered. For instance, in agile software development, a key part of the process includes users, in describing their needs, through to testing products at various stages of completion to make sure their needs have been met. As part of this agenda, we also see a greater integration and openness between customers and suppliers. Company information that would previously have been a closely guarded secret (typically costs) can often be shared in a move towards partnership rather than adversarial relationships.

Competitiveness is normally associated with repetitive operations activity, but it is increasingly common to hear project leaders from both business and government, talking about how they have to compete for resources to do projects. In order to justify their resources, they are often required to commit to:

- Do it faster: the time it takes before the benefits from a project can be critical to its justification and most often, the faster the better.
- Be flexible: commit to be willing to change the requirements at short notice and possibly without further resources, as requirements are identified.
- Do it better: do it better than it was done last time, faster and with less resource.

Means to provide this including better use of people (engaged, motivated, individual and collective creativity), and engagement of non-traditional ways of working (e.g. lean and agile). These ideas will be expanded upon in later chapters. Most importantly though first, we need means to make sense of the project itself.

The project itself

Moving inside the project, there are many **structures** or **frameworks** that assist in making sense of the reality that project managers have to cope with. One approach that we have found to work well in describing projects is the **7-S**. It is described here in principle and in usage in the Project Management in Practice section at the end of this chapter. The 7-S framework provides a comprehensive set of issues that needs to be considered. The 7-S framework of management issues was promoted by McKinsey and Co., management consultants. Their original 7-S is amended for the project environment, with a description of each of the elements, as shown in Table 2.1.

Rather than being simply an outcome or a statement, *strategy* is a process. It involves a high-level consideration of objectives, which can be seen as points of principle rather than activity-level details. Success starts with a rational strategy process, which then guides and informs the decisions made in all areas of the project. The element of strategy will be discussed further in Chapter 3, along with the means by which organisational strategy is pursued through activities, including projects.

Structure is the arrangement of human resources relative to lines of command and control. A key question for the project manager concerns the nature of this structure. For example, should the project team be a dedicated, full-time team or one where staff are 'borrowed' from other parts of the organisation or other organisations, only as and when needed? This is elaborated in Chapter 11.

Systems are 'the way we work'. Both formal and informal systems will need to be designed or at least recognised for key tasks, including communication and quality assurance. Formal systems can be demonstrated through statements of procedure – simply put, 'under these conditions, we carry out this action'. Informal systems, particularly for information transfer, are far less easy to describe and control, and it is often the case that in practice knowledge is transferred around groups socially rather than through formal process, and this needs to be recognised and considered. A theme within the systems element is the focus of organisations on 'process' or prescriptions for the ways that work is to be carried out. Systems are a recurring theme throughout this text.

Staff need to be selected, recruited and then managed. How they respond to their treatment will have a large impact on the success or otherwise of the project. Yet this element has traditionally not been a strength of both the subject and practice of project management. The role of the manager in the element of staffing is discussed in Chapter 11, in addition to a consideration of the *skills* they require.

Skills are required in the technology, the team, the task and its coordination. Ideally, a project team will be populated by SQEPs – suitably qualified and experienced personnel. A consistent feature of projects is the ongoing professionalisation of project management, with significant roles played by the professional institutes (see **resources** at the end of Chapter 1), the projects function within organisations (where such exists) and learning and development functions.

Table 2.1 The 7-S of project management

Element	Description
Strategy	The high-level requirements of the project and the means to achieve them
Structure	The organisational arrangement that will be used to carry out the project
Systems	The methods for work to be designed, monitored and controlled
Staff	The selection, recruitment, management and leadership of those working on the project
Skills	The managerial and technical tools available to the project manager and the staff, and how these are developed
Style/culture	The underlying way of working and inter-relating within the work team or organisation
Stakeholders	Individuals and groups with an interest in the project process or outcome

Style/culture is part of the 'soft' side of management. Indeed, it cannot be managed in the short term in the same way that the finances of a project, for example, can be managed. This element will also be discussed in Chapter 11, in particular with reference to the cross-cultural nature of many projects.

Stakeholders are a major consideration for project managers. Their importance in project delivery has resulted in increasing interest in the project management literature, with methods for the management of expectations and perceptions developed. Issues concerned with stakeholders are considered further in Chapters 4 and 9.

These 7-S headings provide one view of the issues that project managers will be faced with.

2.2   Describing the project process: activity models

'Improve constantly and forever every activity in the company, to improve quality and productivity and thus constantly decrease costs.' (Dr. W. Edwards Deming)[3]

Making sense of the project as a system: the ICOM model

For many years, the most basic **model** of any operating system has been the input–output model.[4] This applies well here as the basic unit of analysis of project activities and follows process-based thinking, identified in Chapter 1.

The project is viewed as a controlled conversion or transformation of input into output, under a set of constraints and utilising a set of mechanisms to make the project happen. As Figure 2.2 shows, the inputs include some form of want or need which is to be satisfied through the process. The project will take place under a set of controls and constraints including any assumptions or limitations placed on the project. The mechanisms are those resources that make the transformation process possible.

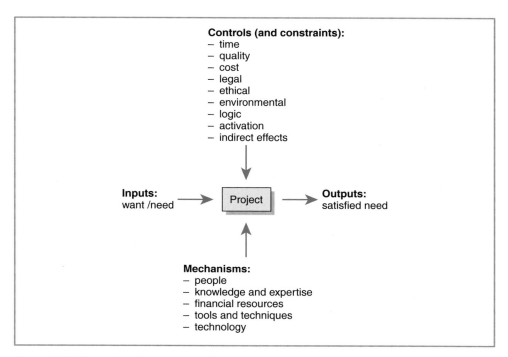

Figure 2.2 The project as a conversion process

Inputs

The desire to develop a new bagless vacuum cleaner was the starting point for James Dyson's highly successful product range. The project did not start with any formalisation, just the want to develop a product that would not suffer from the drawbacks associated with a paper bag being the filter for particles passing through a vacuum cleaner.[5]

For many organisations there has to be a limit to the number of projects that are started and this need will be encapsulated into a *brief* – a document describing the nature of the work to be undertaken – before the resources will be released to do even the most preliminary work. For the project manager, there will be both explicitly stated requirements (original needs) and those that emerge during the course of the project due to the customer's changing needs or perceptions (emergent needs).

Controls (and constraints)

The brief will also set out the constraints, which principally focus on time, cost and quality, but will also have a wider range of issues for the project manager to reconcile with the wants or needs. The most basic constraints for projects, which impact how those projects are to be controlled, are associated with:

- *time* – all projects by definition have a time constraint. In practice, it is often found to be the most challenging to meet;
- *cost* – the value and timing of financial resources required to carry out the project work;
- *quality* – the standards by which both the product (the output of the process) and the process itself will be judged.

In addition to these three, the following constraints can prove limiting on the project:

- legal – this may not be explicitly stated but there will be legal constraints, e.g. a building may not be constructed unless the planning permission for it has been obtained;
- ethical – a major area for many organisations today, particularly those where the ethics of their organisational policies have been questioned in the past. This includes the supply chain, and brands can be publicly admonished and held responsible for undesirable activities their suppliers undertake. The fast-fashion industry is also increasingly targeted for the unsustainability of its products, such as cheap cotton t-shirts which need a great deal of water in the manufacturing process but are discarded after being worn only a few times;
- environmental – the deluge of environmental legislation that has been generated by governments has changed the role of environmental control from a subsidiary issue to one which is at the forefront of management thinking in many sectors. Being ahead of major trends can be advantageous, for example we are seeing the development of net-zero buildings as a response to climate change;
- logic – the need for certain activities to have been completed before a project can start;
- activation – actions to show when a project or activity can begin;
- indirect effects – it is practically impossible for any change to take place in isolation. There will be ripple effects, which cannot be foreseen fully at the outset. For example, the increasing data rates available on mobile phones enable new services to proliferate, which then in turn require more and more data, in a self-reinforcing cycle. Not that long ago, text messaging was an innovation, and livestreaming was the stuff of science fiction.

Outputs

Figure 2.2 describes the output as a 'satisfied need'. This will usually be in the form of:

- converted information, e.g. a set of specifications for a new product;
- a tangible product, e.g. a building;
- changed people, e.g. through a training project, the participants have received new knowledge and so are part of the transformation process as well as being a product of it.

Mechanisms

The means or mechanisms by which the output is achieved are as follows:

- people – those involved both directly and indirectly in the project;
- knowledge and expertise – brought to the project by the participants and outside recruited help (e.g. consultants) of both technical specialisms and management processes;
- financial resources;
- tools and techniques – the methods for organising the potential work with the available resources;
- technology – the available physical assets that will be performing part or all of the conversion process.

From this Inputs, Constraints, Outputs and Mechanisms **(ICOM)** model one of the major roles of project managers becomes apparent. They are required to be the **integrator** of the elements of the project – the need or want with the available mechanisms or resources under the conditions imposed by the constraints. This is a key skill of the project manager. The nature of this task will change during the life of a project, and this will be described in the following section.

Continuously improving the system: the 4-D model

Two parties to a contract, a county council and a construction contractor, ended up taking their claims[6] and counter-claims to court following the construction of a new leisure centre. Seven years later, the same two parties were in court again, to settle their claims and counter-claims, following the construction of an almost identical facility and very similar claims being made. How did this happen? Why had the parties not learned from their earlier, expensive mistakes? The only people with an interest in this kind of process are the lawyers.

This is depressingly common in many organisations (particularly those that use a large proportion of contract staff who leave once the project is completed) and is termed *hedgehog syndrome*.[7]

We see this problem regularly on our roads, where the unsuspecting hedgehog encounters a car and the result is fairly predictable. Worse, as long as there are hedgehogs, roads and cars, we will continue to find our little flat friends. Why, then, don't hedgehogs learn from this? The reason is that there is no feedback to hedgehog-kind of the knowledge that the road is a dangerous place for them to be, so that they can amend their behaviour accordingly. All too often the same applies to projects – the same mistakes are repeated again and again. Unless there is an opportunity to develop the project processes and provide the feedback to the organisation, the knowledge is lost.

World-class organisations use previous projects and their reviews as the starting point for new pieces of work. Some become known for their ability to do this, but sustaining such high performance appears to be particularly difficult. Exemplar companies eventually stumble, and demonstrations of such excellence over decades are rare. However, their focus on the lessons from both good and bad experiences means that there is some path for continuous improvement in projects. We will consider this in some detail in Chapter 16. For now, it is worth noting that while many organisations do carry out 'lessons learned reviews' (aka post mortems) for their projects, it is a real challenge for project managers to get this learning transferred to subsequent projects. One recently noted that his organisation had stopped calling the last phase the 'lessons learned review' and had instead decided to call it 'the lessons identified review'. Because, as he noted, 'we don't learn'. However, while this shows that such a learning process is challenging, that does not alter the objective that the approach to future projects should be based on the opportunity to learn from previous projects.

Source: Arterra Picture Library/Alamy Stock Photo

Hedgehog syndrome

One approach is to consider a project as being structured into four identifiable phases. These were shown in Chapter 1; they provide the basic structure for this book and are repeated here in Figure 2.3.

The four phases are described in more detail in Table 2.2, but before continuing there are three points worth noting.

1 Projects involve a lot of pre-project work to be done to justify resources, prepare documents, evaluate options, and there is considerable diversity of opinion as to whether this work should be included in 'the project'. This will likely include a 'project initiation document' (PID). It should be noted that killing the project before it has really begun ('failing fast') can be beneficial as it is relatively easy and cheap to do at this stage. Once it is fully underway, cancellation becomes harder.

2 Projects are, though, terminated prior to completion for all sorts of reasons. For instance, a project to move a bank to new and larger premises was scrapped as a result of an economic downturn. The project was going well but the additional costs and facilities were deemed unnecessary as customer demands had changed.

3 There are often many stages within each of these main phases. Indeed, for large projects, the project lifecycle can be replicated within each phase, as each of them becomes a mini-project in its own right. This *cycles-within-cycles* is common to many other project processes. Such an approach does represent the reality of many projects well, as they are more akin to cycles of activities rather than the linear progression indicated by Figure 2.3. The real world is rarely so well defined!

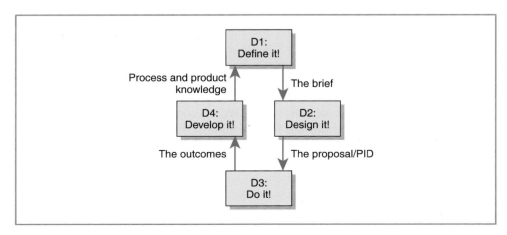

Figure 2.3 Four phases of project lifecycle

Table 2.2 The four phases of project management

Phase	Key issues	Fundamental questions
Define the project	Project and organisational strategy, goal definition	What is to be done? Why is it to be done? What are the benefits?
Design the project process	Modelling and planning, estimating, resource analysis, conflict resolution and justification	How will it be done? Who will be involved in each part? When can it start and finish? What methods and structure are going to be used?
Deliver the project (Do it!)	Organisation, control, leadership, decision-making and problem-solving	How should the project be managed, measured and evaluated on a day-to-day basis?
Develop the process	Assessment of process and outcomes of the project, evaluation, changes for the future	How can we learn from the work? How can the project process be improved?

The **4-D** structure is as follows:

- **Define the project** – this is the time when it is determined what the project is about, its reasons for existence and the intentions that it intends to progress. It is a time to explore the possibilities, and find alternatives to the problems presented.
- **Design the project process** – construct models to show how the requirements will be gathered and turned into an organisation that will deliver them.
- **Do It!** or **Deliver the project** – carry out the project in line with the models or plans generated above.
- **Develop the process** – improve the products and processes in the light of the experience gained from the project.

There are a number of tasks and issues to be addressed in each phase. Using the analogy of a project as a *chain*, it is important that there is general competence across the phases. This is preferable to there being excellence in one area, with other areas falling down.[8]

The generic lifecycle for a project involves consideration of how the level of activity varies with time. This is illustrated in Figure 2.4 and shows how the level of activity is

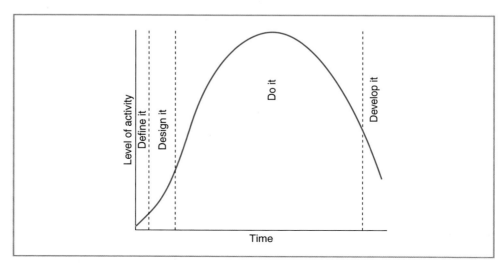

Figure 2.4 Graph showing how level of activity varies with time

relatively low during the early phases, increases through the doing phase when the major volume of work is done, and decreases through the development phase.

This pattern is reflected in the graph of cumulative expenditure against time (Figure 2.5). Outgoings are generally low in the early stages but grow rapidly during the execution phase. However, future expenditure can be committed in the early stages, so it is vital to get it right. Consider a product development when new parts with a six-month lead time are ordered. If the designers find later that there is a mistake when full-scale production is underway, this becomes exceptionally difficult to recover. Changes are relatively easy (and cheap) to make in the definition and design stages, but far more painful later. The graph also demonstrates why the *'develop it'* phase is so vital – by the time the majority of the doing phase is completed, the probability is that in excess of 98 per cent of the total project expenditure will have been incurred. The last phase is the time when the project team themselves can benefit from the process and ensure that lessons (good and bad) are applied in the future. The excuse is often used that organisations cannot review projects because there is no budget for the review work. Given that mistakes are observed to occur repeatedly (hedgehog syndrome), organisations seem perfectly prepared to pay when things inevitably go wrong. This last phase is therefore an investment in future performance, just as spending money on a new piece of equipment would be.

Shell – consistent with other major energy companies – has some key rules for its projects. One of these is that as the project progresses, changes to the specification for the project are not allowed. This allows the team stability in what they are targeting. The rules only permit changes to the specification of the project, if there are legal, operational or safety reasons. A frequent cause of change was that it would provide performance enhancement. However, various studies showed that due to the complexity of the systems that are typical in the industry, making a change in one part of the system had knock-on effects on other parts of the system and the logistics for the system. While this does appear to be a sensible rule, for some engineers this is a challenge. They argue that this constrains their innovation.

As an extreme example, consider the planning for the London 2012 Olympics, including the Olympic Route Network for the Games (the routes athletes and officials would take across the city to get to their events) and the telecoms requirements to support the event. There were years of hard, detailed, planning running up to it. The route details would change daily to reflect the different events going on at different venues, so preparation was absolutely key. For the telecoms and technical equipment, as much testing as possible was done beforehand (including many 'test events' with the athletes to simulate as much as possible before summer 2012). During the Games, there was only a small window of time to carry out their plans, when there was relatively little that could be done to change anything. 'Success' here was taken to be smooth operation and no disruptions or negative headlines.

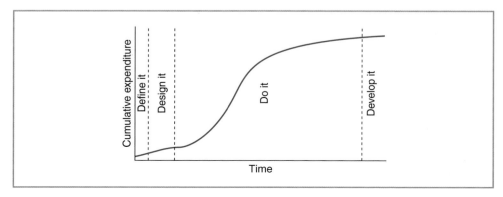

Figure 2.5 Graph of cumulative expenditure against time – the S-curve

The generic lifecycle may be further broken down as shown in Table 2.3. Key additional features include some explicit analysis of the idea during the definition stage, and the focus on a business case being prepared for the project right from the outset. This is expanded during the justification activities of the second-stage processes.

This is still generic, however, and the practice of phasing the project is best illustrated by an application. Table 2.4 shows how a new management information system was supplied to a hospital through a software company with the description of how the project was broken down and the activities that were undertaken in each phase. It illustrates the early structuring that took place within the project. This had a number of plus-points for both the hospital and the IT firm, not least in the clarity that the phasing presented to each side. At a high level, the activities could be tracked to see progress (or lack of it).

Table 2.3 Development of the project lifecycle

Stage in project lifecycle	Activity	Description
Define the Project	Conceptualisation Analysis	Generate explicit statement of needs. Identify what has to be provided to meet those needs – is it likely to be feasible?
Design the project process	Proposal Justification Agreement	Show how those needs will be met through the project activities Prepare and evaluate financial costs and benefits from the project Point at which go-ahead is agreed by project sponsor
Deliver the project (do it!)	Start-up Execution Completion Handover	Gather resources, assemble project teams Carry out defined activities Time/money constraint reached or activity series completed Output of project passed to client/user
Develop the process	Review Feedback	Identify the outcomes for all stakeholders Put in place improvements to procedures, fill gaps in knowledge, document lessons for the future

Table 2.4 Supply of a management information system to a hospital project

Sub-phase of project	Activities
D1 – Conceptualisation	Software house receives an outline from the Information Systems (IS) department of the hospital; various pieces of information and points of clarification are requested.
D1 – Analysis	The concept is converted into the terminology of the software house (every organisation has its own jargon). An initial feasibility check is carried out to see what could be achieved at what cost. Objectives are set for the system to be developed and the interfaces with other systems studied. The analysis phase is completed by an appraisal of the capability of the company to provide what was being asked for by the client.
D2 – Proposal	The proposal document is submitted for approval by the client's IS department in terms of whether or not it would meet the requirements set out in the initial request. The client organisation is offered the opportunity to visit the software house's premises and existing clients to view their systems.
D2 – Justification	There are two parts to this process. First, the software house carries out a financial analysis to show whether or not it is feasible for it to undertake the project. Second, the IS people at the hospital need to provide evidence that the new system will provide a return. This has to be agreed by the financial managers.

→

Table 2.4 continued

Sub-phase of project	Activities
D2 – Agreement	After the justification has been prepared by both sides, the formal act of preparation and signing of contracts can take place. This is the basis of the agreement between supplier and customer. The terms and conditions will have to go through each of the party's legal advisers (see Chapter 14).
D3 – Start-up	The software house starts to gather resources as soon as the contract looks likely to go ahead. Formal commitments are not made until the deal is formally signed. A project manager within the company is allocated to provide a single point of contact for the customer. The project team is gathered, external programmers hired and resources (development computers, pre-written software) procured. The project elements are allocated to individuals and specifications are written for what each of the elements must achieve.
D3 – Execution	The project team starts work on the system – this is a mixture of importing existing code, modifying other parts and writing totally new elements. At the completion of each section of the work the modules are tested to ensure integration. Gradually the system is pieced together and debugged. The client is involved in the process, with modules being demonstrated as they are completed, so that amendments are made at the time rather than at the end of the entire process.
D3 – Completion	Towards the end of the development the units being tested are getting larger and more complex. The in-house specialist staff are kept on and the programmers who were hired in continue to other jobs. The major task to be completed at this stage is the documentation of the system.
D3 – Handover	The software is transported to the user's site and installed on the machines. The software specialists are on hand to see that any problems can be resolved quickly. Staff are trained in the usage of the system and the IS staff are taught to deal with its maintenance and support. Ongoing support is to be provided by the software house.
D4 – Review	The way in which each of the modules was developed is documented to provide a rich picture of the process. Mistakes and good practice are identified and customer perceptions of the system are canvassed. The results to the company in financial terms are compared with the proposal.
D4 – Feedback	Where deficiencies were highlighted, e.g. in the documentation of the system, the company puts in place new procedures and practices that will ensure (a) that the problem for the customer is resolved in this case and (b) that it does not occur in subsequent projects.

The four phases each have different characteristics and different management requirements. Some points are of note here. The first is that many project managers will not be involved in the early stages and will be handed a brief for the project after the initial definition work has been done by another party. There are many reasons why this causes problems, not least because the project manager cannot be involved in problem-avoidance measures at the early stage.

REAL WORLD **IDeA in Armenia**

IDeA is a charitable foundation based in Armenia which seeks to generate long-term social and economic benefit. It uses a structured approach to run its projects, from initial ideas through to concept development, detailed planning, execution and operation. After each stage of the project a 'gate' process is used to evaluate the deliverables and ensure that the project is sufficiently well-developed to continue. The purpose of each gate review (discussed in more detail in Chapter 5) is to be an official decision point where the participants and sponsors review what has been done and evaluate progress against the requirements of the gate. At Gate 0 in Figure 2.6, the project idea is evaluated with only rough order of magnitude (ROM) estimates at this stage. As the work progresses, more detailed plans are developed. Importantly, the gates provide regular opportunities to stop the project if it is deemed no longer valuable. As time goes on, what initially seemed a viable project may no longer be so if, for example, the original assumptions are found to be incorrect, or the world moves on and it is no longer required. It is worth noting that in practice, projects that have started and have funding and momentum can in fact be surprisingly hard to stop.

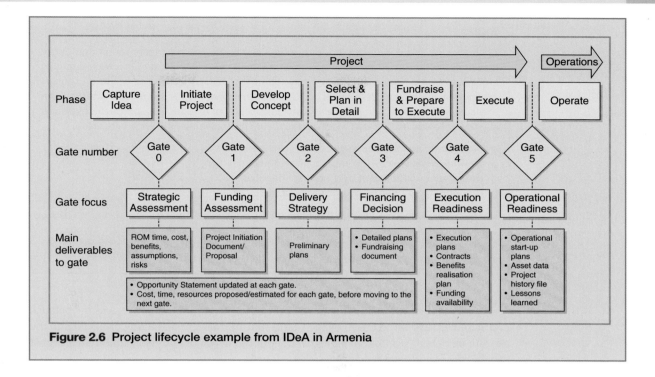

Figure 2.6 Project lifecycle example from IDeA in Armenia

It is important to distinguish between the **'project' lifecycle** (the development and delivery of the project itself) and that of the **product** or service being developed. There are as many different versions of the lifecycle as there are organisations running projects, but they all broadly follow the same pattern. The useful life of a mobile phone will likely be only a few years and will require limited servicing. Military equipment or a new passenger aircraft needs to be supported for decades, and major infrastructure is intended to benefit multiple future generations. This needs to be central to the planning process, as the costs of servicing or maintaining the product may be significantly more than its production cost, so lifecycle costs are vital to consider in the earliest phases.

The role of Agile

There is much debate within the project management community about the most effective way to run projects. The more linear approach, with the idea of steps within the project that follow one after the other (as indicated in Figure 2.6, above, and discussed in more depth throughout this book) is often referred to as the 'waterfall' model. We can envisage this as being high-level requirements that flow down into detailed design and planning, then controlled development and thorough testing. Throughout the development of project management as a discipline, this has been a key idea. However, it is not the only way. Recognising that often this is an unrealistic goal, it is perfectly feasible to run a more iterative ('agile') approach, where ideas are tested and knowledge gained throughout the project. It is a contested area, with some viewing these as incompatible ways of managing projects. The Introduction of the 7th edition of the APM Body of Knowledge says, 'Avoiding any simplification of this matter by referring to "waterfall vs agile", we outline the choices that leaders can make and acknowledge the reality that many project-based endeavours now adopt some sort of hybrid linear / iterative life cycle approach.' This is the line of reasoning we follow also. Different ways of running projects are available in the manager's toolbox, and it is reasonable that different sections of the project can, and should, be run in different ways.

> **Agile**
>
> Agile evolved in the software industry, where engineers and managers found that better results could be gained by solving problems during development, and incorporating new requirements and feedback during the development phase. By working as a team and ensuring frequent interaction, developers could ensure that what they ended up with was what the end customer wanted and prioritised. This philosophy of an adaptive approach developed into the *agile manifesto*,[9] and a set of practices. This states that the engineers value:
>
> - *individuals and interactions* over processes and tools;
> - *working software* over comprehensive documentation;
> - *customer collaboration* over contract negotiation;
> - *responding to change* over following a plan.
>
> That is, while there is value in the items on the right, we value the items on the left more. These points are important, though represent a shift of emphasis rather than a wholesale movement away from previous thinking. Any project with a low regard for process, documentation, contracts or planning is unlikely to be successful!

The key challenge for software development, as the originators saw it, was the balance of disciplines (as characterised by the traditional approach to managing projects) and the need to be able to respond to change – in both the needs of end-users and the emergent capabilities of software products.

Without going into the technicalities of that environment, some of the features of the practicalities of agile include the following:

1 Work broken into time boxes or *sprints* – typically of 1–4 weeks in duration. This keeps works packages short and visible.
2 Output of each sprint is to be a *working software release* – something that can be seen and tested by the end-user – vital in keeping the users engaged and developers connected with the purpose of their work.
3 Intensity maintained by daily stand-up meetings or *scrums*. Standing up is important because it tends to keep the meeting short (15–20 minutes is the maximum) and focused on removing barriers or obstacles to progress.
4 Programming sometimes carried out in pairs – claimed to dramatically reduce programming errors – one person working on the keyboard coding, the other watching, then regularly swapping over.
5 Programmers urged to write the testing protocols before the software.

What does this mean in practice? In one study we were involved in, a large organisation was involved in writing safety-critical software. Historically their client would draw up a long list of detailed requirements, taking many months to refine. The development team would then spend many more months working to implement and test the code, and then deliver the final result back to the customer. Often there were misunderstandings, key elements not as anticipated, unforeseen difficulties that caused delays, and opportunities for improvement missed because of the inability to discuss fully. A move to an agile development approach meant a very different way of working. The client and the developers met weekly, allowing ideas and options to be discussed regularly rather than only at the end. The daily stand-up meetings for the development team allowed everyone to know what was going on, and individuals understood better how their work fitted with the 'bigger picture'. Several key points came out:

- The greatly increased informal social contact allowed technical problems to be raised and addressed far more rapidly than was previously the case in a more 'formal' working arrangement.

- Customer involvement allowed discussions to be had throughout, capitalising on opportunities for improvement and avoiding the recriminations and blame that had characterised the end of previous similar projects.
- The conversations between experts in different disciplines allowed new ideas to be implemented that had not previously been considered. Software engineers raised the possibility for new functionality that the end users had not realised was possible. By bringing together different specialisms, beneficial ideas were trialled and implemented that had not been identified at the outset. Similarly, users spotted implementation problems at an early stage when they could be fixed more easily, saving difficult and time-consuming fixes later.

Overall, the new way of working was hailed as a success by all concerned, allowing faster development with far fewer difficulties. Is it a panacea for all projects? Absolutely not. However, a more flexible, exploratory and 'social' approach can be extremely beneficial if the context warrants it.

The potential for agile approaches does need careful evaluation, but it has been adopted with great enthusiasm by organisations across the world. Some of the ideas (scrums, rapid prototypes, focused working) are useful tools for the project manager. In an environment of uncertainty, iteration can certainly be a sensible approach. In other scenarios (such as a clearly defined, relatively straightforward and unchanging specification) iteration can be viewed as a waste and a 'right first time' approach would be more suitable. The two approaches are contrasted in Table 2.5, based on Dybå and Dingsøyr (2008).[10] This indicates that they are two quite different ways of thinking, yet the reality may not be quite so clear-cut. Nevertheless, it is an instructive way of thinking about your particular project and considering the best way of running it.

A mixed or 'hybrid' approach should be considered when some aspects of a project would benefit from an agile approach but other aspects are deemed inappropriate for its application. Some pieces of work or phases of the project may contain more 'standard', repeatable, elements, and these should be treated as such. Other aspects might be more

Table 2.5 Comparison of approach (adapted from Dybå and Dingsøyr, 2008)

Dimension	Traditional Development	Agile Development
Fundamental principles	Systems are specifiable, predictable, and are built through meticulous and extensive planning	High-quality adaptive software is developed by small teams using the principles of continuous design improvement based on rapid feedback and change
Management style	Tendency towards command and control	Tendency towards leadership and collaboration
Knowledge management	More focus on explicit knowledge	More focus on tacit knowledge
Communication	More formal	More informal
Desired organisational form/structure	Mechanistic (bureaucratic and formalised) aimed more at large organisations	Organic (flexible and participative encouraging cooperative social action) aimed more at small and medium organisations
Quality control	Heavy planning and strict control. Late, heavy testing	Continuous control of requirements, design and solutions. Continuous testing

novel and uncertain, and these should be run with this in mind. Alternatively, early stages of the work may be more exploratory and iterative, later ones more certain and controlled. Managerial judgement remains vital in defining the appropriate way of operating, and the APM BoK (2019) discusses this:

'Context matters: there is no universally-applicable one-size-fits-all life cycle. The choice often hinges on what the organisation is trying to achieve and what is important. . . Hybrid life cycles enable a pragmatic mix of philosophies, typically fusing together elements from predictive and adaptive perspectives to create a new model or approach.'[11]

This is a rapidly evolving aspect of project management and the implementation of agile is an important area. Its adoption in the IT sector is well-established, but outside this the evidence is limited. How to scale it effectively to larger projects and programmes is, as yet, unresolved, although this is currently a major aspect of investigation.

Design Thinking

One of the enduring features of Agile and its proponents, is the view that it is 'something new.' This is certainly not the case, as there is clear evidence that the principles were in use from the 1970s. Indeed, if one looks more broadly for evidence of the application of the key principles including iterative design and user involvement, these were clear in new product development practices from around the same time. However, as with many aspects of business and management, just because they were popular in the past, does not mean that the ideas cannot have currency today. We just hope that they are applied with the wisdom that should come with repeated use, rather than in a continuous search for novelty. The 2019 edition of the APM Body of Knowledge takes an approach which is worth noting here. Rather than joining in the tussle between the proponents of Agile and its objectors, the pragmatic line taken considers that all projects will involve iterative steps – that is – they will involve looping back a re-working of past outputs, in the light of new experience, as well as some notion of linearity from start to finish. This is a *hybrid* approach.

Design Thinking[12,13] itself has many values that would apply more generally to projects including integrating the requirements of the needs of the end users, the available resources and the constraints imposed by the organisations involved. But one of the key differences in approach is the discipline of holding off on a solution, until the problem is properly understood. The apocryphal tale is told of the first space missions, where NASA spent heavily developing a writing instrument that worked in space, producing the biro. The Russians took pencils. It is not hard to imagine that the Russian approach would have been more akin to the design thinking philosophy, where time was invested in understanding the needs, rather than in imposing a solution. Indeed, it is notable how many teams when faced with problems, will solutionise before having a deep understanding of the problem. The creativity encouraged by design thinking is more broadly needed in projects, and not just in terms of the product (the project output) but also the project process. Working across both dimensions is a real strength of this approach.

2.3   Describing the project management challenge: managerial complexity

The range of tasks called 'projects' has already been shown to be very wide and as you would expect, not all tools, techniques and management ideas are universally applicable across this range. The examples below illustrate two contrasting projects, how we can describe their **complexity** and hence the **managerial challenge** associated with each.

Book launch

As one of the few remaining privately owned bookstores, book launches were a major occasion. David Smith, the owner of the store, took charge of them personally so that he could maintain contact with both authors and his regular customers. Looking ahead to his next launch, he described it as 'a project of the utmost importance'. He had started planning this one six months in advance. He would need to liaise between the publishers, the author's agent and his own team to generate interest in the event and to use it to turn that interest into much-needed sales.

Scientific research project

A Nobel prize-winning scientist from a world-renowned institution, the Karolinska Institutet in Sweden, was considering how he would manage a major new research grant for which he was the principal investigator. The grant funded a network of scientists to pursue work that would assist in the understanding of major diseases, was worth many million euros per year and involved no less than 24 partners from all over Europe. The legal agreements between the parties ran to hundreds of pages, and that was before the discussions about the science even started. Managing groups of academics has been described as 'like herding feral cats', then add in any international dimensions, and that many will know little or nothing about managing a project, and the scientist suddenly found he had huge complexity to work with.

In each case, how would you approach the project? The book launch has little complexity and some basic plans and documentation would be appropriate. This could be achieved with a small number of written pages and would be unlikely to require professional project management assistance. The shop manager has done this before anyway and is confident of handling the requirements of this project. In the scientific research project, the financial and legal aspects of that work on their own are likely to keep not just the scientist but a small team of project support people busy for some time before, during and after the project. It is clearly of much higher complexity and would require a more structured and formalised approach to its management.

In assessing the complexity of a project, we are asking the question, *'how complex or difficult will it be to manage?'* While there are a number of approaches commonly used (e.g. Shenhar & Dvir's diamond model)[14] to answering this question, few of these have been grounded in both empirical and theoretical studies. One approach that has been developed in this way, categorises the answers to this question in terms of whether they are structural, socio-political or emergent complexities.[15]

Structural complexity is associated with size, variety, breadth of scope, the level of interdependence of people or tasks, or the pace of the work. It is the most easily recognised of the complexities, and is also described as *complicatedness* or the *level of interconnectedness*. For instance, in the development of a new product for a large firm, the programme manager commented, *'We're talking about 450,000 end users, which doesn't necessarily make it complex, but when all of those 450,000 have different requirements, then that does make it quite complex.'* In addition, the complexity associated with *pace* can be particularly challenging as the faster the pace, the greater the resource intensity (a lot of people working on the project for a relatively short time) and therefore the more complex it is to manage, albeit for a limited time. Pace would be typical in developing a new piece of consumer electronics or some events management.

Socio-political complexity is associated with a project's importance, its people, power, and (P)politics, in both the project team and wider. For instance, in the delivery of a new piece of software to a large bank, the programme manager noted, *'You've got multiple relationships within the bank... they've all got their own agendas, they never look at the thing in the whole...'* The number of people involved represents a structural complexity, but their different agendas (wants or purpose for wanting something) cause socio-political complexity. It represents the relational issues of projects.

Emergent complexity comprises uncertainty and change. Uncertainty is typically the result of novelty of technology or process, a lack of experience, and (non)availability of information on which to make decisions. This emergence is a characteristic of so many projects today and is a change or instability in either structural or socio-political complexity. As an example, one project manager commented on her project, *'We said to our client, "in terms of technical direction we haven't got a clue which way you're going." And they said, "no, you're right, because we really don't know either."'* This lack of clarity on the requirements in practice is not that unusual. However, it provides a particular set of challenges or complexities to the project manager, in how they adapt or respond to the uncertainty and change.

These three complexities, structural, socio-political and emergent, provide a means to distinguish between projects. While this is useful, they may not be fixed and can change as the project progresses. A recent $US multi-billion project to develop a new oil field by Shell, was initially structurally complex – the sheer scale of the project meant that this was the major complexity. During the development of the field, the government of the country in which it was taking place claimed some of the assets and, overnight, became a partner in the project. The complexity shifted – having to work with that partner provided another dimension to the complexity of the project – it now became far more socio-politically complex. Staying with the oil sector, the requirement to exploit energy reserves in increasingly hostile environments (e.g. from the arctic or the deep ocean), increases the levels of emergent complexity in such projects. The rapidly decreasing costs of renewable energy (e.g. wind and solar) also adds another layer of uncertainty.

In order to describe these complexities and allow for the classification of projects, Table 2.6 provides definitions.

Using this framework and the examples of issues allows us to compare the book launch (labelled A in Table 2.7) and the scientific research project (labelled B). The results of this assessment are shown in Table 2.7, with issues that are expected to make the project complex to manage ticked or crossed.

Table 2.6 The complexity framework

Element of complexity	Examples of issues that make management complex
Structural	Lack of clarity of requirements
	High level of interaction required across multiple technical disciplines
	Large scale, high value, high importance, high urgency
	Large number of constraints – legal, health and safety, security
	High level of interaction and interdependency with other projects
Socio-political	Problematic communications in the project team
	Large number of customers with differing requirements
	Lack of commitment to the project by key people or groups
	Interference in the project by key people or groups
	Lack of good relationships with key people or groups
Emergent	Uncertainty in the requirements
	Changes in the requirements
	Changes in the resources available to deliver the project
	Uncertainty in the key decision-makers
	Changes in the political support or business case for a project

Table 2.7 Assessing project complexity

Element of complexity	Examples of issues that make management complex	A	B
Structural	Lack of clarity of requirements	✗	✗
	High level of interaction required across multiple technical disciplines	✗	✓
	Large scale, high value, high importance, high urgency	✗	✓
	Large number of constraints – legal, health and safety, security	✗	✓
	High level of interaction and interdependency with other projects	✗	✓
Socio-political	Problematic communications in the project team	✗	✓
	Large number of customers with differing requirements	✗	✗
	Lack of commitment to the project by key people or groups	✗	✗
	Interference in the project by key people or groups	✗	✓
	Lack of good relationships with key people or groups	✗	✗
Emergent	Uncertainty in the requirements	✗	✗
	Changes in the requirements	✗	✓
	Changes in the resources available to deliver the project	✗	✓
	Uncertainty in the key decision-makers	✗	✓
	Changes in the political support or business case for a project	✗	✓

If you were to fill in a similar table for your own project, you would be able to create your own profile for that project and probably be able to add some elements of your own. Any complexity assessment is **subjective** – it is based on what an individual perceives would make that difficult to deliver. It is clear that the projects are of different orders of complexity and that the project manager for the scientific research project will have to take measures to deal with the specific complexities that are identified here. For instance, the 'high level of interaction and interdependency with other projects' was identified. In response, it would be appropriate to put in place a system for monitoring those other projects to ensure that the impact of changes in those projects is known. It is a core skill of a professional project manager that they have a range of responses to such complexities.

A complexity profile is a useful framework if used at the outset and then at various times during the project to identify particular difficulties and formulate a response to them. When considering these elements of complexity, it is worth considering their *interdependence* – for instance, the impact of structural aspects on socio-political aspects, and that complexities change over time. Changes can of course be positive (e.g. the cancellation or delay of another project releases resources which can be used to speed up your own work), but organising to deploy those additional resources usefully does, at least temporarily, increase the complexity faced.

Preparing the profile is the first step in complexity management – *understand*. As we progress through this book, we will be working on the remaining two elements – *reduce* and *respond*. The opportunity exists for most projects once there is this understanding, to undertake some complexity reduction.[16] This can be a hugely beneficial process. The residual complexities are what the project leader then has to work with, and become the subject of the response. The response can be for instance in the specific type of people to employ or the process to be used for the project. Complexity then, is a key variable that describes the fundamental nature of the work to be undertaken.

Summary

■ The world in which projects operate grows in complexity. This places additional challenges on project leaders in delivering and at the same time has increased expectations about delivery. It is no wonder, perhaps, that stories of 'failed projects' seem to have such presence in the media. Having frameworks or mental models enables us to make sense of complexity. This is not to say that we can ever completely describe something that is very complex, just as in the common aphorism: 'All models are wrong. Some are useful.' This is the utility this chapter has sought to provide in an attempt to facilitate the objective identified at the start – *get the thinking right*.

Key terms

4-D *p. 35*

5 Cs *p. 27*

7-S *p. 29*

change *p. 26*

Competitiveness *p. 29*

Completeness *p. 29*

complexity *p. 42*

context *p. 28*

Customer focus *p. 29*

emergent complexity models *p. 44*

framework *p. 29*

ICOM *p. 33*

integrator *p. 33*

issues *p. 26*

managerial challenge *p. 42*

model *p. 31*

PESTEL *p. 28*

project/product lifecycle *p. 39*

sense-making *p. 26*

socio-political complexity *p. 43*

structural complexity *p. 43*

structures *p. 29*

subjective *p. 45*

Relevant areas of the Bodies of Knowledge

Two Bodies of Knowledge are referenced throughout this book as they are used by many organisations as the basis for their own project management systems and as a knowledge base for accrediting their people. For instance, in some UK government organisations they require project managers to be licensed – that is to have passed a basic knowledge test of project management, such as those from the APM.

The standards do not set out to be comprehensive about everything that is known about project management; rather they provide guidance on some of the common ground between projects that covers 'most projects most of the time'. PMI's Standard[17] (American National Standards Institute) is Part 2 of its Guide to the Project Management Body of Knowledge – generally referred to as 'the pimbok guide.' The guide itself is relatively extensive compared with the APM version, but both are valuable and very widely-used resources.

Written by committee, one feature is that they tend to be focused on aspects of first-time projects (see Chapter 1) rather than the vast majority of project management activity that takes place in 'as . . . but . . . ' and 'painting by numbers' projects. They also assume that the relationship between the party carrying out the project and the 'customer' is contractual. Many projects are not 'direct revenue earners', instead being change projects (reorganising a firm, a merger or acquisition, or an individual undertaking a course of study, for instance). As a result of these factors, the application of the Bodies of Knowledge is a long way from universal. However, both are associated with professional qualifications and the contribution of these to the practice of project management and its professionalisation globally is significant.

This section presents an overview of the Bodies of Knowledge. These provide points of reference to the approach and identify some of the areas of overlap with the content of this text. As Tables 2.8 and 2.9 show, the format of the APM document is different from that of the PMI, with the themes arranged into sections, and specific sub-sections within each covering particular topics.

Neither of the bodies of knowledge shows how to decide 'what works where', or even suitable responses to the different complexities as described in this chapter.

Table 2.8 The APM Body of Knowledge 7th edition (2019)[18] and the relationship with topic coverage in this text

Section	Title	Topics covered	Relevant chapters in this text
1	Setting Up for Success	Focuses on available options for managers and the strategic decisions required.	
1.1	Implementing Strategy	High-level view on how to set up the investment in change and the use of projects, programmes and portfolios to deliver benefits. Subsections on: Organisational environment; Strategic implementation; Organisational change; Benefits to the organisation; Structural choices.	1, 2, 3, 4, 5, 8, 11
1.2	Life Cycle Options and Choices	Discusses the options and implications of different ways of structuring project work. There is no single 'best way', there are different approaches available to managers. Subsections on: Life cycle philosophy; Linear life cycles; Iterative life cycles; Hybrid life cycles; Extended life cycles; Product life cycles.	1, 2, 3, 5, 6
1.3	Establishing Governance and Oversight	Covers the mechanisms to enable the achievement of the objectives of the change. Subsections on: Governance principles; Assurance principles; Sustainability; Strategic sourcing; Sponsorship; Investment decisions; Business case; Temporary structures; Talent management; Governance boards.	8, 11, 12, 13, 14, 16
2	Preparing for Change	This looks at the practices throughout the life cycle that are important for the project, programme or portfolio manager to consider.	
2.1	Shaping the Early Life Cycle	Discusses how to set up the work to meet the needs of the stakeholders in a complex environment, including the consideration of the supply chain. Subsections on: Project shaping; Programme shaping; Portfolio shaping; Procurement strategy; Operational adjustments.	1, 2, 3, 4, 5, 14, 15
2.2	Assurance, Learning and Maturity	The ability to assure progress and to create, share and use knowledge is important in managing performance. Subsections on: The PMO; Decision gates; Information management; Audits and assurance; Knowledge management; Communities of practice; Maturity of practice.	5, 9, 11, 13, 15, 16
2.3	Transition into Use	Discusses transforming the outputs of the project(s) into beneficial outcomes for stakeholders and transitioning into organisational business-as-usual (BAU). Subsections on: Business readiness; Transition of project outputs; Adoption and benefits realisation; Unplanned project endings; Administrative closure of projects; Closing programmes and portfolios.	16

Table 2.8 continued

Section	Title	Topics covered	Relevant chapters in this text
3	People and Behaviours	Projects are dependent upon the people that deliver them. Leading teams and working with stakeholders is a necessary skill of an effective, professional, project manager. Sometimes known as 'soft' skills, they can be the hardest to master.	
3.1	Engaging Stakeholders	Understanding, building relationships with, and working alongside stakeholders is a key skill in project delivery. Subsections on: Stakeholders; Social context; Engagement and influence; Facilitation; Conflict resolution.	9, 12
3.2	Leading Teams	Leading teams, often under pressure, is central in project-based working, and it is important to set the right context for the team to develop and work together. Subsections on: Teams; Virtual teams; Team development; Leadership; Organisational culture; Diversity and inclusion; Workplace stress.	12
3.3	Working Professionally	As a chartered profession, there is significant emphasis on professionalism and ethical working. Subsections on: Communication; Negotiation; Time management; Regulatory environment; Ethics and standards; Continuing professional development.	12
4	Planning and Managing Deployment	It is a challenge to manage the end-to-end process of delivery, especially if agility and flexibility are required.	
4.1	Defining Outputs	It can be difficult to move from the initial high-level vision to the practical details of the final requirements document. This may require an iterative approach, but should not negate the discipline of clearly defining what needs to be done. Subsections on: Success and benefits; Objectives and requirements; Options and solutions; Scope definition; Quality planning.	2, 3, 9
4.2	Integrated Planning	Detailed planning is essential, and this covers many of the 'hard' skills expected of project management to make sure that the practicalities of the planning, costing and resource allocation are robust. Subsections on: Contract award; Risk identification; Risk analysis; Estimation; Scheduling – critical path; Scheduling – critical chain; Resource optimisation; Cost planning; Contingency planning; Deployment baseline.	5, 6, 7, 8, 10
4.3	Controlling Deployment	This is a major component of project managers' days, and it involves bringing together the technical and people skills covered in the preceding sections of the Body of Knowledge. Subsections on: Progress monitoring and reporting; Contract management; Risk management; Contingency management; Issue management; Change control; Configuration management; Quality control.	9, 10, 13

Table 2.9 The PMI Body of Knowledge[19] and the relationship with topic coverage in this text

Section	Title	Summary	Relevant chapters
1	Introduction	Sets out the purpose of the guide and the definitions of projects and project management, project lifecycle and the role of the project in organisations.	1, 2, 3
2	The Environment in which Projects Operate	This discusses the internal and external environmental influences on the project, and the organisational systems and structures used to control the work.	1, 2, 3

Section	Title	Summary	Relevant chapters
3	The Role of the Project Manager	This looks at the manager's sphere of influence within and outside the project, and key project management competencies.	1, 4, 11, 12
4	Project Integration Management	Integration management refers to bringing together the different aspects of a project in a coordinated way over the project life cycle. Further, it recognises that there will be trade-offs in the decisions that project managers make and that the task of management is complex.	2, 5, 13, 16
5	Project Scope Management	The scope of the project is defined in terms of a written statement of what is to be included in the project and what is specifically excluded. The main scoping work includes the work breakdown structure (WBS). Scope change control is also identified as a specific item, separate but linked to other aspects of change control.	5, 6, 10, 13
6	Project Schedule Management	Activities identified during scope management processes are compiled into an activity list, sequenced and times assigned to each activity. This then leads to the schedule for these activities – the times at which each must be completed to ensure the project as a whole finishes on time.	6, 13
7	Project Cost Management	Similar to the process for time management, each of the activities is associated with a cost. This becomes the budget for each activity and there will need to be control measures to ensure that deviations from 'the plan' as a result of project problems and customer changes are 'managed'. Measures including *earned value* are suggested.	8, 13
8	Project Quality Management	The focus on the carrying out of planning, assurance and control is comparable in many ways to the intention of ISO 9000[20] – that of providing *conformance*. (As for time and cost, in this text it is considered that conformance is only the minimum requirement of a project and that the current commercial environment for many organisations requires *performance* above and beyond these minimum standards.)	9, 13
9	Project Resource Management	The main areas here are planning the organisational structure in which people will work, documenting their roles and reporting relationships, identifying the necessary individuals and developing and managing the team.	11, 12
10	Project Communications Management	There are three aspects to this area: planning, managing and monitoring project communications. The guide provides a set of practices that are applicable to most projects.	4, 9
11	Project Risk Management	Contains a broad description of risk management processes, from planning to identification to monitoring and control actions. Focus is on administrating the process.	10, 13
12	Project Procurement Management	Covers a wide range of contract administration issues from the perspective of both buyer and seller of products or services.	14
13	Project Stakeholder Management	Looks specifically at identifying stakeholders and then planning, managing and monitoring stakeholder engagement.	4

PROJECT MANAGEMENT IN PRACTICE
The rescue of Crossrail

The brief was nowhere near this simple for Crossrail, but at one level this was what was required. The project team needed to just:

1 Dig a tunnel under the centre of London, of course avoiding all the existing infrastructure (water mains, train tunnels, sewers, burial grounds, reclaimed land,) whether or not we know they are there.
2 Fit the tunnel out with stations, interchanges, rails, power, signalling. Make sure the signalling is up to the latest safety standards.

Source: Guy Corbishley/Alamy Stock Photo

3 Get some trains that will run on the system, work with the signalling to the east of London, the underground, and the west (all completely different).
4 And do not run late or over-budget.

How hard can it be?

As it turns out, it was ridiculously hard. This is a case study worth following as it has been a saga that has claimed reputations, careers and vast amounts of public and private money. It is, of course, nowhere near as good in this regard as the Sydney Opera House or the Canadian Gun Control Register (also worth looking up).

The case came to one of its many crunch points in 2018. The costs of the scheme had already risen from the previous estimate by £2.8 billion to £17.6 billion. It was due to open in late 2018. However, during the summer of 2018, it became clear that this was not going to happen. Following a review, the developing company, Crossrail Limited, had to admit that even up until July 2018 this had been hugely optimistic. They 'reset' the schedule to 'between October 2020 and March 2021'. As of March 2021, this is now looking more like 'sometime in 2022'.

Points for discussion

The following aspects of this case are worth exploring further:
1 Just how optimistic were the original forecasts for schedule and budget?
2 Why did this optimism prevail in Crossrail Ltd.?
3 Who is to blame for this? Is it Transport for London, the UK Department for Transport, Crossrail Ltd., the contractors or individual leaders?
4 What approach should the project have taken, that might have contributed to a better outcome?
5 Will the problems be remembered once it is open and operating?

PROJECT MANAGEMENT IN PRACTICE
Using the 7-S approach in the review of a real project[21]

The Arson Task Force (ATF) was the name given to a 24-month project to reduce the incidence of arson in one area. During the project, the incidence of arson there declined and the team built an extensive knowledge base of cases of arson, its impact, effects and, most importantly, the causes and patterns of occurrence.

This report considers the process by which the project has been managed for the purposes of identifying areas of good practice and improvement. Specific findings are that the project has been a success due to the team that has been put in place, the funding arrangements, flexible and adaptive management and considerable goodwill towards the project. Areas for improvement that have been identified include the project governance structure, project systems, staffing, skills and the management of stakeholders in the project.

Source: Courtesy of Avon Fire & Rescue Service

Terms of reference

This report has been prepared to evaluate the project management practices used by the ATF during the bidding and execution of the project. The baseline for comparison of the processes and practices used is a combination of elements of PRINCE2 and the PMI Body of Knowledge.

Overview of the project

The ATF is an alliance between two fire and rescue services and an area police force. The task force comprises eight full-time staff with the following key objectives:

- To work in partnership with other agencies and private businesses to effect a sustainable reduction in the number of arson incidents.
- To increase the percentage of arson incidents that are successfully detected.
- To reduce the number of arson incidents in schools and other educational premises.
- To produce and deliver educational programmes aimed at addressing the behaviour and attitudes of 7–16 year olds towards fire setting.
- To reduce the incidence of re-offending by working with Youth Offending Teams and developing intervention schemes for young offenders.

The framework for analysis

The 7-S framework will be used in this report. Under each heading, a statement of the understanding of relevant or illuminating events will be included with relevant elements of process. Where appropriate, suggestions will be made for improving the process of running future projects.

Strategy

Two aspects of strategy will be considered:

1 Project success measures – how are they defined?
2 Project strategy – the stated goals and priorities of the project.

Project success measures

The main measure for the success of the project is the reduction in arson in the region. This is an *outcome* measure that the work of the team will predominantly influence through indirect means. The team cannot stop acts of arson directly – they are working to influence the behaviour of those who may be or become arsonists. This outcome measure does little to allow the process that the team have gone through to be evaluated and could easily be influenced by events outside the control of the team (social disorder, for instance, causing a surge in the figures). In order to provide meaningful measures, it would also be appropriate to measure the *process* of the work, e.g. the number of workshops carried out or long-term initiatives established.

→

Project strategy

The project has a fixed time and budget. Any issues in the project would therefore be expected to affect the 'quality' (outcomes, achievements, etc.) of the project. As part of the bidding documentation for the project the high-level objectives for the project were established. These were sufficiently explicit to provide a focused framework for activities and yet still allowed considerable flexibility for dealing with issues that emerged as the research into incidents of arson progressed. There was no priority attached to these objectives however, and no allowance or process for change and assessing the impact of changes on quality.

Structure

The structure of a dedicated project team with permanently committed resources is an entirely appropriate arrangement. However, there are a number of issues.

Location

Co-locating the team was entirely appropriate for this kind of cross-agency working. Indeed, given the need for knowledge-sharing in the team, this kind of arrangement is to be encouraged.

Role of the project management board

The board, meeting quarterly, provided useful and informed views from a wide range of stakeholder groups. Its role was entirely advisory however, and there appears to have been minimal input to the management of the project by this board. The monitoring of progress by this board was not achieved – other than commenting on major milestones. In addition, it was noted that there were no terms of reference for the members of the board. It would be consistent with the declared intention to run the project using the PRINCE2 approach that a managerial board was put in place.

Authority structure

The project had two project managers who operated 'side by side'. This is very unusual, particularly when they come from different agencies. In reality, there were two team leaders, rather than project managers, who retained their line reporting from their own organisations. However, the arrangement appears to have worked. While no single individual had overall responsibility or authority for the project, the shared goals and the efforts of the two individuals concerned have carried this. This practice should be reviewed for future projects as such a structure is more likely to be associated with project failure than success.

Systems

In PM terms, there are not a lot of project systems to report on. The effect of such a low level of systematisation is that the management has been able to be very flexible, unconstrained in many ways by incumbent plans. However, this does have an impact on the repeatability of such a project and does not provide any evidence for future time or resource planning. Indeed, if the project is to be an exemplar for other such projects in other areas in the future (as the organisations involved had hoped), some 'retrospective planning' would be worthwhile – for instance, recording at a high level basic timelines (using a Gantt Chart) indicating the phases of the project and key deliverables in each phase, identification of basic resource requirements (typical activities, time main activities take, job/role descriptions). Such a piece of documentation would add to the utility of the project outputs.

Planning and control

The objectives of the project were very well defined and provided a good basis for the broad categories of work that were followed. However, there was little by way of planning as would conventionally be expected, even in such a project. The effects of this 'it's all in my head' approach appear limited. In the event of the project not having been such a success, the management of the project, and in particular the planning and control, could be viewed unfavourably. Further, the project was unnecessarily 'at risk' from loss of one of the project managers.

In order to enhance the level of performance obtained through the existing approach and provide a level of management consistent with the context, there are a number of devices that could be applied. At the strategic level, these include the provision of basic work breakdown structures linked to stages and gates as an overview plan. These provide a basis for planning and resource allocation, without adding significantly to the bureaucratic workload. In addition, it would help with scoping activities (deciding what is in and what is outside the project) given resource availability and with communicating with the team and other stakeholders the plan for and progress of the project. Basic analysis of the work content of the project could be carried out and likely problems or opportunities identified proactively.

PRINCE2

According to the project proposal, ATF was going to be planned and managed using PRINCE2. While this would have had to have been a selective application, there is no evidence that this standard was used. Unless mandated by the funding authority, it would be worth removing this requirement from future bids and developing basic project strategies, systems, structures etc. that are appropriate to the specific context and complexity.

Staff

Succession planning and knowledge management

There was no succession planning (what is to happen in the event of a team member leaving the team for whatever reason) in place at an organisational level. When a key member of staff was promoted out of the team, a core resource was removed. More importantly for the project was the loss of considerable knowledge as a result of this move, and instability for the team.

Teambuilding and team roles

Teambuilding did not appear as a specific activity in the project and would be worth including in the future. In addition, some personality profiling, as part of the ongoing teambuilding/staff development process, would help.

Recruitment

Recruitment and retention of team members is always going to be a challenge where there are uncertainties over funding beyond the life of the project. The approach taken here appears to have been highly pragmatic, with the scale and scope of work being flexible depending on resource availability. In future, it is likely that more specific task identification will be required and in such a case appropriate allowances must be made in the plans for the challenges of recruiting team members into specific roles and retaining them.

Skills

Not training the project managers in PRINCE2 until well into the execution phase of the project was a major oversight. In addition, there was no oversight of the management tasks being undertaken. In this case, it does not appear to have been detrimental to the performance of the project, although it does represent an unnecessary risk.

Style/culture

From the comments of the interviewees, the can-do culture of the team appeared to be entirely consistent with the goals of the project and has been encouraged by the team leaders.

Stakeholders

Managing stakeholders, particularly those who have an influence in the outcome of the project and the future of the team, is widely recognised as a core task for a project manager.

Stakeholders include:

- funders – Arson Control Forum (ACF) (central government, which would also fund any future work including continuation of the ATF);
- each of the partner organisations;
- local authorities;
- the project team;
- the project board;
- local businesses and residents;
- insurance companies (hoping to get reduced exposure to the risk of arson fires);
- other organisations looking to use the approach in their areas in the future.

There was no evidence that a communications plan/strategy was in place and this should form an integral part of the work packages in such a project. Marketing the project to stakeholder groups is again part of the role of a PM, particularly in a case such as this, where ongoing funding is required.

Points for discussion

1 How useful is the 7-S framework in the evaluation of this case?

2 How else could you review the management of such a project?

3 How complex is the ATF project?

4 The ATF received funding for a further two years. What would you recommend that the management of the ATF does to ensure success?

Topics for discussion

1 Identify a personal project that you have completed in the recent past – this may be a piece of coursework, a DIY project, etc. Consider the way in which the project was planned, carried out, the results analysed and then acted upon. What would you do differently if you were doing it all over again?

2 Taking the example of a personal project that you have recently completed (as for question 1), identify the inputs, outputs, constraints and mechanisms for the project. What is the importance of defining the nature of constraints on a project prior to starting work on it?

3 How would you describe the competitive environment of the following organisations?

- automotive industry;
- construction industry;
- banking;
- further/higher education.

What constraints does this place on projects being carried out in such an environment?

4 Why is it necessary to define the complexity of a project?

5 Identify the likely complexity of the following projects:

- the development of a new office block;
- the development of a new office complex where a radical new design is proposed;
- a project to put a new telescope in space by the European Space Agency;
- implementing a robotised assembly line in a manufacturing company.

6 Why is it necessary to consider the continuous improvement of the processes by which projects are carried out?

7 Identify the criteria for success or failure of the projects that you discussed in question 1 and question 2.

8 Show how developing a new product, for example a new range of vehicle engines, could benefit through the analysis of previous development projects.

9 Write a commentary on the Bodies of Knowledge, and how they could relate to your own work environment both now and in the future.

10 Explore the possibilities for gaining professional qualification and recognition in project management, through both APM and PMI. How well would these fit with your own intentions regarding your profession?

Further information

APM Assurance Specific Interest Group (2017) *A Guide to Assurance of Agile Delivery*, Association for Project Management, Princes Risborough.

APM Governance Specific Interest Group (2016) *Directing Agile Change*, Association for Project Management, Princes Risborough.

AXELOS (2015) *PRINCE2 Agile*, The Stationery Office, Norwich.

AXELOS (2017) Managing Successful Projects with PRINCE2, TSO, Norwich.

Checkland, P. and Poulter, J. (2006) *Learning for Action: A Short Definitive Guide to Soft Systems Methodology and Its Use for Practitioners, Students and Teachers*, John Wiley and Sons, Chichester.

Conforto, E.C., Amaral, D.C., da Silva, S.L., Di Felippo, A., and Kamikawachi, D.S.L. (2016) 'The agility construct on project management theory', *International Journal of Project Management*, Vol. 34, No. 4, pp. 660–674.

Cooke-Davies, T, Crawford, L., and Patton, J. (eds) (2011*), Aspects of Complexity: Managing Projects in a Complex World,* Project Management Institute, Newtown Square, PA.

Cooke-Davies, T., Cicmil, S., Crawford, L. and Richardson, K. (2007) 'We're Not in Kansas Anymore, Toto: Mapping the Strange Landscape of Complexity Theory, and Its Relationship to Project Management', *Project Management Journal*, Vol. 38, No. 2, pp. 50–61.

Geraldi, J., Maylor, H. and Williams, T. (2011) 'Now, Let's make it really Complex (Complicated): A Systematic Review of the Complexities of Projects', *International Journal of Operations and Production Management*, Vol. 31, No. 9, pp. 966–990.

IPMA (International Project Management Association) *Individual Competence Baseline*, see www.ipma.world/individuals/standard/

Lappi, T., Karvonen, T., Lwakatare, L.E., Aaltonen, K. and Kuvaja, P. (2018) 'Toward an Improved Understanding of Agile Project Governance: A Systematic Literature Review', *Project Management Journal*, Vol. 49, No. 6, pp. 39–63.

Lenfle, S. and Loch, C. (2010) 'Lost roots: How project management came to emphasize control over flexibility and novelty', *California Management Review*, Vol. 53, No. 1, pp. 32–55.

Shenhar, A. and Holzmann, V. (2017) 'The three secrets of megaprojects success: clear strategic vision, total alignment, and adapting to complexity', *Project Management Journal*, Vol. 48, No. 6, pp. 29–46.

Söderlund, J. (2011). 'Pluralism in project management: Navigating the crossroads of specialization and fragmentation,' *International Journal of Management Reviews*, Vol. 13, No. 2, pp. 153–176.

Tam, C., Moura, E. J., Oliveira, T. and Varajão, J. (2020) 'The factors influencing the success of on-going agile software development projects', *International Journal of Project Management*, Vol. 38, No. 3, pp. 165–176.

Turner N., Aitken J. and Bozarth C. (2018) 'A framework for understanding managerial responses to supply chain complexity', *International Journal of Operations and Production Management*, Vol. 38, No. 6, pp. 1433–1466.

Xia, W. and Lee, G. (2004) 'Grasping the Complexity of IS Development Projects', *Communications of the ACM*, Vol. 47, No. 5, pp. 69–74.

Websites

www.agilealliance.org

www.apm.org.uk/ – including many reports on agile project management

www.mindtools.com/pages/article/newSTR_91.htm

www.pmi.org/

References

1 For more on this sense-making approach in business and management, see e.g. Weick K.E., Sutcliffe K.M. and Obstfeld D. (2005) 'Organizing and the Process of Sensemaking', *Organization Science*, Vol. 16, No. 4, pp. 409–421

2 Gareis, R., Huemann, M., Martinuzzi, A., (2013) *Project Management & Sustainable Development Principles*, Project Management Institute, Newtown Square, PA.

3 See Deming, W.E. (1986) *Out of the Crisis – Quality Productivity and Competitive Position*, MIT Center for Advanced Engineering Study, Cambridge, MA.

4 A further discussion of the use of such models in operations management can be found in Slack, N. and Brandon-Jones A. (2019) *Operations Management,* 9th edition, Pearson, Harlow.

5 For a further description of this development see Dyson, J. (2000) *Against the Odds*, Taxere Publishing, London.

6 It is the usual practice in some industries to have a period of claims following a contract completion. In the case of a building, there may be additional work as a result of clients changing specifications during the project or where there were unknowns (for instance, ground conditions) that were the risk of the client, not the contractor. Where these cannot be resolved amicably, a regular occurrence is the trip to court at the end of the project.

7 If not native to you, replace with any other animal that is more likely to be roadkill where you are.

8 This is supported by, among others, the findings of Clark and Fujimoto's study of excellence in the world automotive industry – see Clark, K.B. and Fujimoto, T. (1991) *Product Development Performance: Strategy, Organisation and Management in the World Automotive Industry*, Harvard Business School Press, Boston, MA.

9 www.agilemanifesto.org/

10 Dybå T. and Dingsøyr T. (2008) 'Empirical studies of agile software development: A systematic review', *Information and Software Technology*, Vol. 50, Nos 9/10, pp.

11 APM (2019) *Project Management Body of Knowledge*, 7th edition, Association for Project Management, High Wycombe, p. 22.

12 Brown, T. (2008) 'Design Thinking', *Harvard Business Review*, Vol. 86, No. 6, pp. 84–92.

13 Mahmoud-Jouini, S.B., Midler, C. and Silberzahn, P. (2016) 'Contributions of Design Thinking to Project Management in an Innovation Context', *Project Management Journal*, Vol. 47, No. 2, pp. 144–156.

14 Shenhar , A. J. , and Dvir , D. (2007) *Reinventing Project Management: The Diamond Approach to Successful Growth and Innovation*, Harvard Business School Press, Cambridge, MA.

15 See Maylor H., Turner N., and Murray-Webster R. (2013) 'How Hard Can It Be? Actively Managing Complexity in Technology Projects', *Research Technology Management*, Vol. 56, No. 4, pp. 45–51.

16 Maylor H. and Turner N. (2017) 'Understand, Reduce, Respond: Project Complexity Management Theory and Practice', *International Journal of Operations and Production Management*, Vol. 37, No. 8, pp. 1076–1093.

17 ANSI/PMI 99-001-2017

18 APM (2019) *Project Management Body of Knowledge*, 7th edition, Association for Project Management, High Wycombe.

19 PMI (2017) *A Guide to the Project Management Body of Knowledge (PMBOK® Guide)*, 6th edition, Project Management Institute, Newtown Square, PA.

20 See www.iso.org/iso-9001-quality-management.html

21 This is not intended to illustrate good or bad practice or a good/bad report. The purpose is to show how such a framework is useful in providing a relatively straightforward but comprehensive review in practice. It is a synopsis of a longer report.

3

Projects and organisations

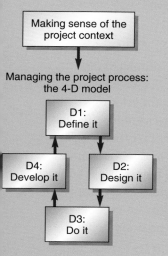

Making sense of the project context

↓

Managing the project process: the 4-D model

D1: Define it

D4: Develop it

D2: Design it

D3: Do it

'After more than 30 years of evolution, from a planning methodology associated with PERT and CPM, project management has finally come of age. No longer simply a middle management tool for planning, organising and controlling human and other resources, project management can now be regarded as an essential means of turning strategic objectives into organisational ventures.'[1]

Principles

1 There should be coherence between the objectives of the organisation and the work being carried out in projects.

2 Resources are scarce: the time, money and effort committed to projects need to be managed.

3 Project management is best carried out in an environment that recognises and supports the needs of the people carrying out the activities.

Learning objectives

By the time you have completed this chapter, you should be able to:

→ define the role of organisational strategy in projects

→ recognise a process for the deployment of strategy

→ demonstrate the role of portfolios and programmes of projects and the possible support roles that organisation can offer to portfolio, programme and project managers.

Contents

Introduction *58*
3.1 Organisational strategy and projects *59*
3.2 Portfolios and programmes[2] *64*
3.3 Project roles and governance *70*
Summary *75*
Key terms *76*
Relevant areas of the Bodies of Knowledge *76*
Project management in practice: *The Airbus A380 development* *76*
Project management in practice: *Selecting a personal project* *79*
Topics for discussion *80*
Further information *80*
References *81*

Following the rise of budget airlines (e.g. Southwest Airlines) in the US, Europe and Australia in particular have seen new carriers emerging as major players in the markets. In Europe, easyJet and Ryanair have been the main players in this burgeoning market.

Source: Steven May/Alamy

A notable feature of easyJet has been its focus. Right from its humble beginnings, its resources (initially limited compared with the established competition at the time) have been focused on achieving results in its key corporate objectives, as expressed in its mission statement:

easyJet's values are publicly available[3] and emphasise their drive for safety, simplicity (a focus on lean operations), teamwork, integrity, passion, and a pioneering spirit.

This provides a good steer for the business: safety is critical – this is the foundation of air travel and cannot be compromised. Good value, or how to move passengers in the most efficient (cheapest) manner possible, is what wins them business. Projects that support this efficiency, for instance by improving the speed with which transactions are handled on the website, or changes that will reduce the amount of time that planes spend on the ground between flights, are readily approved. A clear statement on cutting out the non-essential elements provides clarity for the whole organisation. Anything that does not directly contribute to this is not allowed to progress. The result is that everyone in the firm has a clear sense of purpose – there is no doubt what the firm is about.

Introduction

Walking around some organisations, you get the sense of everything being very purposeful, with people somehow connected, each in their own way, with the organisation in which they work. Such an event is rare, but when it occurs there is always a common element – a clear organisational direction that everyone in the organisation understands, and a demonstrable link between activities and this direction.

The opening quotation in this chapter illustrates the role of project management in creating such a connection. Such a conversion of strategic objectives into operational ventures, and then activities, requires the active participation of project managers in the process. This view has received much more attention recently with phrases like:

Notice that the journey from boardroom to marketplace must pass through project management[4] becoming more common. To achieve such a connection requires that the process, purpose and language of strategy and the organisational strategist be understood. That is the purpose of this chapter. The reason is that behind every organisational strategy there are a huge number of individual decisions that have to be made. As will be shown, these need to carry forward that strategy into the day-to-day activities of a project and also inform the future direction of an organisation through the evolution of that organisation's capabilities.

3.1   Organisational strategy and projects

It has been recognised for a long time that '*the organisation that attempts a narrow mission, will outperform one that attempts a wider* **mission**'.[5] Put another way, don't try to be good at everything. In organisational terms this means that the things that the organisation decides to be good at should be the **focus** of what it does. There are a number of elements to achieving this focus that will be explored in this and section 3.2. These elements build into the **strategy process** shown in Figure 3.1. Each of the elements will be discussed here.

At the top of Figure 3.1, there is the Chief Executive Officer (CEO) or leader of the organisation who is responsible (amongst other things) for providing the **vision** of where the organisation is going. For the organisation, this has been well described as:

'We're standing on this hill here. The vision is that we want to be on that hill over there.'

The description implies that there is knowledge of the organisation's current position and a notion of where its leader(s) wants it to be at a point in the future. The vision is expressed as a **mission statement** for the organisation. Often clichéd, they are nonetheless a good guide to the effectiveness of the strategy process in an organisation.

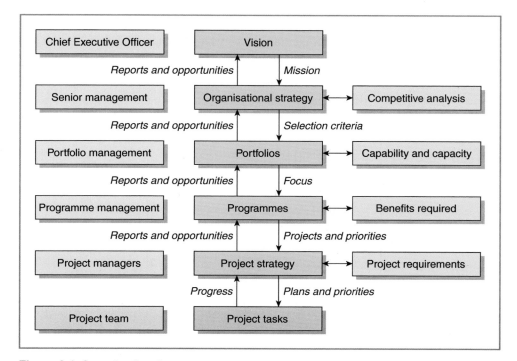

Figure 3.1 Organisational strategy process

Formulating the content of that mission requires input from the current capabilities of the organisation, and analysis of the threats and opportunities that it faces. In this book, we consider two major inputs to the process – the organisation itself feeding in opportunities and the organisation's leadership. Traditionally, **strategy** was considered to be a one-way process – organisational strategy would be implemented from the top down. Figure 3.2 shows the differences between this and the strategy processes of world-class organisations today that combine this with feedback from the organisation.[6]

Using a traditional approach, it is often found that rather than aiming to create competitive advantage through projects, project managers are forced into the mode of trying to 'minimise the negative potential' of projects.[7] In this mode the focus is on **conformance** regardless of the real needs of **performance** of the organisation (this is discussed further below) and an attitude of 'just don't mess up'. Strategy is the concern of senior management only and is implemented in a top-down manner, often regardless of the realities of what is possible at a project level.

The strategic approach has a number of important differentiating features. These include the strong link between strategy and activities at the project level. Strategy formulation is still carried out by senior management in the organisation, but importantly, there are inputs from all levels of the organisation. These include progress reports on existing work, current workloads and capacities, limitations of existing capabilities and potential new capabilities, and in particular ideas as to how new opportunities that have emerged from project activities can be developed.

The notion here is simple – by creating an involving process of two-way communication throughout the organisation, the strategy process becomes more consensual and people are aware of the realities of capabilities and limitations 'on the ground'.[8] Projects become, as described in the quotation at the start of this chapter, the *'essential means of turning strategic objectives into organisational ventures'*. More than this, they will also contribute to developing future strategic objectives.

The nature of the strategy process has changed in many organisations. Returning to the elements of the process identified in Figure 3.1, the mission statement of an organisation is often revealing of the understanding of that organisation about the nature of strategy. For instance, contrast the very targeted approach from easyJet at the start of the chapter with the one seen proudly displayed in the reception office of a small firm:

> *'Our mission is to be the best producer in the world of high-technology solutions which delight our customers.'*

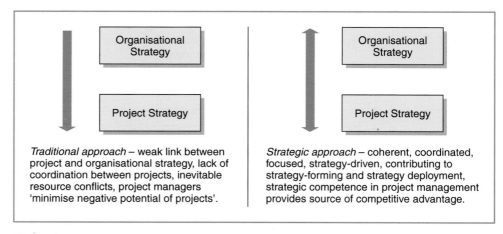

Figure 3.2 Traditional versus strategic approaches

The firm was a small player in a large market, which survived through its ability to supply quickly to local markets. It did not need to be the 'best in the world' – indeed this was not remotely credible, as its larger competitors all had superior technology and delivery capabilities. The employees and the customers all knew this. The firm was excellent at providing capacity for manufacturing complex printed circuit board (PCB) assemblies at short notice. A more appropriate mission might have been:

> *'To be the most responsive supplier of PCBs and associated design services to our customers.'*

Being the best wasn't necessary – the firm didn't have to be the best quality or the cheapest. It did have to be responsive to gain advantage from its geographical position close to a number of original equipment manufacturers (OEMs – the people who make branded electronic equipment). Setting the vision identifies where the organisation is heading. Using the hill metaphor, the direction or course has been set. The next layer down in the strategy process is the *organisational strategy*. In one sense this is 'the route to get to the other hill'. The process here is now concerned with delivery – turning the ideas into reality. This part of the strategy process is known as **strategy deployment** – providing a focused set of activities that the organisation will work on.

In addition to the vision providing an input to the deployment, an analysis of the environment contributes – as described in Chapter 2. Further tools for providing this input include **SWOT** (strengths, weaknesses, opportunities and threats) and analysis of 5-Forces (bargaining power of customers and suppliers, threats of new entrants and substitutes and competitive rivalry between existing players).[9] Henry Mintzberg, one of the founders of modern thinking in strategic management and more recently one of its most ardent critics,[10] defined strategy in terms of 5-Ps[11] – a plan, a pattern of consistent behaviour over time, a position created by an organisation in a market, a perspective or approach that is identified with that organisation ('the HP Way', Ericsson's PROPPS system) and a ploy. The last is reminiscent of militaristic strategy and would be intended to outmanoeuvre a competitor. All of these are evident in the analogy of how to get to 'that hill over there'.

This is not easy. Developing a strategy is one thing, making it happen the way you expect (especially in a large organisation) is challenging. One recent study[12] offered clear advice for top managers regarding this in terms of questions to ask:

1 'What is our vision?' – what is the long-term aspiration we seek?
2 'What are our critical vulnerabilities?' – which areas do we need to pay most attention to?
3 'What should we prioritise?' – doing too many things risks spreading resources too thinly; clear priorities help managers focus.

Deploying strategy results in two key things – the priorities for the way that products and services are delivered today (*direct revenue-earning* activities) and what the organisation will be doing tomorrow (resulting in **organisational change**). The first category includes completing a consultancy assignment, a construction project or any work carried out for a third party for which you or your organisation is paid. The second category would include changes to an organisation's structure, IT system, a merger or a new business start-up. These projects do not directly earn anything, though they should be yielding benefits to the organisation, for instance in obtaining cost savings or opening up a new market to the organisation. Their cases do have some overlap, but the strategic aspects of each are essentially different.

Figure 3.3 shows this split and the different approaches that are taken to deploying strategy in each case.

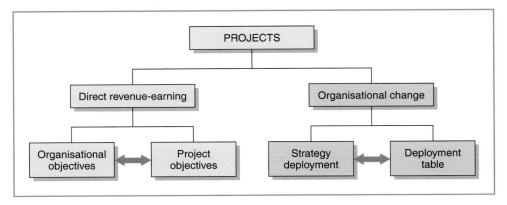

Figure 3.3 Projects and organisational strategy (Adapted from Shenhar, A.J., Milosevic, D., Dvir, D. and Thamhain,H., 2007, *Linking Project Management to Business Strategy*, Project Management Institute, Newtown, PA, where this two-way process is further described)

Strategy and direct revenue-earning projects

The strategic input here is the organisational **objectives**, as Figure 3.3 shows. This would be of the form – we are in business to be the fastest OR the best OR the cheapest providers of these projects. This can then be reflected into the project objectives, usually starting with such time, cost and quality objectives. An organisation that sells itself on being the cheapest should have this as the objective of the project – to deliver the cheapest solution. As will be shown, such a decision has far-reaching consequences and will impact practically every aspect of how the project is managed. This should include the other players in the supply chain – both suppliers and customers. This is illustrated in the following example.

REAL WORLD   Speed is key

Pearce Retail is a lead contractor for several organisations, including Asda/Walmart, Tesco and Marks and Spencer, in the provision of new retail spaces (also called 'sheds' by those less favourably disposed to the aesthetics of such buildings). The design and erection of these buildings is one of its key revenue-generating processes. For its main client, Asda, the time that such projects take, from acquisition of land to the opening of a new store, needs to be as short as possible. It is only once the store is opened that the investment in the facility starts to be repaid. As a result, Pearce has had to develop relationships with its suppliers (suppliers of designs, materials, labour, legal services, site support facilities and so on) consistent with this objective. In addition, all internal processes need to be consistent with this objective. For instance, there is no point having a highly responsive supplier able to deliver materials at 24 hours' notice if it takes 6 weeks to process a purchase order.

Project strategy

The topic of project strategy is covered in much more detail in Chapter 4. For the purpose of this book, the definition of project strategy that will be used is as follows:

Project strategy is the definition of position, the means and the guidelines of what to do and how to do it, to achieve the highest competitive advantage and the best value from a project.[13]

This approach focuses more on the benefits and value of a project than the mechanics of how it is to be delivered. It is a higher-order consideration and one that is fundamental to success in both direct revenue earning and organisational change projects.

Deploying strategy in organisational change projects

The task of strategy deployment is well established in a few world-class organisations.[14] It was a central feature of the Total Quality Management movement and more recently in business excellence models, such as that of the European Foundation for Quality Management (see www.efqm.org). The principle is that the strategies and projects of an organisation should show a high level of **coherence**. This is where, as a minimum, all projects are part of some overall plan for the organisation and form a recognisable contribution to that plan.

Masters of this particular art include the Toyota Motor Company where projects must demonstrate contribution to QCD – Quality, Cost or Delivery performance – as a prime, qualifying requirement. Features of its process of deployment are:

- objectives aligned throughout the organisation by making strategy highly visible and well understood. Conflicts between functional and project objectives are resolved at a high level;
- all members of the organisation are responsible for the process – strategy is no longer the domain of senior management alone and individuals can show the impact of their contribution to organisational objectives through their contribution to change projects;
- progress towards objectives monitored through highly visible measures;
- objectives based on customer needs – retaining the customer-focused nature of the organisation.

The strategy deployment table (Table 3.1) provides a means for project managers to agree objectives for their projects and illustrate how these relate to organisational objectives. This is ideal where an organisation has a large number of projects ongoing and a manager is responsible for more than one project. It can be used both between and within organisations to ensure consistency of objectives.

Table 3.1 Strategy deployment table

Objectives Level 1	Activities Level 1	Objectives Level 2	Activities Level 2	Objectives Level 3	Activities Level 3
Reduce new product lead-time by 20 per cent	1 Establish managed portfolio of projects	Achieve balanced work allocations Close down 80 per cent of projects that are over 2 years old	Determine workload due to current projects Examine potential of all projects over 2 years old		
	2 Re-engineer project processes	Understand current processes Increase level of concurrency in processes	Map current processes Co-locate staff for major projects Train project facilitators	Identify strengths and weaknesses in processes	Conduct review of all major projects over the past 3 years
	3 Implement new design technology	Reduce prototyping time by 80 per cent Reduce product engineering time by 38 per cent	Install rapid-prototyping equipment Install new version of design software		

Table 3.1 shows the deployment of a strategy by a firm to reduce its new product lead-time (how long it takes to bring a new product through from the initial idea to when it is launched into a market) by 20 per cent. It is important that the objective set is quantifiable wherever possible – particularly a higher-level objective. This is then deployed into a series of second-level objectives. These include achieving balanced workloads, that is, a balance between the amount of time available and the amount of work that is required to be carried out. As is the case for 'increase level of concurrency in processes', objectives may have more than one activity associated with them.

Having determined the strategic objectives of the organisation and specifically the nature of both current and future activities that it carries out, the next level in the strategy process shown in Figure 3.1 is the design of *portfolios* and *programmes*.

3.2 Portfolios and programmes

'Managing projects is, it is said, like juggling three balls – cost, quality and time. Programme management (portfolio management, multi-project management) is like organising a troupe of jugglers all juggling their three balls and swapping balls from time to time.'[15]

The previous section showed how organisations were developing current and future activities under the first principle 'it is not possible to be good at everything'. This reflects the reality for both organisations and individuals that they have to make choices about 'what is important'.

The second principle is that 'it is not possible to do everything'. In practice, organisations and individuals have to make choices about what they do, not just how well they are going to do it. This is part of the strategy process known as **portfolio management**. Ideally, an organisation will choose the activities it undertakes such that it will gain maximum benefit from its investment in those activities.

In the Real World box below, we look at the practical challenges organisations can face, and how they can be understood.

REAL WORLD Managing a bank transformation programme

In a three-year study[16] of a transformation programme within a major European retail bank, the researchers sought to understand how such work balanced the rigour and detail expected from a good project management process, with the uncertainty inherent in such an undertaking.

The work included a plan to restructure and redesign most of the physical bank branches, together with a significant push to offer more internet banking. This necessarily entailed major organisational change while continuing 'business-as-usual'. It is not possible to shut down normal bank operations to enable work to be done; the bank functions must remain seamless to the customer at all times. Part of the work was a significant (US$200M per year) investment in IT upgrades, notorious for their dif-

Source: Pavel Losevsky/123rf.com

ficulty. In the retail banking industry, successful IT projects are rarely noticed, but if they go wrong and customers cannot access their accounts, it is headline news and can be career-ending for those in charge.

How was this done effectively? A twin approach was used, including a governance system that required detailed scrutiny of all the different projects. This ensured controlled delivery of the planned work. For example, it meant that branch conversions were 'industrialised', efficient, and repeatable. At the programme level, senior managers realised that it was not feasible to plan in detail over a 3–5 year period, so the high-level programme plan was regularly reviewed, assessed, and modified as required. This enabled the Board to manage the programme over the medium term in light of the current performance of the work, as well as respond to market demands and competitors' actions.

Thinking about how to manage programmes this way is helpful. You do need to ensure that discrete shorter-term projects are defined clearly and monitored and controlled effectively. However, over a complex and multi-year piece of work, flexibility can sit at the programme level. Overall strategy deployment sits with the senior management who choose, authorise and define the detail of the subsequent projects. The projects can then be delivered by the project teams, who can feed their insight back up through the programme. This reflects the strategic approach of Figure 3.2, where learning can be captured and used to refine the programme.

The focus on choosing specific projects and ensuring they are done to plan illustrates the first principle of this chapter and a major reason why 'we can't do everything' is that, as the economists would say, 'resources are scarce'. That is, they are finite, not necessarily flexible or easily transferred between activities, and, particularly where these resources are 'people', are not 100 per cent available. In the bank transformation case, the 'business-as-usual' aspect still required staff to keep all the bank operations running; operations could not be paused because staff were working on a new project. To take account of this, programme management therefore requires the following step: aggregation of resource plans.

The sanity check: aggregate resource plan

'The first time we assessed our total project load, we found that we had scheduled three times as much work in one year as we could reasonably handle. The results weren't very pleasant or productive.'
(Programme manager – automotive supply firm)

The above scenario is very typical of many organisations that have no mechanism for determining their total workload. The 'too many projects' problem is very real.[17] The **aggregate resource plan** is essential to keep control of the activities that the organisation is undertaking, both projects and repetitive operations – aka business-as-usual work. Firms often have a good picture of their repetitive operations – these have a relatively high level of visibility, particularly in a manufacturing setting. Projects, meanwhile, require some overall view to be maintained of what is going on in the organisation. Providing a concise statement of the resource requirements of the expected activities, both project and operational, is the objective of the aggregate resource plan.

An aggregate plan is another step in the process of determining what projects can be undertaken and in what order. It determines the *capacity* of the organisation to carry out projects and allocates this capacity to projects that fit with the organisational priorities. Imagine a production line that can produce 11 000 drinks cans per hour for 23 hours a day. The capacity of that line is $11\,000 \times 23 = 253\,000$ cans per day. In organisational terms, the role of management then becomes to make sure that this capacity is used to generate the best return for the organisation – and schedule jobs on the machine accordingly. If there is a changeover time between jobs on the machine, this needs to be considered too, as such a changeover will reduce the productive time of the machine and therefore the overall capacity. This becomes part of the expectation for the scheduling of the work around that machine – you would not schedule, for instance, 300 000 or 500 000 cans per day without adding new resources (another machine, for instance).

Indeed, where, for instance, a new design of can was being trialled, you might significantly reduce the working capacity of the machine. Therefore, in managing the capacity of the machine, the role of management is to limit the demands placed on it to be less than or equal to the capacity of the machine and to schedule the jobs accordingly, taking account of the needs of the specific job and changeover times.

Organisations that manage their work capacity follow the same approach. The capacity of people and machines is finite, they need to work on the most important jobs first, and there is a significant changeover time between tasks. The following example shows how one organisation treats this capacity issue.

What do you do the rest of the time?

A large engineering consultancy wanted to manage its capacity. Its main and certainly most expensive resources were its people – mostly graduate engineers, designers and planners. Capacity for them would be determined by the availability of those people for work tasks, both within the company (e.g. in operational improvement work) and as part of delivering work to clients. People always seemed very busy in the company and a number of departmental heads had asked for more staff to be able to deal with the workloads. Did they need more people or should they be able to manage with the people they already had? The first stage in determining this was to assess the capacity for work of the people they had. The result was quite a surprise to them – it was considerably less than they had predicted.

In calculating their capacity they calculated that one person would be available for productive work for no more than 40 weeks per year (allowing for holidays, training, sick leave and other disturbances) and in each week would be productive for 30 hours, to allow for meetings, briefings, dealing with administration, emails, etc. This gave a capacity figure of 1200 hours per person per year. Project requirements were always estimated in person hours and the firm now had a basic assessment of the hours required to do the work and what it had available to do it. It was now able to make an assessment of the loadings of the different departments and determine that it did indeed need more people in certain key areas.

Having assessed the workload of project staff (which in many cases will include ongoing work in addition to project tasks), just as the firm in the example did, many firms are surprised to find just how overloaded their personnel are. Keeping track of the workload is an important contribution that programme management can make. The means for this is to keep a log of the available person-hours (number of people multiplied by the hours they are available in a time period) and to allocate these by project. There is frequently a tendency to underestimate the amount of time required for activities (particularly where there is some uncertainty regarding the outcome), resulting in an overcommitment of resources. Where resources are overcommitted, the scope for any flexibility becomes very limited and will stifle innovation – a key component of success for many projects.

The capabilities or competencies required for the project portfolio should also be considered at this level. There may be key resources or people that are critical to the processes. In addition, many firms do not consider their key competencies, trying instead to do everything themselves. This is rarely a successful strategy, particularly where technology is concerned. Where a requirement is outside the firm's set of core competencies, the requirements of external partners or contractors should be discussed.

There is an additional consideration for the aggregate project plan. People rarely know the relative importance of the projects on which they are working or their contribution to organisational strategy. Furthermore, taking on too many projects causes stress for the people carrying them out. This is compounded by confusion about what is urgent and what is important. There should be only a restricted set of activities that any individuals undertake that is both urgent and important. It is the responsibility of the senior management team to ensure this. Otherwise, the changeover time between projects will become significant.

So, just how many projects can a firm undertake at any one time? There is, of course, no universal answer. However, one firm, visited as part of a research project, had 72 development projects ongoing at the time, with one manager and eight staff. The result was an obvious confusion about the relative priorities of the projects and a highly stressful work environment. Furthermore, the task for the manager was enormous. For instance, which projects should each person be working on at any one time? Inevitably, the projects worked on were those where the customers were screaming the loudest. The knock-on effect was that staff would start work on one project and then be moved on to another as the priorities changed, to appease the latest angry customer. The effects of this are very stressful for the individual and highly unproductive for the organisation.

For the development organisation, a move away from the old system of 'whoever shouts loudest' to a clear system of priorities reduced the workload from 72 projects to 12. This sounds draconian, as many projects had to be put on hold or abandoned. The positive effect was incredible – the firm successfully completed twice as many projects that year as it had ever done in the past with the same resources. In addition, the working conditions improved immeasurably and the workload and flow through the department became not only faster but more predictable.[18]

EPM

EPM (Enterprise portfolio/programme/project management) has emerged and grown in importance over the past 20 years. It is defined as:

the capability to lead and manage resources, knowledge and skills in the effective deployment of multiple projects designed collectively to deliver enhanced value.[19]

EPM concerns the resourcing and managing of programmes across an entire organisation. While a small organisation or business unit can manage using spreadsheets for instance, for larger organisations it is usually associated with enterprise-wide software applications, such as Microsoft Project, Primavera, or SAP. These are necessary to integrate the vast amount of data, including the number of projects, the resource requirements and timings of those requirements, and to handle these in a dynamic manner. Schedules, availability of people and resources, priorities and project requirements can all change and frequently do in reality.

Working through the implications of all the changes on the ability of an organisation to deliver a portfolio of projects and routine operations is complicated, and although modern software is powerful it requires skilled operators who understand what they are doing. As with any software, it is the thinking behind it and the way that it is used that will determine whether it provides the solution being sought or just adds another headache for those in the organisation.

Programme management

The photo shown here illustrates beautifully the need for **programme management**. As can be seen, two projects have been completed – the road building and the erection of telegraph poles. However, in order for the community to get any *benefits* from these projects, someone needs to have integrated the work. Clearly this hasn't happened.

Source: Courtesy of Michael Trolove

Programme management provides this layer of coordination between projects, ensuring that the higher-level benefits are realised.[20]

As for project management, the professional institutes have generated considerable discussion around the nature of definitions of a programme. The main ones are shown in Table 3.2.

A summary of the characteristics of these provides the definition for programme that will be used in this book:

> *An [organisational] framework for grouping existing or defining new projects, and for focusing all the activities required to achieve a set of major benefits. These projects are managed in a coordinated way, either to achieve a common goal, or to extract benefits which would otherwise not be realised if they were managed independently.*[21]

However, there is considerable disparity between and even within organisations as to what constitutes 'a programme'.[22] Currently, there is no scientific or rigorous method that would allow us to identify a piece of work as a project or a programme. At one level, programmes can be considered simply as 'big projects'. This is not entirely without foundation – in one organisation, a unit of work that is labelled a 'programme' would be

Table 3.2 Definitions of 'programme' (PMI 'program')

Standard / methodology	Definition
APM BoK (2019)	A unique, transient strategic endeavour undertaken to achieve beneficial change and incorporating a group of related projects and business-as-usual (steady state) activities.
PMI BoK (2017)	A group of related projects, subsidiary programs, and program activities that are managed in a coordinated manner to obtain benefits not available from managing them individually.
Managing Successful Programmes (2020)	A temporary structure designed to lead multiple, interrelated projects and other work in order to progressively achieve outcomes of benefit for one or more organizations.

a 'large project' in another. In general though, the larger the organisation, the larger the unit of work that is termed 'a programme'.

Consistent with this variation in definition of the unit of work, programme management is viewed by some as 'the management of multiple projects', while by others as 'the management of organisational change through projects that bring about change'.[23] The ongoing inconsistency in recent versions of major standards and bodies of knowledge shown in Table 3.2 suggests that clarity is unlikely to be achieved in the near future. Part of this variation is explained by the differences in the nature of the programme. For instance, the projects in a programme may be represented as a chain of projects, one occurring after another, a portfolio of projects taking place at one point in time, or as a network of interlinked projects.[24] These are shown in Figure 3.4.

In reality, large organisations use a blend of these different types of programmes in deploying their strategies.

Organising multiple projects into programmes allows commonalities between projects to be exploited (e.g. knowledge obtained from one project being transferred to another similar project) and coordination of objectives and resources. *Programme management* can also be viewed as a means of management gaining greater control of the activities in the organisation. Indeed, the creation of programme management in many organisations has resulted in a new layer of management being added – an interesting phenomenon at a time when most organisations have been removing layers of management. However, there are instances, such as the bank case shown earlier, where this approach has yielded considerable benefits over and above the additional costs that this extra layer of management activity will incur. Another view of programme management is that it is a *sense-making* process – it is a method by which those running an organisation will seek to understand the complexities of that organisation and its activities, by adding structures that put some order to what otherwise will appear chaotic.

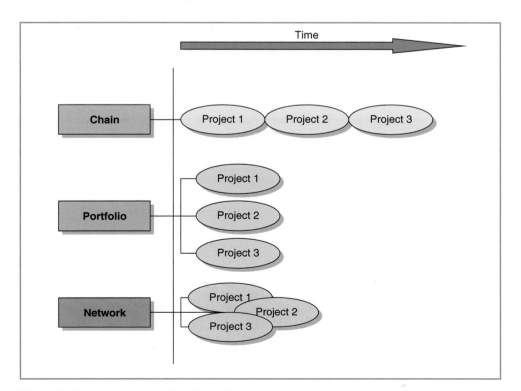

Figure 3.4 Arrangements of projects in programmes

Table 3.3 Strategy matrix

	Objective 1	*Objective 2*	*Objective 3*
Project 1	++	+	
Project 2	— —	++	
Project 3	+	+	++

Key: ++ Strong positive relationship
    + Positive relationship
    — Negative relationship
   — — Strong negative relationship

The issue of project selection is considered in more detail in Chapter 4. The prime issues concern the relation of the potential and existing projects to the organisational objectives and the use of a strategy matrix to balance the objectives.

An example of a **strategy matrix** is shown in Table 3.3. The matrix shows the relationship between three projects and three key strategic objectives. Each of the projects addresses one of the key strategic objectives. However, project 2 will have a negative effect on objective 1. For instance, if objective 1 is 'to improve the quality of customer service' and project 2 is 'cut costs by 20 per cent', it is likely that this objective and this project will conflict. This indicates that the project should be reconsidered to see precisely the nature of this impact and whether the negative effect can be removed. Having determined the project objectives, these are then implemented through the measurement system that is put in place.

The matrix therefore provides a sense of the deployment of the organisation's or even programme objectives into projects and a means of resolving or at least identifying the conflicts that will inevitably arise with a complex set of projects and objectives. In addition, gaps can be identified where objectives have no projects contributing to their achievement.

Having established the programme or portfolio of projects that the organisation will undertake in any given time period, the issue is then how to support these projects in their execution and ensure their continued contribution to organisational objectives.

3.3 Project roles and governance

There are many roles that have been created by organisations in an attempt to facilitate the management of projects. The roles and the structure that they can operate in are well illustrated in PRINCE2 2017, and MSP has more detail considering the programme level, though there are many variants on this. The roles and their relationships as defined by the project organisation are termed the *project governance*.

Governance and projects

The word governance is used here to mean 'providing steering'. Steering a project, both as it begins and then subsequently maintaining it on its course, is viewed as key to success by many organisations. The OECD defines governance as:

> *Good corporate governance helps to build an environment of trust, transparency and accountability necessary for fostering long-term investment, financial stability and business integrity, thereby supporting stronger growth and more inclusive societies.*[25]

This was written for a 'permanent organisation' – a company, charity or government body. These terms are found increasingly applied to the governance of projects or 'temporary organisations'. The increase in usage is in no small part due to governance being part of international standards, and recognition that not all project problems can be solved by the project team; they will often require external support.[26] For example, senior management in an organisation may be asked to support an ailing project by allocating additional resources or to ensure that organisational priorities on resources are maintained. The governance of the project and the organisation(s) involved need to align – no small challenge itself when there are multiple organisations present in a project.

In addition to formal roles. much governance takes place through social means. For instance, managers in collaborating firms who use their relationships to influence each other, rather than resorting to any formal structures. We should also though note the antithesis of this – the kinds of approaches used in for instance the development of Linux where there were few formal structures set out.

Project governance sets out who is responsible for doing what and to whom they are responsible. The structure shown in Figure 3.5 is an expansion of that shown in Figure 3.1.

Project roles

There is little agreement between the various standards on any particular structure or terminology for projects. However, a common feature of both the standards and many projects, is having a **project board** at the top level of the project. This is run by an **executive**, **senior responsible owner (SRO)** or the **sponsor**. The SRO is the person who ultimately wants the result. The sponsor has the budget for the project to be carried out. The **senior user** provides high-level input to the project from those who will ultimately be using the output of the project (e.g. the users of an IT system being delivered through a project). The **senior supplier** is the representative of those who will be delivering the project. For instance, if the work to deliver the project is being carried out by an outside contractor, a senior manager from that firm would be represented on the project board.

A **technical advisory group** may be added where the project is of a highly technical nature. For instance, in scientific research projects, a group of scientists external to the

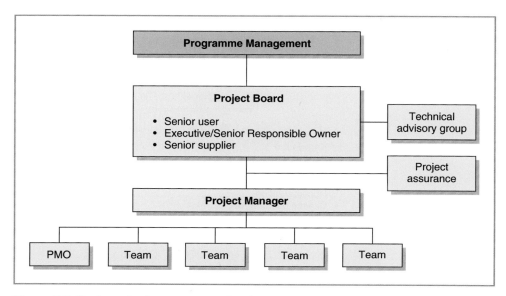

Figure 3.5 Basic project governance structure

project may be asked to provide advice to the project board on the status of the project and the viability of science being considered.

Also reporting into the project board and not under the direct control of the project manager may be a **project assurance** function. This may be as extensive as the project itself, particularly where security or safety is concerned. For instance, in running projects for London Underground (a highly safety-critical environment), all projects have to pass through extensive assurance processes. These will include engineering assurance, ensuring that any potential impact on the working of the underground system has been properly evaluated.

The project manager then has a number of direct reports, including the various teams carrying out the work of the project. In addition, we are increasingly seeing that they will have at their disposal a PMO – a **project management office**.

The project management office (PMO)

Many organisations, particularly from sectors that regularly run large-scale projects, use project offices to assist in all aspects of the management of project work. This is constituted as a function alongside other functions within the organisation. At one time, it was limited to large-scale engineering firms, but the project office is a regular feature in most major organisations globally today. This function has been added to run alongside other functions in the organisation and provides recognition of the importance of project activities, and in particular the need for project management professionals to run projects. The relationship between the project and the project office is shown in Figure 3.6.[27]

The office provides a central facility with the skills and knowledge of how to run project processes. This can be drawn on by the project manager to help ensure that the project is given the best chance of success. The office can provide key project staff, often including the project manager, but also including project planners, accountants, staff to carry out review activities and consultants. Resources that may be under the control of the project office include any project planning software system that is used. The support role includes one of personal support to individuals, including training and mentoring (personal counselling and assistance) and sharing of experience where problems are encountered that have occurred elsewhere. The project office can also provide checks and controls on the

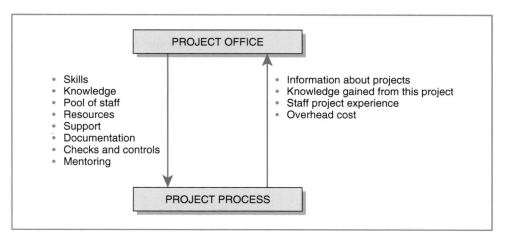

Figure 3.6 Relationship between the project and the project office

project processes, assisting in the establishment of checkpoints (see Chapter 5) and control measures (see Chapter 13).

The project management office can also be called:

- project support office;
- programme management office;
- enterprise project/programme management office.

The role that any PMO covers is incredibly varied – between and within organisations and also over time. Work carried out at the University of Quebec in Montreal has identified 24 roles which have been grouped into five categories, as shown in Table 3.4.[28]

Three further roles did not fit with the other categories shown here:

1 Manage customer interfaces.
2 Execute specialised tasks for project managers.
3 Recruit, select, evaluate and determine salaries for project managers.[29]

All this additional support to the project process does not come free. Organisations that do use this way of working usually maintain that any downside element, including the increased overhead cost, is more than compensated for by the increased project success.

Table 3.4 PMO roles

Category	Role
1 Monitoring and control of project performance	Report status to upper management Monitor and control project performance Implement and operate a project information system Develop and maintain a project scoreboard
2 Development of project management capabilities and methodologies	Develop and implement a standard methodology Develop competency of personnel, including training Promote project management within organisation Provide mentoring for project managers Provide a set of tools without an effort to standardise
3 Multi-project management	Coordinate between projects Manage one or more portfolios Identify, select and prioritise new projects Manage one or more programmes Allocate resources between projects
4 Strategic management	Provide advice to senior management Participate in strategic planning Manage benefits Conduct networking and environmental scanning
5 Organisational learning	Monitor and control performance of PMO Manage archives of project documentation Conduct project audits Conduct post-project reviews Implement and manage database of lessons learned Implement and manage risk database

Experience has also shown that there is considerable benefit from having a consistent approach to running projects and the advice provided prevents problems such as teams overpromising on project deliverables or failing to analyse the risks associated with their work properly. Other contributions from the project to the office include the stream of knowledge and experience that the projects generate. The role of the office in this respect is marshalling and managing this knowledge. People who have been working on projects and show an interest in a project management career can use the project office as a way of moving to take a greater role in future projects. For example, a marketing person may enjoy the project environment more than the day-to-day activities of the marketing function and wish to become more involved with projects. The professionalisation of the role through the project office provides a route for such an individual to progress within the organisation and research has shown that this should be a separate career path from that of either a project or programme manager, as it requires a distinct and different skillset.

Given the importance of the PMO to project-based organisations, we might expect a standardised approach to have been developed, but this is not the case. Indeed, the wide range of forms and functions available and implemented[30] appear to highlight that one size definitely does not fit all. Large, small, client- or company-funded, high-level strategic departments or administrative support systems, all of these variations can be identified. To make matters perhaps even more difficult, PMOs are often set up to support particular projects, especially if supporting a particular customer. In this scenario, the PMO will likely undergo a lifecycle in parallel with the project itself. Under these circumstances, learning from different projects becomes even more difficult as both the projects and their PMOs are relatively isolated and neither continue their existence beyond the end of the project duration.

REAL WORLD Connecting project offices in an IT-services company

We were involved in an interesting study[31] within Hewlett Packard Enterprise Services (HPES). Senior managers did not know how many PMOs the company had supporting their various client-facing projects, but estimated it to be around 200 worldwide. At the time there was no directory, and no specific job code by which PMO managers could be identified. Their view was that the organisation would be strengthened if peer-to-peer visibility could be enhanced to enable PMO members to share practices and experiences.

To support this, HPES set up a virtual Community of Practice (CoP) to connect staff. This was run by a programme manager who initially reached out to his contacts, but relied on them to tell other PMO staff whom they knew. The CoP itself consisted of regular monthly presentations and live webinars (also recorded for later viewing by those in different time zones), a document repository and a LinkedIn group. Through these relatively straightforward mechanisms members learned directly from others, but also made new contacts they could talk to directly. Tools, effective practices and ideas were shared freely, with staff gaining recognition for their expertise in key areas. Over several years, membership grew and the perception of those taking part was that they found it valuable and worth their time to participate. Over 50 people typically attended the meetings, with a total membership of over 300.

It is hard to quantify the benefits of the CoP, and HPES did not try to put a financial value on the work. Instead, they identified successful instances of knowledge-sharing, and considered that if busy people took time out of their day to participate then that is evidence that they must have found it to be worthwhile. Our interviews of participants found that they identified benefits in terms of best practices, interactions with professional peers, new knowledge and skills, and a greater understanding of where the organisation was going and why.

It is apparent that organisations and projects implement and use PMOs to meet their objectives in many different ways, and configuring the PMO both to the work and to the particular project phase is now common. Further structural and governance issues are discussed in Chapter 11.

Summary

- The strategy process identified in Figure 3.1 shows how the vision created for an organisation is reflected through to the project activities. The input from competitive analysis might include, for example, an analysis of the organisation's strengths, weaknesses, opportunities and threats (SWOT). It may also consider the impact of changes in technology, new entrants to the market (if a commercial organisation) and other market force changes (e.g. currency movements, legal changes) that will affect the organisation. The other input to this process comes from the organisation itself, demonstrating that strategy is a two-way process.

- The vision is to be realised through the organisational strategy in the first instance. This provides a focus for all the activities of the organisation, including all projects. Focus is an important concept here, which we define as those aspects of our product or service offering into which we are going to invest time, money and effort, with the objective of securing improved/superior performance.

- Having determined the intended focus, it has been observed that many senior management teams make the mistake of assuming that this will automatically be followed through by those who make decisions within the organisation. This does not always happen and results in problems for project managers trying to operate in the middle of interdepartmental conflicts, where different views of the mission and focus prevail. The alternative is to instigate programme or portfolio management. As part of this process of evaluating the strategic contribution of each project, overlaps and gaps in the programme need to be identified. An aggregate resource plan ensures that the capacity and capability exist to do the work required by the strategy and to keep an overview of the many projects going on in an organisation at any one time.

- Programmes consist of a number of projects. These may be externally generated – as direct revenue earners which will require their own set of strategies. This must be in line with corporate objectives regarding the basis on which the organisation will compete in order to meet customer needs. The project strategy in this case would include both conformance and performance objectives. In addition, organisational change projects should be part of the strategy deployment of the organisation and their objectives should be put through a strategy matrix to remove conflicts before the project starts.

- The objective of this process is to clear the way for project activities to be undertaken in a coherent manner with the organisational objectives, focused and with minimal conflict. This process is simple in concept, but very challenging in application. It is notable that in organisations where this does happen, there is an almost palpable feeling of everybody working in the one direction, with many of the stresses and failures that are caused by 'the system' avoided. This is surely a worthwhile objective for our organisations.

Key terms

aggregate resource plan *p. 65*

coherence *p. 63*

conformance *p. 60*

EPM (enterprise project/ programme management) *p. 67*

executive *p. 71*

focus *p. 59*

mission *p. 59*

mission statement *p. 59*

objectives *p. 62*

organisational change *p. 61*

performance *p. 60*

programme/portfolio management *pp. 67, 64*

project assurance *p. 72*

project board *p. 71*

project management office *p. 72*

senior responsible owner *p. 71*

senior supplier *p. 71*

senior user *p. 71*

sponsor *p. 71*

strategy *p. 60*

strategy deployment *p. 61*

strategy matrix *p. 70*

strategy process *p. 59*

SWOT *p. 61*

technical advisory group *p. 71*

vision *p. 59*

Relevant areas of the Bodies of Knowledge

There is little in either of the Bodies of Knowledge concerning the strategic context or aspects of projects. Given the importance of this area and the impact that it has on projects in general, this is a significant omission. There are some points of relevance in the APM version for programme management and these are given in Table 3.5.

The PMI Body of Knowledge covers some descriptions and definitions of the terms used in this chapter, in section 1.

Table 3.5 Relevant areas of the APM Body of Knowledge

Relevant section	Title	Summary
11	Programme management	Defines programme management and some of the tasks that are done under this heading.
20	Project success criteria	Defines some of the terms used here, including requirements, critical success factors and key performance indicators.

PROJECT MANAGEMENT IN PRACTICE
The Airbus A380 development

The 27 April 2005 was a huge day for the Airbus A380 as the brand-new plane took to the skies for its maiden test flight. With six crew and 20 tonnes of test equipment, it successfully completed the first stage in its flight trials, that took several more years to complete before the plane entered commercial service in October 2007 with Singapore Airlines. That it ever flew at all was an enormous achievement on the part of the individuals and organisations taking part in the development. The technical and managerial challenges were significant, not least because of the number of nations involved in both the design and building of the plane.

The plane was considerably larger than Boeing's 747 (see Figure 3.7), in basic form being able to accommodate over 550 passengers in three classes on two decks, up to a version for the Japanese market able to carry 840 passengers. Technically, this additional size does create new constraints.

The wings, for instance, at 36.6 m long, are considerably longer than the previously largest wing that Airbus had built. The fuel capacity of the aircraft is 310 000 litres. On landing, the undercarriage and brake systems have to bring the 560 tonne aircraft to a standstill from over 320 km/h in just 32 seconds. While some of this increase in scale of the product was achieved by incremental innovation, there were limits to some of the technology that was being applied, and new technological solutions, particularly in the avionics, materials and manufacturing processes, had to be developed.

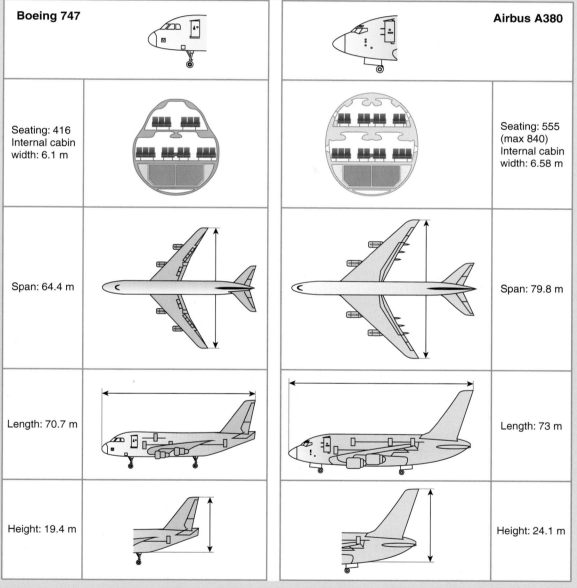

Boeing 747	Airbus A380
Seating: 416 Internal cabin width: 6.1 m	Seating: 555 (max 840) Internal cabin width: 6.58 m
Span: 64.4 m	Span: 79.8 m
Length: 70.7 m	Length: 73 m
Height: 19.4 m	Height: 24.1 m

Figure 3.7 Comparative size of Boeing 747 and Airbus A380 (Adapted from 'Enormous plane takes to the sky', BBC News, 14 February 2007)

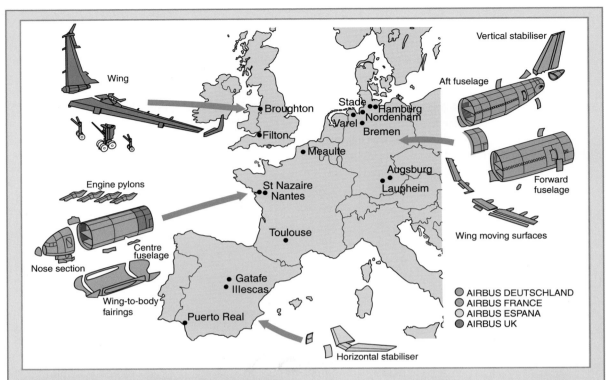

Figure 3.8 Sourcing the components of the A380

It was a significant commercial risk for Airbus, as the business case for the A380's development was hotly contested in the industry – Airbus claiming a market of 1100 planes, Boeing, its main rival, claiming that it is nearer to 300. The latter figure would be commercially disastrous for Airbus, given the development budget of US$13 billion. Up to October 2012, Airbus had received orders for 257 aircraft, and their CEO was claiming break-even on the project by around 2015. This had been pushed back significantly due to delays in the delivery of the initial aircraft.

While the technological and business risks were significant for the A380, the organisation of the programme added another dimension to the risks. Firstly, there were in place existing agreements for the percentage of value of the work that would be undertaken by the countries that were part of the Airbus consortium – the UK, France, Germany and Spain. These had to be incorporated into the new organisation set up to run the A380 programme. Within each organisation, there were a variety of procurement mechanisms for each of the major systems. For instance, Rolls-Royce (which developed the Trent 900 engines for the plane) provided most engines to airlines on a 'power by the hour' basis – the owner of the plane will not actually own the engines but will buy the capability that they provide on an hourly chargeable basis. Other major components are provided, as shown in Figure 3.8.

All the components had to be transported to the assembly plant in Toulouse, France, with the completed planes then flown to Hamburg, Germany for fitting out. The logistics of moving the major aircraft components alone were huge – and significant projects in their own right. While much of the manufacture took place in Europe, many sub-assemblies were brought in from all over the world.

This was to make sure that local manufacturing content requirements were kept up to ensure saleability of the aircraft, particularly in China, and Boeing's own backyard, in the US. Wing tips, for instance, came into Broughton in the UK. These were assembled onto the wings and then loaded onto specially adapted barges. They met with parts of the fuselage that had been pre-assembled in Germany at Mostyn docks for the journey to Bordeaux. En route the ship stopped at St Nazaire in France to deliver one forward section of fuselage and collect a completed forward and nose assembly. From Bordeaux, the assemblies were transferred to barge and then road to Toulouse for final assembly.

However, on 14 February 2019, Airbus announced that it would cease production of the A380 due to lack of sales. At the time, *The Economist* said that the development costs would be unlikely to be recouped. The 2020 pandemic meant that its high-capacity passenger offering was not wanted, and resale values plummeted. Despite the magnificence of the aircraft and the hugely impressive engineering and manufacturing behind it, the case shows the difficulty of predicting how a multi-decade investment will play out in a competitive market.

Points for discussion

1 Was the A380 development a project or a programme?

2 Using the notation of Figure 3.5, how has the development been managed?

3 Suggest what the 'challenges to the management of this development' might be.

4 Review the performance of the plane to date using relevant websites. Has this been a success to date, and, if so, to whom?

5 Suggest the role that project/programme offices could take in such a development.

PROJECT MANAGEMENT IN PRACTICE
Selecting a personal project

A group of students, as part of their coursework, has to carry out a group project where they run an event or perform a particular task to demonstrate their ability to plan, execute and review a project. They are assessed on the basis of originality of their idea, the quality of the planning process and the content of a report following the project that reflects on their experiences of the project. They had a meeting and came up with a number of ideas. These were:

- produce a yearbook for their class group;
- develop a short video promoting the course that they are studying;
- run a formal ball for the entire department;
- organise a treasure hunt one Sunday;
- organise an 'accident awareness' day for schoolchildren.

The group then had to consider which one of these was the first choice. The next activity was to establish the decision criteria by which each of the proposals would be judged. The first three were given by the requirements of the assessment – that of originality of idea, whether the idea would allow demonstration of project management skills and whether it would enable them to produce a good report. The students added some further characteristics that they felt they wanted their project to have. These were:

- it should be sufficiently stretching of the group;
- it should not depend too heavily on other people for its success;
- it must not require them to undertake any large financial risk;
- it must be fun for the group to do.

They then put this together as shown in Table 3.6.

Table 3.6 Decision matrix

	Originality	Demonstrate skills	Produce good report	Stretching	Independent of others	Avoids financial risk	FUN
Yearbook	✗	✓	✓	–	–	✗	✗
Video	✓	✓	✓	✓	✓	–	✓
Ball	–	✓	✓	✓	✗	✗✗✗	✓
Treasure hunt	✗	–	–	✗	–	✓	–
Accident awareness day	✓	✓	–	–	✗	✓	–

You may disagree with the rating that the group gave some of the items, but this is how the students saw the options. They also saw very clearly as a group that there was one clear choice for them: the video. It also told them that the financial risk element (cost of hiring editing facilities and production of the finished product) needed to be minimised.

Points for discussion

1 Under what circumstances might this approach to selection be beneficial?

2 How might the measures of success change over time?

3 Suggest other applications for this approach to decision-making.

Topics for discussion

1 You have been asked to advise the 2028 Los Angeles Olympics team on running the Games. Firstly, is this a project or a programme, and why?

2 What are the impacts at a project level of poor strategy processes?

3 What is coherence and why is it worth pursuing?

4 What is the role of strategy in project management?

5 Do a web search and identify the mission statements of some organisations that you know. Would you recognise that mission statement from the experience that you have of that organisation?

6 What is the difference between programme and portfolio management?

7 Why is an aggregate project plan beneficial for an organisation that pursues a number of projects at the same time?

8 Investigate the potential for EPM – what problems is it claimed to solve for an organisation?

9 Compile a list of project roles based on one of the project management standards (PMI, APM or PRINCE2). Which is the most important role in your view for the success of a project?

10 What are the costs and benefits to an organisation of having a PMO?

Further information

Altfeld, H.H. (2010) *Commercial Aircraft Projects*, Ashgate Publications, London.

APM (2014) 'A Guide to Integrated Assurance', Association for Project Management, Princes Risborough.

APM (2019) 'Developing the practice of governance', Association for Project Management, Princes Risborough.

APM Assurance SIG (2016) 'Measures for Assuring Projects', available at apm.org.uk

Artto, K., Kujala, J., Dietrich, P. and Martinsuo, M. (2008) 'What is project strategy?' *International Journal of Project Management*, Vol. 26, No. 1, pp. 4–12.

Bernstein, S. (2000) 'Project Office in Practice', *Project Management Journal*, Vol. 31, No. 4, pp. 4–6.

Block, T.R. and Frame, J.D. (1998) *The Project Office*, Crisp Learning, Menlo Park, CA.

Brunet, M. (2019) 'Governance-as-practice for major public infrastructure projects: A case of multilevel project governing', *International Journal of Project Management*, Vol. 37, No. 2, pp. 98–116.

Crawford, L., Cooke-Davies, T., Hobbs, B., Labuschagne, L., Remington, K. and Chen, P. (2008) 'Governance and support in the sponsoring of projects and programs', *Project Management Journal*, Vol. 39, S1, pp. 43–55.

Derakhshan, R., Turner, R. and Mauro Mancini M. (2019) 'Project governance and stakeholders: a literature review', *International Journal of Project Management*, Vol 37, No. 1, pp. 98–116.

Hill, G.M. (2013) *The Complete Project Management Office Handbook*, 3rd edition, ESI International, Arlington, Virginia.

Joslin R. and Müller, R. (2015) 'Relationships between a project management methodology and project success in different project governance contexts', *International Journal of Project Management*, Vol. 33, No. 6, pp. 1377–1392.

Klakegg, O.J., Williams, T., Magnussen, O.M. and Glasspool, H. (2008) 'Governance Frameworks for Public Project Development and Estimation,' *Project Management Journal*, Vol. 30, Supplement S27–S42.

Lycett, M., Rassau, A. and Danson, J. (2004) 'Programme Management: A Critical Review', *International Journal of Project Management*, Vol. 22, No. 4, pp. 289–299.

Maylor, H., Turner, N., and Murray-Webster, R. (2015) 'It Worked for Manufacturing. . . Operations Strategy in Project-based Operations', *International Journal of Project Management*, Vol. 33, No. 1, pp. 103–115.

Müller, R. (2009) *Project Governance*, Gower, Aldershot.

Musawir, A., Abd-Karim, S.B., and Mohd-Danuri M.S. (2020) 'Project governance and its role in enabling organizational strategy implementation: A systematic literature review', *International Journal of Project Management*, Vol. 38, No. 1, pp. 1–16.

Pelegrinelli, S. (2008) *Thinking and Acting as a Great Programme Manager*, Palgrave Macmillan, Basingstoke.

Pinto, J, Slevin, and English, B. (2009) 'Trust in Projects: an Empirical Assessment of Owner / contractor Relationships', *International Journal of Project Management,* Vol. 27, No. 6, pp. 68–648.

Website

www.efqm.org for more information on the European Foundation for Quality Management Business Excellence Model.

References

1 Lord, M.A. (1993) 'Implementing Strategy Through Project Management', *Long Range Planning*, Vol. 26, No. 1, pp. 76–85.

2 Throughout this book, the spelling of programme will be with the ending 'me'. North America and Australia in particular use the spelling 'program'.

3 See corporate.easyjet.com/about/our-values

4 Morgan, M., Levitt, R.E., & Malek, W. (2007) *Executing Your Strategy: how to break it down and get it done*, Harvard Business School Press, Boston, MA, p. 6.

5 Skinner, W. (1969) 'Manufacturing – Missing Link in Corporate Strategy', *Harvard Business Review*, May–June, pp. 136–145.

6 It is not intended to provide a detailed consideration of the many and varied views of strategy here. For this, you should refer to dedicated texts, such as Johnson, G., Whittington, R., Scholes, K., Angwin, D. and Regner, P. (2017) *Exploring Corporate Strategy*, 11th edition, Pearson, Harlow.

7 This follows the terminology of Hayes and Wheelwright (1984) in describing the relationship between operations strategy and organisational strategy – see Hayes, R.H. and Wheelwright, S.C. (1984) *Restoring Our Competitive Edge: Competing Through Manufacturing*, Wiley, New York.

8 The nature of this two-way process is further described in Shenhar, A.J., Milosevic, D., Dvir, D. and Thamhain, H. (2007) *Linking Project Management to Business Strategy*, Project Management Institute, Newtown, PA.

9 See Porter, M.E. (2004) *Competitive Strategy: Techniques for Analyzing Industries and Competitors*, Free Press, New York.

10 See Mintzberg, H. (2000) *The Rise and Fall of Strategic Planning*, FT Prentice Hall, Harlow.

11 Mintzberg, H. and Ghoshal, S. (2002) *The Strategy Process*, FT Prentice Hall, Harlow.

12 Sull, D., Turconi, S., Sull, C., Yoder, J. (2019) 'How to Develop Strategy for Execution', *MIT Sloan Management Review*, Special Issue, pp. 1–6.

13 Shenhar, A.J., Milosevic, D., Dvir, D. and Thamhain, H. (2007) *Linking Project Management to Business Strategy*, Project Management Institute, Newtown, PA, p. 65.

14 Another term that is used to describe this process is *Hoshin Kanri* or policy deployment – see Akao Akao, Y. (ed) (1991) *Hoshin Kanri – Policy Deployment for Successful TQM*, Productivity Press, New York.

15 Reiss, G. (1996) *Programme Management Demystified*, E & FN Spon, London.

16 Pellegrinelli S., Murray-Webster R. and Turner N. (2015) 'Facilitating Organizational Ambidexterity

through the Complementary Use of Projects and Programs', *International Journal of Project Management*, Vol. 33, No. 1, pp. 153–164.

17 Hollister, R. and Watkins, M.D. (2018) 'Too Many Projects', *Harvard Business Review*, Vol. 96, No. 5, pp. 64–71.

18 For further examples of this type of change, see Newbold, R. (1999) *Project Management in the Fast Lane*, St Lucie Press, Boca Raton, FL.

19 Williams, D. and Parr, T. (2004) *Enterprise Programme Management*, Palgrave Macmillan, Basingstoke.

20 For a discussion of the emergence of the use of programmes in organisations, see Maylor, H., Brady, T., Cooke-Davies, T. and Hodgson, D. (2006) 'From Projectification to Programmification', *International Journal of Project Management*, Vol. 24, pp. 663–672.

21 MSP is a programme management standard – often referred to as 'the big brother of PRINCE 2'. See Axelos (2020) *Managing Successful Programmes*, TSO, Norwich.

22 Pellegrinelli, S. (1997) 'Programme Management: Organising Project Based Change', *International Journal of Project Management*, Vol. 15, No. 3, pp. 141–149.

23 Murray-Webster, R. and Thiry, M. (2000) 'Managing Programmes of Projects' in Turner, J.R. and Simister, S.J. (eds), *Gower Handbook of Project Management*, Gower, Aldershot, pp. 33–46.

24 Vereecke, A., Pandelaere, E., Deschoolmeester, D. and Stevens, M. (2003) 'A Classification of Development Programmes and Its Consequences for Programme Development', *International Journal of Operations and Production Management*, Vol. 23, No. 10, pp. 1279–1290.

25 See http://www.oecd.org/corporate/

26 Crawford, L., Cooke-Davies, T., Hobbs, B., Labuschagne, L., Remington, K., and Chen, P. (2008), 'Governance and Support in the Sponsoring of Projects and Programmes,' *Project Management Journal*, Vol. 39, Supplement S43–S55.

27 See Axelos' (2013) *Portfolio, Programme and Project Offices*, The Stationery Office, Norwich.

28 Hobbs, J.B. (2007) *The Multi-Project PMO: Global Analysis of the Current State of Practice*, Project Management Institute, Newtown Square, PA.

29 See also Hobbs, B., Aubry, M. and Thuillier, D. (2008) 'The Project Management Office as an Organisational Innovation', *International Journal of Project Management*, Vol. 26, No. 5, pp. 547–555.

30 Darling, E.J. and Whitty, S.J. (2016) 'The Project Management Office: it's just not what it used to be', *International Journal of Managing Projects in Business.*, Vol. 9, No. 2, pp. 282–308.

31 Lee-Kelley, L. and Turner N. (2017) 'PMO Managers' Self-Determined Participation in a Purposeful Virtual Community-of-Practice', *International Journal of Project Management*, Vol. 35, No. 1, pp. 64–77.

Managing the project process:
the 4-D model

D1: Define it

Making sense of the project context

> 1 Introduction
> 2 Structures and frameworks
> 3 Projects and organisations

Managing the project process: the 4-D model

D1: Define it
4 Setting up for success
5 Planning for success

D4: Develop it
16 Completing projects and learning to improve

D2: Design it
6 Time planning and scheduling
7 Making time planning robust: Advanced Project Thinking (APT)
8 Building a business case for a project
9 Engaging stakeholders
10 Managing risks and opportunities

D3: Do it
11 Organising people in the project
12 Leading people in projects
13 Monitoring and controlling the project
14 Procuring, contracting, and working with supply chains
15 Problem-solving and decision-making

4

Setting up for success

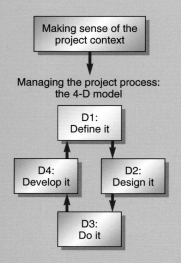

Making sense of the
project context

Managing the project process:
the 4-D model

D1:
Define it

D4:
Develop it

D2:
Design it

D3:
Do it

'*. . . project managers are the new strategic leaders, who must take on total responsibility for project business results.*'[1]

Principles

1 '*Begin with the end in mind.*'[2] Whether a project is a success or failure is rarely universally agreed at the end of a project. However, an agreed statement of what is required provides a good starting point.

2 The perfect result, delivered yesterday and at no cost, is for idealists. The rest of us have to manage the trade-offs between objectives.

3 Projects consume time, energy and resources and in most cases therefore require justification.

Learning objectives

By the time you have completed this chapter, you should be able to:

→ identify appropriate stakeholders and relevant success measures at the outset of a project and recognise their achievement or otherwise at completion

→ demonstrate the need for and the implications of prioritising trade-offs

→ recognise a structured approach to assessing the benefits of and requirements for a project.

Contents

Introduction   85
4.1 Stakeholders: success and failure   86
4.2 Managing strategic choices   95
4.3 Benefits analysis, value and justification   100
Summary   102
Key terms   103
Relevant areas of the Bodies of Knowledge   103
Project management in practice: *Managing stakeholders at European transport infrastructure provider   104*
Project management in practice: *A new campus for the University of Rummidge   105*
Topics for discussion   107
Further information   107
References   108

One of the maddest pieces of architecture we have ever seen is in Barcelona, Spain. Gaudi's Basilica – the Sagrada Familia – is one of those jaw-dropping buildings that belies description and divides opinion. Some think it beautiful, others, a folly. Whatever your view on the result, most have nothing but sympathy for those tasked with building it. The project began in 1882 and Gaudi joined the following year, giving it substantial time up until his death in 1926. It relied on private donations initially, supplemented in recent years by visitors' fees. Progress has

Source: Used with permission from Harvey Maylor

been interrupted by lack of money, the death of Gaudi and the Spanish Civil War, amongst other things. It may be finished in time for the 100th anniversary of Gaudi's death in 2026. On the other hand . . .

Introduction

The case of the Sagrada Familia is included as it is about as far from modern commercial thinking on strategy and success as it is possible to get. Few organisations today will even consider starting projects with very long durations, as it would not be possible to see the benefits of the project realised. Further, problems tend to multiply with time, and the sponsors – those responsible for the provision of the funding and its proper use – are unlikely to be around to see the results. Indeed, short-termism in measuring success abounds as one of the less desirable attributes of our *projectified* world. This is in contrast to many icons we may view as great, from the London Underground (recently celebrated 175 years) to Milan's *Duomo,* where the perspective was very definitely longer term.

Yet even in more conventional projects, *success*, its definition and achievement, provides an interesting challenge for project managers. Ultimate success may be the achievement of political, environmental, economic and social objectives, in the short, medium and long term, to the satisfaction of all concerned. Such a requirement represents the ultimate state of perfection for a project. Managing almost any project requires project managers to take a pragmatic view as to just how close to this perfection can be achieved and where success in one area may have to be achieved at the expense of that in another.

In this chapter, we will examine how and whether stakeholders can be 'managed' and some approaches that project managers have used to try to do this. Also, while some projects, such as those involved in disaster relief, are 'self-evidently needed', commercial projects in particular are founded upon a good *business case*. This provides the rationale as to why the project is being carried out and will remain one of the anchors of a project as it moves from conception to execution.

4.1 Stakeholders: success and failure

The challenge to achieving total success comes from the complexity of the objectives and the requirements of many different groups of **stakeholders** for the project, not least because there will be conflicts between the **requirements** of each. We express these requirements as **measures**. Table 4.1 defines and illustrates these.

Measures and requirements are considered together here, as the measures provide an explicit expression of the requirements.

Furthermore, if for instance initial costs could be reduced by using inferior materials, the impact would be seen on the longer-term objectives – when maintenance costs are likely to be higher as a result. There is therefore a **timing** issue here. Three issues will form the basis for the discussion of success and failure here – stakeholders, requirements and measures, and timing.

Starting from a point that a project is unlikely to meet the requirements of all stakeholders all of the time can provide an uninspiring prospect for the project manager. It could be argued that this can be reduced to managing 'how much you are going to fail'. Indeed, the stakeholder management literature appears to have taken this view. Whatever you do, someone somewhere is going to be unhappy. The PM's role is simply to minimise the critical levels of *unhappiness*.

There is another view. This states that a project is about delivering **value** rather than a *product*. Such an approach considers that the opportunity from a stakeholder analysis is to maximise the overall value of the project. For instance, a project is carried out to change the processes used in a business. During this project, the product (the changed processes) is the main outcome of the process and the project manager should find ways to minimise the level of disruption to members of the organisation. A **value-maximisation** view would take the opportunity to make as many changes as possible in the pursuit of the objective of delivering business benefit from the work being carried out (see section 4.3).

The principle stated at the start of the chapter is from Stephen Covey's *The Seven Habits of Highly Effective People*: begin with the end in mind. In the project environment, mapping the stakeholders and their requirements sets this 'end' and allows focus of the project definition work that follows (Chapter 5) and the quality management of the project (Chapter 9). Such a mapping is worthwhile in most projects. The effort is justifiable as it

Table 4.1 Stakeholders, requirements and measures

Item	Definition	Examples
Stakeholders	Any individual or group with an interest in the project process or outcome	The project customers, the delivery team, the end beneficiaries of the project, anyone affected by the outcome, proponents and opponents of any change
Requirements	What each individual or group wants from the process or outcome	Defined requirements in the form of a specification or contract, implicit requirements (I want this project to be a good place to work), or legal/ethical/moral/commercial/competitive requirements
Measures	The means by which it will be determined during and post project whether those requirements have been met	Level of compliance to specification, customer satisfaction, level of return on investment, staff retention levels

begins the avoidance of the most often-cited causes of project failure. These include lack of user involvement, lack of top management support, unrealistic user expectations, failing to recognise the real requirements of a key customer group or to gain a shared understanding on the outcomes of the project.[3] The project manager has a major role to play in how stakeholders and this success or otherwise play out in the project.

Stakeholders

A stakeholder, as described in Chapter 2, is any party with an interest in the project process or outcome. Most projects have more than one stakeholder or stakeholder group, presenting the project manager with a major challenge – that of resolving their often divergent and potentially conflicting requirements. Key questions posed here include: Who are the stakeholders? What do they want? What influence is this going to have on the project process or outcome? Mapping these factors does provide a basic means of making sense of project requirements and at least in the first instance having a view on how what will be termed the '**stakeholder landscape**' can be managed.

Who are they?

One aspect of project complexity that was defined in Chapter 2 was that of the role of **external stakeholders**. These are people outside the 'project team' or organisation. Typically, these include the people for whom the project is being provided (a customer group, for instance) or the people paying for the process (termed the 'sponsor'). As will be shown though, this can be an extensive group. **Internal stakeholders** are those associated with the process, typically members of the project team or governance structure.

Who are the stakeholders for the football World Cup in Qatar in 2022 (or any other major sporting event for that matter)? A list would include the following:

1 The players, referees, coaches, managers, physios and other team support staff.
2 The players' partners, agents, friends and entourage.
3 FIFA – the governing body.
4 The national football associations.
5 Constructors of the stadia being used for the event.
6 Fans attending.
7 Police and other law enforcement agencies.
8 Media and press attending (huge numbers).
9 The sponsors.
10 People watching or listening to the games.
11 People working in the venues.
12 The organising committee.

Source: TRAVEL by VISION/Alamy Stock Photo

In the context of development projects, the World Bank (1996) provides the following questions to enable identification:

1 Who might be affected (positively or negatively) by the development concern to be addressed?
2 Who are the 'voiceless' for whom special efforts may have to be made?
3 Who are the representatives of those likely to be affected?

4 Who is responsible for what is intended?

5 Who is likely to mobilise for or against what is intended?

6 Who can make what is intended more effective through their participation or less effective through non-participation or outright opposition?

7 Who can contribute financial and technical resources?

8 Whose behaviour has to change for the effort to succeed?

Source: World Bank, 1996 (http://web.worldbank.org)

The challenge that many project managers face with stakeholder identification is not that of making sure that all relevant groups and individuals are included but deciding where to stop the process. As the questions in the World Bank list show, the 'interest' in the project may be unstated or even unknown, and yet there may be a need to show that these interests have been considered, particularly if an organisation is seeking funding for its work.

Returning to the scenario of a major sporting event, the stakeholders could be viewed as a list that comprises a large percentage of the world's population. For instance, the increase in air travel as a result of the event could be argued to contribute further to climate change, with those being affected in the future being stakeholders. The industries that provide souvenirs of the event but have no direct contractual contact with the organisers are another. The list just goes on. As already noted, the initial challenge for the project manager is the identification of stakeholders. The next step is to make sense of the scale of impact of the stakeholders on the project and the project on the stakeholders. As a first sift on the people whom you have identified, Figure 4.1 gives a basic framework. The internal team are always going to be central to your consideration. The next level out is the core external people – people external to the project but who are crucial for its success – ideally containing a few people or groups. The last layer is 'the **rest of the world**' and only requires monitoring to ensure that any new individuals or groups do not unwittingly become core to the project success without appropriate changes being made to the project. For instance, a change of responsibilities between two government departments

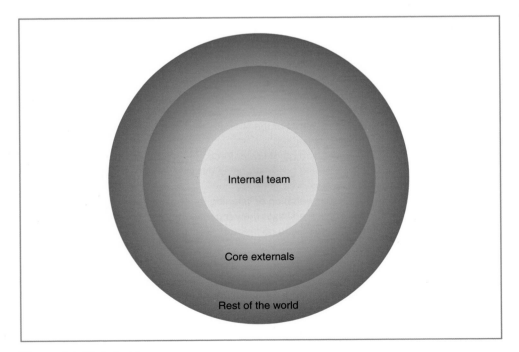

Figure 4.1 Stakeholder groups

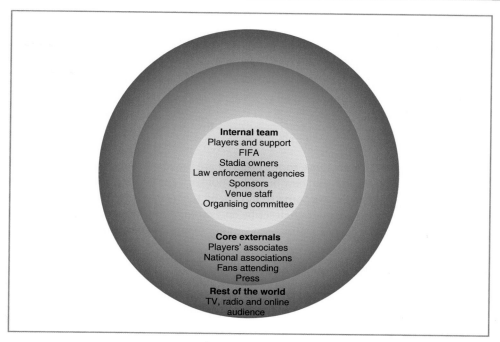

Figure 4.2 Stakeholder grouping for World Cup 2022

dramatically changed the nature of the stakeholder environment, with major implications for an IT project being carried out across a number of departments. This resulted in the stakeholders and their requirements and measures changing significantly.

Applying the framework to the World Cup in 2022 provides the analysis shown in Figure 4.2.

This immediately raises a challenge – whose requirements are paramount? For example, evening games, particularly late evening games, are most popular with the players as the temperature is lower. However, for fans in Asia wanting to watch the games, these would be in the early hours of the morning.

What do they want?

The quotations below illustrate the requirements of different project stakeholder groups.

1 'This product needs to be developed in the shortest possible time – we need it yesterday.' (Marketing manager, automotive firm)
2 'I want a good working solution to the problem, not promises that it will work one day.' (Main client, IT implementation project)
3 'I want to work in a stimulating environment with good people and a manager who knows what they want and sticks to it, not changing things all the time.' (Team member, new product development project)
4 'We want this project to stay out of the news and out of the public eye until it is finished. The last thing we want here is more bad headlines about this project.' (Main client, large defence project)
5 'I want this project to be seen as a success in years to come.' (Project manager, firm relocation project)
6 'I am prepared to make a certain level of investment, but when they (the project team) have spent that, there is no more – we will cancel the project.' (Project sponsor, new business group)

Table 4.2 Input, process and outcome requirements

	Input	*Process*	*Outcome*
Characteristics	Limit on resources provided (quotes 1, 6)	The environment in which the project is undertaken (quote 3); process resource consumption controlled (quote 4)	Product meets certain requirements (quotes 1, 2, 5)

Among these **requirements** are the ideas that they can be expressed as measures of the **inputs** (the new business sponsor), the **process** (the team member, the defence client) and the **outcome** (the IT client, the relocation PM). We have used the basic idea of process in Chapter 1 to describe one view of the project environment, and this is a useful idea in terms of classifying the requirements. Examples of these are shown in Table 4.2.

Measures

At the most basic level, the requirements of a project may be stated in terms of time, cost and quality/specification. This triad of requirements is heavily embedded within the concept of projects and has been used for decades.[4] At a first level of consideration, time, cost and quality are the most frequently used and do provide the opportunity to consider some requirements. Simply stating the requirements is insufficient from a managerial perspective – these must be prioritised to allow for decisions to be made.

There is, however, a much larger set of measures consistent with the diverse requirements of stakeholders as shown in Table 4.3. Regarding the key concept of project outcome, according to various studies that acknowledged the necessity to measure project success beyond project efficiency (cost, scope and time), project managers were asked to what extent the project achieved its purpose, provided satisfactory benefit to the owner, satisfied the needs of the owner, users and stakeholders, met the pre-stated objectives, was produced to specification, within budget and on time, and satisfied the needs of the project team.

Table 4.3 New product development (NPD) metrics[5]

Type of measure	*Characteristic measured*
Process measures	Product development cost, time and conformance to quality procedures
Short-term outcome measures	Product performance level, desirability to market, flexibility of design to be changed to meet emergent customer needs
Longer-term outcome measures	Payback period, customer satisfaction, percentage of business being generated by the new product, market share, customisability for high-margin markets

Beyond the conventional approach[6]

The following demonstrates the influence of the measures and the involvement of stakeholders in two different approaches to their management. Specifically, the measures set up (described here as 'the end') are then used for monitoring and control as the project

Table 4.4 Conventional versus participatory project monitoring and evaluation

	Conventional M&E	*Participatory M&E*
Who plans and manages the process:	Project managers	Local people, project staff, managers and other stakeholders, often helped by a facilitator
Role of 'primary stakeholders' (the intended beneficiaries):	Provide information only	Design and adapt the methodology, collect and analyse data, share findings and link them to action
How success is measured:	Externally defined, mainly quantitative indicators	Internally defined indicators, including more qualitative judgements
Approach:	Pre-determined	Adaptive

progresses. In Table 4.4, the approach of **participatory monitoring and evaluation (PM&E)** is contrasted with the conventional approach.

This example demonstrates a development in the approach to projects more generally. Specifically, the move to 'shared ownership' of the project planning process from one centred on the project manager, from 'telling stakeholders' to 'consulting and adapting according to emergent needs', from success measures (particularly efficiency measures) to a wider range of relevant and often qualitative indicators, and from an approach that suggests that the path of the project can be identified at the outset to one that recognises that the project environment is a dynamic environment.

We must also think of the delivery of projects as a service. Although we want the final output, the journey of creating it is important too. We may develop the new product or build the new office block on time, to budget and to the original specification, but if we irritate the client throughout and antagonise stakeholders, it cannot really be considered a success. Consider an evening spent at a fine restaurant. If the environment is beautiful and the food is excellent but the waiting staff are rude, it will end up being a disappointing experience. As a consequence, we will be unlikely to return in the foreseeable future. The same is true in project delivery, and is especially important for businesses who deliver projects for clients – the 'how' of project delivery, although less tangible, is highly significant in creating customer satisfaction.[7]

These themes will be developed further in Chapter 13.

So not only what do we measure, but how and when do we measure it? There is clearly a range of measures, even within the basic time, cost and quality criteria. Measurement will be discussed further throughout this book, as measurements are vital as the means of checking whether strategy is in fact being implemented.

Timing

It is argued by some that a project manager should not concern themselves with wider issues, that achievement of a limited set of objectives over the project duration alone is sufficient. This may be acceptable in some areas, but we are concerned with project managers having a strategic role as outlined in the previous chapters, and it is consistent with such a strategic role that a wider consideration is appropriate.

So, how do we determine whether a project is a **success**?

REAL WORLD   The Oresund Link

The Oresund Link is a 16.4 km road and rail connection between Copenhagen (Denmark) and Malmo (Sweden). This length includes nearly 8 km of bridge, a tunnel and an artificial island. As a project, completing this link is a significant engineering achievement – a combined four-lane road and twin-track rail bridge, with one of the longest cable-stayed main spans in the world. It was opened on time on 1 July 2000, a major management achievement given the scale and complexity of the project. However, the cost of the crossing (c. €30) was initially blamed for lower than expected traffic figures. This caused the operators some concern, but politically, the idea of a more integrated region as a result of the bridge appears to be a more important long-term objective than any short-term financial issues.

Source: Anders Blomqvist/Stone/Getty image

So, has the project been a success? The timing of the assessment and the perspective of the assessor are critical. Measurement in 2001 would have suggested not, but as of today, how is it doing? In addition, is it more important to consider the view of the operators, or the Swedish and Danish governments, both of whom realise the longer-term regeneration impact of the bridge? The challenge though comes with the implications for the team managing the project. Most of these will be temporary and for them, the project will finish when construction is complete. So, what is their stake in the longer-term success of that project?

The whole issue of the timings and nature of assessments is crucial to focus the work of the project team. During a project, some notion of 'control' must be imposed on the work (see Chapter 13). Post completion, there will be reviews (see Chapter 16) and stakeholders will form opinions over time. The challenge for the project manager here is that such a long-term view is not consistent with the nature of project work. Their performance is assessed over a period longer than the project, yet their rewards are usually linked to performance within the project.

Some projects must be designed at the outset to last for generations. Extreme cases include military platforms (such as ships and aircraft) that must remain operational for decades. At the time of writing, Thames Tideway, London's new 'super sewer' is being constructed, with intended operation for generations to come. Work like this extends well beyond the careers (and even the lives) of the designers, and 'simple' measurement is inappropriate. One measure at one point in time will not capture the performance of most projects, the managers, project teams or stakeholder views. The challenge then is to put in place an appropriate set of measures, to report performance to date and then to guide in the setting of objectives for the future. Crucial to this is the whole issue of whether perception of success is a good performance measure. Sometimes it just takes longer than has been expected for success to be achieved, as the examples below illustrate.

Sometimes, it just takes longer than expected . . .

There is very little evidence from ancient history that time and budget constraints were set for projects. Instead, emergence of requirements (e.g. evident in the construction of the pyramids) and ongoing provision of resources until the desired outcome was achieved was accepted.

Reviewing major projects in recent history from IK Brunel, through all Olympics, to modern rail implementations, there is a consistent theme: *things that change the world usually take longer (and/or cost more) than we think.*

- **IK Brunel** – most of Brunel's more ambitious schemes ran late and over budget. His tunnel under the Thames and the SS Great Eastern went particularly awry in these terms. However, his legacy has been huge – railways, canals and bridges that are still in use today, delivering benefits decades after the original investments had been repaid.
- **The Apollo missions** – for a series of projects where budget was not a major consideration, the programme was frequently delayed. However, the success was not in terms of conformance to budget, it was in the achievement of the exploration of space.
- **Concorde** – delivered years late and cost over five times the original budget.[8] In service, it was operated commercially for 27 years and transformed the face of global travel. When it was taken out of service, it was doubtful whether supersonic commercial flights would be seen again in this generation.
- **Channel Tunnel** – considered a vital political part of 'the European Project' – delivered over two years late and double its original budget. It was disastrous in project terms, particularly as the over-budget project left a mountain of debt for the operating company (Eurotunnel) such that its shares were virtually worthless for many years. In 2009, the company made its first operating profit and declared its first dividend to shareholders in 23 years. Technically, environmentally and in so many other ways, this was a success.

There are many other examples of course, but these do make the point that on a project management level, all of these are examples of **failure** if we consider them in terms of their out-turn compared with initial predictions. Far more important though is their longer-term impact on their stakeholders.

Managing stakeholders

You can't please all of the people, all of the time . . .

REAL WORLD   Jersey and Berlin airports

The construction of a new airport terminal building at Jersey Airport started well. The design was approved by all the necessary authorities and contractors were appointed to carry out the work.

The main concern was the deadline for completion – it had to be in the spring, in time for the island's main tourist influx in the summer. This was achieved and everyone was, for a time, very happy with the new facility. That was until a few problems arose.

These all concerned the impact that the new building was having on the operation of the airport. First, the air traffic controllers (ATCs) complained that they were being dazzled by sunlight reflected from the roof of the new terminal building. No problem, said the Chief Executive of the Jersey Airport Authority – well, at least not during the winter.

A further complaint was that the new building affected the accuracy of the airport's wind speed indicator when the wind was in a certain direction. While a new site for the indicator was being sought, the air traffic controllers were having to advise pilots to use their own judgement regarding the wind speed, when it was blowing in a particular direction. Furthermore, the new building obscured the view of parts of the taxiway to the ATCs (they are responsible for aircraft movements on the ground as well as in the air). The solution – install closed-circuit cameras which would relay the obscured area to the control tower.

When questioned about these problems, the Chief Executive reminded his interviewer that safety was still a top priority. In the light of these problems, the *Financial Times* reminded potential visitors to Jersey that 'they can easily go by boat'.[9]

The latest airports are faring no better. The saga of Berlin's Brandenburg Airport has plagued the city for years.[10] After the fall of the Berlin Wall in 1989 the city resolved to build a new, modern, airport. Construction began in 2006, with a planned opening date in 2012, and a budget of €2.83 billion. Delay after delay saw the opening date slip and slip, and the budget rise beyond €7.3 billion. In late 2019 the new opening date was set for 31 October 2020. At this point, with the story of the build known world-wide, 'success' was not really an option for the team; it was a matter of damage limitation and finally making it operational. Time and budget were not recoverable, and it is hard to imagine what facilities would make up for the years of delay. However, once it has been running for some time, it is entirely feasible that it will be considered a success if it brings benefits to the city. As it turns out, the airport did indeed open at the end of October, in a pandemic where passenger throughput was very limited. To cap the sorry story, the first two planes to land were planned to do so in parallel, but sadly this too was curtailed by fog.

The Real World box shows that the Jersey air traffic controllers were clearly a key stakeholder, but their needs were apparently not considered during the design of the new facility. Or if they were, insufficient modelling of the new work environment took place during the design. Also, they would not have been the only stakeholder in this project and clearly there were other requirements that took precedence. For Berlin, the stakeholder mix is far more extensive, including the city inhabitants, the German government, and the world's press looking on.

In balancing the precedence given to different stakeholders, many project managers talk about a key aspect of their work in acting as 'mediator' between stakeholders. In Chapter 3, we identified a whole category of managerial complexity devoted to 'stakeholders'. How, then, can we attempt to make some sense of this complexity? One approach is to consider the nature of the **power** or **influence** of a stakeholder on the project and the *interest* or **impact** of the project on that stakeholder.

Power in this context can be in the form of direct authority (e.g. through being the CEO of a company in which a project is carried out), through indirect authority (e.g. a legislative change requiring that a project is carried out) or having an important relationship with the project team (as would be the case of a financial or technical audit function). Interest is the measure of how much that stakeholder knows about the project; impact is how much they will be affected by the process or outcome. Either can be used to produce what is termed a *stakeholder map*.

The stakeholder map provides a rough guide to how to 'manage' particular groups. One commonly used framework is shown in Figure 4.3.

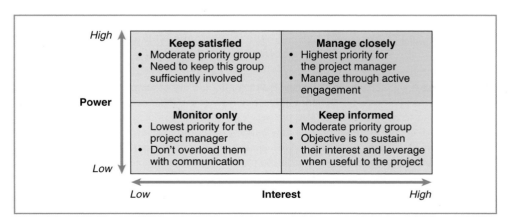

Figure 4.3 Power: Interest stakeholder map

An example of the use of such mapping is included in *Project Management in Practice* at the end of this chapter. Another popular means of mapping stakeholders involves the stakeholder potential for cooperation, with the project being plotted against the potential threat of that stakeholder to the project. This is useful where there is likely to be opposition to a project, for instance as is common with organisational change projects.[11]

4.2   Managing strategic choices

In business, there are strategic choices to be made. These choices focus the organisation on to a limited set of objectives, illustrated in Chapter 3 by the cost focus of easyJet. This is stated as, '*We are in business to be the fastest OR the best OR the cheapest.*' The same prioritisation is necessary in projects, as was demonstrated by the strategy framework in Figure 3.1, and is part of the strategy deployment process in organisations.

As described above, the simplest consideration of a project's objectives can be made in terms of time, cost and quality (TCQ). How do we decide which is/are the most important of these three? First, it is necessary to understand the nature of the **trade-offs** that exist in the project.

Consider the following scenario. Your team has been set a task to carry out a piece of market research, for instance. You have a limited time to complete the report on this market for your director. At the outset of the activity, you are able to plan your activities with the objective of delivering the assignment in the time required. The quality of the outcome is dependent on the time that you have – the longer you have, the more research you would be able to do and the more effort you could put into the presentation of the end result. If you have only a very short time, this clearly limits what you can do. You can buy in additional resource, but this costs. This shows clearly the relationship between three elements of project strategy: time, cost and quality. We say that there is a trade-off between these three – that you can have the task completed very quickly, but unless you are prepared to compromise on the quality, you may have to pay more to recruit additional resources to the team.

An example of getting this wrong was the project to build the ship Titanic – it took to sea after its owners had prioritised time over its quality of design. The 'unsinkable' was compromised because emergent issues (ones that could not have been reasonably foreseen or resolved in early design and planning) could not be accommodated in the schedule.[12]

A trade-off is, therefore, the prioritisation of the objectives of a project. It is important at this stage, as there are two major occasions where it will affect the decisions made. The first is during planning. If a customer indicates that a specification for a set of project activities is non-negotiable, the resources of time and cost will need to be manipulated around this central objective. Furthermore, it focuses the project on what is really important, as many projects start with unnecessary assumptions regarding what needs to be achieved.

Second, it will affect the decisions made during execution. For example, if the most important objective for a project is to achieve a particular level of cost performance, where problems exist and decisions need to be made, time and quality could be compromised to ensure that the cost objective is met. This does look like a poor compromise but it is the reality, particularly where there are inherent uncertainties in the project. Resources cannot be stretched ad infinitum to obtain goals that are passing out of sight due to unforeseen problems. It is vital to know in advance what can and cannot be moved should this scenario arise, no matter how undesirable this is in principle. These form the so-called **iron triangle**, as shown in Figure 4.4.

In some cases, it is clear where the position of the project in the iron triangle should lie. For instance, during recent military engagements, new requirements for the equipment that soldiers were using emerged. These needed to be met with enhanced products in the

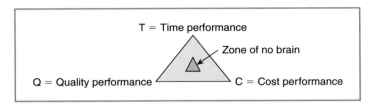

Figure 4.4 Trade-offs in project management

shortest possible time. The suppliers of that equipment were issued with orders for urgent operational requirements (UOR) by the UK's Ministry of Defence – prioritised work that bypassed much of the normal process associated with product orders, in the interests of getting enhanced equipment into use at the earliest possible time. In such a case, location of the project firmly in the 'time corner' meant that trading off cost and in some instances quality (particularly of process documentation) was necessary (Figure 4.5).

In March 2019 the Boeing 737 Max fleet was grounded worldwide after two fatal crashes that were traced back to design issues in the automated control system. Expectations of the date by which they would be recertified kept slipping, and in December 2019 production of the plane was halted. This cost Boeing billions of dollars, and Chief Executive Dennis Muilenburg his job. The location (finally) of the project in the 'quality' corner was an appropriate response (Figure 4.6), although internal documentation released by the company seemed to show that safety and quality had not been sufficiently supported in the design phase. It was not cleared to fly again until November 2020.

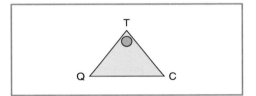

Figure 4.5 Time priority project

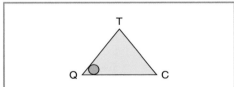

Figure 4.6 Quality priority project

There is a whole category of projects that is cash-limited. For instance, many EU-funded scientific research projects have an absolute maximum funding. Researchers are not allowed to go over that funding limit. Any additional spend has to be funded by their institutions, so there is considerable incentive to stay within allocated budgets resulting in the position shown in Figure 4.7. Similarly, many international development or aid projects are characterised by fixed budgets.

Lastly, on the location of the basic priority, many projects have dual requirements. The Olympic Games is perhaps the best example of a major project that absolutely cannot be late. The organisers cannot have athletes and spectators turning up at the Games and ask them to 'come back next month, the facilities are not yet finished'. The opening ceremony timings are set years in advance, with an audience of billions anticipating a spectacular show. Quality is therefore similarly non-negotiable. A shoddy event would reflect very badly on the country hosting the biggest event in sport. Cost is therefore the only variable, and it is noteworthy that all Olympics in modern times have been on time, but with major cost overruns (see Figure 4.8).

A highly impressive example of both speed and quality was in early 2020 when Huoshenshan hospital was constructed in just 10 days in Wuhan city. This 1000-bed facility was built in response to the escalating coronavirus outbreak in China, and time-lapse footage of the project was watched around the world. Cost data were not released, but the project showed what could be done if resources could be mobilised and coordinated swiftly and effectively.

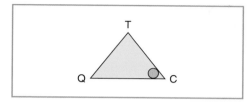

Figure 4.7 Cost priority project

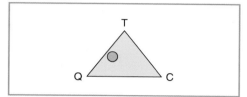

Figure 4.8 Time AND quality priority

It is important to note that the strategic choices are communicated effectively to the project team. Although the cases above are clear-cut, most real-world projects are not so obvious. In a new product development, if some of the team are aiming for the lowest production cost possible, others want to create the highest quality they can, and still others are rushing to be fastest to market, the competing tensions will lead to greatly increased complexity in the work. If this happens it is likely that all three dimensions will be compromised. The project leader needs to ensure that the team are clear on the actual priorities if or when trade-offs need to be made, and that there is a common, shared, view.[13]

Some authors have claimed that the necessity to consider trade-offs has been removed by modern management practices.[14] The evidence for this is not as convincing as suggested and the pragmatic project manager is still faced with making these decisions. Before committing to a course of action, the manager should, however, consider the assumptions that underlie each of the criteria. For example, if a project is running up against time constraints, it may be worth considering the sequence of activities to see whether their rearrangement will yield the necessary time savings. This is before any compromise is made on the cost element (reducing time by other means could incur additional costs).

However, such an approach is limited. We will look at whether there is a need to consider the further element of **flexibility** and whether a wider range of measures would, in fact, be beneficial.

The first consideration is to determine the nature of the three key objectives. These have been at the heart of consideration in project management for many years, and while limited on their own, are still the basis for any consideration of project objectives. As a minimum, the project manager must define these and then put in place a project process to ensure that these objectives are met. This approach stresses **conformance** to the stated objectives as being the most important for measuring project success. This is a measure of the *reliability* required of the project system, expressed as:

- Can the project be guaranteed to deliver on time?
- Will the project finish within budget?
- Will the project meet the specified level of quality?

Such reliability measures are a 'good place to start' for many individuals and organisations as they attempt to make sense of a project.

Table 4.5 Conformance versus performance: attributes of time, cost and quality

	Time	*Cost*	*Quality*
Performance	Shortest possible	Cheapest possible	Highest level
Conformance	As planned	As budgeted	As specified

Going beyond this minimalist approach is consistent with the emphasis in many business projects today which has shifted away from just achieving conformance. Still focusing on our three basic criteria of time, cost and quality, excellence is defined in terms of real **performance**, expressed as:

- What is the shortest possible project duration?
- What is the lowest cost?
- What is the highest level of quality that can be achieved?

The mechanisms by which the project manager assures conformance are different from those that ensure performance. For example, by selecting low-cost suppliers, the project manager may attempt to ensure that the project is delivered at minimum cost (performance). Whether it is in fact deliverable is determined by the actions of that manager to secure guarantees that the price (in addition to delivery and quality) will be achieved in practice (conformance). Table 4.5 summarises these characteristics.

Time and cost criteria are relatively straightforward concepts. In practice, determining whether key objectives have been achieved can be a matter of some argument and commercial significance. One of the least understood concepts in projects is *quality*. There are a number of manufacturing and service definitions which we will explore in Chapter 9, including the relationship between expectations and perceptions of customers (and other stakeholders) of both the project process and its outcomes.

What lies beyond TCQ?

Looking at the work covered so far, it can be seen that for most projects there are diverse stakeholders with diverse sets of requirements at various stages during and beyond the project lifecycle. Therefore we can say that time, cost and quality are incomplete as a statement of requirements for a project. We cannot assume that such objectives are fixed and known in advance of the project starting and that such diversity of requirements can be reduced to only three measures. In an ideal world (and many project managers' dreams), this would indeed be the case. The process of developing strategy for projects would be easier if customers always knew exactly what they wanted at the outset and were able to communicate this. As will be discussed later, it is the responsibility of the project manager to ensure that customer input is obtained by the project and there are a number of methods available for doing this.

The GTO framework[15]

When dealing with major or complex projects, simple frameworks such as the iron triangle, no longer provide much help to project leaders, and a greater set of objectives and considerations is required. Under such circumstances, we find it helpful to classify objectives into three categories:

1 Givens – these are objectives that must be achieved and cannot be traded or given up. A typical 'given' is legal requirements – a project must comply with all relevant laws. It is simply not an option to do anything else. However, there are many other objectives that might fall into this. For an Olympics or an event, the timing might be a given. Or for an increasing number of organisations, the societal or environmental impact will be a given (see Real World below).

2 Tradeables – these are desirable for the project and are objectives that could be given up if there were more important objectives. For instance, the scope of a project may be classified as a tradeable, if there are elements or features of the project output, that could be compromised. For some organisations, cost may become a tradeable where the project is urgent or its achievement means a continued license to operate in a particular place.

3 Optimisers – these are the objectives that the stakeholders want more of and it might be worth compromising on the tradeables (but of course, not the givens) to achieve. For instance, 'the benefits to the citizen' might be an optimser for a government project, or minimising disruption to the business for a change project.

Crucial for the project leader then, is what objectives fit into which category, and to make sure that there are some tradeables. Using the GTO framework has been found to encourage much more meaningful conversations with stakeholders, who otherwise are likely to operate under the illusion that projects can be delivered 'perfectly, yesterday and for nothing'. In addition, making objectives a matter for discussion is helpful; one leader noted that before we discussed the objectives, they had been under such pressure that 'staff wellbeing' had inadvertently become a tradeable. Once discussed, she agreed with the team that this should, quite rightly, be placed in the 'givens' category and managed accordingly for the rest of the project.

Flexibility

There are, however, many occasions when the requirements of the customer are likely to change as the project progresses. The ability of the project system to address this change is expressed by its flexibility. Such flexibility needs to be accounted for at the outset, as there are penalties in relation to the other objectives – flexibility costs. For example, a firm that makes custom-engineered components is contracted to supply parts to an automotive assembler. It is asked to provide a quotation for new parts, but the specification requires some flexibility, as it will not be determined exactly until the last minute. With this required flexibility, the firm will need to hold back the making up of tooling, requiring this to be made by an express service rather than its normal supplier. This design flexibility therefore has potential cost implications, which, unless built into the estimates, will cause the firm to perform poorly on the cost conformance aspect.

The emergence of givens

By no means the least important factor for stakeholders, is the consideration of *ethics* and *health and safety*. As the Real World box below demonstrates, this is a non-tradeable aspect for many organisations and this is fed through to project staff. Failure to meet the necessary requirements in these areas is likely to have serious consequences, increasingly including fines and jail-terms for staff who are negligent. Apocryphal tales in this area include a project manager who delivered a major infrastructure project in one country, but was jailed when he arrived home. He had made payments to local officials to ensure that parts of the project could progress unhindered by the notorious local bureaucracy.

REAL WORLD   **Shell and Goal Zero**

Shell considers Health, Safety, Security and the Environment (HSSE) the prime objective for its projects. Within the Health and Safety area, *Goal Zero* is the target that nobody will be harmed or injured by one of its projects or facilities. In complex construction, this is a significant challenge, as people are often working in hazardous conditions, at height, with large loads, or under considerable pressure to increase the speed of work. However, when deciding on its project objectives (*project promises* in Shell), increases in speed, reductions in cost or changes in specification cannot be achieved at the expense of HSSE.

Project performance mapping

Having determined the nature of the trade-offs in the project (and which elements cannot be traded), the most important ones are determined by our organisational strategy. As stated earlier, this provides the guidance that we compete in a market or market segment by offering projects as the fastest or best or cheapest supplier. If the organisational objective is to be the fastest, then this is a *performance objective*, while the cost and quality criteria are *conformance objectives*. As a minimum, we must hit our conformance objectives. We will focus on improving on our performance objectives. Other objectives can form part of the conformance requirements of the project – not just time, cost and quality. These may be environmental, ethical, legal, health and safety – indeed any of the constraints identified at the start of Chapter 2 can become objectives and as discussed above, may also be non-tradeable.

4.3 Benefits analysis, value and justification

In Chapter 3, we explored the idea that it is neither possible nor desirable for an organisation to undertake all of the projects that present themselves. Programme and portfolio management provide the mechanisms by which organisations can reconcile the demands and the capacity to deliver these demands. The objective here is to consider the principles by which projects may be evaluated.

The fundamental idea is that a project should yield value: value to someone at some point in time. Decorating a house may yield value in terms of personal gratification about its improved ambience and may also add financial value, by increasing the price that someone is prepared to pay for it. A social project may not yield any return on the investment, yet may deliver perceived value to those that it tries to help. Business projects will usually have to be justified in hard financial terms, by justifying the timing and **payback** from an investment.

At a high level, the logic behind this is good – payback or **return on investment** should be criteria for determining which projects go into the portfolio of work to be carried out and which should be deferred, amended or rejected. A principle from the previous chapter is that an organisation cannot carry out every project proposed. Determining the kind of benefits that a project can deliver is not always completely straightforward, however. A framework that many organisations use to determine the nature of the return on an investment is the **balanced scorecard**.[16]

The balanced scorecard links four perspectives on business projects. These are:

1 *Shareholders* – what are the intended financial benefits in the short, medium or long term of the project?
2 *Customers and suppliers* – what are the benefits that they will receive from the project, be it direct benefit (reduced costs, for instance) or simply increasing goodwill? Will it enable the organisation to work with a different market of customers or suppliers?
3 *Internally* – how will the project improve our business processes?
4 *Innovation and learning* – how much will we learn from the project?

The last one is particularly interesting and often missed. For instance, the Apollo (and the preceding Mercury) missions were late and budget was 'not a major consideration'. In the development of the Apollo programme, with each successive project in that programme there was considerable learning. There was learning internally for NASA scientists and astronauts. There was learning for the supply chain, both in terms of what worked and what didn't, technically and in process terms.

It is worth considering that often a 'failed' project may in fact be of value. A product development that fails financially may still offer insight into new technical innovations or what customers actually require. If companies 'pivot' to a new approach using this knowledge, the longer-term outcome can still be positive.

Overall, these combine to provide a notion of the **value proposition** from a project. Such terminology has become commonplace in the justification of time, energy and resources on business projects. The originators of the balanced scorecard promote a logical cause–effect building of benefits from project work, with the objective to demonstrate how each project will impact organisational strategy. Such construction is consistent with the approach shown in Chapter 3.

Demonstrating such benefits is the purpose of an approach known as **benefits mapping**.[17] Using this, it is possible to work back from the business benefit required, see how this maps to organisational objectives and then determine the changes and supporting actions required to yield those benefits.

One organisation used this approach to demonstrate how an initiative to improve its programme and project management (PPM) capability would benefit the business and produced the map shown in Figure 4.9.

Starting on the right of the figure, the organisational drivers for the change are shown. At the most basic level, improving the organisation's PPM capability is necessary for survival and continued investment in that company and its projects. This drives the benefits requirement – organisational benefits. Externally, it needs to be able to deliver projects in the way planned – its markets and customers are unforgiving when projects are delayed or otherwise compromised. Internally, it wants to demonstrate how improved capability will help the people in the firm who would need to be key participants in any change. It was also noted how it was often forgotten why projects were started – not uncommon in organisations. The next box to the left is the organisational changes that

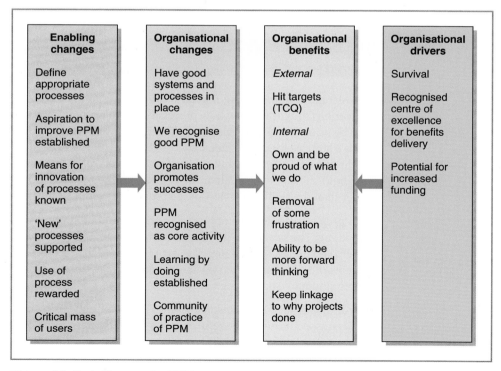

Figure 4.9 Benefits map for PPM capability improvement

are required – each one can be linked to an element in the organisational benefits box. Similarly, the far left box has elements which are linked to the changes. For instance, before you can have good processes in place (organisational change) it is necessary to define appropriate processes (enabling change).

From intangible to quantifiable

While there are some benefits that do not require justification (e.g. implement a regulatory change in a bank or be prevented from trading), many project managers struggle with intangible benefits. There are a number of strategies for dealing with this *quantification problem*.[18] These include:

- carrying out a pilot study – determine on a small scale the costs and benefits of the work being proposed before launching into a full-scale project;
- benchmarking and reference sites – other organisations which have carried out similar projects and their costs incurred and benefits gained;
- modelling – build a simulation of the proposed changes – use the data from these to provide evidence of costs and benefits.

One area to be wary of is when a major undertaking is argued based primarily on the inputs, rather than the details of the expected benefits. It is common for politicians to promise, for example, to recruit 10,000 nurses or police, or to ensure that a certain percentage of gross domestic product is spent on aid or defence. This gets the headlines, but is it the right way round? What benefits are actually desired? Thinking in terms of real patient care requirements, late-night patrols, future equipment requirements, and disaster relief, focus the mind on what needs to be achieved. Spending money is relatively easy; thinking through what you are really after is normally a lot harder. This is one of the reasons delivering complex projects is challenging. It is good practice to establish the benefits you are looking for, then work back to the ways of setting up the work.

Summary

■ Welcome to some of the inherent complexity that goes with running projects. This chapter has sought to show how professional project managers cope with such complexity. The principle of 'beginning with the end in mind' is a good one, and determining this end is a key role for project managers. In doing so, they will need to wrestle with the often indeterminate and conflicting needs of different stakeholder groups. In reality, managing stakeholders can be as much art as science – often referred to in terms of 'herding cats' rather than the traditional view of the process as 'optimising'.

■ In projects, the science and art can and should be mutually reinforcing rather than competing. The science helps with the identification and provision of numbers in an effort to help with decision-making. The art recognises that projects and the accompanying 'systems of stakeholders' or stakeholder landscapes, as they have been termed here, are people systems – social systems.

■ Working in social systems, it becomes clear that the basic measures of time, cost and quality or specification are useful only to a point in determining project objectives. Beyond the most simple of projects, the key performance indicators (KPIs) used should reflect the broader requirements of stakeholders over different time periods. These requirements can be mapped to help understanding of the project and the requirements.

Key terms

balanced scorecard *p. 100*

benefits mapping *p. 101*

conformance/
performance *pp. 97, 98*

failure *p. 93*

flexibility *p. 97*

impact *p. 94*

influence *p. 94*

input/process/outcome
requirements *p. 90*

internal/external
stakeholders *p. 87*

iron triangle *p. 95*

measures *p. 86*

participatory monitoring and
evaluation (PM&E) *p. 91*

payback *p. 100*

power *p. 94*

requirements *p. 86*

rest of the world *p. 88*

return on investment *p. 100*

stakeholder landscape
p. 87

stakeholders *p. 86*

success *p. 91*

timing *p. 86*

trade-offs *p. 95*

value *p. 86*

value-maximisation *p. 86*

value proposition *p. 101*

Relevant areas of the Bodies of Knowledge

Both Bodies of Knowledge have improved their coverage of these areas with their latest editions (see Tables 4.6 and 4.7). Part of the reason they were previously weak is due to the definition that they use of project work – that the project doesn't start until such work as is included here has been completed, a business case prepared and the project 'signed off'. The reality for most project managers is that they will and indeed should be involved in the earlier discussions, as described here as phase D1, and not simply pick up the project fully formed in D3.

Table 4.6 Relevant areas of the APM Body of Knowledge

Relevant section	*Title*	*Summary*
1.3.7	Business case	The formal document that pulls together the rationale for undertaking a project.
3.1	Stakeholder management	The section discusses systematically engaging with stakeholders.
1.1.4 and 2.3.3	Benefits management	The process that takes benefits from identification as part of the business case through to their delivery – benefits realisation.

Table 4.7 Relevant areas of the PMI Body of Knowledge

Relevant section	*Title*	*Summary*
4.1	Develop project charter	Recognises that the creation of a project charter provides a justification of the project in terms of its link with the strategic objectives of the organisation.
10.1	Communications planning	States requirements for plan to communicate in an appropriate manner with all necessary stakeholder groups.
13	Project stakeholder management	The use of a whole section recognises the importance of stakeholders to the success of projects.

PROJECT MANAGEMENT IN PRACTICE
Managing stakeholders at European transport infrastructure provider

In the development of a strategy for major projects, this organisation spent some time considering how it would work with each of its stakeholder groups. The first stage was to identify these groups. These were:

1 Government – owned the company.

2 Managers – worked in the company.

3 Supervisory board – acted in the role of a regulator of the company's activities.

4 Public authorities – local government organisations.

5 Strategic partners – other transport providers, construction companies.

6 Employees – worked in the company.

7 Suppliers – many organisations, from utility companies to consultants.

8 Press and media – always trying to find a good story.

9 Associations and organisations – groups of interested parties.

10 Local communities – impacted by both the project and the outcomes of the project.

11 Customers – those who actually paid to use the services provided.

Having done this, it then mapped its power and interest, as shown in Figure 4.10. Each stakeholder was represented as an oval on the diagram, with the size of the oval representing the scale of that

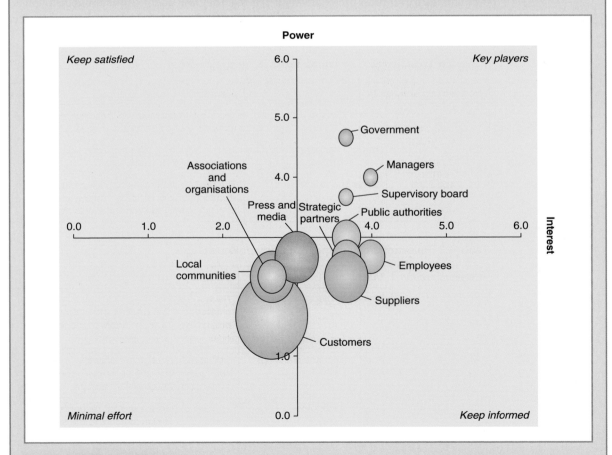

Figure 4.10 Stakeholder map

stakeholder group. 'Government' in these terms is relatively small scale – they were controlled through one single government department that reported directly to a government minister. The press and media were on a larger scale as there were more individual organisations involved: journalists, media companies, etc. The largest group, represented by the largest oval, was the customers.

The company was concerned about the placement of some of its stakeholders as it moved forward. For instance, it appeared that the press and media had more power and influence than one of the most important groups, the customers. As the company developed plans for a major new infrastructure project which would affect all of the groups and particularly customers, it was contemplating whether this arrangement was appropriate.

Points for discussion

1 Outline the role that a government-owned company might take in its management of a major piece of transport infrastructure (could be a road, railway or airport, for instance).

2 Should it be concerned about the placement of customers so low down and in the 'minimal effort' quadrant?

3 Suggest three stakeholders whose positions you would change and outline a strategy for doing so.

PROJECT MANAGEMENT IN PRACTICE
A new campus for the University of Rummidge (with apologies to David Lodge)[19]

A chance meeting between the leader of the town council of Splot and the Vice-chancellor of the University of Rummidge started a project that would lead to the opening of a new campus in Splot.

This appeared to be an ideal opportunity for both parties – the university was unable to expand further on its existing site, due to local planning restrictions. This was despite having a well-known brand name in the market, particularly for management education. The town was in the process of applying to become a city, a status that would confer additional prestige on the area and almost certain political success for whoever could make it happen. It had been the recipient of around €5 billion of investment in recent years, from leading-edge companies in the automotive and electronics sectors. These new firms were providing a major demand for a wide variety of higher education services that the existing institutions were incapable of providing. Local unemployment was virtually zero and firms were having problems recruiting for all types of work.

A number of opportunities presented themselves to the Splot council. These included setting up their own university, in conjunction with local businesses, and developing a range of specialist training through a virtual campus. The first was rejected on the grounds that they did not have the expertise to do this and the second on the basis that they could not identify the unique advantage they would be bringing to the market. The availability of school premises in the middle of the town, which could be readily converted into a campus and which were in an area prioritised for redevelopment, sealed the decision. Shutting down the school was a decision eased by the falling numbers of pupils.

For the University of Rummidge, there were likewise other options. Expansion into areas that would relieve the dependence on government funding was always a priority, and operations beyond the physical limitations of the campus were increasingly attractive. Internet-based activities were an option for investment, but there were other initiatives in place to promote these. In addition, forming direct relationships with one or more of the large companies in the area for provision of integrated higher education services was considered. The university's management team favourably viewed the opening of a new campus.

In order to progress the work, a joint venture organisation entitled 'The University of Rummidge in Splot' was established with the brief to 'explore all the various options that will permit the establishment of a permanent and physical presence by the University of Rummidge in Splot'.

Six months later, the joint venture organisation reported, recommending to both the university and the council that the school premises be converted ready for courses to be run the following September. A budget for the conversion of the premises and establishment of the campus (including provision of library and IT facilities) of €25 million was suggested and funding was underwritten by both organisations, subject to grants being approved from central government and sponsorship being obtained from local companies.

The main part of the project is now about to start and the team has 12 months to get the new facility, staffing and all the necessary support services ready. Academic staff at Rummidge are not impressed by this move as much of the negotiation has taken place without their input. Moreover, Splot is around a one-hour drive from Rummidge, traffic permitting. There are also significant reservations about the location of the campus in a relatively run-down district of the town and whether there will be sufficient buy-in from local people to make it worthwhile. In addition, there was debate as to whether courses (both undergraduate and postgraduate) would be run at both sites and whether there would be resources available to assist with the workloads of the departments (both academic and administrative) caused by the new courses. Some of the administrative departments were also unclear as to how the new campus would affect their workloads.

The organisational structures are shown in outline in Figure 4.11.

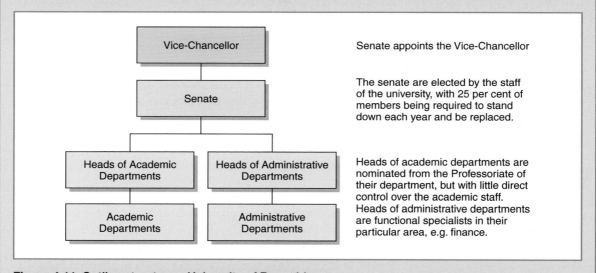

Figure 4.11 Outline structure – University of Rummidge

Points for discussion

1 What are the strategic objectives for each of the organisations involved? Provide a high-level benefits map to structure the objectives and necessary changes.

2 Who are the key stakeholders in such a project? Show how each group should be managed.

3 What would appropriate success measures be for the project?

Topics for discussion

1 Consider the last Olympics and Paralympics and identify the list of major stakeholders. How did the Games 'project' perform for each of these stakeholders?

2 What are the implications for a project manager of not having any clear prioritisation of objectives in terms of time, cost and quality?

3 What are the implications for a project manager of being told that the cost of the project was the most important objective for them to achieve?

4 Time, cost and quality measured at project completion have been widely used as performance measures for projects. When might this be useful and how is this a limited approach?

5 How would the use of the balanced scorecard approach to project performance management help a project be 'successful'?

6 Why should 'ethics' be a non-tradeable entity?

7 A couple have decided to get married. Being professional project managers, they decide to analyse the stakeholders in the 'wedding project' and to work out any conflicts in advance. List the stakeholders, and provide an interest/influence matrix to determine the strategy for managing the stakeholders in this project.

8 In the launch of a particular product, two key stakeholder groups were identified – the customers and the marketing department of the firm launching the product. As the project manager for this project, identify what the requirements and likely measures are for these two groups and any problems you might face managing these two groups.

9 If a project should be assessed on its long-term performance (beyond the end of the project itself), but project managers have only short-term appointments (usually only up to the end of the project), how should the performance of project managers be measured?

10 What is the purpose of a benefits map? If it showed that a project was not, in fact, contributing to organisational benefits, what would you do?

Further information

Atkinson, R. (1999) 'Project Management: Cost, Time and Quality, Two Best Guesses and a Phenomenon, Its [sic] Time to Accept Other Success Criteria', *International Journal of Project Management*, Vol. 17, No. 6, pp. 337–342.

Baccarini, D. (1999) 'The Logical Framework Method for Defining Project Success', *Project Management Journal*, Vol. 30, No. 4, pp. 25–32.

Carroll, A., and Buchholz, A. (2015) *Business and Society: Ethics, Sustainability and Stakeholder Management*, 9th edition, Cengage, Stamford, CT.

Christenson, D. and Walker, D.H.T (2004) 'Understanding the Role of "Vision" in Project Success', *Project Management Journal*, Vol. 35, No. 3, pp. 39–52.

Freeman, R.E. (2010) *Strategic Management: A Stakeholder Approach*, Cambridge University Press, Cambridge, UK.

Frooman, J. (1999) 'Stakeholder Influence Strategies', *Academy of Management Review*, Vol. 24, No. 2, pp. 191–205.

Gareis, R., Huemann, M., Martinuzzi, A., Weninger, C. and Sedlacko, M. (2013), *Project Management and Sustainable Development Principles*, PMI, Newtown Square, PA.

Joldersma, C. and Winter, V. (2002) 'Strategic Management in Hybrid Organisations', *Public Management Review*, Vol. 4, No. 1, pp. 83–99.

Maylor, H., Turner, N., and Murray-Webster, R. (2015) 'It Worked for Manufacturing. . . Operations Strategy in Project-based Operations', *International Journal of Project Management*, Vol. 33, No. 1, pp. 103–115.

McManus, J. (2011) *Managing Stakeholders in Software Development Projects*, Routledge, Abingdon, Oxon.

Mitchell, R., Agle, B. and Wood, D. (1997) 'Towards a Theory of Stakeholder Identification and Salience', *Academy of Management Review*, Vol. 22, No. 4, pp. 853–887.

Rasche, A. and Esser, D. (2006) 'From Stakeholder Management to Stakeholder Accountability', *Journal of Business Ethics*, Vol. 65, No. 3, pp. 251–267.

Scott J., Schultz, F.C. and Hekman, D.R. (2006) 'Stakeholder Theory and Managerial Decision-Making: Constraints and Implications of Balancing Stakeholder Interests', *Journal of Business Ethics*, Vol. 64, No. 3, pp. 285–301.

Turner, R., and Zolin, R. (2012) 'Forecasting Success on large Projects: Developing Reliable Scales to Predict Multiple Perspectives by Multiple Stakeholders Over Different Time Frames', *Project Management Journal*, Vol. 43, No. 5, pp. 87–99.

Winstanley, D., Sorabji, D. and Dawson, S. (1995) 'When the Pieces Don't Fit: A Stakeholder Power Matrix to Analyse Public Sector Restructuring', *Public Money & Management*, Vol. 15, No. 2, pp. 19–26.

Wolfe, R.A. and Putler, D.S. (2002) 'How Tight Are the Ties that Bind Stakeholder Groups?' *Organisation Science*, Vol. 13, No. 1, pp. 64–80.

Websites

http://web.worldbank.org – many publications concerning managing stakeholder participation in development projects in particular.

References

1 Shenhar, A.J., Dvir, D., Levy, O. and Maltz, A. (2001) 'Project Success – A Multidimensional Strategic Concept', *Long Range Planning*, Vol. 34, No. 6, pp. 699–725.

2 Covey, Stephen R. (1990) *The Seven Habits of Highly Effective People*, Free Press, New York.

3 Pinto, J. and Kharbanda, O. (1996) 'How to Fail in Project Management (Without Really Trying)', *Business Horizons*, July–August, pp. 45–53.

4 Pollack, J., Helm, J. and Adler, D. (2018) 'What is the Iron Triangle, and how has it changed?' *International Journal of Managing Projects in Business*, Vol. 11, No. 2, pp. 527–547.

5 For a fuller list of measures see Griffin, A. and Page, A.L. (1996) 'PDMA Success Measurement Project: Recommended Measures for Product Development Success and Failure', *Journal of Product Innovation Management*, Vol. 13, pp. 478–496.

6 Estrella M. (1999) *Learning from Change: Issues and experiences in participatory monitoring and evaluation*, ITDG Publishing.

7 Geraldi J., Kutsch E. and Turner N. (2011) 'Towards a conceptualisation of quality in information technology projects', *International Journal of Project Management*, Vol. 29, No. 5, pp. 557–567.

8 In 1962 the total bill was expected to be between £150 million and £170 million. In December 1974, a written Parliamentary answer disclosed that the cost to Britain and France of developing Concorde up to the point at which it entered service would be £974 million.

9 *Financial Times*, 15 October 1996.

10 *CNN*, 5 December 2019.

11 There are many variants on this approach and many sources claiming authorship. One easily accessed source is www.mindtools.com/pages/article/newPPM_07.htm

12 For more on this, see Kozak-Holland, M. (2004) *Titanic Lessons for IT Projects*, Multi-media Publications Inc., Chicago; also http://lessons-from-history.com

13 Maylor H., Turner N., and Murray-Webster R. (2015) 'It Worked for Manufacturing...! Operations Strategy in Project-Based Operations' *International Journal of Project Management*, Vol. 33, No.1, pp. 103–115.

14 Notable but not alone in promoting this view was Schonberger, R. (1985) *World Class Manufacturing*, Free Press, New York.

15 This section includes original unpublished work carried out by Harvey Maylor and Alexander Budzier.

16 See also Kaplan, R.S. and Norton, D.P. (2001) *The Strategy Focused Organisation: How Balanced Scorecard Companies Thrive in the New Business Environment*, Harvard Business School Press, Boston.

17 Ward, J., Hemingway, C.J. and Daniel, E.M. (2005) 'A Framework for Addressing the Organisational Issues of Enterprise Systems Implementation', *Journal of Strategic Information Systems*, Vol. 14, No. 2, pp. 97–119.

18 Ward, J. and Daniels, L. (2012) *Benefits Management: Delivering Value from IS and IT Investments*, 2nd edition, John Wiley, Chichester.

19 Lodge, D. (2002) *Changing Places*, Penguin, Harlow.

5

Planning for success

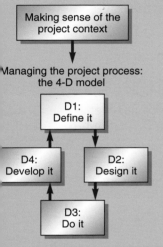

Making sense of the
project context

Managing the project process:
the 4-D model

D1:
Define it

D4:
Develop it

D2:
Design it

D3:
Do it

Even the longest journey begins with a single step.

Principles

1   The approach to planning determines the nature, role and ultimately
the utility of the plan.

2   It is just as important to know how and why to stop a project as to
start one.

3   Making sense of a complex project can be assisted by encouraging a
high level of visibility in the process.

Learning objectives

By the time you have completed this chapter, you should be able to:

→ define the requirements of initial planning, including the role that managing scope plays in this

→ identify characteristics of the planning process and approaches to
planning

→ set up a basic project outline with stages and gates, with the overview
of the process mapped out.

Contents

Introduction   *110*
5.1 Models of planning   *111*
5.2 The planning process   *116*
5.3 Basic project landscapes: stages and gates, activities and maps   *123*
Summary   *132*
Key terms   *132*
Relevant areas of the Bodies of Knowledge   *133*
Project management in practice: *Norway's QA process for major project
procurement   134*
Project management in practice: *The Mini project – the brief and
the PID   135*
Topics for discussion   *141*
Further information   *141*
References   *141*

Launching a new vehicle is an important moment for any manufacturer. Sales depend on that first impression created by the launch. So, launching a new Range Rover, a key model for UK-based Jaguar Land Rover, had to be special. In the event it was special. It captured the imagination of the media around the world and created attention no amount of advertising spend could hope to match.

Bringing Manhattan, New York to a standstill to have Daniel Craig (aka James Bond) drive the new car as part of the New York Motor Show was

Source: Pacific Press Media Production Corp./Alamy Stock Photo

a huge event, and demonstrated that while at one time it may have been enough simply to pull the cover off a new car, today launches are far more complex events.

Consider this as a project. How long would you want to organise such a launch? Who are the major stakeholders? How would you make sure all of the parts of the project came together 'on the night?' How would you deal with the inevitable changes and challenges that would occur along the way? Even when the physical launch event was complete, how would you make sure that publicity was maximised from the event? Oh, and don't forget that there will have to be a business case provided for every part of the cost incurred!

Introduction

A project may begin in many ways: a flash of inspiration on the part of an individual or group; a response to a stated need on the part of a particular client; an exploration of an issue for personal interest; or a project which forms part of a larger programme of organisational change. Chapter 4 described processes for setting the performance requirements for projects. Interestingly, for the Range Rover launch, while the immediate project was completed on the launch day, major elements of its success or failure will be measurable only many years afterwards in how well the vehicle sells.

Having outlined the requirements, measures and benefits required, the next step in a project comes with the construction of an initial plan. These are vital for all projects, not just ones as complex as a major vehicle launch. An initial plan will take in the context, the organisational strategy and the project idea and then demonstrate in outline the product, the process by which it will be delivered, the tasks involved in its delivery, the people and organisation involved, and pull these together to provide an estimate of cost, as shown in Figure 5.1. This high-level planning will facilitate the detailed planning, which will be described in Chapters 6–10. Just as importantly, the outline plan needs to provide a means to decide whether any further work on the project should be carried out or the fledgling project terminated. Continuously checking the viability of a project is a core organisational discipline and vital for effective programme and portfolio management.

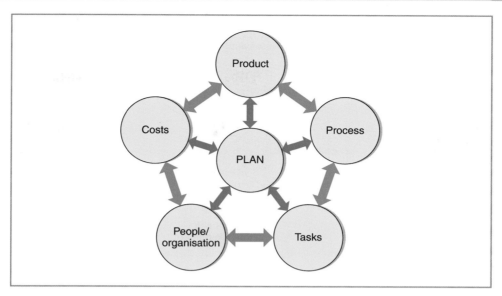

Figure 5.1 Initial planning

5.1 Models of planning

Whatever the root of the project, for years the study of excellence in projects[1] has shown that they are characterised by a combination of **order** and **chaos**. Ideally, the chaos comes first, followed by the order or system that a well-developed process can bring. Such order and chaos will always exist in tension to one degree or another in projects, and this tension is one of the fascinating balances that has to be achieved.

From personal projects to new product development

Many students have to produce a dissertation or similar piece of work. The early stage of this often causes particular challenges as topics for study are sought out. Adding chaos here is vital to a good piece of work. This increases the number of concepts under consideration, which can be narrowed later. Typically, this can be done from looking at practice, theory or both for greater insights, and considering the range of possibilities that a general area of interest has opened up.[2] After this initial stage though, there has to be a filtering down of the ideas to produce a more focused piece of work. **Filters** include:

- interest – after the chaos, whether it is still sufficiently interesting to the student;
- feasible – whether it is researchable with the time and resources available;
- theoretical – is there sufficient already written to underpin such a study?

Writing a dissertation is a creative process and it is rare to find a dissertation that has ended up in exactly the place that was envisaged at the outset. There are many parallels with commercial new product development.

Commercial new product development (NPD) is carried out through projects and likewise is rarely a linear activity, with the outcome logically following the intention at the start. In the early stages of the work, there will be an increase in the number of possibilities as new ideas emerge. This is highly desirable, provided that the scope of the project is maintained (see following section). At some point, however, the ideas will have to be

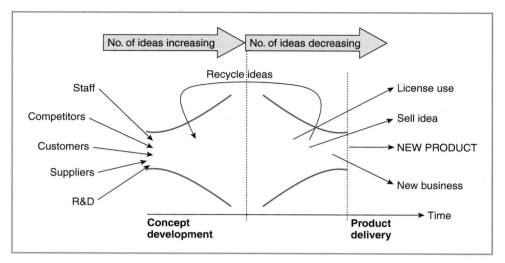

Figure 5.2 Concept development in NPD

narrowed down, as it is unlikely they will all be feasible. This is done by *screening*, where the ideas are gradually filtered by, for example:

- marketing assessment of the ideas – which ones are most attractive to the market?
- financial appraisal, such as potential to develop a good rate of return on the investment required of it;
- strategic – does this product fit with our current mission?
- technical – is it technically possible to develop and deliver?

This process is illustrated in Figure 5.2 and filtering is developed through the stage-gate process described in section 5.3. The figure shows the inputs to the process, including research and development (R&D), suppliers (see Chapter 14), customers and competitors. Staff also have a big input to the process, and this is not just applicable to physical products. The Disney Corporation, for example, employs 'imagineers' who have the job of creating new ideas in entertainment – they are there to 'blue-sky', a term which implies that they spend the day gazing skywards waiting for inspiration as to what the next *Despicable Me* or *Frozen* will be.

At the output side, a new product, service or solution to the problem being studied may emerge, but there are other routes for exploitation of ideas. These include licensing (another organisation paying for the use of your idea), selling the idea or, an approach adopted by many firms today when a new idea comes along, starting a new business to exploit it. Some ideas will also be rejected and some will need to be recycled, possibly into development projects of their own at a later date. Pharmaceutical companies, for whom the costs of a new product increase exponentially with time as a formulation moves through its development, are rated as the benchmarks in this kind of process.[3] They typically have a **pipeline** of work with products at various stages in development. However they too have struggled in recent years, as smaller firms have consistently used their flexibility to be more innovative – they can and will often tolerate greater degrees of chaos for longer than the larger firms.

So what are the characteristics of highly creative processes for **concept development**? There have been many attempts to develop sets of rules and some common elements are as follows:

- Allow time and space for individuals to carry out the exploration. 3M famously allows its development staff up to 15 per cent of their working time to pursue 'personal projects' – work that is not necessarily directly related to their normal role. The result has been a stream of new products, which include the ubiquitous Post-it note, and a turnover in the sale of these ideas that is predicted to exceed sales of the company's own products.[4] There is therefore clearly a financial case for such innovation.

- Protect ownership of ideas. If people feel that the organisation is simply trying to take their ideas from them, they are unlikely to contribute much.
- Encourage **rapid prototyping** to try ideas right at the start and see how they work. This approach to test ideas rapidly and rehearse them – walk through the process and see how the ideas work in practice – should become a cornerstone of modern project management practices.
- Have people at a senior level in the organisation prepared to act as **project champions** who will promote particular ideas and attempt to obtain the necessary resources from the organisation to progress projects with good potential.
- Have a rapid development process ready to take on such ideas and see them through to fruition. This must include clear criteria as to what will be supported by the organisation and what will not.

While these factors are not new discoveries, we still see organisations limiting rather than encouraging innovation through over-restrictive processes. There are also still some organisations where there is no process for innovation projects, and no path for development. Either of these is a considerable difficulty. For instance, during work with scientists undertaking European Union funded projects, the scientists stated on many occasions that the vast majority of interesting opportunities (in excess of 95 per cent) that emerged from research projects could not be pursued due to the lack of any process or resource to do so. Given that the projects in question were pursuing understanding of and potential cures for life-threatening diseases, this was clearly a major loss.

Sony, Nintendo, Apple and other world-class organisations not only have this **creativity** present but also an effective process that follows from that. This is well planned and directed (not at all as chaotic and unstructured as some sources would lead you to think) and includes the elements of process planning that are described in the rest of this chapter.

REAL WORLD   Lockheed Skunk Works

In seeking to overcome product development bureaucracy, Lockheed (now Lockheed Martin), the US defence manufacturer, is famous for setting up what it called its 'Skunk Works' in 1943. Here, scientists and engineers were given the opportunity to work on exciting (and secret) projects, focusing on rapid development of new technologies. Radical new aircraft were developed in record time by small teams, often achieving performance that was previously thought impossible.

Source: PJF Military Collection/Alamy Stock Photo

The Skunk Works operated with limited constraints, but was backed by the considerable technological and financial muscle of the larger organisation. The move was highly successful, with many (now famous) world-beating products developed over the years including the U2 spy plane, SR71 Blackbird and F117 Stealth Fighter. Its experts were given the freedom to try completely new ideas and they achieved huge successes. Ironically, one of the most secretive major product development groups ever assembled is now famous for its unconventional approach.

Scope management

Within projects, we have already noted the tension between order and chaos. The forces pushing for order require a well-defined product, process, set of tasks, organisation and costs. Those pushing chaos would like to leave these out entirely, or at least leave them until much later in the project. And even when order appears to have prevailed, someone will come along and change their minds about what they want. While being innovative and flexible may be desirable, the costs of change can be considerable. This is another project tension – between setting out a defined path and following it, regardless of the consequences, and allowing change. In large, complex projects, there are considerable data to demonstrate that changes can be one root cause of projects failing to meet their objectives. A project engineer for a major oil and gas company described a situation they faced:

> *'We were ready to start the detailed engineering design for the refurbishment of part of our plant. The outline designs and costs had already been signed off and used technology very similar to what we had already. Just as we were about to place orders with our contractors, we were made aware that another plant had developed an improved technology. The benefits would be tens of millions of dollars a year in reduced operating and maintenance costs. The problem was that it was going to delay the project, as we would need to re-engineer much of the existing work we had done.'*

So what do you do?

The product of the project, the outcome or output, is described as 'the scope'. Both APM and PMI Bodies of Knowledge and PRINCE2[5] recommend the dedication of significant quantities of effort to scope management at the outset and throughout the project. One of the reasons may be seen in the Real World box below.

REAL WORLD   The Sinclair C5

Initially conceived in the mid-1970s as a four-seater, electrically powered vehicle for under £1000, the concept of the Sinclair C5 grabbed a lot of attention. Because it came from such a renowned inventor – Sir Clive Sinclair, famous for one of the first calculators and personal computers – it was a highly popular idea and had no shortage of backers, including Hoover, which kitted out part of its factory for its manufacture. The result at the end of the process was rather differ-

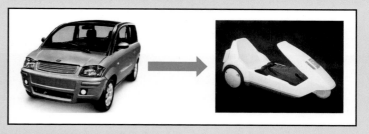

Figure 5.3 Scope creep

Source: Oleksiy Maksymenko/Alamy Stock Photo and Motoring Picture Library/Alamy Stock Photo.

ent, as shown in Figure 5.3. In this case the scope was significantly downgraded, cutting the specification to what the designers believed might be the minimum viable product. However, history tells us that the final design was not accepted by consumers and the C5 is a famous case study sadly for all the wrong reasons.

Figure 5.3 shows the results of the phenomenon known as product **scope creep**. The original purpose was subtly changed on many subsequent occasions until it no longer resembled the original concept. The result was disastrous – the product was a flop and all the firms involved lost substantial sums of money. Quite how an electric car evolved into an electrically assisted recumbent tricycle is one of those sets of decisions that probably made perfect sense at the time, but in hindsight appear unfathomable. The conversation when the product went from having four wheels to only three, for instance, must have been an interesting one.

Managing product scope to avoid creep is a role for the project manager. Similarly, the process scope needs managing right from the start – see *Get it in Writing* below. One decision is where in the process the scope will be **frozen**. This means that it will not be changing and that the project can progress with this as an assumption.

Get it in writing!

A sponsored student project started well enough. A Merchant Bank from the City of London offered a well-paid position for 3 months to allow a Masters student to carry out some work for them that would fit with the intended subject of his dissertation – organisational change in a financial services organisation. In return, the student offered a number of executive briefings in addition to reports on the changes that had been implemented.

At the start, verbal promises were made on both sides, the firm offering the support of managers and the provision of data, the student on the scope of the work to be undertaken. Within weeks of starting the project though, there was evidence of discontent on both sides. The student complained about promised access to people and data not being given and the company complained about the lack of visible progress towards the first major milestone, an executive briefing. These issues were never dealt with at this stage and the project rumbled on to its natural conclusion. The student left the company after 3 months and submitted a poor dissertation based on very limited data. Then the letters started arriving for the student from his sponsor. Initially, these simply asked the student to submit the report on the work that he had done, which he duly did. Then the letters started arriving from the solicitors of the merchant bank stating that he had failed to carry out the required project to an acceptable standard and they were intending to sue him for this.

In the first meeting that the supervisor arbitrated to try to reach an agreeable solution, the firm produced documents which were purported to be the requirements of the project. The student had never seen them before. Indeed, it became clear that his immediate boss in the company had written them only after the project had got into trouble to 'cover his own back'. The requirements were for a very different project to the one that the student had carried out. It was going to be very difficult for him to address the 'new issues' – he simply didn't have the data to do this.

The result was a messy compromise, which cost everyone involved considerable additional time and resources. The lesson was clear though – if you don't produce a clear statement of scope that can be discussed and agreed by the key stakeholders, one will almost certainly emerge that will not be what you thought it would be.

Given the lesson of the above example, it is clear that the last but by no means least important part of the scope management is to obtain acceptance. This may be via a formal **sign-off** process where a paying client is involved or simply that a meeting is called where everyone agrees to the scope statement as written. As discussed in the previous chapter, in principle it is useful at least to start with agreement on where the project is going and what it is going to do.

The scope management and control aspects will be discussed further in Chapter 13. For now, it is useful simply to recognise that there will be tension between the wish to keep the scope the same and pressure to make changes. In order to avoid a repeat of the C5 case and to recognise that change costs, some systematic means is necessary to maintain the project benefits in the light of the changes.

Having outlined the content and the purpose of the product through the concept and scope development activities, the next consideration will be the process by which the project will be delivered.

5.2 The planning process

To call project planning a 'process' could imply that there is a well-defined route for the planner to take. This is not always clear, and a generic model of planning is difficult to construct. Planning as a process involves the consumption of resources – it has costs associated with it. The project manager has to decide on the balance between the costs incurred in the process and the benefits that will be reaped from it, as illustrated by Figure 5.4. Costs associated with the planning process include:

- labour (time) and associated expenses (travel, subsistence, etc.);
- planner's tools – may include computer assistance and new software;
- cost of preparing the written plan;
- opportunity cost – what the planner and others drawn into the planning process could have been doing otherwise (e.g. working on an existing project).

In order for the planning process to be value adding and not just cost adding, the benefits of the activity have to be shown. These include:

- avoiding the costs of the chaos that would otherwise take place with an unplanned activity;
- providing a basis for a formalised evaluation process – described above as 'filtering';
- identifying problems in advance.

The time that a planner spends preparing the plan should reflect the potential benefits of the planning activity. The UK's National Audit Office recognise this, and in their 2019 strategy stated: *'Our interventions now look at programmes earlier in their lifecycle and at the planning stage as failure can become built in at an early stage of a project.'*[6] However, the effects of a plan do go beyond the purpose of justification for a project being continued. Figure 5.4 shows the positive and negative effects that the plan can have on project activities.

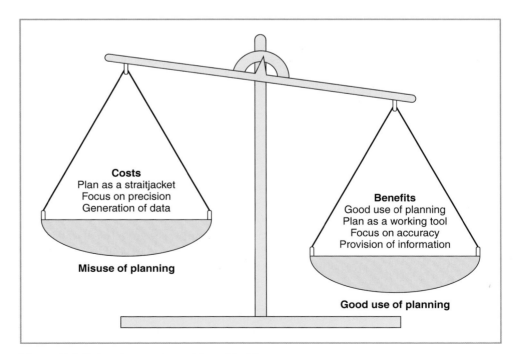

Figure 5.4 Balancing costs and benefits (1)

One of the paradoxes that the project manager has to address is whether the output of the planning process remains a working tool or becomes a form of organisational 'straitjacket'. As a working tool, plans are used to help decision-making and guide future activities. A well-balanced plan will guide the actions of the project team, without the need to define to the absolute detail level what each person will do for every minute of every day. We will discuss this issue further later in this chapter. Similarly, project plans should change as circumstances change. People can get so involved in the plan that the project objectives are forgotten, with the planning becoming an end in itself rather than a means to an end. If the techniques that follow are applied intelligently, changed circumstances can be matched by a new course of action. The phrase 'because it says so in the plan' is the defence of a person who, wrongly, does not use the plan as a working tool. Similarly, there is a phrase well known in military circles:

'A plan never survives first engagement with the enemy.'

This is useful to remember – a plan is a representation of a future state, and that future is uncertain. This is not to jettison plans in favour of wishful thinking or to devalue the planning process, but to encourage a pragmatism about its usage and the level of certainty that it holds. Similarly, the phrase

'The plan is nothing. Planning is everything'[7]

is still well used. There is considerable benefit in the process of planning, not least the insight that the planner gains into the project by working through the plans. Such insight is beneficial. It is important to recognise that there are a number of approaches to gaining such insight and the role of this in the development of the plans.

Planning and uncertainty

Progress with a project and you never know what will happen. Take, for instance, the IT project where the requirements were changed as the product was being developed or the drug that when tested generated benefits beyond those originally predicted. This is **product uncertainty**. Similarly, consider the construction project that during excavation for foundations uncovered a well-preserved Roman villa (archeologically significant but caused months of delays for the project), or the marketing project team that found they could not work together due to 'irreconcilable differences'. These are **process uncertainties**. Both of these cause variability in performance that impact on our ability to plan and then schedule work. The planning approach needs to take account of such variability, but frequently does not. Approaches to planning fall into four broad categories:

1 Claim we know everything.
2 Acknowledge we know nothing.
3 Both of the above – the nearer the point in time, the more we know about it.
4 Claim to work in an *agile* manner.

The first approach works well for a 'painting by numbers' project – the level of variation if studied over time can be reduced and the project can be made to function like a repetitive operation. The case of the construction of the McDonald's drive-throughs described in Chapter 1 is a good example of this. The organisations concerned had carried out such projects on many occasions and had worked out ways of working with the product and the process. The key issue here is to test whether there really is the knowledge to claim that such things are known or whether it is simply subject to **optimism bias** – the level of uncertainty being understated to make the results of the planning activity appear more credible.[8]

The second approach can result in a kind of 'wishful thinking' approach – just set up some basic milestones (dates on which key deliverables will arrive) and hope that these are met. This approach is more extensively used than generally acknowledged. We regularly work with organisations who admit, in private, that their planning is not where it should be and that they are not doing the 'basics' as well as they should. Project managers understandably do not like the label of having acted through 'wishful thinking', but in reality many just expect that people know what to do and when.

The third approach includes so-called **rolling-wave planning**. This is where the level of detail of the plan increases with the proximity to the date. The overall schedule of activities is determined at a high level, with the details being worked out as the project progresses (see Figure 5.5). The detailed planning horizon can be from as little as 1 week up to 90 days (various practitioners) or 'as far as the next milestone'. Pragmatically, the pace of the project and the requirements and lead-times of people and resources determine the time-frame that will work best. It has been used successfully in application at BAA's Terminal 5, where the principle of the **50 per cent rule** applies and in **Last Planner** (see Chapter 14).

The 50 per cent rule states that prior to final approval of each stage of work, cost targets for 50 per cent of the work to be undertaken during that stage must be fixed and for 100 per cent of initial works (within weeks of the start of that phase). This encourages realistic accuracy about the immediate work to be carried out.

The rolling-wave approach is not without its critics, claiming that it simply leads to imprecision in planning and poor delivery against key objectives. The challenge here is that as we have seen, not all objectives can be stated at the outset of every project. The reality is that both processes and products do change and this can be incorporated as part of a managed process.

Agile approaches to planning and managing projects are described in more detail throughout this book as they have become more commonly used since the last edition, notably in the IT sector. In practice, an agile project is broken down into short sprints lasting a number of weeks (1–6 is common) and the list of desired outputs from this is determined at the start of the sprint. Any outputs not completed during the sprint are added to a backlog which may be picked up in future sprints. At the task level, this has simplified planning, as the scope of work is fixed for that sprint and relatively visible. Where

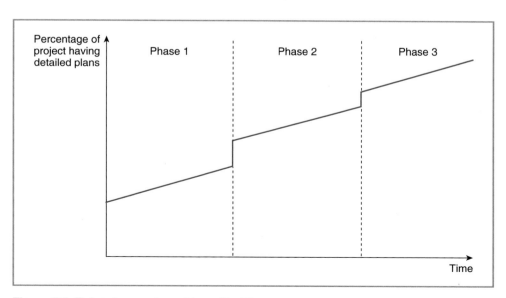

Figure 5.5 Balancing costs and benefits (2)

this work is part of complex projects, the outputs from each sprint need integrating. This, though, is not always successfully achieved.

Do plans provide information or just data?

One of the benefits of modern business systems is the ease and speed with which vast quantities of data can be generated. However, there is a tendency for managers to become overrun with data. **Data** are the numbers on the page. **Information** is the part or summary of that which can be usefully applied. The rest is just noise and clutters the thought and analysis process. One of the major roles of the project manager in projects, other than in the smallest pieces of work, will be to gather data from the relevant sources. Simply passing the data on is unlikely to be a value-adding activity. The project manager therefore needs to be both a collector of data and a provider of information.

The process of project planning – inputs, outputs and the process itself

The process of project planning takes place at two levels. At one level it has to be decided 'what' happens. This, the tactical-level plan, then needs to be converted into a statement of 'how' it is going to be carried out (or operationalised) at the operational level. Figure 5.6 shows an activity model as would be used to analyse systems of activity by considering the inputs, controls, outputs and mechanisms (ICOMs) for the activity. The inputs are the basis for what is going to be converted by the activity – in this case the project brief. The output is the project plan, or more specifically the project proposal. The controls provide the activation, the constraints and the quality standards for the planning process in addition to its outputs, and the mechanisms provide the means by which the process can happen.

At the operational level, the way in which the proposal is generated should not be viewed as a one-off activity but should go through many cycles of suggestion and review before the 'final' document is produced. The first cycles are to provide the major revisions, where significant changes are made. Once these have been done and the project team is happy with the basic format, the last stages are those of refinement, where small adjustments are made.

It is important for the **overview** to be verified first, before further effort is committed to planning at a detailed level, as discussed above. The lifecycle of planning in Figure 5.7 shows the stages that the plan should go through. Cases such as the one given below are examples where the detail was considered before the major issues. As the example shows, this is very wasteful of management time.

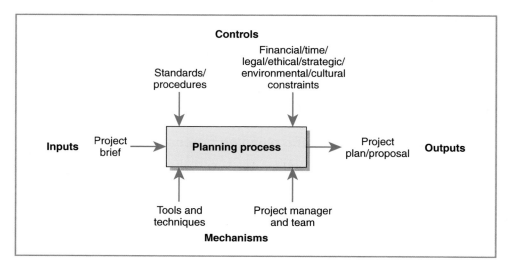

Figure 5.6 Activity model using ICOMs

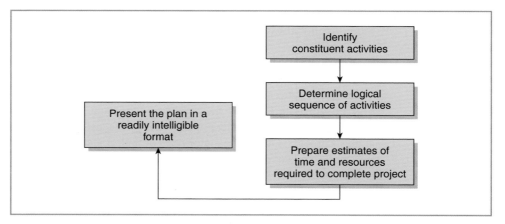

Figure 5.7 The project planning process

The upside-down business plan

Business plan meetings were serious affairs – they always were. The concept was quite attractive: to set up an exclusive nursery school with an appealing teaching method in a smart area of the city. So far so good. This was, however, where the rough planning stopped and the group succumbed to the virus that plagues so many projects at this point – *detailitus*. The discussions were then waylaid by the need to have safety tyres on the school minibus and by the detailed wording of the liability insurance. No matter that the lag between the money being spent on the buildings and equipment and any income from fees received would create interest payments that the company could never hope to meet . . .

Planning accuracy or precision?

So, would you rather be roughly right or precisely wrong? Often, what is termed a 'quick and dirty' approach (with the objective of being as accurate as possible) may be far more beneficial than months of painstaking planning (with the objective of being as precise as possible). There is clearly a role for detailed planning, but not before an overview plan has been worked through. Evaluating the overview reveals fundamental flaws in assumptions. Until this level of plan satisfies basic criteria such as financial or technical feasibility, detailed plans are inappropriate.

The revision/refinement process considers the necessary sub-projects (if any), the results of any numerical analysis (may be financial, resource, risk analysis or some form of mathematical simulation), the element of 'gut feel' (also referred to as the subconscious or back-of-the-mind element) as well as experience. The sponsor and other stakeholders will usually have some input to be considered in this process.

Managing the planning process

Most projects of low complexity will bias the ratio of planning:action heavily towards the action. As complexity increases, so does the necessity for a formalised plan. This is both a systematic analysis of the project (which provides its own set of benefits) and an opportunity to show that the project manager has been systematic in the planning process (by showing the level of consideration that the project manager has given to issues). '**Traceability**' has become a major issue in many companies, allowing products to be traced back to records of their constituent parts. The same is required of a project plan. In the event of an unsatisfactory result, for whatever reason, a good plan can show that the planner took every possible precaution to ensure that the result was positive. Conversely, should the project go particularly well, you will have an assignable cause for this – namely your planning!

The benefits of using a **systematic approach** to planning include:

- breaking down complex activities into manageable chunks (see Chapter 6);
- determining logical sequences of activities;
- providing an input to subsequent project management processes, including estimating the time and resources required for the project;
- providing a logical basis for making decisions;
- showing effects on other systems;
- filtering frivolous ideas and activities;
- providing a framework for the assessment of programmes (the post-project review process relies on comparing the achieved result with the original plan, particularly for the purpose of improving the planning process);
- being essential for the revision/refinement process;
- allowing lessons to be learned from practice;
- facilitating communication of ideas in a logical form to others.

What follows shows how these benefits can be achieved through the application of tried and tested methods within a systematic framework.

Formalised project overview documents

A common format in industries where projects are undertaken for external clients involves the customer or client providing a **brief** or **terms of reference** and the project manager replying with a **proposal** or project initiation document (**PID**). In process terms, the PID is the output of the overview planning process.

PRINCE2 (2017) provides detailed requirements for a PID, which include the following contents:

1 Project definition – explains what the project needs to achieve. This should include: background; objectives and desired outcomes; scope and exclusions; constraints and assumptions; the user(s) and interested parties; interfaces.
2 Project approach – the choice of solution and delivery approach, taking into consideration the operational environment.
3 Business case – a justification of the project based on estimated costs, risks, and benefits.
4 Project management team structure chart.
5 Role descriptions – the roles of those in the project management team, and other key resources.
6 Quality management approach – the quality techniques and standards to be applied.
7 Change control approach – how and by whom changes will be controlled.
8 Risk management approach – describes the risk management techniques and standards to be applied.
9 Communication management approach – defines the interested parties and the means and frequency of communication.
10 The project plan – a basic time plan showing the major activities to be undertaken, their sequence, duration, and required resources.
11 Project controls – summarises the controls such as stage boundaries and monitoring and reporting.
12 Tailoring of PRINCE2 – a summary of how PRINCE2 will be implemented on this project.

To this, it is useful always to add key statements from the stakeholder analysis (what's in it for the PM, the team, the customer, the sponsor, etc.) and key performance objectives – what would constitute success in this instance? An example of the use of a PID is included in the Project Management in Practice case at the end of this chapter.

PMI suggest the use of a **project charter** to set out the requirements for the project. The emphasis is different from a PID – the PID is normally prepared by the project team in answer to a brief or specification. The charter is then the official notification of the start of the project. It is defined as:

> 'A document issued by the project initiator or sponsor that formally authorises the existence of a project and provides the project manager with the authority to apply organisational resources to project activities.'

Formalisation

A PID, followed by a project charter, is one way to capture the requirements of a project and formally authorise its progress to the next stage – D2 project design. As such it is a useful device and one that should have near universal application. We see in many organisations a resentment of such devices; people perceive them as 'needless bureaucracy'. Herein lies an interesting tension: to formalise processes and actions through devices such as a PID, incurring cost and time in doing so, or to allow individuals flexibility in determining what needs to be done as the project progresses and risk important issues being missed.

The level of **formalisation** required differs between organisations and often between projects in those organisations. We have two issues to consider here in determining the level of formalisation required. The first is the level of complexity, as described in Chapter 2. At one level it is useful to consider that the higher the level of complexity, the higher the level of systemisation that is required. The second factor is custom and practice in the industry or organisation in which you are working, whether these are appropriate or not. For instance, in the UK, suppliers of IT systems to government were at one time required to run all their projects using PRINCE2 processes regardless of the utility or benefits of that approach.

Where a formal proposal is required it should be considered in the following light:

- Who is the proposal for – the investment decision-maker or a third party?
- Why is the proposal being requested?

The first part of the analysis in the proposal development should consider the potential customers for the work – are they internal to the organisation or external? In addition, are the customers end-users, investment decision-makers or a third party acting on behalf of one of these? The degree of formalisation will need to be tailored, a bid to an external organisation usually requiring a much higher degree of formality.

In addition, if the project is:

- for an internal customer, there needs to be consistency with the organisation's stated goals or aims;
- for an external customer, the most basic requirement is that they will be able to pay for the work to be carried out. It is pointless generating detailed proposals only to find that the customer is insolvent or the transaction cannot be completed for other reasons. Where the customer is from overseas, it is worth investigating at a very early stage whether or not they are eligible for export credit guarantees, for example;
- going to be appraised by a set of people, it is useful to know their backgrounds. For example, where a client has a detailed knowledge of the subject area, more detail of the nature of the work to be carried out should be included, or for an investment decision-maker, details of the cost–benefit analysis.

The reason for the proposal being requested should also be examined to ensure that the result is appropriate:

- If it is to be part of a full competitive bid for funding, then it is probably worth investing the time to prepare a detailed proposal.
- If it is to be a first examination of the possibilities of such a project, with the customer deciding to find out what would be involved if the project were to be undertaken, then an overview proposal should be submitted.
- If the proposal has been requested as part of organisational policy to consider more than one supplier for any product or service, it is worth finding out whether or not an existing supplier already has the contract before investing your time. Providing a very rough proposal can be dangerous as the impression that is left with the customer may not favour you in the future. It may be worth in such a case declining to put in a proposal, though this again should be determined by the aims of the organisation.

Other scenarios where the supplier may decide not to submit a proposal (also called a 'bid') include when the capability (organisational capability), resource (e.g. if capital is already tied up in other projects) or desirability (e.g. moving into direct competition with an existing customer) is questionable.

The process of preparing and submitting the proposal is the organisation's opportunity to sell itself to the potential customer. You only have one chance to make a good first impression, so basics like ensuring that the proposal document reaches the customer on time, is presented in a way that demands attention and is free from stupid mistakes (particularly spelling and grammatical errors) are essential. This is only part of the process. A 'pre-sell' to a client can involve visits, informal discussions and general information gathering by both parties. The intention, as set out in describing the project environment, is to foster partnership relationships between the two parties.

The proposal itself should contain:

- an executive summary – provides the basic information in a few words, ideally one that can be read in one minute;
- the main body of the report – diagrams and pictures convey information much better than reams of text. In order to ensure that the presentation is consistent, a standard set of forms is often used which also makes it far more difficult to leave items out.[9] Checklists are also of great value in compiling documents;[10]
- appendices – any information that is summarised in the main report can be included in longer form here, along with supporting evidence for any major points made.

The plan is the first step in providing the means of satisfying the requirements of the project owner (the person wanting the outcome) or sponsor (the person in charge of the funding for the outcome). It is the beginning of the project manager's input to ensuring that, wherever possible, potential problems are identified and solved in advance. The plan is an explicit statement of the intended timing of project activities and the basis for estimating the resource requirements. Problem and error prevention, rather than rectification, is one of the main drivers of the planning process.

5.3   Basic project landscapes: stages and gates, activities and maps

At the overview stage in the project it is part of the role of the planner to determine the nature and objectives of each **phase** or part of the project. The use of checkpoints or *gates* between the phases provides the most basic opportunity to review progress (or otherwise). More importantly, you do not have to wait until the project budget or time allowance

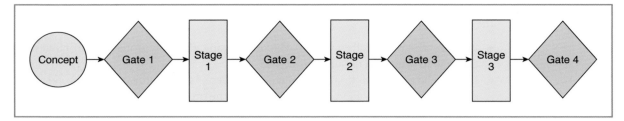

Figure 5.8 Stage-gate model of projects

Source: After Cooper, R.G. (1988) 'The new product process: a decision guide for management', *Journal of Marketing Management*, 3(3): 238–55 but not originating there. Widely applied.

expires to find out that there is a fundamental problem.[11] Figure 5.8 shows the basic arrangement of the checkpoints.

The criteria for passing to the next stage must be laid down in advance. Calling a halt to activities can save future expenditure and must never be discounted as an option, particularly where:

1   the majority of the benefits from the activities have already been achieved by the organisation;
2   the initial plans and estimates have turned out to be wildly inaccurate;
3   a new alternative that is more attractive has materialised;
4   organisational strategy changes and the project outcomes cease to be in line with the new strategy;
5   key personnel leave the organisation;
6   the project requires a higher level of capability than the organisation possesses;
7   to continue would endanger the organisation financially.

All projects require such gates as a fundamental discipline. Some, such as where the project is delivering to a contract, are unlikely to be stopped where problems arise. Others can and should be. The nature of a 'failure' at a gate therefore differs between projects. The options include the winding-up of the activities (which often causes bad feeling among the project team and can lead to future disenchantment) or finding ways of maximising the potential benefit while minimising the risk or expenditure. Many development projects have got to the point where they were about to be commercialised and the large amount of finance required (hundreds of millions of pounds for pharmaceutical products) could not be provided by the originators. Taking on joint partners and licensing are possible remedies in such a case.

Two examples illustrate the broad utility of this approach.

Know when to quit

A scientific research company had been engaged by another company to carry out some work. At the second gate review, it became apparent that the deliverables of the project were never going to be achieved and as a result the research company suggested that the project should be terminated. The client insisted that the research continue with the development efforts in accordance with their contract. The research firm finally bought itself out of the contract, paying a fee to the client to end the work. This was a pragmatic move based on a business case analysis – it was cheaper to do that than to continue and have to pay inevitable penalty clauses at the end of the project. It was also a first for the firm – implementing the stage-gate approach meant that it could have a business discussion about the basis for continuation of the work.

This time it's personal

A former colleague and his wife set up their own business. They invested their life savings to do this, but after less than a year in business the company folded. In discussions after the event, he recognised that they had had reservations about the whole venture, but had continued as 'they had no way to know when to stop'. After covering the stage-gate approach in a course, his words were: 'I wish we had known about that 5 years ago – it could have saved us an awful lot of money.'

The **stage-gate** system derives from NASA's Phases Review Process (PRP). This favours the use of gates between activities of different functions within an organisation, requiring that problems are resolved before 'going through the gate' rather than being passed on to the next phase. This allows cross-functional activities to be coordinated more effectively and is used by many public- and private-sector organisations today.

A pillar of many government procurement strategies today involves the use of a version of a gated process. For instance:

- In the UK, the Government mandates the use of the *Gateway Review* structure – a *peer review* of major programmes and projects.[12]
- In Norway, major procurement is phased and controlled using a process known as QA (1 and 2).[13]

Not all organisations approve of having gated processes, however. For some, the possibility that a project may be stopped does cause instability and a sense of a lack of commitment to the project from the organisation. Also, the downside of a project that is stopped at a gate may be loss of morale by the project team.

REAL WORLD   Use of gated processes at IDeA Foundation

In Chapter 2 we showed the high-level gate review structure at the IDeA Foundation. Within any organisation's gate structure there will be a series of questions and deliverables that need to be addressed and evaluated. The review should be an opportunity to take a step back and establish how well the project is doing, according to pre-established criteria, and ask whether or not the project should be continued. Although each gate should in theory be a go / no-go boundary, in reality most organisations find it very difficult to stop the funding once a project is underway. This is especially the case if stakeholders want the final result and a great deal of money has already been spent. Table 5.1 indicates the types of criteria that are used at each stage.

Table 5.1 Stage gate questions based on the IDeA Foundation

	Gate 0	Gate 1	Gate 2	Gate 3	Gate 4	Gate 5
	Strategic assessment	*Funding assessment*	*Delivery strategy*	*Financing decision*	*Execution readiness*	*Operations readiness*
Focusing question	Do we start this project?	Do we continue with this project?	Do we continue with this project, with current scope?	Do we continue with this project, with current scope?	Do we continue with this project?	Is everything ready for handover?

→

	Gate 0	Gate 1	Gate 2	Gate 3	Gate 4	Gate 5
	Strategic assessment	*Funding assessment*	*Delivery strategy*	*Financing decision*	*Execution readiness*	*Operations readiness*
Opportunity statement	Simple overview	Revised overview	Clear and compelling story for the project Prioritised objectives	Clear and compelling story for the project Prioritised objectives	Continued viability agreed	Continued viability agreed
Project scope	Simple overview	Viable project scenarios	Converge to a single main project scenario	Fully developed statements of project boundaries	Continued viability agreed	Continued viability agreed
Governance, roles and responsibilities		Initial governance and structure established	Governance and structure agreed	Project board identified Full responsibility assignment matrix agreed	Project board verified Updated responsibility assignment matrix	Operations governance agreed
Risks	One line	High level risk log	Risk log	Full validated risk log	Updated full risk log	Operational risk analysis
Issues	One line	High level issues log	Issues log	Full validated issues log	Updated full issues log	Operational issues analysis
Stakeholder engagement		Stakeholder map and high-level engagement plan	Engagement and marketing / communications plans	Engagement and marketing / communications plan	Engagement and marketing / communications plan	Engagement and marketing / communications plan
Socio-economic impact	One line	Evaluated against Strategic Development Goals	Outline impact / benefits management plan, baseline finalised	Full impact / benefits management plan	Full impact / benefits realisation plan	
Costs and funding	High-level, rough estimated costs of the project and next stage Funds approval for next gate	Rough estimates of efforts & costs Funding viability established Funds approval for next gate	Expert and parametric analysis of costs Full funding analysis Next stage costs established Funds approval for next gate	Ground-up costs Benchmarks Funding available Funds approval for next gate	Updated ground-up costs. Funding sustained Funds approval for next gate	Funds approval for next gate (if applicable)
Schedule	Rough Estimate	Estimate based on high-level Work Breakdown Structure (WBS)	Based on mid-level WBS	Based on detailed WBS	Updated schedule	Operations plan agreed

	Gate 0	Gate 1	Gate 2	Gate 3	Gate 4	Gate 5
	Strategic assessment	*Funding assessment*	*Delivery strategy*	*Financing decision*	*Execution readiness*	*Operations readiness*
Monitoring and control		Monitoring & Reporting plan Key Performance Indicators (KPIs) for next stage	Monitoring & Reporting plan KPIs for next stage	Monitoring & Reporting plan KPIs for next stage	Monitoring & Reporting plan KPIs for next stage	Operations monitoring and control plan agreed

There have been various refinements of this basic idea over the years, including the addition of 'fuzzy gates', where a project is allowed to continue working for a period after a gate until a proper review can be conducted.[14] This was introduced to prevent the gates themselves from slowing down project work, but can itself cause confusion over which activities can continue and which can be stopped at a gate.

Activities in phases

In preparation of an overview plan, having set out the phases or stages that will constitute the project, the next part of the planning process is to consider the arrangement of activities within these stages and the relationship between the stages. For instance, should all the activities run **sequentially**, i.e. one after the other, or **concurrently**, i.e. as far as possible, at the same time? There is the issue of logic of the arrangement of these activities (which must be done first) and how the individual activities within the arrangement interact. It is noted that in practice, where different groups are involved in different stages of a project, it is often seen that people focus on their part of the project only, with no consideration of the outcome as a whole. This is illustrated by the conventional lifecycle for a new product development (NPD) project, as shown in Figure 5.9. This suffers from two major drawbacks:

1 The message or customer specification is interpreted by different people at each stage of the process. The information that reaches the manufacturing people telling them what to make is potentially very different from what goes in at the start of the process (Miscommunication – Figure 5.10).
2 Due to the constant process revision that is required, engineering changes are often made very late in the development process. These cause enormous disruption, in particular time delay.

Both of the above issues were seen by many industrialists, academics and consultants who visited Japan during the early 1990s[15] and investigated the world-class players in its automotive industry. Of particular interest to them was the different speed of development of new vehicles. Typically, firms like Toyota, Honda and Nissan were developing vehicles from concept to mass production in times of the order of 14 months, whereas the closest Western competitor was taking at least twice that. One of the causes for this difference was linked to the level of design changes and engineering activity having a very different profile from that being used in the West. The Japanese firms' model was focused on getting

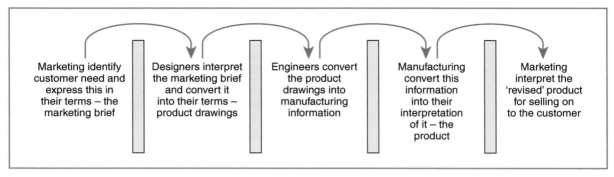

Figure 5.9 Conventional approach to new product development

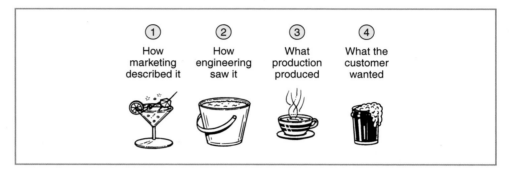

Figure 5.10 Effect of miscommunication on new product development

the product 'right first time', with the result as shown in Figure 5.11. As can be seen, the amount of activity declines as the product nears production. The importance of time-to-market has been shown recently to be responsible for over 30 per cent of the total profit to be made from a product during its lifecycle. The reduction in long-term costs has also been shown to be significant if instead of arranging activities to occur sequentially, as would be the simplest arrangement, they are overlapped. This is termed '**concurrent engineering**' and has become widespread in its application in engineering projects.

The arrangement of product development into a process stream, with all the necessary parties involved at all stages to prevent the cycle of reworking ideas, has the natural effect of allowing activities to run alongside one another (concurrently) as opposed to one after the other (sequentially). This is shown in Figure 5.12.

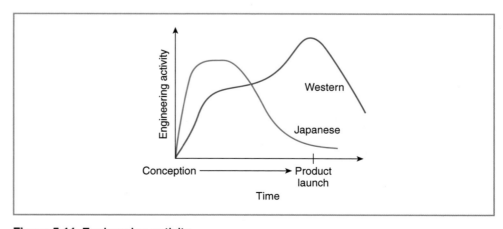

Figure 5.11 Engineering activity

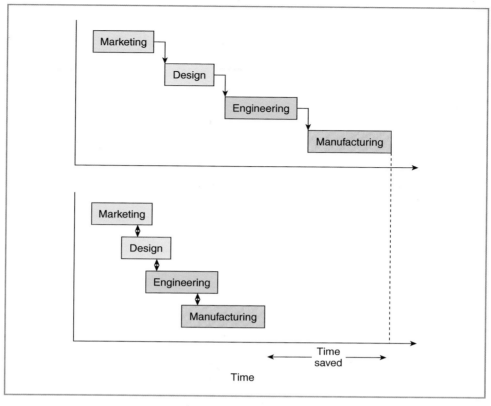

Figure 5.12 Sequential versus concurrent models for new product development

The benefits for projects in general can be summarised as potential for:

- reduced project time;
- reduced project costs, due to the reduction in reworking between each stage.

The disadvantages of applying this method of working include:

- increased overheads – as the teams require their own administration support;
- costs of co-location – people being relocated away from their functions to be with the team with which they are working;
- cultural resistance;
- inappropriate application – it is no panacea for other project problems.[16]

Running activities in parallel requires cooperation during planning (ideally involving co-location of the planners) and high levels of communication during the activity phases. It has proved to be beneficial but as the following Real World example shows, the application needs careful consideration.

REAL WORLD **Chicago's Millennium Park**

The idea of saving time by organising sequential activities to run concurrently is highly appealing. The reality can be far less attractive. Chicago's Millennium Park is one of many millennium projects around the world that ran into problems. It trebled its original US$150 million budget and was delayed by four years, finally being formally completed in July 2004: it suffered from a process that didn't work. The fast-track idea was applied to this pro-

→

ject to allow construction work to start on converting the former railway yard into a park before the design work had been completed. The problem appears to have been that the designers, developers and various contractors before the start of works had not agreed the overall scheme for the park. As a result, features were added, then removed, work had to be done and then redone when the designs were changed, and the city found itself in contractual wranglings with its contractors. The size of the park also expanded during the process, from 16 to 24 acres.

Source: Nick Fox/Shutterstock

The result, however, has been generally viewed as a success – the park is a home for various works of art and has some unique features, including a stainless steel bandstand and various Frank Gehry designed structures. It has since become the top tourist destination in Chicago and the Midwest.[17] Again, this challenges us to understand the nature of a 'successful project'. When is that success evaluated? And success for whom?

As for all 'good ideas', fast-track needs to be considered in context. In such a scenario, there is often great benefit to be gained from having contractors, designers and engineers working together from the outset, to ensure that what is being designed is feasible and can be constructed. There is, however, a logical order to these processes, and continuing without a good basis to work on is futile. The example illustrates what many people know from experience – that the quality of the final job is determined by the level of preparation undertaken. In this case, the inherent conflicts with the project should have been resolved at an early stage and work undertaken based on a clear vision of the intended outcome. This is termed **front-end loading** in projects, and broadly follows the pattern of resource commitments of the Japanese automotive firms shown in Figure 5.12. Indeed, there is a view in some sectors that any project termed a 'fast-track' project is doomed, as the necessary up-front work will not have been undertaken in (paradoxically) a rush to make progress on the development.

Activity maps

The objective of this part of the process is to provide an overview of what the project, should it go ahead, would look like. With the plethora of modern tools available through the medium of the computer, it is easy to forget the objectives of the plan, which are discussed here. Some of the basic techniques for establishing the logic and timing of activities are presented.

How do we describe a process? Many organisations have procedure manuals that run to thousands of pages and are only dusted off for annual quality audits (see Chapter 9). Process mapping techniques, such as those discussed throughout this book, work far better and greatly reduce the amount of documentation required, while improving the usefulness of the end result.

One graphical technique is four fields mapping or deployment flow charting (FFM/DFC).[18] As shown in Figure 5.13, it is a way of relating four information fields:

1 The team members (shown at the top).
2 The logical phases of an activity (sequentially down the left-hand side, the first at the top, flowing downwards).

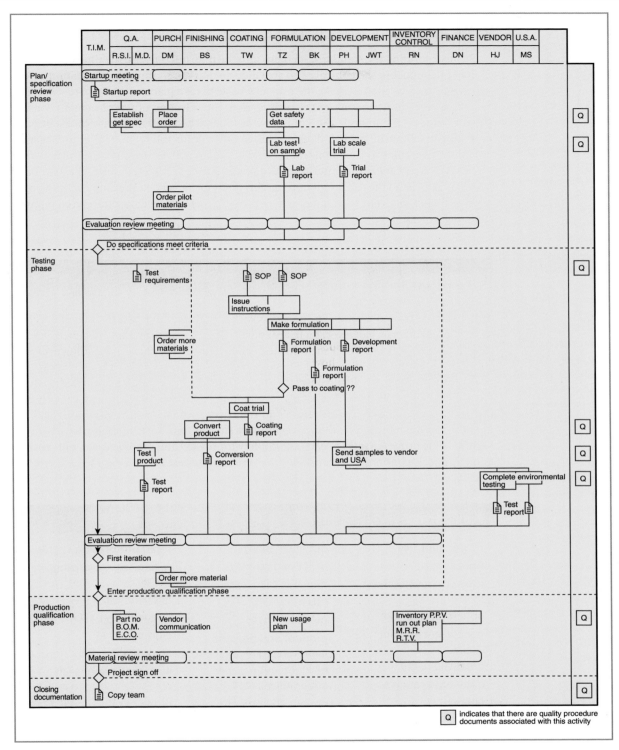

Figure 5.13 The use of FFM/DFC in planning the introduction of a new coating material (Adapted from ElectroComponentCo)

3 Tasks to be performed, including decisions made.

4 The standards that apply for each task.

By incorporating the standards element into the plan not only are the time and activity planned in detail but the controls also specified so that the sharing of information across an organisation needed to make the project work can take place.

Figure 5.13 shows the use of the technique in the selection of a replacement coating product used in the manufacture of a new product. The entry and exit criteria at each phase ensure that the project does not move on without the team having met certain criteria at that point. For example, at the end of the first phase the outcome must be that the specifications meet the criteria set. No phase can be completed until all errors have been corrected and the causes identified. This does not sit very comfortably with the conventional ideas of project planning, where activities just proceed at some stated point in time, regardless.[19]

Summary

■ Projects are started through an enormous variety of means and their manner of progression is no less diverse. However, there are some principal structures that are generic and of benefit to most projects. These include the formal definition of phases, including time and a process to allow creativity into the development of the concept. This is then enshrined into a scope statement, which allows the start of the development of the process by which the project will be delivered. Key elements of initial planning are the product, the process, the tasks, the people or organisation, and the costs. Task and information flow can be modelled through the application of techniques such as four fields mapping to produce a highly visible process. Gates at each stage allow for review and in some cases will prevent failing projects continuing to consume time, energy and resource.

Key terms

50 per cent rule *p. 118*

brief *p. 121*

concept development *p. 112*

concurrently *p. 127*

concurrent engineering *p. 128*

creativity *p. 113*

data/information *p. 119*

filters *p. 111*

formalisation *p. 122*

Last Planner *p. 118*

optimism bias *p. 117*

order and chaos *p. 111*

phase *p. 123*

PID *p. 121*

pipeline *p. 112*

product and process overview *p. 119*

product and process uncertainty *p. 117*

project champions *p. 113*

project charter *p. 133*

proposal *p. 121*

rapid prototyping *p. 113*

rolling-wave planning *p. 118*

scope creep *p. 114*

sequentially *p. 127*

sign-off *p. 115*

stage-gate *p. 125*

systematic approach *p. 121*

terms of reference *p. 121*

Traceability *p. 120*

Relevant areas of the Bodies of Knowledge

Tables 5.2 and 5.3 summarise the relevant sections. Both of these approaches to this phase of the project suggest that proceduralisation is more important than creativity in projects. They also assume that customers know what they want from a project and that this is enshrined in a written document of commitment, such as a contract. This environment is alien to many project managers. The disciplines suggested by both of these can be beneficial, however, even in relatively small projects, as they formalise the process of gaining 'buy-in' from key stakeholders.

Table 5.2 Relevant areas of the APM Body of Knowledge

Relevant section	Title	Summary
2.2.2	Decision gates	Gives an overview of decision gates and the key questions that should be asked.
4.1.4	Scope definition	This section discusses the translation of requirements into outputs for the chosen solution. Scope management is later defined as 'The process whereby outputs, outcomes and benefits are identified, defined and controlled.'
4.2	Integrated planning	This section looks at the aspects that need to be considered when doing detailed planning. These include risk identification and analysis, estimation, scheduling, resource optimisation and cost planning.

Table 5.3 Relevant areas of the PMI Body of Knowledge

Relevant section	Title	Summary
2.3.1	Processes, policies and procedures: initiating and planning	Provides an outline of the processes, methods, templates and supplier contractual agreements needed to start a project.
4.1	Develop project charter	This is the process which formally authorises the existence of the project. It builds on the initial business case and provides a link between the business case and the strategic objectives of the organisation.
5.1	Project scope management: plan scope management	This builds on the **project charter** and the project management plan. It documents how the project and product scope will be defined, validated and controlled over the course of the project.
5.2	Project scope management: collect requirements	Defined as: '. . . the process of determining, documenting and managing stakeholder needs and requirements to meet objectives. The key benefit of this process is that it provides the basis for defining the product scope and project scope.' Note that this is treated as a process that is carried out as part of a formalised project initiation, and assumes that stakeholders know what they want from the project.
5.3	Project scope management: define scope	This activity carries out some appraisal of the project in terms of cost–benefit analysis and the identification of alternatives. The output from this process is in the form of a scope statement ('a detailed description of the project and product') that can be signed off before continuing.

PROJECT MANAGEMENT IN PRACTICE
Norway's QA process for major project procurement

A number of major public investment projects failed by having significant cost overruns, delays and quality standards not being met. In 2000, the Norwegian government installed a Quality Assurance (QA) scheme for planning major projects where the budget was estimated at more than NOK500 million. In 2011, this limit was revised to NOK750 million. Investments in the oil sector and made by state-owned responsible organisations were exempt, as they still are today. In the early days, QA was only concerned with the quality assurance of the cost and benefit estimates before public funding was approved (now known as QA2). Later, a separate quality check of the initial concept (QA1) was added.

Source: Jim Parkin/Shutterstock

QA1 is intended to assure that the choice of concept is likely to be suitable, before any investment into the project proposals are authorised. These have to not only meet certain criteria for the quality of the documentation produced, they also have to pass scrutiny by the political policy makers in government. This is based on the belief that the choice of concept is actually the most important decision for the state as project owner. Documentation is checked for consistency. Reviews are performed investigating decisions in terms of their relevance to needs, strategy and requirements, and to what extent they fully exploit the opportunity. The implementation strategy and plans for the pre-project (D2 phase) are also checked. Additionally, independent uncertainty analysis and cost–benefit analysis are undertaken.

QA2 provides assurance of what is termed 'the management base' and cost estimates. The management base is all of the project definition documents, including all of the aspects of product, process, tasks, people, and costs. In addition, uncertainty analysis is conducted before the project is submitted to Parliament for approval. Gaining accountability and providing government with the necessary control is the purpose of this process. In addition, an assessment of two potential contracting strategies is reviewed in addition to analyses of success factors and a quantification of the uncertainty in terms of cost. On the basis of all this information, recommendations regarding the total cost range for the project as well as the management approach to it are provided.

After a QA exercise is completed and the report delivered, the Ministry of Finance will hold a meeting with the ministry proposing the project and the consultant concerned, to ensure that all relevant experience from the process has been elicited and collected.

As of 2012, more than 150 QAs have been performed and the scheme has been continued. Although well received, the cost (more than NOK8 million annually) and the time it adds to the already long planning phase of public projects (approximately 10 years in some cases) has been criticised. In addition, it is found difficult to involve more entrepreneurial people and practices in the early days of projects as a result (thereby limiting the chaos that can be created at the outset).

Points for discussion

Compare the QA process with that used by other organisations you can find information on. What do you see as the strengths and weaknesses of each? What do you notice about the differences in approach?

1 Why might the long process of approvals reduce the level of enterprise in the project?

2 QA is a highly formalised approach. Consider the range of projects procured by government departments. Discuss the benefits and likely costs of such an approach across this range.

Text provided by Associate Professor Anne Live Vaagaasar, Department of Leadership and Organizational Behaviour at BI Norwegian Business School.

PROJECT MANAGEMENT IN PRACTICE
The Mini project – the brief and the PID[20]

The brief

Your group are to organise a charity event of your choosing that will demonstrate your ability to use the structures and processes of professional project management. The basic rules are as follows:

- You are financially accountable and liable for anything that you do – the University will not take this responsibility. Any profits you make must go to charity and outline accounts must be provided to demonstrate that this has happened.
- Your idea must be approved by the course tutor at the key gates – between D1 and D2 based on your PID, and D2 and D3.
- You cannot use any logos without the explicit permission of the organisations involved.
- Two groups cannot do the same project – the first with the idea to be approved by the tutor is the one that 'wins'.
- You are responsible for managing all group issues, including any conflicts that arise.
- The key product, in addition to your event, is the report on the processes used and reflections on their utility in such an environment.

  In response to this requirement, the group undertaking the assignment put together a PID.

The PID: Mini World Record Challenge

Executive summary

The goal of this event is to break the world record for the greatest number of people in a BMW mini. The official Guinness World Record currently stands at 27 for the classic model and 29 for the new model. The event date and time have been agreed. Teams of 29 or more will be invited throughout the afternoon to make their attempt, with a prize awarded to the team achieving the highest total. Food and drinks will be provided at the venue. A small entrance fee will be charged and all proceeds from the event and food sales will be donated to charity.

Background

As a group of six students, we have been set the task of organising an event that allows the demonstration and utilisation of PM techniques, structures and processes. The dates for the event and submission of the final report have been set and agreed. In response to the brief, the group aim to organise an event for the purpose of breaking the official world record for the most people in a BMW mini.

Outline

The car will be provided by a local dealer and driven to the venue by a member of the team. Insurance has been arranged. The event will be advertised extensively during the two weeks prior to the event and promoted through direct contact with local sports clubs and societies. Participants will be invited to submit a team prior to the day of the event and will be allocated a 10-minute slot to make their attempt, under the supervision of the organisers, with medical staff in attendance. The event will be observed by an independent adjudicator and recorded on video for the purposes of verification. Food and drinks will be served nearby, for spectators and participants. A small fee will be charged for the event and all profits go to our nominated charity.

Key objectives

The objective of the event is to provide a fun event for students. This will be done by providing a unique experience and by allowing them to compete with their friends in something they are unlikely to have tried before. The venue therefore must be amenable to spectators. Secondary objectives are to break the world record and to raise money for charity.

Desired outcomes

- The event takes place on the day agreed
- At least 5 teams enter
- No damage to car or injury to participants
- The world record is broken
- At least £250 is raised for charity.

Constraints

- *Time*: the date is constrained by the due date for the report so the event must take place on the date agreed
- *Cost*: there is no external funding for the event. The maximum loss that the team are prepared to make is £30 per person (£180 in total)
- *Quality*: to be regarded as a success, at least 2 teams are required to participate.

Of these three, the most restrictive is the time, and therefore this becomes the highest priority of our objectives. In addition, the event is subject to health and safety legislation, must be insured appropriately and meet the requirement of the group members not to affect other work in which they are involved adversely.

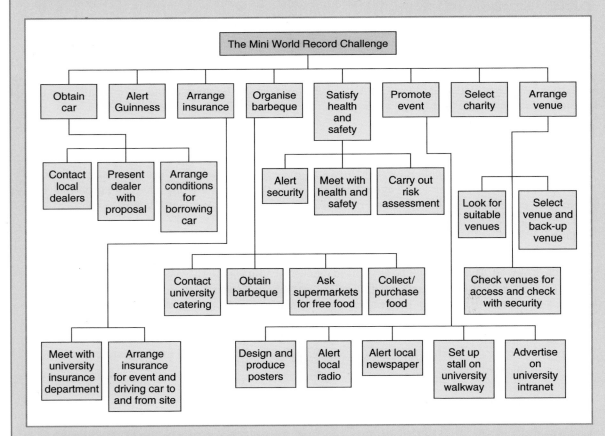

Figure 5.14 Work breakdown structure

Project organisational structure

The group members all have equal authority and power over the project. We will coordinate activities via meetings on a twice-weekly basis, except during vacation times. The group will regularly present progress reports to the course tutor.

Project plan

The Work Breakdown Structure (WBS) is shown in Figure 5.14.

The tasks are then presented in a four fields map, indicating who is responsible for each task and the exit criteria for each stage. This is shown in Figure 5.15.

The Gantt chart for the project is shown in Figure 5.16. (See Chapter 6 for discussion of Gantt charts.)

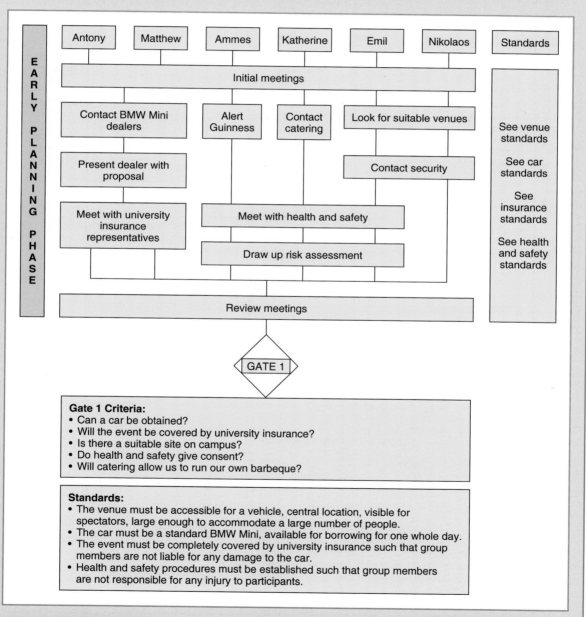

Figure 5.15 Four fields map

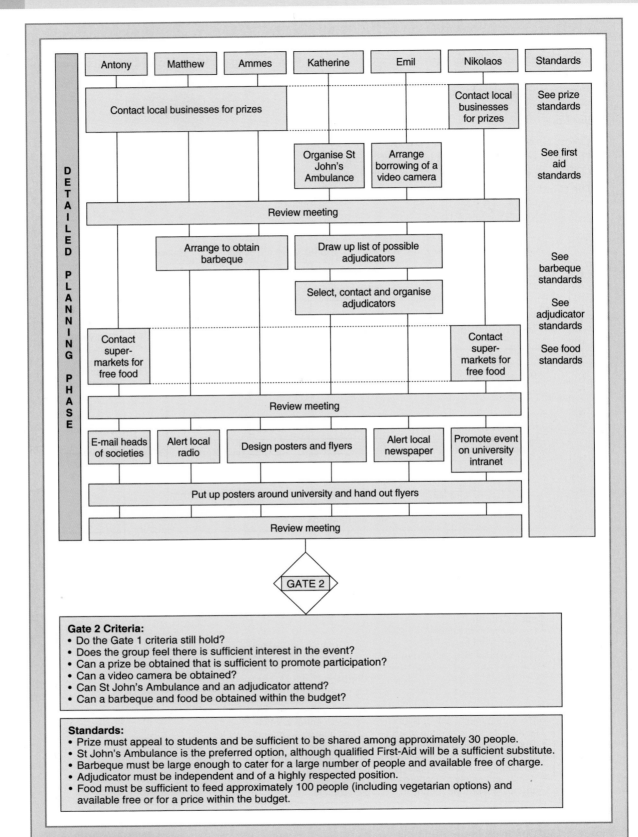

Figure 5.15 continued

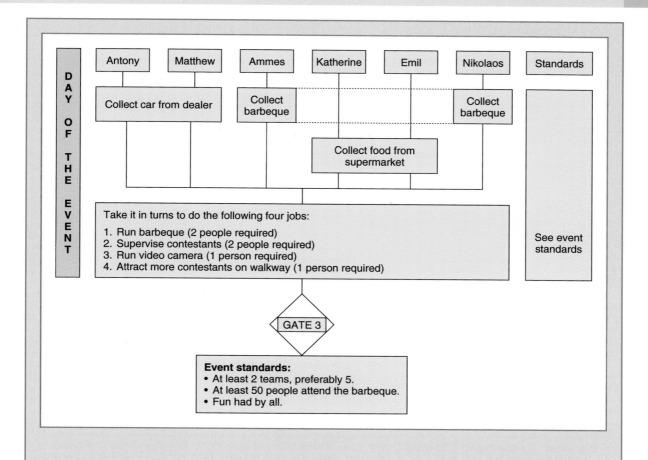

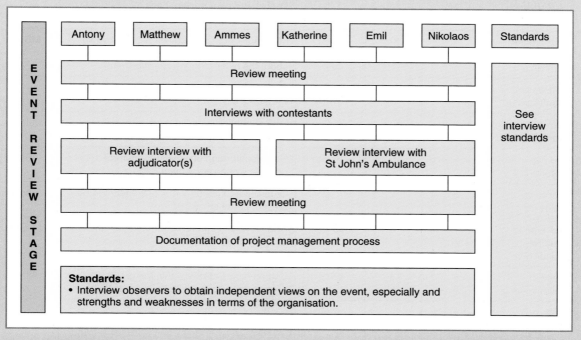

Figure 5.15 continued

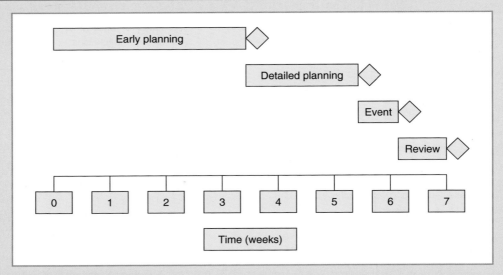

Figure 5.16 Gantt chart

Risk assessment and management

A full assessment of the risks associated with the project and the steps that will be taken to manage these risks are shown in Table 5.4. (See Chapter 10 for more on risk assessments.)

Table 5.4 Risk assessment and management

Risk Event	Likelihood	Severity	PRN (rank)	Mitigation	Owner
Advertising not ready	1	10	10 (5)	Design and print posters early.	AP
Car breaks down/not available	1	10	10 (5)	Make sure insurance covers for breakdown and have written confirmation with the garage about the hire of the mini for the event.	MB
Witnesses don't turn up	2	9	18 (4)	Create a reserve list of on campus alternative witnesses e.g. staff.	
No participants	2	10	20 (3)	Lots of publicity early in the summer term.	All
No car insurance	1	10	10 (5)	Organise through university. Construct a detailed written agreement.	AS
Personal injury	5	2	10 (5)	Organise a St John's Ambulance team to be present at the event.	KA
Adverse weather conditions	7	8	56 (2)	Find university umbrellas for the event and possibly hire a marquee.	
Lack of teamworking	8	8	64 (1)	Communicate clearly within the group. Share work and make decisions together.	All
Loss of one group member	1	2	2 (9)		

Topics for discussion

1 Why would creativity be essential in a personal project, such as an assignment or dissertation? How might this be incorporated into your plan of work?

2 Why should the plan be viewed as a value-adding activity?

3 Identify the costs and potential negative effects of the misuse of plans.

4 Why is getting scope 'sign-off' so important?

5 To whom does the project manager have to 'sell' a proposal?

6 When is it important for the brief to be highly precise and when should it be left as loose as possible?

7 Why is it important to know the customer for a proposal document?

8 What is the benefit to be gained from mapping a process before proceeding with the detailed planning?

9 From a project with which you are familiar, how might providing gates and gate criteria have helped in its management?

10 Should the activities in a project be run sequentially or concurrently? Choose a project and analyse the options for the outline plan.

Further information

Andriopoulos, C., Gotsi, M., Lewis, M.W., and Ingram A.E. (2017) 'Turning the Sword: How NPD Teams Cope with Front-End Tensions', *Journal of Product Innovation Management*, Vol. 35, No.3, pp. 427–445.

Cooper, R.G. and Edgett, S.J. (2012) 'Best Practices in the Idea-to-Launch Process and Its Governance', *Research-Technology Management*, Vol. 55, No. 2, pp. 43–54.

Cooper, R.G. and Sommer, A.F. (2016) 'The Agile-Stage-Gate Hybrid Model: A Promising New Approach and a New Research Opportunity', *Journal of Product Innovation Management*, Vol 33, No. 5, pp. 513–526.

Drucker, P.F. (1998) 'The Discipline of Innovation', *Harvard Business Review*, November–December, pp. 149–157.

Papke-Shields, K.E. and Boyer-Wright, K.M (2017) 'Strategic planning characteristics applied to project management', *International Journal of Project Management*, Vol. 35, No. 2, pp. 169–179.

PMI (2006) *Practice Standard for Work Breakdown Structures*, 2nd edition, PMI, Upper Darby, PA.

Sobek, D.K. II, Liker, J.K. and Ward, A.C. (1998) 'Another Look at How Toyota Integrates Product Development', *Harvard Business Review*, July–August, pp. 36–49.

Websites

https://www.axelos.com/best-practice-solutions/ prince2/prince2-templates – downloads of PID documents. See also prince2.wiki

www.teamflow.com – FFM/DFC software.

References

1 Nonaka, I. (1990) 'Redundant, Overlappping Organisation: A Japanese Approach to Managing the Innovation Process', *California Management Review*, Spring, pp. 27–38.

2 Much fuller discussion of this can be found in Maylor, H. and Blackmon, K. (2015) *Researching Business & Management*, 2nd edition, Palgrave Macmillan, London, Chapter 2.

3 GSK's pipeline can be seen at https://www.gsk.com/ en-gb/research-and-development/our-pipeline/

and Pfizer's at https://www.pfizer.com/science/ drug-product-pipeline

4 Von Hippel, E. et al. (1999) 'Creating Breakthroughs at 3M', *Harvard Business Review*, September–October, pp. 47–57 and interview with 3M VP Innovation.

5 See www.prince2.com

6 National Audit Office https://www.nao.org.uk/report/ national-audit-office-strategy-our-strategy-2019-20-to-2021-22/

7 Variously attributed to Admiral Lord Nelson and General Eisenhower.

8 Flyvberg, B., Bruzelius, N. and Rothengatter, W. (2003) *Megaprojects and Risk: An Anatomy of Ambition*, Cambridge University Press, Cambridge.

9 PMI Body of Knowledge.

10 PMI (2017) *The PMI Book of Project Management Forms*, 3rd edition, PMI, Upper Darby, PA and also for instance www.projectmanagement.com for downloadable standard forms.

11 Cooper, R.G. (2005) *Product Leadership: Pathways to Profitable Innovation*, Basic Books, New York, Chapter 7.

12 https://www.gov.uk/government/collections/ infrastructure-and-projects-authority-assurance- review-toolkit

13 An excellent comparative review of the procurement approaches of the UK and Norway is Klakegg, O.J., Williams, T.J. and Magnussen, O.M. (2010) 'An investigation of governance frameworks for public projects in Norway and the UK', *International Journal of Project Management*, Vol. 28, No. 1, pp. 40–50.

14 Calantone, R. and Di Benedetto, C.A. (2000) 'Performance and Time to Market: Accelerating Cycle Time without Overlapping Stages', *IEEE Transactions on Engineering Management*, Vol. 47, No. 2, pp. 232–244.

15 See for instance Clark, K.B. and Fujimoto, T. (1991) *Product Development Performance*, Harvard Business School Press, Boston, MA.

16 A full review of this can be found in Maylor, H. (1997) 'Concurrent New Product Development: An Empirical Assessment', *International Journal of Operations and Production Management*, Vol. 17, No. 12, pp. 1196–1214.

17 See https://www.chicagotribune.com/entertainment/ ct-millennium-park-visitors-ent-0406-20170406- column.html

18 Dimancescu, D. (1995) *The Seamless Enterprise, Making Cross Functional Management Work*, Wiley, New York.

19 Further graphical techniques can be found in Forsberg, K., Mooz, H. and Cotterman, H. (2005) *Visualizing Project Management*, John Wiley & Sons Inc, Hoboken, NJ.

20 See www.prince2.com.

Managing the project process: the 4-D model

D2: Design it

Making sense of the project context

> 1 Introduction
> 2 Structures and frameworks
> 3 Projects and organisations

Managing the project process: the 4-D model

D1: Define it
4 Setting up for success
5 Planning for success

D4: Develop it
16 Completing projects and learning to improve

D2: Design it
6 Time planning and scheduling
7 Making time planning robust: Advanced Project Thinking (APT)
8 Building a business case for a project
9 Engaging stakeholders
10 Managing risks and opportunities

D3: Do it
11 Organising people in the project
12 Leading people in projects
13 Monitoring and controlling the project
14 Procuring, contracting, and working with supply chains
15 Problem-solving and decision-making

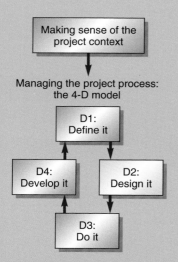

6

Time planning and scheduling

'*If you fail to plan, you plan to fail!*'
(Benjamin Franklin)

'*Planning is an unnatural process. It is much more satisfying to do something and the nicest thing about not planning is that failure comes as a complete surprise rather than being preceded by a long period of worry and depression.*'
(John Harvey, c.1800)

Principles

1   The first principle of planning is deconstruction: break the product and the work into tasks.

2   A time plan requires the arrangement of the tasks into a sequence for the purpose of analysis.

3   The most recognised way to communicate a time plan is as a Gantt chart.

Learning objectives

By the time you have completed this chapter, you should be able to:

→   use the basics of product, task and organisational breakdown and recognise the limitations of these

→   arrange tasks in a simple project into a sequence, and calculate the project duration and critical path

→   display the results of a time plan for communication purposes.

Contents

Introduction   *145*
6.1   Deconstruction of a project   *146*
6.2   Constructing a time plan   *150*
6.3   Using Gantt charts   *159*
Summary   *163*
Key terms   *164*
Relevant areas of the Bodies of Knowledge   *164*
Project management in practice: *The Balti Experience*   *165*
Project management in practice: *The mobile phone development*   *167*
Topics for discussion   *167*
Further information   *168*
Reference   *169*

The Glastonbury Festival has become one of the largest of its kind in Europe. In addition to the performing acts, there is a huge operation to make the festival work, in the management of the media, tickets, security, retail units and general care of the location. Each of these requires a different approach to planning – not just to make sure that all of the acts arrive on a constructed stage at a given time, have all their kit and are able to be heard by the paying guests. In addition to the considerable scale and complexity of the festival, there are always intrinsic uncertainties – will the bands turn up, will the rain turn the place into a mire or be so hot that people are passing out with heatstroke? How will the organisers respond in case of a major security alert? Might it have to be cancelled or postponed for a reason outside the organisers' control? All these things are vital considerations for the planners.

Source: Samuel Wordley/Alamy Stock Photo

Introduction

In Chapter 5, the initial or master plan was constructed and various means provided to communicate and evaluate it. In this chapter, we move into the second major phase of the project process D2: detailed process design. As the opening case demonstrates, this is not a trivial process, as the planner will have not only to deal with the most likely scenarios, but also plan for eventualities – to answer the question 'what happens if . . . ?'

The most basic approach is to deconstruct the project into its constituent products, processes, tasks, people and costs as part of the compilation of the project management plan. Having prepared a plan (not date dependent), the next stage is to compile the schedule (e.g. we will start on this date). The Gantt chart is just one way to display this all-important schedule.

The opening quotations illustrate a tension between the need to plan a project, and the need to get on with it. The phases of D2 and D3 need to be balanced and on this point there is little to guide the manager as to what constitutes 'sufficient planning'. In extremis, no planning could be sufficient or the team spend the entire time and budget working up a 'perfect plan.' This tension, between no plan (just do it) and all plan, requires judgement. This is where the 'art' as well as the 'science' of the professional project manager is critical.

6.1 Deconstruction of a project

Having prepared the overview models, it is now the task of the project team and its planners to put in place the detail. High-level consideration of the objectives of the various stakeholders and resolution of potential conflicts of the project provide a strong foundation on which to build. This chapter presents the means by which the first part of these details can be put in place. Graphical techniques are preferred, as these create the greatest potential for involving others to gain their insight and commitment. However, the objective of such detail must remain at the forefront of the planner's mind. In itself it has little merit. The strength that it offers is in the ability to probe the plans to identify potential improvements to the methods, which may present opportunities for either better performance or risk avoidance (hence *the plan is nothing, planning is everything*).

For the project manager, this is one of the most developed parts of the subject – the methods have been formalised for over 70 years, though in reality have undoubtedly been in use in one form or another since the beginning of civilisation. They must, however, be considered in the light of experience, and this is discussed in the following chapter.

The production of plans is often treated as an end in itself. This misses the point and the value that such an activity can add. Its objectives are twofold. First, it must provide an opportunity for the planner to analyse the project system, to reveal opportunities for improvement and problem prevention, and setting out the basis on which the project will proceed. Second, the benefits of plans are only realised when they are communicated. These two objectives create the rationale for what follows.

In the previous chapter, we identified the five elements that form the basis of a plan. These are not an exhaustive list but they are the most common. Figure 6.1 shows how these are developed in to five more detailed elements, the **product breakdown structure**, the **detailed process map**, the **work breakdown structure**, the **organisational breakdown structure** and the **cost breakdown structure**. All of these are interdependent; in the simplest case, the product determines the work to be done, which determines who will be required to do it, which will determine the costs. Similarly, any change in the product will be reflected in a revised product breakdown, which will impact the work breakdown, the organisation and the cost breakdown. We will look at the PBS, the WBS and the OBS in this section. The CBS will be discussed further in Chapter 8. The detailed process maps can be produced using the approaches shown in Chapter 5.

Work breakdown structure (WBS)

With some small projects, many people are able to break these up into lists of 'things to do' in their heads. This has the advantage of being relatively quick and in many cases works as long as the scale and complexity of the project is relatively limited. The two major downsides of this approach are the vulnerability of the project to that one person, and the inability of this 'plan' to be analysed or communicated. In an attempt to be more systematic about this, the most basic approach for the medium-to-large project is to use a work breakdown structure.

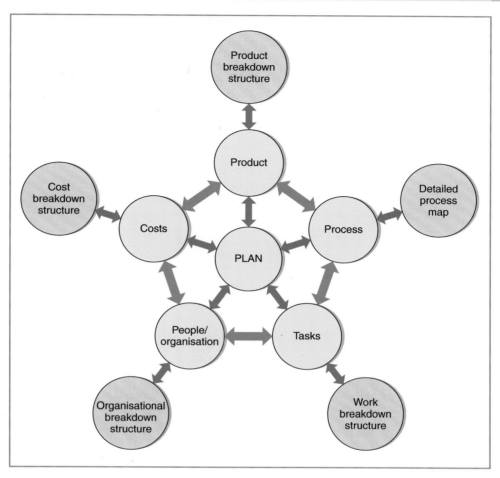

Figure 6.1 Core planning elements

> *'So how do you eat an elephant*
> *(or vegetarian equivalent)?'*
> *'Just one slice at a time.'*

The breaking down of large activities (the elephant) into comprehensible or manageable units of work (the slices) is a fundamental part of project management. Figure 6.2 shows how a systems project – the installation of a new computer system – was broken down into elements that one person or one department could tackle as an activity in its own right at the lowest level in the project. In principle, what could be simpler?! The reality, of course, is never quite so straightforward.

Source: Image by Chris Nierhaus at TinBug Design Studios (tinbug.com)

WBS is also known as 'chunking' or 'unbundling'. This is attractive as it gives people responsibility for a manageable part of the project. Each activity description is in the form of a verb.

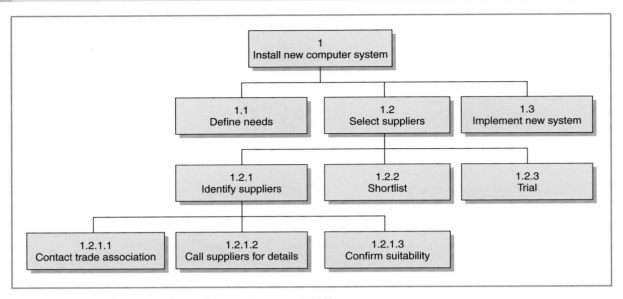

Figure 6.2 Example of a work breakdown structure (WBS)

The role of a WBS is to create a hierarchical series of activities, which are independent units, but at the same time still part of the whole, and here lies the major problem with WBS. The breakdown of work into **work packages** is only part of the challenge; the main challenge is to join all of these pieces up. Returning to the elephant analogy, the challenge is not about eating the elephant, but how do you join all of the pieces up to make a working elephant. This is a much trickier proposition. While this is stretching the metaphor, it does illustrate the reality of the challenge for the project manager. They will not only need to manage the delivery of the individual activities or work packages, but also coordinate between the different parts of the breakdown. Practically, this has been achieved through having a liaison person, exchanging staff, or through changing the scheduling of activities to run more of them in parallel. This requires much greater interfacing and team-working. Generating the WBS looks like such a simple set of activities, yet the decisions made here are fundamental in achieving success.

Organisational breakdown structure (OBS)

The purpose of the OBS is to identify the human resources needed to carry out the project. In Figure 6.3, the same IT installation project is broken down into the three relevant groups of people involved – the finance department, the IT department and some contractors. Under each of these headings, a further breakdown identified the individuals concerned with the project. For instance, not having the necessary resources internally to do the training or to manage the project, this will have to be done by contractors. This OBS simply identifies potential people. We will discuss how those people are allocated to tasks and the structures in which they can work further in Chapter 11.

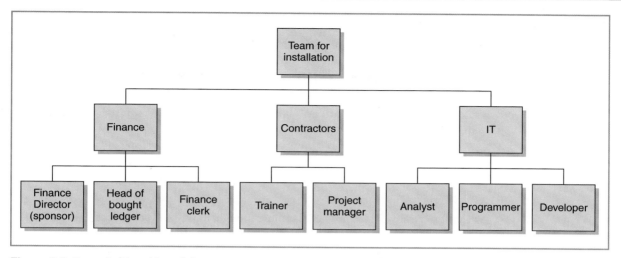

Figure 6.3 Organisational breakdown structure

Product breakdown structure

The product breakdown structure is the physical deconstruction of a required product into its constituent parts. In the example of the IT system, the simplest breakdown is into hardware and software. How the product is broken down though, can make a difference – as shown in the Figure 6.4.

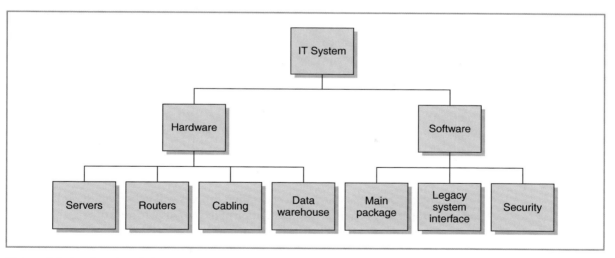

Figure 6.4 Product breakdown structure

Does it matter how you structure the hierarchy? Err, yes

During a line refurbishment for London Underground carried out during the 1980s, the project was broken down into track/tunnel units and train/rolling stock units. Communication between the two was problematic, and when the refurbished trains were delivered they did not fit into the refurbished tunnels. Nobody had been assigned to manage the interfaces between the teams during the project, as a result of which everybody relentlessly pursued their own part of the work – regardless of the consequences that it would have elsewhere.

6.2 Constructing a time plan

How long will it take you to complete a major report for your boss, or a 3000-word assignment for a course of study? Many questions then arise, including:

- How precise do you need to be – is a rough/ballpark figure required, or are we using this for detailed planning?
- Do we have any previous experience of doing this? If so, how long did it take last time?
- What are the likely pitfalls that may arise that would cause significant delay?
- What other tasks are going to get in the way of doing this (see *Multi-tasking* in Chapter 7).

Estimating is a key part of project planning, though, as we shall see, it is one that is subject to more games-playing and delusion than almost any other field of human activity. The basics of estimating are discussed here, but it should be remembered that estimates unless based on good data (this is how long this task normally takes) are better termed 'guesses'. We should therefore be careful how scientifically we treat the numbers that come from this process, and in particular, not be committed in a hurry to making rough estimates that we later get held to.

> HM was walking to the lift in the offices of a major IT contractor with his host, a senior manager in that business. They met one of his clients. After greetings and introductions, his host was taken aside by the client and asked, *you remember that proposal we discussed to update our security system?* His host did remember the proposal – it had been discussed for a total of no more than five minutes at their recent management board meeting. *How much do you think it would cost and how long would it take?* His host considered for a minute and then said, *based on what I think we would need to do, about £120 000 and six weeks, but don't hold me to it, I need to check with that team.* Promising not to, the client departed. Next morning a purchase order arrived on the desk of his host, commissioning the project, to take no longer than six weeks and cost no more than £120 000. Subsequent detailed planning showed that his initial guess was only 40 per cent of the cost of what the team thought it should be. Motto: be careful providing an estimate before you have worked out what is involved.

The project manager's role in the estimation process will vary from the collection of estimates from other people in the preparation of the proposal to the provision of detailed financial cost–benefit analysis. It is imperative that this function does not operate in a vacuum – that the feedback from previous plans and estimates is used to guide the process. Estimation is an activity which continues during the project lifecycle. As the project nears completion, the manager will have more certainty of the final times, resources and therefore costs. The accuracy of the estimates is therefore going to get better. The types of estimates, their nature, role and accuracies are shown in Table 6.1.

Having the estimates of times and resources required is one part of compiling the plans. In modelling time, these then need to be built into models of the likely project system that will enable key variables such as project duration and then schedules to be established.

Many projects require a planning method, which lends itself to analysis. The most commonly used of these is the '**activity-on-node**' technique. In this, activities from the WBS are represented as tasks on a relatively simple-to-understand diagram, to indicate the way the project is expected to work. The *estimates* have been obtained and a logical analysis of the work packages will usually determine their *sequence*.

Table 6.1 The nature, role and accuracy of estimate types

Name	Nature	Role	Accuracy
Rough/finger-in-the-air/ballpark	Much uncertainty as to what is involved	Early check on feasibility of brief	Very low
As-buts	As was carried out previously, but with the following amendments – some quantitative data exists	With an appropriate contingency factor – can be used for proposals	Moderate
Detailed estimates	Some initial work is carried out to determine what the likely problems are going to be	Proposals	Moderate
. . . to finish	Much of the project is completed and additional funding is needed to complete the tasks	Additional funds request	High

Activity-on-node diagrams and critical path analysis

Using the A-o-N technique, the construction of the project plan combines the work breakdown structure to identify all the constituent activities, the sequence in which they need to be performed, and the estimated duration for each activity.

If the logic of the project can be identified, the project manager can develop a diagram to represent it, allowing better analysis of the activities. Firstly, then, we need to represent the logical sequence in which the activities take place.

Consider a simple example. Figure 6.5 shows two activities, A and B, represented by simple boxes. B cannot start until A has finished and the times for A and B are 6 and 7 days respectively. This logic is known as **dependency**. This dependency means that the total duration of the two tasks is 13 days.

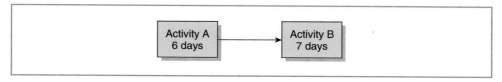

Figure 6.5 Task dependency

The visual clarity of denoting activities as boxes and linking them together is appealing. However, for any two activities, A then B, there are four ways in which they can link (see Figure 6.6). Precedence is indicated by arrows going from:

- the start of an activity (top left-hand or bottom left-hand corner of the box);
- the finish of an activity (middle of right-hand edge of box);

to:

- the start of an activity (middle of left-hand edge of box);
- the finish of an activity (top right-hand or bottom right-hand corner of the box).

The four ways in which activities therefore can link are:

- finish-to-start – the second activity cannot start until the first has finished;
- start-to-start – the second activity cannot start until the first has started;
- finish-to-finish – the second activity cannot finish until the first has finished;
- start-to-finish – the second activity cannot finish until the first has started.

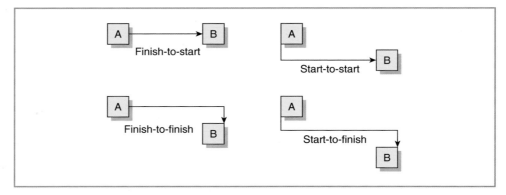

Figure 6.6 Logical activity linkages

Sometimes several things all need to be complete before the next stage can be started (even a simple meal will generally consist of a number of elements to get ready before you actually sit down to eat it). This can be represented as shown in Figure 6.7. Activity C cannot start until both A and B are complete. These are finish-to-start activities, and the distinction is important. A delay in either A or B means that C will be late.

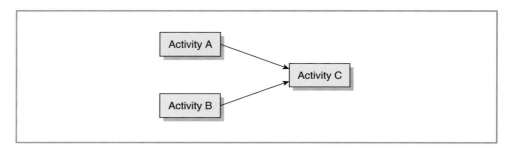

Figure 6.7 Representing multiple dependencies (1)

If the project has multiple activities that need to be completed before another task can start, that can be represented also. Consider the more complicated set of activities in Figure 6.8, which shows that the final activity, H, cannot start until all of E, F and G are finished.

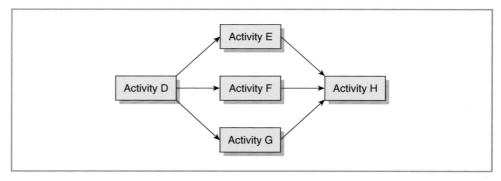

Figure 6.8 Representing multiple dependencies (2)

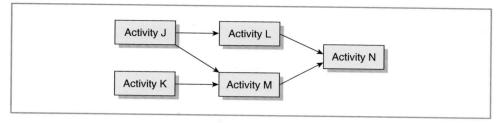

Figure 6.9 Representing multiple dependencies (3)

The plan can be made slightly more complicated. For example, taking the statement that 'activity L is dependent on activity J but activity M is dependent on both activities J and K' would lead to Figure 6.9. In this sequence, L can start once J has finished, but M cannot be started until both J and K are complete.

In order to complete the project with activity N, the project manager needs to schedule the predecessor activities. To understand how best to achieve this, we need more information about the activities within the project. To do this, we add additional information to the activity 'box' and the full detail of the activity-on-node technique becomes apparent. Considering the **network** of Figure 6.9, we already know the activity names (J, K, L, M, N) and we can estimate the time duration that each task will take. Knowing the way the tasks are linked, and the duration of each, we can perform a valuable analysis of the project.

Analysing the network – Critical Path Analysis (CPA)

We can amend the activity boxes of Figure 6.9 to add more information. Specifically, stating the expected duration of the task is the first stage in being able to analyse the project more completely. This addition is shown in Figure 6.10.
There are also three new terms to be introduced to the diagrams:

- **earliest start time** (EST) – determined by the activities preceding the event and is the earliest time at which the activity on this node can start;
- **latest start time** (LST) – is the same or later than the EST and is the latest time at which all the previous activities need to have been completed to prevent the whole project being held up;
- *total* **float** – the difference between the LST and the EST.

How is this used in practice? If we look at the example of Figure 6.11, we see the logic of the activities within this project, and the dependencies between the activities. Bottom-left in each box shows the duration of each activity, and we can use this to determine how

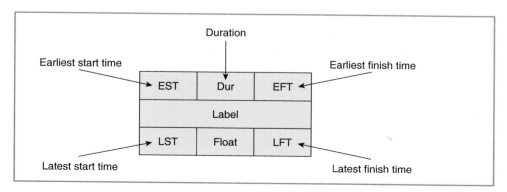

Figure 6.10 Activity notation

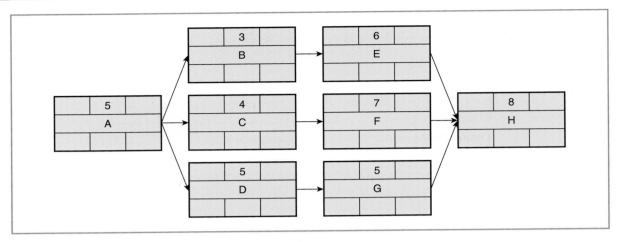

Figure 6.11 Activity network with durations included

long this project is going to take. The path through the activities which takes the longest is known as the 'critical path' – the longest sequence of dependent activities that need to be completed in order for the project as a whole to finish.

We firstly determine the overall project duration. There are three paths between the start and finish points that need to be examined – A–B–E–H, A–C–F–H and A–D–G–H. This first stage of the analysis is known as the **forward pass**. The subsequent calculation is the **reverse pass** to determine the critical path through the activities.

The forward pass

The forward pass determines the ESTs and EFTs, and starts at the left-hand side of the diagram with the EST for the first activity. This is zero. Activity A has a duration of 5 days and so the EFT for A is 5 days. It started on day zero, took 5 days, so now we are at day 5. The EFT for one activity becomes the EST for immediately following linked activities. For B, C and D the ESTs are all 5.

The EFTs for B,C and D are:

EFT (B) = EST (B) + duration of B = 5 + 3 = 8

EFT (C) = EST (C) + duration of C = 5 + 4 = 9

EFT (D) = EST (D) + duration of D = 5 + 5 = 10

EST for the E, F and G are as follows:

EST (E) = EFT (B) = 8

EST (F) = EFT (C) = 9

EST (G) = EFT (D) = 10

EFT (E) = EST (E) + duration of E = 8 + 6 = 14

EFT (F) = EST (F) + duration of F = 9 + 7 = 16

EST (G) = EST (G) + duration of G = 10 + 5 = 15

These are now entered onto the diagram. Activity H presents a small challenge in that there are three possible ESTs. These are the three EFTs of E, F and G.

Activity H cannot start until all three preceding activities have been completed – in this case at time 16 (the *latest* of the ESTs).

Following this through to the end of the network gives the EFT (H) as 16 + 8 = 24. This is the project duration. The completed forward pass is shown in Figure 6.12.

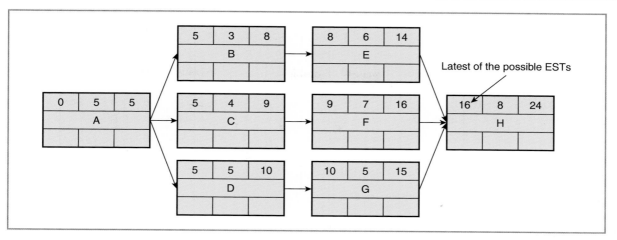

Figure 6.12 Results from the forward pass

The reverse pass

The reverse pass starts from the end of the network and assigns the LSTs and LFTs for each activity. The LFT for the last activity is taken to be the same as the EFT for that activity – meaning that we want the project to be completed as soon as possible. Working backwards, the LST for H is the LFT minus the duration of H. That is, it is the latest time that H could start without delaying the entire project. This is $24 - 8 = 16$.

Following the logic backwards, the LFTs of E, F and G must all be the same as the LST of H. The LSTs and LFTs for E, F and G can now be calculated.

> LST (E) = LFT (E) − duration of E = $16 - 6 = 10$
> LST (F) = LFT (F) − duration of F = $16 - 7 = 9$
> LST (G) = LFT (G) − duration of G = $16 - 5 = 11$

and similarly for B, C and D, where:

> LFT (B) = LST (E)
> LFT (C) = LST (F)
> LFT (D) = LST (G)
> LST (B) = LFT (B) − duration of B = $10 - 3 = 7$
> LST (C) = LFT (C) − duration of C = $9 - 4 = 5$
> LST (D) = LFT (D) − duration of D = $11 - 5 = 6$

The LFT for A is another case where there is more than one possibility. The three possible LFTs are:

> LST (B) = 7
> LST (C) = 5
> LST (D) = 6

The choice is the *earliest* of the LSTs – 5. Checking back to the LST for activity A shows that the LST (A) = LFT (A) − duration of A = $5 - 5 = 0$. The resulting analysis is shown in Figure 6.13.

The remaining task is to calculate the *float* for each activity. An activity has float if there is a difference between its EST and LST. That is:

> Float = LST − EST

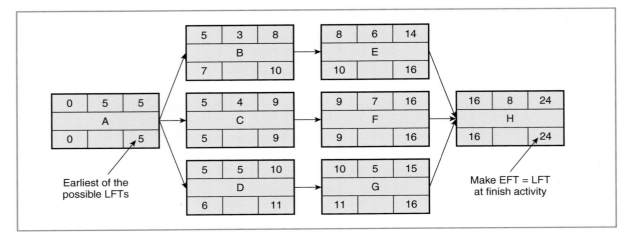

Figure 6.13 Results of the forward and reverse passes

This can be calculated for each activity. Where there is no float, it means that the activity is *critical*, and any delay in this activity will delay the project as a whole. The **critical path** through the network is therefore:

A – C – F – H as these are the activities with zero floats.

The final network, complete with floats and with the critical path highlighted, is shown in Figure 6.14.

Knowing the critical path has significant implications for project managers. In the example of Figure 6.14, we now know the elements of the project that can tolerate no delay without impacting the end date. This means that the project manager should focus more attention on activities A, C, F and H to ensure they go smoothly. The floats on tasks B, E, D and G mean that they can tolerate a delay of *up to* the float value before they start to impact the critical path.

However, projects rarely run exactly to plan, and if activity C goes better than expected and only takes three days, but task D is delayed by two days, then D's float is lost, and the critical path *changes* to A–D–G–H. In this case the overall expected duration increases by one day as well, so it is vital that the project manager does not focus *all* their attention on the critical path and lose track of how the other elements are progressing.

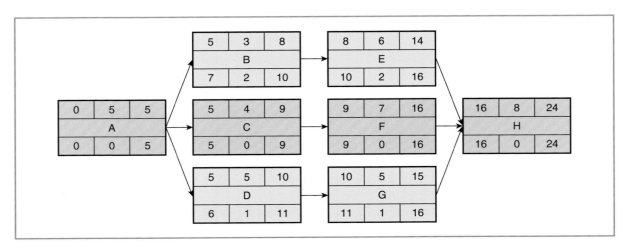

Figure 6.14 Completed network analysis including floats and highlighted critical path

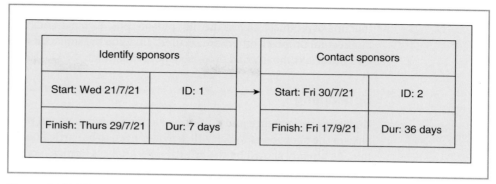

Figure 6.15 Microsoft Project output

The most used package for project planning, Microsoft Project, uses a slightly different format for its A-o-N diagrams as it takes absolute dates rather than relative times for EST and LST. An example of the format is shown in Figure 6.15.

In Figure 6.15 the activity description is given in the top of the box. The right hand side contains the activity number (simply a label) and the activity duration. The left hand side of the box contains the start and the finish times of that activity. In the example, the duration of 7 days does not include weekend working – hence the start on the Wednesday and not finishing until the Thursday of the following week. The calculation is done for you with this package – hence the apparent lack of detail. This presentation does not allow you to see whether there is any float in the activity, though there are other means of doing this, including showing it in the Gantt chart for the project, which will be shown in the following section.

One problem with today's project planning software is that sometimes its level of sophistication can add to the confusion of the project team, not reduce it. One multinational company had teams around the world, each working on their section of the WBS in MS Project. All these plans would then be gathered together in the master programme plan in a different package. It all sounds quite sensible, but because the packages recognised different local holidays and individual planners either accounted for or omitted these local factors, milestones always managed to shift by several days. Because of the complexity of the overall plan, many hours would be required to understand where the errors were and correct them to everyone's satisfaction.

If you are involved in working with multinational teams, it is extremely useful to have a wall planner with all the appropriate national holidays clearly highlighted. The more countries involved, the more pens you're likely to need, but at least you can work around the time when other team members are not available. For instance, it is unwise to try to schedule a key Chinese manufacturing activity over their New Year holiday!

Origin of CPA

The 'invention' of the techniques that have been described here as CPA are variously attributed, depending on the particular book you read. The time of first use, 1957/8, is less debated. The first users/developers are credited as being:

- the Catalytic Construction Company for the planning and control of a construction project for DuPont Corporation;
- DuPont Consulting;
- Kelly of Remington Rand and M. Walker of DuPont.

Whoever instigated its usage, the applications are now far and wide – it is only a shame that unlike products such as the ring-pull on cans, such methods cannot be patented or the intellectual property otherwise secured. Imagine the impact if they were given just 0.1p every time a company had produced a CPA diagram.

Scheduling

Knowing the sequence and duration of activities is a major step. This does not, however, answer the question of 'When will activities need to be carried out?' The schedule provides this. As already shown by the critical path analysis, critical activities have to take place at a particular time or the entire plan will be disrupted. In order for this to happen, the necessary resources need to be in place in time for the critical activity. In an ideal world, this would allow a very simple schedule to be used for critical activities and everything else arranged around these. The reality is far less appealing – people are not available when you need them, resources have a long lead-time and there are likely to be clashes with other project schedules in a multi-project environment. This provides a constraint on the scheduling process, and as a result of trying this, the activities and sequence will often have to be changed. This is where an additional element of complexity enters and makes a mess of your nice plans!

The process of developing the schedule is shown in Figure 6.16.

The arrows for the inputs to the scheduling process are two-way. The network provides the logic for the order in which activities need to be carried out. Having completed this, the input of the time estimates may show that the time that the project requires for completion is longer than is available. This may necessitate a reconsideration of both the network and the time estimates. As was shown in the previous chapter, planning is inevitably an iterative process.

The **resource capability** is the set of tasks that the resources available to the project manager can reasonably undertake. These resources are often referred to as the **resource pool**. For example, where a project is being undertaken by a particular project team, these are the resource pool. If additional staff can be brought in as needed, they should also be considered as part of that pool. This part of the allocation process requires that the project manager has some knowledge of the capabilities and limitations of the resources concerned.

The **resource capacity** depends on the volume of resources available and issues such as the **resource calendar**. For instance, while a machine may be scheduled for utilisation

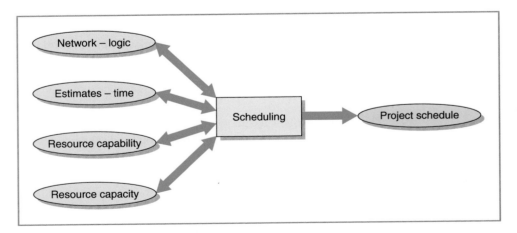

Figure 6.16 Schedule development process

24 hours a day, 7 days a week (with time allowed for maintenance), the same cannot be said of humans. The *calendar* is those times that the resource is available, allowing for all the usual times when no work takes place (e.g. weekends, public holidays, personal holidays, sick leave). This does significantly limit when work can be carried out. Again the process of scheduling is iterative, with the schedule being developed, the resource availability checked and subsequently rescheduled. Where resources are over- or under-loaded, corrections may be made at this point.

This iterative process is often supported for medium and large-scale projects by the use of software – allowing rapid calculation of key project times and evaluation of the impact of difference scenarios. The role of such software is discussed in the following section.

6.3 Using Gantt charts

The purpose of the Gantt chart is to illustrate the relationships between the activities and time as in Figure 6.17. This shows activity A represented by the shaded bar starting at time 1 and finishing at time 3. Multiple activities can be built up on the same chart, using the same timescale.

The following example involves a dissertation planning exercise. The student has a number of options as to how to present the information. The supervisor, being a busy person, has asked for the information to be presented in graphical form. The WBS identifies the activities and the time constraints are imposed by the organisation – the start and end dates. The original statement looked as follows:

Activity	Time
Project start date	2/5
1 Carry out literature review	2/5–20/6
2 Arrange visits	20/6–4/7
3 Prepare questionnaire	4/7–25/7
4 Review questionnaire	25/7–8/8
5 Deliver questionnaire	8/8–26/9
6 Analyse results	26/9–2/11
7 Write up	2/11–9/12
Hand-in date	9/12

The project is not sufficiently complex to warrant a network, so the next step is to present the plan as a Gantt chart. In this case, simply showing a week by a star is possible and requires nothing more than pen and paper, a word processor or spreadsheet, as shown in Figure 6.18.

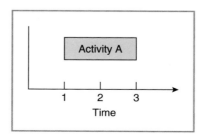

Figure 6.17 Horizontal bar chart: Activity A starts at Time 1 and finishes at Time 3

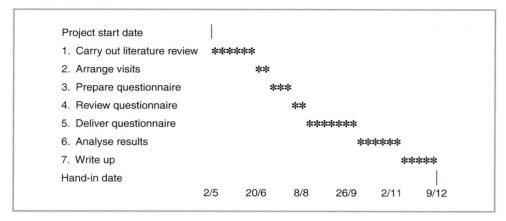

Figure 6.18 Project plan in graphical form

In moving from the WBS to the Gantt chart, there is:

- a level of logic established; and
- conventions used (time goes from left to right, activities are arranged top to bottom in order of their occurrence).

In addition, the student has had to undertake two critical activities:

- **forward schedule** – started the activities at a given date and followed them forwards in time to determine the end date;
- **backward schedule** – looked at the time by which the project needed to be completed and worked the logic of activities backwards.

The tasks have had rough times allocated to see whether they meet the two constraints of start- and end-times. Where there was insufficient time, activities have been shortened. Any excess time (or slack) is used to lengthen activities.

Figure 6.19 shows an alternative presentation to the above. Logical links are indicated by the use of arrows. The head of the arrow points to an activity that cannot proceed until the activity at the tail of the arrow is completed. The diamond shapes on the chart are used to indicate 'milestones', i.e. important points in the life of the project – in this case the start and the hand-in dates.

Such a chart is often referred to as a **Gantt** or **linked-bar chart**, as it is part of a family of techniques developed at the turn of the last century by Henry Gantt. They were originally used in industrial planning. Gantt charts, drawn by hand, are best suited to relatively simple projects, where the number of activities and resources is low, the environment is fairly static and the time periods are relatively long – days and weeks rather than hours.

Their great utility is in their ability to communicate a time plan – they are relatively easy to construct and are readily understood. They do have limitations, however, even when using a computer to generate the charts. Amongst other limitations, the basic charts do not make the link between time and cost and therefore do not provide a method for determining how resources should optimally be allocated, e.g. there are two activities, X and Y, for which the times have been estimated and which use the same resource. If the resource could be shifted from activity X to activity Y, Y could be completed in a shorter time; X would obviously take longer, but how would this affect the project overall? This kind of analysis is at the root of the other techniques covered earlier in this chapter. The one really great weakness of Gantt charts is that there is a tendency for the charts to be perceived as a 'statement of reality' (this task will start on this date and finish on that date)

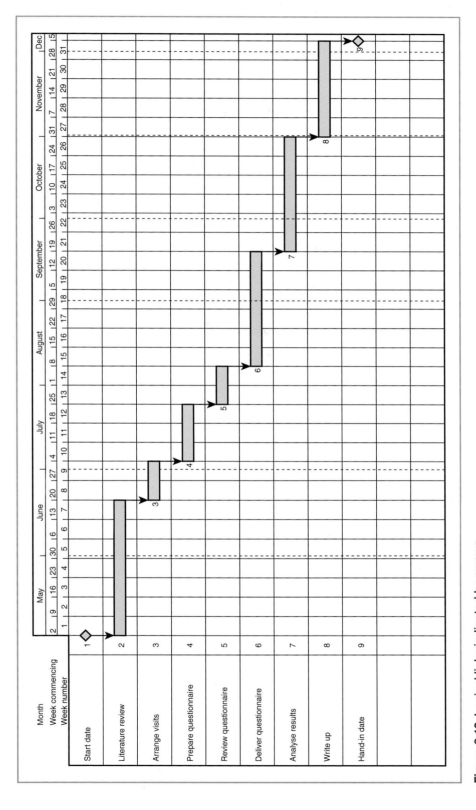

Figure 6.19 Logical links indicated by arrows

rather than a view of 'this is how I would like it to be'. The two are entirely different – one has certainty, the other recognises the fundamental uncertainty that managers in projects have to deal with. In plans prepared using software, the outputs, usually printed in colour, can gain their own legitimacy. Referring back to the start of this chapter, the topic of estimates was discussed. Unless you have substantial data concerning prior projects, these are *guesses*. These provide the inputs to your planning. In IT, the phrase '*Garbage in, Garbage out*' expresses the idea that what you get out is only as good as what you put in. In project planning, there is the danger that we end up with '*Garbage in, Gospel out*', the output being seen in isolation, without concern for the quality of the information that went in to generating it.

Gantt charts – summary

Good points
- simple to draw and read
- good for static environments
- useful for providing overview of project activities
- very widely used
- the basis of the graphical interface for most project planning software.

Limitations
- difficult to update manually where there are many changes – charts can quickly become obsolete and therefore discredited
- does not equate time with cost
- does not help in optimising resource allocation
- can lead to false sense of certainty about the project.

Computer-assisted project planning

At a recent seminar on organisational change, when asked about the biggest influences on the change process, the speaker responded with 'the people who wrote Microsoft Project'. He continued to justify this statement, based on his experience that the first tool that many organisational change planners reached for in such projects was MS Project. This is an interesting phenomenon in itself – how such tools have influenced organisational practices. The experience, though, is not limited to organisational change. In working with many organisations across all sectors, it was notable in the past that when employees request a training course on 'project management', the organisation offers a course for one of the major software packages. More recently, this has been partially replaced by training programmes leading to certification by the professional institutes and PRINCE2.

There are other issues that occur with using software. There is the tendency for the project manager to become not just 'keeper of the charts' but also computer operator. This will often occur in a vain attempt to keep the computer version of the project plan up to date. Many consider the predominance of planning software not to be as helpful to the profession as the vendors of such systems would have us believe. Indeed, as the projects director of a large construction company recently commented, 'I believe that computer-based project management software has set the subject back 20 years.' This presents an interesting paradox – the capability of the packages has never been greater and yet there is a perception amongst some practitioners and academics that this has not been entirely helpful in improving practices. Given the levels of performance of projects reported in earlier chapters, this is not so hard to understand.

Many truly excellent organisations do not use the critical path analysis (CPA) approach to planning projects. One of Hewlett-Packard's UK plants used whiteboards and Post-it notes for project planning at the top level with individual sub-project managers free to use computerised planning software at the task level. This approach is an adaptation of the principle so well demonstrated by Japanese manufacturers in planning and scheduling – that of ensuring **visibility**. To assist in moving towards more visual methods of planning, there are many tools and techniques available to the project manager. Deployment flow charts described in the previous chapter are just one such example, which allow whole processes to be mapped simply. That said, there is significant power in modern planning packages that can be used to some benefit. They have a vital role, particularly where there are large numbers of tasks. Given the discussion of complexity in Chapter 2, it is however interesting to reflect which aspects of complexity are assisted by these planning tools.

Will artificial intelligence prove to be the solution to our planning problems? Academic papers proclaiming this go back to the 1980s, but as yet we have not seen the technology assist as much as we might have expected. It is certainly a hot topic of research in the field, and interest and enthusiasm abound, although there are often complaints that the reality is not living up to early promises[1]. No doubt it makes sense to use data accumulated from previous projects to feed into new plans, and this is an area to keep a watching eye on.

Summary

■ The objectives of the planning process are to optimise the project process and to prevent problems in the process. This is achieved through the systematic evaluation of the project's constituent activities, their duration and logical linkage (sequencing). The use of graphical techniques helps in the presentation of the plan and facilitates its review and revision.

■ Having identified the activities through the WBS, the next step is arranging them in a logical sequence and then estimating their time requirements. Estimates become more uncertain the further ahead in time the situation is being considered, and range from rough (usually least accurate) to to-finish (usually most accurate).

■ The most widely used tools for development of schedules are Gantt charts and network techniques. A Gantt chart is a time-scaled graphical planning tool, which gives a static representation of the relationship between activities and their duration. Network techniques provide a graphical means of expressing more complex projects and include activity-on-node (A-o-N) methods of representation of the verbal statement of activities.

■ The application of these methods must be in line with the objectives for the process and in themselves they have little merit. The first level of analysis that can be applied to the network diagrams is CPA. This allows determination of the path of activities where, if there is any delay, the whole project will be delayed. The critical path should therefore be the initial focus for management attention – for the purposes of both shortening and control.

■ Scheduling is the process that converts the plan into a specific set of dates for individual activities to be started and finished.

Key terms

activity-on-node *p. 150*

critical path *p. 154*

dependency *p. 151*

earliest/latest start times *p. 153*

float *p. 153*

forward/backward schedule *p. 160*

forward/reverse pass *p. 154*

Gantt or linked-bar chart *p. 160*

network *p. 153*

resource capability/pool/capacity/calendar *p. 158*

visibility *p. 163*

Relevant areas of the Bodies of Knowledge

The Bodies of Knowledge (Tables 6.2 and 6.3) are very different in this respect, with the PMI being relatively comprehensive concerning the nature of the processes involved here and the accompanying tools and techniques. It would be possible in either to lose the reason for carrying out the planning process – to enable optimisation of the project processes and the prevention of problems.

Table 6.2 Relevant areas of the APM Body of Knowledge

Relevant section	Title	Summary
4.2.5	Scheduling – critical path	A short section looking at the development of the critical path using a Gantt chart.

Table 6.3 Relevant areas of the PMI Body of Knowledge

Relevant section	Title	Summary
5.4	Create WBS	As the title suggests, the section focuses on the creation of the WBS. However, it is notably different from the APM BoK in that the PBS is not distinguished from the WBS. Indeed, their WBS examples use few verbs.
6	Project schedule management	This is a general description of the planning process within which the topics covered in this chapter of the book sit.
6.1	Plan schedule management	This section discusses how the schedule management is to be done, and how the procedures and associated documentation are to be used to control the schedule.
6.2	Define activities	This process takes in the scope and all the other project information compiled up to that point. This work generates a list of activities, their attributes, and the key milestones. The project management plan is correspondingly updated.

Table 6.3 continued

Relevant section	Title	Summary
6.3	Sequence activities	In this chapter we have covered what is described in this section of the Guide in identifying the sequence or precedence of the tasks identified in the WBS (e.g. finish to start).
6.4	Estimate activity durations	Techniques identified for estimating include *expert judgement*, *analogous* estimating (based on historical data from similar work) *parametric* (quantitatively based) estimating, and *three-point* (most likely, optimistic, and pessimistic) estimating.
6.5	Develop schedule	This looks at developing a detailed schedule based on A-o-N techniques to identify the critical path, and also Monte-Carlo simulation techniques and the use of Agile release planning.

PROJECT MANAGEMENT IN PRACTICE
The Balti Experience

In new product development, time to market can be a key determinant of the success of a product. In the packaged food business, this is especially true, as in excess of 95 per cent of new products last less than 6 months. In this case, the firm concerned were not just launching a new product but a new range of products, to meet Europe's burgeoning appetite for Indian Balti-style ready meals. These were intended as a replacement range for another that had become increasingly difficult to source the materials for, and to meet with environmental requirements of the packaging. Strategically, this was a major change for the company, and required significant investment. The idea had been approved by the board and the firm was now in the phase of detailed planning. The project manager was now tasked by the board with the preparation of plans that would allow them to schedule the launch.

The first step was to prepare a work breakdown structure. The main activities and their sequence were identified, and their durations estimated in weeks. The resulting network is shown in Figure 6.20.

The project manager is now ready to present the plan back to the board. She is determined to make a good impression and have answers to their questions.

Points for discussion

1 What is the project duration and what is the critical path?

2 The board were hoping to launch the new range in the next 9 months. From your analysis, could this be achieved? If so, how?

3 Where would you suggest that gates are put in this process?

→

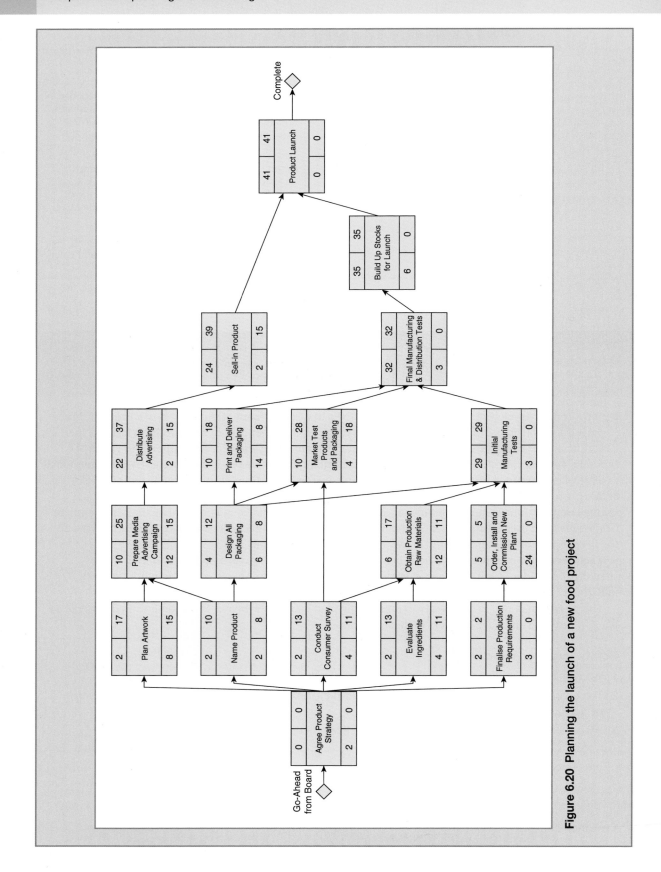

Figure 6.20 Planning the launch of a new food project

PROJECT MANAGEMENT IN PRACTICE
The mobile phone development

The challenge of new product development

A mobile phone company has just promoted a project manager to head up a new product development project.

Developing a mobile phone is a challenging project. Time-to-market is short, the product is technically complicated and there are multiple stakeholders within the phone company. Marketing have strong ideas about new product design, and they have some initial specifications based on their market research. The project is likely to be signed off very shortly, and the finance department are insisting that to be profitable it has to be delivered very quickly, although development funds are tight.

The design team consists of electronics engineers to design the circuitry, software engineers to develop the functionality, interface and features that the customers see, and mechanical engineers to create the unit itself. Additionally, manufacturing engineers need to be involved as soon as possible to ensure that the design is going to be suitable for high-volume manufacture.

Suppliers need to be on board quickly so that they can ensure availability of material when volume production starts. Lead times for some parts can be several months, but often there are design changes throughout the project as the detailed design stabilises. You know there will be technical difficulties with the design, and several prototypes need to be planned in so that the phone can be tested during the design phase.

You have been asked to advise and help the new project manager on the best way of planning this project, and what factors need to be taken into consideration.

Points for discussion

1 Use the work covered in Chapters 4 and 5 to provide an analysis of the stakeholders and the project strategy.

2 Given your answer to (1), how would this affect the nature of the overview plan that should be presented?

3 What are your recommendations to the project manager to ensure that the project is completed as required?

Topics for discussion

1 You have been put in charge of organising a group trip to visit a company in Japan which has expertise that you and your group are interested in finding out more about. Identify the constituent activities, their sequence and estimate the times that each of the activities will take. Show how you have used forward and backward scheduling to achieve this. Display your plan using a bar chart or similar method.

2 Discuss why graphical techniques for displaying plans are superior to verbal statements.

3 Describe what is meant by 'precedence' and illustrate your answer with an appropriate example.

4 Show the dissertation case example (Figure 6.18) as an activity-on-node diagram.

5 Show the information given in Table 6.4 about a project activity as an activity-on-node diagram.

(a) From your diagram identify the total project duration.

(b) Show which activities you feel could be run alongside others (in parallel, rather than sequentially). Redraw the network diagram and calculate the new project duration and the critical path.

(c) What further benefits may arise from using parallel activities, rather than sequential?

(d) Assuming that the completion time is critical, identify which activities you would suggest should be the focus for management attention.

Table 6.4 Project activities, precedence and duration

Activity	Description	Duration (weeks)	Preceding activity
A	Select software	4	–
B	Select hardware	3	A
C	Install hardware	6	B
D	Install software	2	C
E	Test software	3	D
F	Train staff	5	E
G	System run-up	1	F

Table 6.5 Project activities, precedence and duration

Activity	Description	Duration (weeks)	Preceding activity
A	Design course overview and publicity	4	–
B	Identify potential staff to teach on course	2	–
C	Construct detailed syllabus	6	–
D	Send out publicity and application forms	10	A
E	Confirm staff availability	2	B
F	Select staff to teach on course	1	C, E
G	Acknowledge student applications	3	D
H	Identify course written material	2	F
J	Preparation of teaching material	20	G, H
K	Prepare room for the course	1	G

6 Table 6.5 considers the development of a short course in project management. From the information, construct the network diagram.

(a) Determine the ESTs, the LSTs, the project duration and the critical path activities.

(b) Show the slack for each activity.

(c) What further factors should be considered in order to give a better view of the realistic timescale for the organisation of the course?

7 Why might the critical path change during a project? What happens if it does?

8 What aspects of complexity are assisted by the use of computer-aided project planning and which are not?

9 Using MS Project software, prepare a Gantt chart and critical path network for the example projects in Tables 6.4 and 6.5.

10 What are the benefits and limitations of using software to help with presenting plans?

Further information

Badiru, A.B. (1993) *Quantitative Models for Project Planning, Scheduling and Control*, Quorum, London.

Besner C. and Hobbs B. (2012) 'An Empirical Identification of Project Management Toolsets and a Comparison Among Project Types', *Project Management Journal*, Vol. 43, No.5, pp.24–46.

Davenport T.H. and Ronanki R. (2018) 'Artificial Intelligence for the Real World', *Harvard Business Review*, Vol. 96, No. 1, pp. 108–116.

Lock, D. (2013) *Project Management*, 10th edition, Gower, Aldershot.

Lockyer, K. and Gordon, J. (1991) *Critical Path Analysis and Other Project Network Techniques*, 5th edition, Financial Times Pitman Publishing, London.

Reiss, G. (2007) *Project Management Demystified: Today's Tools and Techniques*, 3rd edition, Taylor & Francis, London.

Sapolsky, H.M. (1972) *The Polaris System Development: Bureaucratic and Programmatic Success in Government*, Harvard University Press, Cambridge, MA.

Websites

www.extremeplanner.com

www.microsoft.com – for Microsoft Project and enterprise.

www.primavera.com – Primavera is used by many organisations that run large-scale engineering projects.

www.elecosoft.com – Powerproject and other software tools.

sourceforge.net/projects/openworkbench/ – open source planning and scheduling package.

Reference

1   'An understanding of AI's limitations is starting to sink in', *The Economist*, Technology Quarterly, 11 June 2020.

7

Making time planning robust: Advanced Project Thinking (APT)

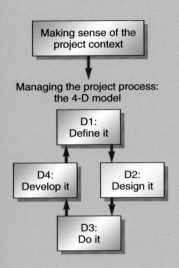

Making sense of the project context

Managing the project process: the 4-D model

D1: Define it

D4: Develop it

D2: Design it

D3: Do it

'Why should there be need for other methods for Project Management to replace or maybe enhance CPM/PERT?[1] *Self-evidently, CPM/PERT frequently does not work.*'[2] *'The best-laid schemes o' mice an' men Gang aft agley; An' lea'e us nought but grief an' pain, For promis'd joy.*'[3]

Principles

1   If you plan using the critical path time, your project is likely to be late.
2   The understanding of constraints in a project is vital to progressing project work effectively.
3   The APT approach works with the constraints to provide a more robust method for planning and controlling projects.

Learning objectives

By the time you have completed this chapter, you should be able to:

→   recognise the limitations of the traditional approaches to planning projects

→   identify the constraints in a project

→   describe the principles of the APT approach.

Contents

Introduction   *171*
7.1 Limitations of current approaches to project planning   *172*
7.2 Managing by constraints in projects   *177*
7.3 Using the APT approach   *183*
Summary   *186*
Key terms   *187*
Relevant areas of the Bodies of Knowledge   *187*
Project management in practice: *A major road project delivered early – success with APT*   *187*
Topics for discussion   *193*
Further information   *193*
References   *194*

A project, delivered early, under budget and with a customer praising the quality of the work? In the construction sector? You sure?

This was the reaction to the news that the new waste-water recycling plant for South West Water had achieved not only success

Source: Tom Meaker/iStock/Getty Images Plus

for the client, but also made 'good business' for the main contractors involved, Tilbury Douglas, OTVB and PFW. The key difference from previous projects that the contractors had been involved in was the use of **critical chain** methods. Moreover, the project didn't end with all the parties trooping off to court to sue each other over claims and counter-claims concerning the work that they carried out.

The implementation of the methods began with a one-day seminar on the methods with key players from each of the contractors attending. When plans were prepared, the principles of critical chain were applied and the accompanying methods of operation reviewed at a further 2.5-day workshop.

Once the project actually started, the implementation was not without its challenges. These occurred when a major sub-contractor who was to provide the highly specialised concrete water tanks went into liquidation just before they were scheduled to carry out their part of the project. Yet despite this, the critical activities went unchanged for the 18 months of the work.

Introduction

Given the level of project failures identified in various studies, the need to find the causes and provide solutions has significant economic importance.[4] Chapter 3 identified some of the strategy-related problem areas. In this chapter, some of the operational problems associated with the current systems for planning and controlling time in projects are identified.

In developing solutions to these problems, we have combined the techniques learned in Chapter 3, with those of the theory of constraints (TOC)[5] and *Lean* management. Both TOC and lean have provided significant performance enhancement over traditional approaches in repetitive operations, and there is growing evidence that the application of principles from these two approaches can yield benefit in project management. Indeed, the case at the start of this chapter illustrates what can happen when the traditional approaches to planning are challenged and a different view of managing time in projects is considered. We begin with the application of TOC to projects, known as the Critical Chain approach. This has been augmented with some of the tools of lean management to deliver the approach we have termed '*advanced project thinking*'. The case study at the end of the chapter provides evidence of the efficacy of APT for the organisation concerned.

To determine whether a different approach is needed, the first step is to identify the problems that individuals and organisations are facing. Following this, the background to TOC and lean is explored, and then their application in the project environment.

7.1 Limitations of current approaches to project planning

The effects

Projects that run late, overbudget or fail to meet key needs of their stakeholders cause considerable problems for businesses, governments and individuals. A basic analysis suggests that either the methods being used for project management, their application, or both must be at fault. In Chapter 3 the problems of what Deming termed 'the system' were considered, and it was demonstrated how many organisations have started to come to terms with these problems through a new approach to strategy. This has the potential to remove one group of problems. It is not sufficient on its own, however, to change project performance radically. That is because the operational problems will inevitably remain where conventional techniques are used.

The causes

Operational problems arise due to two main causes. The first is natural variability where tasks take longer on some occasions than at other times. We shall explore this variability further later in this chapter. The second is the impact of behaviours on the task times, both in planning and execution. As a result, the CPA approach alone is not sufficiently **robust**. Variability results in **emergent complexity** and Chapter 10 considers how this can be included in planning, by including ranges of estimates rather than single figures for the time of each activity. This complements what is being proposed here.

Chapter 6 presented some detailed planning techniques for time – in particular the basics of the critical path method (CPM). Having spent some time getting to grips with these techniques, you now encounter a chapter that states that these techniques do not work (opening quotation). The obvious question arises as to why these were covered at all in the first place. There are two reasons:

- in order to understand the shortcomings of the techniques and search for potential solutions, you must first understand the techniques themselves;
- the logical organisation of tasks and understanding where they occur relative to each other in time, is the same starting point for this approach.

In addition, the statement that 'the techniques of CPM and PERT do not work' requires some justification. Seven issues are identified which demonstrate the problems associated with the CPM approach to planning and controlling. These are:

1 Estimates and reality for activity times: all goals are based on estimates which attempt to provide a model, i.e. a representation of the project. How well does this model reflect the reality of what will happen when the project starts for real?
2 The difference between task and activity times: estimates of activity times often include a large safety margin but this does not help the project in achieving on-time completion.
3 Everything runs to latest start: for critical path activities, this is inevitable as the EST and LSTs are the same for these activities. However, for *non-critical* activities, running to the LST adds to the risk of the whole project running late.
4 Fixed dates: because of this method of scheduling activities, the situation arises where '. . . a delay in one step is passed on in full to the next step. An advance in one step is usually wasted.'[6]

5 The way that we measure progress is in error: generally by the time a project manager is notified of a problem it is already too late to prevent it having an impact.

6 **Student syndrome**: an individual or team don't start an activity until the latest possible time.

7 It is usual in business projects for people to have to multi-task. The effect of this is to increase the lead-time for all the projects.

1 Estimates and reality

Some projects benefit from significant data as to how long each project task will take. Others have to rely on estimates, some on nothing more than pure guesses. Estimates and guesses become the basis for plans and these plans form the basis of the business models for our projects. Yet, when reviewing what actually happened compared to those plans, we find that the assumptions of estimates do not always hold. Notable is the myth of the Gaussian distribution in planning. Activities will have a most likely time and this can be taken as the 'estimated time'. On some occasions, the task will finish early, on others, late. This is the planning assumption. The reality is that activities will sometimes run to time, often late, but almost never early.

Figure 7.1 shows the difference between the planning assumption (an activity has as much chance of finishing early as late) and the reality (on time is as good as it gets). This is worth exploring because it is an unintended consequence of the traditional approaches to managing projects. Consider that in an office environment, one member of the team does finish a task early – say in three days instead of the five that she had planned. We find in practice that in such situations, people rarely hand over their completed work to the next stage. If we investigate further, we see that the reasons are behavioural and that they are discouraged from handing it over to the next activity because:

● they have the opportunity in the remaining two days to 'polish the product' – to make it even better and to be seen to have produced good work;

● they do not want to give the boss an excuse to give them more work to do – in many environments people who do deliver early are 'rewarded' with extra work; we find that over time, they do learn;

● they provided the estimate and do not want to be seen to have overestimated the task time;

● they know that this shorter time will become the 'expected time' for the activity and do not want to have their own margin of safety reduced in future, which might thereby compromise their own perceived performance.

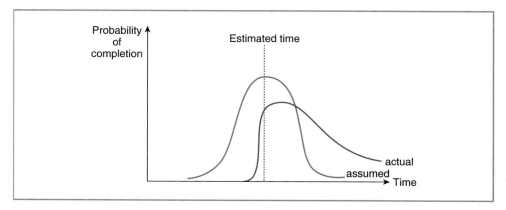

Figure 7.1 Activity completion profiles – assumed and actual

This is a great example of how natural variability (the task finished early) combine with behaviours (I won't hand this work over until the deadline) impact projects operationally and how measures and incentives do not necessarily mean that the behaviours exhibited are beneficial to the project. If they were, any early finish benefits would be passed on in full, and the subsequent task would start immediately. This should contribute to making up for the times when the task, through natural variability, does run late.

2 The difference between task and elapsed times

Ask for a time estimate and it is normal for this to include not just the task (or **takt**) time but other factors that make up the difference between task and **elapsed** time. Figure 7.2 shows some of the other factors that go into making up this difference. If in any doubt about this, consider how long a 3000-word assignment would take to write. Having asked this of many students, the mean time we have been given is around 3 working days. However, while this is the task time, the elapsed time (between being given the work and its submission) is often much longer. Figure 7.2 shows the components of a typical time estimate. The relative proportions of the elapsed time taken by each of these will vary considerably. For instance, in working with a law firm, the takt time for the task being undertaken by one of the partners was two hours compared to an elapsed time of six weeks and this is not the worst example of time lost.

The takt time can be a small part of the overall elapsed time for tasks in a project. The allowances for interruptions (unplanned but known work) such as being called to meetings at short notice, and for other work (just answering emails can take a good part of each day for many people) and the differences become understandable. Given the opportunity, many people will also add a safety margin 'just to be sure' in case anything untoward happens. These give a certain 'comfort' that someone is not going to be shown to be underperforming due to missing deadlines. It is not unusual however, to see safety margins added at many levels in the WBS – at the task level by those carrying out the tasks, and at each level above. As we will see, this not only increases the time (and thereby costs) for projects, it is also unlikely to help the project be delivered on time. Indeed, the presence of such safety can have the opposite effect.

3 Everything runs to latest start

As shown in Chapter 6, where the LST and EST are the same, there is no float and these activities are termed critical – any delay in any one of them will delay the entire project. In practice, it is often seen that business pressures mean that what appear to be non-critical tasks are also pushed to start at their LSTs and in doing so, these activities too become critical.

This is undesirable because the greater the number of critical paths in a project, the greater the chance of failing to meet time goals. Furthermore, one of the benefits of

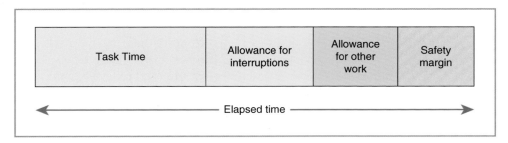

Figure 7.2 Components of a time estimate

knowing the critical path is that a project manager or their controls team can give greater attention to the progress of these most important tasks and less to non-critical ones.

To illustrate the first of these reasons, if one critical path has a 70 per cent chance of being completed within a certain time, adding a parallel critical path with the same chance of completion in that time, means that the project cannot be completed until both paths are complete. The chance of the project now being completed in that time is 49 per cent (70 per cent $\times$ 70 per cent). Add more paths or less certainty of completion by any path, and the numbers get worse.

4 Fixed dates

If we can persuade people to release work as soon as it is completed, then it is possible to start the next task and so gain that early finish benefit. However, there are all sorts of rules and 'established practices' that prevent this from happening, most notably fixing all the dates in the schedule. The reasons for this could be contractual. For instance, in the construction sector, many sub-contracts for tasks will start on a Monday. This is regardless of whether the preceding tasks finished on the previous Monday or Friday. It could also simply be that unless there is an incentive for that next activity to start, it will be ignored. The converse though does not apply and hence the idea that 'early finish benefits are often wasted, whist delays are passed on in full to the next activity'. Worse still, where there are parallel activities, regardless of an early finish in one of the paths, the *biggest* delay is passed on to the subsequent activities.

The alternative is to approach scheduling more like a *relay race*, where the project, like the baton in the race, is passed on not at a fixed time, but at the earliest possible time following the completion of a task.

5 Measuring progress in error

It has been said that 'a project will spend 90 per cent of its time 90 per cent complete'. This is because (as we will discuss further in Chapter 13) ask someone working on a task how their work is going, and it is frequently heard that 'we are 90 per cent complete.' It is possible to ignore problems when measures indicate that progress is satisfactory, particularly those that rely on estimates of per cent complete.

The problems that we see regularly happening are the effects of one single root cause: projects contain fundamental **uncertainties** – particularly in as . . . but . . . s and first-timer projects, but also in some painting by numbers projects. These may be related to the process (how will we deliver this?) or the outcome (what is it that we need to achieve?). The challenge is that in many cases 'we don't know what we will find until we get there'. This applies to technological developments, groundworks (e.g. putting in foundations) on construction sites or even writing books (allegedly).

6 Student syndrome

Student syndrome is where despite having some float in a task, a team or individual chooses not to start it until the LST. At this point, the effect is the same as for point 3 – that task and whatever follows it, becomes critical. The difference from point 3 is that where that has been a deliberate strategy, this has a behavioural cause.

This is an unfair term for some students, who conscientiously start work ahead of time, and work it through to completion with time to spare before a deadline. However, there are others for whom 'last minute' or 11th hour is the only time to start a piece of work. It is by no means limited to students either (we won't share our own or colleagues' scheduling misdemeanours at this point, but many are guilty of this).

7 Multi-tasking

Dr Eli Goldratt,[7] the originator of the critical chain concept, demonstrates this phenomenon in the following example. Imagine that you have three tasks to work on – A, B and C. Each is going to take 10 days for you to do your part of the work. If you do them in sequence, the lead-time (start to finish) is shown in Figure 7.3.

This is simple enough. In the scenario described above, subsequently each of these tasks was being broken down into two smaller units. Let us see the effect of breaking each project in two, doing half of each then returning to finish the remainder, in Figure 7.4.

The immediate effect is to make tasks take considerably longer than they need to. In the case of one new product development team, one can only imagine the effects of having an average of 12 projects per person ongoing at any one time. The reality is, therefore, worse than in the simple example given above as the simple model includes the assumption that people can put down and pick up a project without any loss of time. Where such multi-tasking was evident in a software company (see VCS case, Chapter 16), programmers would regularly lose 1–2 days of work when transferring between tasks. This was caused

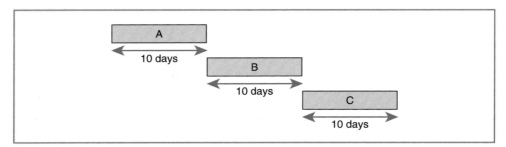

Figure 7.3 Activities completed in strict sequence

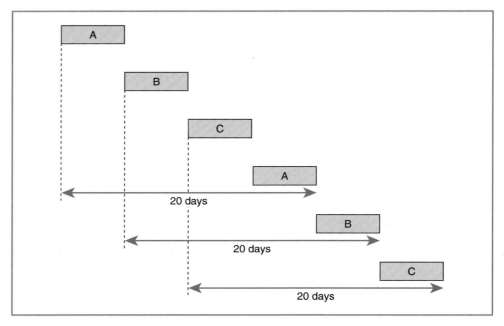

Figure 7.4 The effects of multi-tasking

by the need for refamiliarising themselves with the logic of the task that they were undertaking. These days were lost to the critical path of the project and this occurred on a regular basis, each time incurring the loss. This is waste and its elimination is the focus of the work we will overview on lean.

Multitasking is not only inefficient, it is also not how our brains are wired[8]. Every time we switch from one task to another, there is a cost in terms of brain capacity used up in switching. *In extremis*, it causes stress. Worse, it is addictive. Much productive time is lost by perpetually jumping from one task to another and while it is done in the name of being 'efficient', paradoxically it isn't.

There are, of course, some projects where there are delays in getting information or results, where some multi-tasking is inevitable. For instance, in the lighting industry, fluorescent lamps are typically guaranteed for 10,000 hours of operation. In one year there are 8760 hours, meaning that life-testing takes in excess of a year, with no realistic means to accelerate such tests. It would be pointless waiting for test results to come through before starting on other work – the development team have to move on to other projects.

The above requires us to take account of human behavioural actions in planning and estimating, and to find ways to either amend the behaviour or mitigate its effects. Some further explanation of the problems of estimating are initially discussed, followed by an elaboration of the remaining points raised above.

Further problems with estimates

The reliability of 'estimates' has already been questioned in this chapter, and yet despite such warnings, it is notable how major decisions are made on a less than sound basis. In practice, we also note:

- inappropriate use of estimates – people being asked for rough estimates as to how long a particular activity will take, only to find that this becomes the target time enshrined in a committed plan;
- inappropriate data used to build estimates – people either taking unrepresentative previous experience or not checking whether this was in fact a good representation of the reality of carrying out the task (it is not unusual for such situations to exist for many years where there is a lack of review);
- the estimates are used out of context – having given an estimate of time required to do some work, this is then used despite significant changes having been made to where and how the work is to be carried out.

As commented in the previous chapter, in the absence of good data, estimates are a guess as to how long a task will take. They should not then be imbued with more certainty than they deserve!

The above discussion provides some clues as to why such high proportions of projects are late due to variability and behaviours at the operational level. The challenge now is to analyse these and determine whether there are alternative methods that may have a better chance of success.

7.2   Managing by constraints in projects

The **theory of constraints (TOC)** was the result of the application of a structured logic approach to the problems of a manufacturing environment. Specifically, it targeted the way in which production lines were scheduled and the flow of goods along the line was managed. It worked by focusing on the *constraint* (also termed the **bottleneck**). This is the slowest part in a sequence of activities, and is the one that determines how quickly work can pass through that system. In a production line, the bottleneck can usually be identified by the pile of inventory waiting to be processed by that part of the process. The constraint is important because it determines the ability of the system to process work, which we call **throughput**. It is this idea of focusing on the flow of work that will be carried forward to the next section to examine the potential application in projects.

Before considering whether such an approach will yield benefits, some understanding of the principles of its application is necessary. The five steps of the TOC approach, as set out in the *The Goal*[9] are as follows:

1 Identify the constraint.
2 Exploit the system constraint.
3 Subordinate everything else to the constraint.
4 Elevate the constraint.
5 Go back and find new constraints, repeating the process.

In a production situation, identifying the constraint provided an immediate benefit. New manufacturing technology requires significant investment, and there is no point in adding this to a part of the system that is not a constraint. The focus on the constraint provided an alternative to the conventions of line balancing. Many firms applied the principles to a range of scenarios, with apparent benefit. So did it work? There were many successful applications, but many where no improvements were gained. This does provide a warning against an uncritical approach to the application in project management, but there are as many lessons for implementation of such changes, as for the changes themselves.[10]

Application of TOC to project management

The situation of manufacturing scheduling at the time of publication of *The Goal* has a number of similarities with project management today. First, there was the tendency to try to solve all perceived practitioner problems using increasingly complex mathematics. This led to the promotion of MRPII[11] (manufacturing resource planning – a resource planning and scheduling tool) in manufacturing, and ever more complex planning and scheduling software for project managers. Second, manufacturing was a subject that was unfashionable and rooted in a reactive rather than a strategic mode. The success of the first of these was undoubtedly limited, and to a great extent the problems were removed through the application of TOC and *Just In Time* manufacturing. The second of these was tackled by the creation of a set of strategic frameworks for manufacturing, which would bring the discussion to the boardroom. In project management, journal articles regularly promote one or other new algorithm or method for planning, but without any real attempt to solve the root causes of the problems that project managers face. These are enshrined in the popular software packages that have become the focus of so much project management activity.

The five focusing steps applied to projects are as follows.

Step 1: Identify the constraint

In a project system, the constraint is whatever determines the project duration, in other words, what is stopping the project being carried out faster? This can be:

● the critical path of the project;
● the availability of resources;

- dates that are fixed into the schedule and cannot be moved;
- behaviours, policies or rules.

One of the particular challenges for projects is that 'the constraint' will probably be different things at different times during the project. Indeed, it would be appropriate here to use the phrase 'identify the constraints' to reflect this.

The critical path

The critical path was identified in the previous chapter as the most basic determinant of project duration. It is:

The longest series of dependent activities in a project.

The availability of resources

In reality, this is only the starting point for the calculation of project duration. Considering the project as a system of constraints, further constraints are added when resources are added to the discussion. Consider the following example.

Example

A marketing firm has two main teams, A and B, to carry out different parts of their projects. The firm has two projects to plan, each having a number of activities that need to be undertaken. In this case, two activities simultaneously need the same resource – Team B in weeks 14–16, as shown in Figure 7.5. This is a **resource contention/conflict**. There is a further resource contention with Team A during week 18.

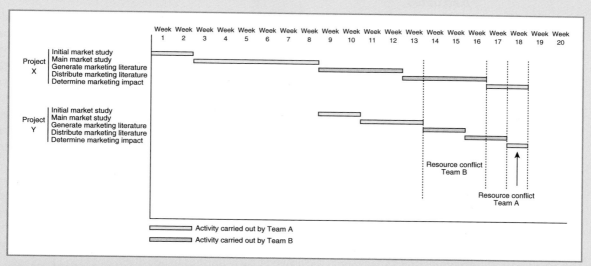

Figure 7.5 Resource contention

Removing the resource contention requires initially that the choice be made as to which of the projects has priority over Team B. Taking Project X as the priority, Figure 7.6 shows the effect of removing that resource contention. The impact is to make Project Y finish later, at the end of week 21 rather than the end of week 18.

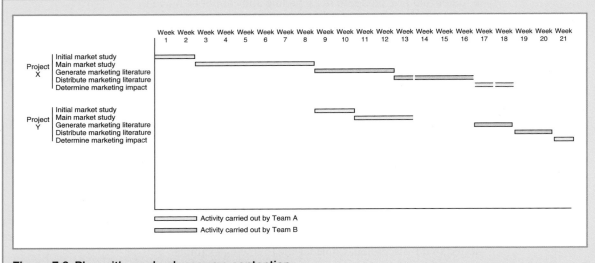

Figure 7.6 Plan with resolved resource contention

Removing the resource contention now causes delay itself – in this case 3 weeks. This kind of situation is clearly made more complicated the more projects and the more interdependencies there are between activities. This is the reality of the modern project environment, though – projects are rarely carried out in isolation and a stakeholder group for projects should now be identified as 'other projects which will share the same resources'.

Fixed dates

After determining the constraint of resource availability, the next constraint to be considered are any fixed dates in the schedule. For instance, during a large IT project, each phase had to be signed off by the company board before progressing to the next phase. Given that board meetings were only every 2 months, this meant that a delay of one day to hit a phase deadline prior to a board meeting would result in the project being suspended for 2 months. Similarly, a large construction project required the installation of a large lift. The arrangements for getting the lift delivered involved the police closing local roads, the presence of large cranes and key installation staff, and the site being clear of other construction workers at that time. This resulted in the date for the installation having to be fixed significantly in advance and not being movable – hence being a constraint.

Many projects run entirely on scheduled dates with every activity fixed in advance. The effect of this is that every activity becomes a constraint. This is not a happy situation and the result is often significant lateness in many activities and poor performance of the project overall. Despite this, many organisations still seem deeply committed to the system of scheduling everything by fixed dates. It merely compounds the problem of delays accumulating and prevents the usage of early finishes in activities.

Behaviours, policies, rules

The last and most general type of constraints are those that are imposed by the organisation and individuals, as rules or 'custom and practice'. For instance, one contracts manager noted that in 800 contracts that he had let, every single one started on a Monday. Starting every activity on the next available Monday may sound convenient, but what are the chances that the preceding activities will all finish on the Friday before? The result is that this 'rule' would cost delays due to the gaps between one activity finishing and another starting. A further example of a rule or process-based constraint is that one activity may have to be finished in its entirety before the next can start, preventing overlap between activities.

These will change through the life of the project, but as the examples will show, projects often take significantly longer than they need because of the failure to consider the impact of one or other of these constraints on the project.

Step 2: Exploit the constraint

'The most important thing is to keep the most important thing the most important thing'[12]

The most important thing in the project plan is the constraints. Having identified these, exploiting means removing anything that prevents a constraint performing to its maximum potential.

> ### How could that be important?
> In the last phase of a road-building project, final surfacing was identified as a critical activity and the machine that could do this as a constraining resource. In other words, any delay to the work that this machine carried out delayed the project, which would cause significant additional costs.
>   In this case (and we will revisit this subsequently), this became the constraint – the most important thing during that phase of the project. Whatever else happened on the site, it was imperative that the machine was kept running doing its surfacing work. This had implications for the way that the site was run, as we shall see in subsequent steps.

Step 3: Subordinate everything to the constraint

A project was being held up as a great success before it was finished. The project manager had managed to achieve a very high rate of 98 per cent completion of activities to schedule. However, the project finished late and was shown to have lost money for the firm that carried it out. How could this be? The reason is that the 2 per cent of tasks that finished late were critical tasks, but the measurement system focused attention on the 'less important' things – activities that were non-critical. Hence, the next step is *subordination* – make the constraint the focus for our measurement and control. **Any delay to the constraint is a delay to the entire project.**

Where the constraint is a resource, it needs to be kept as the most important thing. For instance, a firm that analysed their processes found that a particular designer was the constraint for many projects – all projects required at least some work to be undertaken by him. In order to make sure that he was best used, it was imperative that work was ready for him and that he was not kept waiting or disturbed during this work. Another firm highlighted critical resources or people performing critical tasks by placing a bright orange beach ball on the desk of that person. This seemingly ludicrous practice made the tasks highly visible, and indicated that that person must not be interrupted until the task was complete. It sounds extreme, but at least no one was in any doubt as to what was going on.

> ### Back on the road . . .
> The surfacing machine would frequently break down. On one occasion it was seen to be sitting idle awaiting the attention of the site maintenance person. He was on another part of the site doing repairs on a digger – a resource that was definitely not a constraint. Every hour that the surfacing machine was idle was delaying the project by an hour. At an average day labour and equipment rate for the site of £5500 plus £3000 per day penalties if the project ran late, this meant that one hour of delay was worth over £1000.

Step 4: Elevate the constraint

Elevating the constraint means increasing the flow through that part of the system – removing it as a constraint. In the two examples given above, the road surfacer and the designer need to have their work capacities increased if the system is required to work any faster – either through working longer or through adding extra help to them (e.g. adding another active machine or designer). In the case of the road surfacer, the project manager decided to have another machine available on site on stand-by, should the first break down. Repairing the first while work was able to continue with the second elevated the constraint, and the cost overall for the rental of the machine was shown to be considerably less than the potential delays the previous approach was causing.

Step 5: Go back to step 1

In a repetitive operation, the last step is to go back and find the new system constraint, which will probably now be elsewhere in the system. In projects, the constraint changes routinely as the project progresses through activities but will always be identifiable as a logic path, a resource, a date or a rule. In practice this means that a project manager will need to check progress and recognise where constraints change. This will require the way that activities and resources are treated to be adapted accordingly.

The application of the five focusing steps to projects is summarised in Figure 7.7.

There is much to assist in managing throughput by focusing on the constraints and in the following section, further refinements are made to improve the robustness of plans.

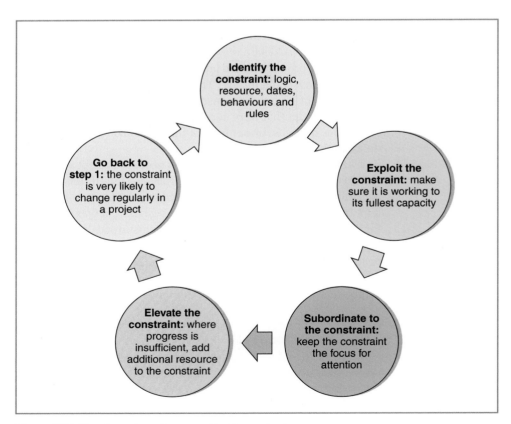

Figure 7.7 Five focusing steps applied to projects

Are there any differences in the planning process under APT? We normally see the application starting once a project has been evaluated and some preliminary estimates for time and cost have been prepared.

1 Evaluate the potential costs / benefits of a late / early finish.
2 Plan in detail ensuring that the logic of the activities is properly established.
3 Review the estimates provided for the durations of each activity, noting the behaviours associated with each and the differences between the takt and elapsed times.
4 Time saved from the review should be taken from individual tasks and used to provide a buffer or series of buffers.

1 Evaluate the potential costs / benefits of a late / early finish

This is carried out to provide the business reason for such an approach to be used. The full consequences of a late finish should be properly evaluated in financial terms, along with any upside benefits from an early finish. It is often not a simple process, as the boxes below show.

More construction

A project to refurbish bridges over a stretch of motorway was being planned. It had been allowed a 4-week duration and the client had required that the project finish on the last working day before the Christmas break. This gave the team planning the project very little time to do any pre-preparation or any of the normal surveying work before the project started. It was handed to the project manager as a 'Just Do It' project. The project was costing the client £300 000 and the industry norm for the profit to be made on it was in the region of 6 per cent. The potential profit was therefore £18 000, provided it was completed on time. If it was not, the penalty clauses in the contract specified £3000 per day to be paid to the client. In addition, the costs of keeping the site going were £3000 per day. This was not unusual, but the Christmas break (the industry closes down for 2 weeks) meant that if the project was running even 24 hours behind schedule the losses would be a minimum of 14 days of penalty clauses (14 × £3000) plus the additional site days. This represented a minimum loss of £42 000, and the chances of running late were substantial. This more than outweighed the potential profit on the project. There was a pressing need to do something different in the management of this project to ensure that it would be completed on time.[13]

A leisurely finish is not always bad. . .

This does prove that there is not always a penalty for a late finish. A leisure centre was being constructed for a district council and was completed 2 months late. The council incurred the displeasure of the voters of the region and wanted some redress from the contractors. The problem was determining the extent of the loss that the council had suffered as a result of the lateness. Leisure centres usually require a substantial ongoing subsidy from local government to remain viable. The late opening meant that the council had not had to start paying the subsidy, so the late opening had in fact saved them a considerable sum of money. They lost the claim for compensation.

Determining these costs provides the justification for the additional work that follows in the planning stage – and there is extra work to be done.

2 Plan in detail ensuring that the logic of the activities is properly established

A significant challenge for many projects is gaining a detailed plan down to a level of detail that makes the analysis that follows meaningful, and there is frequently resistance from those doing the work to such planning. This is understandable for instance in a change project, where the exact order of what will happen can only be established as the project progresses. In technology projects, notably IT, less so. Indeed, it is frequently seen that major projects progress without this detail being understood.

Such detail is part of the **Front End Loading** that has been associated with higher levels of project delivery. The lack of detail at this stage is a significant cause of ambiguity or uncertainty, and itself causes complexity. For instance, without the detailed plan, there can be a lack of common understanding of what needs to be done and by whom to achieve a particular task. However, this is not universally accepted as necessary, and particularly by the proponents of agile planning methodologies.

3 Review the estimates provided for the durations of each activity

Estimating

Estimates (both initial and to-finish) should ideally be based on the activity times only, with no **safety** added. The components of an activity time were shown in Figure 7.2. Estimates can be given as a single point, as a range and or a point with a certainty. For instance, how long to finish this task could be expressed as:

- 12 days (single point)
- From 8–16 days (range)
- A P50 of 11 days (number with a probability – in this case 50 per cent).

We find here a behavioural constraint – that people will want to have longer to do a task, and so will provide an estimate with more like an 80 per cent chance that they can complete the task in the promised time.

Where these longer times are given, and with the impact of student syndrome and **Parkinson's law**,[14] the tasks will take the 80 per cent time or even longer.

In order to change this behaviour, it is possible to plan using the P50 – where there is a 50 per cent probability of a task finishing early and 50 per cent chance of it finishing late. The difference between the 50 per cent and the 80 per cent times, are added to your project **buffer** (see below). In addition, a better understanding of the takt and elapsed times can show opportunities for removing time – particularly if the activities are on a critical path.

This relies on a number of underlying changes (see later discussion) including buy-in from all people estimating and a commitment to acceptance that 50 per cent of activities will finish early and 50 per cent late. Finishing late is therefore to be expected for half of all activities, necessitating removal of any punishment for a late finish.

4 Time saved should be used to provide buffers

Rather than adding a safety margin to a single activity, safety should be included at the end of a critical path – not before. Where there are feeder paths (parallel activities that lead on to the critical path), the safety buffer should be placed at the point where the feeder joins the critical path (see Figure 7.8).

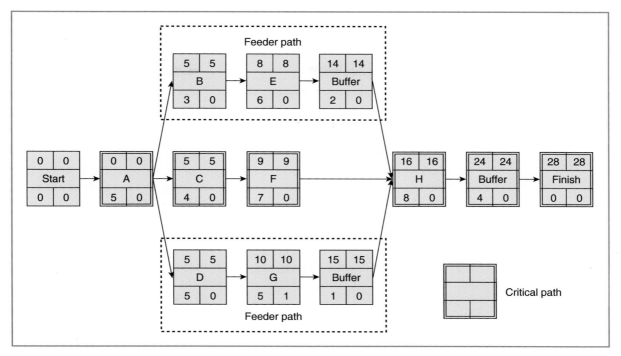

Figure 7.8 Buffering the feeder paths

The nature of project management needs to reflect the dynamic of the actual situation, and accommodate changes as they occur. Furthermore, given the **uncertainty** of plans, it is vital that all the parties involved are given regular updates on when their input is required. This statement, albeit trite, reflects the need for greater communication to ensure that critical activities can proceed without incurring any delay.

As for traditional approaches, progress should be monitored by the critical path; a time to finish is now required from task managers. This is then aggregated into the live project buffer. The application is shown in the case at the end of this chapter.

It is worth noting that the constraint may be outside the firm – for instance, with suppliers or customers. It is not unusual in construction or software engineering for delays to be caused by work provided by the client not being ready on time. Suppliers may have a similar problem – unable to start their part of the project until they have been provided with the necessary information. Using the same approach provides benefits to all parties – we identify that there may be a constraint and **buffer** it accordingly.

One of the major challenges for a project manager is in keeping plans up to date. They may re-plan the project on a daily basis and reissue copies to everyone in the project whenever there are changes. This can become very unsettling for everyone concerned, as the whole situation lacks any stability and is not robust to the inevitable changes that will start the minute the project commences. Plans with buffers as described and due-date constraints removed from activities wherever possible are far more stable. This stability (as demonstrated in the opening case at the start of the chapter) is a major benefit of critical chain scheduling.

Moreover, when a non-critical activity becomes critical it is only necessary to reconsider the criticality as far as the point that the paths merge. Non-critical activities can become critical due to resource contentions. These resources (a person, a department, an external organisation or a piece of technology) are now the constraint, and should be protected by a buffer (some time-slack in front of them). The same rules of managing constraints apply to these constraints, and they should be managed by going through the same five steps.

This added complication to the critical path represents the formation of compound series of activities – often involving different paths – which has been termed *the critical chain*.

Control

So what is the role of the project manager in control, and how is it different under APT? The answer to the first part of the question is that the project manager has ultimate responsibility for control – by determining the issues of importance, their measures and then devising the system by which they will be monitored and corrective action implemented where necessary. A full description of this process is contained in Chapter 13.

The break with due-dates has been identified as one of the features of APT. Rather than waiting for a due-date to arrive before starting an activity, it continues directly from the completion of a preceding activity. The analogy that describes this best is that of a relay race, where the runners are lined up ready to receive the baton before continuing with their leg of the race.

Where due-dates are used, there is neither requirement nor incentive for an early finish. Under APT, this must be used and any early finish added to the buffers. The role of the project manager therefore changes. Far from watching the dates, the issue becomes one of managing the hand-overs between activities – ensuring that early finishes are encouraged and that subsequent activities are ready to start. This is a major information-handling and communications role, and is one that many project managers undertake anyway, albeit without the framework to gain benefits from the early finish.

The last part of the APT approach is to monitor continuously what is causing delays and disruptions to progress. As discussed in Chapter 2, at the activity level in a project, there is a good chance that the work is of a repetitive nature. Being repeated means that each subsequent practice of that work has the opportunity to be improved. Further examples are included in the Project Management in Practice at the end of this Chapter, and in Chapter 16.

Source: Pete Saloutos/Getty image

Summary

■ Traditional approaches to planning and scheduling work in projects have both strengths and limitations. Understanding these limitations demonstrates the need for enhanced solutions to gain more reliable project delivery.

■ The Theory of Constraints is applicable to planning and controlling the flow of work through projects. The constraints in projects are continuously moving (unlike in most manufacturing plants) and consist of logic, resource, dates and behaviours or rules. The constraint determines how quickly a project can progress at any one time.

■ In practice, APT requires that the costs / benefits of late / early completion are known, that detailed plans are developed and that each task has no buffer or safety margin for time associated with it. The buffer is used to protect key resources and the end of the project.

■ The approach to planning and controlling projects described here is sufficiently different from previous approaches to warrant some further attention, and uses the same logical basis that has been successfully applied in manufacturing. References to the details of applications are increasing, with Critical Chain applications in use in firms like Boeing, Intel, and Phillips, and full APT in organisations such as Transport for London.

Key terms

bottleneck p. 178	resource contention/ conflict p. 179	Theory of constraints (TOC) p. 177
buffer p. 185	robust p. 172	throughput p. 178
critical chain p. 171	safety p. 184	uncertainties p. 175
multi-tasking p. 176	student syndrome p. 173	
Parkinson's Law p. 184		

Relevant areas of the Bodies of Knowledge

The Bodies of Knowledge differ in this with regards to critical chain, with the APM including the concept, whereas it is notably absent from the PMI's discussion.

Table 7.1 Relevant areas of the APM Body of Knowledge

Relevant section	Title	Summary
4.2.6	Scheduling – critical chain	A short section looking at the critical chain approach, with an emphasis on resource management.

PROJECT MANAGEMENT IN PRACTICE
A major road project delivered early – success with APT

The original organisational driver behind Transport for London (TfL)'s initiative to apply APT was the need to improve project performance. A centre of excellence had been established and some common problems with project delivery recognised, including many projects that overran, some substantially. When this happened the press was usually withering in its condemnation of TfL and sometimes directly of the Mayor of London, an elected position. Consequently, projects that made headlines were very unpopular. The centre of excellence established a range of training and development opportunities for staff, and identified the opportunity for more senior project managers to undertake a course in APT to address directly some of the delivery problems.

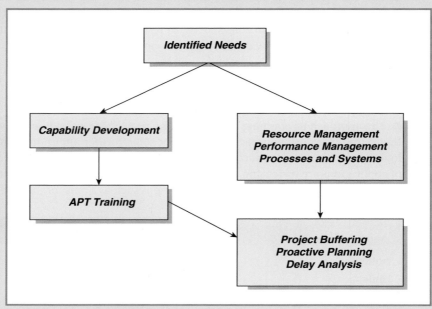

Figure 7.9 APT implementation

In conjunction with this training, tools and techniques were also recommended as part of a practical implementation plan. TfL management briefings were given on the approach, the content of the APT work and the potential business benefits. It was highlighted that these had been used elsewhere successfully, yet had been customised to meet the challenges of TfL's environment.

East London Transit (ELT1A) was the first major application of APT in TfL, was praised by all the participants interviewed, and most importantly for the organisation was delivered early, and under budget while accommodating additional work, uncovered as the project progressed.

Activities undertaken within APT – project history

The construction contract was awarded with the stipulation that a new project management process would be implemented. The APT process was introduced to the ELT1A project team with a 2-day workshop at the beginning of the work. This was attended by the main TfL team, the designer and supervisor, Parsons Brinkerhoff, and the contractor Skanska (including their commercial team). This enabled both the introduction of the proposed techniques, but also the development of a 'team spirit' at the beginning of the work, together with the setting of key goals and objectives for all parties.

There was understandable concern at the beginning of the project since the proposed techniques were counter to usual industry practice. However, senior management support from all parties ensured that the trialling of the new system was implemented. This was particularly challenging due to the rapid mobilisation, difficulties with the initial design and the fact that the work straddled two different London boroughs. The combination of these factors meant that it was a more difficult start than anticipated, thereby increasing the complication and risk of trying a different system. The success of the project under these circumstances is therefore even more noteworthy.

At the start of the process, the participants admitted to scepticism in the new approach. There was low trust at the start, with staff admitting that they could see how it *could* work, but were not sure that it *would* work.

However, initial team-building was successful and this was supported by a mutually supportive attitude amongst all the project participants, with a desire to 'get the job done'.

Four key APT features were implemented on the ELT1A from the outset:

- Implementation and monitoring of a time buffer on the critical path of the nine different work areas. The planned activities had the time contingency stripped out and all that time was added to the end of the project and carefully monitored.

- Weekly (cross-functional) walk of the route to update on progress and resolve issues, followed by:
- A proactive 'look-ahead' planning meeting to discuss upcoming work, together with
- A one-week 'look-back' to analyse any delays and identify and remove their causes.

This was a significant change in the work practices of those involved. Feelings at this time were that this left 'nowhere to hide' for the contractor, and there was also suspicion that the new approach would be 'gone in a month'. From the client side, there was the feeling that it was a good sign if the contractor would open up about their use of buffers in activities, although the contractor felt as if the client had a 'big stick'. The use of this language in the interviews shows that the impact of these changes should not be underestimated. All parties were apprehensive, and the use of an independent external facilitator was beneficial in trying to mediate between the parties.

The removal of time from activities and placing it in buffers required the recognition of where such safety lay and was described by the contractor as a process of 'baring our souls'. Since this is not accepted practice within the construction / civil engineering industry, it was a major step to move to that level of planning. Physically walking the route each week and looking ahead to ensure that adequate preparation had been made for upcoming activities meant that the whole team (TfL and contractors) were required to be open in terms of sharing knowledge, identifying problems and providing solutions. Similarly, the forward planning meetings and the delay and disruption analyses required that risks and issues be acknowledged so that they could be addressed. This was the physical manifestation of the collaborative working, in terms of successful practices.

Benefits

The ELT1A project was completed 4 weeks early, £2m under budget, and included a significant increase in the scope of work. Benefits were observed by the participants within 4–6 weeks of starting the project. The use of the buffering technique was also beneficial. In conjunction with the other techniques, this enabled the project to be tracked against a potential early completion date, with a realistic chance of it being achieved.

In terms of process, at the early stages of the project, significant time was spent in the weekly walk and planning meetings, so this was a considerable investment. However, as the project progressed, the time required diminished. So, although the project completed early, this took time investment throughout the work to achieve it. However, it could be considered as a successful and worthwhile investment, given the time, cost and quality outcomes.

A key consideration is that there was an alignment in incentives for TfL, the contractor and the designer. The early finish was mutually financially beneficial, with the suppliers also aiming to gain reputational benefit by association with a successful new approach.

The external benefits were therefore that the project was deemed successful by all of the organisations involved, and could readily be measured as such. However, we should not underestimate the other internal benefits also. The participants were proud of the work, and morale remained high. The ELT1A project offered a win-win approach with benefit-sharing amongst participants, and the significance of this must be appreciated.

Enablers of the process

It is apparent from the interviews on these projects that there were multiple mutually-reinforcing enablers within the ELT1A project.

Firstly, the people involved were open to the APT approach. The general feeling was that the individuals were highly professional, 'all can, and do, appreciate the bigger picture', and the contractor acknowledged the fact that the client would 'get stuck in' to help. The fact that the client was resident on site alongside the contractor was also beneficial.

Other feedback was that the project team had a 'good attitude' and wanted to 'get the job done'. The high calibre of staff was acknowledged, people who had knowledge of what needed to be done, were all willing to assist, acted proactively, with the right personalities.

→

There was also an appreciation that the site managers had pride in their work, had a certain amount of internal competition between them, and they wanted to 'look good' at the Tuesday planning meeting with work completed. This was a weekly milestone at which accomplishments and problems could be shared. The project manager leadership was also acknowledged, the individual in that position has to be someone who can deal with a style of operation that may be outside industry norms, and make the decisions necessary.

Secondly, the social aspects of the team working were important to identify and acknowledge. The 'good atmosphere' was instrumental in providing the context for successful operation, and this was supported by the initial group training and ongoing regular social events. The phrases 'collaborative working' and 'good attitude' were prevalent in the interviews; these appeared to be major contributors to success in the minds of the respondents. The co-location and on-site presence of the staff appeared to reinforce the social aspects of the work, meaning that the participants from different organisations were 'joined at the hip' and mutual trust contributed to the positive outcome.

Thirdly, the operational work processes aligned with the project goals and reinforced the previously discussed aspects. Although Key Performance Indicators were in place to track both project performance and inter-firm relationships, the contractor was keen to build a good relationship and this is likely to have also contributed to the superior performance.

The team social aspects also enabled effective organisational processes. The proactive planning facilitated successful procurement, and, for example, traffic management meetings were set up early, resulting in smooth results. Sharing of ideas meant that everything was in the open. It was remarked that when everyone is looking forward, it negates the ability to build a financial claim, since all the information is readily available to all participants. Some examples of early 'silly pricing' and confrontation were curtailed by intervention from the contractor's senior management, preventing escalation of issues that could considerably sour the relationship.

Feedback was that TfL utilised highly effective, equitable, pragmatic and sensible financial approaches to issues that arose. Specifically, if alternative (relatively inexpensive) solutions were proposed that were appropriate, there was sufficient financial flexibility to ensure that the 'right thing was done', and that 'common sense prevailed'. Processes were tailored to the situation, and a mature approach was taken.

In terms of the weekly walk and planning sessions, this ensured that the team were sufficiently focused, with no multi-tasking. The purpose was to formalise and coordinate, and this appears to have been successful. TfL also paid for an observer and independent facilitator, 'a different pair of eyes', which may have helped smooth any tensions. He also acted as the planner, since the overhead of running and tracking the APT buffer concepts means that this does take more time than using a more straightforward, predetermined, Gantt chart approach.

The use of the buffer system in the planning process also enabled a simple buffer chart to be put on the office wall showing the red/green status of each aspect of the project. People wanted to do well, and this enabled a clear visual indication of progress. In conjunction with this, the meetings brought issues out in the open so that they could be resolved early, so 'you know where you stand'.

In essence, the new processes implemented were not particularly radical. They can be identified in three stages: plan the work, look forward to identify any issues that are coming up, then review the work to assess how well it went, and how it can be improved. The process flow of the weekly project management activities is shown in Figure 7.10.

Evidence of the success of the process is captured in the project data. Figure 7.11 shows the disruption analysis results over three three-month periods. As can be seen, the percentage of tasks completed as planned increases in each period, and in the third period by far the most significant issue was outside of the project manager's direct control.

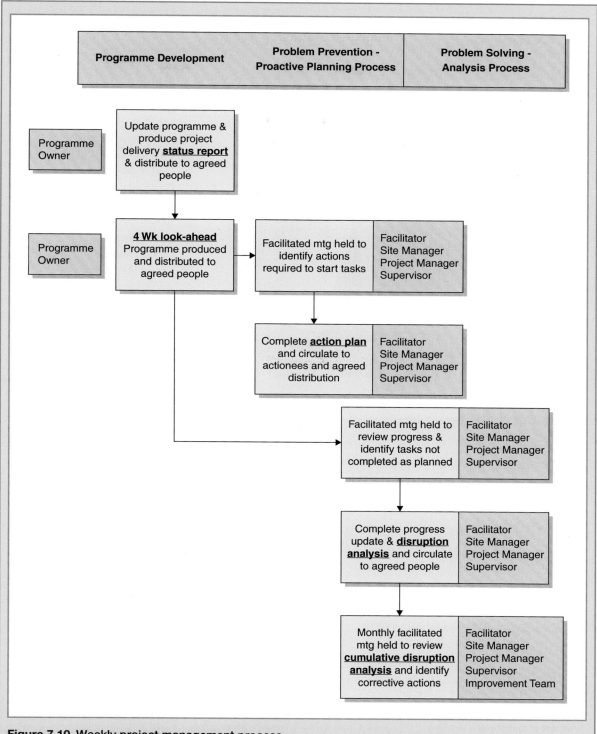

Figure 7.10 Weekly project management process

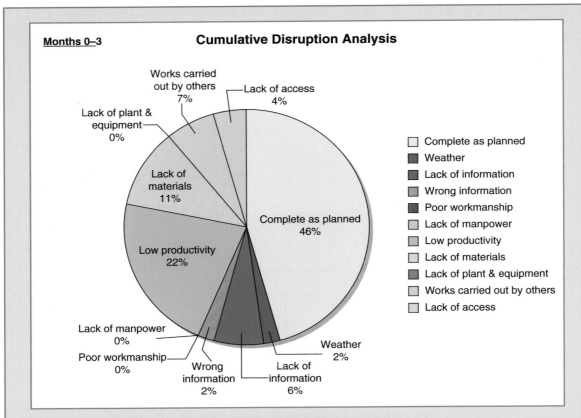

Figure 7.11 Improvement effect throughout the project – Months 0–3

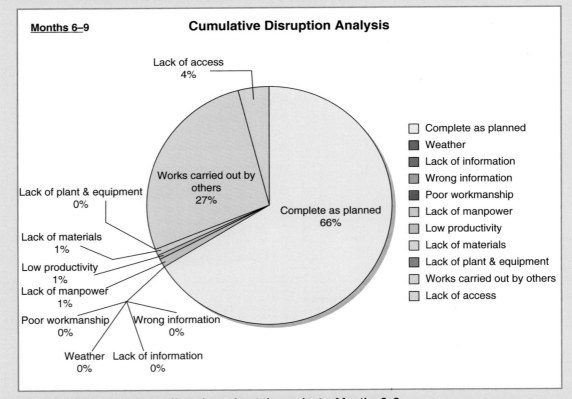

Figure 7.12 Improvement effect throughout the project – Months 6–9

Points for discussion

1 What is the evidence to support the claim that this project was a success?

2 Identify the key changes in this project. How did this contribute to the success?

3 What was the role of the support provided to the project by TfL? Would this success have been achieved without such organisational support?

Topics for discussion

1 Why is there a need for a new consideration – such as through APT?

2 What are the constraints in projects? How would you recognise them?

3 Carry out estimating on some tasks that you do regularly – the trip to work or place of study, for instance. Compare your estimates with the times you actually take. What do you notice about your estimates?

4 What is the evidence for student syndrome? How might you encourage people to move away from such behaviour?

5 Why might it be necessary to shorten some activities, even if someone has given you an estimate for their time?

6 Where should buffers be placed? Using an example of a personal project, show how the use of a buffer would help.

7 How would you deal with the argument that 'our project is too short to be including buffers in it'?

8 If this is such a good idea how come every project organisation is not using it?

9 What happens to a constraining resource when it is required by more than one project at any one time? Which project should it be working on?

10 If one project has a large buffer remaining, but another has depleted its buffer, what action could be taken to help the project with the least buffer?

Further information

Jacob, D., Bergland, S. and Cox, J. (2015) *Velocity: Combining Lean, Six Sigma and the Theory of Constraints to Achieve Breakthrough Performance*, Simon and Schuster, New York.

Coman, A. and Ronen, B. (2007) 'Managing Strategic and Tactical Constraints in the Hi-tech Industry', *International Journal of Production Research*, Vol. 45, No. 4, pp. 779–788.

Cox, J.F. III and Schleier, J.G. (2010), *Theory of Constraints Handbook*, McGraw Hill, New York.

De Meyer, A., Loch, C.H. and Pich, M.T. (2002) 'Managing Project Uncertainty: From Variation to Chaos', *MIT Sloan Management Review*, Winter, pp. 60–67.

Dettmer, H.W. (1998) *Goldratt's Theory of Constraints: A Systems Approach to Continuous Improvement*, McGraw-Hill, New York.

Gupta, M. and Boyd, L.H. (2008) 'Theory of Constraints: A Theory for Operations Management', *International Journal of Operations and Production Management*, Vol. 28, No. 10, pp. 991–1012.

Herroelen, W. and Leus, R. (2005) 'Identification and Illumination of Popular Misconceptions About Project Scheduling and Time Buffering in a Resource-constrained Environment', *Journal of the Operational Research Society*, Vol. 56, pp. 102–109.

Leach, L. (2014) *Critical Chain Project Management*, 3rd edition, Artech House Publishing, Norwood, MA.

Lechler, T.G., Ronen, B. and Stohr, E.A. (2005) 'Critical Chain: A New Project Management Paradigm or Old Wine in New Bottles?' *Engineering Management Journal*, Vol. 17, No. 4, pp. 45–58.

Luiz, O.R., de Souza, F.B., Luiz, J.V.R. and Jugend, D. (2019) 'Linking the Critical Chain Project Management literature', *International Journal of Managing Projects in Business*, Vol. 12, No. 2, pp. 423–443.

Luiz, O.R., de Souza, F.B., Luiz, J.V.R., Jugend, D., Salgado, M.H. and da Silva, S.L. (2019) 'Impact of critical chain project management and product portfolio management on new product development performance', *Journal of Business & Industrial Marketing*, Vol. 34 No. 8 pp. 1692–1705.

Newbold, R. (1997) *Project Management in the Fast Lane*, St Lucie Press, Boca Raton, FL.

Nokes, S. and Kelly, S. (2007) *The Definitive Guide to Project Management: The Fast Track to Getting the Job Done on Time and on Budget*, 2nd edition, FT Prentice Hall, Harlow.

Rahman, S. (1998) 'Theory of Constraints: A Review of the Philosophy and its Applications', *International Journal of Operations and Production Management*, Vol. 18, No. 4, pp. 336–355.

Raz, T., Barnes, R. and Dvir, D. (2003) 'A Critical Look at Critical Chain Project Management', *Project Management Journal*, Vol. 34, No. 4, pp. 24–32.

Schonberger, R. (1981) 'Why Projects Are Always Late: A Rationale Based on Manual Simulation of a PERT/CPM Network', *Interfaces*, Vol. 11, pp. 66–70.

Schragenheim, E. (1999) *Management Dilemmas: The TOC Approach to Problem Identification and Solution*, St Lucie Press, Boca Raton, FL.

Trietsch, D. (2005) 'Why A Critical Path By Any Other Name Would Smell Less Sweet? Towards a Holistic Approach to PERT/CPM', *Project Management Journal*, Vol. 36, No. 1, pp. 27–36.

Websites

www.goldratt.com

www.prochain.com – good website with lots of discussions of critical chain and applications. Promotes its software to construct buffered schedules.

www.sciforma.com – sells Scitor software which works with the critical chain ideas.

References

1 PERT – Programme Evaluation and Review Technique is described in Chapter 10.
2 Rand, G. (2000) 'Critical Chain: The Theory of Constraints Applied to Project Management', *International Journal of Project Management*, Vol. 18, pp. 173–177.
3 Robbie Burns.
4 Evidence from as early as Morris, P.W.G. and Hough, G.H. (1987) *The Anatomy of Major Projects*, Wiley, Chichester, onwards questions the efficacy of current planning methods.
5 The theory of constraints (Goldratt, E.M. (1990) *Theory of Constraints*, North River Press, New York) is arguably not a theory and this approach should be called 'management by constraints' (Ronen, B. and Starr, M.K. (1990) 'Synchronised Manufacturing as in OPT: From Practice to Theory', *Computers and Industrial Engineering*, Vol. 18, pp. 585–600). For the purposes of this text, we have stuck with the more well-known Theory of Constraints.

6 Goldratt, E.M. (1997) *The Critical Chain*, North River Press, New York, p. 121.
7 As reference 6.
8 Levitin, D. (2015). *The Organized Mind*. London: Penguin Random House.
9 Goldratt, E.M. and Cox, J. (1984) *The Goal*, North River Press, New York.
10 Leach, L.P. (1999) 'Critical Chain Project Management Improves Project Performance', *Project Management Journal*, Vol. 30, No. 2, pp. 39–51.
11 For a description of MRPII, JIT and the application of TOC in manufacturing see Brown, S., Blackmon, K., Cousins, P. and Maylor, H. (2001) *Operations Management: Policy, Practice and Performance Improvement*, Butterworth Heinemann, Oxford.
12 Curly in *City Slickers*.
13 Predictably, the project ran considerably over time and cost what the firm termed 'a significant amount of money'.
14 Parkinson, C.N. (1957) *Parkinson's Law*, Riverside Press, Cambridge, MA.

8

Building a business case for a project

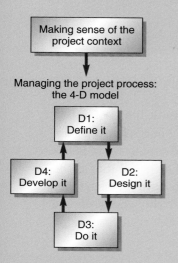

Making sense of the project context

Managing the project process: the 4-D model

D1: Define it

D4: Develop it

D2: Design it

D3: Do it

'The method I use to estimate costs, is think of a number and double it.' (Project Planner)

'The only people who give reliable estimates are depressed, or worse.' (Professor of Accounting)

Principles

1   Costs should be justified in terms of payback or return on investment as part of a business case.

2   In order to provide an assessment of plans it is vital to understand the costs associated with activities and projects and to have a realistic cost plan.

3   Determining the magnitude of the costs and benefits of projects needs to be carried out critically.

Learning objectives

By the time you have completed this chapter, you should be able to:

→   identify elements of cost and a process for construction of cost plans

→   recognise methods for the development of a business case

→   identify causes of failure in cost and benefits analysis.

Contents

Introduction   *196*
8.1   Basics of a cost planning process   *198*
8.2   Business case development   *206*
8.3   Challenges for the received wisdom   *213*
Summary   *216*
Key terms   *217*
Relevant areas of the Bodies of Knowledge   *217*
Project management in practice: *Justify IT!*   *218*
Topics for discussion   *218*
Further information   *219*
References   *219*
Appendix: Present value of £1   *220*

Signature projects, business cases and reality, or 'if we had known how much they would cost, would we have done them?!'

Holyrood: The construction costs of Holyrood, the Scottish Parliament building, increased from an early estimate of £10–40 million in 1997, to an actual £414 million by the time it was finished and occupied in 2004. The *Scotsman* newspaper produced a 2019 retrospective[1] entitled 'Scottish Parliament at 20: £414m, endless recrimination, and finally, an iconic building'. It has become justly famous for this massive overspend, and, despite winning a major architectural award and becoming a top tourist attraction, it is hard to think of a project where such an outcome could be more public.

HS2: As an ongoing project, High-Speed 2 (HS2) is the new UK rail upgrade, linking London to Manchester and Leeds. The budget in 2009 was anticipated to be £32 billion, yet this rose progressively over the years. The Oakervee Review[2] in late 2019 anticipated a total cost of £80.7 to 87.7 billion, although admitted it could be over £100 billion. It should be noted that at the time of writing, preparatory works have started, but no new tracks or tunnels have yet been built. With the formal approval for construction work being given in April 2020, the whole scheme is not expected to be operating until 2032–33, so it will be some time before we can assess the benefits of this investment.

Introduction

The business case is an important artefact in the life of a project; it defines the project and its rationale, the value or benefits that are sought by carrying out the project, the costs of doing so and the risks associated with it. Compiling a formal business case is a key part of the governance required by organisations so that they can demonstrate that (in the case of businesses) shareholders' investments are being appropriately safeguarded. As the project progresses, it provides the **base case** for the project to evaluate both progress and the impact of any changes to the project or its deliverables.

Such documented justification is not just required by businesses, it is standard practice in many public-sector organisations too. For instance, a road bridge in London was in urgent need of having its bearings replaced. The benefits would be that the road would continue to stay above the railway line that it was crossing. The costs were substantial and the disruption would be painful during the project. The only other option was to close the bridge permanently. Despite the urgency and the lack of any viable alternative, the project team were required to compile a full business case for the work, which took many months. Such cases then do cost time and money to compile, which may be better spent on developing the project itself. However, used well they can provide benefits. For instance, in contrast to the problems faced by Holyrood, the original plans for the building for the Welsh Assembly were scrapped, when it became clear that the estimates were hopelessly understated. This early recognition is a good example of the application of gated processes (the project was stopped at a gate) because the business case was not approved by those with responsibility to the public for that money.

The objective of this section is to demonstrate how such an analysis can be constructed to determine whether an investment is favourable or not, and some of the challenges that such a supposedly 'objective process' can face.

The APM BoK defines the business case as:

> '. . . *justification for undertaking a project programme, or portfolio. It evaluates the benefit, cost and risk of alternative options and provides a rationale for the preferred solution.*'[3]

This assumes that there are always definable benefits and costs, that risk can be assessed, that there is a well understood problem that needs 'solution' and that there is a defined sponsor – a named individual who 'owns' the business case and will be held accountable to the leadership of the organisation for the benefits being delivered. Where processes are well developed and projects are routinely executed, this may indeed be the case. But where there is a compelling need (disaster relief, for instance) or it just has to be done (banks having to make changes to comply with new legislation, or the replacement of safety-critical infrastructure), then an assessment of the options and costs, rather than detailed analysis of the benefits may be more appropriate.

The example of the Holyrood Parliament Project demonstrates some of the challenges with cost estimating and the process of delivering to plan. It does show that such costing processes are rarely objective, due to the influence of stakeholders determining what is *politically acceptable* in the evaluation of costs and benefits. In this case, even when these began to be determined, there was little political will to make them public. However, there is no such thing as the *perfect estimate*. The estimate is an attempt to predict the status of spend at some point in the future (sometimes decades) and as such is subject to that fundamental property of projects – uncertainty. It may sound straightforward, but in practice it is an extremely difficult endeavour.[4]

A fundamental principle of economics is that resources are scarce. In practice, this means that it is not possible to attempt every idea or opportunity that comes along, as, in any organisation or environment, there are insufficient resources to undertake them all. The implication of 'some can be done, some can't' is the need for choices to be made by organisations as to which projects are pursued and which are not. These decisions form part of the process of portfolio management (Chapter 3) and filtering (Chapter 5). During the D1 phase of a project, it becomes necessary to evaluate the likely costs and benefits of the project – providing *an* input (but note – not *the* input) to the process of selection and then providing a baseline for the project if approved. Preparing a **business case** as a statement of predicted costs, benefits and risks is a process common to most large organisations and is a key role in the D2 phase for project managers.

The challenges for the business case include the estimation of costs and the identification of benefits. These are particularly challenging where the benefits may not be purely financial, as will be shown. For instance, the Holyrood building has provided a landmark that has been described as an emblem of Scottish independence and heritage (bamboo cladding and all). It is certainly a challenge to derive a monetary benefit from something iconic, whatever its costs.

This chapter considers the basics of obtaining an estimate of project costs, the preparation of the business case, and some challenges for the received wisdom in this area, including some of the issues raised by Holyrood, HS2 and the other cases. And it is recognised that there are some projects that are completely inappropriate for a business case.

8.1 Basics of a cost planning process

As a **process**, **cost planning** resembles the iterative steps of the time planning process described in Chapter 5. It differs in that there is a further uncertainty with projects of several years' duration – we cannot know exactly what activities will be required that far into the project or how long they will take, but we also are susceptible to the vagaries of changes in costs over time as a result of currency fluctuations, inflation and base material costs. We also need to know the basis of the relationship between cost, price and profit in the project that we are undertaking. This will be determined by the context in which we are working.

The role of costing

The basic relationship between price, cost and profit can be expressed in a number of ways:

$$\left.\begin{array}{l} \text{price} = \text{cost} + \text{profit} \\ \text{cost} = \text{price} - \text{profit} \\ \text{profit} = \text{price} - \text{cost} \end{array}\right\} \text{ same equation different meaning}$$

Which one applies depends on whether price, cost or profit is fixed first. These differences can be explained as follows:

- in the first case the price is fixed through legislation, for example, or in the case of a **target costing** system (see below), through market analysis;
- in the second the cost is fixed, generally through contract purchase which guarantees that goods will be supplied to you at a particular price. This fixes your costs while your selling price and profits can be varied;
- some agreements state the profit that a company is allowed to make through the system known as **cost-plus** or **reimbursable pricing**.

Target costing is being used increasingly in the automotive and aerospace industries, among others. The target price for a complete vehicle or aircraft is established that will give it competitiveness in the intended market and the margin determined by corporate decision. That leaves a figure of the target cost. Designers work back from that figure to the individual component or system costs. The main implication is for component suppliers, who are subsequently set target costs to achieve on their components or systems.

It was normal in the defence industry until a few years ago for everyone to work on a cost-plus basis. This required very detailed time and material cost estimates (and subsequently, records) for a project to be submitted to the purchaser for vetting. Should a supplier be awarded a contract it would be on the basis of direct costs plus a percentage towards overheads and profit. The procedures were lengthy, involved massive bureaucracy and, most importantly, did not encourage suppliers to improve their performance. If costs overran they would still be paid. The changes in the relationships between the various national military procurement agencies and their suppliers mean that contracts are now most likely to be awarded on the basis of competitive tendering with fixed costs for the delivery required. The supplier knows how much they will be paid if awarded the contracts, and has a vested interest in ensuring costs are minimised.

Not everyone welcomed the demise of cost-plus – as one veteran of the era said: 'When we worked to cost-plus, you would do the job properly and know you'd get paid for doing a proper job. Now we have to watch every bean. Previously, the engineers had control over these projects, now it's the accountants.' Reimbursable contracts are still in evidence in some sectors, particularly construction.

As stated at the outset, cost planning is an iterative process that will be refined during the D2 phase. Indeed, it is likely to be ongoing, as planned costs become baselines, budgets are turned into activities and outcomes, and requirements change as the project progresses. The elements of this process are unpacked in the discussion that follows.

Approaches to costing

There are two basic approaches to the preparation of costing information:

- **ground-up costing** – the estimates of each level in the work breakdown structure are compiled and added together by each level of supervision in the project hierarchy, as would be the case for reimbursable contracts;
- **top-down costing** – you are allocated a certain amount of money to complete the project activities and this has to be split between the sub-projects. The allocation is based on either senior management's estimates or the use of target costing.

The two systems are illustrated in Figure 8.1. The advantage of ground-up costing is that the estimates are prepared by the people who will carry out the activities, or their supervisor. In principle, this may give some notion of commitment to achieving these figures if the costs are accepted unmodified by the project manager. In practice, some organisations find that it is common for costing proposals to be cut by project managers or other decision-makers. As a result, the activity level costs may become artificially inflated, as staff try to remove the effect of such cuts. The process consequently loses its apparently straightforward motives and purpose.

Top-down costing involves the allocation of the costs to the sub-activities. This creates a degree of competition between the supervisors of the activities for resources which many view as being beneficial.

Having determined the nature of the costing process it is now necessary to identify the elements of cost. The methods for putting numbers to these elements are then discussed, leading on to how they are accumulated into a final cost estimate.

Elements of cost

The major elements of cost are:

- **time** – the direct input of labour into activities;
- **materials** – consumables and other items used in the process;
- **capital equipment** – the purchase of the means of providing the conversion process, or part of its cost, maintenance, running and depreciation offset against activities;

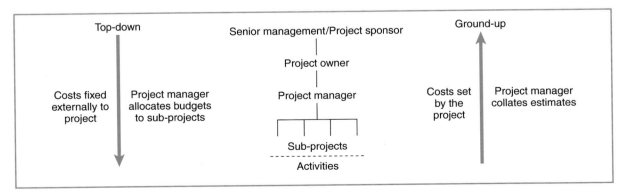

Figure 8.1 Top-down and ground-up approaches to costing

- **indirect expenses** – e.g. transportation, training;
- **overheads** – provision of an office, financial and legal support, managers and other non-direct staff;
- **contingency** margin/allowance for minor changes, unknowables (sometimes it is impossible to assess the condition of part of a system e.g. a condenser or storage vessel on a chemical plant, until it is taken apart as part of the project), errors and uncertainties (e.g. fluctuations in material prices).

Materials can be included in the costings, either at the cost to the company or with a margin added. Capital equipment may have to be purchased specially, in which case its entire cost, or part of it, will need to be offset against the project. Where the equipment will have potential further use after the project has finished with it, it may attract a residual value. Indirect expenses are those not directly related to the value-adding activities, but which are considered necessary to support the project. Overheads are carried by all organisations and include the running of the headquarters and the provision of central services.

In some industries, a margin is allowed for contingencies under the control of the project manager. A margin of 10 per cent of the budget is not unusual in such cases, but much larger contingencies may be held by the organisation centrally to cover a smaller number of bigger problems across a portfolio.

OPEX and CAPEX

OPEX – is the **operating expenditur**e of a piece of equipment or a system and is not a project cost. However, the effectiveness of a project, may have a significant impact on the OPEX. For instance, in the construction of wind turbines, one firm noted that they could increase their project spend (known as the CAPEX or **capital expenditure**) in order to reduce the future OPEX – a change in the speed control housing design would cost extra on the project, but would reduce the annual operating cost of the turbines. This trade-off between CAPEX and OPEX is a common challenge for project teams.

Estimating techniques

In the material covered so far, the approach has been to build up the costs from the elements of the WBS and to add to them the elements identified above. In addition to this ground-up approach, there are various techniques that are used. These include:

- **parametric estimating**;
- as . . . but . . . s;
- forecasts;
- **synthetic estimation**;
- using **learning curve** effects;
- **wishful thinking**.

Parametric estimating

This type of estimating works well where there is considerable experience of a particular type of project. The project is broken down into a unit that can be readily estimated – for instance, this could be lines of code in a computer programme, hours of contact for a training programme or cost per mile of resurfacing a road, or relaying track in the rail sector. This provides a number to start from with your estimates as shown in the following illustration.

Parametrics provide a means to estimate costs from knowledge of the work being undertaken and can be used at different levels in the product breakdown. In the example below, this was evident from the different approaches taken by the builder (from experience of previous projects) and simply based on floor area, and by the QS based on product and work breakdown. This recognises the principle described in Chapter 1, that projects are rarely totally unique and that at the lowest level of the WBS there is usually a high degree of repetition in activities.

How much?

A builder was asked to provide a cost estimate for an extension to a house. The architect had estimated £60 000 for the building works. The builder worked on the basis of £2400 per square metre of additional ground area. The additional ground area was 60 square metres equating to a cost in the region of £144 000. For the customer, this difference was unacceptable for their purposes, and so they sought out another source for an estimate. In this instance, they turned to a quantity surveyor (QS). A QS is a specialist in providing such estimates, and had a much more detailed set of parametrics that they used. These included rates per square metre for walling, hours taken to dig foundations, and standard costs per metre for timber. The result was that the QS confirmed the builder's estimate, allowing the client to make a well-founded decision on whether to go ahead with the project or not.

As . . . but . . . s (also called comparative estimates)

As . . . but . . . s are where you or your organisation has experience of doing a similar job previously. The use of previous costs as a baseline for future estimation assumes that these were in some way validated by the previous experience. Given the statement made in Chapter 2 that so many projects are not reviewed in any meaningful way, this is an assumption worth challenging. Indeed, unless there is some method of tracking the actual costings and these are compared with the originals there is considerable doubt as to the validity of such records. Hedgehog syndrome will rule the day. Provided there is some logic to back the continued use of such estimates, they are a good basis from which to start.

Forecasts

In many instances, there will be a degree of uncertainty in cost elements and these can only be **forecast** – a real 'best guess'. In some instances parametrics or **proxies** can be used, as shown in the example below.

Forecasting a conference

Specialist academic conferences are held each year on specific topics, and generally the location will vary annually. For example, some move around Europe or the US, others have a more global span and will cross continents. They can be attended by tens, hundreds or even thousands of academics who have submitted papers, and are often hosted by local universities. This becomes a major organisational challenge to put together the promotional material, the paper reviewing process, the agenda, guest speakers, accommodation, catering, and so forth.

An issue is that it is never clear how many will actually attend, as formal registration can be quite late in the process. So, although the event is an annual occurrence and many of the attendees are regular participants, a high degree of variability can be experienced, which makes it difficult to plan for. The number of participants can be affected by the ease of travel (a major city is easier to fly to than an out-of-the-way location), the travel and accommodation costs, any potential clashes with other scheduled events, and the availability of funding for individuals to attend. Sometimes extreme events occur, such as the Icelandic volcanic eruption of Eyjafjallajökull in 2010 causing huge flight disruption across Europe, or the Covid-19 pandemic of 2020 which curtailed all travel.

Whenever you attend any event and it goes smoothly, spare a thought for all the effort that went into it – it is never a simple process behind the scenes!

There are a number of issues in this case. The first is the difference between fixed and variable costs. In a case such as a conference, the fixed costs would include the venue and the administration – they will not change no matter what the number of delegates (within certain ranges). The variable costs include the food costs, which are usually charged per delegate.

Secondly, as we note, it is not possible to determine accurately the numbers of delegates in advance – people rarely book a long time in advance, yet the venue and facilities would need to be booked months in advance. Instead of this actual data, it is often the case that the number of delegates would be roughly the same as the number of abstracts (outlines of papers) that were submitted for the conference. This number provides a *proxy* – an indirect best guess of the final number of delegates.

Thirdly, there is sometimes another fundamental uncertainty – the exchange rate. The conference fee may be paid in a currency different from that of the hosting university. In this case, there may be no easy way to deal with such risk, but a series of estimates can be fed into a spreadsheet model to see the impact of these on the budget. For very large projects it may be necessary for the organisation to become involved in currency speculation – either buying the necessary amount of currency when the rates appear favourable, or agreeing exchange deals at particular rates. Where key materials are commodities they may also take an interest in the relevant commodity market. Whatever the case, projects having a currency risk have to factor this into their risk analysis (see Chapter 10).

Synthetic estimation

Where there are considerable items of repetitive work in a project the times for people to carry out certain activities can be analysed to provide a generic set of actions and consequent timings. New activities can be deconstructed into these generic actions and the timings added accordingly. Little or no direct measurement of the workplace needs subsequently to be carried out. This is based on the practices of work measurement, and can be used with some reliability off-line to give indications of the scale of effort required to perform particular tasks.

Time estimation – learning curve effects

Watching a skilled craftsperson at work shows how a highly intricate task can be learned and carried out so that it is made to look easy. Gaining such a level of skill requires years of training and practice (and many mistakes). A project rarely has such an opportunity to gain advantage through repetition. There will, however, be repetitive elements to any project – and usually at the lowest levels of the WBS. Where these occur, the time taken each time the task is carried out will decrease as the person becomes familiar with the methods. Subsequent improvements in speed are seen to become smaller over time. This can be quantified using the following formula:

$$Y_x = Kx^n$$

Where

x = the number of times the task has been carried out

Y_x = time taken to carry out the task the xth time

K = time taken to carry out the task the first time

n = log b/log 2 where b = learning rate

Learning curves and painting by numbers projects

A team is set up to carry out a quality audit of 10 departments. The first audit takes 4 days as the auditors are unfamiliar with the procedures. The second audit takes 3. After a period of time, the minimum audit time is reached, and very little further improvement is seen. We can plot this progression as shown in Figure 8.2.

If we wish to find out how long the eighth audit will take we need to calculate the learning rate, b. The following values can be assigned from the above information:

x = the number of times the task has been carried out = 2

Y_x = time taken to carry out the task the xth time = 3

K = time taken to carry out the task the first time = 4

n can be calculated.

Putting these values in:

$$3 = 4(2)^n$$
$$2^n = 3/4$$
$$n \log 2 = \log (3/4)$$
$$n = -0.1249/0.4149$$
$$n = \log b/\log 2 = -0.4149$$
$$\log b = -0.1249$$
$$b = 0.75$$

From this we can say that the project has a 75 per cent learning curve.

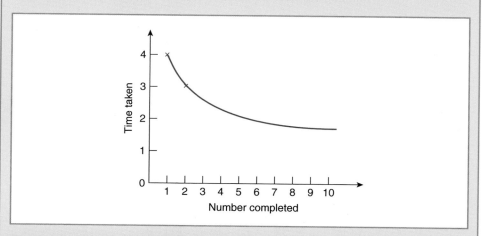

Figure 8.2 Learning curve effects on time taken

Table 8.1 Improvement over time

Audit no.	Time taken (days)
1	4
2	3
3	2.54
4	2.25
5	2.05
6	1.90
7	1.78
8	1.69

This can also be seen intuitively, as another way of expressing the learning curve is to say that every time the total number of audits completed doubles the time taken for the last audit will be the learning percentage multiplied by the original time. In this case as the number of audits doubled from one to two, the time decreased from 4 to 3. The percentage is therefore 3/4 = 75 per cent. As the number of times the audit is done increases, the times taken will decrease as shown in Table 8.1.

To complete this example, the time figures can then be put into the kind of cost build-up calculations described in the following section.

Cost build-up

We decided to employ a researcher for 6 months to do some data collection and analysis. The direct cost of employing the person was calculated at £18 000. The expenses involved in carrying out the work were in the region of £5000. The total mini-project budget ended up at an incredible £52 000 by the time overheads, sundry expenses, administrative assistance and office space costs had been taken into account. How do we end up with the final cost? As this shows, relatively small pieces of work can look very expensive once they have been fully calculated. The elements of cost are added as shown in Figure 8.3.

The following example illustrates the cost build-up principle and the use of this in determining the level of benefits needed to make the project worthwhile.

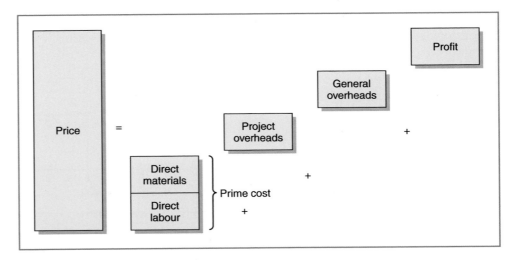

Figure 8.3 Elements of cost

Training course – how much should I charge?

A course coordinator wishes to advertise the course but needs to know how much will have to be charged in order to make a profit. The time estimates are made based on the proposed course length – determined by first considering what it could usefully achieve in given times. These are correlated with the necessary labour input to ascertain the direct cost. The programme requires a consultant to do three days' training which costs £500 per day, to be supported by an administrator, whose time is costed at £180 per day. The direct costs (fixed, i.e. regardless of how many delegates attend) are therefore £2040. The course requires the provision of printed materials and stationery, which are a variable cost (the more delegates, the greater the cost) of £120 per delegate. Assuming the course is fully subscribed and can accommodate 15 delegates, a further £1800 needs to be added to the estimate. The total of these is the prime cost. Indirect labour and materials include administrative time arranging the course (say eight days at £180 per day), and general overheads would be the ongoing 'fixed costs' of providing the building, heating, lighting and functions such as finance to provide the funds, and procurement in raising the necessary purchase orders. The overhead is added to the total cost at a rate of 60 per cent.

The cost build-up is as Figure 8.4. This does not include the profit for the organisation. The minimum rate per delegate should be the total cost (£8448) divided by the number of delegates (15). This gives £563.20. To this should be added a profit margin and a contingency figure in case the course is undersubscribed.

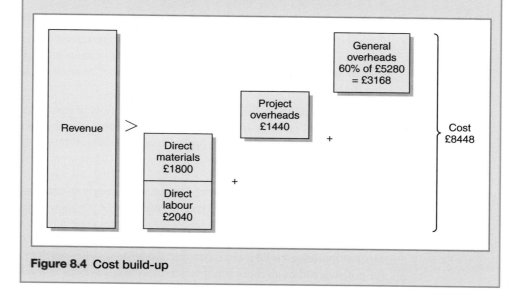

Figure 8.4 Cost build-up

Reliance on this form of allocating overheads does cause anomalies in costing, which can be very damaging to the profitability of the organisation as a whole. For instance, if a department has the overhead allocated to its budgets as revenue (income to that department) then there is little incentive to improve the methods or reduce the amount of time that an activity takes, as this would reduce the apparent income to that department. This is unlikely to encourage improvement, to say the least. Such anomalies raise questions about the merits of conventional cost accounting, though it is still the most-used system.

Use of cost estimates

A consistent theme in planning is its evolutionary or iterative nature. At the outset of the project initial cost plans will provide a rough idea as to whether the project is viable

– that is, the returns will justify the investment. As the project progresses to detailed planning, these estimates will have to be revised to show the increased level of consideration that has gone into compiling the estimates. If approved, this spend becomes the budget, though often not without being 'trimmed'. It is this budget that is the subject of the next section, and the basis for control – in particular through earned value (see Chapter 13).

8.2 Business case development

The following considers some basic approaches to financial appraisal.

Financial appraisal

The financial appraisal of project proposals will consider the potential rewards of carrying out a project against the predicted costs. The form of this evaluation will depend on:

- the size of the project being considered;
- the timespan over which the costs and benefits are going to be spread.

Once the cost of completing the project has been determined from the WBS (ground-up) or senior management (top-down) system the justification is that the return will at least exceed the amount spent. This return or payback can be analysed in a number of ways to determine feasibility or net benefit:

- **payback analysis** – simply considers the cash flow of costs and benefits;
- **discounted cash flow** – considers the 'time value' of cash flows;
- **internal rate of return** – sets basic return criteria on time value of money.

Payback

The most basic method of financial evaluation is simply to compare the income that will be generated with the initial investment. From this a payback period can be determined, i.e. the amount of time the revenue will need to be generated to cancel out the investment. For instance, an initial investment of £30 million will be paid back in 5 years if the revenue generated is £6 million per year. Some companies set this time period as a hurdle for projects, although more sophisticated analyses are more common.

While this method has inherent simplicity it ignores:

- the total lifecycle cost of an item and only considers costs within the payback period (if there are major items outside this period to be considered, e.g. high disposal or decommissioning costs, the analysis does not provide a good financial model of reality);
- the time value of money (see below).

Discounted cash flow

Where the timespan extends over more than one financial period and certainly where it is over many years, this 'time value of money' will need to be taken into account, through techniques known as *discounting*. The basis of the technique is the comparison between the value of the return on an investment and the value of the same sum of money had it been deposited in a bank account at a given rate of interest for the same period. The technique therefore considers the opportunity cost of the project (i.e. the cost of not doing something else with the resources).

Example

A project proposal aims to spend £100 000 on information technology and £20 000 a year to maintain it for four years. The return is £50 000 per year in terms of labour savings and extra profit generated. Would the project be worth pursuing or should other options be considered?

The payback model shows that the project would generate £200 000 in revenue from an expenditure of £180 000, and so looks plausible. However, if the money was deposited in a bank account, at say 2 per cent interest p.a., the account would show a balance of £194 837 at the end of year 4 (see later work for how the calculation was carried out). It appears better to carry out the project than to leave the money in the bank.

This is part of the consideration. Given the number of times IT projects overrun or do not deliver as expected,[5] would you consider this a sensible investment? The potential benefit is relatively small, the possible downside if a major IT catastrophe occurs may be enormous. There is no 'right' answer here, but it highlights the wider discussions that should be encouraged around investment decisions.

The concept of discounting is applied to the cash flows (not just profits) to determine whether or not the projected costs and benefits are going to yield the necessary results and is called discounted cash flow.

Compound interest or 'to those that have shall be given . . . '

When a sum of money is left on deposit in a bank account it accrues interest. If the interest is paid into the account then in the following period there will be interest paid on the original amount plus interest on the first period's interest. As time progresses the amount on which interest is being paid grows, hence in the following period more interest is paid, and so on. This phenomenon is known as **compound interest** and was described by Einstein as the eighth wonder of the modern world! If you are in a situation where you have money in the bank it is a great invention. Of course, the converse is also true, that if you borrow money, you will accrue interest charges not only on the capital amount but also on any unpaid interest levied on the amount.

Discounting is the opposite of compounding. All values are considered in today's terms – called the present value (PV). We can calculate the value of the sum that would have to be deposited at a given rate of interest for a certain period to yield a stated end value.

NOTE: It is important to highlight that we are using interest rates in this chapter that many readers will consider very high. Since the Financial Crisis of 2008, bank rates have been at a historic low (and even negative in some cases). At the time of writing this state shows no sign of changing, but we cannot foresee the future and it is likely that at some point the rates will return closer to the long-term average. For many people, these are numbers they have never encountered in their careers, so it is worth becoming familiar with the effects of higher interest rates and the impact it has on investment decisions. In the examples given, try working out the impact of very low rates as well, and observe the difference. If you are working on a multi-year (or even multi-decade) project, the possibility of major interest rate fluctuations can have a significant impact on the work.

Example

If you wanted to have a final value of £2012 in 12 years' time with a rate of return (called the discount rate) of 6 per cent, the present value (the amount that would have to be deposited) is £1000. The calculation is done through:

$$PV = \frac{C_n}{(1 + i)^n}$$

where

C_n = future value of the investment n years hence
i = discounting rate

(Check the above example by putting C_n = 2012, i = 0.06 and n = 12.)

This basic calculation is applied to the benefits, which must then be offset against the costs. This figure is called the **net present value** (NPV):

Net present value = present value of benefits − present value of costs

Example

If a project requires the expenditure of £100 000 now and will yield £200 000 in 6 years, how will the manager evaluate whether or not this is viable (assuming a 10 per cent discount rate)?

$$\text{The PV of the benefits} = \frac{200000}{(1 + i)^n}$$

$$= \frac{200000}{(1 + 0.1)^6}$$

$$= 112800$$

The PV of the costs = 100000
∴ the NPV = 112800 − 100000 = 12800

The minimum criterion for project selection is that the NPV $\geq$ 0 at a given discounting rate. The project therefore meets this basic criterion and could be allowed to proceed.

The discounting rate can be taken as the interest rate which could be earned from a bank. It is more usual for the rate to be stated according to the type of project and allied to the cost of borrowing that money. A consequently higher rate than the normal bank rates is set, for example one manufacturing company had a discounting rate of 12 per cent. The effect was that it was correspondingly harder for projects to meet the minimum criterion of having an NPV of zero.

It is usual for the revenues and costs to be occurring over a period of years. More complex examples such as the following can be evaluated.

Example

You have been asked to evaluate the following proposal. Apply the technique of discounted cash flow to the figures to show whether or not this is worth pursuing. The applicable discount rate is 12 per cent.

	Now	Year 1	Year 2	Year 3
Start-up costs	£50000			
Running costs (rent, rates, staffing, etc.)		£30000	£45000	£45000
Revenues		£40000	£50000	£60000
Sale of business				£70000

NPV(project) = NPV(year 1) + NPV(year 2) + NPV(year 3)

$$= (-50000) + \frac{(-30000 + 40000)}{(1 + 0.12)^1} + \frac{(-45000 + 50000)}{(1 + 0.12)^2}$$

$$+ \frac{(-45000 + 60000 + 70000)}{(1 + 0.12)^3}$$

$$= -50000 + 8928 + 3986 + 60501 = £23415$$

The project on this basis is worth pursuing.

(*Note*: this does assume that there is no competition for this investment – that this is the only project being considered.)

Future value (FV)

The **future value** of an investment is the value of that money C if deposited for n years at an interest rate of i and is given by:

$$FV = C(1 + i)^n$$

There is a 'rule of thumb' called the 'rule of 72'. If you invest at a per cent for b years, where $a \times b = 72$, your money will roughly double, e.g. if you invest £1000 at a fixed rate of 6 per cent for 12 years, the balance at the end of the 12th year ($6 \times 12 = 72$) will be roughly £2000 (actually £2012), and if the rate was 18 per cent and the term 4 years the balance would be the same (actually £1938).

The internal rate of return (IRR)

A related technique is to calculate the IRR of a project, i.e. the discount rate for which the NPV = 0. This can be done mathematically involving a number of iterations (working out the NPV with a variety of discount rates and gradually getting to the point where NPV = 0), or graphically. This does depend on the problem to solve being limited.

Example

A sum of £100 000 is invested over 6 years with a potential yield of £200 000 at the end of the sixth year. What is the IRR of the project? As a starting point, an arbitrary rate of 10 per cent is chosen.

$$NPV_{10\%} = \frac{20000}{(1 + 0.1)^6} - 100000 = 112895 - 10000 = 12895$$

The discount rate in this case is clearly too low (the PV of the benefits is too high); try 14 per cent:

$$NPV_{14\%} = \frac{200000}{(1 + 0.14)^6} - 10000 = -8883$$

This rate is too high (the PV of the benefits is too low). Having two points for the NPV, each on either side of the zero NPV target, the value must be somewhere between the two. This is shown graphically in Figure 8.5. As can be seen, the relationship within small changes in the discount rate can often be approximated to linear. Over a larger range, the change is as shown in Figure 8.6. As the number of benefit points and payout points increases, there will be multiple IRRs. This is shown in Figure 8.7, there being one change in direction of the curve (point of inflection) for each change in the sign (+ to −, or − to +) in the NPV analysis.

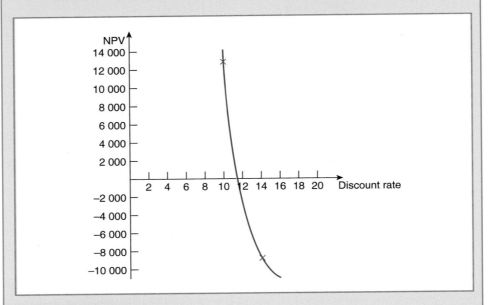

Figure 8.5 NPV profile

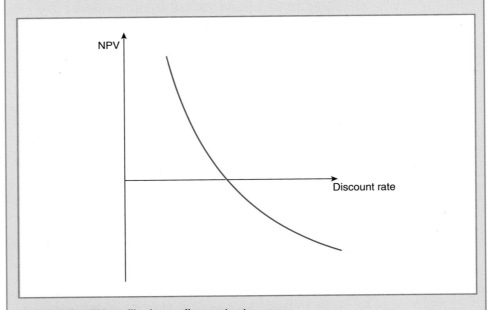

Figure 8.6 NPV profile: large discount rate range

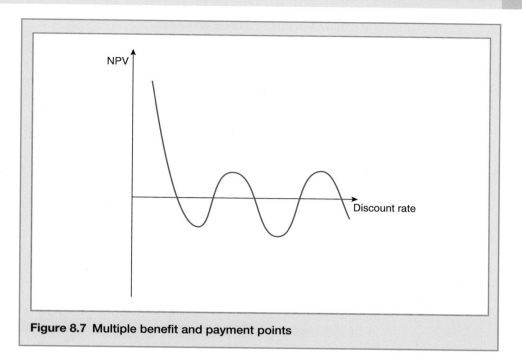

Figure 8.7 Multiple benefit and payment points

Using IRR

Using the percentage rate from an IRR calculation has a certain appeal. It also gets over the need to choose a discount rate for a project, which can save considerable debate. On the other hand, two projects may have the same IRR but yield very different NPVs, e.g. if two proposals have the same IRR but one has a much higher NPV, the one with the high NPV is clearly preferable (risk and availability of funds allowing). The IRR also cannot cope with changes in the discount rate over time. This would have been particularly problematic during periods such as the early 1990s, when rates changed rapidly and by over 10 per cent. We reiterate the fact that, at the time of writing, interest rates have been low since 2008, and this may lead to complacency in terms of project financing. What would your project financing look like if rates suddenly jumped by 10 per cent? It is a valuable question to ask, and it is worth having a plan in case it happens.

Using discounted cash flow (DCF)

Originally it was only accountants who would be given the knowledge for the use and application of DCF, and would be the ones to accept/reject projects. Its use is now widespread and built into most financial appraisal systems and there are powerful functions in most spreadsheets to assist in this analysis (see Appendix at end of chapter). Almost anyone can run a project through the financial constraints without needing to submit a project plan formally. This has numerous benefits to the project manager, as they can build not only time-based models of the project but also financial ones. The use of financial models has similar benefits to written project plans:

- the model can be interpreted by a non-financial expert to make changes where necessary to components of the model and evaluate the impact of those changes;
- no third-party intervention is necessary until a well-developed plan has been constructed.

It does have certain limitations, however:

- how to determine the interest rate to use – for how long might today's rate be valid? It is relatively easy to model the effects of sudden spikes in rates, and this may be time well spent.
- the process of forecasting cash flow years into the future involves a high degree of uncertainty;
- defining the **cash flows** – they are different from the data generally presented in a balance sheet – write-off values, for example, are treated very differently.

For many firms, this is an important area of intersection between the financial controllers, management accountants and project managers. In order for everyone to understand the process of financial evaluation of projects better, many organisations provide simple spreadsheet-based evaluation packages, available on intranets or online, that can be used by project managers for the purposes of doing initial financial evaluation to see if ideas are worth pursuing. Having such models readily available for people to try out ideas quickly and easily is one of the keys to innovation in both products and processes.

However, the upshot of having such evaluation packages is that it is quite straightforward to 'game' the numbers. If your organisation has specific IRR or NPV hurdles, then slight tweak to the revenue expectations or cost assumptions can move the project into the 'viable' category quite easily. Given that in the very early stages these numbers are often fairly loose estimates anyway, the incentive to nudge the figures in the manager's favour is understandable. Obviously we do not endorse such activity, but if you are reviewing project proposals it may be worth looking closely at those that come in just above the minimum requirements!

Determining cash flow figures for DCF and IRR calculations

In order to present the most accurate picture of the financial health or otherwise of the proposal the following rules should be applied:[6]

- cash flows, not profit figures, should be used;
- **sunk costs** (those already incurred) should be ignored;
- only **variable costs** arising directly from the project should be included (**fixed costs**, which would be incurred whether or not the project goes ahead, should be excluded);
- **opportunity costs** must be taken into account (developing one area of a business to the detriment of another).

Determining the discount rate

It is more usual for the project manager to have discount rates set as part of organisational policy. There are a number of methods for obtaining values for the discount rate – this one determines the risk adjusted discount rate (RADR).

There are three factors that determine the discount rate:

(a) = the rate charged for the use of the capital;
(b) = the rate due to inflation (so that the purchasing power is not reduced);
(c) = a premium factor due to the fact that the investor is taking a risk that the capital amount may never be repaid.

These are selected as follows:

$$(\text{overall rate}) = (1+a)(1+b)(1+c)$$

Cash flow considerations

The rejection or deferral of a project proposal may have nothing to do with its intrinsic merit. The decision will be based on the availability or otherwise of the necessary cash in the context of an organisation that has to meet both its current liabilities and future investment requirements. A project is almost certain to be competing against others for scarce resources, and as the project manager will have to balance the trade-offs inherent in a project, so the project sponsor will have to balance the cost–benefit trade-offs of a number of proposals.

In large projects, the timing of payments may be critical for both the project organisation and its customers. For this reason it is necessary for both to know when expenditures are going to be made. In order to ease cash flow, projects may involve stage payments. This is common both in construction and large-scale engineering. While all the necessary credit checks can and should be carried out, it is still a matter of risk for both parties when large contracts are entered into.

8.3   Challenges for the received wisdom

It started all so well. . .

So far in this chapter, the nature of the business case, various approaches to obtaining costs and then for comparing them against the proposed benefits from the project, have been set out. It all appears on reading it back to be a wonderfully rational process. However, for all but the simplest of projects, there will be behavioural interventions here too which will have a significant impact on the business case.

These include:

- *optimism bias* – as will be demonstrated later in this chapter, a common activity in preparing and assessing estimates is to be over-optimistic in how much can be achieved in a project and how much or little it will cost;
- *politics* – for instance, in The Channel Tunnel project, the total cost escalated from £5 billion to £10 billion. Some of the people who worked on the estimating for that project always maintained that the costs would be £10 billion, but that such a figure was not politically acceptable on either side of The Channel. The need to have the fixed transport link was believed by some to be a key requirement of European integration. As for the Oresund Link in Chapter 4, sometimes that objective is placed above the costs. This issue is expanded in the next section;
- *strategic misrepresentation* – while optimism bias can be argued to be unintentional, strategic misrepresentation is deliberate.[7,8] In order to get their projects approved, managers underestimate the costs and risks, whereas they overestimate the benefits. It is worth thinking about the incentives here. Getting a major project funded is a big career achievement, so clearly people want to do this. The longer the project is (years, decades), the less likely it will be that the initial estimates will be accurate and, importantly, the less likely that the particular manager will still be there to have to explain why expectations are not being met. It is surprisingly common to meet project managers who have been handed unrealistic project requirements to deliver that they had no part in developing. As a general rule it is always helpful to engage those who will be doing the work to develop the plan, as they have both the specialist knowledge and 'skin in the game'. Where possible it is also advisable to have the manager in charge of the initial bid actually run the project and deliver it. Knowing you will be accountable later on focuses the mind very effectively!
- *improper use of estimates* – where 'ballpark figures' become official estimates without any checking or further development (what Eric Verzuh calls an 'on the way to the lift' estimate)[9]. For instance, you are asked by a colleague how much time it would take to do a particular task just so they can do some preliminary costings. Without any further

referral to you the original request is changed, but your figures are still used in preparing a detailed estimate. The latest version of the work is far more involved than you had been led to believe and it is too late to change the figures. This is known as anchoring bias, where people rely heavily on the first piece of information (the 'anchor') they have and fail to update their expectations when new and better information becomes available;

- *failure to be systematic about planning* – through either complacency or certainty that they will not actually be called on to do the work being discussed, people are vague and give an unqualified estimate to 'get the request off their desks'.

There are many other reasons for wishful thinking in costing. Various techniques have been demonstrated, with the objective of avoiding wishful thinking. However, as has been said many times already, the answers from even the best techniques are only estimates, and errors made at this stage can be multiplied many times.

So far, we have considered the relatively straightforward case, where there is a well-defined benefit for a well-defined investment. Reality is rarely so simple and while rational investment appraisal based on 'objective criteria' is often held up as an ideal, there are many instances where judgement as to the benefits of a project will have to be made on a qualitative basis. In particular, conventional approaches are problematic where:

- there is no guaranteed return;
- the benefit is made in terms of reduction of labour – some companies do not see this as being in line with their philosophy;
- the project is considered to be 'strategic' in nature;
- the organisation is in a not-for-profit sector – e.g. government or charity.

A good example of a *strategic investment* is in organisational change. Very often the justification will be made in terms of increased flexibility or capability of the organisation – both of which are very difficult to assign a monetary value to. Likewise, a new computer system may help speed the transfer of information and encourage an organisation to become more integrated, but will be challenged to show a cash return.

Also, some projects do have to have a 'leap of faith' attached to them – the founder of Kentucky Fried Chicken presented a proposal that was not attractive to hundreds of banks (over 600 said 'no'). There are many other pieces of business folklore that initially did not meet the conventional criteria. Indeed, as companies strive to find competitive advantage, conventional solutions are less likely to provide them. This is far more likely to be provided by those that challenge the limits of appraisal systems, though as the bursting of the dot-com bubble showed in the late 1990s, there is no getting around some business basics concerning expenditure and return.

When the organisation carrying out a project does not have the profit motive, assessing projects can be far more difficult. What is the financial benefit of a development project, for instance, which improves the quality of life of a group of people, or has an environmental benefit? How would you justify choosing a more expensive supplier because of their ethical stance despite making the project more expensive? Such questions are becoming more rather than less common for project managers, as the requirements of ethical and environmental policies produce considerable impacts for the context of their work.

The financial argument for provision of social goods can be much harder than for a more 'straightforward' decision, for example over whether to invest in a certain piece of factory equipment. Hospitals, parks, education, social care and a range of other benefits do not fit the same logic of NPV and a readily quantifiable financial return. Governments and local councils do, of course, have to argue the financial case for spending on one project over another, but these arguments are often as much political as financial, with a very wide range of stakeholders holding strong opinions. Sometimes there has to be a 'just do it' decision. In the extreme example of the Covid-19 crisis of 2020, governments around the world supported workers to stay at home to avoid spreading the disease. This would be unthinkable in 'normal' times, but the only sensible choice at the time was to do and spend whatever was necessary to save lives, and work out later how to deal with the consequences.

Factoring for optimism bias

Another challenge for the organisation trying to assess the business case for a project is demonstrated by Flyvberg's work on **optimism bias**.[10] Headline findings from his work include the critique of project approval processes that:

Understated costs + overstated benefits + understated environmental impact + overstated economic impact = project approval

This is fairly condemning of the approach that has been outlined for assessing costs and benefits. Indeed, further work carried out for the UK Treasury[11] yielded the guidance shown in Table 8.2 for budget assessment of infrastructure projects.

Table 8.2 shows the levels of uplift (increase in the budget) of a project that would have to be added, for a given level of confidence. There is a four-step process to follow. First, identify the sort of project being undertaken. In a programme with multiple projects of different types, each should be assessed separately. Second, consider the optimism bias adjustment and reduce the upper bound according to the extent risk has been identified and mitigated. Third, apply the optimism bias adjustment. The example given is that of work costing £10 million with an optimism bias of 40 per cent. The adjusted costs should therefore be £10 million + 40 per cent, i.e. £14 million. Importantly, the fourth stage is to review these numbers at different stages of the appraisal process, according to objective and transparent evidence of risk mitigation or avoidance.

This demonstrates some key principles about business case analysis. Firstly, that experience shows that budgets are usually conservatively estimated. Secondly, that the results of the analysis will depend on the level of *risk* that the organisation is prepared to accept. Risk will be discussed further in Chapter 10. Lastly, while there may be uplift on the cost side, a similarly critical approach should be taken to the benefits side.

Table 8.2 Recommended cost uplift for different project types

Spending Type	Optimism Bias Adjustment (%)			
	Works Duration		Capital Expenditure	
	Lower	Upper	Lower	Upper
Standard buildings	1	4	2	24
Non-standard buildings	2	39	4	51
Standard civil engineering	1	20	3	44
Non-standard civil engineering	3	25	6	66
Equipment/development	10	54	10	200
Outsourcing	n/a	n/a	0	41

Source: The Green Book: appraisal and evaluation in central government, HM Treasury and Government Finance 18 April 2013, Retrieved from https://www.gov.uk/government/publications/the-green-book-appraisal-and-evaluation-in-central-governent

Benefits realisation

An important part of the business case is that the target benefits of the project should be clearly stated, and the project should be able to be evaluated as to whether or not these were actually achieved in the end. In reality, though, this is normally more difficult than it sounds. One recent study[12] aids in this by offering three key dimensions on which they should be assessed. The first is *specificity* – clarity with regards to numerical targets that can be measured (e.g. a 10 per cent reduction in operating costs), and a dedicated owner. The second is *attainability* – goals should be challenging, yet attainable, and have a clear timeframe. The third is *comprehensiveness* – the target benefits should reflect the organisation's strategy, and be relevant to the project's stakeholders. These are very helpful. As we have seen in this chapter, there are well-established financial techniques for business case analysis, but these become less valuable if the initial ideas and overall purpose of the project are not clearly articulated. Considering specificity, attainability, and comprehensiveness aids our thinking when setting these ideas out, helps those doing the work focus on what is important, and allows a more thorough evaluation of the effectiveness of the work at the end.

One bank's commercial director stated that when they analysed their business, the combined benefits claimed by their projects meant they were heading for 110 per cent of the retail mortgage market in the UK. Clearly simply adding together the benefits claimed by projects is not going to give the best overall picture – such projects rarely act in isolation, and are frequently subject to overstated benefits, as mentioned above.

The conclusion of this discussion of optimism bias in both costs and benefits should not necessarily be to dispense with the method of business case analysis altogether. The challenge for project managers and appraisers is to use the experience of similar projects to provide a critical approach to costs and benefits, and be aware of the levels of risk or uncertainty attached to either.

Summary

■ For cost planning the issue here is to determine its importance, and through the iterative process outlined to come to some decisions as to the likely costs (and hence price and profit) on the project. This also determines the project viability. There are many techniques for cost estimation, although there is a 'wishful thinking' element to some estimates. Through the idea of cost build-up, all the elements are integrated and may become the budget against which your project will be assessed. Combined with the analysis of the benefits, starting qualitatively (as Chapter 4), and moving to a quantitative basis where possible, the business case can be developed. While there is an apparently rational process in operation here, there are considerable behavioural interventions in this process (e.g. optimism bias) that provide an added complication. Unless these are considered, they are likely to have a significant negative impact on the project as it progresses.

Key terms

business case *p. 197*	indirect expenses *p. 200*	payback analysis *p. 206*
capital equipment *p. 199*	internal rate of return *p. 206*	proxies *p. 201*
cash flows *p. 212*	learning curve *p. 200*	reimbursable pricing *p. 198*
compound interest *p. 207*	materials *p. 199*	sunk costs *p. 212*
contingency *p. 200*	net present/future value *pp. 208, 209*	synthetic estimation *p. 200*
cost planning process *p. 198*		target costing *p. 198*
cost-plus *p. 198*	opportunity costs *p. 212*	time *p. 199*
discounted cash flow *p. 206*	optimism bias *p. 215*	top-down and ground-up costing *p. 199*
fixed/variable costs *p. 212*	overheads *p. 200*	
forecast *p. 201*	parametric estimating *p. 200*	wishful thinking *p. 200*

Relevant areas of the Bodies of Knowledge

Table 8.3 Relevant areas of the APM Body of Knowledge

Relevant section	Title	Summary
1.3.7	Business case	High-level look at the justification for the business case, covering the strategic context, economic analysis, commercial approach, financial case, and management approach.
4.2.8	Cost planning	Discusses different costs incurred, and their timing over the life of the project.

Table 8.4 Relevant areas of the PMI Body of Knowledge

Relevant section	Title	Summary
7	Project cost management	This section looks at planning, estimating, budgeting, financing and managing costs over the project.
7.1	Plan cost management	This discusses the processes of cost management, and the details of how this will be done.
7.2	Estimate costs	The inputs to the process include the project documentation at the time, and it is advocated that costs are updated periodically, since new or updated information will become available. Standard published commercial costs can be used as an input, as well as expert human judgement.

PROJECT MANAGEMENT IN PRACTICE
Justify IT!

IT investment

A 2018 European Union report[13] stated that the EU Information and Communication Technologies (ICT) sector provided a Value Added (VA) of €581 bIllion, employed 5.8 million people and spent €30 billion on R&D. These are massive numbers, and our lives have been transformed in recent years by advances in technology which have made our lives and work easier. However, investments in IT are notorious for being late, over budget, and not delivering the benefits anticipated. Sometimes they are headline news, such as when a bank software update goes wrong and customers are locked out of their accounts for days.

With IT projects especially, the benefits can be advantageous, but if it goes wrong it can be absolutely catastrophic for an organisation. When looking at a major technology undertaking, it is sensible to consider the extreme events – what happens if it goes over budget by 400 per cent and only delivers 25–50 per cent of the anticipated benefits?[14] This does happen, what would you do if it happens to you? These are important conversations to have in the early stages of the work. As we saw in the example earlier in this chapter, if the benefits are relatively small, it is prudent to ask if it is really worth it. If you are proposing the project, be prepared with good answers here, and if you are on the approval committee it is your responsibility to ask those hard questions.

Points for discussion

1 Identify the nature of the costs and benefits that might be derived from such significant investments in both IT and R&D.

2 What levels of risk might be attributed to both IT and R&D projects?

3 Given the potential for optimism bias in business case development, how might organisations respond to this?

Topics for discussion

1 Identify the different roles that cost, price and profit can play in determining project costs.

2 In costing proposals, discuss the differences between top-down and ground-up approaches.

3 Describe the major elements of cost in a proposal to:

(a) implement a new computer system for the administration of a college or university
(b) construct a new theme park
(c) introduce a new range of non-paracetamol headache tablets.

4 Identify the benefits and potential disadvantages of a budget system.

5 'Evans the Steam' has set up a new business and secured a contract to build 32 locomotives for mountain railways, which are being reopened as tourist attractions. The order is to be fulfilled in two batches of 16. The first locomotive takes 30 days to assemble with seven people working full time on it. The daily rate for a locomotive fitter is £160 and the overheads are estimated to be 50 per cent on top of the labour rate. Evans is confident that an 80 per cent learning curve is possible. The first batch has been priced with a labour estimate of £32 000 per locomotive and the last 16 with a labour cost of £20 000. Comment on the pricing of the labour content and show whether the rates per locomotive are sufficient to cover the likely actual costs.

6 Draw up a table of potential costing methods, and show where each might be appropriate, giving examples.

7 Evaluate, using discounting techniques, which option, lease or buy, is most financially beneficial in the scenario given in Table 8.5. You should consider the discount rate to be 10 per cent and the period of consideration to be five years.

Table 8.5

	Buy	*Lease*
Purchase/lease cost	£50 000	£10 000 per year
Annual operating cost	£4000 per year	£4000 per year
Maintenance cost	£2000 per year	Maintained by leasing co.
Salvage value at the end of five years	£20 000	not applicable

8 The purchase of new office furniture for a boardroom has caused conflict between two factions within a company. One faction argues that the company should buy modern furniture, which will cost £24 000, and can be scrapped (replaced with zero salvage costs) in six years' time. The other favours the purchase of antique furniture which costs £60 000, but can be sold for £60 000 in six years' time. The modern furniture will cost £1000 in maintenance and the antique £2000. You have been asked to arbitrate the decision and resolve the conflict using financial methods (calculate the net present value of each scheme, using the company discount rate of 12 per cent).

9 Discuss the three main pricing strategies and indicate which one you feel provides the greatest benefits to customers and which to suppliers.

10 Holyrood (again). How did this project go so massively over its original budget? A cost overrun of 10 per cent, for instance, suggests that natural variation was present – it is not unreasonable. A cost overrun in excess of 900 per cent indicates some more fundamental issues with the whole costing process. Suggest where the process might have failed in this case given the material covered in this chapter.

Further information

Ashta, A. (2007) 'Behavioral Influences on the Calculation of Expectations in Project Appraisal', *The Icfai Journal of Behavioral Finance*, Vol. 4, No. 2, pp. 7–31.

Kahneman, D. and Lovallo, D. (2002) 'Timid Choices and Bold Forecasts: A Cognitive Perspective on Risk Taking' in Kahneman, D. and Tversky, A. (eds) (2002) *Choices, Values, and Frames*, Cambridge University Press, Cambridge, pp. 393–413.

Lovallo, D. and Kahneman, D. (2003) 'Delusions of Success – How Optimism Undermines Executives' Decisions', *Harvard Business Review*, July, pp. 56–63.

Mishan, E.J. and Quah, E. (2007) *Cost Benefit Analysis*, 5th edition, Routledge, Oxford.

Myddleton, D.R. (2007) *They Meant Well. Government Project Disasters*, Institute of Economic Affairs, London.

Ward, J. and Daniel, E. (2012) *Benefits Management: How to Increase the Business Value of Your IT Investments*, Wiley, Chichester.

Websites

www.maxwideman.com/pmglossary/PMG_C11.htm – useful glossary of project cost management terms; wider in scope than this chapter.

www.gov.uk/government/major-project-management

References

1 https://www.scotsman.com/news/scottish-news/scottish-parliament-20-ps414m-endless-recrimination-and-finally-iconic-building-1418185

2 www.gov.uk/government/publications/oakervee-review-of-hs2

3 APM (2019), *APM Body of Knowledge*, 7th edition, Association for Project Management, High Wycombe, UK.

4 Flyvbjerg B. et al. (2018) 'Five things you should know about cost overrun', *Transportation Research Part A*. 118, pp. 174–190.

5 Flyvbjerg, B. and Budzier, A. (2011) 'Why Your IT Project May Be Riskier Than You Think', *Harvard Business Review*, Vol. 89 No. 9, pp. 23–25.

6 Hogg, N. (1994) *Business Forecasting Using Financial Models*, Financial Times Pitman Publishing, London.

7 Flyvbjerg B. (2008) 'Curbing Optimism Bias and Strategic Misrepresentation in Planning: Reference Class Forecasting in Practice', *European Planning Studies*, Vol. 16, No. 1, pp. 3–21.

8 Flyvberg, B., Bruzelius, N. and Rothengatter, W. (2003) *Megaprojects and Risk: An Anatomy of Ambition*, Cambridge University Press, Cambridge.

9 Verzuh, E. (2003) *The Portable MBA in Project Management*, Wiley, Chichester.

10 As reference 7.

11 www.gov.uk/government/publications/the-green-book-appraisal-and-evaluation-in-central-goverent

12 Zwikael, O., Chih Y-Y, and Meredith J.R. (2018) 'Project benefit management: Setting effective target benefits', *International Journal of Project Management*, Vol. 36, No. 4, pp. 650–658.

13 The 2018 PREDICT Key Facts Report, see https://ec.europa.eu/jrc/en/predict

14 As reference 5.

APPENDIX
Present value of £1

Year	Discount rate												
	1%	2%	3%	4%	5%	6%	7%	8%	9%	10%	12%	14%	15%
1	0.990	0.980	0.971	0.962	0.952	0.943	0.935	0.926	0.917	0.909	0.893	0.877	0.870
2	0.980	0.961	0.943	0.925	0.907	0.890	0.873	0.857	0.842	0.826	0.797	0.769	0.756
3	0.971	0.942	0.915	0.889	0.864	0.840	0.816	0.794	0.772	0.751	0.712	0.675	0.658
4	0.961	0.924	0.889	0.855	0.823	0.792	0.763	0.735	0.708	0.683	0.636	0.592	0.572
5	0.951	0.906	0.863	0.822	0.784	0.747	0.713	0.681	0.650	0.621	0.567	0.519	0.497
6	0.942	0.888	0.838	0.790	0.746	0.705	0.666	0.630	0.596	0.564	0.507	0.456	0.432
7	0.933	0.871	0.813	0.760	0.711	0.665	0.623	0.583	0.547	0.513	0.452	0.400	0.376
8	0.923	0.853	0.789	0.731	0.677	0.627	0.582	0.540	0.502	0.467	0.404	0.351	0.327
9	0.914	0.837	0.766	0.703	0.645	0.592	0.544	0.500	0.460	0.424	0.361	0.308	0.284
10	0.905	0.820	0.744	0.676	0.614	0.558	0.508	0.463	0.422	0.386	0.322	0.270	0.247
11	0.896	0.804	0.722	0.650	0.585	0.527	0.475	0.429	0.388	0.350	0.287	0.237	0.215
12	0.887	0.788	0.701	0.625	0.557	0.497	0.444	0.397	0.356	0.319	0.257	0.208	0.187
13	0.879	0.773	0.681	0.601	0.530	0.469	0.415	0.368	0.326	0.290	0.229	0.182	0.163
14	0.870	0.758	0.661	0.577	0.505	0.442	0.388	0.340	0.299	0.263	0.205	0.160	0.141
15	0.861	0.743	0.642	0.555	0.481	0.417	0.362	0.315	0.275	0.239	0.183	0.140	0.123
16	0.853	0.728	0.623	0.534	0.458	0.394	0.339	0.292	0.252	0.218	0.163	0.123	0.107
17	0.844	0.714	0.605	0.513	0.436	0.371	0.317	0.270	0.231	0.198	0.146	0.108	0.093
18	0.836	0.700	0.587	0.494	0.416	0.350	0.296	0.250	0.212	0.180	0.130	0.095	0.081
19	0.828	0.686	0.570	0.475	0.396	0.331	0.276	0.232	0.194	0.164	0.116	0.083	0.070
20	0.820	0.673	0.554	0.456	0.377	0.312	0.258	0.215	0.178	0.149	0.104	0.073	0.061
25	0.780	0.610	0.478	0.375	0.295	0.233	0.184	0.146	0.116	0.092	0.059	0.038	0.030
30	0.742	0.552	0.412	0.308	0.231	0.174	0.131	0.099	0.075	0.057	0.033	0.020	0.015

	Discount rate												
Year	16%	18%	20%	24%	28%	32%	36%	40%	50%	60%	70%	80%	90%
1	0.862	0.847	0.833	0.806	0.781	0.758	0.735	0.714	0.667	0.625	0.588	0.556	0.526
2	0.743	0.718	0.694	0.650	0.610	0.574	0.541	0.510	0.444	0.391	0.346	0.309	0.277
3	0.641	0.609	0.579	0.524	0.477	0.435	0.398	0.364	0.296	0.244	0.204	0.171	0.146
4	0.552	0.516	0.482	0.423	0.373	0.329	0.292	0.260	0.198	0.153	0.120	0.095	0.077
5	0.476	0.437	0.402	0.341	0.291	0.250	0.215	0.186	0.132	0.095	0.070	0.053	0.040
6	0.410	0.370	0.335	0.275	0.227	0.189	0.158	0.133	0.088	0.060	0.041	0.029	0.021
7	0.354	0.314	0.279	0.222	0.178	0.143	0.116	0.095	0.059	0.037	0.024	0.016	0.011
8	0.305	0.266	0.233	0.179	0.139	0.108	0.085	0.068	0.039	0.023	0.014	0.009	0.006
9	0.263	0.226	0.194	0.144	0.108	0.082	0.063	0.048	0.026	0.015	0.008	0.005	0.003
10	0.227	0.191	0.162	0.116	0.085	0.062	0.046	0.035	0.017	0.009	0.005	0.003	0.002
11	0.195	0.162	0.135	0.094	0.066	0.047	0.034	0.025	0.012	0.006	0.003	0.002	0.001
12	0.168	0.137	0.112	0.076	0.052	0.036	0.025	0.018	0.008	0.004	0.002	0.001	0.001
13	0.145	0.116	0.093	0.061	0.040	0.027	0.018	0.013	0.005	0.002	0.001	0.001	0.000
14	0.125	0.099	0.078	0.049	0.032	0.021	0.014	0.009	0.003	0.001	0.001	0.000	0.000
15	0.108	0.084	0.065	0.040	0.025	0.016	0.010	0.006	0.002	0.001	0.000	0.000	0.000
16	0.093	0.071	0.054	0.032	0.019	0.012	0.007	0.005	0.002	0.001	0.000	0.000	
17	0.080	0.060	0.045	0.026	0.015	0.009	0.005	0.003	0.001	0.000	0.000		
18	0.069	0.051	0.038	0.021	0.012	0.007	0.004	0.002	0.001	0.000	0.000		
19	0.060	0.043	0.031	0.017	0.009	0.005	0.003	0.002	0.000	0.000			
20	0.051	0.037	0.026	0.014	0.007	0.004	0.002	0.001	0.000	0.000			
25	0.024	0.016	0.010	0.005	0.002	0.001	0.000	0.000					
30	0.012	0.007	0.004	0.002	0.001	0.000	0.000						

9 Engaging stakeholders

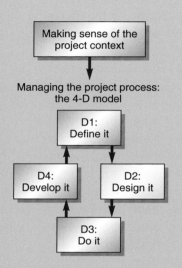

Making sense of the
project context

Managing the project process:
the 4-D model

D1:
Define it

D4:
Develop it

D2:
Design it

D3:
Do it

Principles

1 Achieving a certain level of quality is one of the primary objectives of most projects, and there are costs associated with this.

2 Quality is a subjective property and is judged by each of the project stakeholders. The outcome has an important impact on customer retention and future trust in projects.

3 Some elements of quality will require conformance, others provide the opportunity for real performance to be demonstrated, while still others provide the opportunity for business improvement.

Learning objectives

By the time you have completed this chapter, you should be able to:

→ identify various definitions of quality of product and service

→ recognise a process for managing a basic level of quality achievement through the concept of the quality bridge

→ identify the benefits of improving quality performance.

Contents

Introduction   *223*
9.1 The concept of quality and quality management   *224*
9.2 Quality performance and conformance   *230*
9.3 Towards quality improvement   *236*
Summary   *238*
Key terms   *239*
Relevant areas of the Bodies of Knowledge   *239*
Project management in practice: *Adopting a standard for project planning – useful discipline or unnecessary constraint?   240*
Topics for discussion   *241*
Further information   *241*
References   *242*

Universal Credit

Universal Credit was initiated in 2010 by the UK Government with the aim of digitising and streamlining the UK's benefits payments system. This was intended to be a major transformation of the social security system, both in terms of a change in the way of working, and also in a major technical IT investment to support it. The pro-

Source: Logo used with permission from Universal Credit

gramme subsequently became embroiled in very public delivery issues, with the work becoming significantly late and over budget. Technical issues hampered the project, not least because the contracts to develop hardware, software, networks and communications infrastructure were given to different firms and coordination was challenging. Newspaper articles were sometimes scathing, and at one point the programme went through five leaders in two and a half years. However, a new leader took over in 2014 and since then the delivery improved substantially and roll-out has been progressing at pace.

This is an example of a piece of work with major stakeholder challenges. As a multi-year government initiative costing billions of pounds, it will always be under relentless scrutiny from Parliamentary committees, individual ministers, the media, advocacy groups, not to mention the millions of benefits recipients. It is one of those programmes that gets relatively little press coverage when it is going well, but issues can be flagged up and become prominent (e.g. stakeholders can make their views known via social media) very quickly. In 2020 a BBC documentary series[1] showed the working of the system as it was being rolled out. This focused on the staff responsible for the delivery and the high-level rationales for some of the decisions, along with the experiences of the Job Centre employees supporting welfare recipients in their search for work, and the lives of some of those on the receiving end of the benefit system and how they perceived the practicalities of its working.

Delays in payment and difficulty in accessing support have very real consequences for the members of society that the system serves. As a project leader, whatever the nature of the undertaking, it is important to have the key metrics that you are responsible for achieving, but never forget that there are stakeholders who are relying on you to deliver an outcome for them. Take time to understand their real needs, and try to make sure that the targets you are working to still align with what they are expecting.

Introduction

Projects have stakeholders – those with an interest in the process of the project or its outcome. A project such as the development of Universal Credit has a huge array of stakeholders, many with different requirements. The quality of the development project will be judged by those stakeholders, in different ways and at different points in time. It is not sufficient for a project leader to leave this process of judgement to chance. Instead, managing the engagement of stakeholders, their perceptions and expectations of quality, is a key role of the project leader.

In a simple world, the quality of a project would be assessed by the output of that project – did you deliver the report, change, bridge, IT system, school, hospital or whatever, as was specified in the project brief? In the world of most modern projects, this is only the starting point for considering how a project will be appraised. It is not sufficient, in all but the simplest projects, to consider the product: the process by which it was delivered and the implications for the reputations of those involved are at least as important. This triumvirate of quality; health, safety, security, environment; and the impact of the project on the reputation of those involved, are part of the conversation about success.

In Chapter 4, a process for the identification and engagement of stakeholders was described. Key to this process is how 'quality' is managed. This will involve initially understanding the concept of quality – what it is and why it is so important to projects. It is notable that quality can be both a positive and negative construct. For instance, in the case of Samsung's Galaxy Note 7, viral videos of phones bursting into flames caused significant damage to the brand and ended a product life cycle, virtually overnight. The quality of the product may have been assured in the factory, but in use, a clear defect had emerged. The project leader has the challenge then of trying to maximise the positive aspects of the project's quality, while minimising the negative.

In quality planning, the definition of the relevant characteristics for the project is followed by the management of both conformance and performance aspects. Treating the project as a service rather than just a product can have benefits here, and a key role for project managers is to manage both the expectations and perceptions of stakeholders in the process.

9.1   The concept of quality and quality management

In the planning that has been discussed in previous chapters, inputs to the plans have included product breakdown structures, and these have then been turned into activities or work packages – the process by which the product will be delivered. Traditional approaches to managing quality have focused on the output – the product – regardless of the wider issues of stakeholders and their needs that were identified in Chapter 4. Many of these stakeholders will not receive a product, but a service – something that is intangible, is not durable and is more appropriately judged by assessing perceptions of the quality rather than objective measures. The three main concepts of this chapter concern the product, the process and the service quality for stakeholders.

REAL WORLD   What is quality? The 'Minimum Viable Product'

The IT industry is replete with tales of major projects that had detailed specifications and a long development phase, only to find out later that it wasn't what the users wanted or needed. Here even if the final system is developed on time, on budget, and meeting every specification, it is hard to call the project a success if it is not adopted by its end users. It is often unclear exactly what the market actually wants, and here the concept of the 'Minimum Viable Product' (MVP) is useful. Eric Ries[2] advocates a 'build-measure-learn' loop, and defines the MVP as 'that version of the product . . . with the minimum amount of effort and the least amount of development time'. If you are unsure exactly what the customer will value, build a prototype that you trial with them to find out. He tells the story[3] of Dropbox, the file-storage and sharing application. Started by engineers, they struggled to convince potential customers of their ideas and did not want to invest huge sums of money into a system if there would be little return. Instead, the CEO, Drew Houston, made a short demonstration video of how the technology would work and how seamless the functionality would be. This showed users what they could expect, and, as they say, the rest is history. Dropbox is a huge Silicon Valley success story.

The MVP concept serves several purposes. It allows an inexpensive demonstration of the product without the risk of the full-scale investment. This enables rapid learning – what does the customer want? Which aspects are most valuable, and which aren't necessarily required? What else would the customer like it to do? This is most frequently used in software products; it is straightforward to set up an initial webpage or app with basic functionality which customers can try for themselves. Early feedback enables development with a degree of confidence that it is going in the right direction. These preliminary versions may be sufficient for early adopters to pay for, bringing in some initial revenue as well. In addition, any potential customer who has their ideas adopted and incorporated into the next version is likely to be more positively disposed to the final product – everyone likes having their ideas implemented.

This can also apply to hardware. The advent of cheap 3D printing enables companies to make physical prototypes to show customers. One company we visited had such a printer to manufacture example housings for their electronic equipment. These could be taken to meetings to show what the final product would look like. This is in contrast to seeing a representation on screen, where scale and usability is hard to judge. Customers could handle the physical model and make any recommendations for changes, whereas the normal investment in tooling meant not only a delay of weeks between design and first product, but that any subsequent changes would be both time-consuming and expensive.

If you are starting a new development, ask yourself what the minimum initial product needs to be to enable you to trial it with customers. This enables you to learn about any improvements while they can be incorporated relatively easily. That way you can build quality into the product with confidence that the end user agrees. It can be an excellent way of building stakeholder support.

In the Universal Credit example, different stakeholders will have different views of quality. For Parliament, lateness and overspend in the development phase will be viewed very negatively. For Job Centre staff, the processes and IT need to work efficiently so that they can deliver a service to the public, since they are the 'face' of the system to the end users each day. The recipients of benefits need to be confident that they will receive the right money at the right time. Any IT budget issues or delayed milestones are not high on the priorities of most people here, they are more concerned with the delivery of the services they are expecting. 'Quality' thus incorporates a working system, rolled out smoothly over a long period of time, to enable new services to be delivered to end users with as little disruption to their lives as possible. Different stakeholder groups will have different views on quality, and making sure everyone is happy is a difficult, if not impossible task.

As can be seen, then, there is no single definition of quality. A lack of agreed definition on the term causes a problem for the project manager, in that if they cannot describe what it is (the precise quality) they are aiming for, it is very difficult to design a project system that will deliver it. The first step then is to recognise that there are many **definitions of quality**, and to determine which is/are most appropriate for the project being considered.

It helps to recognise that there is a set of well-used definitions that can be applied to facilitate the project manager in developing such an enhanced definition of quality. Initially, definitions can be focused internally and therefore be the prerogative of the project team (such as the technical specification of the final product), or focused externally and be in the domain of the marketers or other business managers. Success lies not in choosing one of these routes, but in the combination of the two. The effectiveness of the quality management is determined by the combination of these two views (**the bridge**), as shown in Figure 9.1. The *caveat* with this discussion of definition is that no matter how far we explore this area, there will always remain an element of quality that is elusive and as individual as people are.

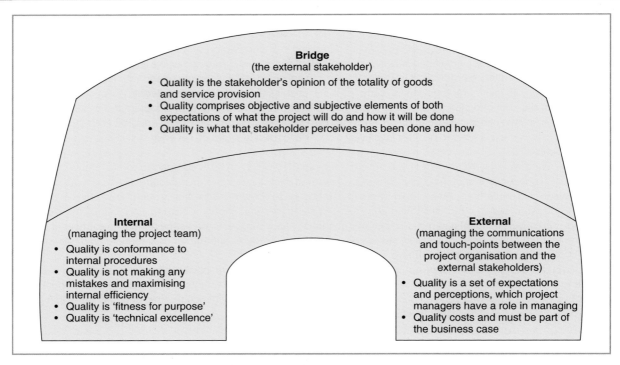

Bridge
(the external stakeholder)
- Quality is the stakeholder's opinion of the totality of goods and service provision
- Quality comprises objective and subjective elements of both expectations of what the project will do and how it will be done
- Quality is what that stakeholder perceives has been done and how

Internal
(managing the project team)
- Quality is conformance to internal procedures
- Quality is not making any mistakes and maximising internal efficiency
- Quality is 'fitness for purpose'
- Quality is 'technical excellence'

External
(managing the communications and touch-points between the project organisation and the external stakeholders)
- Quality is a set of expectations and perceptions, which project managers have a role in managing
- Quality costs and must be part of the business case

Figure 9.1 Bridge model of project quality management

One view states that quality is a definable and measurable set of characteristics, such as legally stating a product as 'fitness for purpose' or 'conforming to specification' or even 'being technically excellent'. This is a *product-based* view. Likewise, the *process* by which the project was delivered could be considered as being of a high quality if it was defect free, or conformed to a pre-determined plan. Such views are internally focused as this is irrespective of what any external stakeholder actually wanted.

There is a view that quality is the result of **expectations and perceptions** that can be managed through two-way communications.

The link between these two views occurs in the minds of the external stakeholder as a synthesis of objective and subjective elements of both product and process. This will include a judgement of *value* – the level of quality expected and perceived relative to both time and cost.

The approach of this chapter is to concentrate on those manageable elements within this model – the internal (project team) issues and the external (communications) ones. In doing so, we maximise the likely positive impact on the external stakeholders. The two perspectives, that of the internal (team-focused) and external (communications-focused) approaches comprise the definitions from a number of different approaches to quality, its meaning and a related approach to its management. Table 9.1 shows these, the definitions of quality that they support and a short description of the approach.

For many years, the **mathematical approach** was the only tool available to managers in pursuing quality improvement – the output of a process would be checked and corrected if statistically significant variations were seen to have entered the production system. This has been incorporated as an element of other approaches and is now seen as a very limited approach if used alone. Moreover, its use in projects is limited to where there are highly repetitive elements in the WBS.

Table 9.1 Perspectives on quality management

Perspective	Definition supported	Description of approach
Mathematical	Conformance to specification	The management of quality is limited to the assurance of the 'goodness' of a mechanical product or process. Activities are based on statistical tools, such as Statistical Process Control.[4]
System-structural	Conformance to procedure	This is encapsulated in the approach of the bureaucratic quality system as used as the basis for the ISO 9000 model of quality management. The achievement of a level of quality relies on the development and following of a hierarchical set of procedural documents.
Control-organisational	Continuously meeting customer requirements	In this approach, employees and customers are viewed as key determinants of project quality. This is particularly useful where there are high levels of contact with particular external stakeholder groups during the project.
Economic	Cost of (un)quality	The financial costs and benefits of quality management are assessed against the costs of failure.
Holistic	Continuously meeting customer requirements at lowest cost	The Total Quality approach – relies on a change in the entire way the operation approaches its project processes, from senior management to the front-of-house staff.
Strategic	Quality as competitive advantage	The additional responsiveness that can come from successfully pursuing product and process improvement is treated as part of the competitive strategy of the firm.

The **system-structural approach** is where procedures are defined by a particular standard, possibly ISO 9001[5] or any one of a number of customer-specific sets of guidelines. While there are marketing benefits to be gained from organisations becoming accredited to such standards, the measures they incorporate are also limited as they focus on what are termed the *conformance aspects* of quality, as will be discussed in the following section and Project Management in Practice at the end of this chapter. Rather than being used in isolation, the conformance system should be one part of a much wider quality management improvement effort if real benefit is to be gained by the system.

In the **control-organisational approach**, employees and customers are viewed as key determinants of quality. This idea is particularly relevant in organisational change projects, where there are very high levels of contact during the execution of the project between the transforming team and the organisation. In considering the degree of control that the organisation can exert over the actions of individuals, training and systems of pay and reward are the main 'behaviour modifiers'. The imposition of control through excessive chains of command is shown to be ineffective in many studies. However, developing the concept of 'internal customers' within organisations has been effective. An internal customer is someone who receives work from another person (the supplier) within the organisation. This ensures that *back-office* staff (those who have little or no contact with the external or final customer) are connected to the project delivery process, as their input will inevitably have an effect on the ability of the front-of-house staff to deliver service quality. For instance, in the IT industry, some firms now encourage their programming staff to visit customer staff, whereas previously they would have been isolated from the customer. Similarly, social contact between members of a project team can enhance the level of commitment to objectives.

The approach to quality management from an **economic** perspective is vital in providing a driver for improving performance and will be described further in Section 9.3.

For the **holistic approach**, the whole organisation needs to see quality as vital to their operation, and implement systems that support this. There are several well-established approaches here. Six-Sigma was established in Motorola in the 1980s initially as a way of measuring and controlling process defects in manufacturing operations but was taken up by many organisations, notably including General Electric. The sigma refers to standard deviations within any operation, and achieving six sigma levels of quality means that there is only one defect per 3.4 million operations. By focusing on measuring process variations and using statistics in manufacturing, dramatic improvements in quality could be achieved. The DMAIC ('Define-Measure-Analyse-Improve-Control') system gives a clear structure to process improvement, applicable to internal operations beyond just manufacturing, and thus can be used across the organisation. Staff knowledge of these systems could be graded similarly to martial arts expertise, with 'white belt' for a basic understanding, through 'green belt', up to a much longer formal course for 'black belt' (as one of the authors can attest).

'Lean' has a similar objective, but the primary focus here is on eliminating waste. The Lean Enterprise Institute[6] specifies a five-step process for implementing lean techniques. First, specify value from the viewpoint of the end customer – what do they actually require? Second identify the steps you take in delivering that value, and eliminate steps that do not add value. This is where wasted time, movement, or unnecessary stock can be removed. Third, make the value-creating steps occur in a smooth sequence so the product will flow towards the customer. Fourth, use a 'pull' system from the next activity (rather than 'pushing' product to the next stage). Finally, repeat the process, improving it further. This is discussed further in Chapter 16.

To consider quality as a **strategic approach** may seem odd. Who doesn't want quality? However, it makes sense when we consider that producing a quality product or service inevitably involves trade-offs. In Chapter 4 we considered the trade-offs between time, cost and quality with the 'iron triangle'. A strategic approach to project management involves thinking carefully about what the stakeholders really want, and managing the project according to that. Inevitably, customers always want the best product possible, immediately, and at zero cost. Clearly this isn't possible, but what realistic steps can we take? Consider the diagram in Figure 9.2, which expands the iron triangle a little further.[7] There are a number of options here that need to be considered. First, time. There is a distinction between speed of delivery (how fast can it be done?) and delivery reliability (can we guarantee a delivery date?). Consider, for example, the manufacture of aircraft wings. The project plan will specify when wings need to be delivered to complete the manufacturing. Delivering early is unhelpful – where would they be stored? How important, then, is speed? Should the project be delivered as fast as possible, or is a delivery date critical (left-hand side of Figure 9.2), or is it really not that vital? Note that you simply cannot have all the options on the left-hand side of the scale, and working out what you do really need is a valuable exercise.

Next, what about price? Is a cheap solution really what the customer wants, or does the work just have to be competitively priced? Obviously price is important, the question is *how* important. Often it is not the overriding factor – people will pay extra for speed and service.

The quality aspect is more nuanced, as there are a number of factors that can be considered. First, the product quality itself – does the customer want the very best possible? It will cost more, and may well take longer. The service quality (discussed shortly) is also important to consider. We need to consider the value of *how* the project

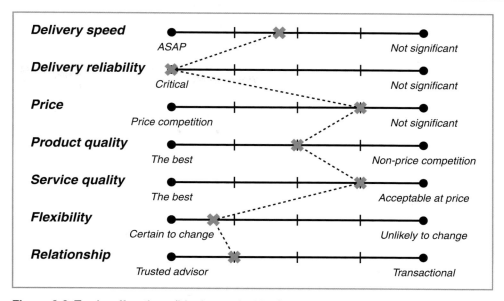

Figure 9.2 Trade-off options (Maylor et al., 2015)

is delivered, as well as *what* is delivered. The final two options may not be immediately obvious, but they can be significant. How much flexibility is expected? Sometimes the requirements are clear and straightforward, but often they are not. In a new product development, for example, lots may change and so flexibility is valuable. This may end up costing more and taking longer, so the trade-off is against those factors. The relationship aspect may also be key – is this a transactional piece of work where the parties are unlikely to work together again, or might it lead to a longer-term relationship with more projects in the future?

A practical example of this based on one organisation we worked with is shown in Figure 9.2. This was a client undertaking an important software project. Speed itself was not essential, but reliability and hitting the delivery date was vital as it was part of a much bigger upgrade. Because of this, price was not so critical (e.g. to allow for more staff, and any overtime required to hit to the due date). A key aspect, though, was that flexibility and relationship were rated highly since this work had to fit within the bigger programme and aspects could change.

This is how a strategic approach can be considered to meet a wider interpretation of 'quality' and ensure stakeholder satisfaction. Trade-offs do need to be made (you cannot be the fastest, cheapest, have the highest product and service quality and be the most flexible at the same time), and understanding what the customer needs and tailoring the project approach to this may be a route to project success.

Quality and stakeholder satisfaction

The nature of satisfaction

Some general principles of **stakeholder management** come from an appreciation of basic customer behaviour. One part of this concerns the nature of **satisfaction**. Here, Maister's[8] first law of service is useful, namely that:

$$satisfaction = perception - expectation$$

That is, the satisfaction is determined by the difference between how the project is perceived or viewed by a stakeholder and how they expected it to perform. One of the greatest causes of dissatisfaction is the creation of unrealistic expectations. As was seen in the previous chapter, where competitive tendering is required for obtaining a contract, firms have to push the limits of what they could achieve in order to win the business. The levels to which the bidders should go to win needs to be carefully considered, as it does set the level of expectations against which they will later be judged. Even where there is no competitive element of bidding for resources, many people still take a very optimistic view of the project outcome. This needs to be considered carefully.

In one study we were involved with[9] in the IT-services industry, one of the managers complained that they were 'green' on all their key metrics, but their client still wasn't satisfied. Digging deeper, we found that the client wanted the work to be completed in compliance to the specification (as you would expect), but that the 'service' aspect of the delivery was also very important to them. This emphasises the 'how' as well as just the 'what' of the project. Aspects such as integration (bringing everything together and emphasising stakeholder engagement), adaptability (identifying and manging changes effectively) and adding value (contributing to long-term success) were found to be significant, beyond just the required items in the contract.

In order to deliver quality in the eyes of the customer, we need to understand the gap between the expectations and the perceptions of stakeholders. This gap is identified as:

- between the actuality of customer requirements and the perceptions of managers who try to ensure good capture of the requirements;
- between this perception of the requirements and the written specification of the requirements of the project;
- between the specification as written and the actual product and process delivered during the execution phase of the project;
- between that quality of service received by the customer and that which they were led to expect from communications.[10]

Tools to help manage these gaps include process mapping (Chapter 5).

9.2 Quality performance and conformance

The quality planning process should follow the structure shown in Figure 9.3. There are a number of elements to this figure, revolving around the first step in any quality process – that of definition. Quality is a term that has so many different meanings for different people that it must be subject to some further definition before we can in any sense manage it. The two major inputs are from organisational strategy and from customer requirements. Customer requirements may be explicitly stated in direct value-adding projects through the terms of the contract or, in many cases, will have to be determined through discussions. The strategy input should help to determine the kind of quality that we are trying to achieve – for instance, technical excellence or meeting certain external standards. These two inputs can be put into context by considering the alternative approaches to defining and managing quality and can be summarised in the **manufacturing and service paradigms** as shown in Table 9.2.

The manufacturing approach to quality championed conformance to specification as the metric for success. This relied on quality being definable through a precisely measurable set of characteristics. This is applicable to large-scale engineering projects, for

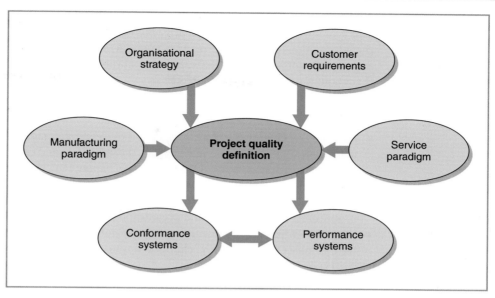

Figure 9.3 Quality planning process

Table 9.2 Manufacturing and service approaches to quality

	Manufacturing	*Service*
Definition	Product-based – a precise and measurable set of characteristics	Based on stakeholders' expectations and perceptions
Attributes	Performance, conformance features, reliability, durability, serviceability, perceived quality and aesthetics	Access, communication, competence, courtesy, credibility, reliability, responsiveness, security, tangibles, understanding/ knowing the customer

instance. Outside this environment, there are many types of projects that require a much higher degree of customer orientation, considering management of both perceptions and expectations. Furthermore, many modern projects do not just have **tangible** outputs. An office move, for example, is conceptually straightforward (transfer furniture and facilities from point A to point B), but it is notoriously difficult in practice. It is disruptive, people are never satisfied with where they end up, everyone wants a corner office, and so on. Instead of doing it 'to' the staff, it is more effective to do it 'with' them and consider their experiences of the move. Rather than applying product-based measures of quality in such instances, service-based definitions and derived measures are far more appropriate. These feed into the two sets of actions that have to be planned at this stage – developing systems that ensure conformance and performance.

Quality conformance planning

Since the 1950s quality conformance planning – otherwise referred to as quality assurance – has been used to ensure that minimum standards are maintained in a wide array of activities. There is considerable literature on it (see Further Information at the end of this chapter). The discussion here will focus on the use of a **project manual** as a means of not only planning for achieving what you have set out to do in quality terms but also demonstrating that you have planned to achieve what you set out to do in quality terms. This is no small difference, particularly when it comes to legal liability issues or preparing the information for a review process. The project manual, as the contents list below demonstrates, is not just about quality. It is about bringing all project information – including that about time and cost – into one place.

A contents list might include the following:

- Introduction – the reasoning behind the project.
- Planning – including the objectives, priorities, scope statement and WBS (as described in Chapter 6) and all the detailed plans – those for time and cost, both in summary and detail, contingencies and risk analysis (see Chapter 10). These are the basis for reference when decisions are required.[11]
- Execution details – including the schedules, the responsibilities (see below), relevant procedures, standard forms and organisational structure that will be used.
- Records – minutes of relevant meetings, notes of problems that have arisen and how they were dealt with, changes requested and made, status reports, other correspondence.
- Miscellaneous information – including contact points for all people involved in the project, and sources of technical reference material.

For relatively small, low-complexity projects such a definition may seem excessive, and indeed it can be reduced to a minimum. As one events manager who used a project manual routinely for her work commented, 'If I fall under a bus tomorrow, someone could walk in here and pick up the project, and get up to speed with it fairly quickly.'

Responsibility allocation

A major task for the project manager concerns the allocation of resources to different parts of the project. These may be to different parts of their own firm or even to different organisations. Before plans can go forward for analysis it is vital that each part of the organisation has the resources available to carry out the tasks that have been assigned to them. Inevitably, some parts of the organisation will have little problem meeting the objectives with the resources under their control. Others will be put under considerable strain. If the plans are to have any credibility, they must consider the limitations imposed by the availability of people and equipment. Allocation of responsibility is certainly important, but project work is generally more complex than whether an individual is responsible or not. This is where a RACI chart is helpful, it shows who is *R*esponsible (needs to do the actual work), *A*ccountable (often the decision-maker, likely the project manager), *C*onsulted (who needs to be asked about key issues, such as technical experts, end users, or department heads) and who needs to be *I*nformed (may be the project management office, and/or senior management). Working out how the various stakeholders map onto each category for the various activities is a useful exercise and does clarify the role each plays in the project. An example **RACI matrix** is shown in Figure 9.4.

All the above provides the basis for having the necessary documentation in place to demonstrate that you have done everything possible to ensure that the project delivers as conforming to the stated requirements. Many organisations do legislate the type and style of documentation required, and this is demonstrated in the Project Management in Practice at the end of this chapter. For large-scale projects the documentation is a significant workload in itself – and one potential role for a project office. The compilation and sharing of information through a project manual is a task that can easily be shared using online tools.

Person	Activity					
	1	2	3	4	5	6
A	RA	A	A		A	A
B			I	A	R	R
C	C	I	C	R	C	I
D		R	I	I		
E		I	R	I		
F	C	I	I	C	I	C

Figure 9.4 RACI matrix

One of the challenges in justifying the bureaucracy that goes with such quality plans – for instance, as required by PRINCE2 – is the question, 'does all this make your stakeholders – customers in particular – happy or delighted?' The answer to this is that if you do not have it, it will make them very unhappy, but it does not in itself cause satisfaction or delight. As a result, there will have to be other aspects of the product or process that will have to address this issue. Specifically, having satisfied the conformance requirements, what can the project manager do to ensure good-quality performance?

Quality performance planning

Consider the challenge of planning the Olympics in a major city. There is a large and diverse stakeholder group, all with different requirements. Compare, for example, the requirements of those residents of the area in which the stadia are being constructed with those of the athletes. For the athletes, having their residences as close to the stadium as possible is convenient, but does mean that there is additional construction traffic and congestion immediately in the vicinity. Locating the residential accommodation further afield would spread the impact of the project. There are two further aspects that need consideration here:

- the nature of satisfaction;
- how then to manage the process by which the service provided by the project is delivered.

Perceptions can to a certain extent be managed. A useful consideration of this element is to provide customer **cues** – points where the stakeholder's attention is drawn to favourable aspects of the project process or outcome. These are from the stakeholder's own experience, but importantly can be reinforced by external factors such as publicity material. Rather than relying on the assumption that 'quality speaks for itself' and that customers are able unambiguously to evaluate the quality of the outcome or the process, the project manager has a number of channels of communication that can be used to 'manage' consumer perceptions. The publicity element of the marketing communications programme potentially affects the information available to stakeholders, as demonstrated by the following example.

Stakeholder management – the road builders

It seems that wherever you go in the world people moan about the state of their country's roads. The UK is no different in this respect. When a local council decided to resurface the road leading to a major tourist area in the height of the summer the anger turned from the state of the road to the stupidity of doing such work during the period of highest demand. For weeks the road was in turmoil, with significant delays being encountered during very hot weather. Local residents were horrified at the amount of work being done during 'anti-social hours' – creating noise from the works and substantial additional heavy traffic bringing in machinery and materials to the site. Yet this all seemed to be forgotten when the project was completed and notices were posted at the side of the road stating that:

'XYZ contractors, working in conjunction with your local council, are pleased to announce the completion of the road up-grade scheme, 6 full weeks ahead of schedule.'

Even the local paper was impressed. How about this for stakeholder management?!

A further level in the consideration of the management of perceptions was identified at the start of this section. This concerns the nature of the attribute of the outcome of the project as either a product or a service. As was shown then, services can be considered to have a wider array of characteristics that a customer or group of customers will consider. For instance, the outcome of a project may be the construction of a building or the preparation of a document. Both of these have tangible qualities that can readily be assessed and will form part of the expectations and perceptions of stakeholders. There are also intangible elements of the process. Specific elements from Table 9.2 for projects include:

- **responsiveness** – the speed of reply to requests for information or changes;
- **communication** – how readily the project team provided information;
- **competence/professionalism** – the apparent ability of the project organisation to deliver the outcomes;
- **courtesy** – the style of the treatment received by stakeholders;
- **accessibility** – the ease with which individuals could be identified and contacted when information was required.

These elements may not represent the **core product** of the project – the building or the document. There may be **peripheral** elements – documentation for the building or support information from a document on a website. Project managers therefore also need to consider which elements of the project are core and which are peripheral. While the core should take the majority of the resources, you may find that provided it is achieved in a satisfactory manner, it is the peripheral product of the project on which you will be judged.

Table 9.3 provides a summary of these issues for the project manager. It shows elements of the process and outcomes from the project, and how the expectations and perceptions can be managed in each case. This is a major improvement on the normal system, where managers simply use customer complaints as a measure of the success or otherwise of their actions. However, even if your project performs satisfactorily, do not expect customers to be pleased. You will have to find elements – maybe of the peripheral product – which can

Table 9.3 Management of expectations and perceptions

	Process	*Outcome*
Expectations	Provide samples of process documentation; use of accreditations of processes (e.g. ISO 9000, PRINCE2 2009)	Determine actual requirements; do not over-promise
Perceptions	Provide regular reports of progress; build on issues important to the stakeholders – e.g. through senior management involvement in the project.	Promote positive aspects of outcome – cues; in some cases, use 'selective over-delivery'.

be used to provide the excess of perception over expectation. If project management is to move to a more proactive approach to such issues, it is vital that they are considered at the strategy stage.

So how do we ensure that we communicate with stakeholders and that key individuals are kept 'in the loop'? Four-field maps/deployment flow-charts do help with this process, and ensure that those directly affected are included. Many project managers also like to include a specific **communications plan** as part of the planning process, and indeed this is part of both PRINCE2 methods and the PMI Body of Knowledge. As a tool, it is probably most useful for medium/large-scale complexity projects, particularly where there is a diverse stakeholder group.

Communications planning

A common technique for communications management centres on the use of a table to identify the nature of the communication (what will be told to whom and in what format), the timing and who is responsible for doing it. We are not considering daily communication or simple information-sharing activities, which while vital, are not the type of 'grand communications' being considered here – typically key reports, announcements of achievements, technical updates, etc.

To help structure this the basic stakeholder analysis carried out as part of the project strategy formulation process is expanded in Table 9.4.

While IT can assist in the distribution of information, many managers suffer from e-mail overload, restricting not only their efficiency but also the effectiveness of the communication. Other, more visible, methods of reporting are therefore preferable, as will be shown in Chapter 13.

Table 9.4 Communication plan

Stakeholder	*Communication*	*Timing*	*Format*	*Distribution*	*Person responsible*
Project sponsor	Monthly	Week 1 each month	Short report	E-mail	Project manager
Accounts department	Monthly spend schedule	2 weeks before start of month	Short budget	E-mail	Administrator
Client department	Monthly	Week 1 each month	1-page report	E-mail and noticeboard	Liaison officer

9.3 Towards quality improvement

The idea that quality performance has both direct and indirect effects on the financial performance of the organisation is quantified and used as the basis for management activity. Directly, we can say that 'quality is not free, it costs'. Precisely how much it costs is a matter for the managers of the system. Comparable companies in the same sector routinely have widely differing approaches to quality, and very different assessments of their quality costs. It is not reported on balance sheets, but can have a major impact on profitability.[12]

Quality costs include elements of prevention, appraisal and failure as described in Table 9.5.

The management of quality should involve the calculation of these costs – an activity that is by no means a simple one. Quality costs, it seems, like quality have a large number of definitions, and the elements that are included under each heading in the table below are often subjective and vary from organisation to organisation. Typically, compiling cost reports is the mechanism for measuring these costs. The objective is not the keeping of further legions of 'bean counters' in work, rather allowing a process of self-investigation to follow, i.e. the purpose is that of reducing quality costs, not simply measuring them. It has been found that a company with a well-developed quality system will have quality costs in the region of 2 per cent of turnover. A company with a poorly developed quality system will devote in excess of 20 per cent of its turnover to quality costs. The impact on bottom-line performance from this consideration alone is clearly significant. This establishes the importance of quality management in the costs of the service provision. The role for management in this is the control and reduction of these costs.

Management of failure

The **management of failure** is required where, for whatever reason, a stakeholder and particularly a customer becomes dissatisfied with the service encounter that your organisation has provided or is in the process of providing. Customer perceptions are transitory (they change with time) and it is a key element of the responsiveness element of the service encounter how the problem is resolved. Failure management, or recovery as it is more

Table 9.5 Quality cost categories[13]

Category	Characteristic being measured	Examples
Prevention	The costs of ensuring that the required level of quality of service is met	Planning Risk management Stakeholder management
Appraisal	Measuring what level of quality of service is provided	Stakeholder surveys Random inspection/checks Performance data gathering and analysis
Failure	The costs of getting it wrong and putting it right – can be categorised as either internal or external failure	*Internal failure*: mishaps or errors that are resolved without the customer ever seeing them *External failure*: occurs in the interaction with the customer, may result in loss/withdrawal of business or rectification/rescue being required

correctly termed, is not a fashionable issue. Organisations that recognise that failures will occur, no matter how well planned the system, do have some chance of not only rescuing the current situation, but also learning from it, and improving in the future. As one organisation noted, customer complaints in the first instance were directed to the person who was responsible for that area. Any repeat customer complaints were routed to the firm's managing director. This attempt to eliminate these 'repeat concerns' was highly effective and showed a level of commitment to the issue of quality at a high level. Moreover, it is a realistic approach – mistakes do happen – most customers accept this (albeit grudgingly). It is the actions that follow that determine whether or not the event becomes a cause for 'consumer terrorism' (customers who gladly tell everyone the problems that they had with a firm) or an opportunity to get closer to the customer. The organisation does have a choice in this respect. The stages in the management of failure are as follows:

- identify that something has gone wrong;
- contain the situation – accept that there is a problem, prevent further damage or escalation of the problem;
- put in place recovery actions to regain the customer's confidence;
- ensure that practices are changed so that this incident does not occur again.

The first step – identification – considers that there will be some cue from the customer that all is not well. This may be through a verbal comment made to a member of staff, or direct observation of customer behaviour.

The second stage is that of recognition and containment. For a customer, the rejection of their query by an organisation can be the first stage in a downward spiral. Front-line staff need to be aware of the need to be accepting of customer views, rather than defensive about their organisations. Having done so, it is vital that this is followed through to some resolution that is acceptable to both the organisation and the customer. Containment is where the problem is prevented from spreading – customers of tourism products are notorious for spreading dissatisfaction, by drawing attention to (providing cues to other customers) elements of poor quality.

The third stage is the recovery action. This undoubtedly needs to consider the technical and interaction needs of the customer. Firstly, the technical needs should be addressed, ensuring that a solution is found that is mutually acceptable. The second is the interaction – the customer should be left in little doubt that their needs were considered and that everything possible has been done to rectify the situation.

Finally, it is vital that the organisation learns from the problems. Typically this would include some analysis of the root causes of the problems and remedial action through, for example, training or amendment to procedures. Further methods of problem-solving are described in Chapter 15.

The discussion of such failure entails much additional work for an organisation, which cannot be cost-justified in conventional terms. If, however, an approach is taken which considers all costs – in this case quality costs (see below) – the justification becomes far easier.

Variability

Service projects, due to the involvement of the customer in their delivery and the reliance on staff for their quality, exhibit a far greater variability in their delivery than manufactured products. This is not necessarily a problem where the service delivery is a high-margin, customised service. Variability becomes a problem where, due to volume throughput requirements, a standardised service is required. Staff may take more time processing each project than is allocated, and queuing or other form of delay results. For instance, an accountancy firm decided that each of its major audits would be termed 'a project'.

Each project was relatively standardised as the audit trail was defined by law. However, where there were discrepancies between the standards and the findings of the audit, this introduced variability into the process – it was not known where it would be found or how serious it would be.

The economic argument for organisational quality improvement is based on direct cost-saving, as demonstrated through the arguments of the cost of quality. This is a *productivity-based* argument – you will get more out for the same input of resources. Another argument exists – the *competitiveness-based* argument. This maintains that, consistent with the resource-based view of an organisation,[14] improving the levels of quality in an organisation and its ability to deliver projects effectively will improve its overall level of strategic competitiveness. Make sure to consider what the customer finds important, though. As we saw in Figure 9.2, trade-offs are a fact of life, and prioritising the right aspects can be very important in ensuring stakeholder satisfaction.

Project quality costs – large and very famous electronics company*

Assessing the costs of quality is never a straightforward process, but as suggested already, does generate a very good insight into the nature of costs being incurred by an organisation. Sometimes, though, it does provide news that people simply don't want to hear. During a study to start to identify some typical figures for costs of quality in this firm, a small task team was established. They piloted a basic method for the identification of quality costs in their environment.

The project started well, gathering some useful data that showed a cost of quality around 8 per cent of project budgets. This was not good news in the firm, and caused some issues with senior managers. However, that was just the pilot study. On one project, further investigation into the costs of failure revealed that the initial 8 per cent figure was significantly understated, and that 28 per cent was more likely to be realistic. This was 'not politically acceptable', and the project to assess quality costs was abandoned.

* Cannot be named due to non-disclosure agreement.

Summary

■ In this chapter we have considered the two main inputs of strategy and customer requirements, and translated these into a process to consider assurance – or conformance to requirements, and a process to work towards customer satisfaction/delight. This would be through first considering the definition of quality that the organisation had as relevant and the needs of the customers. This definitional issue is highly significant due to the diversity of meanings of 'quality' and this is facilitated through the application of both product and service definitions to core and peripheral outputs from the project. In managing conformance, the importance of documented systems including the use of a project manual was covered. The managing of perceptions includes the use of active cues and a communications plan.

■ Finally there is, to use the language of Chapter 8, a 'business case' for quality improvement activity. The assessment of quality costs provides a justification for such improvement. It is found that investment in prevention and appraisal issues will, in the medium term at least, reduce failure costs. Given that these are usually by far the largest categories of cost, the opportunity exists to return some of that wasted cost of failure to the bottom line of the project.

Key terms

accessibility *p. 234*

communication *p. 234*

communications plan *p. 235*

competence/
professionalism *p. 234*

conformance and
performance *p. 231*

control-organisational
approach *p. 227*

core product *p. 234*

courtesy *p. 234*

cues *p. 233*

definitions of quality *p. 225*

economic approach *p. 228*

expectations and
perceptions *p. 226*

holistic approach *p. 228*

management of failure
p. 236

manufacturing and
service paradigms *p. 230*

mathematical approach
p. 226

peripheral *p. 234*

project manual *p. 231*

quality costs *p. 236*

RACI matrix *p. 232*

responsiveness *p. 234*

satisfaction *p. 229*

stakeholder
management *p. 229*

strategic approach *p. 228*

system-structural
approach *p. 227*

tangible *p. 231*

the bridge *p. 225*

Relevant areas of the Bodies of Knowledge

Table 9.6 Relevant area of the APM Body of Knowledge

Relevant section	Title	Summary
4.1.5	Quality planning	Emphasises ensuring that the outputs delivered are in line with the customer's requirements. Gives a broad outline of what should be in the Quality Plan.

Table 9.7 Relevant areas of the PMI Body of Knowledge

Relevant section	Title	Summary
8	Project quality management	Breaks the quality management into planning, managing and controlling quality.
8.1	Plan quality management	This looks at how quality requirements / standards will be identified, and how the project will demonstrate compliance with them. Conformance and non-conformance costs are discussed, along with key data and metrics.
8.2	Manage quality	This section addresses practical tools and techniques to use within the project, including checklists, root cause analysis, data representation techniques, audits, and problem-solving.
8.3	Control quality	This covers the verification that the project outputs are in line with the expectations of the customer. Activities that can be used include statistical sampling, inspection, and product testing.

PROJECT MANAGEMENT IN PRACTICE
Adopting a standard for project planning – useful discipline or unnecessary constraint?

Should all the project plans produced and used in an organisation conform to a particular set of rules and processes, such as:

- the notation used in diagrams;
- the units to be used;
- the requirements to use any default estimates for regularly used work packages;
- the requirements to review lessons-learnt documents and 'plan-versus-actual' data from previous similar projects;
- who can construct the diagrams;
- the procedure used for checking the plans prior to their issue;
- the regularity by which they are reviewed and updated (e.g. weekly);
- the filing, storage and control of plans to ensure that only the current version is being worked to;
- the number of versions kept, and for how long;
- the documentation required to support changes and keep a history of the deviation from the original plan;
- the format of reports;
- the structure of project documents on the company intranet;

. . . or is this just creating unnecessary bureaucracy?

There was a clear divide among the project managers who were questioned on this issue, which can be summarised in the following composite cases.

Example 1 Makesure Electronics

There are very tight controls as to how project plans may be drawn up. The bureaucracy of the company is considered necessary to ensure that the end-customers of the projects are kept happy (generally military procurement agencies). The correct paperwork is essential to the project and would be returned to the originator if all the boxes on the accompanying forms are not fully completed. It is generally felt that the process prevents any dynamic activity taking place, but that is appropriate for their market. Updating the plans and tracking progress is done throughout the project execution and allows a detailed history to be retained. Although these controls can be perceived as onerous and time-consuming, it does allow close scrutiny and provides detailed information on the performance of the many projects they run, from which trends can be observed and insight obtained.

Example 2 Internal consultancy in a public service industry

The role of the consultancy is one of a team that moves in to help a department solve a particular problem before moving on to the next. The team is required to be dynamic and respond quickly to changes. Plans are mainly for the use of the team in structuring how they tackle the problem. No particular convention is adhered to and there are no rules which the team believe would constrain the problem-solving process. This often causes problems with their 'customers', many of whom believe in the benefits of the more formalised approach but who nonetheless are generally satisfied with the results of their work.

Points for discussion

1 When might such formalisation of a project process be necessary?
2 How would you assess the business benefit of such procedures?
3 Under what conditions would such procedures be inappropriate?

Topics for discussion

1 What is 'quality'?

2 Select a product and a service that you have recently purchased. For each of these, what does quality mean?

3 How well do the definitions that you applied in answering (2), apply to projects?

4 Taking a project that you are familiar with such as an assignment, what aspects of quality of the process and the outcome would be relevant?

5 Who are the stakeholders for your assignment, what are their expectations and how are you going to manage these?

6 For the project you have identified, how in practice can you manage the perceptions of a key stakeholder of the project? What will be the aspects of the core and peripheral product that you could consider?

7 Investigate the application of ISO 9000 in an organisation with which you are familiar. What are the implications of the standard for that organisation? How does this application compare with the processes described in ISO 10006?

8 What is the use of a project manual and in what types of projects would you suggest that it would be most beneficial?

9 Carry out a web search of companies to see if you can find their quality policy and any relevant quality documentation. What do you notice about the procedural documents?

10 A firm has very poor quality performance and is contemplating what it must do next to improve its situation. Devise a 10-point plan to improve its quality performance.

Further information

Aaltonen, K. and Kujala, J. (2016) 'Towards an improved understanding of project stakeholder landscapes', *International Journal of Project Management*, Vol. 34, No.8, pp. 1537–1552.

Abdelsalam, H.M.E. and Gad, M.M. (2009) 'Cost of Quality in Dubai: An Analytical Case Study of Residential Construction Projects', *International Journal of Project Management*, Vol. 27, No. 5, pp. 501–511.

Bartlett J. (2017) *The Essentials of Managing Quality for Projects and Programmes*, 2nd edition, Abingdon, Routledge.

Barber, P., Graves, A., Hall, M., Sheath, D. and Tomkins, C. (2000) 'Quality Failure Costs in Civil Engineering Projects', *International Journal of Quality and Reliability Management*, Vol. 17, No. 4/5, pp. 479–492.

Bicheno, J. (2002) *The Quality 75, Towards Six Sigma Performance in Service and Manufacturing*, Picsie Books, Buckingham.

Dale, B.G. and Plumkett, J.L. (1991) *Quality Costing*, Chapman & Hall, London.

Eskerod, P., Huemann, M. and Savage, G. (2015) 'Project Stakeholder Management—Past and Present', *Project Management Journal*, Vol. 46, No. 6, pp. 6–14.

Feigenbaum, A.V. (1956) 'Total Quality Control', *Harvard Business Review*, November–December, pp. 93–101.

Gummesson, E. (1991) 'Truths and Myths in Service Quality', *International Journal of Service Industry Management*, Vol. 2, No. 3, pp. 7–16.

International Journal of Quality & Reliability Management, Emerald Press.

Johnston, R. and Clark, G. (2005) *Service Operations Management: Improving Service Delivery*, FT Prentice Hall, Harlow.

Kloppenborg, T. and Petrick, J. (2002) *Managing Project Quality*, Project Management Institute, Darby, PA.

Mishra, A., Sinha, K.K, Thirumalai, S. (2017) 'Project Quality: The Achilles Heel of Offshore Technology Projects?' *IEEE Transactions on Engineering Management*, Vol. 64, No. 3, pp. 272–286.

Rose, K. (2014) *Project Quality Management*, 2nd edition, Ross Publishing, New York.

Srivastava, S.K. (2008) 'Towards Estimating Cost of Quality in Supply Chains', *Total Quality Management & Business Excellence*, Vol. 19, No. 3, pp. 193–208.

Tague, N. (2004) *The Quality Toolbox*, 2nd edition, ASQ Quality Press, Milwaukee, WI.

Williams, P., Ashill, N.J., Naumann, E. and Jackson, E. (2015) 'Relationship quality and satisfaction: Customer-perceived success factors for on-time projects', *International Journal of Project Management*, Vol. 33, No. 8, pp. 1836–1850.

Websites

www.asq.org – the American Society for Quality Control – some useful publications.

References

1 'Universal Credit: Inside the Welfare State', BBC.

2 Ries, E. (2011) *The Lean Startup*, London: Penguin, page 77.

3 Reference 2, pp. 97–99.

4 See Chapter 17 in Slack, N. and Brandon-Jones, A. (2019) *Operations Management*, 9th edition, Pearson, Harlow.

5 www.iso.org/iso-9001-quality-management.html

6 See lean.org

7 Maylor H., Turner N., and Murray-Webster R. (2015) 'It Worked for Manufacturing...! Operations Strategy in Project-Based Operations', *International Journal of Project Management,* Vol 33, No. 1, pp. 103–115.

8 Maister, D.H. (1993) *Managing the Professional Service Firm*, Free Press, New York.

9 Geraldi J., Kutsch E. and Turner N. (2011) 'Towards a conceptualisation of quality in information technology projects', *International Journal of Project Management*, Vol. 29, No.5, pp. 557–567.

10 Parasuraman, V. et al. (1985) 'A Conceptual Model of Service Quality and its Implications for Future Research', *Journal of Marketing*, Vol. 49, Fall, pp. 41–50.

11 ISO 10006 (2017) 'Quality Management – Guidelines to Quality in Project Management'. Contains specifications for the content of quality plans.

12 Crosby, P. (1983) *Quality is Free*, Mentor Press, New York.

13 BS 6143 (1992) *Guide to the Economics of Quality – Part 1: Process Cost Model*, British Standards Institute, Milton Keynes. [Note – standard now withdrawn]

14 Wernerfelt, B. (1995) 'The Resource Based View of the Firm: 10 Years After', *Strategic Management Journal*, Vol. 16, No. 3, pp. 171–174.

10 Managing risks and opportunities

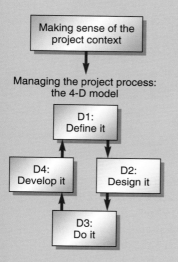

Making sense of the project context

Managing the project process:
the 4-D model

D1:
Define it

D4:
Develop it

D2:
Design it

D3:
Do it

'. . . as we know, there are known knowns; there are things we know we know. We also know there are known unknowns; that is to say we know there are some things we do not know. But there are also unknown unknowns – the ones we don't know we don't know.'
(Donald Rumsfeld)

Principles

1 Risk and uncertainty are fundamentals of projects.
2 There are well-developed approaches that can be applied to the management of risk.
3 While there is always downside potential for a project, there is always upside too. Opportunities are just as important as risk.

Learning objectives

By the time you have completed this chapter, you should be able to:

→ recognise the nature of risk
→ apply basic quantitative and qualitative tools to managing risk
→ recognise the importance of considering the opportunities that a project presents.

Contents

Introduction   244
10.1 The nature of risk and risk management   245
10.2 Qualitative and quantitative approaches   249
10.3 Opportunities management   258
Summary   259
Key terms   260
Relevant areas of the Bodies of Knowledge   260
Project management in practice: *It's a risky business*   262
Topics for discussion   263
Further information   264
References   265
Appendix: PERT factor tables   266

On the morning of 1 February 2003, NASA's space shuttle Columbia was returning to earth from a routine mission. Damage to the heat-resistant panels on the left wing of the shuttle sustained shortly after take-off allowed superheated air to reach the aluminium structure of the shuttle, melting it and causing the disintegration of the craft during re-entry into the earth's atmosphere. All seven crew died.

The official investigation report recognised that space flight is still inherently risky, but was clear that the risk here was the result of some particular organisational issues. Specifically, the report states:

Source: Dennis Hallinan/Alamy Stock Photo

> *The organizational causes of this accident are rooted in the Space Shuttle Program's history and culture, including the original compromises that were required to gain approval for the Shuttle, subsequent years of resource constraints, fluctuating priorities, schedule pressures, mischaracterization of the Shuttle as operational rather than developmental, and lack of an agreed national vision for human space flight. Cultural traits and organizational practices detrimental to safety were allowed to develop, including: reliance on past success as a substitute for sound engineering practices (such as testing to understand why systems were not performing in accordance with requirements); organizational barriers that prevented effective communication of critical safety information and stifled professional differences of opinion; lack of integrated management across program elements; and the evolution of an informal chain of command and decision-making processes that operated outside the organization's rules.[1]*

Introduction

In Chapter 1, the concept of uncertainty related to projects was discussed as one of the key features that distinguishes projects from repetitive operations. In this chapter, we consider the nature of this risk and how it can (and in some cases can't) be managed. The example of the Columbia disaster is an extreme case for considering risk, not least because of the loss of human life involved. Although it is old, it is often cited because it is so instructive, and a powerful lesson for managers. The report cited does illustrate well the complex nature of risk, and elements of its management that are often beyond the consideration of a single project, reflecting political, social and other organisational issues. These are, however, always present in projects, and provide sources of risk beyond the consideration of purely technical issues.

An evaluation of risk is important as it shows at an early stage whether or not a project is worth pursuing. Furthermore, there are well-developed procedures for managing risk as an ongoing process throughout a project. The practices are most well developed in industries where the projects are typically very large (such as heavy engineering), or where there is a significant technical risk element (e.g. aerospace projects). There is also a significant Body of Knowledge on financial risk management, which is separate from the discussion here. Instead we will focus on managing process and outcome risks. The application of active risk management is applicable and beneficial to all projects – right from small, one-person projects up to the very large complex projects that were the origin of many of the techniques. Many eventualities, given the right framework, can be identified in advance to give the project manager a chance to determine the necessary course of action.

The consideration of risk is only one aspect of managing uncertainty. On the upside, as will be seen, there are usually opportunities that arise from a project. At the project level, this may be the development of new capabilities by the organisation as a result of the project or unexpected uses for the project outcome. At the task level, an early finish may result in the opportunity for another activity to start early, or for the development of a better way of completing that task.

Traditional project management has focused on this downside element only. Today's projects require that this broader view is taken. As will be demonstrated, it is reasonable to think that wherever risk is considered, opportunities should be considered too.

10.1   The nature of risk and risk management

The quotation from Donald Rumsfeld, the former US Defense Secretary, at the start of this chapter, is often held to be of great comic value. Without wishing to detract from this, there is a useful consideration of the nature of risk here. The first category (of risk) that he identifies is the *'known knowns'* – the things we know we know. This is the basis for the planning that we have covered in the book to this point. The second category is the *'known unknowns'* – those things that we know are uncertain. For instance, this may be uncertainty as to how long a particular task will take – we know it is uncertain. The third category is the *'unknown unknowns'* – those things that come from out of the blue and we could not have known about. The pandemic of 2020 caused chaos across the world. Notwithstanding the horrific loss of life, whole industries experienced extended turmoil and business plans were rapidly thrown into disarray.

Definitions

Three relevant definitions of **risk** are:

> *'An uncertain event or condition that, if it occurs, has a positive or negative effect on one or more project objectives.'* (PMI, 2017)[2]

> *'Uncertain event or set of events with a potential positive or negative impact.'* (BS 6079, 2017)[3]

> *'The potential of situation or event to impact on the achievement of specific objectives.'* (APM, 2019)[4]

ISO 31000[5] defines risk as the 'effect of uncertainty on objectives'.

These are broad definitions and cause some issue as to what then can be managed. 'Negative effects' can involve significant harm or loss, even for small projects. Risk management therefore needs to incorporate some means of not only identifying potential risks but also analysing the potential of each so that the most significant ones can be 'managed' on an ongoing basis. The positive aspect is equally important – fortune can work in your favour as well as against you. Generally the word 'risk' is used in terms of the negative implications, but it does also apply to opportunities that may arise, so managers need to be mindful of these throughout the project as well. We must also accept that when looking into the future – as happens in project planning – that there is necessarily **uncertainty**. The objective here is not to eliminate uncertainty or risk. Indeed, an accepted notion in many aspects of business life is that risk is proportional to return. The greater the risk that you run, the larger the return could be (if all goes well, etc.). However, this does apply in some respects to projects and their management.

For instance, we can view risk as a **trade-off**. Saving money on one activity by using a cheaper method of performing that activity, for instance, may result in the work having to be redone. There is the chance, of course, that it won't. The saved money trades off against the increased risk that the cheaper method presents. This trade-off can be identified with other objectives – time and quality. It is the job of the project manager, through identification of the organisational objectives or product objectives, to take some of the decisions.[6] There is also the personal view of risk – what are you as an individual prepared to accept in terms of the potential costs and benefits of taking that risk? The costs to you of a high level of risk may be much greater stress levels during the project, as you have to deal with the consequences of your decision. Whatever the process, this is one area where, outside relatively few projects where any project risk is considered unacceptable (e.g. some nuclear industry projects), the treatment of risk is based less on fact but more on partial knowledge and instinct of the project manager and those around them. Science it certainly isn't, but there are some frameworks and tools to help.

Framework for risk management

We shall divide the activity of risk management into three main areas – **identification**, **quantification** and **response**. There are many accompanying tools and techniques for each part of this, and some attributes of each are shown in Figure 10.1.

The first element of the framework is risk identification, the process of predicting the key risk outcomes – indicators that something is going wrong in a project. For example, if an interim report is not received from part of the project team, the likelihood is that there are problems with that part of the project. These are identified from a wide range of sources. In addition to in-house brainstorming and consultation activities, it is possible to seek wider opinions from the stakeholder community and other parties with experience of the product or process. During the evaluation of research grant applications, for instance, experts in the relevant subject area will be asked for their opinions of the application and its chances of success. While such a **peer review** process can work against proposals that are more speculative in nature, it is one way of getting expert input. This is only at a high level and is unlikely to be sufficiently systematic on its own. Reference to the WBS provides a further way to identify risks systematically, and then looking to the time, cost and quality plans can provide more detailed analysis of potential issues.

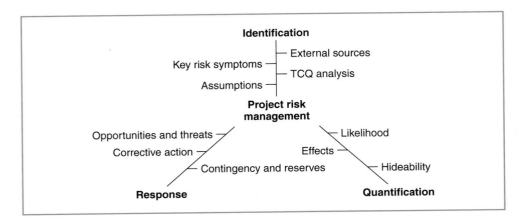

Figure 10.1 Risk management schema

Categories for risk analysis

As a first level of analysis, the likely outcomes are that there is the possibility of missing key objectives, (unexpected) changes from stakeholders, technological problems or staffing changes. These can be generated by a brainstorming exercise with the team – though they are generally fairly gloomy affairs! An alternative is to consider how it could be made to go wrong – looking at the behaviour that would conspire to cause the failure. This is generally far more productive as people are required to consider how parties to the project might behave, rather than simply what might happen almost passively to the project. Some particular aspects to consider are:

- *time* – the critical path or critical chain provides one unit for analysis, as do activities where there is uncertainty, particularly where there is novelty involved. Other key areas to check are time plans for the risky activities that might not even be on the critical path at the start but could easily escalate if there are problems;
- *cost* – the estimates have uncertainty attached to them. How good are they – for instance, if the project is a first-timer?
- *quality* – do we have assurance of all our processes or is a key part of the project (e.g. work being carried out by a supplier or customer) outside our control systems?

In addition, it is now common to see two further risk categories added:

- *health and safety* – what are the risks to people or things of activities being carried out by the project?
- *legal* – the level of risk posed by the project to the legal or financial standing of the organisation.

Indeed it is worth noting that without objectives, there are no risks (as we have defined them here). For instance, if money was not a concern to a particular project (does happen), then there is no financial element to the risks of the project.

Assumptions

Key assumptions are also worth checking at this point. A project that will change the way a company operates and is therefore going to save itself some money needs to ensure that it does not simply add the cost somewhere else. The logistics firm that installed satellite tracking devices on its vehicles because it was useful to keep track of them at all times did not factor in the costs of operating the satellite system, which more than outweighed any cost advantage that came from the availability of such information. The system, once installed, was left switched off. The assumptions of ongoing costs had not been checked.

The trick is not to stop here, however, as the box below shows.

It's going to be OK – we've done the identification . . .

VCS was developing a new software product. Having produced a specification for the product, they went through a risk identification activity, where all the development team went off-site to a hotel for a day, and came up with 152 risk events. These included many features of the product not being to the customers' liking to problems with the process, such as not recognising risks early enough and not controlling the specification as the project progressed. This would have been highly productive had the process been followed through with some quantification and response. Unfortunately, this having been achieved, the team left the hotel where they had brainstormed this and during the next two years over 80 per cent of their risk events actually occurred! The project was a disaster of such proportions that it finished the company.[7]

Stating risks or 'when is a risk not a risk?'

One key challenge for project leaders is to provide a set of risk statements that are actually helpful to the process of managing risks. It is not unusual when reviewing project risks, for us to see a significant number that are ISSUES – that is, there is no uncertainty associated with them – they are facts that the project team is having to deal with. Some more then will be WORRIES – concerns that the team has, but are not actual risks. What is left, usually a much smaller set, then need to be expressed in a format that is helpful. We suggest the discipline of Hillson and Simon (2020)[8] who set out the following:

[As the result of a fact] [a risk event may/might/could occur] [which will have the following effect on the project objectives].

For instance, in a construction project the price of steel is known to vary. A risk then for the project is:

[As the result of the price of steel being variable] [we may have to pay more for the steel we buy] [which will increase the cost of the project].

For leaders, checking that risks start with that fact is always a good start – many do not and so are not risks. Also, if there is no may/might/could element in the risk event, then this could be an issue, not a risk. And if there will be no impact on a specific project objective, again, there is no risk. Note that there could also be an upside of this – steel price may also go down.

One of our delegates provided the following difference between risks and issues – in his company, they used the phrase 'if you can smell it, it is a risk. If you are standing in it, it is an issue.'

The output of the first phase of this risk management process is a list of key risks that will be passed on to the next stage – assessing their magnitude. This assessment is covered further in section 5.2, as it is a large body of work in its own right. However, before leaving this area it is worth re-visiting the Columbia case. While it is normal to consider physical or technical issues that will cause problems for the project, it is clear from the case that there were considerable wider risks, resulting from the organisation, its history and risks that had become 'normal', and were therefore no longer challenged.

Response

Having identified the risk elements to be managed, some procedures are required to ensure that either the likelihood is reduced of that event occurring or the effects managed in some way. For example, the risk of a critical activity running late can be reduced either through reduction in the scale of the activity or by ensuring that there is sufficient buffer at the end of the project to deal with the outcome – the project being delayed. These two approaches cover the main items in Figure 10.1 of corrective action, and contingency and reserves.

In addition, some organisations are not willing to accept risk and *outsource* it – requiring contractors to take on the risks and uncertainties of projects. This has been the case in construction and other sectors, though, as will be discussed in Chapter 14, is often considered to have been of limited success. Undesirable events may also be the subject of insurance – a common response when an organisation wants to limit its risk in any one project.

A common approach that reduces some of the guesswork in risk assessment is to conduct limited trials. This was used very successfully in assessing the risks of the assembly of the roof structure in Heathrow's T5 project, and is a fundamental of the agile/extreme approaches to managing software projects (see Chapter 14).[9]

It is not possible to envisage every possible action or turn that the project might take, but some evaluation of the top 20 per cent of risks (those that are likely to cause 80 per cent of the delays or overrun) is going to be beneficial. When a significant risk is encountered, it is normal for some form of contingency plan to be put in place for that eventuality. Such plans should form part of the project proposal and must fit in with the staged approach described in Chapter 5.

Formal use of risk analysis techniques may be required by:

- company policy;
- clients (especially for defence contracts).

The benefits are considered to be:

- providing a vehicle for improving project plans and better reflecting reality;
- highlighting areas for attention and contingency planning at the planning stage;
- attempting to harness much of the 'gut-feel element' of risk assessment and use this vital intuition as a starting point for further analysis;
- allowing the quantification of risk to build up experience in a structured way and allowing this factor to be traced historically for future benefit in other projects.

The following section considers some of the most widely used techniques for risk quantification, though it is stressed that this is only part of the process. It needs to be followed through with response, and by ensuring that this is not a one-off activity, as risks inevitably emerge during a project.

Other fundamental risk processes

The management of risk doesn't stop at this point. Many organisations claim benefit from it being an ongoing process throughout a project. Typical documentation to support this ongoing process includes the use of a **risk register** or **risk log**. These are lists of the identified risks, their occurrence, actions taken and results of the actions taken. As a project progresses, new risks are added to the register, and ones that have passed or expired are removed. It is important that the risk register be thought of as a 'living document', reflecting the current state of affairs.

In practice, this should be an ongoing activity, with staff looking out for problems, preparing for possible eventualities, 'bouncing back' from the unexpected, and learning from their experiences to improve performance next time.[10] This, though, is difficult to do effectively and it is hard to turn into a 'standard procedure'.

10.2 Qualitative and quantitative approaches

The question that we are trying to answer here is: 'Just how risky is an event or activity?' The traditional approach to this includes a number of techniques to assess the level of risk. They have a similar approach of:

- assessing how likely the event is to occur – somewhere on a scale from improbable to highly likely;
- determining the extent of the effect of the event – for instance, is the effect likely to be:

    – critical – will cause the total failure of one or more parts of a project?

    – major – will hold up or increase costs in one or more areas?

    – minor – will cause inconvenience but not set the project back financially or in time?

These can be done in many ways and the techniques described in this section allow for the project manager to determine which of the risk events are going to be managed (it is improbable that all can be managed).

Qualitative approaches

The majority of risk management activity is based on qualitative data. That is, by gathering peoples' perceptions of the levels of risk involved in a particular activity, some assessment is made of the ranking of that risk for the project.

Typically, this will assess the *likelihood* or **probability** of that risk occurring, and its **impact** or *severity*. These may be expressed as low–medium–high, on a 1–3, 1–5[11] or 1–10 scale.

Obtaining ratings for each criteria is a matter of gathering opinions – often done as part of planning meetings. A method used by many organisations assesses each on the basis of low–medium–high ratings. Figure 10.2 shows the application of a basic grid to show the positioning of the risks and the action that should be taken as a result. In this case, anything highlighted in red will need to be actioned.

The ratings themselves can be used to identify anything that has a high probability or impact as requiring *response* or where both impact and probability are rated as medium. It is often the case that this analysis is done, but then no further action is taken. If a named individual (the risk owner) is responsible and has to report regularly on progress, then it is far more likely that steps will actually be taken. If no one owns the problem, it often gets left. Clear accountability and reporting drive the behaviours that are required. 'Hoping someone else will fix it' is rarely the best strategy here.

An extension of this basic analysis which has been used in industry for many years (particularly in technical developments) and is readily applied to projects is **failure mode, effect analysis (FMEA)**. We can consider three elements of each activity or path through the activities. These are likelihood, severity (as above) and **hideability**. This is because it is often noted that the reasons for failure of projects are not the mainstream risks that were identified during analysis but ones that have emerged because their progress, for instance, was not visible. This factor measures how easy it would be for one party to conceal the fact that things were going very wrong with their part of the project. This would mean that the problems cannot be detected until it is too late.

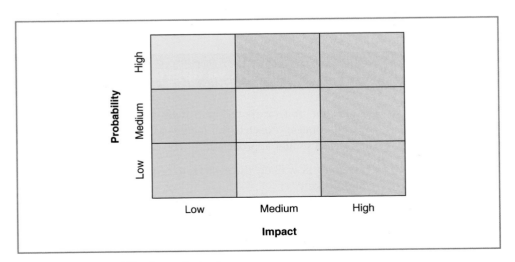

Figure 10.2 Probability impact chart

Each of the three factors can be analysed individually, though a practical method is to consider the total risk to be the product of these three elements. Each can be rated on a 1–10 scale and the total risk (the RPN or risk priority number) is:

$$(likelihood) \times (severity) \times (hideability)$$

Two activities are analysed as in Table 10.1.

Table 10.1 Numerical analysis

Activity	Severity	Hideability	Likelihood	RPN
Development carried out by contractors	8	9	2	144
Development carried out in-house	8	2	7	112

The opportunity exists for development work to be carried out in-house or by contractors. The risk analysis shows that there is potential for failure here – and that the failure would be severe to the project.

The criteria in the example are relative to quality objectives. The method works equally well for time plans. Activities from the critical path (or those with little slack) can be subject to the same criteria and then action taken based on the activities' relative totals. This is the basis of the team-based risk assessment, described in the Project Management in Practice at the end of this chapter.

Whatever criteria are applied, the same criticism of this method prevails – that it takes a list of perceived risks, and for each finds a perceived level of probability and impact. Even putting numbers to these does not make it science, or equivalent to quantitative analysis (as below). However, in the absence of other data, this is one approach to establishing the ranking of a risk.

Quantitative approaches

As for planning, risk analysis is an attempt to provide a mathematical model of the scenario in an attempt to allow the brain to comprehend the effect of a large number of variables on the outcome. Some organisations do have the data to allow them to put together quantitative models of a project, and provide useful guides for decision-making. For instance, one organisation needed 80 per cent certainty of delivery within the specified time as a policy requirement for a project to go ahead. The project manager had to present plans that met this basic criterion. Such an '80 per cent certainty' is arrived at through the use of a variety of differed techniques. Risk quantification techniques that will be discussed here are:

- expected value;
- sensitivity analysis;
- Monte Carlo simulation;
- PERT.

Expected value

The expected value of an event is the possible outcome times the probability of its occurrence, e.g. if a project has a 50 per cent chance of yielding a profit of £30 million, the expected value is 0.5 × £30 million = £15 million. This provides a basic tool for evaluating different project proposals as an investment decision-maker. Two projects require funding – one has a potential return of £200 million and the other a return of £150 million. The first has a 50 per cent chance of yielding this, while the second has a 70 per cent chance.

The expected value calculations yield £100 million for the first and £105 million for the second – on this basis the second is more attractive. The per cent chance can be estimated or calculated using **Monte Carlo analysis**.

Sensitivity analysis

This works similarly to PERT analysis (see below) – an expected value for the main inputs (e.g. costs) to the project is put into the calculations of the outcome as well as an optimistic (in this case $+n$ per cent) and pessimistic ($-n$ per cent) value (value of n is often 10). This will show the effect on the outcome of a change in the variable considered and can show where management control attention should be focused.

The price of materials and labour for a project is likely to fluctuate. As the contract price needs to be fixed in advance, the project manager needs to see the effect of fluctuations on bottom-line performance. The materials are one of the major contributors to the cost of the project. Overheads are calculated on the basis of 175 per cent of direct labour.

Costs:

Materials – £0.60m

Direct labour – £0.20m

Contribution to overheads – £0.35m

Revenues: fixed at £1.2m

The calculations are carried out in Table 10.2 as follows:

revenue

− material costs

− combined labour and overhead costs

= profit

As can be seen, the effect of the changes in costs means that although on initial inspection this looks viable, the figures indicate that should materials increase by 10 per cent, unless there is a drop in the labour costs of the project it will make a loss.

Table 10.2 Sensitivity analysis

		Materials		
		−10%	Expected	+10%
Labour + overheads	−10%	1.2 −0.54 −0.495 +0.165	1.2 −0.6 −0.495 +0.105	1.2 −0.66 −0.495 +0.045
	Expected	1.2 −0.54 −0.55 +0.11	1.2 −0.6 −0.55 +0.05	1.2 −0.66 −0.55 −0.01
	+10%	1.2 −0.54 −0.605 +0.055	1.2 −0.6 −0.605 −0.005	1.2 −0.66 −0.605 −0.065

Monte Carlo simulation

This is a computer-based method and uses a range of values of distribution, rather than single values, for time, cost and other estimates, and then shows the effect on the finances or other critical project factors.

Monte Carlo simulation is available as an extension to most popular spreadsheet packages (including Excel), as well as dedicated pieces of software.

The principle of Monte Carlo analysis is demonstrated in Figure 10.3.

In the example shown in Figure 10.3, there is a revenue (income) stream generated by a project. This is potentially anything between £750 000 (the organisation already have committed revenue of this much) and £1 150 000 if the outcome is good and more can be sold. It is thought equally likely that it could be any value in this range. The materials cost is less certain. The figure of £250 000 is thought to be the most likely, but if there are problems, it could be considerably more. It is unlikely to be less than this. The labour cost could be more or less than £550 000. Normally, the profit would be considered as (revenue–materials–labour) – and the figure of £150 000 emerges. The reality is that if you add the uncertainties together the result is another distribution. In the last line of Figure 10.3, it can be seen that there is a probability that the project will make a loss. As it stands, the project has only a 15 per cent chance that it will make £150 000 or more profit. The organisation now has to consider if it is prepared to accept this level of risk.

The calculation is done by the software selecting values according to each of the distributions and performing the necessary additions/subtractions. This is performed, say, 1000 times, and the resulting distribution given. The result is that a level of confidence can be given for any desired profit figure (in this case).

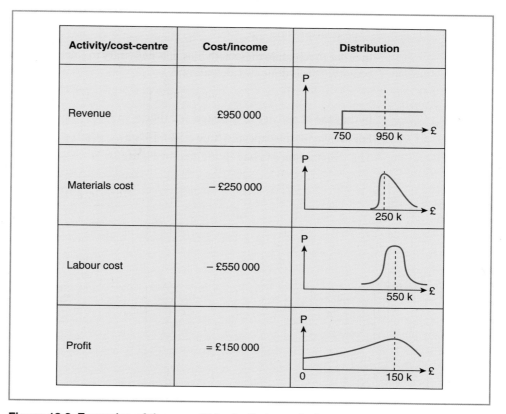

Activity/cost-centre	Cost/income	Distribution
Revenue	£950 000	
Materials cost	– £250 000	
Labour cost	– £550 000	
Profit	= £150 000	

Figure 10.3 Examples of the use of Monte Carlo analysis

Programme evaluation and review technique (PERT)

Programme evaluation and review technique (**PERT**) was developed for use in the Polaris project in the USA in 1958. Due to the claimed success of the technique in this case, it was for a long time held up as the model that everyone should work to in planning projects (though see the note on PERT in Chapter 7). The technique is intended to deal with the likelihood that the single value given as the estimated time for completion of activities is going to have a degree of error associated with it. Instead of taking a single time, three time estimates for each activity are required:

- optimistic time – how long the activity would take if the conditions were ideal;
- most probable time – time if conditions were 'normal';
- pessimistic time – how long the activity would take if a significant proportion of the things that could go wrong did go wrong.

There are an infinite number of possibilities as to how this range is distributed, e.g. optimistic and most probable times may be close together with the pessimistic time considerably different from the other two, or all three may be very close together. This flexibility in the distribution that is applied is one of the major appeals of the technique. The analysis that can be applied can be very simple or go into complex statistics that require the use of a computer. The following example can be done without the need for this. The project that was planned in section 7.3 was further examined, and the times estimated for each of the activities expanded to include an optimistic and a pessimistic element. The result is shown in Figure 10.4.

The activity arrows now have three figures associated with each in the order optimistic, most likely, pessimistic, e.g. for activity A:

optimistic time $= o = 3$

most likely time $= m = 5$

pessimistic time $= p = 7$

In order to schedule these activities, it is necessary to calculate the expected time for each activity. This is done by calculating:

$$\text{expected time} = [o + 4m + p]/6$$

In the case of activity A, the expected time $= [3 + [4 \times 5] + 7]/6 = 5$

For activity B, the expected time $= [2 + [4 \times 3] + 10]/6 = 4$

This distribution can be represented by Figure 10.5.

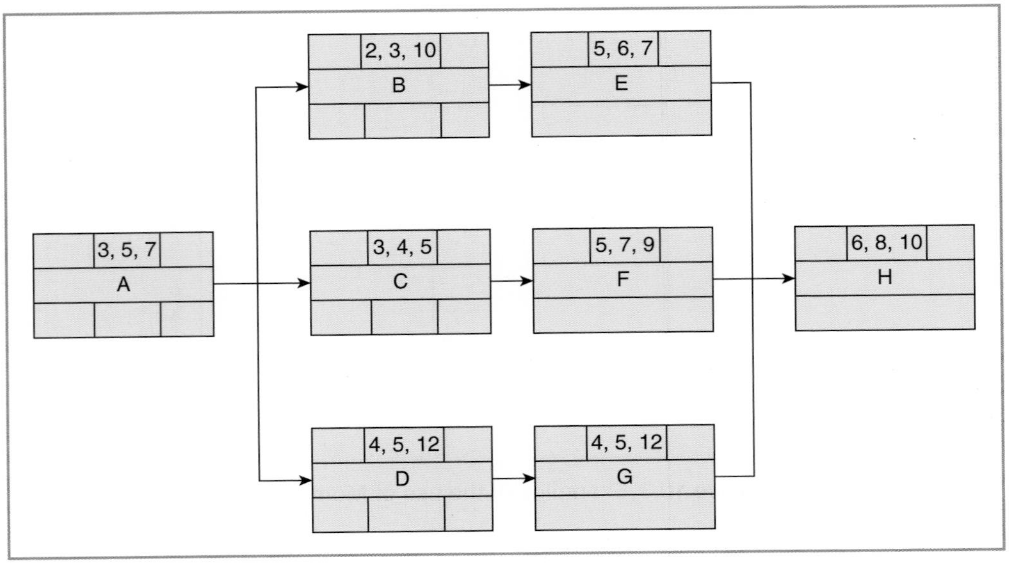

Figure 10.4 Network showing optimistic, most probable and pessimistic times

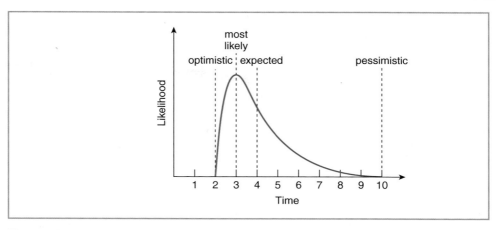

Figure 10.5 Distribution of estimated times for an activity

Table 10.3 Three-point estimates for tasks

Activity	Optimistic time o	Most likely time m	Pessimistic time p	Expected time
A	3	5	7	5
B	2	3	10	4
C	3	4	5	4
D	4	5	12	6
E	5	6	7	6
F	5	7	9	7
G	4	5	12	6
H	6	8	10	8

The example is now completed using the expected times shown in Table 10.3 instead of the most likely times and a critical path analysis carried out. Putting these figures into the network diagram and carrying out the forward pass gives a project expected duration of 25 days. This is not considerably different from the 24 days that the original analysis revealed. The reverse pass reveals that the critical path has changed. Originally it was ACFH, but with the consideration of the ranges of times, it is now ADGH.

In order to save drawing the distribution each time, it is possible to compare activities in terms of a variance measure. This is calculated as follows:

$$\text{variance of activity time} = [[p-o]/6]^2$$

Explanation

The standard deviation of each activity's time is approximated to one sixth of the difference between the optimistic and pessimistic times. The variance = [standard deviation]^2. The standard deviation is the normal measure of spread in a set of numbers, and is represented by the Greek symbol σ or sigma. It is a characteristic of a normal distribution that 99.7 per cent of the numbers being analysed (called the 'population') fall within $\pm 3\sigma$ of the mean (the average of the population).

In this case, the extremes of the distribution are represented by the optimistic and pessimistic times. The normal distribution is applied and the approximation is made that between these two values, 99.7 per cent (practically all) of other values will lie. The upper limit ($mean + 3\sigma$) and the lower limit ($mean - 3\sigma$) are equated to the pessimistic and optimistic times respectively. The distribution that is being considered is the beta distribution, a generic form of which the normal distribution is a special case. Unlike the normal distribution (represented by a bell-shaped curve) the beta distribution need not be symmetrical about the mean, i.e. it can be skewed. It therefore encompasses the effects of one of the values of o and p being further from m than the other.

Applying this to the example:

$$\text{variance for activity B} = [[10 - 2]/6]^2 = 1.78$$
$$\text{variance for activity A} = [[7 - 3]/6]^2 = 0.44$$

Thus we have a mathematical measure for what can be seen from the figures, that the variance (as a measure of uncertainty with this activity) is much higher for activity B than for A, i.e. there is more uncertainty in the completion of B than A.

Figures such as the variance are of greatest practical use in estimating the likelihood that a set of activities will be completed within a certain time. The steps involved are as follows.

1 Calculate the variance for each activity.
2 Calculate the variance for each path (a sequence of activities that will take you from the first event to the last – there are generally many paths through networks) in the network diagram. This is done by summing the variances of all the activities on the path.
3 Calculate the standard deviation for that path:

$$\sigma_{\text{path}} = \text{square root of the variance}$$

4 Identify the time within which you wish to complete the activities.
    Calculate the value for z determined by:

$$z = [\text{specified time} - \text{expected time}]/\sigma_{\text{path}}$$

5 Refer to the Appendix at the end of this chapter – the value of z corresponds to a probability (expressed between 0 and 1). This is the probability that the activity path will be completed within the time identified in 4.
6 The probability that all the paths that have been considered will be finished in the given time is found by multiplying the probabilities for each of the paths together.

This method is best illustrated by an example. If the middle section of the previous example is used, and activities B–G considered, the steps are as follows:

1 Calculate the variance for each activity (shown in Table 10.4).
2 Now it is necessary to identify the paths. There are several rules regarding the selection of paths for this process:

– Each activity must be on only one path – where activities are shared between several paths, the one that is the critical path should be used;
– Activities on different paths need to be independent – there should be no unwritten logic relationship between activities on different paths.

With these in mind the three paths that need to be considered here are:

B–E

C–F

D–G

Table 10.4 Three-point estimates and variances for tasks

Activity	Optimistic time o	Most likely time m	Pessimistic time p	Variance
B	2	3	10	1.78
C	3	4	5	0.11
D	4	5	12	1.78
E	5	6	7	0.11
F	5	7	9	0.44
G	4	5	12	1.78

Table 10.5 Probabilities of completing tasks

Path	Path variance	Standard deviation	z	Probability of completion in 11 days
B-E	1.78 + 0.11 = 1.89	1.37	[11 − 10]/1.37 = 0.73	0.7673
C-F	0.11 + 0.44 = 0.55	0.74	[11 − 11]/0.74 = 0.0	0.5000
D-G	1.78 + 1.78 = 3.56	1.87	[11 − 12]/1.87 = −0.53	0.2981

The following steps are calculated in Table 10.5. The variances are then summed for each path.

3 The standard deviations are then calculated.

4 The time required for completion is arbitrarily 11 days.

5 The z values are added.

6 The probabilities are derived from Table 10.4.

7 The probability of each of these times being achieved is clearly highest where the expected time was less than the time required for completion (path B–E). These values are now required to find the probability that all three paths will be completed in 11 days. This is achieved through the multiplication of the three probabilities. In this case, the probability that the three paths will all be completed in 11 days is:

$$0.7673 \times 0.5000 \times 0.2981 = 0.1144$$

i.e. there is less than a 12 per cent chance that this part of the project will be completed in 11 days.

Many authors choose to use PERT as the generic title for network techniques. This is perfectly valid – the original CPA that was carried out using a single value for the estimated time can be taken as a special case of PERT, where the most likely = optimistic = pessimistic time.

The use of PERT in practice

PERT provides an in-built level of risk assessment, considering as it does three values for time estimates (optimistic, most likely and pessimistic). It does not tell you how likely these are to occur or their effects. Considering this alone results in only a partial picture of the situation. The objective of the risk analysis is to enable the project manager to include **contingencies**, that is, having identified the most risky elements of the project, to put some actions in place to make sure that the risk is minimised.

PERT was very popular in the 1960s. It appears to be less well used today as many project managers feel that the additional complexity is not justified by the return in the accuracy of the plans produced. Also, it was suggested that in organisations where this kind of planning is prevalent, the use of PERT can encourage people to be less accurate in their forecasting. This said, for many very large scale projects and particularly in the defence sector, this technique remains popular. It can be used very effectively in *managing up* – giving senior managers the opportunity to accept or decline a level of risk with a particular project.

One project demanded by a senior manager was thought to be 'difficult' and 'challenging'. The designated project manager was unhappy about what he was being asked to take on, believing that the failure of the project was a high risk and could be 'career limiting' – he might no longer have a job if it did fail as the firm were very good at finding scapegoats for failures. A basic analysis of the chance of success through PERT demonstrated that with the level of resources allocated, he had less than a 5 per cent chance of succeeding in making the delivery date for the project. Communicating this level of risk and requiring senior management acceptance of this level of risk resulted in the opportunity to re-scope the project and a much higher chance of success that was acceptable to both the project manager and the firm.

10.3 Opportunities management

> '*On a recent multi-million pound project, my team spent two days trying to reduce a £50 000 risk. I would much rather they had spent that time looking to see how the project could yield an extra £50 000 of business benefit.*'
> (Project Director, Rolls-Royce)

One of 3M's most successful and enduring projects has been the Post-it note. It is well described in 3M folklore how this was the by-product of another research project which produced an adhesive that was not sufficiently sticky. Had there not been a process for exploiting such a finding the discovery might have been lost. One of their developers applied the glue to small pieces of paper, which he then used to mark the very thin pages of his hymn book. Other people started asking him to make some for them for a whole range of different applications. Again the invention might have stopped there had 3M not had a process for developing such ideas. As it was, they did have such a process, and the new product was rapidly brought to market. Many great ideas are lost every day by teams and individuals because there is no route for them to be exploited. And yet, it is noted by many people who specialise in the management of innovation that it is rare that great products are the result of a development process that started out with that objective in mind. They are the result of there being some scope in the process for such development, and have been discussed in Chapter 4. At this stage, it is worth reconsidering the issue, as it is essential that there is a route not only for threats to the project (as is the negative side of risks) but also for the exploitation of **opportunities**.

There are many approaches to assessing the opportunities. One framework is:[12]

1 *Negative to positive* – where a risk does not materialise, that is a benefit and can be capitalised on, e.g. where a technology proves it can do more than originally thought, the contingency allocated in case it could do less, could be used to develop it further for other applications. Similarly, if a task takes less time than expected, there should be the opportunity to use that early finish benefit to move the rest of the project on faster (as Chapter 7).

2 *Opportunities of response* – where a risk is deemed too high and a response is needed, this itself presents opportunities. For instance, using an existing (known) supplier to reduce the risk of unknown suppliers being involved in the project, does present the opportunity for further learning based on previous experience in running projects.

3 *Random good fortune* – be alert for opportunities presented by breakthroughs that could not have been expected. The 3M story above is a classic example of this.

Whatever approach is taken to identify opportunities, it is possible to put the potential benefits through a process similar to the qualitative risk management process identified in section 10.2. Indeed, there are an increasing number of sources recommending precisely that. However, managers we ask often admit (rather sheepishly) that it is not an approach that their organisation adopts. Most large organisations have extensive and mandated risk management processes, but the ability to capitalise on the positives they may encounter is often far less developed. Sadly, worldwide a huge amount of benefit is likely being missed because of this, so always take the time to consider the effect of managing the opportunities you encounter, as well as the risks. Again, like having a risk owner, identifying a named individual responsible for delivering the benefits is a positive step, otherwise action may not be taken.

Summary

■ The issue of risk is central to the consideration of projects. There is always risk with any endeavour, and how this is managed will have a large impact on the success or otherwise of the project. The basic process of identification, quantification and response provides a structure for this activity, and the main tools for risk management have been described. One area where there has been considerable development over recent years is in the concept of enterprise risk management, where, rather than consider the risks of each individual project in isolation, a risk portfolio is established – with some overall desired pattern of high- and low-risk projects being included. This is typically the approach taken by companies like GSK in pharmaceutical drug development.

■ Risk management is one area where no amount of text and anecdote will give real insight into the process. It is strongly recommended that you try using the kind of framework illustrated in the Project Management in Practice at the end of this chapter in a project of your own – ideally in a group setting. This will provide a point of reflection on the processes you have read about here.

■ Finally, do all the risk processes work? Recent research[13] suggests that their success is limited. As will be discussed in Chapter 16, the risk and indeed opportunities management process is only part of the story. It appears to be just as relevant how organisations respond to risks, including Rumsfeld's unknown unknowns, as much as how they try to manage them in advance. Further, as has emerged in just about every other chapter, consideration of processes for risk and opportunities management is necessary for success, but not sufficient. Sufficiency requires much greater attention to the behaviours that are being promoted in the project.[14]

Key terms

contingencies *p. 257*

failure mode effect analysis (FMEA) *p. 250*

hideability *p. 250*

identification *p. 246*

impact *p. 250*

response *p. 246*

Monte Carlo analysis *p. 252*

opportunities *p. 258*

peer review *p. 246*

PERT *p. 254*

probability *p. 250*

quantification *p. 246*

quantitative and qualitative approaches *p. 249*

risk *p. 245*

risk log *p. 249*

risk register/log *p. 249*

sensitivity analysis *p. 252*

trade-off *p. 246*

uncertainty *p. 245*

Relevant areas of the Bodies of Knowledge

Both Bodies of Knowledge in Tables 10.6 and 10.7 are clear about the nature of risk and risk management, and the importance that this issue has for the successful management of projects. The PMI Body of Knowledge is far more extensive in its coverage of specific techniques and the role of systems to deal with risk on an ongoing basis. In other respects, neither of the Bodies of Knowledge is particularly strong on the analysis of plans, though both make clear the need and role of a business case.

Table 10.6 Relevant areas of the APM Body of Knowledge

Relevant section	Title	Summary
4.2.2	Risk identification	Project managers need to be clear what is 'at risk', and what constitutes tolerable and intolerable outcomes. Recommendation is to use a wide range of stakeholders so that multiple viewpoints are used, then to define the risk owners.
4.2.3	Risk analysis	Demonstrates the use of a 5x5 probability / impact grid with example numerical scales.

Table 10.7 Relevant areas of the PMI Body of Knowledge

Relevant section	Title	Summary
11	Project risk management	Overview of the risk process
11.1	Plan risk management	This discusses how risk management is to be undertaken, including aspects such as methodology, roles and responsibilities, timing, and risk categories (using a risk breakdown structure). Example of a 5x5 probability / impact grid incorporating opportunities as well as threats.

Relevant section	Title	Summary
11.2	Identify risks	From the risk plan, there are number of methods that can be employed for risk identification, including brainstorming, checklists and interviews. The output is a risk register showing risks, risk owners and potential responses.
11.3	Qualitative risk analysis	The quality of the data provided through the risk identification is first established. Then a number of techniques are applied to determine in qualitative terms (low, medium, high, for instance) the nature of the severity and likelihood of occurrence. The final stage of this process can be to turn these into a quantitative assessment, to feed into a quantitative analysis.
11.4	Quantitative risk analysis	This section focuses on the use of quantitative techniques to determine the magnitude of particular risks and their impact on the schedules and costs. Monte Carlo simulations and sensitivity analyses (to understand the relative impact of different aspects of the project) are discussed, as is the use of decision trees to assess relative costs and benefits.
11.5	Plan risk responses	The objective of this part of the risk management process is to ensure that there is some action as a result of a particular risk being identified. By assigning an 'owner' to each risk, and then putting in place plans to escalate, avoid, transfer, reduce or accept that particular risk outcome, the outcome is a risk response plan. This may include the apportionment of contingency funds or time, or changes to plans, contracts or initiates after actions.
11.6	Implement risk responses	This ensures that the planning leads to action when required, as often effort is expended in analysing risks but then they are not actively managed when required. Resources need to be allocated to respond to the risks, and this may involve updating cost and time expectations.
11.7	Monitor risks	This section reinforces the nature of risk management as an ongoing process, linked in to the control systems for other objectives of the project. The compilation of a risk database is suggested, as is the use of checklists to manage the feeding of risk knowledge gained to future projects.

PROJECT MANAGEMENT IN PRACTICE
It's a risky business

Four friends wanted to start a business. After much discussion, they had hit upon the idea of launching an online toys and games delivery business. They were in the development stage of their business plan and wanted to be sure that they had been thorough with their planning. To reinforce this, they had just received a letter from a group of venture capitalists, agreeing to fund the start-up. It concluded its review of their plan by stating:

> *The business plan presents a credible opportunity for all involved and we are prepared to approve the funding request, subject to a risk analysis being carried out on the project to start the business.*

The group were stunned – the funding that they had been hoping for was suddenly a reality. Just one thing stood in their way – that damned risk analysis process. They started with identifying the key risk elements that could face the business during its start-up phase. They considered the process between the time that they received the funding and day one of trading. What could possibly go wrong? Lots of things. They brainstormed the possibilities and recorded them. They then considered the effect that these would have on the project as a whole. The list they generated provided them with too much to do – they would spend all their time trying to prevent things going wrong and not enough making sure that the positive steps towards the business opening were happening. They needed to prioritise the events. As importantly, what would happen when they eventually occurred? Who would be responsible for each of them? On what basis could they rank each risk, in order to identify the most important risks for which they would develop response and ownership?

They decided to use a table to show the risk event, its likelihood and severity, and then multiplying the two ratings together to provide a risk priority number (RPN). This would then allow ranking of the risk elements. For the three highest ranked elements, the group then generated a response process with someone in the group taking ownership of that process. The result of their deliberations is shown in Table 10.8.

As can be seen, the top three risks were identified and tasks put in place either to prevent the risk event happening or to reduce its effect. The initials of the 'owners' of that risk in the last column show who has agreed to monitor that set of events and ensure that the response is put into place before the project suffers from that event occurring.

Table 10.8 Simple risk management table

Risk event	Likelihood	Severity	RPN (rank)	Response	Owner
Advertising material not ready in time for business launch	4	8	32 (2)	Identify marketing firms; develop artwork early	AL
Website not ready in time for business launch	4	9	36 (1)	Website to be ready 3 weeks prior to launch for testing; use simple version first	SL
Banking facilities not ready	2	10	20 (5)	Place orders immediately for opening stock	KM
Initial stock not ready	3	8	24 (3)		
Group cannot agree on items to be sold	3	7	21 (4)		
Loss of one of group members	1	10	10 (6)		

Points for discussion

1 What further methods could have been used to generate ideas for the identification part of the risk process?

2 How scientific can the method that was used to rank the risks claim to be?

3 What should happen as the project progresses to manage risk? Suggest a plan for the remainder of the project (the three months up to the business launch).

Topics for discussion

1 What is risk?

2 Why should risk be a fundamental part of the consideration of a project manager?

3 Which other stakeholders would have an interest in the level of risk that a project presents?

4 When would a quantitative approach be appropriate and when would you use a qualitative approach to risk assessment?

5 What are the benefits and limitations of the quantitative and qualitative approaches to risk assessment?

6 Is risk assessment the same as risk management?

7 The Covid-19 pandemic of 2020 devastated many organisations. For an organisation or industry with which you are familiar, consider whether better risk management could have helped, or were the impacts outside managers' control?

8 Considering the critical path alone for the project in Table 10.9, calculate the activity variances and the total variance of the critical path. From this, calculate the standard deviation. Determine the probability

Table 10.9

Activity	Optimistic time	Most likely time	Pessimistic time
A	3	4	11
B	1	2	3
C	3	10	11
D	8	10	18
E	1	2	3
F	1	3	5
G	2	3	4
H	2	6	10
J	16	20	30
K	1	1	1

of the project being completed within the following times:

(a) 30 days.
(b) 40 days.
(c) 42 days.

9 A construction project requires five major pieces of work to be completed which are independent. These five paths have variances as given in Table 10.10.

Table 10.10

Path	Expected duration (weeks)	Variance
A	10	1.21
B	8	2.00
C	12	1.00
D	15	2.89
E	14	1.44

Determine the probability that the project will be completed within:

(a) 18 weeks.
(b) 16 weeks.
(c) 13 weeks.

10 You are in charge of a new product launch. This will be a formal press launch, where the product is introduced by your Managing Director and the press and major customers have the opportunity to see the product for the first time.

The formalities are to be preceded by a buffet. Before hiring the catering service it is necessary to identify the guest list and invite them to determine numbers. Because of tied arrangements between certain venues and the caterers, you will have to select the venue, then select the caterers. The launch publicity materials will

Table 10.11

Activity	Description	Optimistic time	Most likely	Pessimistic time
A	Select launch venue	1	2	3
B	Design launch publicity	2	3	4
C	Have artwork prepared	2	3	5
D	Print brochures	1	2	4
E	Construct promotion stand	1	2	3
F	Order sound system	0.5	1	1.5
G	Select caterers	1	2	3
H	Develop invite list	1	1	1
J	Invite and get replies	2	3	5

need to be designed, and artwork carried out before brochures can be printed. These must be available on the day. The promotional boards to be placed around the launch room should be constructed once the publicity materials have been designed. No artwork is required for these. A sound system is required and must be hired once the venue has been identified.

The activities are included in Table 10.11, together with the best estimates for optimistic, pessimistic and most likely times. The MD has asked you to set the launch date (all times are in weeks). Show the criteria that you have used, and include the network diagram.

11 Choose a project with which you are familiar. For that project, identify the opportunities that such a project presents for performance or outcome over and above what has been expected or required.

Further information

APM Risk Management SIG (2010), *Project Risk Analysis and Management Guide*, 2nd edition, APM, Princes Risborough.

Atkinson, R., Crawford, L. and Ward, S. (2006) 'Fundamental Uncertainties in Projects and the Scope of Project Management', *International Journal of Project Management*, Vol. 24, No. 8, pp. 687–698.

Axelos (2010) *The Management of Risk: Guidance for Practitioners*, Office of Government Commerce, London.

Barton, T., Shenkir, W. and Walker, P. (2002) *Making Enterprise Risk Management Pay Off: How Leading Companies Implement Risk Management*, FT Prentice Hall, Harlow.

de Carvalho, M.M., Rabechini R. (2015), 'Impact of risk management on project performance: the importance of soft skills', *International Journal of Production Research*, Vol. 53 No. 2, pp. 321–340.

Chapman, C. and Ward, S. (2003) *Project Risk Management: Processes, Techniques and Insights*, 2nd edition, Wiley, Chichester.

Flyvberg, B., Bruzelius, N. and Rothengatter, W. (2003) *Megaprojects and Risk: An Anatomy of Ambition*, Cambridge University Press, Cambridge.

Hillson D. and Murray-Webster R. (2012) *A Short Guide to Risk Appetite*, Routledge, Abingdon.

Pender, S. (2000) Managing Incomplete Knowledge: Why Risk Management Is Not Sufficient, *International Journal of Project Management*, Vol. 19, No. 1, pp. 79–87.

Willumsen, P., Oehmen, J., Stingl, V. and Geraldi, J. (2019) 'Value creation through project risk management', *International Journal of Project Management*, Vol. 37, No. 5, pp. 731–749.

Websites

https://sma.nasa.gov/sma-disciplines/risk-management – NASA's risk process.

www.risk-doctor.com

References

1   For further information, the full investigation report can be found at https://www.nasa.gov/columbia/home/CAIB_Vol1.html

2   PMI (2017) *A Guide to the Project Management Body of Knowledge (PMBOK® Guide)*, 6th edition, Project Management Institute, Newtown Square, PA.

3   BS 6079:2019, Project management – Principles and guidance for the management of projects, BSI Standards Publication.

4   APM (2019) *Project Management Body of Knowledge*, 7th edition, Association for Project Management, High Wycombe.

5   ISO 31000:2018 Risk Management. International Organization for Standardization.

6   HM is grateful to Paul Walley of Warwick Business School for sharing his thoughts on this subject.

7   See Project Management in Practice – the VCS case – at the end of Chapter 16.

8   Hillson, D. and Simon, P. (2020) *Practical Project Risk Management: The ATOM Methodology*, 3rd edition, Management Concepts, London.

9   Turner, J.R. (2005) 'The Role of Pilot Studies in Reducing Risk on Projects and Programmes', *International Journal of Project Management*, Vol. 23, No. 1, pp. 1–6.

10 Turner N., Kutsch E., Maylor H. and Swart J. (2020) 'Hits and (near) misses. Exploring managers' actions and their effects on localised resilience', *Long Range Planning*, Vol. 50, No. 3, pp. 1–17.

11 APM (2019) Body of Knowledge and PMI (2017) PMBoK both suggest a 5-point scale from very low to very high, with numerical guidance for each point.

12 Hillson, D. (2003) *Effective Opportunity Management: Exploiting Positive Risk*, Dekker, New York.

13 Kutsch, E. and Maylor, H. (2009) 'From Failure to Success: An Investigation into Managers' Criteria for Assessing the Outcome of IT Projects', *International Journal of Manufacturing Technology and Management*, Vol. 16, No. 3, pp. 265–282.

14 Hillson, D. and Murray-Webster, R. (2007) *Understanding and Managing Risk Attitude*, 2nd edition, Gower, Aldershot.

APPENDIX
PERT factor tables

Table 10.A.1(a) Areas under the standardised normal curve for $z \leq 0$

0.09	0.08	0.07	0.06	0.05	0.04	0.03	0.02	0.01	0.00	z
0.0002	0.0003	0.0003	0.0003	0.0003	0.0003	0.0003	0.0003	0.0003	0.0003	−3.4
0.0003	0.0004	0.0004	0.0004	0.0004	0.0004	0.0004	0.0005	0.0005	0.0005	−3.3
0.0005	0.0005	0.0005	0.0006	0.0006	0.0006	0.0006	0.0006	0.0007	0.0007	−3.2
0.0007	0.0007	0.0008	0.0008	0.0008	0.0008	0.0009	0.0009	0.0009	0.0010	−3.1
0.0010	0.0010	0.0011	0.0011	0.0011	0.0012	0.0012	0.0013	0.0013	0.0013	−3.0
0.0014	0.0014	0.0015	0.0015	0.0016	0.0016	0.0017	0.0018	0.0018	0.0019	−2.9
0.0019	0.0020	0.0021	0.0021	0.0022	0.0023	0.0023	0.0024	0.0025	0.0026	−2.8
0.0026	0.0027	0.0028	0.0029	0.0030	0.0031	0.0032	0.0033	0.0034	0.0035	−2.7
0.0036	0.0037	0.0038	0.0039	0.0040	0.0041	0.0043	0.0044	0.0045	0.0047	−2.6
0.0048	0.0049	0.0051	0.0052	0.0054	0.0055	0.0057	0.0059	0.0060	0.0062	−2.5
0.0064	0.0066	0.0068	0.0069	0.0071	0.0073	0.0075	0.0078	0.0080	0.0082	−2.4
0.0084	0.0087	0.0089	0.0091	0.0094	0.0096	0.0099	0.0102	0.0104	0.0107	−2.3
0.0110	0.0113	0.0116	0.0119	0.0122	0.0125	0.0129	0.0132	0.0136	0.0139	−2.2
0.0143	0.0146	0.0150	0.0154	0.0158	0.0162	0.0166	0.0170	0.0174	0.0179	−2.1
0.0183	0.0188	0.0192	0.0197	0.0202	0.0207	0.0212	0.0217	0.0222	0.0228	−2.0
0.0233	0.0239	0.0244	0.0250	0.0256	0.0262	0.0268	0.0274	0.0281	0.0287	−1.9
0.0294	0.0301	0.0307	0.0314	0.0322	0.0329	0.0336	0.0344	0.0351	0.0359	−1.8
0.0367	0.0375	0.0384	0.0392	0.0401	0.0409	0.0418	0.0427	0.0436	0.0446	−1.7
0.0455	0.0465	0.0475	0.0485	0.0495	0.0505	0.0516	0.0526	0.0537	0.0548	−1.6
0.0559	0.0571	0.0582	0.0594	0.0606	0.0618	0.0630	0.0643	0.0655	0.0668	−1.5
0.0681	0.0694	0.0708	0.0721	0.0735	0.0749	0.0764	0.0778	0.0793	0.0808	−1.4
0.0823	0.0838	0.0853	0.0869	0.0885	0.0901	0.0918	0.0934	0.0951	0.0968	−1.3
0.0985	0.1003	0.1020	0.1038	0.1056	0.1075	0.1093	0.1112	0.1131	0.1151	−1.2
0.1170	0.1190	0.1210	0.1230	0.1251	0.1271	0.1292	0.1314	0.1335	0.1357	−1.1
0.1379	0.1401	0.1423	0.1446	0.1469	0.1492	0.1515	0.1539	0.1562	0.1587	−1.0
0.1611	0.1635	0.1660	0.1685	0.1711	0.1736	0.1762	0.1788	0.1814	0.1841	−0.9
0.1867	0.1894	0.1922	0.1949	0.1977	0.2005	0.2033	0.2061	0.2090	0.2119	−0.8
0.2148	0.2177	0.2206	0.2236	0.2266	0.2296	0.2327	0.2358	0.2389	0.2420	−0.7
0.2451	0.2483	0.2514	0.2546	0.2578	0.2611	0.2643	0.2676	0.2709	0.2743	−0.6
0.2776	0.2810	0.2843	0.2877	0.2912	0.2946	0.2981	0.3015	0.3050	0.3085	−0.5
0.3121	0.3156	0.3192	0.3228	0.3264	0.3300	0.3336	0.3372	0.3409	0.3446	−0.4
0.3483	0.3520	0.3557	0.3594	0.3632	0.3669	0.3707	0.3745	0.3783	0.3821	−0.3
0.3859	0.3897	0.3936	0.3974	0.4013	0.4052	0.4090	0.4129	0.4168	0.4207	−0.2
0.4247	0.4286	0.4325	0.4364	0.4404	0.4443	0.4483	0.4522	0.4562	0.4602	−0.1
0.4641	0.4681	0.4721	0.4761	0.4801	0.4840	0.4880	0.4920	0.4960	0.5000	−0.0

Table 10.A.1(b) Areas under the standardised normal curve for $z \geq 0$

z	0.00	0.01	0.02	0.03	0.04	0.05	0.06	0.07	0.08	0.09
0.0	0.5000	0.5040	0.5080	0.5120	0.5160	0.5199	0.5239	0.5279	0.5319	0.5359
0.1	0.5398	0.5438	0.5478	0.5517	0.5557	0.5596	0.5636	0.5675	0.5714	0.5753
0.2	0.5793	0.5832	0.5871	0.5910	0.5948	0.5987	0.6026	0.6064	0.6103	0.6141
0.3	0.6179	0.6217	0.6255	0.6293	0.6331	0.6368	0.6406	0.6443	0.6480	0.6517
0.4	0.6554	0.6591	0.6628	0.6664	0.6700	0.6736	0.6772	0.6808	0.6844	0.6879
0.5	0.6915	0.6950	0.6985	0.7019	0.7054	0.7088	0.7123	0.7157	0.7190	0.7224
0.6	0.7257	0.7291	0.7324	0.7357	0.7389	0.7422	0.7454	0.7486	0.7517	0.7549
0.7	0.7580	0.7611	0.7642	0.7673	0.7703	0.7734	0.7764	0.7794	0.7823	0.7852
0.8	0.7881	0.7910	0.7939	0.7967	0.7995	0.8023	0.8051	0.8078	0.8106	0.8133
0.9	0.8159	0.8186	0.8212	0.8238	0.8264	0.8289	0.8315	0.8340	0.8365	0.8389
1.0	0.8413	0.8438	0.8461	0.8485	0.8508	0.8531	0.8554	0.8577	0.8599	0.8621
1.1	0.8643	0.8665	0.8686	0.8708	0.8729	0.8749	0.8770	0.8790	0.8810	0.8830
1.2	0.8849	0.8869	0.8888	0.8907	0.8925	0.8944	0.8962	0.8980	0.8997	0.9015
1.3	0.9032	0.9049	0.9066	0.9082	0.9099	0.9115	0.9131	0.9147	0.9162	0.9177
1.4	0.9192	0.9207	0.9222	0.9236	0.9251	0.9265	0.9279	0.9292	0.9306	0.9319
1.5	0.9332	0.9345	0.9357	0.9370	0.9382	0.9394	0.9406	0.9418	0.9429	0.9441
1.6	0.9452	0.9463	0.9474	0.9484	0.9495	0.9505	0.9515	0.9525	0.9535	0.9545
1.7	0.9554	0.9564	0.9573	0.9582	0.9591	0.9599	0.9608	0.9616	0.9625	0.9633
1.8	0.9641	0.9649	0.9656	0.9664	0.9671	0.9678	0.9686	0.9693	0.9699	0.9706
1.9	0.9713	0.9719	0.9726	0.9732	0.9738	0.9744	0.9750	0.9756	0.9761	0.9767
2.0	0.9772	0.9778	0.9783	0.9788	0.9793	0.9798	0.9803	0.9808	0.9812	0.9817
2.1	0.9821	0.9826	0.9830	0.9834	0.9838	0.9842	0.9846	0.9850	0.9854	0.9857
2.2	0.9861	0.9864	0.9868	0.9871	0.9875	0.9878	0.9881	0.9884	0.9887	0.9890
2.3	0.9893	0.9896	0.9898	0.9901	0.9904	0.9906	0.9909	0.9911	0.9913	0.9916
2.4	0.9918	0.9920	0.9922	0.9925	0.9927	0.9929	0.9931	0.9932	0.9934	0.9936
2.5	0.9938	0.9940	0.9941	0.9943	0.9945	0.9946	0.9948	0.9949	0.9951	0.9952
2.6	0.9953	0.9955	0.9956	0.9957	0.9959	0.9960	0.9961	0.9962	0.9963	0.9964
2.7	0.9965	0.9966	0.9967	0.9968	0.9969	0.9970	0.9971	0.9972	0.9973	0.9974
2.8	0.9974	0.9975	0.9976	0.9977	0.9977	0.9978	0.9979	0.9979	0.9980	0.9981
2.9	0.9981	0.9982	0.9982	0.9983	0.9984	0.9984	0.9985	0.9985	0.9986	0.9986
3.0	0.9987	0.9987	0.9987	0.9988	0.9988	0.9989	0.9989	0.9989	0.9990	0.9990
3.1	0.9990	0.9991	0.9991	0.9991	0.9991	0.9992	0.9992	0.9992	0.9993	0.9993
3.2	0.9993	0.9993	0.9994	0.9994	0.9994	0.9994	0.9994	0.9995	0.9995	0.9995
3.3	0.9995	0.9995	0.9995	0.9996	0.9996	0.9996	0.9996	0.9996	0.9996	0.9997
3.4	0.9997	0.9997	0.9997	0.9997	0.9997	0.9997	0.9997	0.9997	0.9997	0.9998

Managing the project process:
the 4-D model

D3: Do it

Making sense of the project context

1 Introduction
2 Structures and frameworks
3 Projects and organisations

Managing the project process: the 4-D model

D1: Define it
4 Setting up for success
5 Planning for success

D4: Develop it
16 Completing projects and learning to improve

D2: Design it
6 Time planning and scheduling
7 Making time planning robust: Advanced Project Thinking (APT)
8 Building a business case for a project
9 Engaging stakeholders
10 Managing risks and opportunities

D3: Do it
11 Organising people in the project
12 Leading people in projects
13 Monitoring and controlling the project
14 Procuring, contracting, and working with supply chains
15 Problem-solving and decision-making

11

Organising people in the project

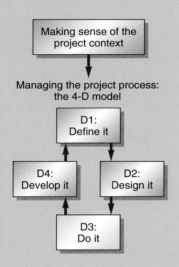

Making sense of the project context

Managing the project process: the 4-D model

D1: Define it

D4: Develop it

D2: Design it

D3: Do it

'To get around the world in 80 days, I needed to average 240 miles a day. Imagine pedalling from the Forth Road Bridge to Liverpool, or London to Plymouth, or more than New York to Boston, every day for two and a half months. To make this sustainable, every day you'd have to be in the saddle for sixteen hours and get about five hours' sleep. . . I want to acknowledge properly that, like the front man in a band, I get the lion's share of the profile and credit for what was actually an amazing team performance.'[1]
(Mark Beaumont)

Principles

1 Projects are rarely delivered by individuals but by groups or teams.

2 The arrangement of these groups or teams and their relationship to the larger organisation contributes significantly to their success or failure.

3 A key role of a project manager is organising human resources.

Learning objectives

By the time you have completed this chapter, you should be able to:

→ recognise the role of teams in achieving project objectives

→ understand the impact that the choice of structure will have on the achievement of project objectives

→ provide a framework for the project manager to guide understanding of some of the human resource issues that they will face.

Contents

Introduction   *271*
11.1 Teams   *272*
11.2 Structures   *279*
11.3 Managing people   *283*
Summary   *288*
Key terms   *289*
Relevant areas of the Bodies of Knowledge   *289*
Project management in practice: *Matrix management at Cardiff Bay Development Corporation   290*
Project management in practice: *Alternative options for problem solving – open innovation and crowdsourcing   291*
Topics for discussion   *292*
Further information   *293*
References   *293*

On 18 September 2017, Mark Beaumont cycled into the Arc de Triomphe in Paris, having ridden round the world in 78 days, 14 hours and 40 minutes, surpassing the previous world record by an amazing 45 days. Jules Verne's 'around the world in 80 days' idea had been accomplished on two wheels in an incredible feat of human endurance. The 18 000 miles of cycling is itself astonishing, but behind this was also a huge feat of organisation.

Source: Ian Langsdon/EPA-EFE/Shutterstock

The planning, preparation (including raising the sponsorship to fund the trip) and training required was immense, and with such limited margin for error and the clock ticking throughout, the logistics of the trip in terms of transport, equipment, food, border crossings, flights and medical support were remarkable. On top of this, the whole trip was documented daily on social media for a worldwide audience to follow Mark's progress. To achieve such an outcome requires a significant team effort.

Introduction

The gathering together of individuals with the aim of making them a cohesive whole and ensuring the benefit of all stakeholders is a fundamental role for most project managers. This is at best likely to be a very hit-and-miss process (very few will naturally achieve both good social interaction and commercial success) and, at worst, financially disastrous. However, there are some excellent examples, and sport and extreme events are often used to demonstrate how teams can work together to achieve exceptional goals. There have been many attempts to describe the best mixture of personalities that will ensure that the group dynamics are right and some of these will be discussed here. These are project issues. A strategic issue is how the project management structure fits in with the structure of the organisation as a whole. The various forms of matrix are also discussed.

Project teams are increasingly being formed not just from within one organisation but from multiple organisations (such as in joint ventures) and often geographically separate locations, forming *virtual teams*. This presents an extra set of challenges to the project manager and the team. Some of the ways that organisations have dealt with these challenges are covered.

11.1 Teams

The role of teams

The organisation of people into *ad hoc* groups takes advantage of bringing together individuals from different specialisms (marketing, engineering, etc.) as needed for a project task. The key characteristic of a team is that they are intended to achieve something collectively that would not be achievable individually.

This collective approach requires organisation from leaders, and greater specialism from team members. Indeed, it is notable that as organisational size increases, the degree of specialism of individuals is increased. Since the days of Henry Ford, large organisations have been organised by **functional** specialism into 'chimneys' or '**silos**' (see Figure 11.1). The notion is that, by grouping all the specialisms together, the arrangement is very efficient, as when you need that function to be performed there is an obvious resource to draw on. Quite reasonably, from the point of view of the individual, career paths are well defined and basic administration systems are geared to this way of working. Give a group the task of setting up and running their own business and, 99 per cent of the time, the first task they set themselves is to allocate roles as heads of the various line functions. This arrangement prevails in many traditional industries, but has been shown to be detrimental to the creativity of individuals and the responsiveness of the organisation to changing market needs.

However, as discussed in Chapter 1, one single function will rarely provide a customer's entire need or want. To do this requires **cross-functional activity**, i.e. the linking of the activities of more than one functional area. Functional arrangements tend to lead individual managers to build their own empires by creating work for themselves – regardless of whether this is value-adding for the organisation as a whole. Departmental head-count is considered to be a measure of the status of the individual manager and the importance of their function.

The conventional management **hierarchy** or **pyramid** (see Figure 11.2) has provided the basis on which the majority of organisations are ordered. The style is militaristic and there may be many layers in the chain of command (the British Army has 16 layers of leadership from the first rung of the leadership ladder at Lance Corporal up to the most senior at General).

For many organisations today, this has been the subject of recent change, with de-layering and corporate restructuring attempting to minimise the number of layers in the organisation. These 'flatter' structures may only have three to five levels (instead of many more previously). Organisations that have done this claim that it simplifies decision-making, as well as removing a considerable overhead cost to the organisation.

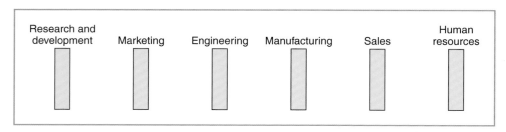

Figure 11.1 Management silos

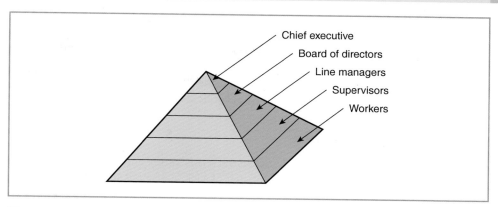

Figure 11.2 Classic hierarchical pyramid

Other structures include organisation by:

- product group;
- customer type (e.g. military/civil);
- geographical area (of their operations or the customers they serve);
- the function they perform.

It is common to see a mixture of these forms of organisation being employed, depending on the nature of the business and the degree of vertical integration in the supply stream (how many of the suppliers/customers are owned by the same organisation).

Where a project can be defined as having more than one function involved (which systems and strategy projects are almost bound to have) it is emerging as one of the roles of the project management specialist to define possible organisational forms. Many authors note that project managers themselves rarely have a choice about how the project organisation is arranged and, consequently, have to use what are often inappropriate structures. The emerging strategic importance of the project manager means that they are likely to have more input in determining the structures within which they work in the future.

The nature of the work organisation is important as it:

- defines **responsibility** and **authority**;
- outlines **reporting arrangements**;
- determines the **management overhead** (costs);
- sets the structure behind the **organisational culture**;
- determines one group of stakeholders in project activities.

As organisations have expanded, so the functions have often become less integrated by, for example, geographical separation. Walls, both literal and metaphorical, are constructed around them. In order to try to enforce communication between departments, many organisations use **dotted-line responsibility**. Here an individual may have a responsibility to one functional manager, with a dotted-line responsibility to another. This device has been used frequently to ensure that certain individuals do not engage in empire-building. In the manufacturing industry, this was done by manufacturing directors who wanted to ensure that they retained responsibility for the running of the entire manufacturing operation. Consequently, when it became fashionable to employ a quality manager they were not given any direct staff but inspection and other quality staff would work for the manufacturing manager while given a dotted-line responsibility to the quality manager (indicating that they were linked to the goals of this part of the operation). It did still leave power in the hands of the manufacturing people.

In addition to the dotted-line responsibility, detailed administrative procedures are introduced to ensure that some form of integration takes place. Often involving interminable meetings and mountains of bureaucracy, they are an attempt to make the organisation perform acts which it is not designed to do, i.e. integrate. Sloan's General Motors in the USA of the 1930s was run using considerable 'command-and-control' structures – based on the premise that 'whoever holds the purse strings, commands'.

Teamwork

The distinction between the terms '**team**' and '**group**' is made to indicate the differences in operating characteristics of each. A group is simply a collection of people. A team meets the following criteria:

- the output of the group is greater than the sum of the outputs of the individuals, e.g. a team can engage in creative processes (idea generation) far more effectively than a collection of individuals;
- a greater range of options can be considered by exploiting differences in individual thought processes;
- decision-making by the team is likely to be better (see Chapter 15).

The purpose of studying the role of **teamwork** in the project environment is:

- to help the project manager in the design and selection of the workgroup;
- to enable the monitoring of the degree to which the team is functioning effectively;
- to provide feedback to the team to help improve effectiveness.

The above assumes that in the first instance the project manager has the luxury of a free hand in the selection of who should form their project team. In reality, the team or group is more likely to be 'inherited' rather than designed. The study of teamworking will raise awareness of what is possible through teaming and the symptoms and consequences of the process not being managed to best effect.

Other characteristics of teams include:

- more openness to taking risks, as the risk is shared between the team rather than carried by one individual;
- higher overall level of motivation, as there is an inherent responsibility to others in the team and a desire not to let them down;
- better support for the individuals within the team, who are more likely to be included in a greater range of activities than they would normally be exposed to, but without their having to work alone.

Typically, a team consists of two to twenty people, though many managers suggest that effectiveness will decrease once the numbers go above ten. Larger teams are managed in the same way as large projects – by breaking down the big team into smaller, more manageable groups. As for the work breakdown structure, such an **organisational breakdown structure (OBS)** must have the appropriate coordination mechanisms in place between the smaller teams.

The value of diversity and inclusivity

As we see throughout this book, project teams undertake myriad difficult challenges in their work and serve a wide range of stakeholders. Given the rate at which projects underperform expectations, we need all the help we can get. There are two reasons why we need to make sure we have a diverse and inclusive team. The first is a clear moral one –

discrimination toward any group is morally reprehensible. Negative behaviour towards someone because of a particular characteristic is unacceptable and is the mark of a very poor leader. If you are in charge of a project then a large part of the role is bringing people together and getting things done through others. Racist, sexist or any other sort of discriminatory behaviour will drive people away and your leadership career will likely be a short, painful, and unsuccessful one. That argument itself should be enough, but there is a wealth of evidence that diverse teams also perform better, both in terms of innovation[2] and with regards to investment choices.[3] This makes sense – a wide range of backgrounds and experiences gives a deeper reservoir of ideas to draw on. When faced with complex problems, this is what project managers should seek to build. This point summarises the argument succinctly:

> 'Studies show that well-managed diverse groups outperform homogeneous ones and are more committed, have higher collective intelligence, and are better at making decisions and solving problems.'[4]

In the project world this is being recognised and promoted. A 2020 report by PMI[5] identifies that 88 per cent of survey respondents thought that cultural and gender diversity increased project value. Project managers improve society through the projects that they undertake. Make sure you contribute to this by building and leading your team professionally.

Lifecycles of teams

Teams, like projects, can be seen as having various stages of development. These can broadly be defined as **collection, entrenchment, resolution**/accommodation and **synergy**, followed almost inevitably by **decline**. At some point, the team will **break-up** because either they have reached a point at which it is no longer feasible for them to carry on working together or the task they are working on has been accomplished. The characteristics of each phase are shown in Table 11.1 and the effectiveness profile during the lifecycle is shown in Figure 11.3.

Using this knowledge, the project manager can identify the stage at which their team is operating, ensuring that the decline phase is held back for as long as possible. This may be done through changing the composition of the team to take the development back a little or expanding the range or scope of the tasks being undertaken to add a new challenge. The important point is, though, that teams do have a natural lifecycle and this should be recognised and used to advantage.

Lifecycle of quality circles

'Quality circles' went through a phase of being a very popular management tool for encouraging people from all parts of organisations to work together to solve problems. They were a move to get people who only previously had limited responsibilities to use their natural creativity and have the opportunity to innovate. The idea was promoted very heavily during the 1980s by the UK's Department of Trade and Industry for use in all organisations, and the idea became popular and was taken up rapidly. The frequently quoted example was that of a trade delegation to Japan who were amazed to find the extent of the use of quality circles in industry, and even more to find it in service industries – including a restaurant where the waiters had formed their own quality circle.

The initiative was taken up by a large number of companies. Quality circle meetings would often take place in the workers' own time, though generally they were given work-time at the start to set up the circles. It was notable that within a very short period (often less than 12 months) these project teams were being disbanded and the idea of quality

Table 11.1 Team lifecycle

Stage	Characteristics
Collection	The bringing together of individuals into a group with a collective task or problem to solve. The participants have a degree of eagerness and initial enthusiasm and generally rely on the authority and hierarchy to provide a degree of certainty in this uncertain environment. They will use this initial phase to establish themselves and find what is expected of them.
Entrenchment	As the group starts work they begin to find out where each person stands on various issues. The entrenchment comes when people arrive with preconceived ideas as to how the project should be proceeding and are unwilling to be persuaded of the merits of allowing the group to decide on the course of action. This phase can be very destructive and is generally fairly unproductive. The reasons for this unproductiveness are issues such as disillusionment with the goals of the project, competition for power or attention within the group, or general confusion as the work being undertaken bears little relationship to the goals of the project.
Resolution/ accommodation	The disagreements begin to be resolved, and characteristics such as mutual trust, harmony, selfesteem and confidence are seen. This is where the team starts to put aside the negative social effects and move to being more productive.
Synergy	On the basis on the work of Igor Ansoff,[6] synergy is defined as when the output of the whole is greater than what would be obtained from the component parts, otherwise stated as 2 + 2 = 5. This is the peak of effectiveness of the team, leadership is shared and there is a new motivation to complete the tasks at hand.
Decline	At some point the team will meet an event when its effectiveness starts to decline – this can be through the nature of the task being undertaken not changing or the focus of the activities being allowed to move towards a social group.
Break-up	If this occurs naturally before the task is finished, there can be problems in getting a new team to take up the remaining work. They will be expected to get 'up to speed' very quickly and have an additional pressure on them. Where the group finishes its task and it is during one of the earlier stages of development, either in resolution or synergy, the effects on future projects can be highly beneficial as the participants go away with good memories of the work they have done.

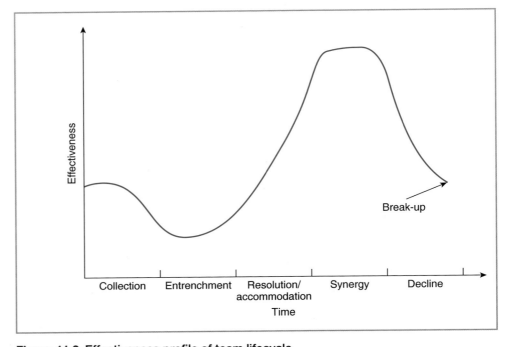

Figure 11.3 Effectiveness profile of team lifecycle

circles discontinued. Initial results were generally found to be excellent – the biggest problems were tackled first by the newly integrated groups and considerable savings were made. Then they started to decline. As was found:

> During this period, groups meet less often, they become less productive, and the resources committed to the program dwindle. The main reason the groups continue at all is because of the social satisfaction and pleasure the members experience rather than the group's problem-solving effectiveness. As managers begin to recognise this they cut back further on resources. As a result, the program shrinks. The people who all along have resisted the program recognise that it is less powerful than it once was, and they openly reject and resist the ideas it generates.[7]

As demonstrated by the above, the idea of using quality circles over an extended timeframe neglects to take account of the natural lifecycles of teams. That terminology has now faded, but the requirement is still there to use knowledgeable groups to solve pressing problems. The alternatives are as follows:

- Have the team assembled for the purpose of solving one single problem, then to be disbanded once it has been solved. These can be labelled as 'Tiger teams', or similar.
- Provide a path for the development of the role of the team from solving one or a small number of low-level problems into semi-autonomous workgroups. This will require other changes (in management reporting arrangements, for example) and considerable development of the team through education and training.

Effective teamwork

You have cleared some of the structural barriers to success – as identified in previous chapters. You have planned the project using the best available methods. You now want to make sure that the project teamwork makes a positive contribution to the success of the project. Eight characteristics, most of which are under the control of the project manager, have been identified.[8] These are as follows:

- a clear, elevating goal – a sense of mission must be created through the development of an objective which is understood, important, worthwhile and personally or collectively challenging;
- provide a results-driven structure – the structure and composition of the team should be commensurate with the task being undertaken (see section 11.2);
- competent team members – need to balance personal with technical competence;
- unified commitment – create the environment of 'doing what has to be done to succeed';
- foster a collaborative climate – encourage reliance on others within the team;
- standards of excellence – through individual standards, team pressure, knowledge of the consequences of failure;
- external support and recognition – where good work is performed, recognise it. It is likely to be absent from the other stakeholders, so it will be the responsibility of the project manager to provide it;
- institute principled leadership – see Chapter 12.

The first point is stated in virtually every consideration of this subject. Indeed, many go as far as to say that demanding performance which is challenging is an integral part of the way of creating a team. In addition, the first tasks that the team carries out will set the scene for the entire project, in particular through the definition of roles and rules of behaviour.

The structure of the team and its composition are broken down into three basic categories – creative, tactical and problem-solving. The use of each can be related to the appropriate or most likely phase in the project lifecycle. The requirements of the structure of each are shown in Table 11.2.

How teams/groups work can be seen in Figure 11.4. At one end of the spectrum is the disintegrated group, where there is no agreement between the team members and complete breakdown of the decision-making processes. At the other end is the integrated team, which has complete consensus on all matters, but which has 'gone over the edge' in terms of effectiveness. Their processes can be categorised by what is termed **group-think**, otherwise described by 'they've beaten the defence, but no one can bang the ball into the back of the net without discussing it with the group first'. Generally this results in ludicrous decisions being made – the ill-fated charge of the Light Brigade resulted from a group of generals who sat around and agreed with each other, rather than upset the working of the group by disagreeing with the decision!

Table 11.2 Requirements of team structure

Category	Likely phase of project lifecycle	Characteristics of team structure
Creative	Planning	Needs to have a high degree of autonomy in order to explore the widest range of possibilities and alternatives. Needs to be independent of systems and procedures and requires independent thinkers and people who are self-starters.
Tactical	Doing	Needs a well-defined plan, hence unambiguous role definitions and clarity of objectives for the individual members. The team members should have loyalty and a sense of urgency.
Problem-solving	Doing (when problems arise)	Will focus on problem resolution rather than any predetermined conclusions – these must be eliminated. The desirable characteristics of the people involved are that they are intelligent and have people sensitivity.

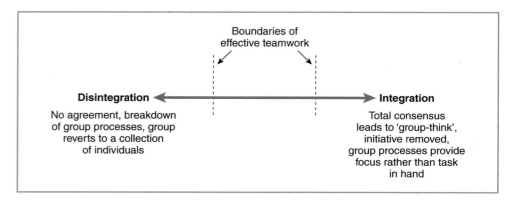

Figure 11.4 Spectrum of team/group performance

11.2 Structures

The pure project organisation

To move away from the functional silo to the project-based organisation is a major step. It is a structure that predominates in the construction industry (see Figure 11.5). At the highest levels in the organisation there are staff posts – senior managers, directors, administrative staff, etc. (called the 'project board'). The next level down is a series of project managers who have control over one or more projects at a time. The constitution of the project team depends on the stage in the lifecycle of the project, e.g. at the planning stage there will be architects, structural engineers, quantity surveyors and various other technical specialities such as groundwater engineers and legal advisers. These will be replaced by various contractors who are brought in to carry out specific tasks (such as steel fixers, electricians and heating/ventilation engineers) as the project moves through the operational phase. Once the particular task is completed, the team in each case is disbanded. The project manager may be retained to move on to other projects.

The advantages of such an arrangement are that:

- the labour force is highly flexible – labour can generally be attracted as and when required, without providing a labour burden or overhead for the rest of the time;
- the main company only has to administer the employment of its own staff – saving on the costs of directly employing others.

The disadvantages are significant:

- the project team is only temporary and so these people have no commitment to its success. The pay on a piece-rate basis may encourage the speed of work, but does little to ensure high quality or solve problems ahead of time. Paying on a time rate only encourages people to drag out jobs over a longer period of time. The only one who has an interest in the achievement of time:cost:quality objectives is the project manager;
- when there is a boom in a particular area in an industry, there is a shortage of labour, increasing labour rates and making hiring of the necessary resources problematic;
- where there are significant events occurring in a project, it is very hard for the lessons of these to be passed on to future projects as the people who have carried out the 'do' part of the project are not around for the 'review'. They cannot benefit, therefore, from the review process. Progress in improving work methods is likely to be slower.

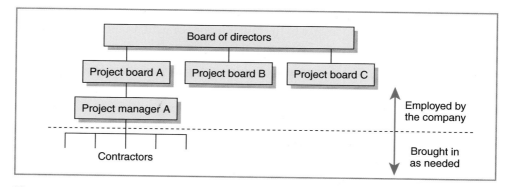

Figure 11.5 Project organisation

Matrix management

Matrix management was invented as a way of achieving some of the benefits of the project organisation without the disadvantages. There are three situations where a matrix management structure is appropriate:[9]

- where there is more than one orientation to the activities of the operation, e.g. multiple customers or geographical differences in markets served;
- where there is the need to process simultaneously large amounts of information;
- where there is the need to share resources – one function or project cannot justify the expenditure on a dedicated resource.

A matrix organisation can be defined as:

$$\text{matrix structure} + \text{matrix systems} + \text{matrix culture} + \text{matrix behaviour}^{[10]}$$

The matrix structure and the variations on the theme are included below. Matrix systems include the activities of management in planning, organising, directing, controlling and motivating within the structure. The culture requires acceptance of the system by the people who have to work within it, and the behaviour required is the ability to understand and work with overlapping boundaries.

The organisation of the matrix follows one of three models:

- *The lightweight matrix*. In this arrangement the project manager acts as a coordinator of the work of the project and chairs meetings of the representatives of all the departments involved. Responsibility is shared for the success of the project between the departments. This is regarded as being the weakest form of matrix structure, as there is little commitment to project success from anyone and the project manager is relatively impotent compared to the functional managers. The project meetings can be either led off-course or totally discredited by the inclusion of people of too high/low levels of authority respectively in the group.
- *The balanced model*. This is an attempt to balance the power of the project manager with that of the line manager. The administration of the organisation is such that the line manager needs the activities of the project manager to balance their resources, i.e. the project provides a means of securing part of the income of that function. The emergence of a second line of command – the project and the line manager – over any member of the team is the crucial drawback of this model. The person will have project responsibilities in addition to their line responsibilities.
- *The 'heavyweight matrix'*. Functional departments have the role of providing resources through seconding people on a full-time basis to the project team. On completion of the project, they return to the line function. In this way it is possible to have the resources available to bring in technical specialists without the project being saddled with their cost on a continuous basis. Such an arrangement is feasible where the project is of vital importance to the organisation. Drawbacks include the discontinuity of tasks for the individual and the resident department.

The success of application of the above models depends on:

- the training given to both managers and team members on working in such environments;
- the support systems – administrative, informational and career-wise;
- the nature of the individual – in particular, their tolerance level for role ambiguity.

Working in the uncertain environment of the project, and with career progression allied to the department rather than the project, means that there are often conflicting priorities.

Selecting the best structure for a project

It was noted in Chapter 2, in the discussion of the 7-S of issues facing the project manager, that the selection of structure was important. It is not uncommon, however, to find projects run using structures that are wholly inappropriate for their importance to the organisation. The previous discussion has outlined the options available. The choice should refer to the critical objectives of each project that an organisation is undertaking. A summary is provided in Table 11.3 of the relationship between structure and objectives for the project.

While Table 11.3 implies a degree of certainty on the choice of structure, there are additional factors to be considered. These include the predominant technology of the firm and the potential resource conflicts that heavyweight teams cause. The choice of structure is therefore a decision that should not be taken in isolation. This again highlights the importance for an organisation of the aggregate project plan and the project being given a definable priority. It is neither feasible nor practical for all projects in the firm to have a heavyweight matrix structure. As a simple rule, those with the highest levels of priority should have the heaviest weight structures.

One of the drawbacks identified in Table 11.3 is the *two bosses problem* – a team member must report to the project manager in addition to the line manager of the function in which they normally work. This leads some[11] to the conclusion that matrix management is unwieldy and practically unworkable and even the comment that 'matrices become hopelessly complicated bureaucracies and gut the emotional energy and ownership of those closest to the marketplace'.[12] The dual command leads to power struggles between the two managers and a selection of the following problems:[13]

- anarchy – people perceive that as soon as a team actually starts to work together, they are disbanded to go to work on another project;
- groupitis – decision-making is removed from the individual who will not take a decision without group approval;

Table 11.3 Relating project structures to project objectives[14]

	Functional organisation	Lightweight project organisation	Heavyweight project organisation	Project organisation
Example of usage	Minor change to existing product	Implementing change to work organisation, e.g. IT system	Major innovation project	Large construction projects
Advantages	Quality through depth of specialisation possible within functions, possible to 'hide' project costs	Quality maintained	Speed and quality (improvement) through use of relatively 'stable' organisation as a base	Speed highest through dedicated resources; organisation design dependent only on project strategy
Disadvantages	Relatively slow as a process	Some cost disadvantage due to additional coordination expense of the matrix	Adverse reaction from line managers; additional coordination and administration costs	Can incur significant additional cost due to the relative expense of contractors; quality may not improve over time; instability for staff
Issues for the project manager	Integration of functions within the organisation	Two bosses problem	Two bosses problem	Management of knowledge

Source: Adapted from Ulrich, K.T. and Eppinger, S.D. (2000) *Product Design and Development*, 2nd edn, New York: McGraw-Hill, p. 29. Reproduced with permission from the McGraw-Hill Companies.

- overhead that is imposed is excessively costly – heavyweight structures in particular often have their own coordination and administration alongside that of the functions in an organisation;
- decision strangling – so much time is spent trying to get consensus that any individual flair is stifled and the group becomes a barrier to any rapid progress.

Having stated all these potential problems, it is understandable that many organisations avoid the matrix form. There are, however, others who use it to good effect, proving that there is not one single way of managing a project that is applicable in all situations. The model that is chosen must be on a contingent basis, i.e. it responds to the needs of the organisation at that moment in time.

Process mapping, as discussed in Chapter 5, is part of the toolkit that can enable the management of cross-functional teams. It is decided at the planning stage who needs information and who needs to be involved at the various stages in a project. This is by nature an integrator – a tool that can be used to keep the overall objectives in view. It can also point to the kind of structure that will be appropriate during the different phases.

Mixed organisational structures and coordination

The above discussion considers the options open to the project manager where a single, homogeneous team is needed. Increasingly, particularly where a project has a high degree of organisational complexity, project managers are being required to use mixed organisational structures and additional coordination mechanisms to help make the structures effective. A recent product development project had the structure shown in Figure 11.6 which allowed the project manager a high degree of flexibility in resourcing the requirements of the project, but also good use of internal expertise – particularly product knowledge.

In Figure 11.6 the project manager has direct control over the heavyweight team working within the organisation and the contractors being employed on the project. They will have less direct control (usually) over staff members of other organisations, though this devolved authority does form part of some joint-venture contracts. In such a case, staff from one organisation may be working directly for a manager from an entirely different organisation.

The other issue arising from such complex structures is how to ensure that parts of the project being undertaken by different functions will actually work together. In the case of the London Underground refurbishment where the new trains would not fit into the tunnels (see Chapter 6), the two functions clearly did not work together on aspects of

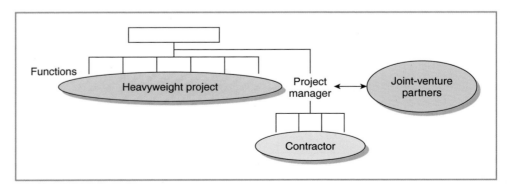

Figure 11.6 Mixed organisational structure

mutual interest. While it is an additional overhead for the project, many projects use an *integrator* – someone who works with both functions and ensures that areas of overlap are addressed. Functions may also swap staff or temporarily relocate them as another means of ensuring that this happens.

11.3 Managing people

Human resource management

The practice of human resource management is perhaps slightly trickier in a project-based organisation. Bredin and Söderlund (2011)[15] offer the concept of the 'HR quadriad', highlighting the interplay between HR specialists, line managers, project managers and project workers. It is worth noting that project managers typically do not have the domain expertise of particular professionals within the project. It is common for technical specialists to be brought in for a specific phase of the project, whereas other staff may be contributing to several different projects at once. This does require distinct skills on the part of the manager to keep the overall team motivated and productive.

Projects, by definition being temporary endeavours, may not represent the culture and dynamics of the parent organisations, especially as the project might draw on staff from outside the wider organisation. This is a challenge in terms of HR,[16] and it may take new entrants to the project time to get 'up to speed'. This is an important area of research,[17] as is the nature of project managers' careers.[18] However, given the increasing importance of projects within organisations and the representation of staff within and by professional bodies, it is likely these issues are going to be addressed more often at the highest levels of management.

Innovation and collaboration

One of the roles of the manager is to make sure the group behaviour suits the needs of the project. Generally, there needs to be some level of innovation (all projects have an element of novelty and problem-solving as part of the work), and collaboration between the participants. Getting these to work in practice, though, can be quite difficult. Pisano (2019)[19] argues that an innovation and experimentation culture requires a tough, disciplined side, and identifies five tensions that the manager needs to consider:

- Tolerance for failure, but no tolerance for incompetence.
- Willingness to experiment, but highly disciplined.
- Psychologically safe, but brutally candid.
- Collaboration, but with individual accountability.
- Flat but strong leadership.

These are not easy, and require ongoing action to ensure that standards remain high. The collaboration aspect is similarly difficult. Gino (2019)[20] offers tools to support successful working together:

- Teach people to listen, not talk.
- Train people to practice empathy.
- Make people more comfortable with feedback.
- Teach people to lead and follow.
- Speak with clarity and avoid abstractions.
- Train people to have win-win interactions.

When managing people, leadership behaviours are very important. You need to demonstrate and support the behaviours you wish to see, and be consistent in how you operate.

Personalities and roles

The project manager can benefit from an understanding of the ways in which individuals behave in group situations. These situations have been studied by social scientists for a long time and the results of these studies form a significant part of the sociological and management literature.

In order to determine the character of an individual (the **personality profile**) there are many commercially available psychometric tests that can be used. Many claim to be the 'definitive and only possible test you will need to find that ideal candidate for your team', but most can be bluffed by an intelligent candidate and few are totally applicable to people other than graduates. They can also be expensive to administer and often require expert guidance to interpret the results. The *curriculum vitae* and interview, though maligned, is still the normal mode for recruiting in most project environments. For leaders, recent ideas on the assessment of character are very interesting and can also provoke valuable reflection.[21]

In designing your team there are certain basic requirements you may wish key players to have, e.g. qualifications or relevant experience. These determine their eligibility for the job. The suitability can be determined through assessing how they are likely to fit in with the rest of the team, and whether or not the team has a balanced portfolio of characteristics relative to the task being undertaken. Meredith Belbin[22] has shown that a structure based on a greater number of classifications than those given above can prove useful in both the selection and ongoing management of the project. The characteristics that Belbin identifies are shown in Figure 11.7.

Having categorised the individual's personalities, it is worth considering the effect this has on their behaviour. Belbin cites this as consisting of six factors:

- personality – as determined through testing;
- mental abilities – e.g. critical reasoning;
- current values and motivations (determined by all sorts of personal factors – the weather, family situation, how well the Blues did on Saturday, etc.);
- field constraints – those rules and procedures that affect behaviour from the environment in which you are working;
- experience – prior events which have left varying degrees of impression on the individual;
- role-learning – the ease with which an individual can take on one of the roles listed in Figure 11.7, but which is not their natural role – this increases their role versatility.

The effects on the design of the team are that there can be a degree of scientific method applied to the selection of individuals – though how *scientific* tests (like the Belbin role profiling) are is open to debate. They are liked by many project managers not just for their use in selection (making sure that there is the right balance of people in the team) but also as part of team development. Understanding the roles of individuals in the team can have a very positive effect on the interactions between team members.

Belbin Team Role		Strengths	Allowable Weaknesses
	Resource Investigator	Outgoing, enthusiastic. Explores opportunities and develops contacts.	Might be over-optimistic, and can lose interest once the initial enthusiasm has passed.
	Teamworker	Co-operative, perceptive and diplomatic. Listens and averts friction.	Can be indecisive in crunch situations and tends to avoid confrontation.
	Co-ordinator	Mature, confident, identifies talent. Clarifies goals.	Can be seen as manipulative and might offload their own share of the work.
	Plant	Creative, imaginative, free-thinking, generates ideas and solves difficult problems.	Might ignore incidentals, and may be too preoccupied to communicate effectively.
	Monitor Evaluator	Sober, strategic and discerning. Sees all options and judges accurately.	Sometimes lacks the drive and ability to inspire others and can be overly critical.
	Specialist	Single-minded, self-starting and dedicated. They provide specialist knowledge and skills.	Tends to contribute on a narrow front and can dwell on the technicalities.
	Shaper	Challenging, dynamic, thrives on pressure. Has the drive and courage to overcome obstacles.	Can be prone to provocation, and may sometimes offend people's feelings.
	Implementer	Practical, reliable, efficient. Turns ideas into actions and organises work that needs to be done.	Can be a bit inflexible and slow to respond to new possibilities.
	Completer Finisher	Painstaking, conscientious, anxious. Searches out errors. Polishes and perfects.	Can be inclined to worry unduly, and reluctant to delegate.

Figure 11.7 The nine team roles

Source: Belbin, R.M. (1993) *Team Roles at Work*, Butterworth-Heinemann, Oxford. Reproduced with permission from Belbin Associates

Managing people: meetings

Manager 1: 'I'm really not in favour of the Scorpion Project – it certainly won't do what my department wants.'

Manager 2: 'Mine neither. Don't worry, I'll just make sure that the meetings go nowhere. They'll soon drop it!'

The project manager will often have to chair **meetings**, so a discussion of the good practice concerning how they should be run is very relevant. This is an exceptional management skill, yet it is so basic that most people assume that they know how to do it. In practice, this is rarely the case and meetings often break up without any progress being made – as is occasionally intended and demonstrated by the quotation at the start of this section. This short section is intended to provide only a few guidance notes as to what constitutes good practice.

- Confirm the purpose of the meeting – there has to be a reason why you need to bring people together. This should be very specific so as to help eliminate spurious issues that can detract from the main purpose.
- Deciding who should be invited, with the minimum requirement of including anyone who would be offended if they were left out. It is often worth checking by asking the individual concerned if you are in doubt.
- The pre-meeting preparation – the location and timing, agenda and any reports providing background information on the topic under discussion should be circulated in advance.
- Running the meeting – provide a forum for constructive debate while limiting the scope of discussion to the matter in hand. Do not allow repetition of points or any one member to dominate the discussions. Regularly summarise progress and ask for conclusions to be drawn based on the discussions. The project manager should have in mind that the level of attention of most people declines rapidly after the first 20 minutes, and after two hours there is unlikely to be any constructive progress. People will often agree to anything at this point simply to get out of the meeting. Obtaining consensus is an art, which the skilful chair of a meeting will aim to achieve. This ensures that the entire meeting has 'bought in' to a decision and makes carrying it out far easier than with a number of dissenters.
- Post-meeting follow-up – send copies of the minutes with action points and who should carry them out listed against each. Most meetings can have their conclusions and action points stated on one side of A4 paper – they have a high chance of being read in this form, rather than 'filed'. These minutes and action points must then form the basis of the next meeting's early discussions, ensuring that whoever said they would carry out a task has a natural responsibility to the meeting to do it. They also know that should they fail to carry out an action, this will be identified at the next meeting.

There are many excellent management skills courses which develop the above ideas, including some of the more complex aspects such as conflict resolution, and aspiring project managers should avail themselves of these. The Further Information at the end of this chapter contains several texts which provide an expansion of the subject.

Managing people: geographically separated teams

All the above good ideas about working with teams are fine where everyone is 'drinking from the same watercooler/coffee machine'. That is, they are geographically close. Many project managers today, even for projects of medium complexity, are having to work with other organisations, often at a distance. Among the reasons for this is the increase in outsourcing (see Chapter 14) and in the number of collaborative projects as a result of organisations working more closely together. The Covid-19 crisis of 2020 forced even co-located teams to work from home via videoconferencing for a period of time, shifting the group dynamics considerably. Business meetings that used to be formal, shifted overnight to more casually dressed affairs with the participants in their kitchens, living rooms or even bedrooms.

Some projects cross multiple continents. The UK is in a useful geographical position as it shares part of the working day with both the US and Asia. For example, relative to the UK, the US site can be 7 hours behind and the Asian plant 8 hours ahead. This has meant that there is no time in the day when all parties would naturally be at work, so it falls to the UK staff to be the 'go-between'.

Experience of projects with this spread highlights key problems that can arise, including:

- language and culture – expectations and norms can differ greatly, especially when starting the project and teams at the different locations have little experience of working with the other sites. Despite the fact that two of these three nominally have English as their first language, there is sometimes work to be done to ensure that communication is effective. Clarity is key, and building relationships with individuals at the other sites is important;
- where each group place the particular project in their priorities – each operating unit may have its own set of priorities. For example, a UK/US product development may be using a Chinese factory for prototyping, and fast turnaround is vital to keep the development on schedule. However, the Chinese factory may (understandably) be more focused on volume production of current product for existing customers, and low-volume prototype runs can be viewed as less important;
- standards – due to the different requirements of each geographical market, staff at each site may have different expectations with regard to the standards to be met and tests required to certify the product. This has the potential to create technical conflict, confusion, and delay;
- national holidays – when coordinating meetings, it is very easy to miss that other participants have, for example, a local holiday that day. Much time can be expended with half the team waiting fruitlessly for the other half to join a meeting! Best to ensure calendars are organised well in advance and key meetings re-scheduled as required.

As you can see even from such a superficial analysis, there is plenty of potential for problems and it is very difficult to conceptualise the management task in this environment. More generally, problems that arise include:

- obtaining buy-in to objectives from remote teams and individuals;
- poor development and communication of plans;
- no clarity as to who is responsible for what and to whom;
- lack of sharing of problems as and when they arise;
- delays caused by support systems – in particular, incompatibilities between administrative systems (e.g. where procedures for allocating and handling budgets may be very different).

Add these to the feelings of isolation of individuals working in such environments and the effects can be contrary to the expectations of high-performing teamwork. To counter these the first stage for the project manager is recognition that such problems arise and that it is only through more active management that they will be avoided or at least minimised. Typically, other devices that managers use to help in such environments include the following:

- Formal project start-up meeting – North American firms often use an all-singing and dancing roadshow to 'rev the team up'. Quite how effective this is in other cultures is debatable.
- Regular face-to-face meetings to ensure that communications are working and to keep the team engaged with the project. Be mindful that much project communication is actually serendipity (e.g. talking to someone in a corridor and picking up an important

piece of information). In the absence of that opportunity, communication will likely be noticeably less effective so this makes the formal meetings more important to ensure key points are shared.

- Establishing regular video-conferences where face-to-face meetings are not possible – use the same guidelines for meetings as in the previous section.
- Judicious use of e-mail in the circulation of project information, that is, keep people 'in the loop' but don't add to their drowning in unnecessary data. Also being aware of the problems that people 'reading between the lines' in what is a relatively informal communications medium can have.
- Working with senior managers to clear the way for project staff in remote locations to be supported in their project work, including assessment and rewards.
- Establish some rules for dealing with particular scenarios, e.g. where conflicts arise in the team, and how these should be handled.
- Create highly visible progress measures that can be viewed by all the project team in real time (see Chapter 13).
- Don't expect to get full productivity from a team that is so diverse – many managers have found that 75–85 per cent is the most that can be expected, due to all the reasons given above. This may require longer schedules or additional resources to be employed, but is at least realistic.

The above list again shows that project management, far from being a mundane and routine task, is one of the most challenging that we face. There are no hard and fast rules here – just some structures and guidelines that warn of potential problems that are known to arise under particular circumstances, and the actions of some managers in dealing with them. The gap between that and practice is to be filled by the individual manager, using their knowledge and creativity, to find ways of working that fit the context and meet their particular set of challenges.

Summary

■ The conventional approach to designing organisations is to have the key functions arranged into 'silos' with people who perform a similar set of tasks grouped together with their own hierarchies. These are very convenient, but are not the most appropriate for achieving results through projects. The pure project organisation is possibly the most flexible and far removed from the conventional approach to management – people are brought in on a contract basis for the project and no other task. The hiring organisation does not then have a further labour overhead when there is no work to be done. Matrix management is an attempt by conventional organisations to give some degree of authority to the project manager while retaining the benefits of the functional organisation. The three different types of matrix model represent increasing levels of authority given to the project manager – namely lightweight, balanced and heavyweight. Matrix management is extensively used but does suffer from the problem of one person having two bosses. The choice of the structure to be used is dependent on, among other criteria, the strategic objectives of the project.

■ One representation of the heavyweight matrix, called the **seamless enterprise**, exists when the functional silos are seen as being subordinate to key business processes. The use of tools such as process mapping can help to make this a reality by stimulating cross-function communication and activity.

■ Forming groups of individuals into teams is a complex process. There are many productivity and effectiveness benefits (synergy) to be gained from teamwork over that of a group. Teams have a natural lifecycle which has recognisable characteristics to each part. The project manager can have a role in controlling both the emergence of the various phases and the management of negative effects when the team goes 'over the hill'.

■ Belbin, among others, has provided managers with a tool for identifying the personalities of individuals which can provide a guide as to the nature of the person or mixture of people who will be required for particular tasks within a particular team. Classifications such as Belbin's do provide a useful avenue for team development activities. However, in order to get the most from a team, the manager can draw on the experience of others. Providing a clear and elevating goal is one of the most important points. The nature of the team can also be managed through the categorisation of the task to be carried out – creative, tactical or problem solving. Running meetings – as for most of project management – is a skill that can be learned, and there are many issues to be resolved when a team is geographically spread, and becomes a *virtual team*.

■ Overall, getting the most from an organisation of individuals does require that they work in a structure that is appropriate to the task being undertaken, and that their local environment is managed as part of the process. This is a whole area of study in its own right.

Key terms

collection/entrenchment/ resolution *p. 275*	management overhead *p. 273*	reporting arrangements *p. 273*
cross-functional activities *p. 272*	matrix management *p. 280*	responsibility/authority *p. 273*
dotted-line responsibility *p. 273*	meetings *p. 286*	seamless enterprise *p. 288*
functional silos *p. 272*	organisational breakdown structure (OBS) *p. 274*	synergy/decline/break-up *p. 275*
group-think *p. 278*	organisational culture *p. 273*	team and group *p. 274*
hierarchy/pyramid *p. 272*	personality profile *p. 284*	teamwork *p. 274*

Relevant areas of the Bodies of Knowledge

The PMI approach in particular (see Tables 11.4 and 11.5) suggests that there should be a highly planned and formalised process for all these stages. The reality for many project managers is that they are handed a team, an imperfect structure and told to 'get on with it'. These are good guidelines, however, but present a significant upfront workload to the project manager. They do contribute to problem prevention, development of *human capital* and recognition of competence.

Table 11.4 Relevant areas of the APM Body of Knowledge

Relevant section	Title	Summary
3.2	Leading Teams	Introduction to the section, highlighting the importance of leading a group for a project professional.
3.2.1	Teams	Emphasises the function of teams, and the key roles, including sponsor, project manager, and the wide range of specialists that may make up the team.
3.2.2	Virtual Teams	The importance of this subject is reflected in that it has its own section. It stresses the value of relationship-building and trust given the challenge of working virtually.
3.2.3	Team Development	Gives guidance on making the team function. Key points include: being clear about goals and objectives; enabling differences to be aired; providing process and clear roles and responsibilities; promoting openness and honesty; and ensuring team members are transitioned back into the business after the project.

Table 11.5 Relevant areas of the PMI Body of Knowledge

Relevant section	Title	Summary
9.3	Project resource management – acquire resources	The characteristics of the individuals required should be determined to include their experience, interests, characteristics, availability and competencies. They are then recruited through negotiation with functional heads, or procurement from outside sources. It notes that the team may be virtual, in which case this may allow a wider pool of staff from whom to pick.
9.4	Project resource management – develop team	'Teamwork is a critical factor for project success and developing effective project teams is one of the primary responsibilities of the project manager.' Team development should include team-building activities, open communication, trust development, conflict management, and encouraging collaboration.

PROJECT MANAGEMENT IN PRACTICE
Matrix management at Cardiff Bay Development Corporation

As a government-funded body the Cardiff Bay Development Corporation is one of a number of UK regional development corporations charged with the regeneration of specific areas. It is a predominantly project-based organisation – the life-span of the corporation was generally fixed at its inception. Its roles include the promotion of the area and the bringing in of business, housing and the necessary infrastructural changes to make it all work.

Aside from London's Docklands development, the Cardiff Bay development was one of the most ambitious schemes running at the time. It included the construction of a barrage across the estuaries of the rivers Taff and Ely, to form a freshwater lagoon when completed. The 2200 acres of land directly adjacent to the lagoon were under the control of a number of owners, with around 60 per cent of it being under contract or negotiation for redevelopment.

When founded in 1987, the corporation was divided into functional groups – engineering, commercial, finance and administration, each under the control of a director. As the work of the corporation grew, it was decided that this was becoming unwieldy and that in order to simplify matters, a matrix (overlay) structure would be adopted. The directors maintained overall charge and the team members were drawn in as needed. The overlay consisted of eight horizontal functions, divided into geographical areas.

As the engineering director commented:

'This proved to be too complicated as people found themselves on too many teams. They lost sight of the corporate objectives – the teams ended up competing against each other for developers to take plots of land, regardless of who was most suitable for that site. What we needed to do was to maintain that competitive spirit, but channel it more constructively. The sale of sites was also problematic as the revenue generated would technically be earned by the teams, but would go back into a central pot for use by all.'

The experiment with this form of matrix management was abandoned. The current structure keeps the power of the functions intact but looks at four key areas through the business processes that are carried out in those areas. In this way, it now more closely follows the seamless ideas than those of the conventional matrix.

The area is now a vibrant centre, including the Welsh Assembly, with many options for family entertainment. The development has made it a major tourist destination in its own right.[23]

Points for discussion

1 Why should the structure for the organisation or the project (in this case each area to be developed constituted a project) affect the way that people behave?

2 What type of matrix is in use here?

3 What alternative structures could they adopt?

PROJECT MANAGEMENT IN PRACTICE
Alternative options for problem solving – open innovation and crowdsourcing

Many of our ideas on how organisations run projects and perform their standard operations are rooted in the concept that we develop teams, using outsourced resources as necessary, and that we 'own' and control as much of it as possible. Other ideas offer different perspectives. One approach is to look externally for help in solving your difficult challenges.

Crowdsourcing is a technique of putting problems out for the wider world (the 'crowd') to try and solve. Although this may seem new, it is not. In 1714 the British Parliament offered a £20 000 prize to whoever could solve the 'longitude problem'.[24] Sailors could determine their latitude (the north-south location) but the east-west position remained a huge challenge, resulting in shipwrecks due to incorrect determination of a ship's position. Famously, the prize was finally won by John Harrison, a clockmaker, for a stable timepiece. He presented his first solution in 1736, but refined it for a further 23 years. It highlighted how a well-specified problem can be put 'out there' to be solved. If the incentives (typically a monetary reward) are sufficient, then people will try to find a solution.

→

This has resulted in concepts such as the X-Prize[25] which offers multi-million dollar rewards for solving major technical and societal challenges. These techniques work. Websites such as innocentive.com allow companies to put up challenges (generally technical) for solvers to address. A typical one might be an organisation with a particular issue they need solving which can be put out to the community. They specify the problem, and the financial award for the winning solution. This way firms can use their limited resources on the areas they choose to address, putting other self-contained problems out to the market where others with more specific expertise can work on them. Although this idea has been around for years, its use within the project community does not seem as prevalent as might be expected given its suitability within project-based work. Recent research[26] has highlighted the benefits of the opportunities it offers, though.

Proponents of 'open innovation' recommend that this can go the other way, too.[27] The 'outside-in' approach allows ideas to be brought in from external sources, but the 'inside-out' method allows organisations to sell or licence un- or under-used ideas to other organisations. This appears to be less developed, but may well lead to an excellent revenue stream if appropriate.

Technology and novel thinking have led to major developments such as open-source software (e.g. Linux) that do not conform to 'standard' thinking about how companies should develop, market, sell and control their wares. Other techniques, such as 'hackathons' allow groups of software developers to develop code in a very short period of time. These may end up with solutions that were not what you originally expected, and can offer innovative results that had not been considered even just the day before.

These ideas are part of a 'toolkit' of project management. If the project is aligned with your current expertise, they may not be appropriate. However, when you are seeking new solutions, step changes in technology, or a different approach to established problems, they may well be worth considering. There may be someone on the other side of the world with a perfect solution to your problem. Conversely, you may have ideas that help someone else and they might be willing to pay handsomely for a working solution. This can help organisations that are resource-limited to achieve more than they planned, although care must be taken and success is not guaranteed.

Points for discussion

1 How might these approaches benefit your organisation, or an organisation with which you are familiar? What might the risks be?

2 How might these ideas work with your organisation's requirements for project planning?

3 How might implementing these ideas affect the current organisational structure, and what may be the impact on current employees?

4 Compare these approaches to general business outsourcing (bringing in other companies to do particular tasks, catering, cleaning, security, etc.). What are the benefits of each approach?

Topics for discussion

1 Why is the functional organisation prevalent in modern business?

2 What are the disadvantages of the functional organisation?

3 Briefly list the other ways in which an organisation may be structured.

4 Why is the subject of organisational structure so important?

5 Why is the 'pure project' organisation a useful structure?

6 Why do organisations use the matrix structure?

7 Briefly describe the three basic types of matrix organisation.

8 Why should project managers concern themselves with the way the groups they are working with interact?

9 How might a knowledge of the lifecycle of teams help the project manager?

10 Using Belbin's character profiles, indicate which of these you feel best applies to you. You may like to apply this to a group in which you are working by then analysing each other's characteristics.

Further information

Ancona D. and Bresman H. (2007) *X-Teams: How To Build Teams That Lead, Innovate, And Succeed*, Harvard Business School Publishing.

Berne, E. (1967) *Games People Play: The Psychology of Human Relationships*, Penguin, Harmondsworth.

Blanchard, K., Carew, D. and Parisi-Carew, E. (1992) *The One Minute Manager Builds High Performing Teams*, HarperCollins, London.

Dainty A. and Loosemore. M. (2012) *Human Resource Management in Construction: Critical Perspectives*, Routledge, Oxon.

DeMarco, T. and Lister, T. (2016) *Peopleware: Productive Projects and Teams*, 3rd edition, Addison-Wesley, Upper Saddle River, NJ.

Edmondson, A.C. (2013) *Teaming to Innovate*, Jossey-Bass, San Francisco.

Handy, C. (1989) *The Age of Unreason*, Arrow Books, London.

Henderson, L.S., Stackman, R.W. and Lindekilde, R. (2018) 'Why cultural intelligence matters on global project teams', *International Journal of Project Management*, Vol. 36, No. 7, pp. 954–967.

Katzenbach, J.R. and Smith, D.K. (1993) *The Wisdom of Teams*, Harvard Business School Press, Cambridge, MA.

Pullen, P. (2016) *Virtual Leadership: Practical Strategies for Getting the Best out of Virtual Work and Virtual Teams*, Kogan-Page, London.

Scott-Young, C.M., Georgy, M. and Grisinger, A. (2019) 'Shared leadership in project teams: An integrative multi-level conceptual model and research agenda', *International Journal of Project Management*, Vol. 37, No. 4, pp. 565–581.

Websites

www.belbin.com – Belbin Associates' website and online role profiling.

www.hackathon.com

References

1 Beaumont, M. (2018) *Around the World in 80 Days*, Penguin, London.

2 Hewlett, S.A., Marshall, M. and Sherbin, L. (2013) 'How Diversity Can Drive Innovation', *Harvard Business Review,* Vol. 91, No. 12, p. 30.

3 Gompers, P. and Kovvali, S. (2018) 'The Other Diversity Dividend', *Harvard Business Review*, Vol. 96, No 4, pp. 72–77.

4 Williams, J.C. and Mihaylo, S. (2019) 'How The Best Bosses Interrupt Bias On Their Teams', *Harvard Business Review*. Vol. 97, No. 6, pp. 151–155. Quote from p. 151.

5 Project Management Institute (2020) 'A Case for Diversity', www.pmi.org.

6 Ansoff, H.I. (1968) *Corporate Strategy*, Penguin Books, New York.

7 Lawler, E.E. and Mohrman, S.A. (1985) 'Quality Circles After the Fad', *Harvard Business Review*, January–February, pp. 65–71.

8 Larson, C.E. and LaFasto, F.M.J. (1989) *Team Work*, Sage, London.

9 Mullins, L.J. (2016) *Management and Organisational Behaviour*, 11th edition, Pearson, Harlow.

10 Davis, S.M. and Lawrence, P.R. (1977) *Matrix*, Addison-Wesley, Reading, MA, pp. 18–19.

11 See the results of research carried out by Bartlett and Ghoshal (Bartlett, A. and Ghoshal, S. (1990) '"Matrix Management" – Not a Structure, a Frame of Mind', *Harvard Business Review*, July–August, pp. 138–145).

12 Peters, T. (1992) *Liberation Management*, Macmillan, London.

13 As reference 6.

14 Ulrich, K.T., Eppinger, S.D. and Yang M.C. (2000) *Product Design and Development*, 2nd edition, McGraw-Hill, New York.

15 Bredin, K. and Söderlund, J. (2011) 'The HR quadriad: a framework for the analysis of HRM in project-based organizations', *International Journal of Human Resource Management*, Vol. 22, No. 10, pp. 2202–2221.

16 Huemann, M. (2015) *Human Resource Management in the Project-Oriented Organization: Towards a Viable System for Project Personnel*, Gower, Abingdon.

17 Keegan, A., Ringhofer, C. and Huemann, M. (2018) 'Human resource management and project based organizing: Fertile ground, missed opportunities and prospects for closer connections', *International Journal of Project Management*, Vol. 36, No. 1, pp. 121–133.

18 Akkermans, J., Keegan, A., Huemann, M. and Ringhofer, C. (2020) 'Crafting Project Managers' Careers: Integrating the Fields of Careers and Project Management', *Project Management Journal*, Vol. 51, No. 2, pp. 135–153.

19 Pisano G. (2019) 'The Hard Truth About Innovative Cultures', *Harvard Business Review* Vol. 97 No. 1, pp. 62–71.

20 Gino F. (2019) 'Cracking the Code of Sustained Collaboration', *Harvard Business Review,* Vol. 97, No. 6, pp. 72–81.

21 Crossan, M.M., Byrne, A., Seijts, G.H., Reno M., Monzani L. and Gandz, J. (2017) 'Toward a Framework of Leader Character in Organizations', *Journal of Management Studies*, Vol. 54, No. 7, pp. 986–1018.

22 Belbin, R.M. (2010) *Team Roles at Work*, 2nd edition, Butterworth-Heinemann, Oxford and Belbin, R.M. (2000) *Beyond The Team*, Butterworth-Heinemann, Oxford.

23 www.cardiffbay.co.uk

24 Spencer, R.W. (2012) 'Open Innovation in the Eighteenth Century', *Research Technology Management*, Vol. 55, No. 4, pp. 39–43.

25 www.xprize.org

26 Wilson, K. B., Bhakoo, V. and Samson, D. 'Crowdsourcing' (2019) *International Journal of Operations & Production Management*, Vol. 38, No. 6, pp. 1467–1494.

27 Bogers, M., Chesbrough, H. and Moedas, C. (2018) 'Open Innovation: Research, Practices, and Policies', *California Management Review*, Vol. 60, No. 2, pp. 5–16.

12

Leading people in projects

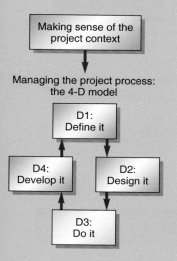

Making sense of the project context

Managing the project process:
the 4-D model

D1:
Define it

D4:
Develop it

D2:
Design it

D3:
Do it

'It is better to lead from behind and to put others in front, especially when you celebrate victory when nice things occur. You take the front line when there is danger. Then people will appreciate your leadership.'
Nelson Mandela

Principles

1   Leadership in projects comprises three facets: managerial, relational and entrepreneurial.

2   There are choices for leaders as to how they lead which greatly influence the performance of the project.

3   Leading starts with leadership of self.

Learning objectives

By the time you have completed this chapter, you should be able to:

→   identify three facets of leadership in projects

→   describe different models of leadership and motivation and their impacts

→   understand a range of choices for your leadership.

Contents

Introduction   *296*
12.1 Leadership in projects   *297*
12.2 Leading and motivation   *300*
12.3 Leading and you   *306*
Summary   *312*
Key terms   *313*
Relevant areas of the Bodies of Knowledge   *313*
Project management in practice: *Doesn't time fly?*   *313*
Topics for discussion   *315*
Further information   *315*
References   *316*

In 2018 the Nobel Committee awarded the Nobel Peace Prize to Nadia Murad and Denis Mukwege for their campaigns 'to end the use of sexual violence as a weapon of war and armed conflict'.[1] Nadia Murad is a war crime victim and member of the Yazidi community from northern Iraq. She was captured by Islamic State in 2014 and subjected to horrific abuse by her captors. After three months she managed to escape, and in 2016 was appointed as the UN's first Goodwill Ambassador for the Dignity of Survivors of Human Trafficking.

Source: Haakon Mosvold Larsen/AP/Shutterstock

Denis Mukwege was awarded for his work to help victims of rape in the Democratic Republic of Congo. He combined being a doctor of medicine with being a campaigner not just to treat women raped during the armed conflict in his country by setting up a hospital, but to prevent such tragedies happening again there and elsewhere. He initially used his technical skills to directly help victims, but then used a much wider set of skills to recruit and nurture the necessary support – financial, technical and political – to extend his reach from treatment to prevention.

Introduction

What does it take to be an effective leader? Is this different from the requirements of a great manager, and project manager in particular? What traits do great leaders such as the two winners of the Nobel Peace Prize have that other leaders could usefully adopt? What also are the implications for each of us in how we work?

The subjects of management and leadership in commercial, military and political settings are all well established and each can contribute some useful thinking to the world of projects. The discussion here will draw on the subjects of organisational behaviour and human resources management in particular, and provide some insight into the impact that the leader or manager can have in a project.

In this chapter, we will consider leadership as part of the response to the complexities facing the individuals charged with delivering projects, programmes and portfolios, as described back in Chapter 2. We consider that leadership is the broad field in which project managers operate, and that their roles comprise three facets in response to complexities: **managerial**, **relational** and **entrepreneurial**. In practice, the terms 'project manager' and 'project leader' are often used interchangeably (rightly or wrongly), but for the purposes of this chapter, we will focus on these three facets. We will be providing an overview and some signposts to further study, as management, leadership and entrepreneurship are huge fields in their own rights. In addition, the need for the manager to show 'leadership of self' at the centre of leadership excellence is noted.

12.1　Leadership in projects

What leaders do

When asked what it is that good project leaders *do*, the replies typically include:

- they get the most out of the team
- they help team members become the best they can be
- they are the holder of the vision for the project
- they are the one who sets the goals and priorities for the team
- they provide the motivation and inspiration for those around them
- they are the focal point for communication
- they are the one with the badge that says 'leader'.

These can be viewed as the skills of a good leader.[2] There are many other attributes that could be added to this list. The last of these is not frivolous, but a recognition that leadership can be a role, appointed by an organisation, and assigned accountability (following the discussion of *governance* in Chapter 11). While there is this formal side to leadership, as our opening example of the Nobel Peace Prize demonstrates, leaders themselves can also emerge unappointed by anyone by simply taking an initiative upon themselves (e.g. as Denis Mukwege did in setting up a hospital). The common element whatever the starting point is that they *take people and organisations with them on whatever is the journey that they are leading.* Unless they take people and organisations with them, they have no **followers**, so can they still be a leader just because they have the badge?

Kirkpatrick and Locke (1991)[3] showed that the successful leaders they studied had the characteristics of having drive and ambition, the desire to lead and influence, honesty and integrity, self-confidence, intelligence and in some cases, technical knowledge. This list is worth adding to from your own experiences of good (and not so good) leadership.

The structure employed for these discussions is shown in Figure 12.1. The assumption is made that leadership has a significant impact on the performance of the project – however such performance is defined (see e.g. Holweg and Maylor, 2018).[4]

We view the project leader as having a set of skills and attitudes that are formed by their education and training (formal and otherwise), their personality, and what we term 'reflected experience'. This last element means that the value of experience (having done something similar previously) is greatly enhanced if the individual has taken time to critically reflect on it.

This set of skills and attitudes then influences the role that they take, which is also influenced by the complexity of the situation being faced (as described by our three complexity dimensions – if in doubt please refer back to Chapter 2). The 'actions of others' recognises that for instance, the involvement of a senior leader from the organisation plays a role – whether they are absent or overly involved and scrutinising. The organisational structure (e.g. matrix or lightweight team, directly employed or contractor) and the norms (in this organisation, project leaders do XYZ, not ABC).

We then describe that role using our three facets. Figure 12.1 shows them as distinct and not interacting, and both of these characteristics do not fit well with reality. However, for the purposes of making a figure that is intelligible, we simply recognise the limitation. The style is the result of all of the above and incorporates whatever that leader does or is perceived to do.

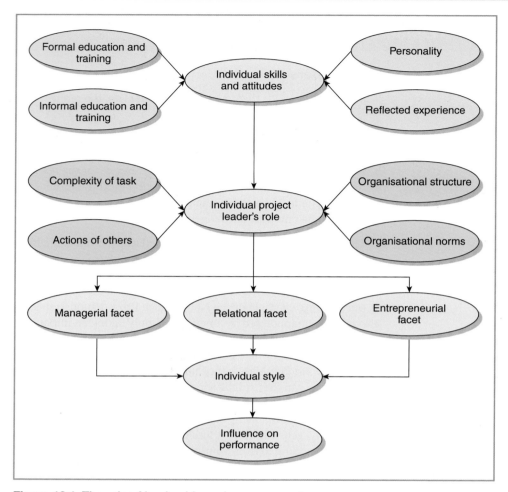

Figure 12.1 The role of leadership and management

We will now explore each of the leadership facets:

Managerial facet

Managing is a term that implies capability to direct and administer the work of others. One of the foundational studies of the role of managers (Fayol, 1950)[5] showed that managers' roles included commanding, organising, planning, controlling and improving. The role may also require technical specialism, but the term 'manager' should imply a knowledge of the issues involved in 'managing'. The definition of management has been stated to include a measure of power or authority given by the organisational structure. Managing is therefore considered to be task-related. As Peter Drucker commented:

> The manager is the dynamic, life-giving element in every business. Without [this facet of] leadership, the resources of production remain resources and never become production. In a competitive economy above all, the quality and performance of the managers determine the success of the business, indeed they determine its survival. For the quality and performance of its managers is the only effective advantage an enterprise in a competitive economy can have.[6]

In classic texts on management, the manager role is typically a response to the hard, structural elements of complexity, and working through this facet, structures, governance and process are put in place.

It is no coincidence that this facet is also the most developed area with the Bodies of Knowledge that we have been using throughout this book. For many years, this was the limit of consideration of the field and is not without its critics as the quotation below notes:

What is the best way to develop leadership? Every society provides its own answer to this question, and each, groping for answers, defines its deepest concerns about the purposes, distributions and uses of power. Business has contributed its answer to the leadership question by evolving a new breed called the manager. Simultaneously, business has established a new power ethic that favours collective over individual leadership, the cult of the group over that of personality. While ensuring the competence, control and the balance of power relations among groups with the potential for rivalry, managerial leadership unfortunately does not necessarily ensure imagination, creativity, or ethical behaviour in guiding the destinies of corporate enterprise.[7]

We note that this consideration of managerial leadership is necessary, but not sufficient, for project leaders. Sufficiency comes when the style incorporates appropriate levels of the following two facets – relational and entrepreneurial.

Relational facet

The relational facet of a leader's role predominantly involves the influencing of others through the personality or actions of that individual. The definition is therefore people-related.

This facet is one of the oldest fields of study within business and management. Some approaches that have been considered over time include:

1. The traits approach – leaders are born not made. They should be tall, posh, usually male and have what was known as 'a commanding bearing.' Mercifully, this lost currency many years ago, but it endured way too long.
2. The situational approach – the best way to lead depends on the situation in which you find yourself. We have adopted elements of this approach by including various contingent factors on the role of the leader in Figure 12.1.
3. Transformational leadership vs transactional leadership. Transactional leadership has most in common with what we termed the managerial facet. The transformational part considers influencing, creating a vision and motivating people for change and is therefore relational.

The notion of this facet being 'relational' involves recognition of the constructed nature of the world in which project leaders generally work – as discussed in Chapter 3, it is the product of human systems and human interactions. In addition, it is notable that project leaders have to work with a range of people, with whom they will often have no direct commercial or structural relationship. That is, they do not have any of the expected 'levers of control' over these people, either through having a contract with them or because of their place in an organisational hierarchy.

Entrepreneurial facet

An entrepreneur is typically someone who is good at creative activities. They see opportunities and then organise themselves and others to pursue those opportunities. Entrepreneurs have been well-studied – indeed some of the more famous entrepreneurs are the subject of books and are prominent in public debates.

We ascribe the entrepreneurial facet to part of the response to emergent complexity. That is, entrepreneurialism is needed when there are high levels of uncertainty or change. Studies of entrepreneurs show that they have one characteristic that is highly relevant to our consideration – they have a very high tolerance for ambiguity, and in many cases, actively seek to work in environments that are highly uncertain. Hence, we see a very good fit with having to live with high levels of emergent complexity.

The entrepreneurial facet is most likely to be of use to a project at the outset, before the project is fully defined and the scope settled. It is also most helpful for the leader to be able to draw on this facet of their leadership when there is considerable change, such as to the scope of the project or to the environment in which the project is being delivered. Being able to re-prioritise and plan your way through challenges is a key attribute for leaders in these circumstances.

In projects, change is normal: the project evolves through its lifecycle and both internal and external circumstances change. The idea that one style of leadership will endure for the life of the project is unlikely to be associated with success. The idea of *situational leadership* was introduced in the seventies[8] but has endured with the clear idea that there is no one best way to lead that will suit all times and places. This is what we term contingency in business and management. Our complexity-response model here is another example of taking a problem, 'what is the best way to manage a project?'; the answer, 'it depends' and then providing some ideas of 'what does it depend on?' (in this case the experienced complexity) and then 'what do you do about it?' (adapt your style, moving between the three facets).

12.2   Leading and motivation

The modern project manager has a responsibility both to the organisation and to the team members to ensure that they are provided with a high level of **motivation**. The rationale for this is straightforward:

> A person will perform their task at a 'normal' level of effort for them. Motivation can increase that level, resulting in the application of what is known as 'discretionary effort'. Conversely, demotivation can result in withdrawal of effort. The difference can be significant for the performance of the project. The level of motivation of an individual is affected by your leadership, the team, the organisation, and their own personal circumstances. For instance, a situation at home that is causing distractions is likely to result in an apparent decrease in motivation. As a leader, you have 'levers' to pull to develop motivation through influencing the individual, the team and the organisational situation.

Motivation and its relationship to leadership is the subject of a huge body of work. The major theories of work motivation are shown in Figure 12.2. The figure indicates the progression of thinking from the early part of the 20th century to date. These are worth considering as part of a portfolio of approaches to leadership that you may wish to draw upon, to determine your own approaches.

Scientific management

Figure 12.2 starts with the work of Frederick Taylor[9] in the development of the principles of scientific management. This is included as its importance is largely historic, but it had an unprecedented effect on management thinking and activity. Despite the principles being

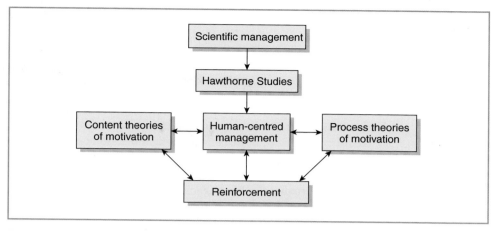

Figure 12.2 Main theories of work motivation

over a century old, they still have some applicability and, importantly, are the foundation of much that followed.

The principles of **scientific management** or '**Taylorism**' are most applicable to repetitive work. They are as follows.

- Work should be studied scientifically to determine in quantitative terms how it should be divided and how each segment should be done. The aim is to maximise efficiency of the activity and is achieved through measurement, recording and subsequent analysis.
- The worker should be matched scientifically to the job, e.g. where a task has a physical input to it, the physique of the individual should match the requirements of that task by, for example, using a well-built person to move heavy loads.
- The person carrying out a task should be trained to do it as per the results of the analysis – it must be carried out exactly as designed and closely supervised.
- The person carrying out the task should be rewarded for following the prescribed method exactly by a substantial monetary bonus.

The result of Taylorism is the separation of the work task from any thinking process by the individual. Any attempt at motivation is purely financially based. Support activities are carried out by trained individuals. The advantage of the system for working is that the task is made very simple, which means that an individual can become very proficient at it and can be replaced with relative ease. The downsides are considerable, however, with the person being alienated from the task they are doing and having no real input to the conversion process. This alienation can be passive in the form of losing interest in the process ('don't care' attitude) ranging to destructive (pilfering, sabotage, deliberate waste, bomb threats, militant union action).

The implications of this for projects are at the lowest levels of the WBS, where tasks are often highly repetitive. Here a choice exists about the nature of work that the manager is going to create for these tasks. The advantages of the scientific approach may yield benefits where, for instance, Taylor's techniques of scientific work measurement and job design can be used by a team to improve their productivity. The construction project where video analysis demonstrated that materials were being moved excessive distances between delivery to the work area and the material being used, allowed the bricklayers to work 20 per cent faster and with less strain injuries, is an example of this.[10] Interestingly, we have noted considerable reluctance to consider the application of such approaches in projects.

Whatever the uptake today, the development of these principles marked a milestone in the evolution of current management thinking.

The Hawthorne Studies

The Hawthorne Studies[11] were carried out to assess the impact of working conditions (temperature, light, noise) on the motivation and hence the productivity of individuals. They focused on a group of production workers and showed that initially, when the lighting level was increased, the level of productivity of the people also increased. The link was made – improving the lighting – improves the motivation – improves productivity. The lighting was increased on subsequent occasions with the same result. The lighting level was now returned to its original level and the productivity still increased. This caused the initial hypothesis to be rejected – there was a much more important factor at work. There is a fundamental rule of measurement – check that the measurement process does not affect the performance of what you are trying to measure. While the measurement process was relatively unobtrusive, what was causing the change was the attention being paid to this group of workers. This finding was far more significant than the finding about physical conditions. There is a clear implication for practical application here which many excellent project managers reinforce, that paying attention to groups improves the likelihood of good performance.

Figure 12.2 shows three paradigms of modern motivation theory/management behaviour:

- *content theories* – focuses on what motivates an individual at work. Key theories include the 'hierarchy of needs' and 'motivation-hygiene';
- *process theories* – focuses on how particular behaviour is initiated, or the process of motivation. Key theories include Vroom's 'expectancy' theory;
- *reinforcement* – focuses on how desirable patterns of behaviour can be reinforced.

We will consider briefly now how each of these may be of relevance to you and your leadership.

Content theories

Maslow published his theory on the **hierarchy of needs** in 1943[12] and these are shown in Figure 12.3. This analysis of needs is based on the notion that individuals will have basic requirements to be content at one level. Once these are met on an ongoing basis, their needs move to the next level, and so on. As Maslow stated:

> *'Man is a wanting animal and rarely reaches a state of complete satisfaction except for a short time. As one desire is satisfied, another pops up to take its place.'*

This theory has intrinsic appeal, as it enables the person designing a working environment to meet the needs of an individual at an appropriate level – providing the elusive motivation through an individual pursuing as yet unmet needs.

The first set of needs are physiological – food, shelter, etc. Maslow argues that until the basics are met, someone will not be looking for higher-order needs, such as recognition. Safety needs are the next level up the hierarchy where the provision of the basic needs is seen to be enduring rather than transitory. Above this is the need to belong, which represents 'the social animal'. This may be to a social group or to a recognisable team, something which will give them an identity. The need for self-esteem and respect comes next, with

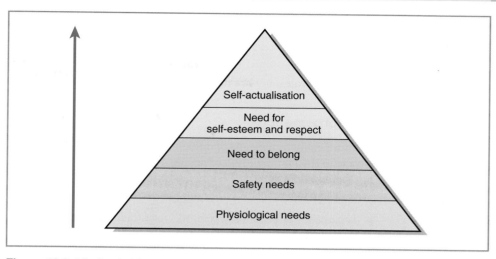

Figure 12.3 Maslow's hierarchy of needs

the thoughts of others about an individual counting in their own self-image. The need for self-actualisation – or to be the best person you can be – is the highest level of needs. Maslow did recognise that this order was not universal and that individuals would have their own hierarchies.

Herzberg's work to produce his 'motivation-hygiene' theory focused on the provision of rewards to the individual. He categorised needs from the task as either 'hygiene' factors or 'motivational'. Hygiene factors are those needs that, unless satisfied, will have a negative effect on motivation. Once a level of satisfaction is reached, increasing the level still further will not increase motivation. Pay is considered to be one such factor for many people. Motivators are those factors which result in higher motivation the better they are met. Recognition is one such factor.

Combining the ideas of Maslow and Herzberg provides a basis for project managers to consider the pay and reward of the project team. It is worth considering in some detail with the objective of finding the reward system that will provide motivating factors for individuals. This consideration has a pay-off in providing great benefits in people's attitudes to their work and willingness to engage with the challenges being faced.

A most useful and instructive example of the application of these theories to motivate people not to greater productivity but to significant levels of safety performance, are shown in Shell's work with the construction of one of the largest gas processing plants in the world.[13]

Process theories

Vroom[14] first developed one of the main theories in this category, that of 'expectancy', published in 1964. The theory considers that people have a choice regarding the amount of effort they expend (termed the 'motivational force') in a certain situation. This will depend on their perception of the likelihood of their receiving a desired outcome from this. The first-level outcomes are performance-related (the results from the task directly – the satisfaction of doing a good job, for example). The second level is the extrinsic benefits that are achieved, such as praise from a colleague or superior, promotion or pay rise. This motivational force is translated into effective work, through the skills and abilities of the individual.

Further revisions of this work have taken place, all building in more or different factors to try to provide a theory which is universally applicable. Human behavioural processes are far more complex than the models can allow, particularly where science dictates that a single exception disproves a rule. Such theories in practical application may help in explanatory roles, but are rarely effective in a predictive mode.

Reinforcement

Reinforcement as a means of influencing behaviour is often, somewhat cynically, related closely to the manipulation of people. It forms a significant part of popular 'how to manage' books and is summarised by the way in which good behaviour can be positively reinforced. The five rules for providing this are as follows:[15]

- *Be specific* – praise should refer to specific achievements and be backed up with current information.
- *Be immediate* – do the praising as soon as the good performance becomes obvious. This will enable the individual to make the link between the good action and the praising.
- *Make targets achievable* – help individuals to break down tasks so that they consist of a series of achievable and recognisable milestones (or even 'inch-stones' or their metric equivalent) and praise on the completion of each.
- *Remember the intangible* – praise may be more of a motivator to future performance than pay or status.
- *Make it unpredictable* – the passing comment of praise can be far more rewarding than the expected 'pat on the back'.

There is, however, an underlying assumption of rationality in the above theories – that an individual's environment can be logically designed and their needs met on an individual basis. While this is clearly desirable, not only the environment but also the system of reward (usually based on promotion and the pay system) have to be designed. Doing so in a large organisation will obviously be an immensely time-consuming activity if the principle that 'the system of reward should be designed to meet the motivation system of the individual' is adhered to. Practically stated, if the individual is motivated by purely financial considerations (which only holds for a relatively small proportion of the population), then their reward system should be financially based. If they are seeking recognition through status or title, then this should be provided (or offered as a potential reward).

Other factors that affect the motivation of the individual include the following:

- Location – motivational systems are strongly influenced by regional and national cultures and by the expectations of people created by their upbringing.
- Length of service of the individual – someone with long service (beyond 2 to 5 years) is going to have different needs from someone new in a job. If a project is being run with a new team, the focus for early management action should be to provide guidance and early feedback so that expectations of the individual are defined. Working with uncertain assessment criteria is very unsettling as you have nothing to rate yourself against. A useful principle in this respect is well stated as:

    'Tell me how you measure me and I will tell you how I will behave. If you measure me in an illogical way, do not complain about illogical behaviour.' (Goldratt)[16]

- Previous work environment – people react and mould to the constraints placed on them. Humans are surprisingly versatile animals, but changes in attitude and roles do not always come with changing jobs or joining a new project team. Previous ways of working become ingrained and moving somewhere new can be a shock that takes some time to get used to.

The literature is probably the most fragmented in the area of motivation. For instance, Vroom cites over 500 different studies on the impacts of various factors on motivation back in 1964. Given the popularity of this area of research, with all its sub-fields and specialisms, the landscape can be bewildering.

Structural implications for project managers

The role of organisational structure has already been discussed in Chapter 11. The following section considers some of the cultural implications of the applications of various organisational structures. The application of Taylorism required a highly developed organisational functional hierarchy. The evolution of the more modern **management paradigms** has changed this considerably. There are implications of the structure for the motivation of the individual. This issue has already been raised of the system of promotion for project managers and how this is often not as clear as for line personnel. However, the subject of Human Resource Management has not completely overlooked the world of projects and there are a number of really useful studies that are worth looking up (see Chapter 11).

Taiichi Ohno is widely accredited as the architect of the Toyota Production System. His role in the development of project engineering has been significant as was shown by comparing the way in which Western car producers organised their product design teams with those of the lean producers (all Japanese). The Western approach was characterised by organising people by functional group, e.g. engine designers would have graduated from being component designers and, if successful, may hope to progress to powertrain design. This provides a clear progression path for individuals, but a designer simply progresses as a designer with no increasing appreciation of the implications of their work on the manufacturing process. As was commented:

> Ohno and Toyota, by contrast, decided early on that product engineering inherently encompassed both process and industrial engineering. Thus they formed teams with strong leaders that contained all the relevant expertise. Career paths were structured so that rewards went to strong team players rather than to those displaying genius in a single area of product, process, or industrial engineering, but without regard to their function as a team.[17]

Organising the resources in the project is therefore a crucial set of choices within the remit of the leader. It is worth reprising the relevant chapters at this point, as we find it is so often overlooked as a powerful means to achieve the project objectives. Before we leave the topic of organisations and project leadership, the subject of promotion is rather cynically summarised by the statement that:

> 'In a hierarchy, anyone will be promoted to their level of incompetence.'

This is known as 'the Peter principle'[18] and was used by its originators to explain why, in their experience, so many managers appeared to be lacking in the basic qualities needed for the task of managing. Their theory relates to the above very closely – they noted that competence in a line task would generally be rewarded by further promotion up the line of authority. The further they were promoted, the further they moved from the specialism for which they had first been promoted for being competent. Project management does not escape this particular principle.

12.3 Leading and you

Recent years have shown a most helpful turn in the study of leadership. There are still many articles written based on very limited evidence (or oversimplified post-hoc justifications of people's careers) which tell you how to be the best possible leader ever. All you need to do is learn the secrets that those people used. Rarely is luck or good fortune mentioned, and there is always the assumption that leadership is a 'good thing'.

In developing our own views on leadership, like so much in projects, there is never 'one best way'. In this chapter, we have sought to outline some ideas that can become a part of your 'leadership toolkit'. Over time, you will develop your own 'heuristics' or simple rules, of when you should use each of them. In developing these, you should note that much of what is written on leadership is based on studies conducted in large, permanent organisations, and therefore does not reflect the rapidly evolving context of the project or temporary organisation. In addition, it is unlikely that an exact set of circumstances will be repeated, and so you will need to combine approaches to find what works for you and your situation at that particular time.

In this final section on leadership we will look at three formative streams of thought that are relevant, and then a set of ideas about how you use one of the most precious leadership commodities of all – time. Firstly, though, three topics in brief that all have had a profound impact on leadership thought.

1 The Incomplete Leader

The paper which set out the ideas of 'The Incomplete Leader'[19] was one of the first that having read it, didn't try to make you believe that all successful leaders had to have a large S on their shirts and be able to fly. Leaders, like the rest of us, are human and therefore have strengths and weaknesses. We all bring a mixture of skills and attributes to a role and this is OK.

In terms of the facets set out in section 12.1, the fundamental idea is that it is not necessary that you must be excellent across all three facets. For instance, if you believe you are more of a managerial leader, but your project has considerable areas of socio-political complexity requiring more relational effort, this is not the end of the world. The really powerful part of the argument made by Ancona et al., is that while the leader is incomplete, the team does not have to be. To return to our example, the socio-politically complex project with the managerial leader would benefit from bringing in people who are more relational to take on this work, coordinated and guided by the project leader. Similarly, if there is a requirement for greater levels of entrepreneurialism that are currently present in the project, then these may be added as a part of the team.

The good news is that you do not need to be a superhero to be a really good project leader. However, it does help . . .

2 The authentic leader

HM was struck during a leadership programme by the discomfort of one of the delegates, a man of considerable personal integrity. We had spent a number of days considering different leadership styles as well as analysing our own style, personality and preferences. He became very concerned that in order to be effective in his current major project, he would have to change his approach and therefore not 'be himself'. This is somebody who was used to being completely themselves at work, being uncomfortable with the thought that they might have to be something else.

In contrast, it is well known that many people have a 'work mask'. In this context we do not mean a Covid-induced face covering but a particular personality or mode that they switch into when they go to work, and is a fundamental part of various personality profiling tools (see e.g. DISC). On another programme, discussions with a group of leaders revealed that they always felt they had to 'wear their work masks' when engaged with work activities. Being authentic was just not something they were comfortable with. Following the programme, several of them did decide that they could begin to drop their masks, and really be themselves to their teams. This was most courageous for them and in each case resulted in much greater commitment from their teams.

The recognition of authentic leadership is not new in the context of studies of leadership development.[20] However, post-Covid, there does appear to be more of a mood in many organisations for 'bringing yourself to work', demonstrating and working through personal values and purpose, understanding your own motivations and continually developing this as your personal approach. Like the incomplete leader, this can be very liberating, not least as it recognises that there is no 'one best way' to be a leader today.

3 Leadership as vice, as well as virtue

One of the enduring features of the literature on leadership is its focus on 'leadership as a force for good'. While many examples, as well as the one at the opening of this chapter, will reinforce this idea, there are plenty of examples at all levels, from despotic leaders of countries, to totally self-obsessed leaders of companies (can you think of any?!) that challenge this 'exclusively good' feature. In extremis, leadership can be highly toxic and create lasting damage for individuals and organisations.

For the project leader, there is a need to understand such behaviour for both sense-making and, we hope, the purpose of avoiding such behaviours. There is plenty written under the headings of 'dark side of leadership',[21] 'destructive leadership'[22] or 'despotic leadership'.[23] Our interest, of course, is in the positive side, and how leadership can lead to beneficial outcomes.

Looking after yourself – the role of personal resilience

It was not necessary for a global pandemic to happen for the benefits of studying personal resilience to become self-evident. However, it has helped raised the profile of this topic for many organisations. One model of leadership depicts the leader holding an umbrella over their team. This is to protect them from all the things that would otherwise fall on them, and prevent them being able to continue working on the project. The things in question are not 'real' but for instance changes to the project scope, or interference with the work of individuals from an external stakeholder.

Resilience involves two aspects:

- Strength – the ability to be able to resist disturbances as the result of events happening around you.
- Flexibility – the ability to be able to accommodate disturbances without being totally disrupted by them.

These two elements are viewed by some as contradictory, but in reality both are needed. Strength as a project leader comes from having a good vision and a plan to achieve it; for instance, many of the criteria of good leadership that we have already discussed. Reaction to crisis is challenging: the 'fight or flight' reaction is rarely effective[24] and yet crises in projects are ubiquitous. Hence, having some tools as a leader to be resilient is a good thing.[25] Lastly, there are many excellent resources which are worth studying further, which can guide you on routines to improve your personal resilience.[26]

Working with time

The model in Figure 12.1 shows the inputs of personality (discussed in Chapter 11), experience (from previous activities within and outside the work environment) and (in)formal methods of training and education. Many of the skills required of the project management are learnable, in particular personal management (the management of yourself, as opposed to personnel management which is the management of people) and the ability to motivate a team.

Many practitioners argue that the best place to start with any improvement is yourself. Most managers would like to have extra time, and no matter what project you are involved in, time is one resource that is not replenishable. The successful project manager has learned to apply some form of structured method to the allocation of that resource. While there are many excellent proprietary **time management** systems, the discussion here will be on the general principles rather than the characteristics of any one particular example.

It is important that a manager's time is used wisely. If they are doing work that could be done by administrative staff, subordinates, or colleagues, they are not using their day as efficiently as they could. There is a shortage of project managers worldwide, so time doing activities that could be passed to others is not fully utilising the rare skills that they have.

Many project managers work long hours, with their own work always being subject to delays and fitting the description 'running to stand still'. This leads to poor decision-making as time is not properly allocated to the analysis and consideration of the issues involved. Their work assumes a pattern where they have no basis for making the decision as to whether to accept or reject further tasks and so undertake more than they can realistically handle. For many people, this is a way of remaining useful as they are seen to be busy, but in reality they are rarely effective.

Time allocation fits three broad categories:

- *proactive* – working on plans that are beyond the timeframe of 'that which needs to be done immediately' with the emphasis on 'problem prevention'. If one considers management to be a process and have a 'management product', the quality of that product will be determined by the effect that it has on both the short- and long-term performance of the project they are managing;
- *reactive* – there is a problem, work to solve it. This is also known as 'firefighting' or 'busy work' and is a style of management which can be very rewarding in that the constant attention of that manager is required, but stress is high and progress on innovative matters haphazard;
- *inactive* – resting between the bouts of proactive and reactive work. Does not include thinking time, but does include time spent outside work.

The basis of any time management system is that it provides a logical base to work from in deciding how to prioritise time between the three categories. The effects of good or bad time management are shown in Figure 12.4, and demonstrated very clearly in the case at the end of this chapter. It is seen that the poor personal management of one person is having major implications for the entire organisation.

One of the major effects of poor performance in management is **stress**. This is pressure which, through the natural reactions of the human body, generates in the individual symptoms ranging from anxiety to physiological symptoms. The body generates adrenalin (for 'fight or flight') which is not worked off by the body – particularly in sedentary

Figure 12.4 Effects of time management on the behaviour of individuals

occupations. While a certain amount of pressure is beneficial and leads to enhanced performance as an individual rises to a challenge, the negative side is 'stress'. One of the upsides of the global pandemic in many workplaces, has been the recognition of the need for wellbeing to be more than just a backup activity when something is clearly going wrong for someone. The stress placed on many people by the changes has had wide-ranging consequences for individuals and led to significant unhappiness, absence, reduced retention rates and worse. Including wellbeing for your team as part of your objectives and prioritising it, for instance over time or cost objectives, is just one way of demonstrating commitment to this as a leader.

However, we find that the advice given on aircraft when oxygen masks are deployed that 'you should fit your own mask before helping others with theirs' is most useful. This means that in order to help others, some amendment of your own routines or practices may be required first. A most helpful guide to the individual managing stress has come in the form of the 'four Ps':

- **P**lan your way out of the situation that is causing you the stress.
- **P**ace yourself – don't try to do everything at once.
- **P**amper yourself – reward yourself for goals accomplished or plans completed.
- **P**ut the joy back – one of the clear indicators of stress is when people stop having fun or at least enjoying what they do.

The approach to improving time management involves taking a little of that commodity to:

- analyse the current situation – the best way of doing this is to chart the amount of time that you spend during a period of several weeks on certain tasks – record it in a table such as Table 12.1. We have found this initially to be a fairly depressing exercise, especially when you refer to the next section (time spent on social media is a major element for some). The priority column should rank the importance of the item being considered from high (will contribute to your long-term objectives) to low (totally irrelevant diversion). However, persevere with it and there are plenty of benefits.
- set goals and targets for short-, medium- and long-term (broken down into professional, financial, personal and any other) objectives, which (according to those who study personal effectiveness) must be SMART:

    S – specific and written down – this is a fundamental starting point for both personal and project management, defining specifically where it is that you want to be (discussion of the need to set objectives often uses the metaphor of a journey – you would not start out unless you knew where it was you were going);

Table 12.1 Time usage analysis

Start time	Activity	Time taken	Priority	Comments
08:00	E-mails	2.5 hours	Low	Why do people always cc me in on stuff?
10:30	Meeting	2.5 hours	Low	Could be interesting in the future, but not now
1:00	Lunch	0.5 hours	High	–
1:30	Planning meeting	2.0 hours	Med	Little progress as, predictably, the client didn't really know what they wanted
3:30	Progress meeting	1.0 hours	Med	Not sure things are really going OK with that project
4:30	E-mails and phone calls	1.5 hours	Low	One of these was very important, rest just added noise

M – measurable – there should be a definable point at which it can be objectively determined that the goal has been achieved;

A – achievable – the objective must be physically possible;

R – realistic – for yourself to achieve this, without being too conservative (goal should be uplifting – see Chapter 7);

T – time-framed – having a limit on the date by which it will be achieved.

To this worthy list (SMART), we would add MOVE:

- **M**otivating – what are the benefits to you of doing this? Can you see yourself with this objective delivered? What will that feel like?
- **O**verseen – who are you going to make yourself accountable to for the achievement of a particular goal? Coaches and mentors are becoming an increasingly important part of project managers' achievements.
- **V**aluable – it both has to fit with your personal values as a leader and be regularly reviewed to make sure it is worth continuing with.
- **E**ducational – contributes to your learning or development in some way.

Where there is a discrepancy between the objectives you have set for yourself and the way in which time is allocated, the plan to achieve those objectives must be changed as follows:

1 Set the plan in place as to how to achieve those goals – there is a certain amount of time that we have to allocate to each of the above areas of activity. This amount of time should reflect the priority that each takes, e.g. the time outside contracted working hours – is that to be spent doing extra work, time with family, in front of the television or on social or sporting activities? Most people can put these in a ranking. The achievement of a certain goal should be associated with the allocation of a certain amount of time to it.

2 Use specific techniques to keep to the above (such as the review of time usage in Table 12.2).

3 Constantly review your performance – the use of a diary along with the repetition of the time evaluation form from time to time can show the magnitude of improvement. Some of the most successful people keep a 'journal'. This is a record of their performance, both good and bad, written at regular intervals (daily/weekly). This

Table 12.2 Techniques to keep to a plan

- Use a diary or other form of time-planner ('the shortest pencil is better than the longest memory') – record activities rather than trying to remember them – this only takes up valuable space in your mind.
- Say 'no' to non-goal-achieving tasks – do not add to your current task list.
- Handle each piece of information (e.g. an e-mail) once only – this rule avoids the little time-bombs (e-mails that required action by a date which is approaching rapidly) that sit in your inbox because you have not got round to tackling them.
- Use checklists and to-do lists to save you having to remember events and to enable you to sequence them rationally. Do not avoid difficult or unpleasant tasks. Get them done (if you do them first thing then the rest of the day you won't be fretting about them) and out of the way so that your time may then be more positively employed.
- Make calls with a fixed duration – e.g. by calling five minutes before a meeting you limit the time of the conversation to five minutes.
- When you talk to someone have your agenda written down and record the results of the discussion. Again – don't handle information twice.
- Allow people to make and implement decisions for themselves – they do not need to bring all basic issues to you – the rules for making the decisions should be established.
- Do not allow interruptions to disturb meetings or periods when you need to be engaged in proactive work. Thinking time is work time.
- Do not be constrained by the normal work practices of time and place (if allowable).

form of honest self-analysis is excellent for charting progress, particularly over a period of years and providing support to the idea that taking charge of your time can yield enormous benefits. As one very successful project manager put it: 'What better way of showing that you are ready for the responsibility of managing other people than by taking effective control of your own time? How on earth can you hope to be an effective manager of other people, if you are incapable of managing yourself?'

One thing at a time – the idea of focus that has been applied to such effect in the development of organisational strategy (the operation that focuses on meeting a narrow range of needs will be more successful than that which tries to meet a wider range) is also applicable to personal time management. Focusing on the goals to be achieved and eliminating distractions can clear the way of unwanted activities. This is illustrated in the following quotation:

'I once read that Charles Schwab, president of Bethlehem Steel in the early 20th century, met with public relations and management consultant Ivy Lee, because he wanted to improve his company's productivity. "We know what we should be doing," explained Schwab. "Now, if you can show us a better way of getting it done, I'll listen to you – and pay you anything within reason." Lee said that he would help him and that it would take only twenty minutes of his time. He handed Schwab a blank sheet of paper and said, "Write down the six most important things you have to do tomorrow." Schwab complied. "Now number them in order of their importance to you and the company." When Schwab had finished, Lee continued, "Now, put that paper in your pocket and first thing tomorrow morning take it out and look at item number one. Don't look at the others, just number one, and start working on it and stay with it until it's completed. Then take item number two the same way, then number three and so on until you have to quit for the day. Don't worry if you have only finished one or two. You'll be working on the most important ones. The others you could have finished with any other method, and without some kind of system, you'd probably take ten times as long to finish them – and might not even have them in the order of their importance." In a few weeks, Schwab sent Lee a

check for $25 000 along with a letter saying that it was the most profitable lesson he had ever learned. Not long after that, Bethlehem Steel became the largest independent steel producer of its day.'[27]

The last two Ps ('Pamper' and 'Put the joy back') are vital if you are to be successful as a project leader. The former takes on the ideas of balance in your life as a whole through sport or other recreation, while having fun is a major spur to better performance as well as a great stress reliever. Back in the early 1990s Tom Peters[28] quoted a Californian marketing company as having a number of strategies to encourage the 'fun' back into work, including regular water-pistol fights in the accounts department. Silicon Valley tech firms have since become noted for the 'fun' elements of their workplaces. These include ping-pong tables, free food, massages, gyms, and so forth, although the markets they work in are highly competitive and long hours are usual so it is not necessarily an easy choice of a place to work.

Having shown these methods for improving your time management, these kinds of skills are only the basis of a longer period of sustained self-improvement. Formal post-experience education for managers is a major industry and most forward-looking organisations promote individuals taking time to study through providing study leave or flexible working arrangements. Many large organisations have gone as far as creating their own study centres. Informal methods of learning are good supplements, through reading new books and journals, in addition to sharing knowledge and ideas with colleagues and other project management professionals. Some organisations have formalised these into communities of practice.

Final word . . .

The following is attributed to Confucius:

'Of bad leaders, the followers say "They were bad leaders."
Of good leaders, the followers say "They were good leaders."
Of the best leaders, the followers say "We did it ourselves."'

Summary

■ So – what are the skills and attributes of a good project manager or leader? The skills and attitudes of the project manager will be determined by personality, experience, and both formal and informal education and training, and there are a number of structures that can be applied to help with the understanding of this area. It is important to the organisation and to individuals as the project manager can have a significant impact on the achievement of outcomes for all stakeholders.

■ Leadership is characterised as the (hopefully) positive influence of the individual on people, whereas management is centred on people being treated as one of a number of resources. For the individual manager or leader, time is a non-replenishable resource and must be managed accordingly.

■ Leadership and motivation are intrinsically linked. Craft-based industries were replaced during the 19th century by organisations with tasks designed according to the principles of scientific management. These relied on financial reward as the prime motivator. However, financial reward is only one means that management can provide as a motivator. Meeting certain other needs through the work task can be more beneficial (Maslow) as well as treating people as individuals rather than automatons.

Key terms

followers *p. 297*	motivation *p. 300*	Taylorism *p. 301*
hierarchy of needs *p. 302*	scientific management	time management *p. 308*
management paradigms	(Taylorism) *p. 301*	
p. 305	stress *p. 308*	

Relevant areas of the Bodies of Knowledge

Section 3 of the APM Body of Knowledge ('People and behaviours') acknowledges the challenges of leadership. It highlights the range of stakeholders who have an interest in the project, and makes clear that '[t]his is not easy work and benefits from a facilitative approach rather than assuming that "command and control" approaches will be effective . . . Leading a group of people so that they become a high-performing team is skilled work and some would argue that it is the most important skill that a project professional needs to develop' (p. 103).

Both Bodies of Knowledge (Tables 12.3 and 12.4) appear to demonstrate that this an emerging area, with far fewer rules than in other areas such as planning, and therefore less ability for either to be prescriptive.

Table 12.3 Relevant area of the APM Body of Knowledge

Relevant section	Title	Summary
3.2.4	Leadership	This section is headed as 'Providing vision, direction, feedback and support so people can do their best work'. It emphasises the need for leaders to change their style to the needs of the team and the nature of the work.

Table 12.4 Relevant area of the PMI Body of Knowledge

Relevant section	Title	Summary
3.4.4	Leadership skills	This focuses on dealing with the wide range of people involved with projects. Relationship management and communication are emphasised, along with influencing and exercising power effectively.

PROJECT MANAGEMENT IN PRACTICE
Doesn't time fly?

It was 7.30 on a Tuesday morning, when John Edwards, general manager of the Jenkins Company's main factory, turned on to the M3 to drive to his office in Basingstoke. The journey took about twenty minutes and gave John an opportunity to reflect on the problems of the plant without interruptions.

The Jenkins Company ran three printing plants and had nationwide clients for its high-quality colour work. There were about 350 employees, almost half of whom were based at Basingstoke. The head office was also at Basingstoke.

John had started with Jenkins as a fresh graduate 10 years previously. He was promoted rapidly and after 5 years became assistant manager of the smaller plant in Birmingham. Almost two years ago

→

he had been transferred to Basingstoke as assistant manager and when the manager retired he was promoted to this position.

John was in good form this morning. He felt that today was going to be a productive day. He began prioritising work in his mind. Which project was the most important? He decided that unit-scheduling was probably the most important – certainly the most urgent. He had been meaning to give it his attention for the past three months but something else always seemed to crop up.

He began to plan this project in his mind, breaking down the objectives, procedures and installation steps – it gave him a feeling of satisfaction as he calculated the cost savings that would occur once this project was implemented. He assured himself that it was time this project was started and mused that it should have been completed a long time ago. This idea had been conceived two years ago and been given the go-ahead but had been temporarily shelved when John had moved to Basingstoke.

John's thoughts returned to other projects that he was determined to implement: he began to think of a procedure to simplify the transport of materials from the Birmingham plant; he thought of the notes on his desk; the inventory analysis he needed to identify and eliminate some of the slow-moving stock items; the packing controls which needed revision and the need for a new order form to be designed. There were a few other projects he remembered needed looking into and he was sure he would find some time in the day to attend to them. John really felt he was going to have a productive day.

As he entered the plant, John was met by the stock controller who had a problem with a new member of staff not turning up. John sympathised with him and suggested that he got Human Resources to call the absentee. The stock controller accepted that action but told John that he needed to find him a person for today. John made a mental note of the problem and headed for his office. His office manager, Mrs James, asked him whether she should send off some samples, or would they need to be inspected? Without waiting for an answer, Mrs James then asked if he could suggest a replacement for the sealing-machine operator, as the normal operator was ill, and told him that Pete, the manufacturing engineer, was waiting to hear from him.

John told Mrs James to send the samples. He noted the need for a sealer-operator and then called Pete, agreeing to meet in his office before lunch.

John started on his routine morning tour of the plant. He asked each supervisor the volumes and types of orders that were being processed that morning, how things were going and which orders would be run next. He helped one worker to find storage space for a container-load of product which was awaiting dispatch, discussed quality control with an employee who had been producing poor work, arranged to transfer people temporarily to four different departments and talked to the dispatch supervisor regarding pick-ups and special orders which were to be processed that day.

Returning to his office, John reviewed the production reports against his projected targets and found that the plant was running slightly behind schedule. He called in the production foreman and together they went through the machine schedules, making several changes. During this discussion, John was asked by someone else to agree several labelling changes to their products and received a telephone call for the approval of a revised printing schedule.

John next began to put delivery dates on important orders received from customers and the sales force (Mrs James handled the routine ones). While doing this, he had two phone calls, one from a salesperson asking for a better delivery date and one from the personnel manager asking him to book time for an initial induction meeting with a new employee. John then headed for his morning conference at the executive offices. He had to answer the chairman's questions on new orders, complaints and potential new business. The production director also had questions on production and personnel problems. He then had to see the purchasing manager to enquire about the delivery of some cartons and also to place an order for some new paper. On the way back to his office, John was talking to the chief engineer about two current engineering projects. When he reached his desk, he looked at his watch – it was ten minutes before lunch.

'Doesn't time fly,' he commented as Mrs James entered his office to put some papers on his desk. 'No,' she replied, 'Time stays, we go.' Wondering about the meaning of this, he headed for the canteen.

After lunch he started again. He began by checking the previous day's production reports and the afternoon followed the pattern of the morning. Another busy day, but how much had he accomplished?

All the routine tasks had been managed, but without any creative or special project work being done. He was the last to leave the plant that night.

As he drove home he pondered the role that he was paid to fulfil and wondered where the time to carry out any innovative thinking had gone today. He was sure that he had planned intelligently and delegated his authority. He acknowledged the need for a personal assistant, but saw that as a long-term project as the chairman was having a blitz on the overhead created by non-direct staff.

Points for discussion

1 What are the effects of John's time management for himself? What are the effects for the company?

2 Identify the tasks which John should have done himself and those which he should have delegated. How effective do you feel John's 'management by walking about' is?

3 How could he improve his time planning? Would employing a personal assistant for John really 'add value' or just be another overhead cost on the company?

Topics for discussion

1 Differentiate between the tasks of leading and managing a project.

2 What are the influences from within an organisation on the role that a project manager takes?

3 Why might the study of time management be fundamental to a project manager?

4 Using Table 12.1, examine your own time-management performance over the period of one or two days. How does this relate to the goals that you have set yourself?

5 From your analysis in (4), show what strategies you are going to use to keep yourself on track to the targets you have set for yourself.

6 Compare the work of the major thinkers on motivation. What influence has each had on modern management?

7 Why is it reasonable to think that as managers, our action can have an effect on a project outcome?

8 Why do people need to have a clear promotion path in their jobs? What other motivators would you provide for people?

Further information

Adair, J. (2009) *How to Grow Leaders: The Seven Key Principles of Effective Leadership Development,* Kogan Page, London.

Bennis, W. (2009) *On Becoming a Leader*, Basic Books, New York.

Drouin, N., Müller, R. and Sankaran, S. (2018) 'Balancing vertical and horizontal leadership in projects', *International Journal of Managing Projects in Business*, Vol. 11, No. 4, pp. 986–1006.

Eom, M.T., Wu, W.W., Preston, D.S. and Luftman, J.N. (2020) 'Effective IT Project Leadership', *MIS Quarterly Executive*, Vol. 19, No. 2, pp. 135–155.

Floris, M., Wiblen, S.L. and Anichenko, E. (2020) 'Senior Project Leadership Skills and Career Stallers: Analysis of Perception Differences and Implications for Careers', *Project Management Journal*, Vol. 51, No. 2, pp. 214–234.

Floris, M. and Cuganesan, S. (2019) 'Project leaders in transition: Manifestations of cognitive and emotional capacity', *International Journal of Project Management*, Vol. 37, No. 3, pp. 517–532.

Forster, M. (2006) *Do It Tomorrow and Other Secrets of Time Management*, Hodder & Stoughton, London.

Grint, K. (2000) *The Arts of Leadership*, Oxford University Press, Oxford.

Herzberg, F. (1974) *Work and the Nature of Man*, Granada Publishing, London.

Havermans, L.A., Keegan, A. and Den Hartog, D. (2015) 'Choosing your words carefully: Leaders' narratives of complex emergent problem resolution',

International Journal of Project Management, Vol. 33, No. 5, pp. 973–984.

Hoegl, M. and Muethel, M. (2016) 'Enabling Shared Leadership in Virtual Project Teams: A Practitioner's Guide', *Project Management Journal*, Vol. 47, No. 1, pp. 7–12.

Jay, A. (1987) *Management and Machiavelli*, revised edition, Business Books, London.

Mullins, L.J. (2016) *Management and Organisational Behaviour*, 11th edition, Financial Times Prentice Hall, Harlow.

Owen, J. (2018) *How to Lead*, 5th edition, Pearson, Harlow.

Sankaran, S. (2018) 'Megaproject management and leadership: a narrative analysis of life stories – past and present', *International Journal of Managing Projects in Business*, Vol. 11, No. 1, pp. 53–79.

Slevin, D.P. and Covin, J.G. (1990) 'Juggling Entrepreneurial Style and Organisational Structure: How To Get Your Act Together', *Sloan Management Review*, Vol. 31, No. 2, pp. 43–53.

Thoms, M. and Pinto, J.K. (1999) 'Project Leadership: A Question of Timing', *Project Management Journal*, Vol. 30, No. 1, pp. 19–26.

www.gov.uk/guidance/how-to-join-the-project-delivery-profession

References

1 See nobelprize.org

2 See, for example, Mintzberg, H. (1973) *The nature of managerial work*, Harper & Row, New York.

3 Kirkpatrick, S. A., and Locke, E. A. (1991) 'Leadership: do traits matter?' *Academy of Management Perspectives*, Vol. 5, No. 2, pp. 48–60.

4 Holweg, M. and Maylor, H. (2018) 'Lean leadership in major projects: from "predict and provide" to "predict and prevent"', *International Journal of Operations & Production Management*, Vol. 38, No. 6, pp. 1368–1386.

5 Fayol, H. (1950) *Administration Industrielle et Générale*, Dunod, Paris (first published 1916).

6 Drucker, P. (1955) *Management*, Butterworth-Heinemann, Oxford (first published in 1955 – many later editions are available and still as relevant to the discussion of the role of management).

7 Zaleznik, A. (1977) 'Managers and Leaders: Are They Different?' *Harvard Business Review*, May–June, pp. 67–78.

8 Hersey, P. and Blanchard, K. H. (1974) 'So you want to know your leadership style?' *Training & Development Journal*, Vol. 28, No. 2, pp. 22–37.

9 Taylor, F.W. (1911) *The Principles of Scientific Management*, Harper, New York.

10 See also Adler, P. (1993) 'Time-and-Motion Regained', *Harvard Business Review*, January/February, Vol. 71, No. 1, pp. 97–108.

11 Roethlisberger, F.J. and Dickson, W.J. (1939) *Management and the Worker*, Harvard University Press, Cambridge, MA.

12 See also Maslow, A.H. (1970) *Motivation and Personality*, 2nd edition, Harper & Row, New York.

13 See https://www.youtube.com/watch?v=ZzxNAsdC-MA

14 Vroom, V.H. (1964) *Work and Motivation*, Kreiger Publishing, New York.

15 Skinner, W. (1985) *Manufacturing: The Formidable Competitive Weapon*, Wiley, New York.

16 Goldratt, E.M. (1990) *The Haystack Syndrome*, North River Press, New York.

17 Womack, J., Jones, D. and Roos, J. (1990) *The Machine That Changed the World*, Rawson Associates, New York.

18 Peter, L. and Hull, R. (1970) *The Peter Principle*, Pan Books, London.

19 Ancona, D., Malone, T. W., Orlikowski, W. J., and Senge, P. M. (2007), 'In praise of the incomplete leader', *Harvard Business Review*, Vol. 85 No. 2, pp. 92–100.

20 See for example: George, B., Sims, P., McLean, A. N., and Mayer, D. (2007) 'Discovering your authentic leadership' *Harvard Business Review*, Vol. 85, No. 2, pp. 129–138; Goffee, R. and Jones, G. (2009) 'Authentic leadership', *Leadership Excellence*, Vol. 26, No. 7, p. 17.

21 See e.g. Schyns, B., Wisse, B., and Sanders, S. (2019) 'Shady strategic behavior: Recognizing strategic followership of Dark Triad followers', *Academy of Management Perspectives*, Vol. 33, No. 2, pp. 234–249.

22 Mackey, J. D., Ellen III, B. P., McAllister, C. P., and Alexander, K. C. (2020) 'The dark side of leadership: A systematic literature review and meta-analysis of destructive leadership research', *Journal of Business Research*, in press.

23 See e.g. Jabeen, R. and Rahim, N. (2021) 'Exploring the effects of despotic leadership on employee engagement, employee trust and task performance', *Management Science Letters*, Vol. 11, No. 1, pp. 223–232.

24 Margolis, J.D. and Stoltz, P.G. (2010) 'How to bounce back from adversity', *Harvard Business Review*, Vol. 88 No. 1–2, pp. 86–92.

25 https://www.forbes.com/sites/joefolkman/2017/04/06/new-research-7-ways-to-become-a-more-resilient-leader

26 Gruenewald P. (2020) *Manifesting Your Best Future Self: Building Adaptive Resilience*, self-published.

27 From Maxwell, J. (2004) *Today Matters: 12 Daily Practices to Guarantee Tomorrow's Success*, Time Warner, New York, pp. 74–75.

28 Peters, T. (1992) *Liberation Management*, Macmillan, London, p. 602.

13

Monitoring and controlling the project

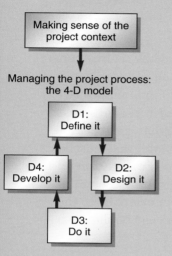

Making sense of the project context

Managing the project process: the 4-D model

D1: Define it

D4: Develop it

D2: Design it

D3: Do it

'I love deadlines. I particularly like that whooshing noise they make as they go flying by.'
(Douglas Adams)

Sir Richard: Standard Foreign Office response in a time of crisis. In Stage One we say that nothing is going to happen.

Sir Humphrey: Stage Two, we say something may be going to happen but we should do nothing about it.

Sir Richard: Stage Three, we say that maybe we should do something about it, but there's nothing we can do.

Sir Humphrey: Stage Four, we say maybe there is something we could have done, but it's too late now.

(From *Yes, Prime Minister*, by Anthony Jay)

Principles

1. A fundamental role of project managers is to monitor and control projects as they progress.
2. There are well-developed methods for monitoring and controlling a project.
3. Despite (1) and (2) the methods require critical evaluation of their effectiveness.

Learning objectives

By the time you have completed this chapter, you should be able to:

→ identify the elements of a monitoring and control system appropriate to a particular project

→ determine the key performance measures that will be monitored and controlled by the system

→ select appropriate tools and techniques to enable such control.

Contents

Introduction   *318*
13.1   The concepts of monitoring and control   *319*
13.2   Techniques of control   *324*
13.3   Limits of control   *334*
Summary   *336*
Key terms   *337*
Relevant areas of the Bodies of Knowledge   *337*
Project management in practice: *The Lifter project*   *338*
Topics for discussion   *340*
Further information   *341*
References   *342*

How hard can it be to control projects?

Ideally we should plan projects well, make sure we follow the plan, and all should come out reasonably satisfactorily. Of course, sometimes things go wrong, but skilled managers can generally bring the work back on track. Occasionally, though, the project becomes catastrophically out of control.

Source: WKanadpon/Shutterstock

One particularly spectacular example is the Canadian gun registry project.[1] This started in 1995 after the government passed new gun control laws, requiring that all firearms be licensed by 2003. The original plan estimated the cost at $119 million, all but $2 million of which would be covered by registration fees. A report in 2000 noted that costs were rising, and in 2001 the spend was estimated at $527 million. It still continued to rise, and by 2002 it had reached $629 million, primarily in computer and programming costs. The Auditor General estimated it would reach $1 billion by 2005, with registration fees only reaching $140 million. What started as a $2 million expenditure resulted in one of the biggest cost escalations known. Surely that must be a one-off; can any other project match it for such a negative impact? Sadly, there are always more.

Was this simply another case of over-optimism in the original estimating or were there fundamental issues with managerial control here? It appears that the optimism extended to the control system as well. This is disappointingly common; many types of project can be shown to be repeatedly over budget, over time, and below the performance anticipated.

Introduction

'So, how's it going?' An innocent enough question, but one that causes all sorts of problems for project managers.

Where projects are of low complexity it may be possible to apply some basic monitoring and control without any of the devices described in this chapter. For medium- and high-complexity projects the role of the project manager in establishing and maintaining some system for control is paramount during this 'Do it' phase of the project. This may sound like a relatively straightforward process, but it is not. Table 13.1 shows the recent research[2] highlighting typical overruns in major infrastructure projects. It does not make easy reading, but shows clearly the challenge of controlling projects so that they go as originally intended.

Table 13.1 Project overrun data

	Roads	Bridges, tunnels	Energy	Rail	Dams	IT	Olympics
Cost overrun	20%	34%	36%	45%	90%	107%	172%
Frequency of cost overrun	9 of 10	9 of 10	6 of 10	9 of 10	7 of 10	5 of 10	10 of 10
Schedule overrun	38%	23%	38%	45%	44%	37%	0%
Schedule length, years	5.5	8.0	5.3	7.8	8.2	3.3	7.0

The nature of monitoring and controlling is discussed here along with the characteristics that require controlling. We shall again see the influence of strategy when we select what to control, and the development of a number of devices that will assist in the control process. Some of these are very simple, others very involved. Whatever the system, the objective is to maximise the visibility of progress and the performance measures that we use should be chosen with this in mind. However, while being totally in control is an idea that has been widely promoted, particularly in the project management literature, the reality is that this is not simple or necessarily always desirable in practice.

13.1 The concepts of monitoring and control

Given that many projects do run late, overbudget or otherwise fail to deliver to customer/ stakeholder requirements, the question is often asked – 'how did this happen?' The answer is often that it happened very gradually, with days being lost and money spent, not in one large block (crisis events tend to get attention quickly) but in small amounts. These amounts gradually add up and over the life of most projects will provide significant problems. The only way that we can deal with this is by having systems that will detect such occurrences, and allow the project manager the opportunity to instigate correction actions to bring the project back on track. This assumes, of course, that we know what the particular track is that we are trying to stay on. Where there has been poor use of planning there may be considerable confusion as to whether progress is indeed acceptable or whether intervention from the project manager is required. Further, as already acknowledged throughout this book, projects are rarely static entities – the requirements, technology and people change during the project, so simply controlling by conformance to a plan that may no longer be relevant is unlikely to be beneficial.

While this work on control predominantly takes place during the execution phase of the project, it should be given careful consideration during the planning phase. It must be careful to add value to the project – so many projects become overburdened by the weight of bureaucratic requirements imposed to try to keep the project in order. Such a burden is counterproductive, as people will resist the additional work required and either ignore or find ways around 'the system'. The alternative is to provide control at different levels within the project that relies on simple and easily understood measures that reflect the objectives of the project.

The basic requirements for a control system include:

- defining system characteristics of importance;
- defining *limits* to their variation;
- *measurement* of those characteristics;
- making progress *visible*;
- *feedback* to the team of performance;
- instituting *corrective action* where required.

This constitutes the most basic model of a control system and is shown in Figure 13.1. In this diagram, the output of a process is monitored by some means to determine the characteristics of the output. These data are interpreted and then fed back in order for the project manager to make the necessary changes to the process. On receipt of this information, adjustments are made to the process. By using this kind of '**feedback control system**', the performance of the process can be guided by the application of corrective actions to keep it within certain limits (having defined 'acceptable deviation' from the desired performance).

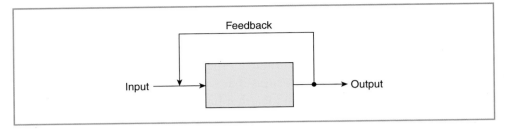

Figure 13.1 Basic model of cybernetic control

Defining system characteristics of importance

So – what characteristics are important? In an ideal world we would be able to say that everything was important and we could devote massive resources to the monitoring and control effort. If you are NASA, this might be the case. In the Covid-19 pandemic of 2020, money and resources were quite rightly given to the response to get the fastest results possible. Temporary hospitals were set up in record time, manufacturers of other products turned their facilities to producing protective equipment as fast as they could. For 'normal' projects, though, we have to prioritise the most important characteristics. The most important aspects that need controlling are those that form part of our strategy – typically time, cost and quality. We will know from our strategy which of these is the most critical, and should therefore have the greatest attention paid to it. Again, here it is vital that project activities and processes are consistent with strategy. If you are planning for a new product launch at a trade fair on a given date, then time and quality would be paramount. A certain amount of cost could be sacrificed should the need arise rather than compromise the other two. The greatest efforts would therefore be placed on ensuring that the time and quality objectives were met through controlling activities.

We must not assume that TCQ objectives are necessarily the only ones that an organisation will have. Other issues of strategic importance were identified in Chapter 2 and these (health and safety, legal, ethical, environmental, human resource) and others may also be the subject of control.

Defining *limits* to their variation

The second requirement is to define limits to the variation of the performance in those key areas. We have seen in previous chapters that performance does vary across people and activities, and various methods have been discussed to deal with this variation (see Chapter 7). So, when does a deviation from a requirement become a problem? Health and safety is usually a *zero tolerance* issue, quite rightly. For some organisations, a 1 per cent deviation from cost targets would be tolerated, while a day's delay would be unacceptable. Others would state their objectives differently. So, what are the limits of variation? The first issue here is that there will always be some variation – but that should be both positive and negative. The theory runs that provided we can harness the positive benefits, they will cancel out the negative issues. That's the theory. For all the reasons discussed in Chapter 7, the reality is that it is often difficult to harness the positive variations, but the negative ones inevitably accumulate. Having accepted this, you immediately put some stability into the process. In reality any negative deviation (activities running over time/cost or failing to meet quality), should trigger further monitoring to ensure that we can keep track of what is happening. There should then be a further zone that triggers action. The critical chain approach uses precisely this approach and is described in section 13.2.

Measurement of characteristics

What we measure has been defined as part of our reconsideration of strategy. A crucial part of control is when to measure. Here, control activities need to strike a balance. Somewhere between finding out too late to take any action and permanently harassing people to find out how they are progressing lies a position that will satisfy both the needs of control and the needs of the project team to keep the work:reporting ratio right.

Imagine that you are driving a car. This is a good example of a control system. You are sensing characteristics of the environment around you (e.g. seeing a corner ahead) and, based on that sensing, making changes to speed and direction to keep the car on the road and away from other cars. While this clearly doesn't apply in the capital cities of most countries, the principle still holds in most other situations. Here you are sensing continuously what is happening around you, unusual for the project situation. What is apparent in the driving case is that you need to assess the feedback and take action without delay. Imagine if you only opened your eyes for a second every 10 seconds, or then waited 5 seconds before reacting to the situation in which you found yourself. How long would it be before your 'control' failed? Not long. These two issues are as important in project management – the timing of your observation and speed of reaction to the situation. Time delay in receiving information or implementing action is a killer for any control system.

There are other aspects to this issue of measurement which need considering. The key structure here is to consider that the measurement of a key characteristic can take place at the **input**, **in-process**, or **output**. In assessing the quality of a construction project, these would include:

- *Inputs*: designs, suitably qualified labour, defect-free correctly ordered materials
- *In-process*: use of appropriate work methods, checks of work carried out
- *Output*: number of defects in the final result, customer/user sign-off.

Making progress visible and feedback of performance

This is an area where there have been many developments in recent years. The principle of visible control was evident in the world-class Japanese manufacturing systems (e.g. *Andon* lights above machines in a factory that would indicate where there was a problem, and continuous monitoring and display of the quantity of output relative to the day's target) and found to be a key factor in their success. The same principles apply very well to project management situations and will be covered in section 13.2.

Instituting corrective action

Finding that there is a deviation from what you expected to be happening is only the first part of the job of the control system. The issue then arises of what to do about it. In some cases, it is clear what action needs to be taken. In others, it may be less clear. An important principle of control shows itself: you can only manage the future – what has happened is history. While knowing where you are is important, it is what you do next that will make the difference.

Example of a control system – corrective actions and stability in a physical system

Try balancing a ball in the centre of a tray – start it moving and try to bring it to rest again 10 centimetres away from the start point. Very quickly the movements of the tray get larger and the movement of the ball will generally become anything other than diminishing as it passes over the point without stopping. The system rapidly becomes unstable as the movement of the ball has passed out of control and soon leaves the tray completely. This is the result of instability in the system – the brain cannot make the necessary corrective action to bring it back to rest and so the control actions get larger as the ball exhibits behaviour which is considerably different from that which is required. The movement of the ball becomes as shown in Figure 13.2.

Programming a machine to do the same task with the application of appropriate control actions can render the system stable in a very short period of time. The pattern of motion is as shown in Figure 13.3. This system is stable – the movement or response of the system does not go off to infinity or cause the destruction of the system (as evidenced by the ball finally running off the edge of the tray in the first test), but settles back to an equilibrium (stationary) after the initial disturbance (the move).

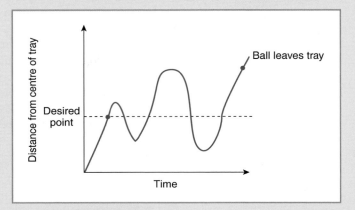

Figure 13.2 Instability

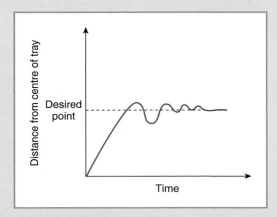

Figure 13.3 Stable system

The control of projects requires the view that although there is a single event being carried out, it is the product of many interlinked smaller events (within the work breakdown structure) which, like the moving of the ball on the tray, can have their progress monitored and appropriate corrective actions applied to keep them on track.

The system for overall control can be viewed as a series of smaller systems of control, which the project manager interlinks. This overall system of control will expand, the larger the project becomes and, as it does so, more of the control actions will have to be devolved. The system of control systems within systems is shown in Figure 13.4. In high-complexity projects, the role of the project office as gatherers and processors of data is fundamental.

The control that will be discussed throughout this chapter is a mixture of feedback control and **feedforward**. A useful way to think of feedforward control is to consider the driving example, where you are not only looking ahead but using your knowledge of the road to make additional changes to speed and direction. For instance, if you knew that there was a particularly dangerous bend ahead, you may take extra care – reducing your speed ahead of the bend. In projects we look ahead to see what problems or situations we will be faced with and make changes to protect the project outcomes from the potential of these events. Part of this feedforward control is risk management – performed at the start and ongoing through the project as was discussed in Chapter 10.

Configuration control

Change happens and it costs. Technology changes, requirements change, markets change and projects are social systems – the people who deliver them change too. As demonstrated in Chapter 5, the change control system will need to be established at a very early stage in the project – indeed, right from the outset. This is not about constraining change, rather being able to recognise it, accommodate it and plan for the eventualities that it creates, both positive and negative.

The state of configuration refers to the **product** of the project, its form (what it looks like), its dimensions and its performance. In a product development, for example an electronic circuit board, the design will change over time as the engineers test and develop the product. Since the list of components (the Bill of Materials) drives purchasing to buy the devices, it is essential both that the right parts are bought, but also that parts that are no longer required are NOT bought. Getting this wrong can lead to delays and/or unnecessary expenditure, so it is important that it is done well.

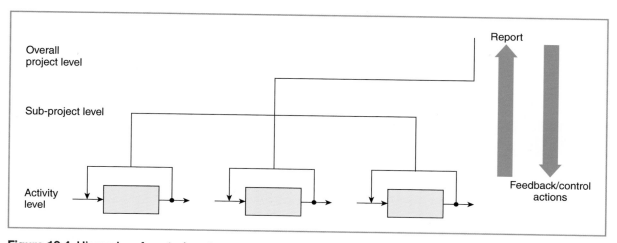

Figure 13.4 Hierarchy of control systems

Tracking lots of changes and updates is important, but sometimes one major issue can derail a project completely. On 2 December 2017, *The Times* reported that a Russian rocket carrying a 2,750 kg Meteor weather satellite, together with 18 other microsatellites, veered off course and plunged to earth. It seems that the staff had failed to change the Soyuz's programming to recognise that it was launching from the new £4 billion Vostochny Cosmodrome in Russia's Far East, rather than the previous launch site at Baikonur in Kazakhstan. Human error is always likely to creep in, so checking and re-checking the really critical aspects of a project is good practice. Little mistakes are a fact of life. This, though, was a huge error, showing even rocket scientists are not infallible.

One of the cases considered in Chapter 3 was the Airbus A380. In this example, it is relatively easy to imagine how many changes there will be in designs as the product is developed. It is also clear that they are unlikely to be simple to resolve. For instance, consider that the firm wanted the plane to be able to travel faster than its planned 652 mph (1050 km/h) maximum cruising speed. This would require an increase in the engine power output, would increase the fuel requirement and reduce the total payload of the aircraft as more fuel would have to be carried to provide the extra speed. The forces acting on the wings and aircraft structures would also increase, requiring more material to be used, again, increasing the weight. Clearly here, the state of each part of the aircraft design would need to be known, and any changes cross-checked to see their implications for other aspects of the design.

This is where the **configuration control** comes in – as making sure that everyone is working to the latest version of the designs. If the proposed speed change were signed off for the aircraft, it is essential that everyone working on the project is aware of the change and its implications. To have a wing designer, for instance, working on an earlier version of the specification could be disastrous. This is the essence of configuration management – ensuring that only the current specifications and designs are being used throughout the project. Again, such a task can be undertaken centrally by a project management office. However executed, it is a fundamental principle of good project management that configuration control is maintained, even on relatively small projects. Writing an assignment in a group can require such a role, for instance, to make sure that only the latest version of a report is edited, eliminating the potential for duplicating work.

A number of considerations are important here. Version control of key documents is critical, whether for a huge multinational, multi-year, design effort, or a group assignment due next week. At best, mistakes are frustrating, at worst they can be disastrous. Information management needs to be considered – where is the necessary information stored, and how easy is it to find? It is quite feasible that different groups can be working on the same problem, unaware that their efforts are being duplicated by others. Who has technical authority? If too many people can make changes, chaos may ensure. Finally, consider having a design freeze after which no further changes can be made. Ongoing changes can cause delay and corresponding costs that far outweigh the intended benefits, so this adds a level of stability to the final phases of the work.

13.2 Techniques of control

The techniques will focus initially on the key issues of quality, cost and time.

Quality

The project manager has two roles in the management and control of quality. These concern the *conformance* of the product and process to agreements (both actual and implied) and the *performance* of the delivery – specifically to manage the stakeholder expectations and perceptions of the project process and outcome (as described in Chapter 9).

Conformance

The establishment and management of an effective system to control the quality of products and services is a role of increasing importance in project management. The quality system contains a number of key elements – policies, system description and procedures. The policies for quality control are determined and set out either as part of organisational policy or as required by contractual terms laid down by a client organisation. The systems are then put in place to meet the requirements of these policies and the procedures are what people at all levels of the organisation carry out on a day-to-day basis. The objective of such quality control is:

> *to provide a formalised system within the project which ensures that the needs of the customer or the stated objectives of the work are continually being met.*

The system needs to be formalised and so requires much of the informality which exists within organisations to be removed. The 'customer' here is anyone who takes the output of the project activities – from an end-user of an artefact or system to a department that receives information from the project team (e.g. accounts or marketing).

There are other reasons for having a quality system in place:

- to protect the project organisation, as far as is possible, from legal liability, most notably professional negligence and product liability claims. The organisation, through its quality system, can demonstrate that it has taken 'every reasonable precaution' to ensure that the project was carried out in a way that ensures that the stated needs were met. This requirement has emerged for many project managers as the business environment in many countries becomes increasingly litigious;
- it is a prerequisite for obtaining business in many markets, including aerospace, defence, public procurement and the motor industry.

The emergence of the importance of quality systems has come as a natural extension of the role of specialisation. In traditional craft industries, the craftsperson would have responsibility for the quality of the output of their process – hence the use of hallmarks in silverware and other forms of labelling of the product, which would allow it to be traced back to the originator. The medieval trade guilds provided a level of quality assurance by regulating their members. As organisations have become more complex and the division of labour has been more extensive (along Tayloristic lines) the role of the quality specialist has emerged.

More recently it has become common to consider not only product (or output) quality but also the 'process' by which that output is delivered. Quality systems provide elements for assuring both of these. One of the recognisable standards for a quality system is ISO 9000.[3] This sets out the criteria for an organisation's quality management system, based on a number of key principles. Organisations, whatever their size, can be certified to this and it is valuable in showing customers that there are appropriate quality processes in place.

Performance

The control of stakeholders' expectations and perceptions has been identified as vital if businesses are to achieve customer satisfaction and retain customer profitably. For a non-revenue-generating project such as organisational change, managing expectations and perceptions is an ongoing challenge. Some issues here are:

- don't create expectations that cannot be delivered – as a minimum a project should have the characteristic of the paint advert that stated: *It does exactly what it says on the tin*;
- measure expectations and perceptions – the issue here is vital for control, that throughout the process we recognise the importance of the stakeholders. Where deviations are uncovered, it is often possible to make very small changes that will bring the perceptions back into line. Like other aspects of control, time here is critical – not leaving it too long to measure or to act where unacceptable deviations are uncovered.

Cost and time

Controlling cost and time requires a considerable input from the project manager in the establishment and execution of processes. The attributes of cost and time are interlinked as previously discussed. The need is for practical tools that will identify when corrective actions are required and what they should be. The role of the project manager in cost control may be stated as:

- setting up the cost control system in conjunction with the needs and recommendations of the financial function;
- allocating responsibilities for administration and analysis of financial data;
- ensuring costs are allocated properly (usually against project codes);
- ensuring costs are incurred in the genuine pursuit of project activities;
- ensuring contractors' payments are authorised;
- checking other projects are not using your budget.

The measurement that is often taken to consider progress using cost as a measure is 'sunk costs'. This is the measure of what has been spent to a particular point in time on activities. It is notoriously unreliable as a measure of how much has been achieved, as it is perfectly possible for a project to be 80 per cent complete but to have incurred 95 per cent of the budget allocated to it. Controlling cost overruns clearly needs more than just a raw figure such as expenditure incurred. The '**earned value**' concept is one attempt to make the measure more meaningful.

Earned value

For projects where warning of problems and an ability to predict final costs and times at completion are required, the use of the tools of earned value management can be helpful. This measure brings together time and cost performance elements into a monetary quantity – a unit that is easily understood.

For instance, a project has ten activities to be performed over a period of 10 weeks. The first stage in the earned value assessment process is to set a budget for each of the activities. The activities are identified and the budget for each estimated, based on the estimated time, materials and overhead element (see Chapter 8) for each. These times and costs are shown in Table 13.2. Each of the activities will run sequentially, one after the other.

The next stage in the measurement of earned value takes place during the project. After a number of weeks, the project manager has a number of ways to address the main question – 'how's it going?' In this case we will consider progress at week five. We need to know how much has been spent on each of the activities (see below for discussion of

Table 13.2 Tasks and budgets

Activity	Time	Budget
1	1 week	€5000
2	1 week	€8000
3	1 week	€7000
4	1 week	€12 000
5	1 week	€14 000
6	1 week	€10 000
7	1 week	€13 000
8	1 week	€11 000
9	1 week	€16 000
10	1 week	€4000
TOTAL	10 weeks	€100 000

the difficulty of calculating amounts spent). We also need to know which of the activities have been completed at this point. After 5 weeks, it is found that activities 1–4 have been completed, and that the spend to this time is €36 000. Using a measure that simply looked at the spend, the target was to have completed five activities during this time and therefore the spend should be:

$$€5000 + €8000 + €7000 + €12\,000 + €14\,000 = €46\,000$$

We have spent only €36 000, so this is good, isn't it? Planned spend of €46 000, actual spend of €36 000 means that we are running €10 000 under budget. Don't start to plan the post-project party just yet. The earned value measures tell us a different story.

The project manager does the following calculations. The first is to determine the earned value. 'Value' is 'earned' by the completion of activities and the budget for each activity is the value that is earned. In this case it would be the sum of the budgets for the completed activities 1–4:

$$\text{Earned value after completion of activities } 1\text{–}4 = €5000 + €8000 + €7000 + €12000$$
$$= €32\,000$$

So now we have an array of measures:

Actual spend: €36 000

Planned spend: €46 000

Earned value: €32 000

How do we interpret these? The first thing is to consider the cost performance. This is done by comparing the earned value with the actual spend. In this case we can see that the earned value is €4000 less than the actual spend – this is not good. We can state that there is a **variance** of €4000 between these two. Another way to state this is to provide a ratio of the two measures – known as the **cost performance indicator** (CPI).

$$\text{Cost performance indicator} = \text{earned value/actual spend}$$
$$= 32\,000/36\,000$$
$$= 0.889$$

Next we can consider time performance. To do this we compare the earned value with the planned spend at that point in time. There is a considerable variance here. Earned value of €32 000 compared with the planned spend of €46 000 – a variance of €14 000. Another way to state this is to provide a ratio of these two measures – known as the **schedule performance indicator** (SPI).

$$\text{Schedule performance indicatior} = \text{earned value/planned spend}$$
$$= 32\,000/46\,000$$
$$= 0.696$$

Both the schedule performance indicator and the cost performance indicator show that there are problems here – as they are both considerably less than 100 per cent. More than this, they provide the project manager with a predictive capability. This will show the likely effect on the overall completion of the project *if nothing is changed*. In this case we can provide a forecast of both the likely cost and time to complete the project.

The cost is calculated from the cost performance indicator and the original project budget as follows:

$$\text{Estimated cost at completion } \textbf{(ECAC)} = \text{Original budget/cost performance indicator}$$
$$= €100\,000/0.889$$
$$= €112\,500$$

Similarly, we can calculate the time of completion as follows:

$$\text{Estimated time of completion} = \text{Original time estimate}/\text{schedule performance indicator}$$
$$= 10 \text{ weeks}/0.696$$
$$= 14.4 \text{ weeks}$$

Both of these are useful calculations and with the assistance of simple spreadsheets can provide good information on the likely effects of the current state of performance on the project overall. The project manager can then decide on appropriate action to take.

These measures can be summarised in the form of reports which provide the input to problem-solving processes (see Chapter 15). The information needs to be collated by a timing coordinator who can do so in one of the following ways:

- obtaining a verbal report on progress from the person or team carrying out that section of work;
- sending out and collecting a form of progress questionnaire, which outlines the activities and the original targets for them which the team members complete and return to the coordinator with the current status recorded;
- detailed internal measure of progress – an assessor viewing progress as a semi-independent arbiter;
- an external assessor carrying out some form of audit on the project, with widespread powers of access to project data.

Clearly the last two are useful where independent checking of information is required, but it tends to imply a lack of trust of the people doing the work. The point is that whatever data are collected must be reliable (it is not unusual for problems to go hidden or undisclosed due to an individual's fear of retribution if poor performance is discovered). Verbal reports are fine but they can obscure important information through either of two extremes – a person who complains about 'problems' even though progress is good, and the person who will say things are OK simply because 'it is not as bad as it could be/as it was last time we did this'. The project manager must be aware of these and look for evidence to corroborate the information received from other sources. Thus the cost information should be matched with verbal reports of time progress from several members of the same team, in addition to gleaning opinion from other teams.

The climate for reporting should be set to provide a balance:

- people require feedback on how they are performing;
- people need to be clear what information to report, in what format (and what to leave out);
- the project manager needs to have a positive statement that progress is being made according to plan;

but the major reports need to be the exceptions – where there is a clear deviation from acceptable performance in meeting any of the constraints imposed on an activity.

This focus on the exception is vital and must be reflected in the importance that the various reports are given. The bureaucracy of 'paying someone to read reports that you have paid someone else to write' is partially eliminated by this focus on exception.

The factor not so far discussed in relation to the reporting and feedback loop is *timeliness*. If the information or feedback is held up for any period of time, the control action will have to be more severe than if the deviation had been spotted and acted on earlier. The analogy of trying to control a car showed this problem.

There are many measures that can be used by the project manager and there are many ways to make these visible. The following shows some methods for doing this.

Control using critical chain

As discussed in Chapter 7, there should be a buffer that can be monitored during the project. At regular intervals – daily in many instances – activity managers are asked 'how long to finish?' Their answers can be simply interpreted in terms of the effect that they will have on the buffer – an early finish will add days to it, a late finish will take days from it. This information provides the project manager with a means of deciding what to do next. One method that has proved highly effective is to divide the project buffer up into three regions. If the buffer was, say, 30 days, each of these regions would have 10 days in them. Once there is any **erosion of the buffer** at all, this puts the project manager into the first zone – that of monitor closely. Use of 10 days of this buffer puts the project into the next zone – plan. Here plans are drawn up to restore the buffer to its original size (or as a proportion of the time remaining in the project). It is only when 20 days of the buffer have been eroded that the plan is required to be implemented. The three zones are shown in Figure 13.5.

Visual control

If you can see what is happening you can control it, runs the theory. There is certainly plenty of evidence to support this, as the measurement and assessment part of the control system is easily achieved. Compare, for instance, the control of the construction of a building with the writing of software. The construction project has one great advantage in terms of control – you can see what is happening (or at least a trained person could determine whether progress was being made). Obtaining some notion of progress when writing a complex piece of software, on the other hand, is more difficult, as the progress will be determined by the finished result only.

To guide progress, the number of lines of code written may be checked or the product modularised so that the unit of control (the element that you are controlling) is made smaller. Either way, the measure is not so easy to construct. How then would you control a scientific research project – say, one of the projects working on the cure for a disease? The result may not be achievable, so this is not a good measure, and is too far away to provide a useful point for control. In such a case, the method of control is on the process rather than the outcome. For instance, the number of experiments performed or the number of ideas generated that would lead to testable formulations for drugs could be monitored. Whatever the circumstance, some measures are needed.

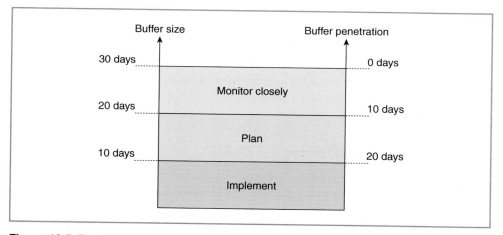

Figure 13.5 Buffer penetration

To make the control visible there are a number of systems used. The Gantt chart frequently has a role to play (see Project Management in Practice at the end of this chapter). As mentioned in Chapter 7, one firm needed to track the progress of critical jobs through an office. They did this by placing a large orange beach ball on the desk of the person working on the critical task at that time. This had a number of effects. First, it made progress highly visible – simply look for the beach ball to determine to which stage the project had progressed. Second, it reinforced the importance of the critical path – that any delay here would delay the entire project. The message to others of 'keep away – this person is working on a critical activity' was most effective. It is a straightforward and effective way of driving the desired behaviours. Other systems include traffic lights and various computer-based '**digital dashboards**'. The latter are particularly effective where teams are spread out over a number of sites or locations. A part of the computer desktop (the working area of the screen) is given over to indicators that show how particular activities and sub-projects are progressing. The data from individual projects can be rolled up (aggregated over many projects) to show performance at programme, portfolio or even business level. Key performance indicators (KPIs) include earned value, aggregate buffer penetration or simply number of projects running on-budget. Useful data can include staff workload, percentage complete of key tasks, upcoming deadlines, key risks, and even to-do lists. There are a wide variety of tools available, and this is a fast-moving field. It should be remembered that these are only displays, however, and that they rely on the timeliness and veracity of the data that are fed into them.

Real-time control

The availability of cost-effective network communications has given rise to the possibility that control information can be reported as it happens, with people making reports on progress several times a day. These data are fed to a central repository (one of the possible roles for a project office) and added to data from other activities. The reporting is far less formal, and the results fed back to the users immediately. This gives the opportunity for small corrective measures to be applied, either where activities are running ahead of time (and subsequent activities should be alerted to the possibility of an early start) or where they are running late (where the application of further resources would bring them back into control).

However, there are other ways of making the progress of a project visible. These include using a whiteboard in the centre of the area in which the project team are working. Ongoing activities are listed and ticked off as they are completed. Here we can also apply the traffic lights idea:

- Project within 2 per cent of time and budget   Green or ☺
- Project within 10 per cent of time and budget   Amber or ☺
- Project not within 10 per cent of time or budget   Red or ☹

These do, however, rely on the information collected through the kind of systems that we have discussed above, and are intended to demonstrate how we are conforming rather than performing.

Last Planner

There are many ways to perform the detailed planning on a project. However, it is often seen to be a weakness and a reason for failure that this was not well carried out. One way to do this detailed planning is to have a central planning office that undertakes such work. Putting the planner at a distance from the work itself is thought by some to provide a degree of independence of the estimate, making it therefore more accurate. Consistent with all the current management thinking and approaches to empowerment, the alternative of allowing the detailed planning to be carried out by those who perform the activities being planned has become popular. This has been promoted by the Lean Construction Institute in the US and published as the **Last Planner**.[4] The method involves the production of look-ahead schedules (consistent with feedforward control) for 4–6 weeks in advance. These contain the details of activities and provide an opportunity to explore the detailed dependencies between activities that are frequently not identified at higher levels of planning. This is of benefit in itself. The main issue for control here is the use of weekly schedules. These are prepared from the look-ahead schedules and contain all the work activities, broken down into half-day units or less. This feature is important – that the work unit size is small (around half a day) and consistent between the different activities. These are listed in a table, and Table 13.3 shows how the preparation of part of a report and presentation by a team with the activities is broken down in this way.

The following week they were able to review their progress simply by taking the same table and adding two extra columns – one for whether the activity was complete or not (just a simple yes (y) or no (n)) and where an activity had not been completed why this was the case. Table 13.4 shows the result that the group achieved for this week.

Table 13.3 Weekly plan

Activity	*When*	*Who*	*Notes*
Write outline of chapter 4	Mon a.m.	All	
Write section 4.1	Mon p.m.	HT & MR	
Complete graphics for chapter 3	Mon p.m.	WF	
Complete telephone interviews	Mon p.m.	KR	
Write section 4.2	Tues a.m.	HT & WF	Relies on 4.1 being complete
Outline presentation	Tues a.m.	MR	
Write section 4.3	Tues p.m.	HT & WF	Relies on 4.2 being complete
Transcribe telephone interview data	Tues p.m.	KR & MR	Relies on interviews being complete
Analyse interview data	Wed a.m.	KR & WF	Relies on transcription being complete
Write section 4.4	Wed a.m.	HT & MR	Relies on section 4.3 being complete
Write conclusion to chapter 4	Wed p.m.	HT & MR	Needs all 4 sections complete
Outline chapter 5 – data analysis	Thurs a.m.	All	Relies on chapter 4 and the data analysis being complete
Write up data analysis	Thurs p.m.	KR & MR	
Extract key findings into presentation	Thurs p.m.	HT & WF	
Prepare graphics for chapter 5 and presentation	Fri a.m.	WF	
Compile report and check flow	Fri a.m.	HT, KR & MR	Needs all sections complete, graphics to be inserted for chapter 5 later
Integrate chapter 5 graphics and print report	Fri p.m.	All	
Practise presentation	Fri p.m.	All	

Table 13.4 Weekly review

Activity	Complete	Reason for incomplete
Write outline of chapter 4	y	
Write section 4.1	y	
Complete graphics for chapter 3	y	
Complete telephone interviews	y	
Write section 4.2	y	
Outline presentation	y	
Write section 4.3	y	
Transcribe telephone interview data	y	
Analyse interview data	y	
Write section 4.4	y	
Write conclusion to chapter 4	y	
Outline chapter 5 – data analysis	y	
Write up data analysis	n	Analysis not completed in time
Extract key findings into presentation	n	Analysis not completed in time
Prepare graphics for chapter 5 and presentation	n	Analysis not completed in time
Compile report and check flow	n	Awaiting chapter 5
Integrate chapter 5 graphics and print report	n	Awaiting chapter 5
Practise presentation	n	Conclusions not yet ready
PLANNED PERCENT COMPLETE (PPC)	67%	

The table shows the basic analysis that can be performed weekly – and the main measure that is used is that of **Planned Percent Complete**. This is calculated as:

$$PPC = activities\ completed/intended\ completed\ activities$$

In this case 12 of the 18 activities were completed this week – giving a PPC measure of 67 per cent.

The PPC measure works well where there are a number of activities going on at any one time. Weekly review meetings provide the forum for discussing progress, but most importantly this tool provides for ongoing problem-solving. Where a group is working together week on week, this provides a means by which review can be carried out every week, and the project process improved as the project progresses. In the above example, the group could meet and discuss the causes of the problems that were faced that week – in this case by the non-completion of the project analysis. Why was this – was it not planned well? Were the time estimates too short? Was the information not made available by someone from within or outside the group? Whatever the reason, the weekly meeting provides an opportunity to make sure that problems are solved at this level, and not left until the post-project review (see Chapter 16) to be resolved. Week by week, we should expect the PPC measure to improve. This is a highly visible and easily understood measure and very powerful in communicating with teams. It is included in the Project Management in Practice case at the end of Chapter 14.

Communicating control information

The control and distribution of information to the project team members and other stakeholders form a significant part of the responsibility of the project manager. They are particularly vital if the stakeholders' expectations are to be managed effectively. The cycle of events that leads to the generation of reports should be as follows:

measure–record–analyse–act

If an attribute is to be measured for control purposes it should be recorded, ideally in the form in which it was collected and without any interpretation. This and other measures should be combined and analysed before action is formalised. Not proceeding with the cycle at any point wastes the previous actions. To prevent this waste, if data are not going to form part of an analysis and subsequent possible action, they should not be collected.

Computer-based PMIS (Project Management Information Systems) are commonly used and allow the regular updating of schedules to provide a basis for management action. The bar charts produced by the planning system are a convenient tool for continuous monitoring and updating of plans (see Figure 13.6). The work completed is shown as the top half of the bars in the chart and is indicated by blue shading. The purveyors of project management software like to help their customers believe that impressive-looking systems can be the panacea in control.

This reliance on computers can lead to the following problems:

- computer paralysis – the project manager spends all day at the computer updating the project data. This is not a value-adding or problem-solving activity;
- PMIS verification – selective treatment of data can hide problems very effectively;
- data overload – there is too much for anyone to make sense of and hence act effectively;
- isolation – the project manager becomes a slave to the computer and detached from what is really happening;
- dependence – apparently removes the role of problem analysis and decision-making from managers, leading to less effective actions and removal of proactive problem-solving;
- misdirection – the effects of problems are tackled rather than the inherent causes.

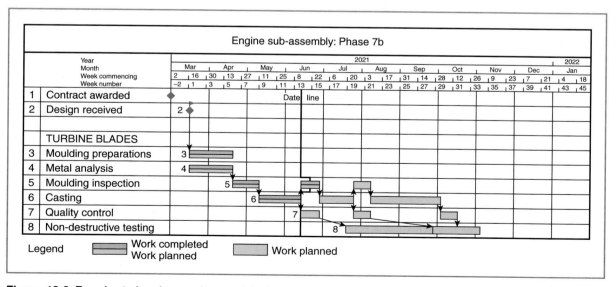

Figure 13.6 Bar chart showing work completed

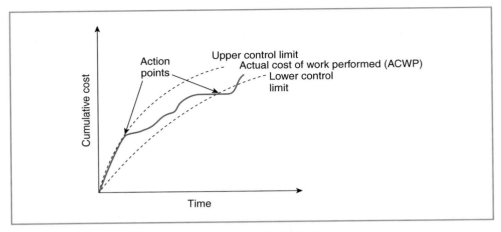

Figure 13.7 Control limits applied to progress in budget spend

The role of the system should be to identify exceptions (as above) and provide timely control information. The decision in setting up the systems should ask 'at what point does the difference between expected and actual performance merit a control action?' This needs to take into account the fact that in any activity there will be a degree of variability. It is the role of the decision-maker to set limits (called 'control limits') at which it is determined that the deviation from desired performance is significant (i.e. would not have occurred through natural variation). The concept of applying control limits to projects is shown in Figure 13.7.

13.3 Limits of control

The concept of control

From the work that has been covered so far, being in control means that you are able to assess the status of a particular activity or set of activities, are able to compare that with a desired position and are then able to make adjustments as necessary to change the state of that system to reduce the gap. This is a limiting idea. If you ask many project managers what it means to be 'in control' they will talk about it in terms of a sense of 'well-being' and that they are in a position to have influence over their worlds. Here the influence to make change may be structural and consistent with the governance ideas of Chapter 11, or through leadership and consistent with those of Chapter 12.

The nature of the baseline

The concept of control requires a baseline to control against for TCQ at least. Here there is an immediate problem as it assumes that a project knows what is required of it and has good estimates of its time and costs. These are then used to compare with the actual. This is not always a reliable point for comparison – it may have been simply a guess that was put in to fill a gap in the plan at the start. To use the classification described in Chapter 1, where a project is a 'painting by numbers' project, such control may indeed be appropriate. For the 'as . . . buts' and 'first timers', it is a different proposition.

The inherent uncertainties in the estimates prepared mean that the controlling actions will be very different in nature and may require not just amending the pace of work or levels of resources being applied, but revisiting the basis for proceeding with the project as it develops.

The nature of the system being controlled

The model of a project that the premise of control has traditionally been based upon is that of a closed mechanical system. Given that most projects are neither closed nor mechanical systems, this does question the approach. Projects are usually open systems in that they are subject to influences from outside parties – political interference, stakeholders changing or simply interacting with other changes in the system. Similarly, projects are better considered as social systems, as described throughout this edition. People rarely respond in the way that, for instance, the thermostat in a room would respond to any changes.

The limits of measurement and assessment

The principles of control established in the opening section of this chapter required that measures could be obtained for the progress of projects. The challenge of assessing the degree of completion of a particular task is often more art than science. Similarly, the information is not always real-time. A project manager recently recounted how he never knew how much money he had in his project budget. His income for the project was recorded when it came in, but expenditures were not recorded when orders were placed, or even when a supplier invoiced them but when the supplier was actually paid. This was on average 3 months after the goods had been ordered.

There is another barrier to assessment of progress. Ask a team member *'How's it going?'* and the reply will often come back *'Oh, fine'*. This is often followed up with, *'90 per cent complete'*. The challenge is that such an assessment of progress is unreliable, and susceptible to the kind of optimism bias that was described in the development of cost plans (Chapter 8).

Control as a paradox

It is often noted in human systems that the more control exerted by the management of that system, the less real control (expressed as ability to influence actual behaviour) the management of that system has over its performance.[5,6,7] For instance, a large multinational computer installer had processes for everything – all well documented and requiring a large organisation and bureaucracy to maintain. This gave apparent control over the work being performed by the organisation. The reality of this was that the staff found the bureaucracy stifling and spent most of their time finding *work arounds* for the system. In other words, there was a considerable counter-process movement in the firm where people would ignore the full rigour of a process in favour of picking and choosing the bits that they thought the most relevant or simply had the resources to do.

Control as a negative idea

The challenge with the idea of control is its negative connotations – we want to be 'in control' but may resist the idea of 'being controlled'. This requires consideration of the issues of management style (cooperation and coercion, for instance) that were part of the previous chapter. There may be times in a project where more control is required than others – for instance, during the execution, a greater degree of managerial control may need to be exerted than at the concept stage. The downside of controlling is that it can lead to a reduction in creativity. As has been discussed previously, this may run counter to the needs of the project. Artists, such as film directors, frequently reject the notion that their work can be controlled – it is a creative process where the emerging process will not conform to some pre-ordained plan. A similar charge has been made against book writers, particularly academics, though obviously not anyone concerned with writing PM texts . . .

In addition, there is an upside to this concept of control. Just as sometimes there will be a deviation from the plan that is negative (e.g. running late or over budget), positive deviations from plan (something going better than expected) will occur. Unless the project manager is in a position to notice and respond (through a 'controlling' action) then the benefit can be lost.

Summary

■ So, how's it going? It probably started as a very simple question at the start of this chapter, but the execution phase of the project is a complex task even in relatively simple projects if control is to be applied effectively. Given the history of projects failing and its incremental nature in the majority of cases, this clearly deserves some attention. There are some approaches that appear to be generating benefits – Last Planner and other methods to increase the visibility of progress, in particular.

■ The most basic approach to control revolves around a feedback control system. This requires monitoring of the project at the activity level, processing the information to determine if there is a significant variation from desired performance, and then instigating corrective action to the process itself. The nature of the feedback determines whether or not the system is stable, and timeliness is essential in the provision of feedback. The focus of control is on those aspects that were defined by the project strategy as being the most important.

■ Among other techniques, costs can be monitored through the application of the 'earned value' concept. Technical performance monitoring provides an ongoing input to future forecasts of the outcome of the project activities and Project Management Information Systems (PMIS) provide the means for achieving the measure–record–analyse–act system for ensuring minimisation of waste in the control system. Change control is needed to check that the effects of changes (in particular, the cumulative effects of many small changes) are considered before they are implemented.

■ As the second of the opening quotes in this chapter showed, the alternative to control is to deny changes, then to ignore them, then to deny that anything can be done about them and then to recognise that it is too late to do anything about them. This is clearly undesirable. Project controls though are not universally regarded as positive. It should be recognised that with social systems, control is often a paradox and unless applied intelligently, can be seen as controlling by the people working in that system. Somewhere between denial and controlling is a good region for project controls to operate in.

Key terms

actual cost of work performed (ACWP) *p. 334*

configuration control *p. 324*

corrective actions *p. 322*

cost/schedule performance indicator *p. 327*

digital dashboards *p. 330*

earned value *p. 326*

erosion of the buffer *p. 329*

estimated cost at completion (ECAC) *p. 327*

feedback control system *p. 319*

feedforward *p. 323*

hierarchy of control systems *p. 323*

input/in-process/output *p. 321*

Last Planner *p. 331*

Planned Percent Complete *p. 332*

stability *p. 322*

variance *p. 327*

visual control *p. 329*

Relevant areas of the Bodies of Knowledge

There is some similarity in the areas considered by the two Bodies of Knowledge (Tables 13.5 and 13.6, with the emphasis on the systemic needs for managing this area. Less emphasis is placed on the visual and communications aspects of control than has been suggested is necessary in this chapter.

Table 13.5 Relevant areas of the APM Body of Knowledge

Relevant section	Title	Summary
4.3.1	Progress monitoring and reporting	Covers how performance can be tracked against the baseline. The concept of earned value is explained, along with the benefits of a PMO to assist, and the use of a 'traffic-light' system.
4.3.6	Change control	This recognises the inevitability of change during projects, and the requirement for this to involve the full array of stakeholders to the project. A documented change control system should be in place to allow the impact of changes to be assessed.
4.3.7	Configuration management	At its simplest level this can mean document version control and information management, but can extend to the digital modelling of, for example, building designs.

Table 13.6 Relevant areas of the PMI Body of Knowledge

Relevant section	Title	Summary
4.5	Monitor and control project work	A system for gathering performance data and then reporting it should be established. This will indicate the current state of the project and provide forecasts for the effects of deviations in performance to the necessary stakeholders.

→

Table 13.6 continued

Relevant section	Title	Summary
4.6	Perform integrated change control	Establish how changes will occur, how they are to be evaluated and accepted or rejected, implemented, and assess their impact on scope and performance. Updated plans to be produced and distributed where changes are accepted.
5.6	Control scope	When a change is requested, from wherever it comes, a set of procedures are required to determine the impact on the original scope statement. This may mean re-working the WBS, for instance.
6.6	Control schedule	Provide a means to keep the project consistent with original objectives, but recognising that changes will occur during the process. This system should be able to show the impact of events, both possible and actual, to assist in decision-making. It should also be capable of keeping stakeholders informed of progress and future plans.
7.4	Control costs	A system is required to track costs, the effects of changes and report these to the necessary people. Typically this might include assessments of the earned value (discussed in detail) of the project and updates to budgets.
8.3	Control quality	The application of the principles of manufacturing quality control to a project processes, including defect prevention, inspection, and reporting of quality issues.
9.6	Control resources	This is concerned with the project's physical resources (not staff) so that they are available when required and released when no longer needed.
11.7	Monitor risks	A system for identifying, quantifying and mitigating risks as they emerge through the life of the project. This will involve the updating of the risk log/register and interface with other control systems – all those given above.

PROJECT MANAGEMENT IN PRACTICE
The Lifter project

In 2020 the Lifter Company saw that the market potential existed for a new model in its range. Following some problems during the project, the plans were redrafted, as shown in Figure 13.8. The decision needs to be made now as to whether the project is likely to be delivered on time or whether the launch dates need to be moved further back. (Homologation is not an issue here, as it will be done in each country in which the product is launched as an ongoing activity.)

At this time (August 2020) it was decided to allocate further resources to the project. However, analysis of the costs incurred was produced for the next quarterly review in October. The effects of the additional resources can be seen on the cost curve in Figure 13.9. The company directors are concerned about the cost overrun, but the project manager thinks that this will be minimal. Again, a decision is required as to whether this is realistic, as it will have significant implications for the budget of the firm.

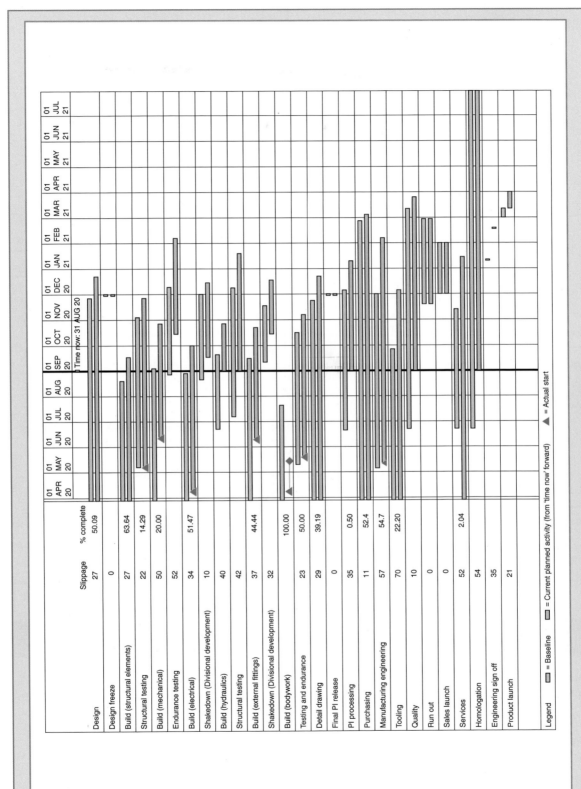

Figure 13.8 A summary of the project against the baseline set on 31 August 2020

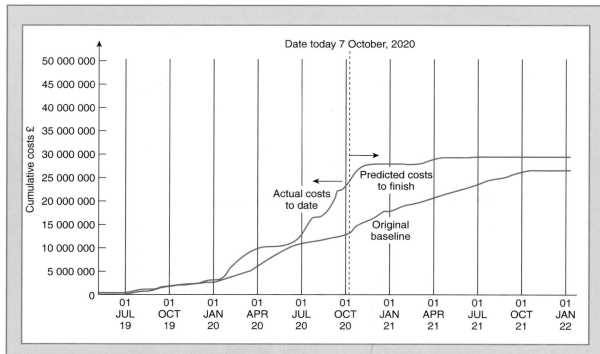

Figure 13.9 Cost control curves for Lifter project

Points for discussion

1 From the plans of Figure 13.8 and the history of the project to date, is it realistic to think that the project will be completed with only a small amount of slippage? How do you know and could you say this with any certainty?

2 You have been asked to advise the board of the company on the status of this project. What further data would you need to be able to present a more complete picture of the project?

3 What information would you want to see presented in future to a board in reporting the progress of such a project?

4 How might a project dashboard help managers monitor and control the project more effectively? What information would you include on the dashboard?

Topics for discussion

1 What is monitoring and *control* in the context of project management?

2 Why is making progress visible so important?

3 How do measures of *conformance* and *performance* differ?

4 Carry out an internet search for examples of *earned value* being used in practice. What are the limitations of this technique?

5 What are the potential advantages of the *Last Planner* approach to project control? Are all members of a project team likely to be so happy with such *micro-level* planning and control? If not, what would you do about this?

6 Why is configuration management and change control so important to the project manager?

7 Should all projects have control systems?

8 Select a project with which you are familiar – an assignment or some other piece of work that you have done. How could such a project be controlled better were you to do it again?

9 Google 'digital dashboards' and review some of the products available. How useful would you rate these as being, in project environments?

10 How do you feel about the statement, *'Being in control is good. Being controlled is not so good.'* Consider this in the context of a career as a project manager.

Further information

APM Earned Value Management Specific Interest Group (2013) *Earned Value Handbook*, Association for Project Management, Princes Risborough.

APM Planning Monitoring and Control Specific Interest Group (2015) *Planning, Scheduling, Monitoring and Control*, Association for Project Management, Princes Risborough.

APM Planning Monitoring and Control Specific Interest Group (2015) *Introduction to Project Controls Guide*, Association for Project Management, Princes Risborough.

Archibald, R.D. (2008) *Managing High Technology Programs and Projects*, 3rd edition, Wiley, Chichester.

Brandon, D.M. Jr (1998) 'Implementing Earned Value Easily and Effectively', *Project Management Journal*, Vol. 29, No. 2, pp. 11–18.

Fleming, Q.W. and Hoppelman, J.M. (2010) *Earned Value Project Management*, 4th edition, PMI, Upper Darby, PA.

Goldratt, E.M. (1990) *The Haystack Syndrome: Sifting Information Out of the Data Ocean*, North River Press, New York.

Project Management Institute (2019) *The Standard for Earned Value Management*, PMI, Newtown Square, PA.

Kivilä, J., Martinsuo, M. and Vuorinen, L. (2017) 'Sustainable project management through project control in infrastructure projects', *International Journal of Project Management*, Vol. 35, No. 6, pp. 1167–1183.

Kutsch, E., Maylor, H., Weyer, B. and Lupson, J. (2011) 'Performers, trackers, lemmings and the lost: Sustained false optimism in forecasting project outcomes — Evidence from a quasi-experiment', *International Journal of Project Management*, Vol. 29, No. 8, pp. 1070–1081.

Lin, L., Müller, R., Zhu, F. and Liu, H. (2019) 'Choosing suitable project control modes to improve the knowledge integration under different uncertainties',

International Journal of Project Management, Vol. 37, No. 7, pp. 896–911.

Loch, C. and Sommer, S. (2019) 'The Tension Between Flexible Goals and Managerial Control in Exploratory Projects', *Project Management Journal*, Vol. 50, No. 5, pp. 524–537.

Pellerin, R. and Perrier, N. (2019) 'A review of methods, techniques and tools for project planning and control', *International Journal of Production Research*, Vol. 57, No. 7, pp. 2160–2178.

Scoleze Ferrer, P.S, Galvão, G.D.A and de Carvalho, M.M. (2020) 'Tensions between compliance, internal controls and ethics in the domain of project governance', *International Journal of Managing Projects in Business*, Vol. 13, No. 4, pp. 845–865.

Taylor, T.P. and Ahmed-Kristensen, S. (2018) 'Global product development projects: measuring performance and monitoring the risks', *Production Planning & Control*, Vol. 29, No. 15, pp. 1290–1302.

Vandevoorde, S. and Vanhoucke, M. (2006) 'A Comparison of Different Project Duration Forecasting Methods Using Earned Value Metrics', *International Journal of Project Management*, Vol. 24, No. 4, pp. 289–302.

Websites

www.cmbok.com/ – Wikipedia site for configuration management – particularly relevant to IT projects.

https://www.projectmanager.com/blog/3-must-have-project-dashboard-tools

https://www.openproject.org/collaboration-software-features/dashboards/

https://www.projectmanager.com/software/dashboard

https://www.softwareadvice.com/resources/best-project-tracking-software-dashboards/

References

1 CBC News, 9 October 2009, 'The gun registry debate'.

2 Flyvbjerg, B., Budzier, A. and Lunn, D. (2020) 'Regression to the tail: Why the Olympics blow up', *Environment and Planning A: Economy and Space*, in press.

3 https://www.iso.org/iso-9001-quality-management.html

4 Ballard, G. (1994) *The Last Planner*, available at: https://leanconstruction.org.uk/wp-content/uploads/2018/09/LastPlanner.pdf

5 Gittell, J. (2000) 'Paradox of Coordination and Control', *California Management Review*, Spring, Vol. 42, No. 3, pp. 4–117.

6 Streatfield, P.J. (2001) *The Paradox of Control in Organisations*, Routledge, New York.

7 Lenfle, S. and Loch, C. (2010). 'Lost roots: How project management came to emphasize control over flexibility and novelty', *California Management Review,* Vol. 53, No. 1, pp. 32–55.

14

Procuring, contracting, and working with supply chains

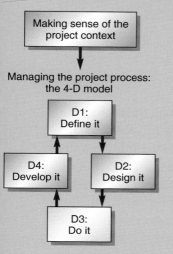

Making sense of the project context

Managing the project process:
the 4-D model

D1:
Define it

D4:
Develop it

D2:
Design it

D3:
Do it

It's just shopping, really . . .

Principles

1 A project may be delivered by a team that includes resources from outside the coordinating organisation.

2 These resources need to be included in all the discussions of 'managing the project' as they do have a major impact on its effectiveness.

3 In addition to contractually-based relationships, partnerships and trust-based relationships between parties in a supply chain form a range of options for how projects will work with their suppliers and customers.

Learning objectives

By the time you have completed this chapter, you should be able to:

→ identify the role of the supply chain in project management and its importance in ensuring project success

→ discuss the evolution of the approaches to the provision of bought-in products and services, from purchasing to the current state of supply chain management

→ describe the nature of the supply chain relationships and contracts that can exist.

Contents

Introduction   *344*
14.1 The supply chain   *345*
14.2 Purchasing and contracts   *347*
14.3 Modern approaches to supply chain management   *355*
Summary   *360*
Key terms   *360*
Relevant areas of the Bodies of Knowledge   *360*
Project management in practice: *Heathrow Terminal 5*   *362*
Topics for discussion   *366*
Further information   *367*
References   *368*

When it comes to enormous investments, sometimes the scale and risk is so huge that only governments can take them on. Examples of this would normally include endeavours such as crewed spaceflight. The Apollo missions of the 1960s and 1970s, for example, were undertaken by NASA at the behest of the US government and represented a spend that could not realistically be matched by any private sector organisation. Although a large number of contractors, in a complex web of suppliers, did the bulk of the detailed design and development, NASA owned the programme. A similar argument can be made for the Space Shuttle development and operation, until that was retired in 2011.

Source: Bill Ingalls/NASA

A major shift occurred in May 2020, when astronauts Bob Behnken and Doug Hurley took off from Florida's Kennedy Space Centre in a ship designed and operated by the private company SpaceX. The Dragon ship and its Falcon-9 rocket enabled the two to travel to the International Space Station (ISS), and return safely in August 2020. This was a radical departure for NASA. As well as being a newsworthy event in itself, it signalled that NASA had successfully moved to a model whereby they purchased the 'taxi-service' from private suppliers, at lower cost than they could manage themselves. The crewed flight was the culmination of an earlier development, the Dragon 1, which successfully flew 20 missions delivering cargo to the ISS.

This illustrates a challenge all organisations face. How much do we do internally, and how much should we rely on external parties for? What expertise do we need to cultivate, and what is appropriate for others to do? Rarely is there a clear-cut answer to this, and the answer will likely change over time. Managerial judgement is essential in taking a sensible approach to these difficult questions.

Introduction

Many of the goods and services that we buy are not the result of one individual or firm but the product of a supply chain. The same applies to a large proportion of project work – and hence the importance of the area; many organisations choose to outsource major parts of their business (have it provided by external firms, rather than direct employees). Indeed, for many organisations today the relationships that are developed between themselves and other parties in their supply chains are vital to their survival.

The basic principles of these arrangements between buyers and suppliers, are explored in this chapter, culminating in the Project Management in Practice where the classic case of the design and construction of Heathrow's Terminal 5 is presented. This project captures many of the principles of supply management discussed here.

14.1   The supply chain

A project is only as good as the weakest part of the process. We can commit considerable resources to ensuring that the processes within our organisation are the best they can be, but the outcome will be poor if this excellence does not also exist in our supply chains.

The subject of supply chain management has evolved considerably in recent years. Forty years ago, the relevant issue for organisations was called 'purchasing', and many firms had specialist buyers and purchasing staff. This function was almost entirely reactive and usually had a very simple objective – obtaining the necessary goods and services at the lowest possible price. While this appeared to provide the necessary short-term needs of the firm, it was becoming clear that there were many different approaches being used. In particular, the performance of the Japanese automotive producers was being studied, including the work of the International Motor Vehicle Program (IMVP) at MIT in the USA. They showed that the Japanese automotive producers had significantly different **relationships** with their suppliers from their Western counterparts. These were much closer – relying far less on contracts for control and far more on trust and long-term relationships. These differences were resulting in a much higher level of performance of the supply chain – shorter development times for new products, much lower levels of inventory and higher levels of quality. These differences are illustrated through the examples given in the boxes below and throughout this chapter we will consider how these issues from repetitive (manufacturing) industries can be applied in the project environment.[1]

> ### Scenario A – The construction manager
>
> 'The contract is everything to us. It defines what we will do and how we will do it. We rely on it because the client will always change their mind, which results in "extras". These extras are where we make our money. We also regularly end up in court at the end of a project to see who will pay for different things (called *claims*).'

> ### Scenario B – The sales manager – aerospace components company
>
> 'For us the contract is a formality. It is kept in the bottom drawer. We know that if we have to resort to the contract terms and conditions, we are in trouble. We rely on mutual goals – we help the assembler (their immediate customer) to develop their product, and then supply, fit and help maintain those components and systems over the life of the aircraft. In many cases, we are the sole supplier of particular products to that firm. We need them, and they need us.'

As demonstrated in these cases, the approach to the role of purchasing and supply management is very different. This is reflected in the differences in the role and scope of influence of the purchasing and supply professionals and departments. These are shown in Figure 14.1.

As the figure shows, there is a large scope difference between the different roles. At one extreme, the traditional purchasing department is purely concerned with the relationship with first-**tier** suppliers – those who supply the project organisation directly. **Materials management**, though restricted to a concern with physical goods, does look after the logistics aspects of the flow between first-tier suppliers, through the project organisation, through to the first-tier customers. In materials management, a

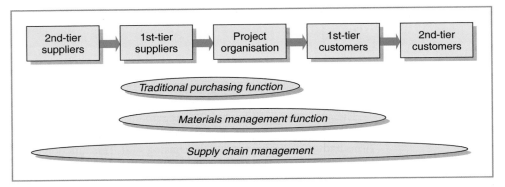

Figure 14.1 Scope of influence of purchasing, materials management and supply chain management

product breakdown structure (PBS) will provide the physical material requirements for the project, in the same way that the work breakdown structure provided the activity list for the project. This product breakdown structure is also called a **bill of materials** and will often be managed through a system of materials requirements planning.

At the most extensive, supply chain management involves issues concerned with project strategy and operations, from primary industry (where applicable) to end-user. Its influence can go beyond the second-tier suppliers indicated in Figure 14.1. Table 14.1 shows examples of supply chains in some medium- and high-complexity projects.

Having identified the supply chain that is relevant to the project, how important is it to the success of the project?[2] The answer to this depends on the following:

- the value of the bought-in products or services relative to the total value of the project;
- the criticality of the items being purchased – do they represent key parts of the project outcome?
- the timing of the work being purchased;
- the impact of the quality level of work purchased.

Table 14.1 Examples of supply chains

Project	Second-tier supplier	First-tier supplier	Integrator	First-tier customer	Second-tier customer
IS implementation project	Computer components supply	Hardware supplier	System implementer	IT department of client firm	Users in client firm
Construction of new houses	Raw material extractor	Material manufacturers	House-building firm	Sales department of house-building firm	House buyers
New product development in pharmaceutical firm	Private research institute	Formulation testing firm	Pharmaceutical firm	Distributors of drugs – shops and pharmacies	End-users
Consulting firm advise a firm on improving customer service	Providers of knowledge, e.g. research firm, regulatory bodies	Contracted consultants	Consulting firm	Immediate client wishing to improve customer service	Customers of immediate client

Some organisations today conduct relatively little of their own project work, preferring to have it carried out by specialist consultants or contractors. This is typical in many parts of the IT industry, construction and manufacturing. The level of importance of the supplier can therefore be rated according to the above four characteristics. Where a firm is using or has the scope to use the same suppliers over a period of time, and the suppliers rate highly on these four characteristics, the organisation should be investing considerable time and effort in developing their relationships with the suppliers.

Where large firms are being supplied by relatively small firms, this may include direct investment and knowledge-sharing. Many automotive and electronics firms require their suppliers to undergo particular training and to have particular processes in place. This is highly intrusive for the suppliers, but results in a very different relationship between themselves and their customers.

Before we consider the nature of the relationships between different parts of a project supply chain, we shall discuss the fundamentals of purchasing.

14.2 Purchasing and contracts

As identified above, there are many instances where a significant part of the value of a project is spent with suppliers and contractors. Indeed, some organisations only exist as 'management shells', having no direct capability to deliver the projects from which they earn their revenue. These include businesses from most sectors. The ability to coordinate the delivery of the project and take part of the revenue for this service provides the business rationale. This increase in the role of **outsourcing** is also not limited to large projects. Many organisations have reduced the size of their human resources function significantly by buying in training resource from consultants rather than trying to maintain it in-house. Similarly for IT – there was a trend during the 1990s (since reversed in many organisations – see e.g. Holweg and Maylor, 2018) to outsource all the IT provision and support. Therefore, not only are direct costs the subject of outsourcing, but also many of the indirect or overhead costs – including project managers in some firms.

Who does the purchasing and what is involved? The diversity of activities covered by this term is illustrated by the following example. In one firm, £20 million of purchases were made each year by a purchasing department of two people. In another, it took 20 people to achieve the same value of purchases. Why should this be so? The traditional purchasing process involves the steps shown in Figure 14.2. It is the number of these steps that they are involved with that determines the workload, in addition to the size of each order (several large or many small orders), the size of the supply base and the ease of placing an order (electronic data interchange versus having to create vast quantities of paperwork).

As shown in Figure 14.2, only authorised staff can make purchases – this provides the central point of control for many projects. A formal request for a purchase leads the purchasing department to carry out a search for a suitable supplier. Where this is a regular item purchased or one that is part of a standard range, this may be a relatively short process. For large capital purchases, the process of seeking and selecting suppliers is extensive. Having determined the supplier and negotiated prices an order is placed. As a minimum, most organisations require an **order number**. This is a unique identifier for the order that allows its origin and all other information relating to it to be traceable. On arrival of the materials, another document is triggered – the goods inwards note. This must be **reconciled** with the delivery note from the supplier, the purchase order and eventually

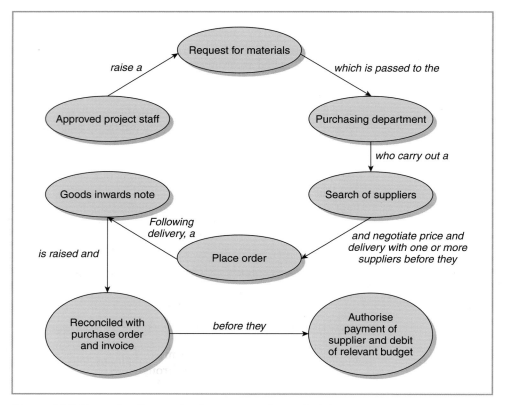

Figure 14.2 Example of a purchasing process for materials

the **invoice** or request for payment from the supplier. Provided these all agree, the invoice can be passed for payment. When the process is largely automated and the suppliers consistent, it is possible for the scenario with two people to be feasible. With the number of activities that need to be carried out and pieces of documentation that must be reconciled, there is clearly scope here for twenty to be perfectly feasible too.

This can get more complicated, though. Invitations to tender (ITT) are quite normal where large contracts are to be placed. The contracting organisation will issue an ITT to potential suppliers or advertise it, for instance for the public sector in the OJEU (Official Journal of the European Union), or (since January 2021) the UK government's 'Find a Tender' service. The ITT document will set out either the detailed requirements or the problem to be solved through the delivery of the contract. Typically this will require potential contractors to provide details of not only how they will meet the requirements, but also the costs, time required and placement of risk.

Rather than place individual contracts for pieces of work, which can be time-consuming and expensive to set up, it is common practice to see organisations offer a broad brief for work and a fixed amount of money in total against which individual projects can be carried out. These are known as framework agreements for the provision of goods and services.

There are many decisions to be made and issues to be understood with regard to purchasing in projects. These include the nature of the organisation that can carry out the purchasing role, the purchasing objectives and the nature and role of contracts established.

Table 14.2 The advantages of centralised and localised purchasing

Centralised purchasing	Localised purchasing
• Purchasing power due to aggregation of orders • Better materials utilisation and stock management • Economies of staffing • Standardisation of purchasing procedures	• Local knowledge of suppliers • Low organisational inertia • Local management control • Enhanced supplier relationships

The organisation of purchasing

For organisations involved in large projects, the decision will have to be made as to the nature of the purchasing organisation. While the design and control of the purchasing function is clearly a management specialism in its own right, the project manager should be aware of the implications of the design chosen for the organisation. The two extremes of purchasing organisation are shown in Table 14.2 – **centralised** and **localised**. For a firm, centralising the purchasing organisation means that each project places its requirements through one purchasing office that has control of all the requirements for the whole business. At the other extreme, a project manager can employ or use the services of a local purchasing officer. In other cases, the purchasing function may be outsourced to an external provider.

It is not uncommon for there to be mixed purchasing arrangements. For instance, large or standard items can be purchased through a central office. Where local knowledge or a rapid delivery is required, these items can be sourced through local arrangements made by project staff. This does reduce the level of central control that many organisations seem to like, but it can provide a closer meeting of project needs. In addition, for large capital projects, a *purchasing agent* is often used – an intermediary who specialises in the purchasing of those particular items.

At the most local level, some firms have allowed their employees to purchase materials and services up to certain values, using a company credit card. This allows direct contact between the buyer and supplier, significantly increasing the effectiveness of the information transfer, and simplifies the purchasing process considerably. Billing is also simplified as accounts are provided on one monthly statement, rather than every item having to be processed as a separate transaction.

The potential for cost savings through simple, on-line, purchasing has grown significantly in recent years due to the ease with which it can be done. The project environment does present some problems here – not least that items and services purchased may be unique. While automation of the purchase of standard or commodity items through this channel provides clear benefits, the case still needs to be made for one-off or special items. This said, there are many project-based industries that do purchase large quantities of standard items, and the opportunities for fast information transfer may actually help in the sourcing of unique items. Online auctions also provide some firms with opportunities to source products and services globally, for instance buying programmers' time from around the world or increasing the range of products that may be considered for a particular application. In addition, as was demonstrated by the processes of Figure 14.2, there is considerable potential for automation of the process, and the use of the web provides one way of doing this.

REAL WORLD   **Procurement in times of Covid-19**

One of the strategies used in the fight against Covid, was for the rapid deployment of mass-testing. Crucial in the provision of this, was the ability to be able to gather high numbers of samples from potentially infected people, before sending them in bulk to labs for testing. This 'gathering' capability, in the first half of 2020, would come in the form of adapted vans, that could set up quickly for instance in supermarket carparks. The normal routes for procurement for such items would take months. The issuing of tenders, preparation of bids, scrutinising of bids, contract negotiation and award (all of the processes described above) had to be completed in hours, with multiple government departments, multiple commercial organisations and each wanting something different. It should have been a disaster. However, it was one of the major successes in the UK, with the procurement and conversion of hundreds of suitable vans. This was achieved over the Easter weekend in the UK – traditionally a time of national holiday. It involved large purchase orders being placed directly on suppliers (in this case a large vehicle rental firm) for used vehicles, and the ownership of these being transferred to the UK government. The role of the British Army was central to both the organisation and the logistics of conversion in days of these vans into mobile testing centres. These formed the backbone of the testing capability. This demonstrated how procurement in a national emergency could be achieved, and likewise, just how much time and energy was usually spent trying to make sure that 'best value' was obtained for the citizens of the UK.

Purchasing and project strategy

The objectives of the purchasing activities should be consistent with those of the project. In project strategy (Chapter 4), we considered the objectives for the project to be broadly stated as having time, cost or quality as the primary objective, with the other objectives arranged in priority. In purchasing terms, the strategy is converted into the **'five rights'**. These are interdependent characteristics of a supplier or contractor depending on their ability to deliver:

- the right quantity;
- the right quality;
- at the right price;
- at the right time and place; and be . . .
- the right supplier.

Quantity

The quantity of goods or services (contractors are generally assumed to deliver a service) is determined from the schedules drawn up with the plans. Where there have been changes these are built in and the quantity calculated. At one time, it was considered best to order in large quantities, as these incurred large discounts and so you bought as much as possible at one time. As will be shown in the following sections, the notion that prevails today tends to be that the necessary goods should be provided at the point of need in the quantity required for that piece of work only. This requires very different systems for conveying orders and managing the supply and resupply process in projects where there are repetitive elements of work than where there are single large or high-value items.

Quality

The quality of goods and services may be determined through:

- trial supply of goods or services;
- prior reputation;
- certification or assessment of a supplier's quality system.

There are also other issues to consider, such as where contractors are hired on an individual basis, the recruiter may also seek membership of a particular professional body and possibly ask the contractor to provide their own legal indemnity insurance. However, these issues all presume that conformance to standard is the quality that is required. There are many other definitions of quality, such as the quality of service that is provided, the speed of response to enquiries and other indirect features of a purchased product or service that have a great impact on the overall quality of the project. For instance, the suppliers of hardware for an IT project may have a great influence on the outcome of the project not only through the hardware that they provide but also through the technical support that they give to the software producers and the installers.

The important quality issues for the project manager with purchasing are therefore:

- *assurance* – managing the conformance of the supplied goods and services to the necessary levels of quality (technical and service quality);
- *performance* – working with the suppliers and customers to obtain the best possible result.

Price

Achieving a purchasing decision at the right price is a challenge. In project organisations there is often the need for long-term relationships to be built up between buyer and supplier, though the relationship for that particular project may be fairly short. There are clearly gains to be made by applying pressure on the price to obtain the cheapest supply. In the long term, however, the supplier may go out of business or may simply economise in ways that cost you money elsewhere. Indeed, Deming's fourth point is:

> *End the practice of awarding business on the basis of a price-tag. Purchasing must be combined with design of product, manufacturing and sales to work with the chosen supplier: the aim is to minimise total cost not merely initial cost.*[3]

The best supplier may not then be the cheapest, as there is often a trade-off in other areas. As for project strategy, this may be against time, cost or flexibility.

It is also worth considering the incentives that are put in place by the buying organisation. With one engineering development company we worked with, the Purchasing Department were given aggressive cost-reduction goals each year. The staff then found cheaper suppliers, who often struggled to meet the demanding quality goals for the specialist parts (despite claiming that they could). Having alternative suppliers for parts is a good approach, but they do have to be able to deliver. The end result was sometimes very expensive line stops (often costing millions of dollars in lost production) with manufacturing halted as the end product failed its final conformance tests. The demands for cost reductions also significantly soured relationships with suppliers, so when extra support was needed on key projects, often their incentive to 'go the extra mile' was heavily reduced. This hit new product development (e.g. for bespoke or modified component requests) as well as manufacturing (e.g. a request for early delivery of the next order). Purchasing may have met their annual targets; it is not clear whether the business really saw any benefit, though.

Further parts of this discussion are concerned with the relationship between cost and quantity. For instance, will a supplier of materials assess the discount given depending on the value of each order, or will they simply consider annual volumes of business? Other issues include the cost of purchasing – typically larger than you might think. To work out the impact, organisations need to divide their total purchasing costs by the number of orders placed with suppliers, and this gives the average cost per order. This can be a considerable overhead cost to a project, and section 14.3 considers some of the ways that firms have tried to reduce this.

Time

Achieving the right time and place is the basis of much literature and the predominant complaint that industrial purchasers have about suppliers. The rating of suppliers and regular performance reviews can keep this as an issue for them. It is also one advantage that a degree of centralisation can have for the purchasing function – that of being able to track supplier performance on the basis of criteria such as late delivery. A major point to note is that it is no good blaming a supplier for late delivery if paperwork to place the order takes six weeks to be processed by the purchasing function. Giving suppliers the longest possible time in which to fulfil an order is going to be beneficial to both parties in the long term.

Supplier

Being the right supplier clearly has dependence on the other four categories, but is included to start the discussion as to the way in which one selects suppliers. The choice based on price alone has been shown to provide possible short-term gains, which can be more than countered in the longer term. There are several other factors that should be considered.

Are choices made on the basis of a 'free lunch'? The expansion of the corporate hospitality industry in the 21st century in most countries has been immense. Interestingly, this has been paralleled by efforts by many companies to be seen to be behaving ethically and state publicly that their staff will not accept gifts, however small, from suppliers. There is clearly a contradiction between these two facts. In the UK, The Chartered Institute of Purchasing and Supply (CIPS – see Further Information at the end of this chapter) has a code of conduct for their members which expressly prohibits the acceptance of gifts from suppliers, and other national regulatory bodies do likewise. To avoid any suspicion of impropriety, as a general rule it is better to avoid accepting any gifts, or at least to document formally any you do receive, regardless of your employer's official policy. This way you cannot later be accused of anything untoward, although it is not clear who in reality would actually give a contract in return for a branded coffee mug.

How are orders conveyed, with what frequency and how do the suppliers really know what your requirements are? Also, they often have expertise in both the design of their products and their application, which, as Deming suggests, should be used as a source of knowledge and improvement.

It is obviously not possible to treat the purchase of the smallest-value items in the way suggested above (through partnership rather than adversarial relationships with suppliers). The use of a version of Pareto analysis (Chapter 15) can identify the 20 per cent of bought-in goods and services that take 80 per cent of the project spend. It is on these that the focus of purchasing attention will rest as they are the areas that will have greatest scope to impact the project's costs. However, where time is the key issue, the consideration of the value of the products or services being provided may be immaterial if they are critical to the project. In such cases the cost focus can be misguided.

One of the activities that many project managers need assistance with is in the negotiation of deals with suppliers and customers alike. In this respect, purchasing staff have often proved invaluable, as, having heard sales pitch after sales pitch, they are less likely, in theory at least, to be influenced by the shine over the substance of the deal. Also, unless you are aware of the games of negotiation, it is a minefield. Some considerable assistance can be provided through the study of some of the specialist publications in that area (see, for instance, Acuff, 2008; Fisher et al., 2011).

The details of the establishment of contracts between suppliers and purchasers is a topic that concerns many specialist books. Not only are there obvious and large national differences between practices in contract law, there are many sectoral idiosyncrasies with which project managers should familiarise themselves. The books on contract law are filled with horror stories of how contracts drawn up by non-experts have only worked well if they were never questioned or tested. The safest advice, in a commercial environment where litigation is becoming more common, is to rely on professionals in this field. There are some issues that can safely be discussed at a general level that will facilitate understanding of some project environments. The comment will be made again that many industries have reduced their reliance on contract as a means of control.

Contracts

The role of **contracts** in many industries has changed. The process by which contracts are awarded depends on the nature of the task being contracted, the relationship between the purchaser and supplier and the relative size of each. In addition, industry norms apply, e.g. in construction, the allocation of contracts for trade services, while following basic rules, may be at the discretion of the site manager. There are two issues here for the project manager. The first is the type of contract that they may be working with, and the second is the process for working with contracts, which will be compared between large and small projects.

Some contract types are listed below:

- *Fixed price* – just what it says – there is this much money agreed for the job to be done, there is no more.
- *Time and materials* – the customer agrees to pay a particular hourly or daily rate and the cost of the materials. This separation of labour and material may increase the transparency of the costings, particularly where materials are a large proportion of the activity cost.
- *Target cost* – where the customer sets a target cost for an item (see Chapter 8) and the supplier is required to work back from this to see what they can provide for that cost. Incentives can be added to encourage the supplier to come in below the target cost.
- *Revenue share* – this has been used with some success in the aerospace sector, where the selling price of a finished aircraft is determined by its performance. The better it performs, the more it is worth. In an effort to get their systems suppliers (major components, e.g. navigation, instrumentation, flight control etc.) working together, deals were agreed where systems would be sold to the firm on the basis that they would attract a percentage of the final selling price of the aircraft. The more it sold for, the greater the price that the systems suppliers would receive.
- *Cost-plus* – this is where the customer agrees to reimburse whatever costs the supplier incurs on a project, plus a margin for profit. This was until relatively recently the preferred form of contract for many military development and procurement projects (see also the cost estimating processes in Chapter 8).

The process

Where a contract is being placed for the supply of a major part of the project spend the process shown in Figure 14.3 may be used. This is a single-stage process – unlike that recommended by the World Bank for development projects, and the major high street banks for human resource development projects. Here a two- or more stage process may be beneficial with a first call to see who has the technical capability and capacity to deliver the project. This identifies potential bidders and may provide considerable insight into how what is being requested can be improved, for instance to reduce cost by making small changes to the requirements. A second phase may then ask the potential bidders to

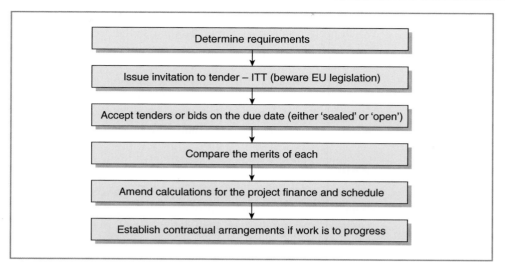

Figure 14.3 Establishment of contracts

provide detailed costings of their proposals. Such a phased approach does take more time to complete, as there will have to be several rounds of bidding, but it does save time by pre-filtering the bidders by technical capability.

There are further rules – for instance, public contracts (central government, purchase/lease of goods or services) are subject to strict controls and processes. For example, the European Union spends around €2 trillion per year on public procurement, and sets out harmonised rules to create a level playing field.[4]

When the **bids** or tenders arrive, they may be treated as either 'sealed' (not opened until a given time) or 'open' (where the information contained in the bids becomes public at the time the bids are received). The system of sealed bids is often felt to be fairer for larger contracts. The information contained in the bids should be fed into the project's financial and time calculations and any amendments to budgets or schedules made on this basis. Contractual arrangements are usually based on standard terms and conditions, but establishing whether the supplier's terms and conditions or those of the purchaser apply is a role for legal advisers, due to a process known as **battle of the forms**:

Customer: 'We place the order subject to our terms and conditions.'

Supplier: 'We accept, subject to our terms and conditions.'

The main objective is to ensure that the contracts can be met on both sides. Breaches of contracts and the ensuing litigation rarely benefit either party greatly but the legal industry gains considerably.

Various bodies have compiled standard forms of contract, which can eliminate some of the wrangling between suppliers and purchasers. For example, the New Engineering Contract (NEC) is used within the construction industry. It is a family of standard contracts, initiated by the UK Institution of Civil Engineers and aimed at making the contracting process between parties more straightforward. These are specialist areas, and experts in each particular industry will be involved in drafting contracts. For large organisations, this is part of doing business and departments are in place to handle the requirements. However, for small businesses or those looking to break into a new (for them) industry, this can be a significant hurdle to overcome and a potential barrier to entry, requiring expert (and likely expensive) advice to avoid the pitfalls of getting it wrong.

Other contract issues that project managers should at least be aware of include:

- The role of penalty clauses – used in many sectors to encourage suppliers to do what they said that they would do. In practice, it does appear that these are treated as the point of last resort if they have to be invoked, which leads on to:
- The role of bonds and insurances – if you are providing goods and services to a larger project, the effects of your part of the project going wrong could have implications way beyond the scale of your part of the project. (For example, a building contractor, contracted to do the concreting of the ground floor of a skyscraper, used concrete that didn't cure properly, resulting in a 4-week delay to the opening of the building. The contract value: £80 000. The damages as a result of their 'misfortune': £2.8 million.) Before being awarded contracts, many firms will require insurances to be in place and bonds to be provided. These may require certain quality procedures to be in place as well.
- Retention money – on completion of large projects there are often final pieces of work to be carried out. These may not delay the completion of the contract and payment of the majority of the agreed contract fee, but the customer may insist on retaining some of the money to ensure that the final jobs are completed to their satisfaction.
- Stage payments – in order for suppliers to stay afloat financially, it is usual in many projects for there to be interim payments made on delivery of particular objectives.
- Contracts may get in the way of project start-up. Where days or even weeks are crucial, a supplier who will not start work until a contract is in place may hold up the project considerably. More flexible means of proceeding (letters of intent are often used) do not replace contracts, but may overcome the initial problems.

A final thought before moving on. The most basic piece of contract legislation in place in many countries is that goods and services provided should be what they say that they are, and do what they say that they should do. This may come as a surprise to many firms which have purchased large IT packages. The systems that they were promised at the usually very glitzy sales promotions do not turn up until very late and then only partly work – the remaining features that you needed being 'still in development'. This being the case for so many IT projects, it must be asked how the firms selling such goods manage to do so without any apparent fear of legal action. The answer appears to lie in the nature of what you buy. In the case of software, you usually do not buy the product, which would be subject to such law, but you buy a licence to use the product. This apparently circumvents the usual laws. The lesson from this is to be careful to understand exactly what you are buying and work with your contract specialists to make sure you are getting what you expect.

14.3 Modern approaches to supply chain management

There have been big changes in the nature of the relationships between buyers and suppliers in some sectors. As will be shown, this has moved from short-term arrangements based on contracts to long-term relationships based on trust. This change is by no means universally applicable nor desirable, but the project manager should be aware of the implications of the intentions of the arrangement for decisions and processes in the project.

There are many classifications of relationship available. For the project manager, we shall simply consider three basic types:

- Traditional **adversarial** – characterised by the reliance on contract, competitive bidding, short-term relationships (as long as the contract), and little by way of process cooperation between the buyer and supplier. The focus of the choice of supplier will be on cost and short-term gain on each side. There will often be several suppliers for each item.

- **Partnership** – here two firms enter into a long-term agreement, whereby the purchaser agrees to award a firm sole-supplier status in return for process developments being undertaken and closer cooperation on costs and information transfer. Orders may be exchanged by electronic data interchange (**EDI**) or call-offs from a pre-agreed quantity ('we don't need all of it, this is the amount that is needed now'). Where there is a small supplier for a large firm, this may take the form of direct investment, e.g. in particular equipment or research and development.

- Relationship management – this is where one of the parties in a complex supply network takes on the role of coordinating and developing the entire supply network. This goes way beyond managing a partnership, but may consider all the elements of the supply chain from primary industry to customer. The British Airports Authority is a good example of a project customer taking control of the supply network and getting involved with firms way down the supply chain to ensure that any weak links are strengthened.

Table 14.3 describes the differences between the traditional adversarial approach and the partnering approach that many firms are at least aspiring to today. The key points of note are the differences in the practices applied in the execution of the work being carried out. Instead of looking around to many suppliers, it is likely that under partnering, a firm will have one supplier for each category of purchase. This has resulted in a significant rationalisation of the supply base by many firms, and a simplification of the purchasing process, as described in Figure 14.2. There is another side to this type of relationship that is evident in repetitive industries, and has become apparent in certain project environments.[5] This concerns the intrusive nature of the relationship and the tough requirements that are often placed upon suppliers for improvement. As one project-based supplier of components to the automotive sector commented:

'The first year they demanded a 5 per cent reduction in our costs from one project to the next. That was just about achievable – we totally rethought our processes and managed to hit our targets. The second year, we were asked to do the same again. That was really

Table 14.3 Adversarial versus partnership relationships

Feature	Adversarial	Partnership
Temporal basis	One-off purchase	Ongoing
Commodity	Product	Product, service, knowledge support
Contractual basis	Each purchase negotiated – competitive basis	Long-term deals agreed in advance, trust-based rather than contractually reliant
Communications and involvement	Limited to 'information as necessary' as determined by contract terms; use standard communications – telephone, e-mail	Involved at all relevant stages of the project, as determined by impacts on all parties; may involve staff loan; suppliers involved in scheduling and planning; communicate through linked networks and regular information-sharing sessions
Focus	Our bit of the project is most important – maximise the return from that bit	The performance of the project as a whole is most important

hard and we struggled. The third year, the same was asked again. We asked them to suggest ways to do this, but did not receive any further help from them. We made a loss on the business that year and took the decision to end the relationship. It was all one-way. Possibly, it was because they were a big firm and we were a small one. We have moved out of this sector and concentrated elsewhere, and are now making three times as much profit as we used to make, without any of the aggravation!'

As can be seen, the management of relationships is not all win-win, and while the principles are admirable, there is clearly considerable effort to be expended with application. As for other 'good ideas' there is plenty of case material on the application which is worth referring to (see Further Information at the end of this chapter).

Modern techniques in supply chain management

Open-book accounting

This has been widely used in the automotive industry, particularly where firms are first-tier suppliers to the automotive companies. The principle is that by opening up the accounts of a supplier, the customer can see how much profit is being made out of them. Too little, and the supplier is going to be unable to have the investment necessary to improve its processes in the future. The customer may suggest ways to reduce costs in such a situation. Too much profit, and the customer will be looking for price reductions.

The use of open-book agreements is not universally popular, with many, particularly small, suppliers resenting the intrusion of accountants from the large firms into their business. They also reduce significantly the bargaining power of a supplier in price negotiations, as the customer is privy to their data. In principle, therefore, this is a nice idea, with helpful customers ensuring that their suppliers remain financially healthy. The reality is often far from this, with the costs data simply being a tool for beating suppliers with, rather than helping them directly. For the project environment, the notion of greater transparency of costs does apply, as it does in repetitive operations.

Vendor-managed inventory

For many organisations the only way to obtain goods for projects was to buy them in bulk in advance of need. For instance, if a building project needed 400 pallets of bricks for the whole job (say, 10 weeks' supply), these would be ordered and delivered at the start of the job – which looks good, at least in the short term as the materials are there ready for use, and the goods were obtained at a discount price as they were bought in bulk. If we look closer, this presents a number of problems for both supplier and customer. For the supplier, they have a sudden surge in demand. In order to meet this demand, they may have staff working overtime, and thereby increasing costs. For the customer, what do they do with 400 pallets of bricks? They store them, count them, move them and probably have to guard them. Theft of such stocks is common. Also, because of the bulk ordering issue, the materials planners have probably over-ordered to make sure that there are enough for the job. In the construction sector there are many countries where it is normal to over-order by a minimum of 10 per cent. Any materials left at the end of the job are either 'removed' for other jobs by the staff or the firm has to pay to have them taken away.

Such a scenario is common in many sectors, not just construction, and results in considerable waste (see Chapter 16). The principle of **vendor-managed inventory** (VMI) is that the supplier will work with the customer to determine the amount of that particular type of material that will be needed during different phases of the project. This is made available on-site, and the material is taken as needed for the job. The supplier owns the material (and may even have to pay the customer rental for site-space to store it) until it is used. The supplier will then invoice the user regularly for the material used. The supplier becomes the sole supplier for those items and in doing so gains the maximum share of that business. As importantly, as the sole supplier they will be involved in the planning process to ensure that the necessary materials are available at the time they are needed, and may also provide technical support for the products and advice (for instance, if the same product is available from another manufacturer at a better price). Such arrangements are used in automotive and electronics projects and manufacturing, and are increasingly being used in retailing. It appears to be a win-win for both supplier and customer as:

- the customer now pays only for the material actually used;
- the customer pays only for material when it is used – no advance purchasing costs;
- the number of transactions is drastically reduced – only one bill for all the materials supplied, instead of many (overhead cost reduction);
- the customer eliminates the costs of storage, checking and moving materials;
- the supplier can provide regular small deliveries rather than having to arrange small numbers of large deliveries;
- the possibilities for partnership between the firms is increased.

The supplier clearly now has a bigger role, managing material as opposed to just being the intermediary between the manufacturer (or their agent) and the user. This is not a transition that many make without problems, but there are plenty of instances of existing practice for them to draw on for knowledge of how to make it work. It appears to have been highly successful in areas of supply such as stationery – see the example below.

The Rapid Pencil Company

When the firm decided to carry out an audit of annual spend they were horrified at the value of stationery purchases in the year. Some parametric estimating, based on the number of people and the type of work the firm carried out, showed they were buying roughly three times the amount of stationery they thought they would need. This was being passed on to individual projects in the form of overhead costs, so it was considered worth monitoring. In addition to the costs of the items being bought, there was significant time dedicated to the ordering, storing and distribution of items. A short investigation revealed that because the supply line was considered to be unreliable, almost everyone in the organisation kept their own stock of materials. Once 'theirs', these stocks would be far more likely to end up at home.

The Rapid Pencil Company offered the firm the opportunity to remove most of the stocks from the system and to eliminate ordering costs. They did this by providing cupboards on each major office level. These contained an agreed level of stock and were replenished each week. In addition, where there were special requirements, these could be ordered directly via a website. The firm submitted one invoice per month to the firm, rather than one for each separate order. As the financial director of the firm commented: 'It was a step of trust to let them take over this activity from us, but it has worked really well. No more ordering for things that we have run out of – that used to happen almost daily – and just one invoice a month. We now know roughly what the spend should be, and we can simply check against that.'

'Good' supply chain complexity?

For most organisations, added complexity is to be discouraged. Any difficulties that cause delay or extra costs are, of course, bad, and as a general rule we want to make our projects less complex, not more. However, there is a line of thought[6] that some level of 'strategic' supply chain complexity is actually beneficial, and indeed necessary. Consider a project to develop a new consumer product. Offering a variety of different options to meet a broad range of consumer demands may be beneficial, and give you a significant advantage in the market. It might mean working with a wider range of suppliers, developing a more complicated manufacturing process with a higher requirement for configuration control, and with more coordination then needed in the final distribution system. However, this extra complexity may make your product range not only more appealing for customers, but harder for competitors to replicate. Simplifying your offering may be inappropriate in this instance. As with many such problems, there is no 'right' answer here, but it is an important area for managers to consider. The ability to deal with a higher level of complexity than your competitors is a valid business strategy that can be a competitive advantage if you can achieve it.

Rethinking the supply chain for the 2020s?

The Covid-19 pandemic of 2020 has thrown some established supply chain principles into doubt. The just-in-time supply of goods relies on efficient transport of the required materials at the right time with the right quantities. Organisations have become very skilled at this, resulting in very efficient production and corresponding reduced costs for end consumers. Similarly, expertise in crafting supply networks has resulted in goods being sourced from around the world, with exporters and importers benefitting from specialisation and trade. Again, all good for the customer. Until it all goes wrong. In 2020 this reliance on global transportation was highlighted when vast swathes of world production were hit by closures and lock-downs. Supply chains had become wonderfully effective, yet this was seemingly accompanied by a rise in fragility. Although many organisations made heroic efforts to keep serving their customers, the lack of resilience to such an extreme shock was apparent. Projects were derailed rapidly when much of the world ground to a halt. Might our view of what a 'good' supply chain looks like change? At the time of writing it is unclear. However, managers impacted will never forget the impact it had on their projects, and it is likely that it will be a consideration in their future planning for many years to come. There is the possibility that crowdsourcing (asking the wider world – see Chapter 11) may gain more favour as a way of keeping supply options open and gaining access to new ideas. The fact that it is so hard to predict the future is a sign that what worked in the past is not necessarily the best indicator of where organisations should be looking going forward.

The issue of trust is central to more recent approaches to managing supply for projects. An article in *Harvard Business Review*[7] starts with the blunt assessment:

> 'Traditional purchasing contracts don't work in complex strategic relationships where the parties are highly dependent on each other, future events can't be predicted, and flexibility and trust are required. Instead of promoting the partnership-like relationships needed to cope with uncertainty, conventional contracts undermine them.'

Instead, they recommend that:

> 'A formal relational contract lays a foundation of trust, specifies mutual goals, and establishes governance structures to keep the parties' expectations and interests aligned over time.'

They give examples of how major, hard-nosed, organisations have found that formal contracts can lead to an adversarial mindset and a lack of innovation. Instead, by defining what the relationship should be, performance can be significantly improved to the benefit of both parties. This is especially important for project-based organisations, where uncertainty is a fact of life and not all eventualities can be specified. It remains to be seen whether this will be taken up widely, but since one of the authors of the paper won the Nobel Prize for his work on contracts, it is certainly promising.

Summary

■ The value of goods and services purchased can make up a major proportion of a project budget, and this has been the case for many project-based industries for some time. The role of purchasing or procurement in organisations has changed to incorporate the management of both suppliers and customers with the objective of maximising the performance of the project. This has led to the area being referred to as supply chain management, rather than simply purchasing or procurement. The activity of purchasing is still important, however, and the stages involved in a typical purchasing process have been described with the accompanying documentation that is required by many systems.

■ A feature of the work of many in the supply chain management area has been the negotiation of contracts. There are many standard procedures to follow and legal issues to navigate – particularly where international trade is concerned. The contract is still the formal basis of some projects, containing the criteria by which it will be assessed. In other projects where the basis of the relationship is different between the parties the contract takes the role of a document 'just in case' it all goes wrong. This is just one feature of the different styles of relationship that can exist between suppliers and customers. At the extremes, the relationship can be adversarial or run on a partnership basis. While the potential advantages of partnering between organisations are clear, there is a considerable downside element to these, particularly where one of the parties is significantly more powerful than the other.

Key terms

adversarial/partnership *pp. 355, 356*

battle of the forms *p. 354*

bids *p. 354*

centralised/localised *p. 349*

contracts *p. 353*

EDI *p. 356*

five rights *p. 350*

invoice *p. 348*

materials management *p. 345*

open-book accounting *p. 357*

order number *p. 347*

outsourcing *p. 347*

product breakdown structure (PBS)/bill of materials *p. 346*

reconciled *p. 347*

relationships *p. 345*

tier *p. 345*

vendor-managed inventory *p. 357*

Relevant areas of the Bodies of Knowledge

Both Bodies of Knowledge (Tables 14.4 and 14.5) cover the role of sourcing and look at how this can be achieved within the project.

Table 14.4 Relevant areas of the APM Body of Knowledge

Relevant section	Title	Summary
1.3.4	Strategic sourcing	As the title suggests, this discusses the strategy for choosing different types of procurement for different products or services. Non-critical ones can be transactional; more important ones in terms of profit or risk impact need a more considered approach.
2.1.4	Procurement strategy	Looks at various contracting strategies and how these can be used with regards to project complexity (low-high) and timescale (1 to 25+ years).
4.2.1	Contract award	Considers the steps needing to be taken before awarding a contract. These include narrowing down potential suppliers, competitive tendering, and shortlisting.
4.3.2	Contract management	This covers the monitoring and management of supplier performance over the contract. It includes making sure both parties understand the contract obligations, regular progress reviews, formal reporting methods, and the potential of risk-sharing.

Table 14.5 Relevant areas of the PMI Body of Knowledge

Relevant section	Title	Summary
12	Project procurement management	This chapter is devoted to the procurement of goods or services from outside suppliers.
12.1	Plan procurement management	Including what to buy (as opposed to do in-house), how much, and when to buy it. Produce specifications for products and services and agree the type of contract to be used.
12.2	Conduct procurement	Provide documents that will invite potential suppliers to tender for the work, and determine how they will be selected. Invite potential suppliers to tender for the work, answer queries related to the work, gather the bids, then select suppliers and negotiate contracts.
12.3	Control procurements	Manage the relationship over the course of the contract, ensure the contract is adhered to and modify it if necessary, and close the contract on completion.

PROJECT MANAGEMENT IN PRACTICE
Heathrow Terminal 5[8]

Introduction

Construction of Heathrow's Terminal 5 was a £4.2 billion programme comprising 16 major projects, including airport infrastructure, all service tunnels, road and rail links. The programme included the construction of the main terminal and two satellite buildings, 60 aircraft stands (some already operational), a new air traffic control tower, a 4000-space multi-storey car park, the creation of a new spur road from the M25 motorway, a 600-bed hotel, the diversion of two rivers and over 13 km of bored tunnel, including extensions to the Heathrow Express and Piccadilly Line services.[9] It was given the go-ahead in November 2001, construction started on site in September 2002 and phase one went into service on time and on budget in March 2008. The project itself involved 60 main (first-tier) contractors. Although the terminal has now been operating successfully for a number of years, it still remains an excellent example of how to build such a daunting undertaking.

Source: Dan Kirkwood/Getty

The vision for the project was ambitious – not just completion on time and within budget, but to 'create a new standard for project delivery in the UK' – a requirement of the process. In addition, the principles of 'fair reward for achievements of our partners' (the contractors) and 'no surprises for BAA shareholders' were established.

Contracts

The basis of the contract between BAA, its main client (BA) and its 60 main suppliers was the 'Team Handbook'. The contracts were reimbursable, with open-book accounting and sampling audit. The contracts were also incentivised, with payments for saving made based on a share of a reward fund – a pooled fund of the benefits gained, which would be distributed on the achievement of key milestones in the construction phase and on the achievement of key objectives during the operational phase.

The claim is 'closer to fewer' with long-term contracts awarded based on good past working relationships and willingness to innovate practices. Where suppliers, particularly materials suppliers, were having problems meeting the requirements of the project, 'parachute teams' were made available to enable improvement. These were funded as part of the contract by BAA, as was the enterprise database – the real-time information system.

The contract was described as behavioural, setting out the values, norms and expectations for the project. Values included statements of mutual respect and the principles of recognition for performance. Norms were set out as processes that would be followed, for instance in getting approval for changes. Expectations included training standards – minimum 2 per cent of people's time with an expectation of 5 per cent. In the team handbook it was stated that: 'When both our company and your company sign the agreement at the end of the team handbook, the handbook is also our contract; our agreement to work to achieve success, together.' The contract therefore was rather different to the conventional work arrangement, where detailed specifications are set out in an attempt to ensure delivery. It was clear that here the principles were completely consistent with the 'Beyond Partnership' approach. These were the principles of operation.

In practice, the arrangements appeared to have worked well. During a site visit to prepare this case, all the interviewees stressed the reality of the high levels of collaboration and cooperation between parties, whatever their role or employing firm. Of particular impact were the performance measures used which were deliberately designed to ensure the necessary levels of collaboration were achieved. Indeed, there was a notable loss of individuals' company identity in the people interviewed, and higher levels of apparent empowerment and acceptance of personal responsibility. People defined their team roles in terms of 'belonging to the T5 project'.

Risk

The fundamental of the project was that 'BAA holds all of the risk, all of the time'. This was in contrast to the conventional construction approach, which requires that risk is 'contracted out', thereby in principle reducing the project risk.

There was a strong rationale for BAA's approach. It claimed that this allowed the contractors to focus on the project, problem-solving and enhancing the product, rather than being concerned about avoiding litigation for time delays, for instance, or relying on post-completion claims for making the work profitable. This approach required a high degree of openness on the part of the contractors and removal of local buffers – both of time and cost – to a central pool. Such pooling of risk and contingency has been shown to be superior to localised arrangements.

Moreover, and in many ways unique to the industry, the opportunities were treated in the same way. Conformance to the expectation was the minimum requirement. BAA realised the ambition of allowing structured flexibility, enabling changes and problem-solving, without losing control of the end-product or costs. The aspiration is described in Figure 14.4.

Hierarchies of risk registers (at project, delivery team, functional team and task level) were maintained, as would be expected. Opportunities were managed on an ongoing basis, with the focus being product enhancement and the removal of waste from the value-stream.

Prototyping and in-project learning

A feature of the process was the extensive use of CAD to work out performance and interface issues in advance. Members of delivery teams were required to work on the same software, for instance, and

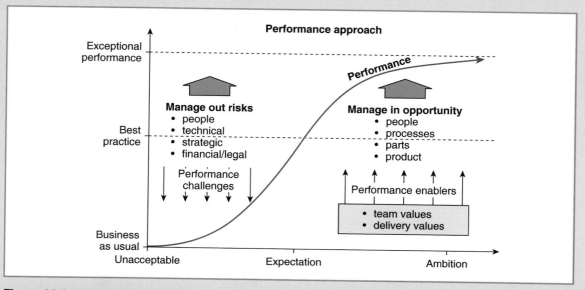

Figure 14.4 BAA's approach to risk

were co-located. In addition, there was extensive use of trialling. The first fixed link – an elevated passenger walkway necessary to link the terminal to aircraft – was installed at the satellite building as a trial study. The result was a considerably streamlined construction process. Indeed, this is just one example of where the repetitive nature of the activities undertaken at the activity level was recognised and treated as a manufacturing process would be.

Confidentiality and Intellectual Property (IP)

The team handbook stated that IP was owned by the provider where it was developed outside the T5 project. A key to teamworking within the project was the sharing of information, and where IP was developed during the project, it became the joint property of BAA and the developer.

The claimed approach was a blend of lean (elimination of waste) and agile (ability to respond to change) project management. The team manual, the integrated process approach adopted, and the extensive use of proactive risk management and intelligent planning led to the conclusion that this programme exhibited a high level of project and programme management maturity, under any set of metrics. Indeed, the environment more closely resembled projects carried out in the automotive, rather than the construction, sector.

Conventional approaches included the use of earned value measures to provide basic financial and progress control, and quality assurance as per ISO 9000. Looking further into the quality management practices, there were many contributory elements, including the product and interface modelling mentioned above and early conflict resolution. The latter of these involved resourced planning – the planning time was considered as a contribution to value-adding activity, and simulation of project as well as product plans was used extensively. Ongoing value definition, engineering and analysis also took place.

The following area of the project scheduling represented a departure from conventional practice.

Scheduling and Last Responsible Moment

In scheduling project activities, including those described above under technology transfer, the information flow in the project was mapped. It was demonstrated that there were many decision points which were critical – if these decisions were delayed, the whole project would be delayed or additional resources would need to be added to downstream activities. In order to make all the parties (including the client, BAA) involved in the process aware of key decision points and this criticality, the team used an approach called the Last Responsible Moment (LRM) for key decisions. This had an additional objective – that the project plan could stay flexible and responsive. The LRM is calculated by backwards scheduling and when established these become 'milestones for information transfer'. These key points of information transfer recognise the reality of design (iterative rather than linear) and provide a visual signal that the next phase of detailed planning is to be commenced by the relevant teams. Such 'planning in waves' again appears to fit well with the reality of the project environment.

Such an approach is an enhancement rather than a radical change of traditional methods of planning and control. It provides a 'managed postponement' of key decisions, particularly those involving trade-offs. Information emerges as the project progresses, and in principle, the later the decision can be made, the more complete the information on which to base that decision is likely to be.

The 50 per cent rule

Prior to final approval of each stage of work, cost targets for 50 per cent of the project must be fixed and for 100 per cent of initial works. This is consistent with the agile planning model. It provides the basis for earned value methods to be used in control, but does not require artificially accurate estimates to be in place before the necessary information is available.

Last Planner

It is reasonable to expect the project to accelerate as it progresses, with Last Planner providing ongoing low-level performance reporting and problem-solving.[10]

Case appendix: Key players

Sponsors	BAA, private investment, HM Government
Lead architect	Richard Rogers Partnership
Strategic planning and design services	Halcrow Group Ltd
Cost consultant services	E C Harris Group Ltd
Cost consultant services	Turner and Townsend Group
Planning supervisor	Bovis Engineering Ltd
Structural tunnel and rail consultant	Mott MacDonald Ltd
Project management and support services	Parsons Brinckerhoff Ltd
Fire engineering services	Warrington Fire Research Consultants
Land surveying services	Mason Land Surveys Ltd
Landscape architect for the project	Hyland Edgar Driver
Design and engineering of the refuelling system	Air BP
Mechanical and electrical contractor services delivery	Carillion Construction Ltd
Airfield pavements delivery	AMEC Civil Engineering Ltd
Civil construction infrastructure and logistics delivery	Laing O'Rourke Civil Engineering Ltd
Design of road infrastructure	KBR (formerly Kellogg, Brown & Root)
Design consultant for campus and airfield pavements	TPS Consult Ltd
Building service delivery team	AMEC Building and Facilities Services
Structural design consultants	Ove Arup & Partners Ltd
Architectural retail design services	Chapman Taylor
Services (mechanical and electrical) design and engineering consultants	DSSR
Roofing design and construction delivery services	Hathaway Roofing Ltd
Architectural station design consultant, architectural production and brief development	HOK International Ltd
Escalator and passenger conveyor services delivery	Kone Escalators Ltd
Construction management	Mace Ltd
Ductwork services delivery	Hotchkiss Ductwork Ltd
Fit-out contractor and fixed links and nodes	Mansell Construction Services Ltd
Production architectural consultant	Pascal & Watson Ltd
Building frame services delivery	Rowen Structures Ltd
Lift services delivery	Schindler Management Ltd
Curtain walling service delivery	Schmidlin (UK) Ltd
Fit-out contractor (interiors)	Warings Contractors Ltd
Signalling communications and control services	Alcatel Telecom Ltd
Building services delivery team	AMEC
Deep bored tunnels delivery	Morgan/VINCI
Track and tunnel (mechanical and electrical) rail design and delivery	Balfour Beatty Rail Projects Ltd
Construction project management services logistics and security	Taylor Woodrow
Environmental monitoring	AEA Technology plc
Archaeological services delivery	Framework Archaeology
Occupational health service	Duradimond Healthcare
Communication infrastructure services delivery	NTL Group Ltd
Temporary accommodation/logistics	Elliott Group

Bussing	Menzies Aviation Group
Catering	Compass Services (UK) Ltd
Raw materials supplier	Foster Yeoman Ltd
Raw materials provider	Baggage Systems
Raw materials provider	Lafarge Cement UK
Track transit design and delivery services	Bombardier Transportation (Holdings) USA Inc
Fixed ground power services delivery	Axa Power
Software assurance services	CSE International Ltd
System integration services	Ultra Electronics Ltd (Ferranti Air Systems Ltd)
High voltage power supply delivery	EDF Energy (Services) Ltd
Supply and installation of building management systems	Novar Projects Ltd
Building structure	Rowen Structures Ltd
Temporary steelwork design	Rolton Group
Lifting jacks	Fagioli PSC
Jacks and hydraulics	Dorman Long Technology
Steelwork manufacture and erection	Watson Steel
Software assurance services	TA Group Ltd (Advantage)
Loading bridge and apron services delivery	ThyssenKrupp Airport Systems SA
Washroom facilities	ADSM plc

Points for discussion

1 How is the approach that BAA has taken here with this project different from the traditional approach to working with suppliers?

2 Why does the company want to 'own all of the risk all of the time'? Surely it is better to outsource risk?

3 Review the press coverage of the opening in March 2008. How did it all go so wrong?

Topics for discussion

1 Consider the way that you make purchases for yourself. How do you decide from whom to buy? Are there examples of your personal purchasing where you have frequented a particular business and formed a partnership-type relationship?

2 Why is the process for procurement so involved? Figure 14.2 contains significant bureaucracy that surely does not help the objective of getting the project completed. Suggest why these processes are in place and how they might be simplified.

3 Why the trend to outsourcing? Suggest how this might or might not be beneficial to a project organisation.

4 Surely it would be better for project managers simply to deal directly with suppliers? Under what circumstances would such an arrangement be beneficial and when would it be inappropriate?

5 You have been offered tickets to your favourite entertainment event of the year by a major potential supplier. The offer includes full corporate hospitality treatment. Should you accept this offer?

6 What are the likely trade-off issues in the purchasing decision, and how would you resolve these?

7 How is the Internet changing the role of the purchasing function? Carry out a search of software vendors and investigate the kinds of features that are being offered here. What are the possible benefits for project managers of these?

8 What is the responsibility of organisations to their suppliers? How might it extend beyond just paying the bill?

9 How successful are government contracting arrangements? How do these compare, for instance, with the arrangements BAA had with their suppliers in

the construction of T5 at Heathrow (Project Management in Practice, this chapter)?

10 Supply chains are complex and can involve many parties. How might you factor in emergencies such as pandemics into your choices of suppliers?

Further information

Aaltonen, K. and Turkulainen, V. (2018) 'Creating relational capital through socialization in project alliances', *International Journal of Operations & Production Management*, Vol. 38, No. 6, pp. 1387–1421.

Acuff, F. (2008) *How to Negotiate Anything With Anyone Anywhere Around the World*, 3rd edition, Amacom, New York.

APM Contracts and Procurement Specific Interest Group (2017) *'APM Guide to Contracts and Procurement'*, Association for Project Management, Princes Risborough.

Baily, P., Farmer, D., Crocker, B., Jessop, D. and Jones, D. (2015) *Procurement Principles and Management*, 11th edition, Financial Times Prentice Hall, Harlow.

Daghar, A., Alinaghian, L. and Turner, N. (2021) 'The role of collaborative interorganizational relationships in supply chain risks: a systematic review using a social capital perspective', *Supply Chain Management: an International Journal,* Vol. 26, No. 2, pp. 279–296.

Fisher, R., Ury, W. and Patten, B. (2011) *Getting to Yes*, 3rd edition, Arrow Books, London.

Harland, C.M., Lamming, R.C. and Cousins, P. (1999) 'Developing the Concept of Supply Strategy', *International Journal of Operations and Production Management*, Vol. 19, No. 7, pp. 650–673.

Holweg M. and Maylor H. (2018) 'Lean leadership in major projects: from "predict and provide" to "predict and prevent"', *International Journal of Operations & Production Management*, Vol. 38, No. 6, pp. 1368–1386.

Meng, X. (2019) 'Lean management in the context of construction supply chains', *International Journal of Production Research*, Vol. 57 No. 11, pp. 3784–3798.

Meng, X. (2020) 'Proactive management in the context of construction supply chains', *Production Planning & Control*, Vol. 31, No. 7, pp. 527–539.

Mishra, A., Sinha, K.K. and Thirumalai, S. (2017) 'Project Quality: The Achilles Heel of Offshore Technology Projects?' *IEEE Transactions on Engineering Management*, Vol. 64, No. 3, pp. 272–286.

Modi, K., Lowalekar, H. and Bhatta, N.M.K. (2019) 'Revolutionizing supply chain management the theory of constraints way: a case study', *International Journal of Production Research*, Vol. 57, No. 11, pp. 3335–3361.

Nevstad, K., Børve, S., Karlsen, A. and Aarseth, W. (2018) 'Understanding how to succeed with project partnering', *International Journal of Managing Projects in Business,* Vol. 11, No. 4, pp. 1044–1065.

von Branconi, C. and Loch, C. (2004) 'Contracting for Major Projects: Eight Business Levers for Top Management', *International Journal of Project Management*, Vol. 22, No. 2, pp. 119–130.

Websites

www.cips.org – The Chartered Institute of Procurement and Supply.

www.ciria.org – Construction Industry Research and Information Association

www.icheme.org/knowledge/forms-of-contract/

www.nec.contract.com – for details of NEC3.

www.nao.org.uk – National Audit Office for analysis of UK Government projects.

References

1   Maylor H., Turner N., and Murray-Webster R. (2015) 'It Worked for Manufacturing...! Operations Strategy in Project-Based Operations.' *International Journal of Project Management,* Vol. 33, No. 1, pp. 103–115.

2   Kraljic P. (1983) 'Purchasing Must Become Supply Chain Management', *Harvard Business Review*, Sept–Oct, pp. 109–117.

3   4th point from Deming, W.E. (1986) *Out of Crisis*, MIT Centre for Advanced Engineering Study, Cambridge, MA.

4   See EU directives on public procurement, https://ec.europa.eu/growth/single-market/public-procurement_en

5   Nevstad, K., Børve, S., Karlsen, A. and Aarseth, W. (2018) 'Understanding how to succeed with project partnering', *International Journal of Managing Projects in Business*, Vol. 11, No. 4, pp. 1044–1065.

6   Turner N., Aitken J. and Bozarth C. (2018) 'A framework for understanding managerial responses to supply chain complexity', *International Journal of Operations and Production Management*, Vol. 38, No. 6, pp. 1433–1466.

7   Frydlinger, D., Hart, O. and Vitasek, O. (2019) 'A New Approach to Contracts. How to Build Better Long-Term Strategic Partnerships', *Harvard Business Review*, Sept–Oct, pp. 116–125.

8   Case prepared in conjunction with Dr David Hancock of Cranfield School of Management.

9   Data from BAA.

10 For a description of this see Chapter 13.

15 Problem-solving and decision-making

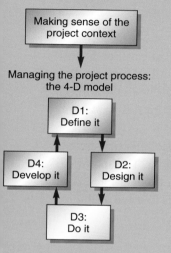

Making sense of the project context

Managing the project process: the 4-D model

D1: Define it

D4: Develop it

D2: Design it

D3: Do it

Principles

1 It happens. What matters is how you deal with it.

2 Complex situations benefit from basic tools to help with sense-making.

3 Establishing basic principles and 'rules of thumb' dramatically improves the success of decision-making processes.

Learning objectives

By the time you have completed this chapter, you should be able to:

→ provide a structure for the identification, definition and solution of problems

→ identify appropriate tools which can be brought to bear at different stages of the problem-solving process

→ show the implications of some of the changes in modern management thinking in the area of decision-making.

Contents

Introduction *370*
15.1 Structuring problems *371*
15.2 Problem analysis *377*
15.3 Decision support *382*
Summary *385*
Key terms *386*
Relevant areas of the Bodies of Knowledge *387*
Project management in practice: *The use of cause–effect–cause analysis* *387*
Topics for discussion *390*
Further information *390*
References *391*

Houston – we have a problem . . .

Preceding one of the most famous landings of all time, pilot Chesley Sullenberger III took off from New York's LaGuardia Airport on 15 January 2009 in an Airbus A320 with 150 passengers on board. Shortly thereafter, US Airways Flight 1549 then suffered an 'impossible' accident, when they hit a flock of Canada geese that disabled both the aircraft's engines. Despite assistance from air traffic control offering a return to LaGuardia

Source: REUTERS/Alamy Stock Photo

or an alternative landing site at nearby Teterboro Airport, Sullenberger and his co-pilot Jeffrey Skiles managed to glide the powerless jet to ditch safely in the Hudson River. All passengers and crew were recovered safely shortly afterwards. The 'Miracle on the Hudson' has been the subject of numerous documentaries, and in 2016 the major film 'Sully' directed by Clint Eastwood and starring Tom Hanks took the story to a worldwide audience.

Pilots have checklists and procedures for eventualities that may occur, but when crisis strikes they have to rely significantly on their experience and judgement in the moment. This expertise is hard to quantify, but it becomes critical at times like these. We hope that you never have such a dangerous moment in your career, but as a project manager part of the role is to solve problems and make decisions under difficult and often fast-moving circumstances.

Introduction

During the execution phase of a project, the project manager will be faced with the need to solve problems and make decisions rapidly and effectively. As it will not be possible to pre-plan all eventualities, the objective of this chapter is to show how such situations can be handled. Some of the techniques are simple enough to be used by almost anyone, though some are considerably more involved. Decision-making is considered as part of a generic problem-solving process.

Price (1984) describes one of the challenges for managers:

> *Business is a risky undertaking. According to those who have devoted their lives to the proper study of mankind, Man is a risk-evasive animal. From what I have seen, risk addicted seems closer to the norm. There is excitement in taking risky decisions and it is possible to get hooked on it; it makes you feel good.*
>
> *Risk, unnecessary risks, are taken by the thousand every day. Often they are unnecessary simply because they are made in the light of inadequate knowledge, but it boosts somebody's self-esteem to make them with an air of omniscience, which is one of the reasons why we are on the whole, such poor quality performers.*

There is another view, namely that the modern project manager is overloaded with data rather than information; the information revolution has provided the means to access large quantities of numbers quickly, often without the means to assimilate them. Handling such a volume of complexity without succumbing to 'data paralysis' is a significant task and one of the value-adding roles that management can play.

The project manager should have the option either to try to provide a structure for making 'rational' decisions or rely on gut-feel and experience and hope that this is appropriate. Much as we would like to have a systematic approach to problems and offer a 'best way', it is notable that the PMI PMBoK Guide calls for 'expert judgement' throughout in dealing with the multiple aspects of project management. Yes, there are many powerful techniques to draw upon, and these are highly beneficial, but professional experience and judgement is also needed in knowing when and how to use the tools in the managerial 'toolbox'.

15.1   Structuring problems

One of the key roles of a manager is to handle problems that challenge them in their own role, as well as being a resource for members of the project team to turn to for help. Problem-solving is a core management skill but, like leadership, one that too often is assumed to be an inbred attribute rather than an acquired skill.

For the purposes of this discussion, a problem is defined as:

The gap between an actual situation or the perception of it and the required or expected situation.

The two properties, expectation and perception, are subjective and based on the viewpoint of the individual (see also the ideas of quality in Chapter 9). Many issues presented to managers fail this definition; people perceive that there is a problem without identifying the gap. Clarifying the reality of the situation with objective measures is a precursor to the problem-solving process. Part of the role of the project manager in this process is the gathering of the possible worldviews. This requires the skill of being involved yet objective.

The nature of the problem determines the point of departure for the manager. This can be categorised as:

- *requiring an immediate reaction* – the timescale of a decision requires a 'conditioned reflex' rather than a 'considered response'. Such a situation would include the threatening of the wellbeing of an individual;
- *response to a crisis* – the problem can be considered within a relatively short time period, i.e. an undesirable state of affairs has occurred – you need to do something about it soon;
- *emerging problem* – some undesirable state of affairs appears likely to happen – what are you going to do to resolve it?
- *response to an opportunity* – speculative problem-solving or avoidance in advance of an undesirable situation (missed opportunity);
- *strategy formulation* – the plotting of a course to a desired situation over a period of years.

The time period of the first kind of problem means that the response or intended solution must be either instinctive (such as to run away) or ingrained through training (to remove the source of potential danger). There is scope in the latter for a major component of any discussion on problem-solving, that of proceduralisation. This is not restricted to emergency situations but is a major component of any work situation today. This proceduralisation or systematisation can be defined as:

The enaction of a predetermined response to a given set of conditions.

The systematisation of problem resolution depends on identifying the situation. The **programmed response** is then initiated, as shown in Figure 15.1.

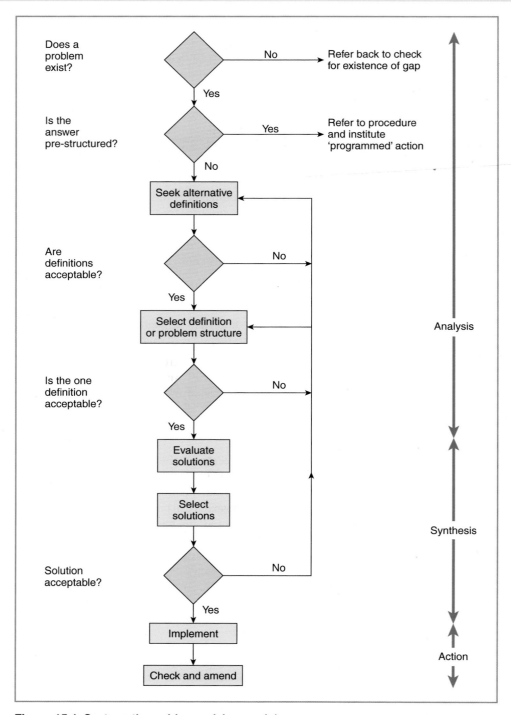

Figure 15.1 Systematic problem-solving model

The preprogramming of actions has a number of advantages:

- once a method has been defined for resolving a situation, it can be refined and improved;
- by removing thought processes from the actions they are, to a great extent, independent of the individual carrying them out;
- if a predetermined procedure is followed, actions are traceable back to the people who carried them out;
- the actions are then the responsibility of the organisation rather than the individual;
- should the procedure fail, the identification of the fail-point is helpful, as the steps can be retraced.

If our organisational procedure manuals are sufficiently detailed, this may suffice. We will have the carefully though-out rules we need, and these can be followed by the staff. However, the reality in projects is that the rules only take you so far, the human element and situation-specific judgement are needed too.[1]

The alternative is that the **problem-solving cycle** is invoked. As for the planning process, the cycle is iterative (involves repetition of steps if the output does not meet recognised or emerging conditions). The remainder of this chapter will consider the possible approaches to problems with a degree of novelty – those that are being solved for the first time and those that are being considered for proceduralisation. There is a downside, not least of which is the removal of the individualism in the performance of that part of the task. No one has yet achieved an effective procedural description for carrying out the job 'as if you cared personally about the outcome'.

The problem-solving model (Figure 15.1) shows the process moving from determining whether a standard procedure exists, to choosing a definition for the problem. Classical problem-solving focuses very heavily on providing a definition for the problem – indeed, it is often stated that 'if you can define the problem you are working with, you are half-way to a solution'. The definition must include the statement of the gap between the two states: actual/perceived situation and desired/expected situation. Without these two, the **problem** is said to be '**unbounded**' and, to all practical purposes, is not amenable to 'problem solving' in the conventional manner.[2]

However, once the problem has been defined, the process can move on to the next stage – the construction of various alternatives. At this point the process leaves the **analysis** of the problem, at least temporarily, and moves to the **synthesis** phase. This transition involves the first major piece of decision-making. The logic of the process is fairly simple at this point – there needs to be a decision made only if there is a choice of definitions or solutions. Where only one exists the implications need to be considered, but without wasting time on non-decisions.

Management styles can be identified at or between the extremes of 'coercive' and 'cooperative'. The natures of the decision-making processes are different. For the former, the project manager would be the key decision-maker. In the latter, many of the decisions would be devolved, either to the individual with the most knowledge or responsibility for this part of the project or to the group as a whole. This devolution removes a large part of the decision-making role of the manager. Part of the process of devolution involves seeking ideas from others. This ensures that the set of possible solutions can bridge the problem gap – and includes '**brainstorming**'.

Brainstorming

Taking a group out of their normal work situation to ponder a problem can be immensely beneficial to both the organisation and the group. The dynamics of the brainstorming process are aided by adherence to a few rules:

- Provide a basic structure to the task of decision-making – groups are generally very bad at looking for structure or logic in decisions.
- The benefit is from the extraction and combination of ideas from a variety of people – the object of the exercise is therefore to facilitate this.
- Give people the opportunity to do some pre-thinking on the problem – the subconscious mind has an enormous capacity and can provide solutions without the input of conscious effort.
- At the start of the meeting an ice-breaking exercise will help people to relax and provide a 'safe environment' for the generation of ideas.
- All ideas must be written down – use whiteboards and 3M's Post-it notes, for example. If the meeting is remote then this can still be done on the screen and shared with all the participants so they can see it.
- Express ideas as the participants state them – paraphrasing removes the original meaning and adds a slant of your own. If in doubt as to the veracity of the point being made, seek clarification.
- Do not allow any criticism of ideas put forward – this will destroy the credibility of that person and you will be unlikely to gain much more from them.
- Do not permit one or a small group of individuals to dominate the proceedings – this will exclude potentially valuable input from others.
- Summarise and record the outcome of the brainstorming session and then circulate it to all those concerned – the after-meeting feedback is a further source of solutions and ideas, as people think of all the things that they would like to have contributed during the session.

Decision-making as a process is the period involving the seeking of alternatives through to the end of the comparative evaluation stage. The inputs to this process are:

- strategic – in order for an organisation to retain coherence the decisions made in the projects that it undertakes need to fit with the overall strategy outlined for the organisation;
- fundamental/political – each person brings their own viewpoint to the decision-making process. This will range in form from bias (often undeclared) to a forthright statement of personal beliefs;
- quantitative modelling;
- subconscious elements – obtaining people's legitimate reservations about a decision can be a preventer of 'group-think' provided that an atmosphere can be created in which people feel free to try to elucidate such thoughts.

The nature of the decision-making process depends on the system that the decision concerns. In Chapter 5 a basic overview of systems was given which showed the application of the input/ controls/output and mechanisms model to a project system. Further examination of this is needed to determine whether it is:

- an open system – having interaction with systems outside through the flows of material or information;
- a closed system – being self-sustaining in informational and material terms, operating in isolation.

It is tempting when considering systems to look for the closed-system model. If this is possible, the modelling process involves defining variables from within the system and then optimising these. In most projects, however, this leads to inappropriate models of behaviour being constructed, as they do not show the dynamic nature of the interchange between the systems and their external environments, i.e. they are open systems.

The use of open-system models is not as attractive, however, as by definition they require the variables from external factors to be continuously introduced and the nature of the environment to be dynamic and inherently unstable. This instability is reflected in a tendency for the behaviour of the system to be unpredictable, and hence the need for the risk and uncertainty management practices developed in previous chapters, and the need for agile approaches.

Modelling systems for decision-making

A study published over 60 years ago[3] identified the reasons for poor decision-making as being:

- data not properly ordered or structured;
- too much time spent developing answers to problems rather than the statement of the problem;
- an inability on the part of the decision-makers to consider all the variables/factors involved;
- an inability to evaluate the impact of extraneous factors.

Given the problems faced by many project managers and the evidence from the case studies covered so far, it appears that not much has changed over this time. While there exists very cheap means of processing large quantities of data, the volume of data that the modern organisation can generate has increased accordingly. Although there appears to be little excuse now for the data not to be properly ordered or structured (the ease of preparation of graphs and other graphical techniques should have removed this as a cause) the sheer complexity of the data that many programme and project managers have to handle can be literally overwhelming. One programme manager we interviewed had so much data coming in from the projects he was overseeing, he spent 3 days each week making sense of it and reporting summaries of it up to his senior management team.

The same argument could also be applied to the third of Drucker's points, as the ability to build more data into decision-making models has been greatly enhanced. The second and fourth of the factors are procedurally linked to the decision-making process and are only removed by:

- increased awareness of the potential of both of these to affect the process;
- focus on the removal of the damaging effects of poor decisions, i.e. make the decisions more robust.

There has been a considerable growth in the use of sophisticated models in decision-making. The application of scientific models to the solving of management problems has developed into a specialist branch of management known as '**management science**' or '**operational research**'. The temptation is to view the output of management science analysis as having a high degree of truth, because the mathematical models that are used are very difficult for a lay person to dispute. In reality, management science is one of the tools that can be employed in decision-making, rather than being the totality of the process.

The model of the system may take on one of many forms, including:

- a descriptive model – using words or graphical means to describe the action or performance of a system, e.g. systemigrams;
- a geometric model – expressing an object in a mathematical form (as used in computer-aided design systems);
- a mechanistic model – determining the inputs to and outputs from a system;
- static predictive – taking a limited picture of the state of a system at a particular point in time and using various mathematical techniques to predict the future performance;
- a dynamic predictive model – a 'real-time system' which takes a constant review of the inputs to a system, providing the most up-to-date forecast of future performance.

Taking a generic view of the modelling process, a model of a system is defined as:

A system which is constructed under controlled conditions, whose behaviour mimics that of another system where it would not be possible for those conditions to be controlled (economically or physically).

The benefits of using modelling during projects are:[4]

- time contraction – it is often possible to speed up events to show the effects of time on a system and use it in the prediction as to what will happen after a period of time, without necessarily waiting that long;
- **what-if** – the decision-makers have the option to manipulate a model and determine a range of scenarios based on their own individual predictions of the conditions as to what the external environment for the system will be;
- error avoidance/detection – there are many systems that can shadow the decisions made by others and act as a coarse filter for marginal decisions or ones where there has been an error. Such systems are often used both in mechanical design and stock-market trading.

In addition:

- it is possible to examine the fundamental assumptions on which a model was based;
- parameters can be optimised without the need for potentially expensive trial and error with reality;
- the sensitivity to external effects can be measured.

Modelling involves a cycle of activities as used in the project planning cycle – that is, the model is designed, built, tested and then amended based on the comparison of the performance of the real system and the model. The model is then updated based on this performance. The process itself involves:

- making assumptions about the behaviour of systems;
- simplification of the system parameters;
- estimation of the likely values of unrelated variables.

A Gantt chart is one model of a project system. Properly constructed, it presents one view of the project. A risk analysis is another view. A cost-benefit model another. A systems diagram, another. All of these are valid and potentially useful models for understanding projects, but each is incomplete. For instance, Chapter 7 showed how the failure to include uncertainty in a basic project plan resulted in instability in the schedule. As a model of a project system, the plan is incomplete. It is ONE view – it must not be THE view. Chapter 1 demonstrated the benefits of using *multiple perspectives* on projects – that is, to take not just a planning view, but also to consider wider issues – stakeholders, politics, team inter-actions, processes, strategy and more.[5] A strategic approach to modelling is therefore part of the skillset of the modern project manager.

Scenario planning

A key tool in the toolbox of the project leader is scenario planning.[6,7] There are many potential approaches to trying to predict the future, and modelling using quantitative data is increasingly powerful, but in reality is less good at preparing a team for the range of outcomes that a project might face. Modelling provides you with **probable** futures. While helpful, this should be supplemented by the consideration of **plausible** futures. Years ago, this was easy to dismiss in many industries, because after all, while technology changes, what is going to completely disrupt the way we do business? Answer: global financial crisis (2008), ongoing social upheaval in so many countries, Brexit for UK and the EU, and (as if we need reminding) Covid in 2020 and beyond. While each of these scenarios had been considered, they were rated as improbable by many. This demonstrates that a tool that focuses on generating plausible options for the future is worthwhile. This may, for instance, encourage the deployment of more flexible strategies for project delivery, or a different form of relationship with stakeholders.

The use of scenario planning requires the participants to focus not on looking forward from today, but to consider the assumptions of the day, and to challenge them. This is not always easy to do, particularly for a project team that may be from a single discipline, e.g. a team of engineers. However, the longer the project and the earlier you can try this, the more worthwhile it is.

15.2 Problem analysis

Uncertainty

There are two approaches to handling uncertainty – dealing with the cause and dealing with the effects. Risk and opportunities management in projects is deliberately structured to take advantage of both of these approaches.

As an example, a company is about to launch a new product onto a market in which it has previously operated. It feels that there is a considerable degree of uncertainty as to whether the new product will be a success. There are a number of possible routes open to it:

- first, analyse the causes of the uncertainty and minimise these, and using the best data available, suggest possible sales scenarios for this product;
- second, look for options for how to respond to the given various scenarios – both good and bad.

The scenarios generated are not 'the picture' – they simply paint 'a number of possible pictures' which the organisation may find itself in. The first looks at handling the cause of a problem, the uncertainty inherent with product volume forecasting, and tries to remove it. The second accepts that variability exists and focuses on the task of pre-evaluating various management strategies given various sets of conditions. The point is that the modelling activity is only the first part of a process of decision-making. As will be shown, there are a number of well-developed techniques to support this activity.

Table 15.1 The use of mathematical modelling techniques

Technique	Description
Simulation	Computer modelling of a scenario
Linear programming	Optimal allocation of restricted resources to maximise or minimise a variable (such as price or cost)
Network analysis through CPM or PERT	Obtaining the logic of both precedence relationships and time requirements in a project environment through graphical means (see Chapters 5 and 6)
Queuing theory	Shows how a system reacts when faced with a random (stochastic) customer who demands the services of that system
Decision trees	Graphical method for describing the flow of decisions depending on the possibilities available at each juncture. May be pursued as a statement of possibilities or with statistical analysis

Mathematical modelling techniques

The use of mathematical models in decision-making is widespread, ranging from basic spreadsheet calculations to the most advanced statistical techniques. Table 15.1 indicates the most-used techniques and a description of their usage. Each of these techniques requires a different level of mathematical skill to use effectively and each would justify a chapter to itself.[8]

Problem-solving tools

The basic problem-solving tools of the project manager include **Pareto analysis** and **Ishikawa/fishbone diagrams**.

Pareto analysis

Vilfredo Pareto was an economist who in 1906 published his finding that 80 per cent of the wealth of Milan was held by 20 per cent of the people. This 80/20 'rule' often recurs – many companies find that 80 per cent of their profits are generated by 20 per cent of their products or services (see Figure 15.2) or that 20 per cent of their clients provide 80 per cent of their business. The Pareto principle applied to problem-solving means that part

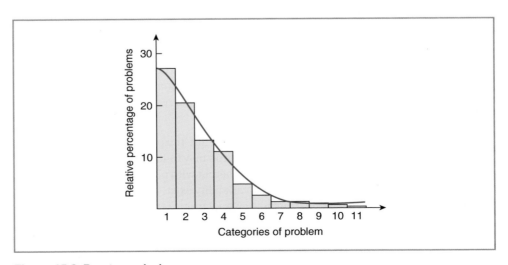

Figure 15.2 Pareto analysis

of the initial analysis is to discover which 20 per cent of causes are causing 80 per cent of the problems. The effort of the problem-solvers can then be focused on establishing solutions to the major factors. The principle is, stated simply, to apply effort where it is going to yield the greatest result.

Ishikawa/fishbone diagrams

The fishbone diagram is a simple graphical technique which can help to structure a problem and guide a team into seeking further information about the nature of the system under consideration. The effect is shown on the right-hand end of Figure 15.3. The causes are then broken down into categories and these are then further deconstructed to show what contributes to that problem from those categories.

The problem of late delivery of software to clients is considered in the example shown in Figure 15.3. The problem is broken down into four main subject areas – management of the team, specification of the software, the people in the development team and the hardware on which they are working. Each of these is then broken down further. The predominant cause is shown by highlighting the particular area – in this case it is the changing of the specification during development.[9]

Cause–effect–cause analysis

Several challenges frequently emerge during the problem-solving process:

- the problem is complex and difficult to structure;
- people enter the discussions with solutions in mind rather than the analysis of the problem itself.

This leads either to stagnation in the process due to the inability to handle the complexity or to inappropriate solutions being given lengthy discussion time. Neither of these is likely

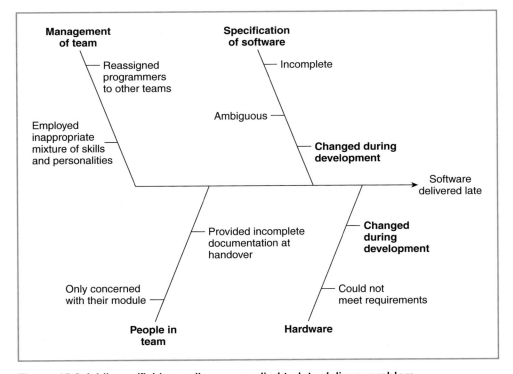

Figure 15.3 Ishikawa/fishbone diagram applied to late delivery problem

to promote good decision-making. Among the problem-solving techniques that have sought to overcome these challenges is **cause–effect–cause analysis**. This is appropriate where:

- a trained, literate and skilful facilitator is available;
- the group is open to consideration of new problem-solving methods.

The objective is to analyse what the group states to be the undesirable effects of the problem (the gap) to find the root cause or causes. These can then be systematically addressed, rather than attention being focused on the effects. This is an excellent way to bound a problem and come up with a detailed description of its nature. Used as above it can be very powerful. It has been found from experience to be less useful for solving tactical problems than for strategic ones, due to the level of input required from team members to keep the logic strong.

One technique inherited from Japanese quality control techniques asks why a problem occurs five times (the 'five whys'). This gets close to the root of the problem, though it is likely to suggest a single root cause rather than, as often happens, several. The process is similar for constructing cause–effect–cause analysis – for the tool to work, the logic has to be preserved in both the reality of the effects listed (do they exist?) and for the linking of causes to effects.

The task order should be completed as follows. It looks odd to start with but, like the construction of network diagrams, will become clear once you have practised using it.

- List the effects of the problem you are tackling – development projects are always delivered late, for example. These must all be real entities, i.e. it must be agreed that these do exist as statements in their own right.
- Start with this as one bubble in the middle of a page (see Figure 15.4).
- Select another of the effects and show how this relates to the first – either as a cause or an effect. Show the result as in Figure 15.5. This should then be read as: IF A THEN B, e.g. IF [it rains tomorrow] THEN [we will not be able to complete the site testing].
- Select other effects and build these round the first two. Many will be interlinked, though at first sight they appeared unrelated. Go as far as you can, again each time checking the links you have made to ensure that the logic is followed.
- Where one cause has a number of effects, this should be drawn as in Figure 15.6.
- Where there is more than one cause linked to an effect, this should be as Figure 15.7, if there is dependency on both of them, i.e. IF [A] AND [B] THEN [C]. If the dependency is on either [A] OR [B] for [C] to exist, this is drawn without the 'banana' linking the two.

It is often necessary during the course of constructing the diagrams both to amend the entities and to add others, e.g. in the example that follows the link between [doesn't allocate time well] and [permanently tired] is not entirely logical. The additional entity [goes to bed late] was added to keep the logic flow. It was obviously necessary to check, as before, that this entity was real. The example shows how a problem concerning the poor performance of a person was analysed. The limited set of effects was listed as:

> [Bill's work performance is poor]
> [He works slower]
> [He has a bad attitude to work]
> [He is often late]
> [He is permanently tired at work]
> [He appears more interested in fishing]
> [He does not allocate his time well]

These are then formed into the diagram shown in Figure 15.8. The additional entities and logic links are a matter of opinion to some degree. A further example of how this technique can be used to structure problems is included at the end of this chapter.[10]

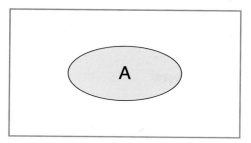

Figure 15.4 Entity A

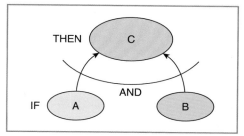

Figure 15.5 IF A THEN B

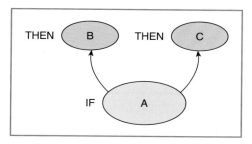

Figure 15.6 IF A THEN B AND C

Figure 15.7 IF A AND B THEN C

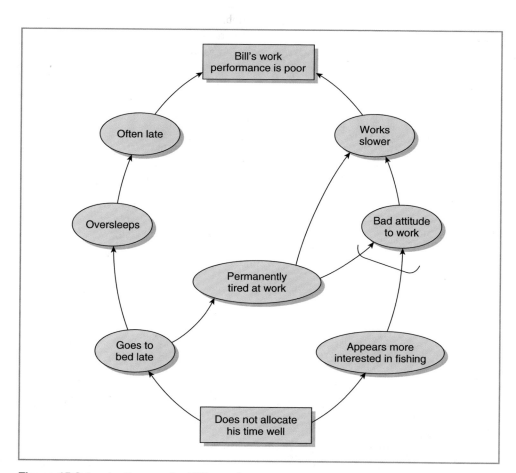

Figure 15.8 Logic diagram for Bill's performance

15.3 Decision support

Decision trees

A technique similar in format to the cause–effect–cause analysis, **decision trees** can be treated at a simple qualitative level or by detailed consideration through the addition of probabilities/distributions to each of the events.

The decision points are shown as squares while possible outcomes are shown as circles. The possibilities and implications of decisions are therefore clearly identified provided that all the decision points are shown. The treatment of the structure has merit in its simplicity and speed of construction. Further analysis of the probabilities of the chance events occurring can be made, providing a means for assessing the likelihood of needing contingency plans. The use of 'expected value' measurements can be both derived from and applied to this tool. The likelihood of the outcome of an event is assessed, and the cost/benefit in monetary terms calculated based on this outcome. The expected value of the branches can then be calculated from the sum of the subsequent expected values. A simple practical example to illustrate this is given below, although most real applications are necessarily more complicated.

Example

A decision has to be made on whether to fund project X or project Y. Each has two possible outcomes. For X, it has a 75 per cent chance of yielding £100 000 but a 25 per cent chance of yielding only £20 000. For Y, it has a 50 per cent chance of yielding £200 000 and a 50 per cent chance that there will be no yield. The decision tree in Figure 15.9 illustrates the problem.

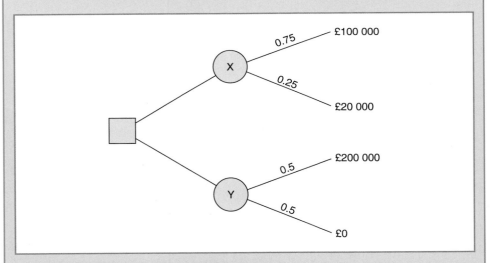

Figure 15.9 Decision tree: project X versus project Y

The financial decision is based on the sum of the expected values of the yields of each branch of the decision tree:

For project X – expected value = (0.75 × 100 000) + (0.25 × 20 000) = 80 000
For project Y – expected value = (0.5 × 200 000) + (0.5 × 0) = 100 000.

The assumption is that we wish to maximise the yield, therefore project Y should be pursued.
This method is attractive in that relatively complex models can be constructed and evaluated quickly. The figures for probabilities and values of return are both a matter of prediction, so the outcome will be determined by the quality of the data with which the model is provided.

Simple decision frameworks

Many complex decisions are best made if they can be broken down into the desirable elements of the outcome of that decision. Techniques for aiding in this process include the use of **attribute analysis** and **force-field analysis**.

Attribute analysis involves breaking down the decision into a set of desirable outcomes. These are then placed alongside the choices in the decision process and rated accordingly. For example, a company wishes to choose a supplier for a project. There are five alternative suppliers (A to E) which are arranged across the top of the table, as shown in Table 15.2. The desirable outcomes are arranged down the table (knowledge and experience, reputation, etc.). The manager of the team can then rate the individual suppliers on their perception of how they will perform on each of those outcomes/attributes. The rating is given out of ten (where 1 = very bad, 10 = excellent), and then totalled for each supplier.

This form of attribute analysis assumes that each of the attributes is of equal importance. Where one is considerably more important than another (e.g. reliability of delivery times may be vital if this is a critical path activity), it can be given an increased weighting, making the score out of 30, say, for that attribute. The totals are viewed in the same way as before. This is clearly a fairly arbitrary means of arriving at the decision, however it is simple to construct and allows a degree of traceability back to how a decision was made. It also enables people to have a discussion on each of the attributes and come up with some relatively objective measure.

Table 15.2 Supplier selection using unweighted attributes

Attribute	A	B	C	D	E
Knowledge and experience	6	7	7	9	8
Reputation	6	6	7	9	10
Prone to strikes/bankruptcy	4	6	9	9	9
Significance of their support	4	8	7	9	9
Design appreciation and conformance	7	7	8	8	9
QA system	5	6	8	9	9
Defects and warranty claims to date	7	6	8	9	10
Reliability of delivery times	6	6	6	9	10
Cost control	7	6	7	6	6
Service level	8	7	8	8	10
Total	60	65	75	85	90

Force-field analysis examines the strengths of different influences on a decision. This is best illustrated through the following example (see Figure 15.10). The decision to stand for election to a representative body (student's union council, parish or town council, club committee, etc.) has a number of implications. First, the time input to get elected may be substantial and the fear of losing the election significant. There is an opportunity cost – other work has to be put off until after the project is complete (which generally proves to be a poor career move, at least in the short term). There are benefits, such as the requirement to take a new view on a subject and to discuss issues that affect your life. It may improve your CV and career prospects. A major consideration is also whether you want to be elected. These influences can then be rated on a 0–5 scale as being positive (stand for election) or negative (find something better to do). The influences with some numbers assigned are shown in Figure 15.10. As can be seen by summing the positive (+12) and negative (−9) influences and subtracting the negative from the positive, the decision was positive.

Decision-support systems

The principle which **decision-support systems** embrace is that there is sufficient knowledge existing for the subject to be considered complex, and therefore can be better interpreted through the abilities of computers to deal with large amounts of information. The knowledge must exist within the system, and this is provided through the contribution of experts in the relevant subjects.

The most basic form of decision-support system is a database. The data is structured in 'fields' which the database system can manipulate and structure as required. One example from the UK is the database of poisons held at Llandough Hospital in Cardiff – the effects of the poison, and its antidote or appropriate treatment, are held on a central computer which other hospitals can access remotely or by telephone. The decision on the appropriate form of treatment is taken without the need for guesswork by the treating doctor. Another use of the information on that database is to track back from the symptoms to the nature of the poison.

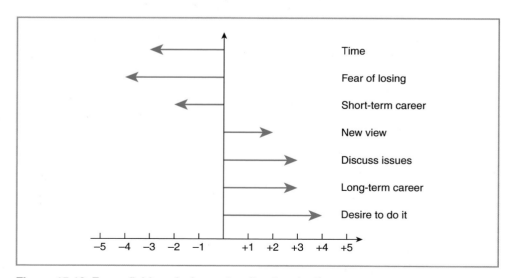

Figure 15.10 Force-field analysis on standing for election

Artificial Intelligence (AI) has been widely called a 'general purpose technology' (Schwab, WEF) and 'the new electricity' (Professor Ng, Stanford) yet its impact in project management is only just being felt.

Today, AI is being used to help project professionals to gain **new insights into** past and current project performance behaviours, **sense** the project environment in real time, make faster and more accurate **decisions** about project activities, **invent** and **optimise** new and richer project scenarios more cheaply, and **respond** more quickly to events.

For instance:

- **Unsupervised machine learning** allows business leaders to group projects by the similarity of their performance and drivers so that they can pin-point and maximise the effectiveness of policy changes.
- **Topic modelling** allows project evaluators to extract critical success and failure factors for completed projects, based on empirical evidence.
- **Internet of Things** sensors provide streaming data from field sensors on construction equipment and personnel to **supervised machine learning classification** algorithms that can perform real-time condition diagnosis. This can improve safety and site productivity.
- **Building Information Modelling, digital twinning** and **augmented reality** are simulation technologies that are supported by artificial intelligence to help project leaders, designers, lenders and end-users to imagine new urban futures, rapidly prototype new energy efficient designs, optimise constructability, streamline end-to-end project activities through object tagging, and troubleshoot more problem scenarios more richly and cheaply.
- **Graph modelling** and **graph reasoning** allows relational project data to be represented in more realistic ways to improve the ability of project managers to predict important project key performance indicators.

The future for AI in project management is exciting with many social and technical challenges to overcome for projects. **Unified AI** models and **expansive training data, including higher quality simulation data** that combine many of the above capabilities will increase both the **strategic** and **operational** value of AI to project-owning organisations. Increasing **model interpretability**, dealing with **data bias** and **minority cases**, improving **privacy preservation** methods, reducing **deep-learning** training data burdens, and increasing the diversity of **people from society** in training data and model development, will improve social attitudes towards AI in project management, for the benefit of all.

Text provided by Cuong Quang, Co-founder and Executive Director,
Octant AI, www.octantai.com

Summary

■ Problems will arise during projects – that is one certainty that you can rely on! As for other project issues, some structure to the thinking and some tools for the process greatly help the project manager in managing towards a successful conclusion. The first stage in this is to define the issue. We defined a problem as the gap between perceptions of an actual situation and that of the expected or required situation. Furthermore, problems may be categorised according to the required reaction time and the nature of the response required – for instance, responses may be predetermined through procedures or reasoned through the problem-solving cycle.

■ To assist the process, a model may be constructed either qualitatively (through descriptive modelling) or quantitatively (through mathematical modelling) to provide one representation of reality which can be tested under controlled conditions. As we saw during the discussion of risk in Chapter 10, uncertainty can be handled either through statistical means, calculating the most likely set of events, or through managerial action to make the system more robust to the effects of uncertainty. Various mathematical tools can be employed to take away the need for subjective decision-making in some areas, while providing decision support in others. Other methods to help in the problem-solving process include the following:

- Ishikawa/fishbone diagrams provide a graphical method for structuring problems; Pareto analysis provides a guide as to which problems to tackle first.
- Cause–effect–cause analysis provides a graphical technique for finding the 'root' of a problem through structuring the logic of the situation.
- Decision trees where the route that actions take can be graphically evaluated and probabilities then assigned to each route if required.

■ Decision-support systems do not eliminate the need for gut-feel and experience, however – indeed they should be better at capturing these elements. They have a vital role to play in decision-making – an area that is central to the discussion of 'what managers do'. Moreover, the increase in the availability of data and sophisticated modelling systems doesn't appear to have made the job of managing projects any easier, or any more successful. Perhaps this is because a modelling process will usually only focus on one viewpoint of a project. The core skill in decision-making is in acquiring multiple viewpoints on an issue – not relying on a single view. Again, the PMI PMBoK Guide is over 750 pages long, and still calls on 'expert judgement' throughout. This highlights that project management is both an art and a science, and we cannot fully outsource these decisions to a system, tool or process. Ultimately it is the manager's decision.

Key terms

analysis *p. 373*

artificial intelligence *p. 385*

attribute analysis *p. 383*

brainstorming *p. 373*

cause–effect–cause analysis *p. 380*

decision frameworks *p. 383*

decision-support systems *p. 384*

decision trees *p. 382*

force-field analysis *p. 383*

Ishikawa/fishbone diagrams *p. 378*

management science/ operational research *p. 375*

Pareto analysis *p. 378*

problem-solving cycle *p. 373*

programmed response *p. 371*

synthesis *p. 373*

unbounded problem *p. 373*

what-if *p. 376*

Relevant areas of the Bodies of Knowledge

While both Bodies of Knowledge refer to decision-making, neither focuses explicitly on the problem-solving process. To some extent, the issue is dealt with procedurally through the risk and quality management processes that have been described elsewhere, but there are no specific sections covering the topic.

PROJECT MANAGEMENT IN PRACTICE
The use of cause–effect–cause analysis

A board meeting was held at the Mighty Sealing Company. There was growing concern about the competitive environment in which the company was operating. Board members were asked to state what they felt the major problems were. They highlighted eight issues. These were:

1 existing market is in decline;

2 sales people do not sell effectively;

3 we have insufficient sales support material;

4 we have an inadequate entry barrier (to the markets in which we operate);

5 we are confused as to which products we should sell;

6 we are unable to exploit new markets;

7 we do not really understand our market environment;

8 there is increasing competition.

These problems or 'undesirable effects' (UDEs) provided the basis for constructing the logic diagram (the 'current reality tree'). Other entities (or logic elements) were introduced to the tree to clarify the logic (see Figure 15.11). The current reality tree shows that there are many effects (including the most significant – the decline in sales volume), but that there is one major cause over which the company has some control – UDE no. 7 [we do not really understand our market environment]. This finding provided the basis for the next steps.

In order to start to resolve the issues faced, the same form of logic diagramming was used. The result: the 'future reality tree' where the root causes are put in place to result in a particular desired effect (in this case sales volume grows). This is shown in Figure 15.12.

The method shown allowed a complex problem to be addressed in a systematic way, and initiatives put in place to help understand the processes that were taking place. How these would contribute to the desired objective could then be mapped.[11]

Points for discussion

1 What is the benefit of constructing a 'current reality tree'?

2 Why is it necessary to insert additional elements into the tree?

3 Why would focusing on 'selling effectiveness' lead to a better understanding of the market?

4 Evaluate the 'future reality tree' – does it resolve the UDEs listed at the start of the exercise?

→

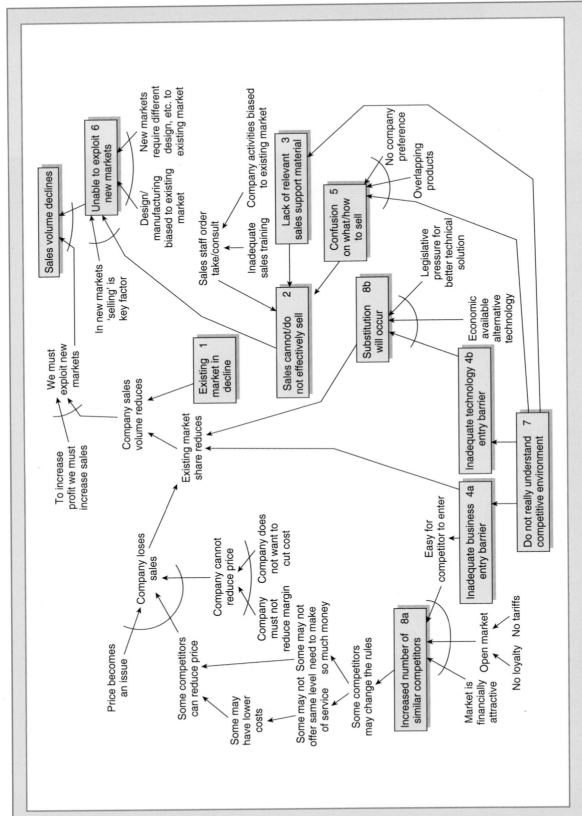

Figure 15.11 Current reality tree

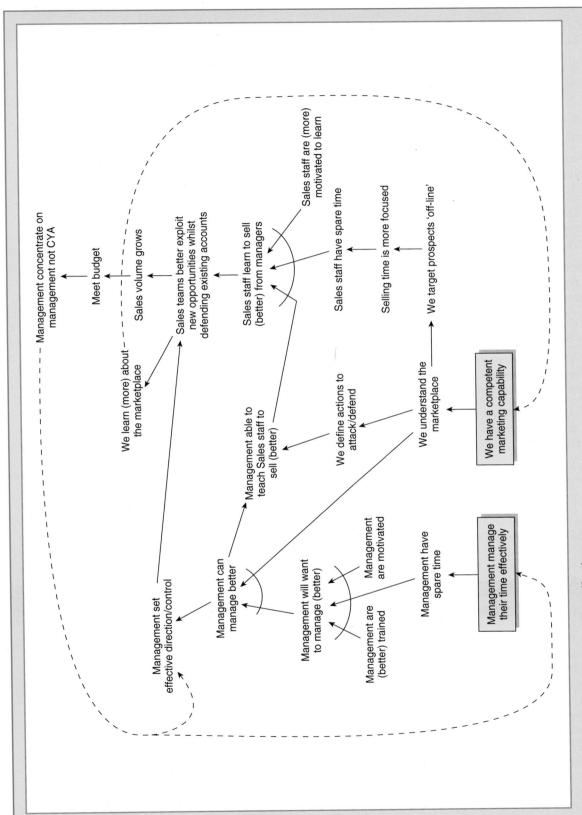

Figure 15.12 Future reality tree: selling effectiveness

Topics for discussion

1 Discuss the statement made by Price in the introduction to this chapter that people are risk-addicted. How do you feel about this personally?

2 How might the tools outlined in this chapter reduce the risk in decision-making?

3 Show the advantages of having preprogrammed actions:

(a) as part of a health and safety policy – for example, in the event of a fire
(b) in the handling of client enquiries
(c) for the installation of new work procedures.

4 Show the effect of time on problem-solving and give practical examples of each of the different timescales.

5 What is the role of 'brainstorming' and how might it be used to greatest effect?

6 What are the major inputs to the decision-making process and how might these be best harnessed to ensure that the decision-making process is effective?

7 What are the basic forms of systems model? Give an example of each and their role in a project environment.

8 As a project manager in a development activity for a new range of computer software, discuss how uncertainty may be handled.

9 You are the coordinator of a moderately complex project. The following problems have arisen during the execution phase of previous projects with the resulting delays as shown. Use an appropriate technique to show which of the problems you would focus your attention on and show the results of your analysis graphically.

Problem	Delay (days)
Late delivery from suppliers	36
Last-minute redesign of assembly due to customer change of specification	7
Suppliers fail to meet the quality levels required in goods supplied	41
Schedule did not leave enough time for testing	5
Components did not fit together when assembled	6
Customer rejected initial trial system	12
Engineer left team during the project	16
Office move was scheduled for during the completion phase	5
Hauliers' firm sacked by customer due to dispute over delivery times	3

10 Select a problem with which you have been involved, and use the Ishikawa/fishbone diagram to structure the causes of the problem. Indicate what you feel to be the biggest causal factor.

Further information

Adair, J. (2009) *Effective Decision Making: The Essential Guide to Thinking for Management Success*, Pan Books, London.

Ahern, T., Leavy, B. and Byrne, P.J. (2014) 'Complex project management as complex problem solving: A distributed knowledge management perspective', *International Journal of Project Management*, Vol. 32, No. 8, pp. 1371–1381.

Goldratt, E. (1995) *It's Not Luck*, North River Press, New York.

Goodwin, P. and Wright, P. (2014) *Decision Analysis for Management Judgement*, 5th edition, John Wiley & Sons, Chichester.

Johansen, A. and Rolstadås, A. (2017) 'Decision process in one-of-a-kind production', *Production Planning & Control*, Vol. 28, No. 10, pp. 802–812.

Kahneman D. (2012) *Thinking, Fast and Slow*, Penguin, London.

Loch, C., Mähring, M. and Sommer, S. (2017) 'Supervising Projects You Don't (Fully) Understand', *California Management Review*, Vol. 59, No. 2, pp. 45–67.

Nutt, P. and Wilson, D. (2010) *Handbook of Decision Making*, Blackwell, Oxford.

Price, F. (1984) *Right First Time*, Wildwood House, London, p. 66.

Rivett, P. (1994) *The Craft of Decision Modelling*, Wiley, Chichester.

Stingl, V. and Geraldi, J. (2017) 'Errors, lies and misunderstandings: Systematic review on behavioural decision making in projects', *International Journal of Project Management*, Vol. 35, No. 2, pp. 121–135.

References

1   Turner N., Kutsch E., Maylor H. and Swart J. (2020) 'Hits and (near) misses. Exploring managers' actions and their effects on localised resilience', *Long Range Planning*, Vol. 50, No. 3, pp. 1–17.

2   Hancock, D.J. (2004) 'What New Skills Must Project Managers Master to Deliver Successful Project Outcomes for the Future?' Engineering Management Conference 2004, *IEEE International*, Vol. 3, pp. 944–948.

3   Drucker, P. (1956) 'How to Make a Business Decision', *Nation's Business*, The Chamber of Commerce of the US.

4   Jennings, D. and Wattam, S. (1998) *Decision-Making: An Integrated Approach*, 2nd edition, Pitman Publishing, London.

5   Winter, M. and Sczepanek, A. (2009) *Images of Projects*, Gower Publishing, Aldershot.

6   Ramirez, R., and Wilkinson, A. (2016) *Strategic reframing: The Oxford scenario planning approach*, Oxford University Press.

7   Ramirez, R., Churchhouse, S., Palermo, A., and Hoffmann, J. (2017) 'Using scenario planning to reshape strategy', *MIT Sloan Management Review*, Vol. 58, No. 4, pp. 31–37.

8   For a detailed discussion of linear and integer programming, and queueing theory, see for example Anderson, D.R., Sweeney, D.J., Williams, T.A., Camm, J.D, Cochran, J.J, Fry. M.J and Ohlmann J.W. (2015) *Quantitative Methods for Business*, 13th edition, Cengage Learning, Boston, MA.

9   Further problem-solving tools may be found in: Bicheno, J. (2002) *The Quality 75, Towards Six Sigma Performance in Service and Manufacturing*, Picsie Books, Buckingham, and Mizuno, S. (ed) (1988) *Management for Quality Improvement: The 7 New QC Tools*, Productivity Press, New York.

10 For further developments of this technique see Goldratt, E. (1993) *Theory of Constraints*, North River Press, New York.

11 For further discussion and elaboration of these techniques see Scheinkopf, L. (2003) *Thinking for a Change*, St Lucie Press, Boca Raton, FL.

Managing the project process: the 4-D model

D4: Develop it

Making sense of the project context

> 1 Introduction
> 2 Structures and frameworks
> 3 Projects and organisations

Managing the project process: the 4-D model

D1: Define it
4 Setting up for success
5 Planning for success

D4: Develop it
16 Completing projects and learning to improve

D2: Design it
6 Time planning and scheduling
7 Making time planning robust: Advanced Project Thinking (APT)
8 Building a business case for a project
9 Engaging stakeholders
10 Managing risks and opportunities

D3: Do it
11 Organising people in the project
12 Leading people in projects
13 Monitoring and controlling the project
14 Procuring, contracting, and working with supply chains
15 Problem-solving and decision-making

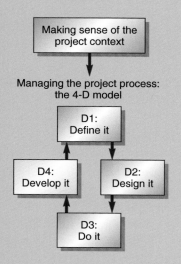

16 Completing projects and learning to improve

'We don't carry out "lessons learned reviews" at the end of projects now. We carry out "lessons identified reviews". We know we don't learn.'
(Programme Manager, major UK government agency)

Principles

1 Ongoing learning and improvement are vital for both individuals and organisations.

2 Projects are excellent opportunities for learning and improvement.

3 Unless planned, scheduled and incentivised, learning and improvement don't happen.

Learning objectives

By the time you have completed this chapter, you should be able to:

→ identify the steps required to complete the project and start the final phase – that of process improvement

→ recognise the mechanisms for learning and process improvement

→ provide a business case to justify such activity through analysing cost of quality.

Contents

Introduction   *395*
16.1   Completion and handover   *397*
16.2   Reviews and learning   *401*
16.3   Improving and maturing   *412*
Summary   *420*
Key terms   *421*
Relevant areas of the Bodies of Knowledge   *422*
Project management in practice: *IT all goes pear-shaped at VCS*   *423*
Topics for discussion   *428*
Further information   *428*
References   *429*

The Vasa Warship

It is a reasonable assumption that organisations should get better at what they do over time. Expertise is developed, ways of working are refined, positive and beneficial practices are promoted, past mistakes are identified and not repeated. Structures can be put in place to do this, and investment in the effort is worthwhile. Reality, though, shows this to be particularly challenging, and it is far from a modern phenomenon.

Source: Kalin Eftimov/Shutterstock

One particularly catastrophic case is from the 17th century. The Swedish King Gustavus Adolphus ordered a huge new warship, the Vasa,[1,2] to be built. Over the course of several years he commanded that the length be increased, a new gun deck be added, and more and bigger guns be fitted. In addition, the delivery date was brought forward. The revised size and weight meant that this was outside of the expertise of the shipbuilder, Henrik Hybertson, who did not have the mathematics to model how the ship would perform and was concerned about its stability. They had no experience of such a large and heavy design. However, who would go against the king's wishes? Despite concerns, the project continued. Hybertson died before completion, leaving the construction in the hands of a less experienced manager. As a final flourish, it was adorned with 700 heavy ornaments and sculptures which it was not designed to carry. At this point it was very much outside the designers' expertise, and there were significant concerns about whether it would remain stable and safe to operate. A simple stability test was performed, with 30 sailors running from one side to the other. This caused huge movements and the test was halted. Despite this vital new knowledge, changes were not made. Shortly thereafter, on 10 August 1628, the magnificent vessel was formally launched to great fanfare. Despite the huge challenges and multiple changes during its construction, 300 sailors sailed out into the open sea. Disastrously, having sailed only 1300 metres, the Vasa keeled over and sunk to the bottom of Stockholm harbour, with the tragic loss of 53 lives.

In the end no individual was held accountable, but there is a lot we can learn. Constant changes, tight deadlines, and untried technology are a dangerous mix in new product development. A lack of knowledge is not necessarily a big problem – that is part of the territory – but a failure to acknowledge the unknown can well be. Learning in and from projects, capturing and sharing knowledge and using this to improve, and ensuring the final product is fit for purpose before handing it over is vitally important. Why aren't we better at it?

Introduction

During a research visit, HM was impressed to see a project manager sitting down with a tatty-looking ring binder. When asked what he was doing, he said that he was looking through the plans and documents from a previous project to see what he could learn for the project that he was about to undertake. He was noting both what had worked well and what had not – the things that he would try to repeat and those that he would then avoid. This was an example of the kind of approach that has been advocated throughout this book – continuous improvement of both individuals (in this case the project manager) and the process (how they go about their work) – what is termed *reflective learning*. Many organisations have invested very heavily in knowledge management systems, but few can be as useful or as effective as the process seen that day. The lesson for organisations is that learning is about what people do, not about what technology you have.

Many studies demonstrate what was described in Chapter 2 as *hedgehog syndrome* – that project teams and project-based organisations don't learn. The apocryphal quotation at the start of the chapter is an example of this. However, the opening case does give some notion that organisations and individuals, under the right conditions, can participate in powerful learning.

Once the main part of the work is completed, it is very tempting to move on rather than ensure that the work is completed and the maximum benefit yielded from it. How the last phases of 'check and act on the results of the checks' are managed will determine to a large extent the views of stakeholders on the outcomes as well as set the chances for future project success.

These final processes carry a number of challenges, which the project manager will have to address:

- trying to make the review process objective while taking into account a rich picture of the events surrounding project performance;
- relating procedural conformance to project performance;
- the establishment of long-term programmes of improvement while being assessed on short-term measures which are predominantly financial;
- satisfying all the relevant stakeholder groups, while looking ahead to the next project.

Such challenges are not easily resolved, particularly where weak guidance is provided from senior management. These same people may be demanding ever greater performance without providing the means to improve. As will be shown, *if* organisations want to take the challenge and significantly improve their project processes, *then* they will have to dedicate some resources in the short term to this. In the longer term, it will be demonstrated that the improvement process becomes self-sustaining, at least in financial terms. Given the poor performance identified during Chapter 1 of many projects and project-based firms, the potential here for financial benefit in the medium to long term is enormous.

Why aren't we better at this?

It sounds straightforward and laudable. However, for businesses whose remit it is to deliver projects, success at this is noticeably elusive. One study[3] we were involved in looked at the operations of a major network and IT provider. Their business was doing huge programmes for clients (a very competitive business), and we looked at how managers actually operated. In theory the fact that many of the programmes were doing similar things meant that they could learn from each other, and an Enterprise Programme Office (EPO) was set up to help do exactly that. In practice, though, things were different. Learning between programmes was often helped primarily by individuals transferring across, rather than through formal mechanisms. That person's knowledge and experience was accessible by virtue of them directly being there. Individuals gain and can share expertise; whether 'the organisation' can capture this effectively is still a matter of some debate. Managers relied heavily on their social networks both in their own programme, and in contact with others (i.e. 'who do I know and trust to help me with this?'). The limitations of the formal systems were apparent. For example, although each programme had extensive documentation on the company intranet, it was deemed quite hard to find and so staff quite often relied on trusted colleagues to point them to the right area and the 'useful information'. The EPO was thought to be more of a reporting structure than a real aid to getting better.

What worked well? Social knowledge-sharing was deemed very important, despite the investment in technical systems aimed at helping this. Barriers to learning and sharing included the time pressure, with staff highly focused on the immediate delivery needs rather than any wider improvement. Practical difficulties of different customer contexts and stakeholders, the specific detailed requirements, and particular complexities encountered in the work also made cross-programme challenging. If other programmes are perceived as sufficiently 'different', the incentive to try to learn from them is diminished, and problems common to multiple pieces of work can be missed.

Finishing projects well, learning from them, and improving long-term performance is hugely important. However, as we shall see, it can be far more complicated than it might seem.

16.1 Completion and handover

There are many reasons that work stops on projects. For some, it is because of the successful **completion** of the project's objectives. Some are stopped by their sponsors, due to changing needs or poor project performance, and others, due to lack of the necessary resources to continue.

Where projects are prematurely **terminated** it is usual for the staff to be dispersed with no provision for a **review**. Where projects are completed, there should be no reason for not reviewing. However, many firms do not allow staff time to review project activities, preferring them to stay busy and simply continue to the next project. In Chapter 2, we identified the result of this – *hedgehog syndrome*. Here, mistakes are repeated over and over again, and the rate of improvement of such organisations is poor or non-existent. For the individuals involved this presents much frustration. This is a very short-sighted view and the costs of hedgehog syndrome are enormous. Before we get to this stage, however, this is the time when completer-finishers (see the Belbin analysis in Chapter 11) become a highly valuable commodity and other role types try to run off to start on the next project! Proper completion of projects requires discipline. Carrying out a worthwhile review requires investment of time and resource. This chapter will consider both of these.

The elements that will require the attention of the project manager during this phase are:

- ensuring there is an incentive for the project to be finished and that activities are completed (all projects);
- ensuring documentation of the process is provided to allow review, and of the outcome to facilitate any future support activities (all projects);
- closing down the project systems, particularly the accounting systems (projects where there has been a medium–high organisational complexity and dedicated systems have been used);
- constructing the immediate review of activities, providing a starting point for all improvement activities (all projects);
- appraisal and relocation of staff who have completed their activities and disposal of assets that are surplus to requirements (some projects);
- ensuring that all stakeholders are satisfied – sell your achievements and maximise the business benefit from your project (all projects) every time!

Completion

The situation the project manager needs to avoid is where a project spends 90 per cent of its life 90 per cent complete. Finishing the activities so that resources can be released for other work and minimising the costs incurred during the close-down phase are vital. There is a trade-off to be considered here: how much time and resource should be put into the closing of activities? At one extreme, there is a temptation to abandon the activities in a great rush to move on to other tasks. Such action risks undue haste and removes the possibilities for maximising the benefit of the review, for example. At the other extreme, a close-down process can become drawn out, nothing is really finished and the overhead costs of the activities remaining keep escalating. Which approach is taken often depends on the success or otherwise of the project – it is clearly much more desirable to spend time closing a project which is an apparent success, whereas a disaster is more likely to be rapidly abandoned. As already discussed, the review process is equally important in either case, as are the other activities listed above.

In the kind of organisation where people are brought in on contract for the duration of that project alone and are paid a time rate (according to the amount of time they spend working on it), there is little incentive for the work to be finished on time. Indeed, it is in their interests to ensure that things go mildly wrong and result in the plan of work being extended. The provision of some form of bonus for early completion should be considered where personnel have an active input to the result. Contractors and sub-contractors should be treated as suppliers in this respect and be eligible for development effort (as discussed in Chapter 14). In addition, as anyone who has had tradespeople working at their house will know, you find yourself saying, 'While you're here, will you take a quick look at the leak/squeaky board, etc.?' This addition to the task list can be a serious extra cost and one that can significantly disrupt the main task. That doesn't mean that they should be avoided, just not taken as 'free'.

Documentation

This subject usually elicits groans from practitioners, for whom this is the least exciting part of the project. Project personnel who are used to being very goal focused often have great difficulty getting to grips with this task, and the quality of documentation is often compromised as a result. The purpose of **documentation** is:

- to provide evidence that the project has been completed in a proper manner – increasingly important given the requirements of ISO 9000, to assist avoidance of litigation and to provide the starting point for review;
- to give guidance to the customer on the operation and maintenance of the item provided – particularly so in the case of a piece of software, a building or a piece of machinery;
- to allow any future work on a similar project to have a good starting point – knowledge of what was done in this project. By definition projects are time-limited and the staff disperse onto new work. 'The project' is not there six months later if someone has a query. You may be able to track down individuals involved, but this is not guaranteed.

In addition the following should be noted:

- If it is left to the end to write documentation much information can be lost, as staff are already reassigned to other activities and the task gets left to certain individuals to complete. As noted above, this task is one that most people dread. Including this activity as part of the work breakdown structure is vital, rather than hoping that it will be carried out as an unaccounted extra. Where time is short, this activity should not be regarded as the one that can be 'squeezed' to provide slack for other hard-pressed activities or this will immediately signal that it is less important than 'the real work of the project'. It is advisable to have key documentation as a deliverable for a gate review; that way, it must be done or the project cannot pass the gate. The documents therefore remain 'front of mind'.
- The nature of the documentation includes the formal items presented throughout the course of the work and the communication documents and notes of individuals. Individuals need to keep their own logbooks of events, discussions and agreements. The professional institutes require these to be kept during training as the basis for assessment of training programmes. Their long-term use is growing more important as the issue of professional liability becomes more pertinent. Such a document might provide valuable material should an individual be implicated in an enquiry involving professional negligence.
- Formal documentation covers all project correspondence, including contracts, permissions, letters and memoranda. All documentation with legal ramifications must be kept and the length of time they are to be held determined (the life of the product or 7 years,

whichever is the longer is standard for many organisations for complex projects). A policy should be established for electronic documents and e-mails as to whether and how these need to be stored, and if they can be consigned to a data warehouse. In this respect, ISO 9001 states the requirement for record storage: that the organisation should provide a filing system for project data, including a guide as to the whereabouts of any item of information.

The close-down activities should form part of the detailed planning. However, it is often difficult to know exactly what will need finishing due to variations in the project schedule. Some further planning is therefore vital during this phase to ensure that there is some system to the activities being carried out and to minimise the temptation for projects to drift on. A major tool here is *checklists*, to provide a highly visible means of ensuring that the finishing tasks are carried out. Such a checklist is:

- an *aide-mémoire* in addition to formal work allocation;
- evidence that the close-down tasks were planned;
- evidence, when completed, that the tasks were carried out, by whom and when.

Closing down the project systems

The activity curve in Chapter 2 shows that, in general, the level of activity falls off as the project nears completion. This is accompanied by a slowdown in the spending rate, on both labour and materials. As people leave the project team it must be remembered that the systems, in particular the accounting and quality systems, are still operational. For the accounting systems, it is likely that people will know the codes against which items could be charged. Rather than deplete new budgets, there is always the temptation to try to get expenditure set against other budgets. In order to stop costs being run up against project codes, the project manager must ensure that further unauthorised expenditure is curtailed. There will, however, be late invoices from suppliers and possibly overhanging administration activities that will need to be charged. These must be paid and are one of the reasons why the financial position at the end of major work does not always provide a good indicator of the financial performance of the project overall. Assessing the committed spend of large projects is a complex task in itself.

A formal notice of closure is issued in many industries to inform other staff and support systems that there are no further activities to be carried out or charges to be made. In contract project activities, the legal termination of activities occurs at the time when the customer '**signs off**' the project. It is often tempting for work to continue after this has occurred and for the team to provide the customer with 'free' consultancy. Many service projects have this element, in particular in information technology. However, no organisation can afford to:

- cut off the customer completely at this point and ruin the possibilities for future business;
- continue to provide services for which they do not charge.

In reality, if this 'consultancy' is required on an ongoing basis, it is likely to indicate that other aspects of the project execution were less well managed. This could be in particular the **handover** process or the failure of documentation to identify solutions to problems. Where the completion criteria for projects are left open, you are more likely to end up providing further benefits with possibly no hope of obtaining payment for them.

Further specifics about the nature of the close-down processes are well documented in PRINCE2 and the Bodies of Knowledge.

Conducting immediate project reviews

The review system contains key elements, providing further control or corrective actions:

- immediate 'post-mortem' on the activities;
- immediate remedial and improvement action;
- long-term audit and review;
- strategic and procedural changes.

The formal long-term review may prescribe major procedural or strategic changes. The one that is carried out as a completion phase activity is intended to provide rapid feedback on the performance of individuals and systems that the dispersing team members can take away with them. It is the basis for identifying short-term needs, such as procedural changes or changes in skills required by individuals. People need rapid feedback on their performance. The organisation should provide this in order that:

- they know what aspects of their performance should be repeated;
- managers can identify training or educational requirements;
- the organisation can assess the utility of individuals to future teams.

A further role of the 'post mortem' is to provide a case history of the project which is then a guide to the documentation that will be required, over and above that already compiled, for the long-term audit.

The assessor or reviewer in this case should be someone who can be brought up to date on the context of the project and the challenges that have been faced – physical, political, environmental, financial and personal. The likely reviewers are the sponsor and the manager, though many believe that the manager could not be expected to be sufficiently objective about the process. Other project managers in the organisation can lead a review and it is a role that can be well taken by staff from the project office (see Chapter 4) or even an external consultant.

One of the tools which is of considerable benefit to short-term improvement is an audit of the management by the team (assumes that the team is managed by an individual rather than being autonomous). Such characteristics as attitude, skills, approachability, openness, ability to delegate authority yet share responsibility, ability to represent the project team to others and willingness to embrace change may be assessed. This kind of management questionnaire can demonstrate very clearly that the manager is serious about improving the 'management product' through continuous self-improvement, rather than just preaching the message to others.

The feedback gained by individuals (both managers and team members) provides reinforcement for good skills and behaviours and a path for change where improvement is required. This information is a vital input to the work of the human resources function in identifying satisfaction levels associated with different ways of working and levels of motivation. This is only one type of review. For low-complexity projects, this is likely to be all that is required to feed onto future improvement activities. For medium- and high-complexity projects, a more formal review of the longer-term aspects of the performance is necessary.

Appraisal and relocation of staff and disposal of surplus assets

Conducting staff appraisal was mentioned above and is a vital part of nurturing the 'human capital' of project organisations. It is one of the management skills that is often assumed to be present in people because they have the title 'manager'. The reality is that this is part of a skillset that is not included in any genetic ability, but needs to be part of a training programme.

Having carried out an appraisal, many project managers will themselves move on to other projects. The relocation of staff is one area where project managers may have little direct influence, but provision of support and help during this process is desirable. Many project managers note the importance of such activities in building a network of good people who can be called upon to carry out particular project activities in the future. Provision of such assistance will strengthen these personal ties.

Assets left at the end of activities include surplus stocks. These represent waste – they were not needed and should not have been supplied. Other project hardware that is not absorbed by the controlling organisation also needs to be disposed of. This is often carried out with the view that as the job is finished, the sooner this hardware is eliminated from the accounts, the site or just from view, the better. Valuable material is put in skips, left to rot or any number of other options that an entrepreneur would baulk at. Trying to encourage people to think of beneficial means of disposal of assets is unnatural for many – they have the attitude that the organisation can afford it and often that 'the paperwork would cost more to raise than would be raised in revenue from its proper sale'. This is, however, more symptomatic of galloping bureaucracy than detachment of the individual from financial results. In such a case, it is possible to outsource the disposal and retain a significant percentage of the market value of such assets.

Ensuring that all stakeholders are satisfied

Marketing influences consumer behaviour, consciously or otherwise, from the clothes that we wear to the brands of groceries we buy. Selling success appears to be an unpopular concept among project professionals, but one that should be considered in enhancing the customers' image of the project organisation. The data for such promotion should come from the review process (for total disasters, the potential and opportunities for improvement come from the same source). The concept of the '**product surround**' should be utilised – actual performance is likely to account for 20 per cent of people's perceptions (and hence impact) but costs 80 per cent of the budget to achieve. The 80 per cent of the impact of the work carried out comes from 20 per cent of the spend. Put simply, 'an ounce of image is worth a pound of performance'. Achieving good publicity can have internal benefits as it is seen that good performance is being both looked for and recognised – organisations are often regarded as only after 'catching you out for doing something wrong'.

Marketing professionals can and should, therefore, be involved at this stage in the process to maximise the business return on the project work. Trade journals, even national newspapers, may pick up on a particular success story following a press release. However, well-executed projects rarely make the headlines, the more newsworthy issues are generally those that go horribly wrong. Although such anonymity at a national level may seem an odd target, it is entirely feasible to promote the story in appropriate professional outlets and on social media. Other professionals are keen to know what you did and it is your chance to tell the story. As a general rule, though, successful project managers who deliver to plan with no drama are rarely heralded as heroes. It went well – what was so hard about it? It is worth noting that getting **stakeholder satisfaction** in your success is more of a challenge than it may initially appear.

16.2 Reviews and learning

Structuring improvement activities

There is much written on the subject of process improvement from almost any perspective you care to imagine. This provides a degree of confusion for the practitioner, often leading to a kind of paralysis where everything looks possible so nothing gets changed. **Management paralysis** is often seen and can usually be linked to poor strategy and policy deployment on the part of senior management. As discussed in Chapter 4, strategy provides the essential focus for improvement activities and all our activities should be geared towards these strategic objectives.

With the focus of a clear strategy, the project manager can carry out activities that will improve the performance of future project processes on these criteria. A useful structure is to separate two elements:[4]

- **learning before doing** – ensuring that the necessary knowledge and skills are available in advance of their need in a project;
- **learning by doing** – those elements that can be learned from previous activities.

The original intention of this structure was concerned with technical elements of processes, though they apply equally to the management elements of processes. It is the *management* of the process that we will be referring to here.

Learning before doing is difficult to manage in practice. Identifying sources of ideas for changes that are likely to yield the results that you are seeking takes time and requires a very clear view of the available sources.

How do you approach the project and identify what knowledge you are going to use, and what you need to generate? One approach is to use the framework in Figure 16.1. This asks some simple questions – what are you going to do, and how are you going to do it? What knowledge do you already have that you can re-use, and what do you need to do differently? This is a really useful conversation for the team to have at the beginning of the project so that everyone has a common understanding, and it is beneficial to repeat at key milestones (such as gate reviews) so that any updates can be incorporated. It is a simple idea, but drives helpful conversations and may unlock different ways of working or opportunities for improvement that had not previously been identified.

Two major sources for ideas around 'learning before doing' are the use of consultants and benchmarking (see Figure 16.2 and the following sections). Many world-class organisations, however, make far more use of the learning from their own projects. Research recently carried out at one of Hewlett-Packard's plants showed that the review information from previous projects provided a starting point for the planning of future projects. This had been done consistently over a long period, resulting in highly developed processes. This internal learning was often missing at firms that had less well-developed processes

	Knowledge we have	Knowledge we need
Output – the 'what'	What can we re-use from before? (e.g. existing designs) - and what should we not use? (e.g. obsolete parts)	What do we need to develop?
Process – the 'how'	What can we take from our 'standard' process set? - and what should we avoid? (e.g. tailoring the process)	What makes sense to do differently in this project?

Figure 16.1 Project knowledge framework (adapted from Turner et al., 2014)[5]

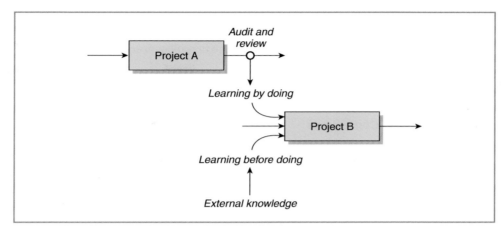

Figure 16.2 Process improvement

and tended to rely on external sources for their process development efforts. As a whole, these were less successful than those generated internally. It is certainly feasible to learn from the past, but this does require a concerted effort to do so, with staff, time, and budget allocated for the task over the long term.

The following considers in more depth each of the issues of learning before doing and learning by doing.

Learning before doing – the role of external knowledge

The main sources of external knowledge that will be considered in this section are through **training** and **education**, and the use of **consultants**.

Training and education

Project management firms frequently run training courses for their people, though with varied rates of success. Having visited the home of a person who had a year previously been on a training course, HM was regaled with the excellence of the hotel and the quality of the course notes. 'In fact,' said the friend, 'I've got them here.' He went to his kitchen and reached up above the kitchen units and pulled down a very impressive-looking file. Blowing the dust from it he remarked, 'Only wish I could have used the ideas. Nobody at work was really interested.' That course had cost the firm the wages of the person for a week, the course fee and the hotel, plus travelling expenses, yet had derived no noticeable benefit.

Sadly, the same story is often heard from MBA and MSc students. Whether self-funded or company-funded, individuals who undertake a part-time Masters learn new ideas and techniques but employers often fail to have the mechanisms to incorporate these into their ways of working. The natural consequence of this is that disillusioned staff may choose to take their new qualification to somewhere where it will be more highly valued.

Training therefore needs to have a relatively immediate application if it is to be worthwhile. This includes a group of people who will be able to work in the new method once the person has been trained. It is rare that one person on their own will be effective in changing methods. They more often are demoralised by the lack of cooperation from colleagues and the processes remain unchanged as a result. Managers must realise that change requires a **critical mass** – that is, it has been suggested that for any change to occur in processes, over 80 per cent of the people working in those processes must be capable and willing to make the necessary changes. This could save a great deal of wasted training time in future and provide a greater focus for improvement activities. Such support and mentoring for change in project processes can be provided by the project office, as noted in Chapter 4.

Another external source of knowledge that is used with varied levels of effectiveness is consultants. The role of consultants is discussed below.

Consultants

There are many large and influential management consultancy firms (e.g. PWC, McKinsey, Accenture) in addition to legions of individuals, but relatively little is written on their roles or how their skills can best be applied. The general role of consultants is in the provision of specific services such as accountancy, strategic analysis, human resource development or information technology. The consultant within the project environment can have the following roles:

- *integrator* – providing an overall project management service as a single point of contact for a customer. They arrange the allocation of tasks between sub-contractors and are responsible for overseeing progress;
- *honesty-broker* – gaining an external 'independent' viewpoint on a situation can be immensely beneficial. As one consultant commented, 'Sometimes people get too close to the work to see the wood for the trees.' People working within the project organisation can be more inclined to accept the views of an outsider on changes than to move from entrenched positions at the behest of a colleague. As importantly, such a solution may allow individuals to 'save face';
- *change-agent* – providing the focus for activities while keeping an overview as to what is happening;
- *knowledge provider* in one or more specific areas or techniques;
- *resource provider* – to allow tasks to be carried out that people from within the organisation would claim that they do not have the time or capability to do (certain documentation activities or specialist technical knowledge);
- *checker* of the way in which the process is being carried out;
- *trainer* – rather than doing the job for the organisation, the knowledge is imparted to the members of the organisation through training. As one consultancy firm advertised, 'Your consultant says "Do this . . . " You do it. Your consultant says "Now do this . . . " You do it. Your consultant leaves. What do you do now?'

The first stage in employing consultants is to decide exactly what it is that they are being brought in to achieve. The means of achieving this must be determined either through having the consultants do the job for you or through training. The evaluation of the suitability of one or other firm can be performed through:

- membership of appropriate professional bodies;
- talking to previous clients;
- closely evaluating their capabilities;
- evaluating the costs for the job, in particular whether there is any financial incentive for them to finish the job in a given time and whether their fee is linked to tangible benefits achieved from their work.

One encounter with a consulting company ended when the two consultants stated that nothing had been written on the area in question. The manager concerned had prepared for the meeting by going to the local university library and locating two large tomes on the subject, which he duly produced for the meeting. The consultants did not get the assignment.

One of the challenges of employing consultants is how to evaluate the benefit of the service that they have provided. Many consultants in the field of total quality management treat it as heresy if a company employing them evaluates their impact in terms of financial cost and benefit. This may be condoned if there is going to be a definable longer-term benefit, but the mechanisms need to be put in place to ensure that this is achieved. Many managers, when viewing the output of consulting assignments, have made the comment: 'If you give them your watch, they will tell you the time!' This does not mean that the findings had little value – getting someone impartial to state the obvious is as good a means as any of starting the debate on such issues.

One of the benefits of a consultant's study is that it is largely impartial. The allocation of tasks to consultants should be fully in the knowledge of any potential conflicts of interest, e.g. if they also do work for a major competitor or if they are employed at various stages in the project. A consultant may be employed to help in the evaluation of a project proposal. The same consultant could quite reasonably be brought in later in the project if it goes ahead. Therefore, they would have a vested interest in its going ahead.

In the future consultants are going to have an important role to play in the management of projects and in the provision of resources that companies are not large enough to have in-house. Their role will need intelligent purchasers of their services if it is to be successful. The lure of the consultant's patter can then be put to good use selling the necessary ideas to those for whom their activities will be value-adding in the longer term. The way that consultants charge for jobs may also be reconsidered. The normal method is currently to work on the basis of a daily rate. This does not offer the consultant much incentive to get the job done at any particular speed. Some firms have included clauses in agreements that they will achieve a return in a given period of so many times their fee for a client. This appears to be moving in the right direction.

Using external expertise can certainly be highly beneficial. However, we have seen numerous cases where consultants are brought in on a long-term basis and the employing organisation lets its own staff expertise wither or leave. It does not take long before they are entirely reliant on the consultants, and this a difficult situation to reverse. Senior managers need to be clear on the nature of the consultant engagement and how this fits in with the organisation's wider strategy. Without careful consideration it is possible to outsource one of your key functions and diminish or lose a previous competitive advantage.

Benchmarking

This is an area which has resulted in a large amount of business for the consultancy industry. As a high-level concept, it certainly seems promising. Organisations are being told, 'How can you be certain that you are as good as you say you are, unless you compare your performance with that of others?' This is a very persuasive logic, but before engaging in any **benchmarking** activities, a deeper understanding of the possibilities and protocols should be explored.

A benchmark is a reference point, some standard by which other phenomena are judged. It is a temporarily fixed point, with the location or magnitude decided by relevant metrics or measures. The original use of benchmarks was claimed by the early map-makers who needed certain reference points by which to judge others – in this case in spatial distance along three dimensions from the reference point. The distances having been assessed, the new point could also be considered to be a reference point, though the accuracy would be diluted the further one went from the original data.

The large-scale commercialisation of benchmarking activities was begun by Rank Xerox in 1979. Managers from its American operations were encouraged to go to view how its Japanese operations were being managed and compare their performance. Where there were performance differences, the methods used were noted to explore the possibilities for adapting the methods to their own plants. Initially fairly informal, the methodology has become more formalised and is viewed as one good way of obtaining ideas for improving both performance and processes.

In project management, the adoption of **KPIs** (Key Performance Indicators) has been tried across a range of sectors to allow some performance benchmarking to take place. In the construction sector, for instance, KPIs of percent of projects delivered on time, budget conformance and customer-satisfaction indices are becoming more widely used, though, as will be shown, this is a very limited approach and one that has not been without its problems.

Indeed, this follows a normal development where the initial approach to benchmarking involves consideration of very basic data, usually financial ratios, which provided a means of comparison of the overall effectiveness of management. Figures without explanation of their means of collection and the meanings of each, with clear bounds established as to what they include, are misleading. This understanding of what lay behind the numbers caused problems at a large UK specialist manufacturer when its German holding company carried out a benchmarking study to compare ratios of direct to non-direct staff. The UK operation appeared to be significantly overstaffed with non-directs compared to other companies in the group. On analysis, however, the comparison was not valid as the definitions of direct and non-direct employees were very different. The German company, for example, counted transport operatives as direct employees, while the UK operation counted them as support (non-direct) staff. The comparison was between unlike sets of statistics – termed 'apples and oranges'. The comparison therefore does not work well.

The numbers can therefore provide useful data, but with caveats. Of much greater interest and potential benefit to the project manager is to consider the processes behind the figures. Mapping processes provides far more useful information on how particular constraints are handled, obstacles overcome and problems solved. These can be collected through benchmarking clubs, established where a group of individuals have a particular interest, and meet to discuss this. This is being used to some effect where project management professionals meet to discuss particular issues. Such networking provides an informal method for benchmarking processes and it is often found that problems being faced by managers were more easily solved by others than themselves.

The generation of benchmarking data does have clear benefits. The nature of the comparison can be with:

- functional projects – those conducted within the same functional part of the organisation;
- internal projects – others conducted by the same organisation;
- generic projects – process-related studies comparing projects with similar processes;
- competitor benchmarking – comparison with competitors.

The objective is to find how the best performers are doing and how these results are achieved. Thus a functional benchmarking exercise is clearly limited to the level of improvement, but it provides a good starting point and is likely to be highly cost-effective. The use of internal studies again develops benchmarking experience among staff and can be considered to be 'safe' as the information is developed and kept in-house. Generic processes are where the most benefit can often be gained, but where the comparisons are likely to be the most difficult.

Consider the project activities associated with publishing a book. If the publisher wished to decrease the time to market, they might consider benchmarking themselves against one of the newspapers, which regularly have to take copy from writers and turn it into printed material within a few hours. For most textbooks, the development process takes months (7 months from submission of manuscript to publication is normal). The methods or processes are similar, the end-product is considered to be very different.

Competitive benchmarking is possibly the most difficult to execute effectively, due to the defensive attitudes of organisations towards their performance. This most certainly should involve a 'code of conduct', including retaining confidentiality of data. The activities do not necessarily involve site visits as much of the information can be collected and exchanged by telephone or e-mail. Other data are often in the public domain and, while it is almost always out of date as soon as it is printed, provides useful indicators, particularly where a project organisation is at the start of its improvement activities.

Any criteria where data are gathered as part of the review process can be used to provide benchmarks. The minimum criteria are that an organisation consistently improves on its own benchmark data, and targets for improvement form an intrinsic part of organisational strategy.

Benchmarking across projects, which by definition have an element of uniqueness,[6] is difficult. One key measure that is often cited in large benchmarking studies is that of productivity. Most simply stated, this is the output achieved per unit of input resources. In operations management, this may be associated with units per hour of output of production lines. In project management, while the measure can be applied to some of the execution phase of the project where repetitive tasks exist, applying it to one-off activities is unlikely to be useful. It is difficult to control activities where there is a non-tangible output, such as in design. As the output and the output rate are very difficult to define (designs produced per month does not consider the quality of the design and can focus attention on the wrong priorities – speed over quality or completeness), productivity at this level is also likely to be meaningless. Overall productivity measures (such as engineering hours per major design activity) are more useful but again focus on speed rather than quality. The achievement of 'right first time' is a worthwhile goal, and so measures of numbers of engineering change requests or manufacturing problems that are accredited to design are more relevant. An organisational culture that supports improvement is, of course, valuable. However, too much of a focus on specific KPIs may drive unwanted behaviours. If goals are set for speed, for example, these may well be achieved, but if the corresponding quality is not measured as well, you may well find later on that there was a downside to being fast. Managers must think through targets carefully and consider all the implications.

In a discussion of this vital aspect of performance assessment, Kaplan and Norton[7] showed how providing a kind of scorecard which contains both process and performance measures can be beneficial (demonstrated in Chapter 4). For each of the following categories, both goals and measures are constructed:

- financial perspectives (how do we look to shareholders?);
- customer perspectives (how do customers see us?);
- internal business perspectives (what must we excel at?);
- innovation and learning perspectives (can we continue to improve and create value?).

This kind of balance to measures can now provide the basis for benchmarking activities as the organisation seeks to improve its scores. A measure of activity-centred progress would be the number of improvement programmes being carried out within an organisation or the number of staff who have been through the quality improvement training programme. Measures of performance include the **percentage improvement** in customer satisfaction as a result of improvement activities and reductions in quality costs, for example.

Learning by doing – the role of audit and review

The process of auditing and reviewing activities at a slight time distance from their execution is a part of normal life in some project organisations and an obvious omission from many others. Carrying out **audit** and **review** sometime after the project has benefit as the results of the actions and the way in which they were undertaken become evident. The return-on-development activities may take even longer to yield the benefits that were attributed to them during the planning process. This should form part of the normal project processes, just as planning does. The process itself requires:

- a reason to exist;
- time;
- information;
- resources;
- credibility.

The reason for reviews is often described as 'praise of the unworthy followed by punishment of the innocent'. The reason must go beyond this and be set out clearly in the terms of reference. The main goal is to ensure that continuous improvement activities are in place and are followed through. It also provides a point at which the responsibility of the project manager can be objectively assessed.

Before continuing to look at some procedural issues associated with review, the first task is to identify the aspects of the project that need reviewing.

Time must be allocated from other activities and an appropriate auditor/reviewer arranged. The project manager should be involved in the process. Information should be provided along with the necessary access and authority to obtain further information. It should be resourced, either from central overhead allocation or from an amount set aside from the project funds to carry it out. As for the manager, the process must be given credibility. The research should be carried out in a manner that is rigorous but fair and there should be no hidden agendas (praise or punishment).

The auditing process involves:

- establishing the procedures – the formal statement of intent as to how activities should be carried out, whether financial, quality or environmental;
- checking documentation and other records of practice to show that they have been followed;
- presenting a report detailing the areas where there are deficiencies or irregularities.

An audit is often viewed as a negative process, i.e. it is trying to catch people out. However, it is responsible for identifying inconsistencies, double-checking information as well as seeking alternative viewpoints on the proceedings. There will regularly be conflict into which the players may try to draw the audit team. In some (albeit rare) cases, the company culture really supports reviews as an opportunity to learn. In one technical organisation we were involved with, the regular project reviews were detailed and sometimes could be viewed as quite aggressive, but everyone involved recognised the need for the best performance and so the focus was on the project outcome, not any individuals involved. That way potentially difficult ideas could be surfaced and discussed, with the emphasis on the work, not individual egos. The participants recognised the value of this approach, but it needs an understanding that is hard to build and easy to destroy if managers become the targets of what they perceive as personal attacks.

The review process involves:

- studying overall performance relative to constraints;
- identifying areas where the procedures failed or have otherwise been shown to be inadequate;
- reporting on the key areas and suggesting improvements.

It is a real skill and art to carry out a worthwhile review process. Getting the truth, or many versions of it, and attempting to make sense of the conflicts (as for audits, but with a more open mandate) are common tests. It is always going to be a subjective exercise – this factor is worth remembering. Two different teams, given the same project, may produce quite different reports. This will depend on the skills and biases of the individuals. The review should differ from the audit in one further dimension – that of the focus. Audits look internally, while reviews should take into account the impact of the project on the environment as a whole. The changes that were impressed by the environment should also be considered.

The nature of the feedback will differ from the post-mortem type of review. Changes are rarely made to procedure-level events at this stage – procedures may have already been changed considerably and the context is unlikely to be completely the same again. Where the greatest impact will be felt is in strategic issues – the role of the project manager, of suppliers and the imposition or relinquishing of controls on activities can be examined. Above all, it is likely that a full picture of performance indicators will be available by this time and provide a more complete picture of the accuracy of forecasts and the veracity of other planning assumptions.

In the execution of a formal audit or review the criteria under consideration will to some extent determine who should be the auditor or reviewer. Expecting someone without accountancy skills, experience or qualification to carry out a financial audit is unlikely to produce usable or credible results. The criteria for the assessor also require a degree of independence. There is often the tendency in formal organisations that run projects in matrix form for one department or function to assess another's projects and vice versa. This arrangement, while being convenient and usually very cost-effective, can be counter-productive as there is the equal chance of complicity or hidden agendas as the departments have old scores to settle. This 'culture of distrust' is perpetuated by such arrangements and simply adds another degree of paying someone to check the work that you have paid someone else to do in the first place. Although it can expose incompetence, the audit/review procedure has to be seen as a value-adding activity rather than simply an opportunity to be negative about the work of others.

The implication of the above is that there can be a worthwhile role for the project audit and review process. An assessor works with the project sponsor and manager to look for areas of improvement. In reality, if you want to find the major areas for improvements, the people who are in the best position to provide this information are those who were directly involved with the activities – the project team themselves. This knowledge is collated with the assessor taking a collaborative role rather than an adversarial one, and utilising their experience to be fair and openly objective, rather than having to indulge in political games-playing. The view should be holistic – no one aspect of the project performance should be considered in isolation and data should be corroborated wherever possible. Substantiating the claims of suppliers (both internal and external) by verification with their customers is always a good check of data. Maintaining a focus which looks externally as well as at the internal data sources ensures that the fundamental objective of 'meeting customer requirements at lowest cost' remains on the management agenda.

Table 16.1 shows the nature of both procedural audits and performance reviews that can be used to assess a project. It shows a variety of criteria and their methods of assessment. As stated during the work on control, if you measure only financial performance measures, do not be surprised if the focus of the project team rests on short-term performance gains. Carrying out such assessment shows the team how seriously the organisation regards the criteria set out. If policy statements at senior management level are not backed up by the allocation of assessment effort *and* resources for improvement as a result of these assessments, the policies will become discredited.

Given that all these are possible, how do you decide which of these is important enough to warrant the effort of a review? The answer comes through the same means as many

Table 16.1 Review and audit criteria

Criteria	Audit	Review
Financial	Accounting systems	ROI, cost variance
Time	Conformance to plan	Customer satisfaction
Quality	Quality procedures	Customer perceptions
Human resources	Conformance to policy	Team spirit, motivation
Environmental	Conformance to policy	EI assessment
Planning	Conformance to plan	Cost, techniques used
Control	Systems for control	Basis for improvement

other decisions of project managers, by reference to the organisational strategy. If time performance is the most important issue for the organisation, then audits and reviews of planning, control and time performance should be carried out. Other aspects of performance can be the subject of particular reviews and it is important that the subject of the review changes over time. This would reflect the changes in strategy and attempts to close performance gaps, as identified in Chapter 4.

Alternative views may also be considered. In Chapter 2 we described the forms of complexity inherent in projects – structural, socio-political, and emergent. It is valuable to assess projects in light of these ideas, too, to get a wider understanding of how well they actually went. Structural complexities can be analysed in terms of timescale, budget and performance, and these are quantifiable aspects that can be discussed. What about the socio-political side? Harder to quantify, but we can ask sensible questions about how well we engaged stakeholders, how satisfied the staff were, and what we could do better next time on the 'people' issues. This is a different question than evaluating the success of a project in terms of our usual 'iron triangle' criteria, but no less important in terms of maintaining a sustainable business. Finally, for emergent complexity, how well did we deal with changes and uncertainty? Were we sufficiently flexible when we needed to be? If not, how might we do better in the future? These are valuable conversations to have as a team and take a more holistic approach than most reviews encompass.

Long-term review

The case where a project was identified as a success at its completion but where the poor quality of the product of the project became recognised only later is not that unusual. Ongoing measurement of project outcomes has been established in the construction and engineering sectors for some time by identification of *whole-life costs* – the initial project cost with the ongoing maintenance and eventual disposal costs of the product. Given the level of many firms' dissatisfaction with their IT suppliers, this would be a useful measure to apply. Other forms of long-term review include individuals reflecting on their experiences of the project. This adds real validity to the concept of experience. It is a feature of many people who participate in regular training on this subject that the training time provides them with an opportunity for this reflection. Some professions require the compilation of a log-book. This type of diary could be highly beneficial to the project management professional as a means of facilitating review of personal experience. This can form a third element of the learning model – learning after doing.[8]

Some further issues concerning how to carry out reviews are included in the following section.

Carrying out reviews

Many firms do not bother to carry out reviews for a variety of reasons. During recent research it became clear that a major reason why this is so is that people resent the fact that reviews frequently become major finger-pointing exercises, simply concerned with allocating blame for shortcomings in the project. Given that this often points at managers, it is perfectly understandable why they are so reluctant to have reviews. However, under some different guidelines it is possible for medium- to high-complexity projects to have very constructive formal reviews. These guidelines include the following.

- Focus on processes, not individuals – Dr Deming suggested, as stated before, that the majority of defects in our workplaces are the fault of the systems that people work in rather than the individuals. Given that this is the case, and that the systems and their design and redesign are under the control of managers, it is reasonable that changes could be expected to the systems rather than simply to the individuals.
- Use factual data wherever possible – it is amazing after even a short period of time how people forget salient points relative to the project. This is a vital role for project documentation to help relieve the problems associated with short-term memory loss or resolve difference of opinion as to what happened and when.
- Allow rehearsal of alternatives, e.g. what would have happened if . . . ? This rehearsal actually can be very useful if allowed for a short part of the review, not to dominate it but to allow some exploration as to how the project system would have responded under different conditions. Given that the objective is the future improvement of the system, this is a legitimate part of the review.
- Use tools and techniques of problem-solving – in particular for ordering data and presenting the findings. This will further help to avoid jumping to conclusions and helps the process of review to be more objective.
- Discourage glib classification – this frequently arises, particularly in the absence of structured reviews and problem-solving activities. People participate in reviews often with very definite ideas of where the problems lie. As discussed in Chapter 15, using a structured cause–effect–cause analysis will yield the root cause rather than simply discussing one of the intermediary effects.
- Use a 'critical friend' – some companies have reviews that are fairly hostile, and the natural reaction is to be defensive. Often these do not produce a great deal of learning. A 'critical friend', such as a colleague doing similar work, who can dig into the project with you and make suggestions about strengths and weaknesses can be valuable. This may be unofficial, but can often give real insight. In return, you can review their projects, and this is often helpful for the reviewer. If done properly, you may pick up some good techniques that you can use as well.

REAL WORLD   **Hewlett-Packard: carrying out a review by following the project**

In new product development it is traditional for the product to be designed, then engineered, then passed to manufacturing for making. The designers would be having battles with the engineers over the need for design features to be preserved, and the engineers with the manufacturing staff over what could and could not be made (these were described in Chapter 5). Hewlett-Packard, as part of the linking process between the different functions, ensures that key staff who do the design work carry the project through. Not just to the end of the project and its handover to manufacturing but to three months into mass production of the designed items. This provides ample opportunity for problems to emerge and for the designer to witness the effects of their decisions on the end product. It is a case of knowledge management of the highest order – people gain great insight from this process and retain this for subsequent projects. It is one thing to hear about a design failure or to read about it in a document later. It is quite another to own the failure you were responsible for implementing and be stuck with the consequences (and angry customers) until you implement a fix! It is very hard to get this level of understanding and motivation if you pass on a dubious product to the customer-support team and start your next design exercise. As a by-product of this, the networks of people they have worked alongside during these extended handovers mean that there is far better communication in the organisation.

As the above Real World example demonstrates, reviews can be an immensely powerful tool for starting process improvement. In themselves, though, they do nothing. As with other decisions, it is how these improvements are followed up with changes in processes and improvements in the individuals and parties to the project that will make the difference in future. It is also worth noting the benefit of short-cycle learning processes *within* projects. These can be exceptionally powerful (such as the 'Last Planner' technique in Chapter 13) yet are often underemphasised. Part of the process of convincing firms and individuals to follow through and make these changes is to provide the business case for them. This is discussed in the following section through the tool of quality costing.

16.3 Improving and maturing

The financial implications of many sorts of failure in performance can be calculated for the purpose of providing the business case for performance improvement activities. The costs are generally enormous and can be expressed as a percentage of turnover.

For the purposes of calculation, quality costs are broken down into three categories – **prevention**, **appraisal** and **failure**. The inclusions in each category are shown in Table 16.2. Failure can be broken down into internal failure (that which is detected by the organisation before the customer does, thus allowing a rapid remedy) and external failure (one that the customer detects after delivery of the product or consumption of the service). Generally, it can be stated that the failure costs are orders of magnitude higher than those of prevention and appraisal.

Table 16.2 Elements of quality cost

Category	Activities included
Prevention	Quality planning, training and auditing, supplier development, costs of maintaining a quality improvement programme or system, maintenance of all testing equipment
Appraisal	Any checking activities (and materials consumed during these), analysis and reporting of quality data, auditing suppliers' quality systems, storing records of quality results
Failure	*Internal* – any wasted activities, be they in the production of an artefact that is scrap or the generation of a document that is not read, changing or rectifying work already done because it was not right first time, downgrading goods or services, problem-solving time
	External – replacement of faulty goods, having to return to a site to redo tasks, complaints and consequent loss of goodwill and repeat business, product and professional liability claims

One famous study researched how the performance of the quality system related to the profitability of the organisation.[9] The findings of this work were that:

For a well developed quality system, the costs of quality can make up as little as 2 per cent of turnover. For an organisation with a poor or neglected quality system, they can make up in excess of 20 per cent.

A recent audit of a project organisation within the aerospace industry showed **quality costs** to be 36 per cent of turnover. This was a surprise for the organisation, given that external failure happened very rarely (as one might hope with aircraft components!). Another study with a construction firm showed quality costs of 38 per cent of turnover. While the aerospace firm could rightfully claim that the precautions that it had to take to prevent failures in service were very costly, whether it justified such a large part of its costs was doubtful. A more realistic benchmark was 15–20 per cent in the medium term. For the construction firm there was no such excuse and the opportunity very large (given that profit margins at the time were of the order of 3–8 per cent of turnover). A benchmark for this firm would be in the range 2–5 per cent.[10]

This is a major driver and source of cost savings if recognised and a system implemented properly. Savings are generally made through the increase of prevention and appraisal activities, which in the medium term will result in reduced failure costs. The project organisation has to accept that in the short term, overall costs are likely to increase as the improvements take their time to work through the system.

Organisational maturity

Learning, improving, benchmarking – these are all valuable, well-documented processes, and few would argue against their value. So, why is it that some organisations have well-developed project processes and others have something that closely resembles chaos? Surely each has the same commercial imperative and desire to be successful? Why also do some organisations become totally bogged down in structures and intensive documentation, losing sight of the reasons for their processes?

There are many ways of characterising organisations, and for the purpose of this discussion we will consider their ability to meet basic objectives of time, cost and quality, and then to improve these over time. Four types of organisation become apparent. They are:

- Group 1 – the **flatliners**. Despite good intentions to improve, these make little or no progress in project performance. Mistakes are repeated and performance stays flat over time.
- Group 2 – the **improvers**. Some improvement actions are put in place and performance shows some increase over time.
- Group 3 – the **wannabes**. This group generally follows every initiative in the book, in an attempt to catch up with the best.
- Group 4 – the **world-class** performers. This small number of organisations set an ever-increasing standard for performance.

These are shown in Figure 16.3. The figure shows a number of features of performance:

- the performance gap between the best and 'the rest' is large;
- the performance gap doesn't seem to be narrowed over time, indeed it appears that 'the best are better at getting better'.

The second of these points shows that there are some fundamentally different mechanisms for improvement in place in the four groups of organisations.

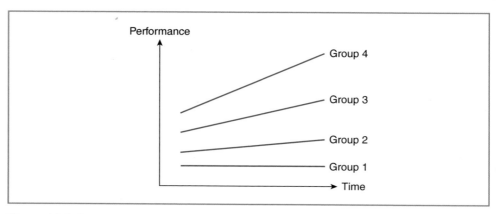

Figure 16.3 Performance groups

Looking more closely, there are some characteristics of each of these types of organisations that can be discerned. This is their level of 'project management maturity'. The characteristics are shown in Table 16.3.

These characteristics enable some prediction of the likely performance of the organisation and also represent a path for improvement. While process changes (see following sections) are needed, a fundamental change in the approach that is taken will be required to move between the groups. Many organisations have moved from group 1 to group 2 – showing the application of some systems to their project management. Moving to group 3 requires considerable discipline, and this is usually imposed through rules and well-defined structures and documentation. While not a good vehicle for improvement, this does instil the necessary disciplines in the organisation. It is only when the procedures are eventually discarded and the organisation has the maturity to be able to take the standard systems and tailor them to each individual project and project team requirements that real improvement takes place. It is usual that a firm will need to move through the stages in sequence. Jumping stages is unlikely, as the disciplines learned at each stage are required later.

Table 16.3 Project management maturity stages

Type	Characteristics
Group 1	Little by way of processes or disciplines. Every project is novel and little learning takes place as a result of project activities. External ideas rejected as being 'not invented here'. Goal of projects poorly established, if at all.
Group 2	Some processes and systems in place, resulting in pockets of acceptable performance. Little learning from one project to another. Goal of projects sometimes established, and focused on conformance to objectives.
Group 3	Processes well documented and systems imposed as to how to run projects. Improvement based on trying to keep up with the best by imitating their processes, but limited by the constraints of system documentation. Goals of projects routinely established and focused on conformance to objectives.
Group 4	Processes mapped and based around a core, which is forever being improved. Learning evident within and between projects. Goal of project is to exceed the objectives and deliver the best project possible (performance).

In moving between the groups, a number of the following topics have been used as the means of generating the necessary changes.

Commercial maturity models

'If you are a project manager, and you suspect that the basic approach to project management in your organization is not ideal, what can you do to convince senior management of the benefits of adopting a different model? Can you trust your own intuition and experience? Where can you look for evidence that there are better ways of approaching the management of projects across an organization?'[11]

Today there are a vast array of maturity models that an organisation can use to assess themselves against. The most commonly used ones are CMMI, OPM3 and P3M3.

CMMI – Capability Maturity Model Integration – one of the more commonly used models in the IT industry. Based on work carried out at Carnegie Mellon University, it is based on a 5-stage model.[12] Although there is a Level 0 ('incomplete', leading to inconsistent performance), Level 1 is 'initial' and comparable to group 1 in Figure 16.3. Level 2 is 'managed, with a basic process for projects. Level 3 is 'defined' – with the emphasis on proactive management of projects, with the project management process ingrained into the institution. Level 4 is 'quantitatively managed' – with a focus on objective reporting and quantification of key measures. Level 5 is 'optimising', where the focus is on continuous and ongoing improvement. Currently, many large IT firms are working to gain accreditation to various levels of the model. In that sector, it is believed that achieving a minimum level (usually 3) will provide some evidence of competence for the firm, while achieving level 5 would give them competitive advantage. Project-based organisations are usually very goal oriented, and it is noticeable that this approach seems to fit well – it allows senior managers to target the organisation on achieving a particular level of accreditation.

OPM3 – Organisational Project Management Maturity Model – commonly used in US-based or large international concerns. OPM3 is a product of the Project Management Institute[13] and is based on an audit of the application of their standards for project, programme and portfolio management. This broad scope has some attraction in that, as we have seen, many of the problems faced by projects are caused by failures elsewhere in the organisation. As for the other standards, the usual claims are made about the ability to determine a route forward for improvement.

P3M3 – Portfolio, Programme and Project Management Maturity Model – developed by the UK's Office of Government Commerce and now available from Axelos.[14] Again there are five levels of maturity (Level 1: awareness; Level 2: repeatable; Level 3: defined; Level 4: managed; Level 5: optimised). This can be downloaded from the Axelos website.[15]

In addition to these, there are many organisations that carry out maturity assessments and use their own scales. Interestingly, our experience is that managers and teams can overestimate their organisation's performance, and often rate it more highly than their customers do, which can lead to overoptimism. Having a clear, externally-validated, goal can thus focus the improvement efforts. Self-reflection and working towards a given target are therefore very effective ways for organisations to improve their performance. However, although improvement is in itself beneficial, it is important to consider what 'good' looks like within the wider industry, and what other organisations are doing.

Securing improvement

The performance and rate of improvement differences described in this chapter provide some interesting material for the management researcher. Why do such differences exist? The answer does not lie with individual project processes but with the fundamentally different approach to change that underlies it. Research showed that these differences were the result of a large number of factors, but that they could be reduced to three main themes. These are shown in Figure 16.4.

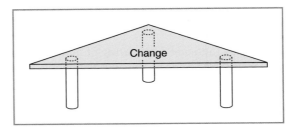

Figure 16.4 The three pillars of change

Figure 16.4 shows that all three of these need to be in place for change in processes to occur. The pillars and their constituent activities are summarised in Table 16.4.

Strategy deployment

This has been discussed in Chapter 3 and throughout this text, with explicit strategy driving the decision-making processes of the organisation. The elements of this include how the organisation determines what to change and thereby avoid the problem of 'change paralysis' discussed previously where there are so many change possibilities that no one knows where to start. Coherence is also vital – strategy ensuring that all changes are moving the processes in one particular direction, and participants understand that direction and work towards it. The nature of the drivers for change here is interesting. Many organisations cannot change until they are on the very edge of extinction. This is an extreme example of a driver. Other drivers for change are more usually internal initiatives or customers demanding improvements.

Managed knowledge

Earlier the role of *learning before doing* and *learning by doing* was discussed. The themes that need to be addressed are relevant to this. Specifically, how do we identify potential improvement targets and the means to achieve them? How do we evaluate the possibilities and identify the limited range of issues that can be addressed at one time? How much of what we know already can be used, and how much of the future state will be new to us?

Table 16.4 Key change issues

Strategy deployment	*Managed knowledge*	*Implementation*
Strategy/policy deployment	Organisational learning	Measurement of impact of changes
Prioritisation of changes	Explicit structure for sources of change ideas	Implementation methodology
Drivers for change (internal/external)	Systematic evaluation of new ideas pre-implementation	
Coherence		

Implementation

As a result of pressure from their customer, a large automotive supplier, a firm implemented a number of new tools and techniques. At least their procedure documents said that they had implemented those tools and techniques. People were trained in their use and pilot projects established, but it never went further than that. Why? Very simply, the measures by which people were assessed were not changed. Therefore, after the hype, the practices reverted to normal. In this case, the **implementation** failed also because there were problems, and there was no one around with the necessary expertise to assist in finding solutions.

Organisations trying new ideas almost always adopt the 'poke-it-with-a-stick' method. If they don't get bitten, they may pursue it further. Or they may not. This is hardly the kind of systematic trial and evaluation that would lead to some conclusion as to whether the changes:

- were a success and should seek wider application;
- were a limited success and should be developed further;
- were a complete disaster and should be ditched forthwith.

Without relevant measures in place, practitioners are unable to be objective about the change.

The message from the implementation themes is that measures should be put in place to identify if the strategic objectives of the change are being met, and that implementation includes full training and support for changes. Such support may be required for a considerable period after the initial implementation. Incentives also help. When promotions and bonuses depend on the desired actions happening, they tend to happen. Hoping that busy people add the required implementation to their 'to-do' list is far less likely to result in change.

The three pillars of change must all be in place for any change process to be successful. Indeed, any change is in itself a project, and one that is consistent with the approaches discussed in this text can show significant benefits from being managed in a way that shows people in the organisation what good project management looks like.

The role of 'lean'

Although we always wish to improve performance, any definition of 'world-class' as an aspiration is inevitably open to some debate, and evaluation is not always totally objective. More than one company can be world-class at any one time in any one sphere of activity, though the gap between the world-class performers and the others can be considerable. This is difficult to evaluate in the project management environment, and it is hard to say who are 'the best'. Given the wide variety of work that can constitute a project, this is perhaps understandable. However, given the evidence for the superiority of **lean** practices (as introduced in Chapter 9), it is worth considering whether the way in which operations have been improved can be adapted to the project environment. In any case, the original studies on lean also noted that the lean Japanese producers were also superior in project performance – developing new vehicles in roughly half the time of their Western counterparts.

The fundamental characteristics for being progressive can be compared to conventional organisations as follows:[16]

- Organisational structures are flexible rather than rigid to accommodate changes in customer requirements. This must be within the context that has been discussed of change/configuration management. As discussed in Chapter 4, flexibility is not free.
- The organisation focuses on optimisation of the entire flow of projects through it, rather than through a single area or department (see below).

- Open communication flows within flat organisational structures as opposed to tall hierarchies leading to long chains of command (where messages are interpreted and changed at each link in the chain). This is a particular challenge for project managers, where they may not have direct authority over the individuals in their 'team' on whom they have to rely. Making important projects heavyweight matrix organisations is consistent with this objective.

- Agreements between parties (including suppliers) are trust-based rather than contractual; this reiterates the principles discussed in Chapter 14. As stated, there are particular problems with this approach for certain project-based sectors.

- The skills base of the teams is wide to allow flexibility rather than narrow and specialist. The cross-training of individuals allows them to spend time outside their normal field of work. This also recognises the need for processes and process-thinking rather than functional thinking.

- Education and training are significant parts of work activity rather than inconvenient distractions from the work in hand. This is an area where there is so much opportunity for improvement in project management. Training often involves little more than a guide to using Gantt charts, network techniques and some of the basics, and many firms undertake it just so that they can tick the box on the Human Resources Training Record marked 'project management'. Unless this is placed in an appropriate structure, it is unlikely to be beneficial.

As stated, there is little by way of rocket science here, except that it brings together all the themes covered in this book. Is lean project management the same as good project management? There is much to suggest that it is, but that the structures within which the project managers work are different. In addition, there is the treatment of the concept of **waste** not mentioned in either of the Bodies of Knowledge, and, given the costs of quality identified in the previous chapter, presenting a significant improvement opportunity.

A lean approach to management,[17] continues the ideas of Henry Ford who is quoted as saying: 'if it doesn't add value, it's waste'. This principle may be applied to the project environment as shown in Table 16.5. The first of these points concerns the flow of information

Table 16.5 Lean principles applied to project management

Line management	Project management
Integrated single-piece workflow produced just in time	Information treated as inventory and processed immediately rather than spending long periods of time waiting
Absolute elimination of waste	See 'seven wastes'
Focus on global rather than local optima	Focus on achieving the goals of the organisation through this and other project activities and considering the project in this light rather than as a totally independent item (develops idea of the role of the stakeholders)
Defect prevention	Defect prevention
Multi-skilling in team-based operations	Multi-skilling in team-based projects
Few indirect staff	Few indirect staff

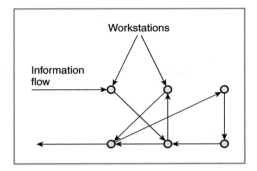

Figure 16.5 Complex information flow around systems

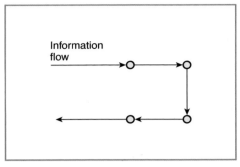

Figure 16.6 Simplified information flow through system

through a project organisation as a manufacturing engineer would plan the routing of a product through a process. The focus is on the simplification of flows so that it becomes visible where problems and hold-ups are occurring. In order not to be seen to be idle, people tend to build up inventories of tasks to be completed, regardless of the consequences of this hold-up in the flow of information being progressed. Consequently, problems get hidden. The role of simplification is to move the type of **information flow** from that shown in Figure 16.5 to that shown in Figure 16.6. In the latter case, there are no inventories. This means that periodically a person may complete their tasks with no further work to be done. In this case, rather than them creating inventory for downstream activities, they may engage in other work through being multi-skilled. Some organisations use 'down time' as the opportunity for extra training, so there is an incentive to finish swiftly to free up time perhaps to learn a skill you had planned for the year.

Apart from becoming faster at processing information, the above leads to improved responsiveness – customer requests and the inevitable changes can be implemented more quickly.

In manufacturing, the seven wastes are: *transportation, inventory (excess), motion, waiting, overproduction, overprocessing, defects* and *skills*, but when lean thinking is applied to projects (as discussed earlier in Chapter 9), the seven wastes are:[18]

- defects and rework;
- inflexibility in responding to emergence;
- lost capabilities;
- interface losses;
- over-checking;
- inappropriate processing;
- failure to capitalise on upside uncertainties

Wherever possible:

- tasks should be simplified – procedures are often needlessly complicated and open to too much interpretation;
- tasks should be combined – putting together tasks through multi-skilling can eliminate the transfer time and reduces the need for handover information;
- non-value-adding tasks should be eliminated, such as bureaucracy, constricting accounting systems and computer-planning systems, which absorb large proportions of managers' time, etc.

The above represents some very basic disciplines which can be applied throughout the project organisation. While it is often tempting to seek technological solutions, 90 per cent of all improvement comes from the application of what is termed 'common sense'.

Further improvement activities need to be focused on the entire value-chain or value-network. It is not unusual for 60 per cent or more of a project spend to be with external suppliers and, unless these are also engaged in improvement activities, the scope for performance improvement of your own organisation is distinctly limited. The concept of removing local optima is applicable here. For example, where a supplier provides you with materials that are required for the execution phase of a project and will be used at a steady rate during this phase, there is little point in their delivering the entire order at the start of work, even though their machines may be geared to produce in such quantities. This would provide a local optimum, namely at the suppliers. The purchaser now has a stock or inventory which will require storing, checking and possibly guarding – all activities that involve costs. The optimum can be redistributed to benefit all parties, with staged deliveries, for example. Helping suppliers to become more responsive is a technique many organisations promote. Better utilisation of their expertise is provided through giving a rough specification for the needs of a product and requiring the supplier to carry out design activities themselves. In this way they can achieve better designs, as their manufacturing processes can be accommodated in the component design.

Summary

■ Chapter 2 answers the question: where do we start? There were structures that would facilitate the thinking for that part of the process. A certainty of the definition of a project is that it will end in one way or another. The question could similarly be asked: how do we end the project? Again, there are structures and ideas to help here. Two basic principles guide this. The first is that there must be a positive statement of closure rather than simply allowing the project to fizzle out. The second is that the knowledge gained by doing the project must be captured. This is achieved through the review and audit process, feeding back into both project process knowledge and technical knowledge. The project may have cost the organisation and individuals dearly – and now is the opportunity to realise some payback from that 'investment'. What was good that we can do again? What was less good that we need to avoid next time?

■ There have been many different improvement initiatives that have tried, and in most cases failed, to revolutionise the ways that we work. Project management is not one of these, whatever people may try to do with it. It is a business basic, a skillset (some say an art) and will be required long after current business forms and firms have ceased to exist. Moreover, it is creative, requiring the greatest personal input.

■ Benchmarking organisational maturity has had considerable repercussions for project management and has considerable real-world value still to offer the vast majority of practitioners and organisations. Comparison of processes will be the area that offers the greatest scope for benchmarking. Lean projects are still few and far between, though the principles are largely already imbedded in 'good project management'. The area that differs is in the treatment of *waste* and its pursuit. These ideas are fine, but are nothing more than 'of theoretical benefit' if they cannot be implemented.

■ Closing out the project involves the shut-down of all project systems, ensuring all activities are completed and preparing for the forthcoming reviews. Audits are there to check conformance to procedure. In short, did you do what you said you would do, in the way that you said you would do it? Reviews look for opportunities for process improvement, at particular aspects of how the project was managed. The aspects of importance are determined by the project strategy – it is not feasible to review every aspect of performance.

■ The learning process from projects was suggested to be at least twofold, through learning before doing (through identification of appropriate knowledge in advance of need), learning by doing (through review and integration of that knowledge into the organisation) and longer-term reflection. This involves self-reflection, not just a written document for the file.

■ The costs of failure were identified above as an 'investment' and these should be calculated as part of a quality costing exercise. This is frequently a good starting point, as the extent of the failures and their costs are usually surprising to most organisations. They also provide considerable insight into what is really going on in the organisation.

■ As part of a longer-term process, how do we get better as an organisation? We need to know how we compare to others, and have a road to improvement and enhanced maturity.

■ In conclusion, for the aspiring career project manager, there is a significant opportunity. With the increased recognition of the contribution of project managers will come greater rewards. Continuously improving our own processes should be the goal of every project manager. The knowledge exists: we need to find ways to apply it, mindful of strategic requirements and in a way that is open to evaluation. In future, we will need to be able to manage not only the improvement process but also its speed. Now there's a challenge that may also turn out to be great fun. Here's hoping.

Key terms

appraisal *p. 412*

audit *p. 408*

benchmarking *p. 405*

completion *p. 397*

consultants *p. 403*

critical mass *p. 403*

documenta'ion *p. 398*

education *p. 403*

failure *p. 412*

flatliners *p. 413*

handover *p. 399*

implementation *p. 417*

improvers *p. 413*

information flow *p. 419*

KPIs *p. 406*

lean *p. 417*

learning before doing *p. 402*

learning by doing *p. 402*

managed knowledge *p. 416*

management paralysis *p. 401*

percentage improvement *p. 407*

prevention *p. 412*

product surround *p. 401*

quality costs *p. 413*

review *pp. 397, 408*

signs off *p. 399*

stakeholder satisfaction *p. 401*

strategy deployment *p. 416*

terminated *p. 397*

training *p. 403*

wannabes *p. 413*

waste *p. 418*

world-class *p. 413*

Relevant areas of the Bodies of Knowledge

Both Bodies of Knowledge (Tables 16.6 and 16.7) focus on the contractual and practical aspects of the completion process, and include the tangible and intangible knowledge within the project.

Table 16.6 Relevant areas of the APM Body of Knowledge

Relevant section	Title	Summary
2.2.3	Information management	Discusses the importance of capturing information (e.g. key documents) and ensuring changes are communicated effectively, and making sure that information is accessible and archived.
2.2.4	Audits and assurance	As discussed in this chapter, independent auditing gives confidence that processes are being carried out correctly.
2.2.5	Knowledge management	Knowledge is understood as being 'intangible and complex' (as opposed to the documented 'information' above), and this section stresses the importance of supporting staff in sharing tacit knowledge. A balance needs to be struck between using existing knowledge and creating new knowledge.
2.2.6	Communities of practice	These are groups which create a social basis for learning in a specific domain, such as project management.
2.3.4	Unplanned project endings	Projects can be ended, for example if the analysis at a decision gate shows that the project is no longer justified.
2.3.5	Administrative closure of projects	The project must be closed properly, including contract completion, team re-assignment, a project review, and the archival of documents.
2.3.6	Closing programmes and portfolios	These should be closed if the outcomes have been delivered, if the expected business case is no longer viable, or if the rest of the work would be better delivered in a different manner.

Table 16.7 Relevant areas of the PMI Body of Knowledge

Relevant section	Title	Summary
4.4	Manage project knowledge	Covers both explicit knowledge (e.g. documents) and tacit knowledge (personal 'know-how'). Also advocates the social aspects such as networking, communities of practice and knowledge-sharing events.
4.7	Close project or phase	Managers need to make sure that at closure all the work is complete, the information is archived, and the team are released to their next piece of work.

PROJECT MANAGEMENT IN PRACTICE
IT all goes pear-shaped at VCS

Introduction

The department that later became VCS was founded to provide computer support in a major firm. Over time, this role expanded, and five years later the function was bought out by three of its managers to begin life as a company in its own right. Two years after that the firm was sold to a plc, which made VCS one of its operating divisions. Two years further on, VCS was sold again to a corporate holdings firm, with interests in a number of software and hardware companies.

VCS's range of products all required regular upgrades to keep them competitive within the market-place. The Time-Track product was undergoing a major revision when a number of problems became apparent. These included areas of the product which were far too complex for the task that was required of them (incurring significant problems elsewhere) and little control over time or cost. As a result, the product arrived late in the market, to the embarrassment of the firm and particularly its new owners. This was given significant attention at board level, and technical specialists conducted a number of internal reviews. Realising that there were more fundamental issues at stake here, the firm's management team was debating the next move.

The product

Time-Track is used as a means of compiling time data from employees as to how they have spent their time, so that clients may be billed accordingly. The product has to work with a company's own account-ing software and is viewed by many firms as 'mission-critical' – if the product fails they are unable to bill their clients and thereby earn revenue. Reliability is therefore essential from the customer's point of view. A major review of the product was required to update its features and capabilities. Moving from Version 2 (V.2) of the software to V.3 meant that, in addition to obtaining upgrade revenue from exist-ing clients, new features could be added to bring new clients in. It was therefore a project of the highest strategic importance for the firm.

The project

Looking back, the V.3 project does not appear ever to have been officially launched. Documents relating to technical aspects of the product were generated, including a 200-page proposal which was circulated to the technical staff, though notably not the sales or marketing people who would be responsible for the income the new product would generate. Two years later, no one on the development team was able to produce a copy of this document.

The project was intended to be a collaborative venture between two companies from the same group, based on potential synergies generated by combining two of their existing offerings. The firms became part of the same owning group during the buyout. They had fundamentally different products but some com-monality in the technology being used. There was significant excitement caused by the potential for the new product – it provided a much-needed replacement for the product sold by one of the firms based in Black-burn (north-west England), by upgrading an established product which was being sold by VCS in Cardiff (South Wales). This opened the market from predominantly public-sector clients to a much wider range including large corporations. Additional sales personnel with corporate sales experience were recruited and began selling the product into the market in expectation that the new product would soon be available.

The timeline of the product highlights the difficulties experienced. At the beginning of year 1, there was a meeting of the project participants from both sites on neutral territory. They considered what could go wrong with the project. A total of 152 potential problems were identified that could lead to project failure. These included the departure of key personnel as well as failures in the technical ele-ments of the process. At the VCS board of directors' monthly meeting in February, the project manager,

Dave Grant, reported that work had started in earnest. He noted then that there were differences in the approaches of the two sites involved in the project, but felt that these could be overcome. He himself was based at the Blackburn site and much of the early project work on adding functionality was being carried out there. At VCS, the main role was detailed coding (programming) of the product.

Problems start to become evident

As early as March, problems between the two sites became evident. VCS's technical director, Steve Timms, reported to the monthly board meeting that things were not going right, that it was hard to know what was going on in Blackburn, and that there was a complete lack of agreement on technical protocols between the sites. Without these protocols, development work lacked any solid foundations on which to build. Dave Grant reported that progress at the Cardiff site had been disappointing. Overruns of the construction of one of the databases necessary for the system were due to overoptimistic estimates and the use of less experienced developers. He further commented in a direct criticism of VCS management that 'work to motivate the team by improving the local supervision of their work is needed to ensure that this slippage is made up'. During the following month, this problem continued, leading to a further report of poor progress on the new product. This time, he identified the problem as 'too many projects for the Cardiff staff to work on. While the staff in Blackburn have one project to work on, Cardiff have a whole list of projects to deliver before the end of the year. The whole of the development department at Cardiff is grossly overcommitted.'

The developers at Cardiff were also starting to become frustrated. As the development coordinator at VCS, Bill Jones, noted: 'When our customer service people have a problem with something they don't understand or with a customer, we just have to go and do it. It's always V.3 that gets dropped. Worse – V.3 work will be the first thing that we get stopped to do something else. It's really hard to keep the team [the programmers] geed up and saying "this is it – everybody's depending on us". It does have an effect on them.' The disruption caused to the programmers by the constant changing of their roles was also noted. 'You can lose half a day easily if something takes you off the train of thought for as little as half an hour.'

The May report continued in a similar vein, with good reported progress at Blackburn and poor or non-existent progress at Cardiff. The addition of a new team member at Cardiff with significant relevant experience gave some hope that the situation would improve from then on. A prototype of the new system was produced and demonstrated to the company's user group (firms which were already using its products) during May. This provided the developers with a first opportunity to gain feedback on their ideas for the new product.

The first target date for completion of the project was announced for August. At the end of May there was still some belief that this deadline could be met. Marketing and sales people were informed accordingly, creating an expectation for V.3 in the market – among existing clients who wished for the promised upgrades and new customers who were interested in the potential new functionality. However, despite the addition of extra staff, there were underlying problems. Mark Small, a member of the development team, commented: 'When I came in in May, programmers were doing things, but nobody could tell you why they were doing them and who had made the decision that they should be done this way. What they were trying to achieve did not seem to be defined anywhere.' Another of VCS's development coordinators noted the result of this to be that 'the development team were making lots of decisions that they should never have been expected to make – they were getting little or no guidance.'

Following concerns about the speed of progress a review of the work outstanding identified a further 90 person-days of work required in one area alone, which had not previously been included in any plans or workload considerations.

Problems come to a head

June of that year was a watershed for the companies and the project. At this time, it became apparent to the Blackburn firm that the product (VCS Time-Track V.2) which they had decided to build upon was nowhere near as sophisticated as first thought. This meant that in order for it to do half of what the existing product did (which it was intended to supersede), there would have to be a substantial rework of the Cardiff product. In addition, there were many problems with the programming quality which required significant rectification work before it could be developed further.

These two problems were a major blow for the project and soon led to the departure of the two members of the team from Blackburn. One of these had been promised a project management role in this project, but was given charge of only one programmer. To make matters worse, there was little management required in this role and he ended up doing much of the coding work, contrary to his expectations. When his management role did not materialise, he started looking for work elsewhere.

The pressure to complete a product (whatever that was) mounted on the Cardiff team. They still had neither design specification nor method of testing the product. Furthermore, their lack of experience of the business processes involved was starting to tell on the product. Steve Timms, technical director at Cardiff, probably sensing the mounting problems and the impending product disaster, decided to leave. He had been noted for his ability to have the whole vision for the product in his head. This led staff to comment that 'we all knew what we were doing, nobody knew why'. His departure caused a significant vacuum within the project team. Meanwhile, Dave Grant at Blackburn was taking active steps to dissociate himself from the project. Indeed, the Cardiff staff perceived that the only time that Dave Grant was interested was just before a board meeting.

By the June report, there was a real sense of growing frustration for the project manager. The newly appointed project coordinator at Cardiff, who now played a pivotal role in the development, was unexpectedly off work due to personal circumstances. Since it was a small firm, replacement cover was provided on a goodwill basis from other areas. With little coordination on the ground, slow progress was being made and the project was increasingly seen as unbalanced. Work carried out at Blackburn was innovative and complete; that at Cardiff was outside any plans that had been laid down (though no one could actually find any detailed plans for the Cardiff work at this stage). Dave Grant continued, in his words, 'to try to manage things from afar', though this was debatable from the Cardiff staff's perspective. Additional developers were added to the team at Cardiff, though at the same time an updated version (V.2.1) of the previous release of the software was sent out. Andy Morgan was brought in as the new development manager and described some of the problems being faced in a report he prepared at the end of June – see the following table.

Proposed work	Planned time	Actual time
General enhancements	15 days	20 days
Specific programming	29 days	6 days
Data structuring	8 days	5 days
Maintenance for V.2.1	15 days	27 days
General support for other products	5 days	5 days

As the table shows, little progress was being made on the specific programming – of the 29 days allocated to it, only 6 were actually used to carry out work on the main programming for the project. This resulted in a significant part of this work being carried forward for completion the following month, which only compounded the time shortage. Andy Morgan stated: 'We've allowed in the plans for a day a week per programmer for maintenance. But it's not working, we're constantly being knocked sideways, in terms of planning, because of the pull from maintenance.' This was indeed a significant issue – customers were demanding that problems in their existing products were resolved, but this resource could come only from the development team.

In June, Andy Morgan was appointed as project manager for the V.3 project and from then on Dave Grant's role was unclear, as Blackburn were no longer very interested in the project – it would not provide them with the product they wanted. The work was completely transferred to the Cardiff site.

In July, Dave Grant noted that there had been some progress with the project and suggested that the software be released for Quality Assurance (QA – the people who will test that the product works before it is released to customers). A separate Cardiff report for July stated that they were on target for a controlled release of the software in late October, though no mention was made of the earlier agreed August deadline. In August, this became 'controlled release in November'. The problem for Andy Morgan in Cardiff was a lack of the resources to carry out the necessary QA of the product and too much work left too late in the project.

In September, Andy Morgan reported that due to further requests for additional functionality from the user group the software would undergo controlled release in January of year 2. In October, this was still 'the schedule'. To facilitate this, he commented that the QA had been set up next to the development office and that a whiteboard had been installed to give the project higher visibility. At this point, concerns were raised about the quality of the final software. This appeared to be vital – that quality was rated 'above all else', to ensure that it was relatively 'bug-free' when put on general release. Not only would the software need to be checked, but any problems found would have to be solved. With such a complex piece of software this would inevitably mean further problems as when you change one area it inevitably affects another. Andy Morgan reiterated his point that 'quality is the most important feature of Version 3 and it will go on general release when we are confident of its quality.' Controlled release was then scheduled for the third week of January.

During QA, it became apparent that the original programming, so highly praised by Dave Grant, was poorly constructed and regularly failed to perform simple tasks, let alone the complex ones it was designed to do. The problems with the coding were exacerbated by an attitude of 'QA is there to find the problems – that's their job'. When this was investigated further, it was found that while some of the programmers were excellent and always checked their work before it went to QA, others were consistently not doing so. This lack of commitment to the project was further noted by one of the board members who stated that 'they [the programmers] just come in at 9:00 and leave by 5:15. Nobody would think we were having major problems with the product.'

Product release

Limited parts of the software were indeed released to a key client at the end of January, though the product was nowhere near ready. Here, the situation was described as 'lose–lose – if we deliver any later, we lose the client, if we deliver and it doesn't work, we lose the client'. The controlled release served one purpose: it showed that there were further problems with the software. On the positive side, the users liked the parts that they saw and even said that they perceived the implementation to be managed well by VCS by not releasing the full version until it was ready.

Commenting on the controlled release, the sales director noted: 'The consultant went on-site at the client and started trying to make the product work. There was no documentation or other help available other than the members of the development team. Even then, there were many parts of the product where nobody knew how they were supposed to work. After three days of trial and error, we had to take the software out again. They are probably our largest client. They wanted V.3 because there were so many bugs in V.2.1 and they wanted fixes for them. We had to stop supporting V.2.1 and told them to go to V.3 to get these things fixed. They do not want a whole load of new features, just the ones they had bought initially to work. The testing was to see that nothing had got worse. This was a shock to me – I thought they wanted the enhancements.'

In addition, one key technical feature (which most users would not be in a position to evaluate anyway) was causing major problems for the developers. The implications of this feature were increased levels of technical complexity, which had been introduced by Steve Timms. As was commented: 'He was technically brilliant – he'll do everything to the nth degree, try to get everything perfect, but half of it won't relate to user requirements. The other problem we've got is that it is an enormous program, it is horribly complex, and every time we fix a bug somewhere, it causes a bug somewhere else. That is the problem for us – the wrong person given too much rope. He built on things we didn't need, but that he thought were a good idea technically.' During the period of uncertainty this one person was able to make all sorts of changes as and when he saw fit. Later comments included: 'One of the things we desperately need to implement is change control throughout maintenance as well as new product development.'

The product was fully released in June of year 2, ten months after the original deadline. It had cost the company dearly. As the sales director commented: 'We've lost £1.5 million worth of business in the past 3 months alone because of these problems.' For a company with a £15 million annual turnover this was a significant amount of revenue. He further noted that the result of the problems with V.3 was that the firm had gone from being a leader in the field to being one that was now pushing obsolete technology and had been overtaken by its competitors. Moreover, it had gained a reputation for being unable to deliver products to the market as it had promised, either at the time or with the full list of promised features.

A final comment on the development process concerned the role of the departments involved with the product and its roll-out to customers. The developers were responsible for the product until it left the firm while a separate function, the consultancy group within the firm, was the one which would take the product to a customer's site, install it and then train staff in its usage. This placed a heavy burden on the consultants, often requiring them to 'fix' problems that became evident with the product during implementation.

After the launch, one of the development team concluded: 'The project was and still is a nightmare.'

The review

Following the project, the management team and the staff at VCS carried out a review. Issues raised during the review included the split-site working where 'the communications simply did not work. There were lots of tests made early on to define standards – ways of doing things, and then latterly to transfer the knowledge of the Blackburn work down to us. There were lots of attempts made, meetings, etc. – it was a struggle all the way along. Towards the end the communications broke down quite badly.'

When they considered the project planning Andy Morgan commented: 'Another problem that we have faced is the constant underestimate made by the guys of the work remaining. What we've tried to do as part of a philosophy of getting the ownership down a couple of levels (development coordinator, etc.) is to try to get the programmers to commit to their own estimates. They do, but they always get it wrong, and fundamentally wrong, particularly in the most complex parts. Part of this is inexperience and part because they do not have any specification to work to. They do not have a technical breakdown – it's pure guesswork.' Related to this, the managing director commented: 'We didn't know until things were going wrong that there was a problem, which is vital for managing customer expectations.' Further planning issues were raised by staff, including the comment that 'we need hands-on project management – regular meetings, not just once a month the day before the board meetings. The team never worked as a team – too much them and us.'

Another member of staff commented: 'A key problem was that there were too few people involved at the start of the project. As a result, when the Cardiff technical director left in June of the first year, so much of the product knowledge left with him. None of this was down in writing, so we lost it. The knowledge base in future must be spread a lot more.' In addition, he noted: 'There was never any business case for the features that were being built into the system. I cannot see how either the existing or future client base is going to benefit from many of the features. The amount of effort we have put into it is disproportionate to the benefit that will be gained.'

$\rightarrow$

The need to start work on V.4 was pressing – many of the clients were demanding updated features that were not available on V.3. As the management team contemplated the review there were clearly a significant number of issues that required attention. 'Above all,' the financial director said, 'this must never happen again.'

Points for discussion

1 What are the root causes of the problems that VCS faced during the V.3 project? Carry out a review of the project to determine what went wrong.

2 How do you suggest that it ensures that these problems 'never happen again'? Use an appropriate framework to structure your arguments.

3 What are the barriers to progress likely to be?

4 How could these be overcome?

5 What additional suggestions do you have for the company?

Topics for discussion

1 Why is there a tendency for individual rather than group projects in particular to spend '90 per cent of their time 90 per cent complete'.

2 Show the activities that must be completed during the final phases of a project.

3 Identify the role that benchmarking can play in improving project performance in organisations. What are the potential drawbacks?

4 Why might compiling project documentation be considered such a burden to the team, yet be so essential?

5 What issues must be considered when deciding how far post-delivery service should extend (such as providing free consultancy with new IT systems)?

6 What are the likely benefits that will be realised from reviews at different times?

7 Construct an audit questionnaire of management performance, which could be given to members of a project team. Test this on someone who has managed you. What areas would you suggest for improvement?

8 What are the criteria that should be taken into consideration when selecting an auditor/reviewer?

9 Considering the very varied nature of the different audits and reviews that can be carried out, is it likely that these can be done at one time by one person?

10 Discuss the role of review in the process of continuous improvement and why this is vital for the survival of organisations.

11 How might an organisation recognise their level of performance and plot a way forward?

Further information

APM Assurance Specific Interest Group (2016) *Measures for Assuring Projects*, Association for Project Management, Princes Risborough.

Argyris C. (1977) 'Double Loop Learning in Organisations', *Harvard Business Review*, Vol. 55, No. 5, pp. 115–125.

Argyris, C. (1993) *Knowledge for Action*, Jossey-Bass, San Francisco, CA.

Baxter D., Colledge T. and Turner N. (2017) 'A study of accountability in two organizational learning frameworks: why accountability for learning is critical', *European Management Review*, Vol. 14, No. 3, pp. 319–332.

Bicheno, J. and Holweg, M. (2016) *The Lean Toolbox: A Handbook for Lean Transformation*, 5th edition, PICSIE Books, Buckingham.

Brady, T. and Davies, A. (2004) 'Building Project Capabilities: From Exploratory to Exploitative Learning', *Organization Studies,* Vol. 25, No. 9, pp. 1601–1621.

British Standards Institute (2018) BS ISO 30401:2018 *Knowledge management systems,* BSI, London: BSI.

Dale, B.G. and Plunkett, J. (2000) *Quality Costing*, 3rd edition, Chapman & Hall, London.

Davenport, T. and Prusak, L. (1998) *Working Knowledge*, Harvard Business School Press, Boston, MA.

Deming, W.E. (1986) *Out of Crisis*, MIT Centre for Advanced Engineering Study, Cambridge, MA.

Edmondson, A. (2008) 'The Competitive Imperative of Learning', *Harvard Business Review*, Vol. 86, No. 7/8, pp. 60–67.

Garvin, D., Edmonsen, A. and Gino, F. (2008) 'Is Yours A Learning Organisation?' *Harvard Business Review*, March, pp. 109–116.

Laudon, K. and Laudon, J. (2016) *Essentials of Management Information Systems*, 12th edition, Pearson, London.

Lee-Kelley, L. and Turner N. (2017) 'PMO Managers' Self-Determined Participation in a Purposeful Virtual Community-of-Practice', *International Journal of Project Management,* Vol. 35, No. 1, pp. 64–77.

McClory S., Read, M. and Labib, A. (2017) 'Conceptualising the lessons-learned process in project management: Towards a triple-loop learning framework', *International Journal of Project Management*, Vol. 35, No. 7, pp. 1322–1335.

Modig N. and Åhlström P. (2015) *This is Lean*, Rheologica, Stockholm.

Oakes, G. (2008) *Project Reviews, Assurance and Governance*, Gower Press, Chichester.

Payne. J., Roden, E. and Simister S. (2019) *Managing Knowledge in Project Environments*, Routledge, Abingdon.

Williams, T. (2008) 'How Do Organisations Learn from Projects – and Do They?' *IEEE Transactions on Engineering Management*, Vol. 55, No. 2, pp. 248–266.

References

1 Kessler, E.H., Bierly, P.E and Gopalakrishnan S. (2001) 'Vasa syndrome: Insights from a 17th-century new-product disaster', *Academy of Management Executive*, Vol. 15, No. 3, pp. 80–91.

2 See the Risk Doctor video at www.youtube.com/watch?v=kmJ59yyYza4

3 Dutton C., Turner N. and Lee-Kelley L. (2014) 'Learning in a Programme Context: An Exploratory Investigation of Drivers and Constraints.' *International Journal of Project Management*, Vol. 32, No. 5, pp. 719–892.

4 Pisano, G.P. (1997) *The Development Factory*, HBS Press, Boston, MA.

5 Turner, N., Maylor, H., Lee-Kelley, L., Brady, T., Kutsch, E. and Carver, S. (2014) 'Ambidexterity and Knowledge Strategy in Major Projects: A Framework and Illustrative Case Study', *Project Management Journal*, Vol 45, No. 5, pp. 44–55.

6 Invernizzi, D. C., Locatelli, G. and Brookes, N.J. (2018) 'A methodology based on benchmarking to learn across megaprojects', *International Journal of Managing Projects in Business*, Vol. 11, No. 1, pp. 104–121.

7 Kaplan, R.S. and Norton, D.P. (1996) *The Balanced Scorecard*, Harvard Business Review Press, Boston.

8 We are grateful to one of the reviewers for this addition.

9 Crosby (1979) *Quality is Free*, McGraw-Hill, New York.

10 These figures were arrived at following an analysis of the elements of quality cost. The majority of the failures in each case were preventable, and these are costs that would be incurred to carry out the necessary prevention and appraisal measures, with a given level of 'inevitable' failure.

11 Cooke-Davies, T. and Arzymanow, A. (2003) 'The Maturity of Project Management in Different Industries: An Investigation into Variations Between Project Management Models', *International Journal of Project Management*, Vol. 21, No. 6, pp. 471–478.

12 www.cmmiinstitute.com/learning/appraisals/levels

13 PMI (2013) *Organizational Project Management Maturity Model (OPM3)* Knowledge Foundation Paperback, 3rd edition, Project Management Institute, Newtown Square, PA.

14 Axelos (2019) Introduction to P3M3, Version 3.

15 Available from www.axelos.com. www.axelos.com/best-practice-solutions/p3m3

16 Suzaki, K. (1987) *The New Manufacturing Challenge: Techniques for Continuous Improvement*, Free Press, New York.

17 Womack, J.P., Jones, D.T. and Roos, D. (1990) *The Machine That Changed The World*, Rawson Associates, New York.

18 Holweg, M. and Maylor, H. (2018) 'Lean leadership in major projects: from "predict and provide" to "predict and prevent"', *International Journal of Operations & Production Management*, Vol. 38, No. 6, pp. 1368–1386.

Index

Headings and subheadings in **bold** refer to key terms.
'PM' is an abbreviation of project management.

3M 258
4-D model 33–9
5-Ps strategy 61
5-stage model 415
7-S framework 29–30, 50–4
50 per cent rule 118, 364
80/20 rule 378–9
5 Cs model 27–8

academic approach to PM 18
accessibility, quality and 234
accidental profession of PM 10–11
activation constraints 32
activity completion profile 173
activity maps 130–2
activity models *see* **models**
activity-on-node technique 150, 151–3
actual cost of work performed (ACWP) 334
Adams, Douglas 317
Advanced Project Thinking (APT) *see* APT approach
adversarial relationships in supply
        chain 355–6
aggregate resource plan 65–7
agile development 40–2
   planning 118–19
agreement in **4-D** model 38
Airbus A380 76–9, 323
analysis
   in **4-D** model 37
   of problems 373
anarchy in teams 281
anchoring bias 214
Ancona et al. 306
APM BoK (2019) 42, 47–9
Apollo missions 93, 100, 344
Apple Inc. 11
appraisal
   in quality costs 236, 412
   of staff 400
APT approach 171, 183–6, 186
   buffers 184–6
   detailed planning 184
   evaluation 183–4

   reviewing estimates 184
   TfL project 187–90
Arson Task Force (ATF) project 50–4
artificial intelligence (AI) 163, 385
as . . . but . . . 's 9, 200, 201
Association for Project Management (APM, UK) 5, 14
attainability of target benefits 216
attribute analysis 383
auditing 408–10
augmented reality 385
Authentic Leader 306–7
authority of work organisation 273

BAA (British Airports Authority) 362–6
backward schedule 160
balanced model 280
balanced scorecard 100
bar charts 333
battle of the forms 354
Beaumont, Mark 270, 271
behaviours 180–1, 184
Behnken, Bob 344
Belbin's Team Roles 284–5, 289
benchmarking 102, 405–7
benefits analysis 100–2
benefits, delivering 6
benefits mapping 101
Bethlehem Steel 311–12
The Big Carpet Company 26
bids 354
bill of materials 346
Bodies of Knowledge 15, 26
   business case 217
   control 337–8
   historical development of PM 15
   leadership 313
   planning 133
   project completion and review 422
   project frameworks 46–9
   purchasing and contracts 361
   quality 239
   risk management 260–1
   stakeholders 103

teams and teamwork 290
time plans 164–5
Boeing 737 Max fleet 96
bonds 355
bottlenecks 178
brainstorming 373–5
Brandenburg Airport 94
break-up of team 275, 276
Bredin, K. and Söderlund, J. 283
bridge, the 225, 226
brief 32, 121
British Standard 6079 (2019) 5
Britspace 8
Brunel, I.K. 93
budgets 96
buffers 184–6
Building Information Modelling (BIM) 385
business case 6
benefits of 196–7
realisation 216
definition 197
financial appraisal 206–13
compound interest 207–9
discounted cash flow (DCF) 206–7, 211–12
future value (FV) 209
internal rate of return (IRR) 209–11
payback 206
importance of 196
improper use of estimates 213–14
optimism bias 213, 215
politics 213
strategic misrepresentation 213

capacity 65–6
CAPEX 200
capital equipment 199, 200
capital expenditure 200
Cardiff Bay Development Corporation 290–1
careers in PM 12, 13
cascading 21
cash flows 212
considerations 212–13
cause-effect-cause analysis 379–81, 387
centralised purchasing 349
change 6, 18, 26, 416
change-agents 404
change programme 26
Channel Tunnel 93
chaos 111, 114
Chartered Institute of Purchasing and Supply (CIPS) 352
check-points *see* gates
checkers 404
checklists 399

closed-system models 374–5
CMMI (Capability Maturity Model Integration) 415
Co-ordinator (Belbin Team Role) 285
coherence 63
collaboration 283–4
collection in team lifecycle 275, 276
common sense 17
communication
control and distribution of information 333
quality and 234
communications plan 235
communications planning 235
comparative estimates 9, 200, 201
competence, quality and 234
competitiveness 27, 28, 29
Complete Finisher (Belbin Team Role) 285
completeness 27, 28, 29
completion in **4-D** model 38
completion of project 395–6, 397–8
closing down project systems 399
disposal of surplus assets 401
documentation 398–9
project reviews 400
relocation of staff 400–1
staff appraisals 400
stakeholder satisfaction 401
complexity 26, 27, 42
in **5 Cs** model 27–8
interdependencies 45
managerial 43–5
reduction 45
compound interest 207–9
comprehensiveness of target benefits 216
computer-assisted project planning 162–3
computers, problems of reliance on 333
concept development 112–13
conceptualisation in **4-D** model 37
Concorde 93
concurrent activities 127, 129
concurrent engineering 128
confidentiality 364
configuration control 323–4
conformance 60, 97, 98, 230–5
control and 324, 325
conformance objectives 100
constraints 31, 32
see also **theory of constraints (TOC)**
consultants 404–5
consumer perceptions 233–4
consumer terrorism 237
content theories 302–3
context 27, 28–9
PESTEL 28–9

contingency 200, 257
contract law 353
contracts 27, 353–5
   battle of the forms 354
   Heathrow Terminal 5 project 362–3
   process 353–5
control 318–19
   baseline, nature of 334–5
   basic requirements for 319
   characteristics, measurement of 321
   concept of 334, 336
   configuration control 323–4
   corrective actions 321–3
   feedback control system 319
   feedback of performance 321
   hierarchy of systems 323
   limits of 334–6
      measurement and assessment 335
   as a negative idea 335–6
   as a paradox 335
   stability in 322
   system characteristics of importance 320
   system, nature of 335
   techniques of 324–34
      communicating information 333
      cost and time 326–9
      Last Planner 330–2
      quality 324–5
      visual control 329–30
   using critical chain 329
   variation, limits to 320–1
   visible progress 321
control-organisational approach 227
conventional monitoring and evaluation 91
core products 234
Corporate Social Responsibility (CSR) 27
corrective actions 321–3
cost and time controls 326–9
cost constraints 32
cost performance 96, 97, 98
cost performance indicator (CPI) 327
cost planning process 198–206
   approaches to costing 199
   CAPEX 200
   cost build-up 204–6
   elements of cost 199–200
   estimating techniques 200–4
   OPEX 200
   role of costing 198–9
cost-plus 198
   contracts 353
costs
   in planning process 116

   in risk analysis 247
courtesy, quality and 234
Covid-19 pandemic 6, 215, 286, 320
   impact on supply chain principles 359
   procurement during 350
Cradle to Cradle (C2C) 26
creative category of team structure 278
creativity 112–13
   stifling of 336
critical chain 171, 186
   control and 329
   methods 171
critical friends 411
critical mass 403–4
critical path analysis (CPA) 14, 153–8, 179
   forward pass 153–4, 156
   insufficiently **robust** 172
   limitations of 172–7
      estimates and reality 172, 173–4, 177
      fixed dates 172, 175
      latest start 172, 174–5
      measuring progress in error 173, 175
      multi-tasking 173, 176–7
      student syndrome 173, 175
      task and activity times 172, 174
   origin of 157–8
   reverse pass 153, 155–7
cross-functional activity 272
Crossrail 50
crowdsourcing 291–2, 359
cues 233
cumulative disruption analysis 192
Cuong Quang 385
customer focus 27, 28, 29
customers 100

data 119
decision frameworks 383–4
decision-making 370
   management science 375
   management styles 373
   modelling systems for 375–7
   open and closed systems 374–5
   poor, reasons for 375
   as a process 374
   see also problems
decision-support systems 384–5
decision trees 378, 382–3
decline in team lifecycle 275, 276
deconstructing projects 146–9
definition in **4-D** model 35, 37
definitions of quality 225–6, 230
delivery in **4-D** model 35, 38

Deming, Dr. W. Edwards 31, 351, 411
dependency logic 151–2
　　multiple dependencies 152–3
deployment flow charting (DFC) 130–2
design
　　in **4-D** model 35, 37–8
　　in Japanese automotive industry 127–8
Design Thinking 42
development in **4-D** model 35, 36, 38
digital dashboards 330
digital twinning 385
direct revenue-earning projects 62
discount rate 208, 212
discounted cash flow (DCF) 206, 206–7,
　　　　211–12
discretionary effort 300
diversity 274–5
DMAIC system 228
documentation 17, 398–9
documentation control 324
dotted-line responsibility 273
Drucker, Peter 298, 375
due-dates 186
Dybå, T. and Dingsøyr, T. 41

earliest finish time (EFT) 153, 154, 156
earliest start time (EST) 153, 154
earned value concept 326–8, 336
East London Transit (ELT1A) 188–9
easyJet 58
economic approach 227, 228
economic influence in PESTEL 28
EDI (electronic data interchange) 356
education 403–4
Edwards, John 313–14
elapsed times for tasks 172, 174
electric vehicles 7
electronic data interchange (**EDI**) 356
emergence 6
emergent complexity 44, 299–300, 410
　　models 44, 45
entrenchment in team lifecycle 275, 276
entrepreneurial facet of leadership 299–300
environmental constraints 32
environmental influence in PESTEL 29
EPM (enterprise portfolio/programme/project
　　　　management) 67
erosion of the buffer 329
error avoidance/detection 376
estimated cost at completion (ECAC) 327–8
estimates
　　in the APT approach 184
　　as guesses 150

imperfect 197
inaccuracy of 124
inappropriate use of 177, 213–14
problems with 172, 173–4, 177
techniques
　　as . . . but . . . 's 200, 201
　　forecasts 200, 201–2
　　learning curve effects 200, 202–4
　　parametric estimating 200–1
　　synthetic estimation 200, 202
　　wishful thinking approach 200
in time plans 150
types of 151
ethical constraints 32
ethics 27, 99
execution in **4-D** model 38
executive 71
expectancy theory 303
expectations 226, 325
　　managing 233–5
expected value 251–2
external knowledge 403–5
external stakeholders 87

failure 93
　　management of 236–8
　　in quality costs 236, 412
　　risk analysis 251
failure mode, effect analysis (FMEA) 250
fast-tracking 130
feedback in **4-D** model 38
feedback control system 319, 336
feedforward control 323
fifth-generation PM 15, 16
filters 111–12
financial appraisal of business case 206–13
first-generation PM 14, 15
first-**tier** suppliers 345
first-timers 9
fishbone diagram 379
five rights 350–3
fixed costs 202, 212
fixed dates 172, 175, 180
fixed price contracts 353
flatliners 413
flexibility 97
　　of objectives 99
float in critical path analysis 153, 155, 156
focus 59
　　of projects 5
followers 297
force-field analysis 383, 384
Ford, Henry 418

forecasts 200, 201–2
formal proposals 122–3
formal systems 30
formalisation in planning process 122–3
forward pass 153–4, 156
forward schedule 160
four fields mapping (FFM) 130–2
four Ps 309
fourth-generation PM 15, 16
frameworks 29–31
front-end loading 130, 184
Fukushima Daiichi nuclear power plant 6
functional silos 272
future value (FV) 209
fuzzy gates 127

Gantt charts 159–62
    good points 162
    limitations 162
gate reviews 38
gates 123–7
general management 5
    versus project management 12
generation of project practices 14
geographically separated teams 286–8
Gino, F. 283
givens 98, 99
Glastonbury Festival 145
globalisation 27
The Goal 178
Goldratt, Dr Eli 176
governance 70–5
    definition 70
graph modelling 385
graph reasoning 385
ground-up costing 199
group-think 278
groupitis 281
groups 274
GTO framework 98–100
guesses 150, 162, 172
gun registry project 317

hackathons 292
handover
    in 4-D model 38
    of project 395–6, 399
Harrison, John 291
Harvard Business Review 359
Hawaii Ironman Triathlon World Championships 9–10
Hawthorne Studies 302
health and safety 99
    in risk analysis 247

Heathrow Terminal 5 362–6
heavyweight matrix 280
hedgehog syndrome 33–4, 36, 396, 397
Herzberg, F. 303
Hewlett-Packard 163, 402, 411–12
Hewlett Packard Enterprise Services (HPES) 74
hideability 250
hierarchy 272, 273
hierarchy of control systems 323
hierarchy of needs 302–3
Hillson, D. and Simon, P. 248
holistic approach 227, 228
Holyrood 196, 197
honesty-brokers 404
HR quadriad 283
HS2 196
human resource management 283
Huoshenshan hospital 97
Hurley, Doug 344
hybrid approach 41, 42

ICOM model 31–3, 119
IDeA Foundation 38–9, 125–7
identification of risk 246
impact
    of risk 250
    of stakeholders 94
implementation 417
Implementer (Belbin Team Role) 285
improvement
    commercial maturity models 415
    lean project management 417–20
    organisational maturity 413–15
    quality costs 412–13
    securing 416–17
improvement activities 401–3
improvers 413
in-process, characteristics at 321
in-project learning 363–4
inactive time allocation 308
inclusivity 274–5
Incompetent Leader 306
indirect effects 32
indirect expenses 200
influence of stakeholders 94
informal systems 30
information 119
information flow 419
information revolution 370
Infrastructure and Projects Authority 18–19
initial planning 110–11
innovation 13, 100, 113, 283–4
input-output model 31

inputs 31, 32, 90
   measurement of characteristics 321
insurances 355
intangible benefits 102
intangible outcomes 234
integrators 33, 404
intellectual property (IP) 364
interest rates 207
internal customers 227
internal rate of return (IRR) 206, 209–11, 212
internal stakeholders 87
International Project Management Association (IPMA) 14
Internet of Things (IoT) 385
invitations to tender (ITT) 348
invoices 348
iPhone 11
iron triangle 95, 96
Ishikawa/fishbone diagrams 379
ISO 9000 standards 325
   ISO 9001 399
issues 26, 248
iteration 41, 42

Japan 163, 345
   design in automotive industry 127–8, 130, 305
   quality circles 275
   supply chain in automotive industry 345
   visible control 321
Jenkins Company 313–14
Jersey Airport 93–4
just-in-time principle 359
justification
   in **4-D** model 37
   of benefits 101–2

Kaplan, R.S. and Norton, D.P. 407
key performance indicators (**KPIs**) *see* **KPIs** (Key
      Performance Indicators)
Kirkpatrick, S.A. and Locke, E.A. 297
knowledge management 41, 53, 395, 422
knowledge providers 404
knowledge-sharing 396
KPIs (Key Performance Indicators) 330, 406
Kranendijk, Stef 26

language and culture 287
Last Planner 118, 330–2, 365–6
Last Responsible Moment (LRM) 364
latest finish time (LFT) 153, 154, 155, 156
latest start time (LST) 153, 154, 155, 174–5
leaders, attributes and skills of 297
leadership
   authentic 306–7

incompetence 306
motivation and 300–5
personal resilience 307–8
in projects 297–300
   entrepreneurial facet 299–300
   managerial facet 298–9
   relational facet 299
time management 308–12
as vice 307
lean management 171, 228, 417–20
learning 100
learning before doing 402, 403–5
learning by doing 402, 408–10
learning curve effects 200, 202–4
legal constraints 32
legal influence in PESTEL 29
legal risk 247
legislation 27
lessons identified reviews 33
lessons learned reviews 33
Lifter Company project 338–40
lightweight matrix 280
limits of variation 320–1
line management 12–13
linear programming 378
linked-bar chart *see* **Gantt charts**
localised purchasing 349
Lockheed 113
logic constraints 32
London 2012 Olympics 36
long-term reviews 410
Lord, M.E. 57

maintenance 13
managed knowledge 416
management 298
   see also leadership
management of failure 236–8
management overheads 273
management paradigms 305
management paralysis 401–2
management questionnaires 400
management science 375
managerial challenge 42–5
managerial complexity 42–5
managerial facet of leadership 298–9
managing people *see* people, managing
Mandela, Nelson 295
manufacturing 178
manufacturing and service paradigms 230–1
margin 200
marketing 401
Maslow, A.H. 302–3

materials 199, 200
materials management 345–6
mathematical approach 226, 227
mathematical modelling techniques 378
matrix management 280, 281
   Cardiff Bay Development Corporation 290–1
matrix organisations 280
maturity
   commercial models 415
   organisational 413–15
   stages in project management 414
Maxwell, J. 311–12
McDonald's 8
measures 86, 90
mechanisms 31, 33
meetings 285–6, 287–8
Microsoft Project 157, 162
milestones 160
Millennium Park 129–30
Minimum Viable Product (MVP) 224–5
Mintzberg, Henry 61
'Miracle on the Hudson' 370
mission 6, 59, 60
mission statements 59, 60
modelling 102
modelling systems for decision-making
   benefits of 376
   descriptive model 376
   dynamic predictive model 376
   generic view of 376
   geometric model 376
   mechanistic model 376
   process 376
   scenario planning 377
   static protective 376
models 31
   4-D model 33–9
   5-stage model 415
   5 Cs model 27–8
   agile development 40–2
   balanced model 280
   closed-system models 374–5
   design thinking 42
   ICOM model 31–3, 119
   input-output model 31
   of planning 111–15
   waterfall model 39
Monitor Evaluator (Belbin Team Role) 285
monitoring *see* control
Monte Carlo analysis 252, 253
motivating-hygiene theory 303
motivation
   content theories 302–3
   Hawthorne Studies 302

   process theories 303–4
   reinforcement 302, 304
   scientific management 300–2
   structural implications for project managers 305
MOVE objectives 310
MRPII (manufacturing resource planning) 178
Mukwege, Denis 296
multi-tasking 173, 176–7
Murad, Nadia 296

NASA
   Apollo missions 93, 100, 344
   Space Shuttle program 244, 248, 344
national holidays 287
net present value (NPV) 208
network analysis 378
networks 153
New Engineering Contract (NEC) 354
new product development (NPD) 90, 97, 111–13
   concept development in 112–13
   conventional approach to 128
   creativity in 112–13
   initial planning 110–11
   inputs and outputs 112
   miscommunication 127, 128
   scope management 114–15
   sequential versus concurrent models 129

Oakervee Review 196
objectives
   classification of 98–9
   conformance 100
   flexibility 99
   givens 98, 99–100
   MOVE 310
   optimisers 99
   organisational 62, 63
   performance 100
   project 62, 70, 97, 281
   quality and 98, 251
   risk analysis 247
   SMART 309–10
   of stakeholders 146, 232
   strategic 60, 64, 70
   strategy deployment 63
   time management and 309–11
   tradeables 99
Ohno, Taiichi 305
Olympic Games 96
open-book accounting 357
open innovation 292
open-source software 292
open-system models 374–5
operating expenditure 200

operational research 375
operations management 5
OPEX 200
OPM3 (Organisational Project Management Maturity Model) 415
opportunities 258–9
opportunity costs 212
optimisers 99
optimism bias 117, 213, 215
optimistic time (PERT) 254
order 111, 114
order numbers 347
Oresund Link 92
organisational breakdown structure (OBS) 148–9, 274
organisational change 61
  deploying strategy in 63–4
organisational culture 273
organisational maturity 413–15
organisational strategy 59–64
  strategic approach 60
  traditional approach 60
organisational structure 272–3
  authority 273
  dotted-line responsibility 273
  management overheads 273
  organisational culture 273
  project-based 279
  reporting arrangements 273
  responsibility 273
outcomes 90
outputs 31, 32
  measurement of characteristics 321
outsourcing 347
overheads 200, 205
overrun data 318
overview 119

P3M3 (Portfolio, Programme and Project Management Maturity Model) 415
P50 planning 184
painting by numbers projects 9, 47, 117, 175, 203
parametric estimating 200–1
Pareto analysis 352, 378–9
Parkinson's law 184
participatory monitoring and evaluation (PM&E) 91
partnerships 356
payback analysis 100, 206
Pearce Retail 62
peer reviews 246
penalty clauses 355
people challenge 7
people, managing 283–8
  geographically separated teams 286–8
  human resource management 283

  innovation and collaboration 283–4
  meetings 285–6, 287–8
  personalities and roles 284–5
percentage improvement 407
perceptions 226, 325
  management of 233–5
performance 60, 98, 231, 320
  control and 324, 325
  in purchasing 351
performance objectives 100
peripheral elements 234
personal projects 111–13
personal resilience 307–8
personality profile 284
PERT analysis 14, 254–7
  factor tables 266–7
  use of in practice 257–8
pessimistic time (PERT) 254
PESTEL 28–9
Peter principle 305
Peters, Tom 312
phases 123–4
  activities in 127–30
Phases Review Process (PRP) 125
PID (project initiation document) 34, 121–2
pilot studies 102
pipeline 112
Pisano, G. 283
Planned Percent Complete 332
planning
  in the APT approach 184
  core elements of 147
  estimating 150, 151
  initial planning 110–11
  limitations of current approaches to see project planning, limitations
  models of 111–15
    new product development (NPD) 111–13
    personal projects 111–13
    scope management 114–15
  project landscapes 123–32
planning assumptions 173
planning process 116–23
  accuracy and precision 120
  costs and benefits 116, 118
  cycles 119
  flexibility 117
  formalisation 122–3
  formalised project overview documents 121–2
  inputs and outputs 119
  managing 120–1
  overview 119
  systematic approach 121
  uncertainty and 117–20

plans
  formal proposals 122–3
  information and data 119
  traceability 120–1
  up to date 185
  as working tools 117
Plant (Belbin Team Role) 285
plausible futures 377
PMI (Project Management Institute) 14, 46, 47, 48–9
PMIS (Project Management Information Systems) 333
policies 180–1
political influence in PESTEL 28
portfolio management 64
portfolio managers 13
portfolios 64–70
portfolios of work 11
post mortems of projects 400
power of stakeholders 94
present value (PV) 207
prevention in quality costs 236, 412
price 198
  in purchasing 351
Price, F. 370
PRINCE2 2017 5
  business cases 6
  requirements for a PID 121–2
priorities 287
private finance initiatives 29
proactive time allocation 308
probability of risk 250
probable time (PERT) 254
problem-solving 371
  cause-effect-cause analysis 379–81
  classical 373
  decision support for 382–5
  systematic model for 372, 373
  tools for
    Ishikawa/fishbone diagrams 379
    Pareto analysis 378–9
problem-solving category of team structure 278
problem-solving cycle 373
problems 370–1
  analysis 377–81
    mathematical modelling techniques 378
    uncertainty in 377–8
  analysis of 373
  brainstorming 373–5
  categories of 371
  definition 371
  proceduralisation of 371
  programming of actions 371–3
  structuring 371–7
  synthesis of 373

unbounded 373
  see also decision-making
procedures 17
process 8–10, 90
  cost planning 198–206
  of planning 116–23
  projects as 31–42
process improvement 401–3
process theories 302, 303–4
process uncertainties 117
procurement 350
product breakdown structure (PBS) 149, 346
product development 323
product surround 401
product uncertainty 117
productivity 407
products 39
professionalism, quality and 234
profit 198
programme and project management (PPM) capability 101
Programme Evaluation and Review Technique (**PERT**) *see* **PERT** analysis
programme management 64, 67–70
programme managers 13
programmed response in problem solving 371–3
programmes 64–70
  definitions 68–9
project assurance function 72
project-based organisations (PBOs) 10, 279
project board 71, 72
project champions 113
project charters 122, 133
project context 27–31
project environments 27–9
project governance 70–5
  structure 71
project initiation document (PID) *see* **PID** (project initiation document)
project landscapes 123–32
  activity maps 130–2
  gates 123–7
  phases 123–4
    activities in 127–30
project lifecycles 34–5, 39
  change 36
  development of 37
  IDeA 39
project management
  as an academic subject 18–19
  accidental profession of 10–11
  careers 12, 13
  versus general management 12

history of 14–16
importance of 10–13
line management and 12–13
managerial complexity in 42–5
perennial issues in 16–18
profession of choice 11
standards 14
Project Management 2.0 16
Project Management Institute (PMI, US) 5, 14
project management office (PMO) 72–5
project managers 10, 13
card-carrying 17
identifying 10
as **integrators** 33
organisational structures 305
as project integrators 16
see also people, managing
project manuals 231–2
project performance mapping 100
project planning, limitations
causes 172–7
natural variability 172, 174
task times 172, 174
effects 172
project/programme support office managers 13
project reviews 400
project roles 71–2
project strategy
definition 62
purchasing and 350–3
Project X 18–19
project(s)
activity models 31–42
change 6, 18
characteristics of 7–8
as a conversion process 31–2
cycles-within-cycles 34
deconstruction of 146–9
organisational breakdown structure (OBS) 148–9
product breakdown structure 149
work breakdown structure (WBS) 146–8
definitions of 4–10, 19
delivering benefits 6
economic contribution of 10
emergence 6
failures 3
focused 5
negative potential of 60
organisational strategy and 59–64
overrun data 318
phases of lifecycle 34–5, 36, 37–8
as a **process** 8–10, 31–42
as **social constructions** 7

stage-gate model of 124
targets 16
temporary 5
uncertainty 6
unique 5, 8–9
promotion 303, 304, 305
proposal in **4-D** model 37
proposals 121
prototyping 363–4
proxies 201
psychometric tests 284
public contracts 354
publishing cycles 16
pull system 228
purchasing 345, 347–53
authorisation of 347
automation of 349
centralised and localised 349
contracts 353–5
five rights 350–3
organisation of 349
outsourcing 347
project strategy and 350–3
of software 355
suppliers 347–8, 351, 352–3
purchasing agents 349
pyramid 272, 273

QCD (Quality, Cost, or Delivery) 63
qualitative approaches to risk 250–1
quality 223–4
competitiveness-based approach 238
conformance 227, 324, 325
definitions 225–6, 230
expectations and perceptions 226
of stakeholders 230
internal and external perspectives 226
Minimum Viable Product (MVP) 224–5
performance 324, 325
product-based view 226
productivity-based approach 238
in purchasing 350–1
in risk analysis 247
stakeholder satisfaction 229–30
trade-offs 229
quality assurance (QA) 134, 351
see also quality conformance planning
quality circles 275–7
quality conformance planning 231–3
see also quality assurance (QA)
quality constraints 32
quality costs 236–8, 238, 413
elements of 412

quality improvement 236–8
quality management
    bridge model 225–6
    control-organisational approach 227
    economic approach 227, 228
    holistic approach 227, 228
    mathematical approach 226, 227
    perspectives on 227
    strategic approach 227, 228–9
    system-structural approach 227
quality performance 96, 98, 230–5
quality performance planning 233–5
quality planning process 231
quality systems 325
quantification of risk 246
quantification problems 102
quantitative approaches to risk 251–8
quantity in purchasing 350
queueing theory 378
quick and dirty approach 120

RACI matrix 232–3
Range Rover Sport 110
Rank Xerox 405–6
Rapid Pencil Company 358
rapid prototyping 113
reactive time allocation 308
real-time control 330
reality of estimates 172, 173–4
reconciliation in purchasing 347–8
reference sites 102
reflected experience 297
reflective learning 395
reimbursable pricing 198
reinforcement 302, 304
relational facet of leadership 299
relationship management 356
relationships in supply chain 345
reliability 97
repetitive operations 9, 27, 65
reporting arrangements 273
reports 328
requirements 86, 89, 90
resilience 307–8
resolution/accommodation in team lifecycle 275, 276
resource calendar 158–9
resource capability 158
resource capacity 158
resource contention/conflict 179
Resource Investigator (Belbin Team Role) 285
resource pool 158
resource providers 404
resources 185

allocation of 232
availability of 179–80
response to risk 246, 248–9
responsibility allocation 232–3
responsibility of work organisation 273
responsiveness, quality and 234
retention money 355
return on investment (ROI) 100
revenue share contracts 353
reverse pass 153, 155–7
review in **4-D** model 38
review of project 397
    benchmarking 405–7
    carrying out reviews 411–12
    continuous improvement 408
    criteria for reviews and audits 410
    learning and 402, 403–5, 408–10
    long-term review 410
    review process 408–9
    structuring improvement activities 401–3
reward system 303, 304
risk
    contingency plans 249
    definitions 245
    evaluation of 244
    Heathrow Terminal 5 project 363
    known knowns 245
    known unknowns 245
    nature of 244–9
    opportunities 258–9
    qualitative approaches to 250–1
    quantitative approaches to 251–8
    statements 248
    unknown unknowns 245
risk adjusted discount rate (RADR) 212
risk analysis 247, 249, 251, 262
risk logs 249
risk management 244–5, 244–9
    assumptions 247
    framework 246–9
        identification 246
        quantification 246
        response 246, 248–9
risk priority numbers (RPNs) 262
risk registers 249
rolling-wave planning 118
Roman Empire 14
rules 180–1
Rumsfeld, Donald 243–5

S-curve 36
safety 184
satisfaction 229–30

scenario planning 377
schedule performance indicator (SPI) 327
scheduling 364
scientific management 300–2
scope creep 114–15
scope management 114–15
screening 112
scrums in Agile 40
sealed bids 354
seamless enterprise 288
second-generation PM 14, 15
Segrada Familia 85
self-actualisation 303
senior responsible owner (SRO) 71
senior supplier 71
senior user 71
sense-making 26, 69
sensitivity analysis 252
sequential activities 127, 129
Shaper (Belbin Team Role) 285
shareholders 100
Shell 36, 44, 99
sign-off process 115
signing off project 399
silos 272
simulation 378
Sinclair C5 114
situational leadership 299, 300
Six-Sigma 228
skills 30
Skunk Works 113
SMART objectives 309–10
social construction of projects 7
social influence in PESTEL 29
socio-political complexity 43–4, 45
software development 40
South West Water 171
SpaceX 344
specialisms 272
Specialist (Belbin Team Role) 285
specificity of target benefits 216
sponsor 71
sprints in agile 40, 118–19
SQEPs (suitably qualified and experienced personnel) 30
stability 322
staff 30
staff appraisals 400
stage-gate system 124–5
stage payments 355
stakeholder landscape 87
stakeholder management 229, 234
stakeholder maps 94, 104
stakeholder satisfaction 229–30, 401

stakeholders 30, 31, 86–95, 223, 223–4
    ethics 99
    expectations and perceptions of 233–4
    external 87
    givens 99
    groups 88, 89
    health and safety 99
    identification of 87–8
    impact on 94
    internal 87
    managing 93–5
    measures 86, 90
    optimisers 99
    power of 94
    requirements of 86, 89, 90
    rest of the world 88
    timing 86, 91–3
    see also quality
stand-up meetings 40
standards 14, 15, 287
    ISO 9000 325, 399
start-up in 4-D model 38
strategic approach 227, 228–9
strategic choices, managing 95–100
    flexibility in 97
    GTO framework 98–100
    iron triangle 95, 96
    trade-offs 95, 96, 97
strategic investment 214
strategic misrepresentation 213
strategy 30, 60
    direct revenue-earning projects and 62
    top-down 60
    two-way communication 60
strategy deployment 61, 62, 416
    in organisational change projects 63–4
strategy matrix 70
strategy process 59
stress 308–9
structural complexity 43, 44, 45
structure(s) 29–31
    of 4-D model 30
    of 7-S framework 30
    definition 30
    of teams 279–83
        coordination mechanisms 282–3
        matrix management 280, 281
        mixed organisational 282–3
        pure project organisation 279
        requirements of 278
        suitability for projects 281–2
        two bosses problem 281
student syndrome 173, 175

style/culture 30, 31
subjective complexity assessment 45
success 85, 91–2
sunk costs 212, 326
supervised machine learning classification
       algorithms 385
suppliers 100
supply chain management 345, 346
   in the 2020s 359
   adversarial relationships 355–6
   complexity 358–9
   modern approaches to 355–9
   modern techniques in 357–8
      open-book accounting 357
      vendor-managed inventory (VMI) 357–8
   partnerships 356
   relationship management 356
supply chains 344, 345–7
   examples of 346
   see also purchasing
supply networks 359
surplus assets, disposal of 401
sustainability 27
Sustainable Development Goals (SDGs) 3, 4
SWOT analysis 61
synergy in team lifecycle 275, 276
synthesis of problems 373
synthetic estimation 200, 202
system-structural approach 227
systematic approach 121
systems 30

tactical category of team structure 278
tangible outcomes 234
tangible outputs 231
target cost contracts 353
target costing 198
targets 216
task times 172, 174
Taylor, Frederick 300
Taylorism 300–1, 305
teams 272–8
   Belbin Team Roles 284–5
   characteristics of 274
   criteria for 274
   diversity and inclusivity 274–5
   geographically separated 286–8
   lifecycles of 275–7
   role of 272–4
   structure of 278, 279–83
   see also people, managing

teamwork 274
   boundaries 278
   effective 277–8
Teamworker (Belbin Team Role) 285
technical advisory group 71–2
technical influence in PESTEL 29
techniques of control 324–34
temporary nature of projects 5
tenders 354
termination of project 397
terms of reference 121
theory of constraints (TOC) 171, 177–82
   application to project management 178
   elevation of 182
   exploitation of 181
   identification of 178–81
   reassessment 182
   subordination to 181
third-generation PM 15, 16
three pillars of change 416–17
throughput 178
Tiger teams 277
time 199
   cost and time controls 326–9
   in purchasing 352
   in risk analysis 247
time allocation 308
time and materials contracts 353
time constraints 32
time contraction 376
time management 308–12
   techniques for planning 311
time performance 96, 97, 98
time plans 150–9
   activity-on-node technique 150, 151–3
   critical path analysis (CPA) 153–8
   dependency logic 151–3
   estimates 150, 151
   scheduling 158–9
Time-Track 423
time usage analysis 310
timing 86, 91–3
top-down costing 199
topic modelling 385
Total Quality Management (TQM) 20–1
Toyota Motor Company 63
Toyota Production System 305
traceability 120–1
trade-offs 95, 96, 97, 246
tradeables 99
traditional development 41

traffic lights system 330
trainers 404
training 403–4
traits approach 299
transactional leadership 299
transformational leadership 299
Transport for London (TfL) 187–90

unbounded problems 373
uncertainty 175, 245
    in planning process 117–20, 175
    in PM 6
    in problem analysis 377–8
    see also risk; risk management
uniqueness of projects 5, 8–9
Universal Credit 223, 225
unsupervised machine learning 385

value 86, 100
value-maximisation 86
value proposition 101
variability of service projects 237–8
variable costs 202, 212
variance 327
variety 8, 9
Vasa Warship 395
VCS 247, 423–8

vendor-managed inventory (VMI) 357–8
virtual teams 16, 27, 271
visibility 163
visible control 321
vision 59, 61
visual control 329–30
volume 8, 9
Vroom, V.H. 303, 305

wannabees 413
waste 418, 419
waterfall model 39
weekly schedules 331–2
Wellington, Chrissie 10
what-if analysis 376
whole-life costs 410
wishful thinking approach 118, 200, 214
Womack et al. 305
work breakdown structure (WBS) 146–8
work masks 307
work packages 148
working software releases 40
world-class performers 413

Yorkon 8

Zaleznik, A. 299

Publisher's acknowledgements

Text:

3 United Nations: The Sustainable Development Goals Report, 2019, United Nations; **5 The British Standards Institution:** BS 6079:2019, Project management – Principles and guidance for the management of projects, BSI Standards Publication; **5 AXELOS LIMITED:** PRINCE2 (Projects in Controlled Environments) 2017; **18 BetterGovProjects:** Project X, six key themes, www.bettergovprojects.com; **31 MIT Professional Education:** Deming, W.E. (1986) *Out of the Crisis – Quality Productivity and Competitive Position*, MIT Center for Advanced Engineering Study, Cambridge, MA; **39, 42, 47–48 The Association for Project Management:** APM (2019), APM Body of Knowledge, 7th edition, Association for Project Management, High Wycombe, UK; **41 Elsevier:** Adapted from Dyba T. and Dingsoyr T. (2008) 'Empirical studies of agile software development: A systematic review', *Information and Software Technology*, Vol. 50, No. 9/10, pp. 833–859; **48-49 Project Management Institute, Inc.:** PMI (2017) A Guide to the Project Management Body of Knowledge (PMBOK® Guide), 6th edition, Project Management Institute, Newtown Square, PA; **57 Elsevier:** Lord, M.A. (1993) 'Implementing Strategy Through Project Management', *Long Range Planning*, Vol. 26, No. 1, pp. 76–85; **58 Harvard Business Publishing:** Morgan, M., Levitt, R.E., & Malek, W. (2007), *Executing Your Strategy: How to break it down and get it done*, Boston, MA: Harvard Business School Press; **59 Harvard Business Publishing:** Skinner, W. (1969) 'Manufacturing – Missing Link in Corporate Strategy', *Harvard Business Review*, May–June, pp. 136–145; **62 Project Management Institute, Inc:** Adapted from The nature of this two-way process is further described in Shenhar, A.J., Milosevic, D., Dvir, D. and Thamhain, H. (2007) *Linking Project Management to Business Strategy*, Project Management Institute, Newtown, PA; **64 E. & F.N. Spon:** Reiss, G. (1996) *Programme Management Demystified*, E & FN Spon, London; **67 Palgrave Macmillan:** Williams, D. and Parr, T. (2004) *Enterprise Programme Management*, Palgrave Macmillan, Basingstoke; **68 AXELOS LIMITED:** MSP is a programme management standard – often referred to as 'the big brother of PRINCE 2'; **69 Gower Publishing Ltd:** Murray-Webster, R. and Thiry, M. (2000) 'Managing Programmes of Projects' in Turner, J.R. and Simister, S.J. (eds), *Gower Handbook of Project Management*, Gower, Aldershot, pp. 33–46; **70 Organisation for Economic Co-operation and Development:** *Corporate governance*, OECD; **73 Project Management Institute, Inc.:** Hobbs, J.B. (2007) *The Multi-Project PMO: Global Analysis of the Current State of Practice*, Project Management Institute, Newtown Square, PA; **77 BBC News:** Adapted from 'Enormous plane takes to the sky', BBC News, 14 February 2007; **84 Elsevier:** Shenhar, A.J., Dvir, D., Levy, O. and Maltz, A. (2001) 'Project Success – A Multidimensional Strategic Concept', *Long Range Planning*, Vol. 34, No. 6, pp. 699–725; **84 Simon & Schuster:** Covey, Stephen R. (1990) *The Seven Habits of Highly Effective People*, Free Press, New York; **87-88 World Bank Group:** The World Bank annual report 1996 ; **90 Elsevier:** For a fuller list of measures see Griffin, A. and Page, A.L. (1996) 'PDMA Success Measurement Project: Recommended Measures for Product Development Success and Failure', *Journal of Product Innovation Management*, Vol. 13, pp. 478–496; **94 The Financial Times Limited:** *Financial Times*, 15 October 1996; **105–106 Penguin Random House :** Lodge, D. (2002) *Changing Places*, Penguin, Harlow; **116 National Audit Office:** National Audit Office (2006) *National Audit Office Strategy: Our strategy 2019–20 to 2021–22*; **117 Dwight D. Eisenhower:** Variously attributed to Admiral Lord Nelson and General Eisenhower; **124 Taylor & Francis Group:** After Cooper, R.G. (1988) 'The new product process: a decision guide for management', *Journal of Marketing Management*, Vol. 3, No. 3, pp. 238–55, Taylor & Francis; **125–127 Idea Foundation:** Based on the IDeA foundation; **125–127 Elsevier:** An excellent comparative review of the procurement approaches of the UK and Norway is Klakegg, O.J., Williams, T.J. and Magnussen, O.M. (2010) 'An investigation of governance frameworks for public projects in Norway and the UK', *International Journal of Project Management*, Vol. 28, No. 1, pp. 40–50; **131 ElectroComponentCo:** ElectroComponentCo; **134 Anne Live Vaagaasar:** Text provided by Associate Professor Anne Live Vaagaasar, Department of Leadership and Organizational Behaviour at BI Norwegian Business School; **144 Benjamin Franklin:** Quoted by Benjamin Franklin; **144 John Harvey:** Quoted by John Harvey, c.1800; **170 United States Navy :** PERT developed by the United States Navy in 1958; **170 Elsevier:** Rand, G. (2000) 'Critical Chain: The Theory of Constraints Applied to Project Management', *International Journal of Project Management*, Vol. 18, pp. 173–177; **172 Robbie Burns:** Quoted by Robbie Burns; **176 North River Press:** Goldratt, E.M. (1997) *The Critical Chain*, North River Press, New York, p. 121; **181 Irby Smith:** Curly in *City Slickers*, 7 June 1991, Produced by Irby Smith; **197 Association for Project Management:** APM (2019), APM Body of Knowledge, 7th edition, Association for Project Management, High Wycombe, UK; **215 Her Majesty's Treasury:** The Green Book: appraisal and evaluation in central government, HM Treasury and Government Finance 18 April 2013; **224 Penguin Random House :** Ries, E. (2011) *The Lean Startup*, London: Penguin, page 77; **229 Elsevier:** Maylor H., Turner N., and Murray-Webster R. (2015) 'It Worked for Manufacturing…! Operations Strategy in Project-Based Operations,' *International Journal of Project Management*, Vol. 33, No. 1, pp. 103–115; **230 American Marketing Association:** Parasuraman, V. et al. (1985) 'A Conceptual Model of Service Quality and its Implications for Future Research', *Journal of Marketing*, Vol. 49, Fall, pp. 41–50; **236 The British Standards Institution:** BS 6143 (1992) *Guide to the Economics of Quality – Part 1: Process Cost Model*, British Standards Institute, Milton Keynes; **243 Donald Rumsfeld:** Quoted by Donald Rumsfeld; **244 NASA:** Report of Columbia Accident Investigation Board, Volume I, NASA; **245 Project Management Institute, Inc.:** PMI (2017) A Guide to the Project Management Body of Knowledge (PMBOK® Guide), 6th edition, Project Management Institute, Newtown Square, PA; **245 The British Standards Institution:** BS 6079:2019, *Project management – Principles and guidance for the management of projects*, BSI Standards Publication; **245 Association for Project Management:** APM (2019) Project Management Body of Knowledge, 7th edition, Association for Project Management, High Wycombe; **245 International Organization for Standardization:** ISO 31000:2018 *Risk Management*, International Organization for Standards; **248 Berrett-Koehler:** Hillson, D. and Simon, P. (2020) *Practical Project Risk Management: The ATOM Methodology*, 3rd edition, Management Concepts, London; **270 Penguin Random House:** Beaumont, M. (2018) *Around the World in 80 Days*, London: Penguin; **275 Harvard Business Publishing:** Williams, J.C. and Mihaylo, S. (2019) 'How The Best Bosses Interrupt Bias On Their Teams', *Harvard Business Review*, Vol. 97; **276 Penguin Random House:** Ansoff, H.I. (1968) *Corporate Strategy*, Penguin Books, New York; **277 Harvard Business Publishing:** Lawler, E.E. and Mohrman, S.A. (1985) 'Quality Circles After the Fad', *Harvard Business Review*, January–February, pp. 65–71; **281 Macmillan:** Peters, T. (1992) *Liberation Management*, Macmillan, London; **281 McGraw-Hill Companies:** Adapted from Ulrich, K.T. and Eppinger, S.D. (2000) *Product Design and Development*, 2nd edition, New York: McGraw-Hill, p. 29; **283 Harvard Business Publishing:** Gino F. (2019) 'Cracking the Code of Sustained Collaboration', *Harvard Business Review*, Vol 97, No. 6, pp. 72–81; **285 Belbin Associates:** Belbin, R.M.

(1993) *Team Roles at Work*, Butterworth-Heinemann, Oxford. Reproduced with permission from Belbin Associates; **295 Nelson Mandela:** Quoted by Nelson Mandela; **298 Elsevier:** Drucker, P. (1955) *Management*, Butterworth-Heinemann, Oxford; **299 Harvard Business Publishing:** Zaleznik, A. (1977) 'Managers and Leaders: Are They Different?' *Harvard Business Review*, May–June, pp. 67–78; **301 HarperCollins:** Taylor, F.W. (1911) *The Principles of Scientific Management*, Harper, New York; **302–303 HarperCollins:** Maslow's hierarchy from Maslow, A.H. (1970) *Motivation and Personality*, 2nd edition, Harper & Row, New York; **304 North River Press:** Goldratt, E.M. (1990) *The Haystack Syndrome*, North River Press, New York; **305 Simon & Schuster:** Womack, J., Jones, D. and Roos, J. (1990) *The Machine That Changed the World*, Rawson Associates, New York; **311–312 WarnerMedia:** Maxwell, J. (2004) *Today Matters: 12 Daily Practices to Guarantee Tomorrow's Success*, Time Warner, New York, pp. 74–75; **312 Confucius:** Quoted by Confucius; **313 Macmillan:** Section 3 of the APM Body of Knowledge ('People and behaviours') Association for Project Management, p.103; **317 Douglas Adams:** Quoted by Douglas Adams; **317 Antony Jay:** From *Yes, Prime Minister*, by Anthony Jay; **318 SAGE Publications:** Flyvbjerg, B., Budzier, A. and Lunn, D. (2020) 'Regression to the tail: Why the Olympics blow up', *Environment and Planning A: Economy and Space*, Sage publication; **359 Harvard Business Publishing:** Frydlinger, D., Hart, O. and Vitasek, O. (2019) 'A New Approach to Contracts. How to Build Better Long-Term Strategic Partnerships', *Harvard Business Review*, Sept–Oct, pp. 116–125; **362 David Hancock:** Case prepared in conjunction with Dr David Hancock of Cranfield School of Management; **370 Wildwood House:** Price, F. (1984) *Right First Time*, Wildwood House, London, p. 66; **385 Cuong Quang:** Used with Permission from Cuong Quang; **402 SAGE Publications:** Adapted from Turner, N., Maylor, H., Lee-Kelley, L., Brady, T., Kutsch, E. and Carver, S. (2014) 'Ambidexterity and Knowledge Strategy in Major Projects: A Framework and Illustrative Case Study', *Project Management Journal*, Vol. 45, No. 5, pp. 44–55; **413 McGraw-Hill Companies:** Crosby (1979) *Quality is Free*, McGraw-Hill, New York; **415 Elsevier:** Cooke-Davies, T. and Arzymanow, A. (2003) 'The Maturity of Project Management in Different Industries: An Investigation into Variations Between Project Management Models', *International Journal of Project Management*, Vol. 21, pp. 471–478.

Photo:

3 United Nations: Sustainable Development Goals (SDGs) by General Assembly resolution A/RES/70/1 of 25 September 2015, United Nations; **8 Alamy Image:** Alex Segre/Alamy Stock Photo; **8 Alamy Image:** Mark Richardson/Alamy Stock Photo; **11 Shutterstock:** New Africa/Shutterstock; **26 Alamy Image:** Tim Scrivener/Alamy Stock Photo; **34 Alamy Image:** Arterra Picture Library/Alamy Stock Photo; **50 Alamy Image:** Guy Corbishley/Alamy Stock Photo; **51 David Bott:** David Bott, Staffordshire Fire & Rescue Service; **58 Alamy Image:** Steven May/Alamy Stock Photo; **64 123RF:** Pavel Losevsky/123rf.com; **68 Michael Trolove:** Michael Trolove; **85 Harvey Maylor:** Used with Permission with Harvey Maylor; **87 Alamy Image:** TRAVEL by VISION/Alamy Stock Photo; **92 Getty Image:** Anders Blomqvist/Stone/Getty image; **110 Alamy Image:** Pacific Press Media Production Corp./Alamy Stock Photo; **113 Alamy Image:** PJF Military Collection/Alamy Stock Photo; **114 Alamy Image:** Oleksiy Maksymenko/Alamy Stock Photo; **114 Alamy Image:** Motoring Picture Library/Alamy Stock Photo; **130 Shutterstock:** Nick Fox/Shutterstock; **134 Shutterstock:** Jim Parkin/Shutterstock; **145 Alamy Image:** samuel wordley/Alamy Stock Photo; **147 Chris Nierhaus:** Image by Chris Nierhaus at TinBug Design Studios (tinbug.com); **171 Getty Image:** Tom Meaker/iStock/Getty Images Plus;

186 Getty Image: Pete Saloutos/Getty Image; **196 Getty Image:** Jeff J Mitchell/ Staff/ Getty Image; **223 Universal credit :** Logo used with Permission from Universal Credit; **244 Alamy Image:** Dennis Hallinan/Alamy Stock Photo; **271 Shutterstock:** Ian Langsdon/ EPA-EFE/Shutterstock; **296 Shutterstock:** Haakon Mosvold Larsen/AP/Shutterstock; **318 Shutterstock:** WKanadpon/Shutterstock; **344 NASA:** Bill Ingalls/ NASA; **362 Getty Image:** Dan Kirkwood/Getty Images; **370 Alamy Image:** REUTERS/Alamy Stock Photo; **395 Shutterstock:** Kalin Eftimov/Shutterstock.